2003

Sharing the Promised Land

Also by Dilip Hiro

Nonfiction
Dictionary of the Middle East (1996)
The Middle East (1995)
Between Marx and Muhammad: The Changing face of Central Asia (1994)
Lebanon, Fire and Embers: A History of the Lebanese Civil War (1992)
Desert Shield to Desert Storm: The Second Gulf War (1992)
Black British, White British: A History of Race Relations in Britain (1991)
The Longest War: The Iran-Iraq Military Conflict (1989)
Islamic Fundamentalism (1988)
Iran: The Revolution Within (1988)
Iran Under the Ayatollahs (1985)
Inside the Middle East (1982)
Inside India Today (1977)
The Untouchables of India (1975)
Black British, White British (1971)
The Indian Family in Britain (1969)

Fiction
Three plays (1987)
Interior, Exchange, Exterior (poems, 1980)
Apply, Apply, No Reply and a Clean Break (two plays, 1978)
To Anchor a Cloud (play, 1972)
A Triangular View (novel, 1969)

Sharing the Promised Land

A Tale of Israelis and Palestinians

DILIP HIRO

OLIVE
BRANCH
PRESS

An imprint of Interlink Publishing Group, Inc.
NEW YORK

First American edition published in 1999 by

OLIVE BRANCH PRESS
An imprint of Interlink Publishing Group, Inc.
99 Seventh Avenue • Brooklyn, New York 11215 and
46 Crosby Street • Northampton, Massachusetts 01060

Library of Congress Cataloging-in-Publication Data

Hiro, Dilip.
      Sharing the Promised Land : a tale of Israelis and Palestinians / by
  Dilip Hiro.
     p. cm.
  Includes bibliographical references and index.
  ISBN 1-56656-320-8 (hardback). —ISBN 1-56656-319-4 (paper)
  1. Arab-Israeli conflict. 2. Israel—Ethnic relations.
3. Israel—Social conditions. 4. Jerusalem—International status.
5. Palestinian Arabs—Israel. 6. Palestinian Arabs—Politics and government.
I. Title.
DS119.7.H535 1999
956.9405—dc21   99-10142
                                                    CIP

With thanks to Macmillan Ltd. for use of seven maps on pages vii-xi.

Printed and bound in Canada
10 9 8 7 6 5 4 3 2 1

Contents

Maps		vi
Preface		xii
Acronyms		xiv
Introduction		xvi
1	The Walled Heart of Jerusalem: A Battleground	1
2	Jerusalem: Yerushalayim/Al Quds	24
3	Mea Shearim: A Fortress of Jewish Ultra-Orthodoxy	38
4	Mizrachim/Sephardim: Coming of Age	48
5	The Secular Center: Pragmatic Politicians	62
6	The Israel Defense Forces (IDF): The Sword and Social Cement	119
7	The Double Marginals: Israeli Arabs	132
8	New Frontiersmen: Zealots on the Hills	146
9	The West Bank: A Diminishing Heritage of Palestinians	161
10	Gaza: The End of the Line	181
11	The Palestine Liberation Organization (PLO): Armed Resistance to Red-Carpet Respectability	200
12	The Palestinian Authority: An Embryo	232
13	Islamist Opposition: Hamas and the Islamic Jihad	256
14	Divine Promises: The Disputing Inheritors	280
15	Summing up the Past, Surmising the Future	286
	Epilogue	304
Appendices		
	Appendix I United Nations Security Council Resolutions 242 (1967) and 338 (1973)	337
	Appendix II Letters of Mutual Recognition by Israel and the PLO	339
Notes		341
Works Cited		355
Index		358

Maps

The Levant under the Ottomans—until World War I (1914-1918)

Palestine 1947: UN Partition Plan

Israel 1948: UN Armistice Lines

Jerusalem 1948: Armistice Lines

Israel and the Occupied Arab Territories 1967

Jerusalem 1967: Under Israel

Israel-PLO May 1994 Interim Agreement: Gaza Strip

Israel-PLO September 1995 Interim Agreement: West Bank

The Old City, Jerusalem

Jewish Settlements in Greater East Jerusalem, 1995

The Tomb of the Patriarchs/Ibrahimi Mosque, Hebron

Emergence of Kiryat Arba Jewish Settlements Complex and Closed Military
    Areas, 1968-95

Israel and the Palestinian Territories of the West Bank and Gaza Strip

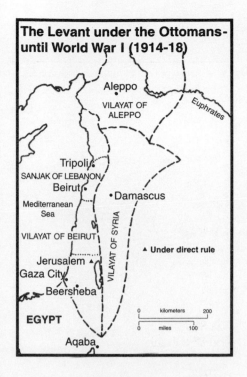

The Levant under the Ottomans- until World War I (1914-18)

Aleppo

VILAYAT OF ALEPPO

Euphrates

Tripoli

SANJAK OF LEBANON

Beirut

•Damascus

Mediterranean Sea

VILAYAT OF BEIRUT

VILAYAT OF SYRIA

Jerusalem ▲

Gaza City

Beersheba

EGYPT

Aqaba

▲ Under direct rule

kilometers 0 — 200
miles 0 — 100

ISRAEL 1949 UN Armistice Lines

LEBANON

SYRIA

Nazareth

Mediterranean Sea

Jenin

Tel Aviv (1)

WEST BANK

Amman

Jerusalem (2)

Hebron

Gaza

GAZA STRIP

Dead Sea

Beersheba

ISRAEL

JORDAN

SINAI / EGYPT

Armistice Lines
(1) Internationally recognized capital of Israel
(2) Self-declared capital of Israel

kilometers 0 — 50
miles 0 — 50

N

Eilat

Aqaba

PALESTINE 1947 UN Partition Plan

LEBANON

SYRIA

Nazareth

Mediterranean Sea

Jenin

Tel Aviv

Jaffa

Amman

Jerusalem

Hebron

Gaza

Beersheba

PALESTINE

TRANSJORDAN

SINAI / EGYPT

International Border of Palestine
Arab Area
International Area
Jewish Area

kilometers 0 — 50
miles 0 — 50

N

Eilat

Aqaba

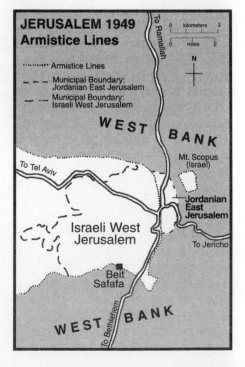

JERUSALEM 1949 Armistice Lines

To Ramallah

kilometers 0 — 3
miles 0 — 2

N

Armistice Lines
Municipal Boundary: Jordanian East Jerusalem
Municipal Boundary: Israeli West Jerusalem

WEST BANK

Mt. Scopus (Israel)

To Tel Aviv

Jordanian East Jerusalem

Israeli West Jerusalem

To Jericho

Beit Safafa

To Bethlehem

WEST BANK

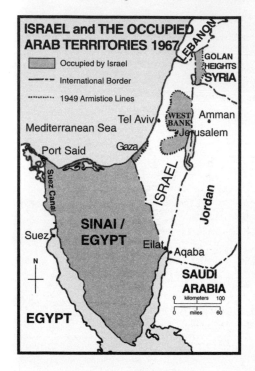

ISRAEL and THE OCCUPIED ARAB TERRITORIES 1967

- Occupied by Israel
- — · — International Border
- ········· 1949 Armistice Lines

LEBANON
GOLAN HEIGHTS
SYRIA
Tel Aviv
WEST BANK
Amman
Mediterranean Sea
Jerusalem
Port Said
Gaza
ISRAEL
Jordan
Suez Canal
SINAI / EGYPT
Suez
Eilat
Aqaba
N
SAUDI ARABIA

kilometers 100
miles 60

EGYPT

ISRAEL-PLO May 1994 Interim Agreement: Gaza Strip

Mediterranean Sea
Erez
Gaza
GAZA STRIP
ISRAEL
Khan Yunis
Rafah
N
EGYPT

kilometers 8
miles 5

- ■ Towns
- ·· — ·· Border of Gaza Strip
- — · — International Border
- ■ Joint control
- Israeli control (Settlements & other areas)
- Palestinian control

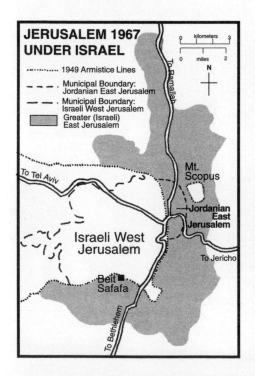

JERUSALEM 1967 UNDER ISRAEL

- ········· 1949 Armistice Lines
- — — — Municipal Boundary: Jordanian East Jerusalem
- — · — Municipal Boundary: Israeli West Jerusalem
- Greater (Israeli) East Jerusalem

kilometers 3
miles 2
N

To Ramallah
Mt. Scopus
To Tel Aviv
Jordanian East Jerusalem
Israeli West Jerusalem
To Jericho
Beit Safafa
To Bethlehem

ISRAEL-PLO SEPT. 1995 INTERIM AGREEMENT: WEST BANK

Jenin
Tulkarm
Nablus
Qalqiliya
Ariel
Tel Aviv
Salfit
WEST BANK
Mediterranean Sea
Birzeit
Ramallah
Beit Luqiya
ISRAEL
Jerusalem
Maale Adumim
Bethlehem
Nahalin
JORDAN
Halhul
Hebron
Qiryat Arba
Abu Harsh
GAZA STRIP
Dead Sea
N

kilometers 30
miles 20

- O Palestinian control (7 Palestinian cities)
- o Joint Israeli-Palestinian control (450 Palestinian villages, selected)
- ✿ Israeli control (128 Jewish settlements, selected)
- Territories occupied by Israel since 1967
- ·· — ·· Gaza Strip Border
- — · — International Border

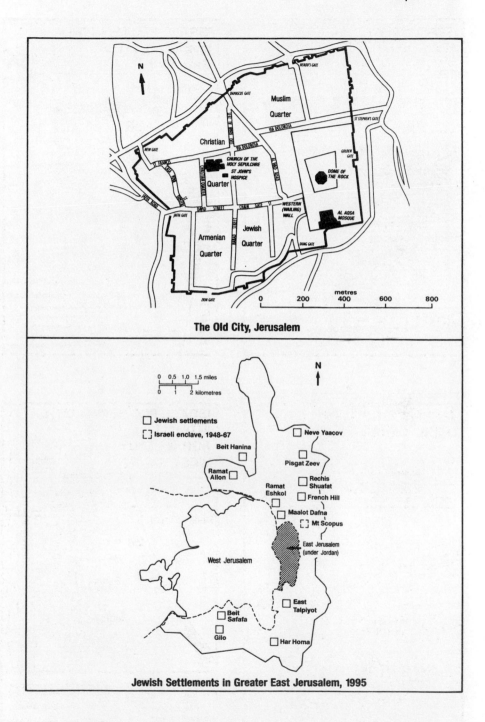

The Old City, Jerusalem

Jewish Settlements in Greater East Jerusalem, 1995

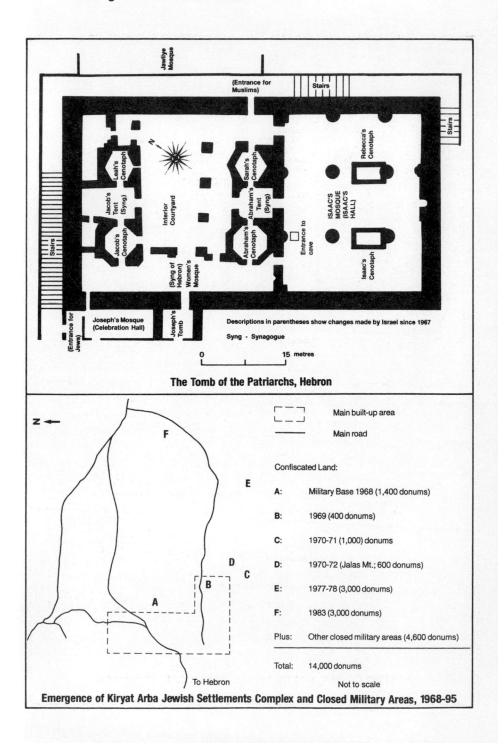

The Tomb of the Patriarchs, Hebron

Descriptions in parentheses show changes made by Israel since 1967

Syng - Synagogue

0   15 metres

Main built-up area

Main road

Confiscated Land:

A: Military Base 1968 (1,400 donums)

B: 1969 (400 donums)

C: 1970-71 (1,000) donums

D: 1970-72 (Jalas Mt.; 600 donums)

E: 1977-78 (3,000 donums)

F: 1983 (3,000 donums)

Plus: Other closed military areas (4,600 donums)

Total: 14,000 donums

Not to scale

Emergence of Kiryat Arba Jewish Settlements Complex and Closed Military Areas, 1968-95

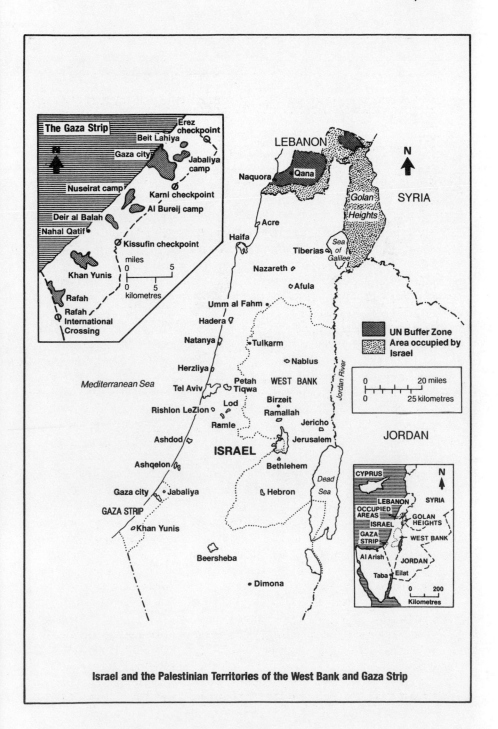

The Gaza Strip

Erez checkpoint

Beit Lahiya

Gaza city

Jabaliya camp

Naquora

Qana

LEBANON

N

Golan Heights

SYRIA

Nuseirat camp

Karni checkpoint

Al Bureij camp

Deir al Balah

Nahal Qatif

Acre

Haifa

Sea of Galilee

Tiberias

miles
0   5

Kissufin checkpoint

Nazareth

Khan Yunis

0   5
kilometres

Afula

Umm al Fahm

Rafah

Hadera

Rafah International Crossing

Natanya

Tulkarm

Nablus

Herzliya

Mediterranean Sea

Tel Aviv

Petah Tiqwa

WEST BANK

Jordan River

Lod

Birzeit

Rishlon LeZion

Ramallah

Ramle

Jericho

Ashdod

Jerusalem

JORDAN

ISRAEL

Ashqelon

Bethlehem

Dead Sea

Gaza city

Jabaliya

GAZA STRIP

Hebron

Khan Yunis

UN Buffer Zone
Area occupied by Israel

0   20 miles

0   25 kilometres

Beersheba

Dimona

CYPRUS

N

LEBANON   SYRIA

OCCUPIED AREAS

GOLAN HEIGHTS

ISRAEL

WEST BANK

GAZA STRIP

Al Arish

JORDAN

Taba   Eilat

0   200
Kilometres

Israel and the Palestinian Territories of the West Bank and Gaza Strip

Preface

The purpose of my book is to describe and analyze Israeli-Palestinian relations, and provide anatomies of the two societies.

There is no better place to examine relations between Israelis and Palestinians than Jerusalem. I therefore open the text with a study of the subject in the historical Old City of Jerusalem, and then move on to the city at large.

Next I anatomize Israeli society, starting at the edges—the ultra-Orthodox in Mea Shearim, Jerusalem—then proceed inward to profile Oriental Jews, also called Sephardim or Mizrachim. In the following chapter, my focus is on the (European) Ashkenazim-dominated secular political center, which includes both left-of-center Labor and right-of-center Likud. At the very core of society is the Israel Defense Forces (IDF), the single most effective cement and homogenizer, the subject of Chapter Six.

I then profile that segment of Israeli society which is excluded from the IDF, Israeli Arabs.

Another section of Israeli society which, though very much part of Jewish life, has chosen to live beyond the 1967 borders: the Jewish settlers in the West Bank and Gaza Strip, a subject I cover in Chapter Eight.

The physical location of the Jewish settlers leads me to examine first the West Bank community, which accounts for nearly half of the Palestinians living within the boundaries of Palestine under the British mandate, and then the residents of Gaza. In the latter case I enclose a history of the Palestinian intifada (1987-93) without which there would have been no mutual recognition of Israel and the Palestine Liberation Organization in 1993.

My focus then shifts to the PLO. Next I turn to the Palestinian Authority and its teething troubles. A study of the Islamic opposition—Hamas and the Islamic Jihad—in the following chapter completes my anatomy of Palestinian society today.

The penultimate chapter in a way reflects the one on Jerusalem's Old City, both being rooted in religion. Here I have Jewish and Islamic fundamentalists debate their respective viewpoints within the context of the Divine Promises as recorded in the Old Testament.

Reflecting the title of the concluding chapter, I close my text with a summary of the past and a surmise of the future.

A word about the terms used. An Israeli citizen's identity document mentions "Nationality: Jew/Arab; and Citizenship: Israeli." Which term should be qualified—Jew or Arab, or Israeli—and when? It is a complex issue; and everyday terminology is far from logical or consistent. The Israeli State emphasizes Jewishness no matter where a particular Jew lives. So Israeli officials describe, say, Saul Bellow, an eminent novelist, as an American Jew rather than Jewish American. At home they apply the same logic when categorizing those Palestinians who stayed behind in Israel in 1948, calling them "Israeli Arabs," not "Arab Israelis." In the media the terms "Israeli" and "Jew" are used interchangeably even though one-sixth of Israelis are not Jewish. In the same way a Palestinian is taken to be a Muslim even though in the Palestinian territories one-twelfth of them are Christian. By and large I have stayed with the prevalent convention despite its deficiencies. But when I discuss Israelis in a religious context, say, I qualify them as Jewish or Muslim or Christian.

Finally, a word about spellings. Since standard ways of transliterating Arabic and Hebrew words require acutes, graves, ogoneks and so on, and these are not used in the English-language news agencies or newspapers, I have opted for the spellings current in the English-language print media. Within this context I have been consistent—using, for instance, Halacha, not Halakha; Muslim, not Moslem; and Quran, not Koran. The "al" or "el" in Arabic and "ha" in Hebrew mean "the." For the sake of consistency, I have used the Hebrew definite article always as a combined prefix—HaAretz, not Haaretz or Ha'aretz.

This edition is a bit shorter, but more up-to-date, than the one published in Britain earlier.

I revisited Israel and the Palestinian territories in September 1998. The concluding chapter and the Epilogue are partly informed by that trip.

Dilip Hiro
London
April 1999

Acronyms

ADP	Arab Democratic Party
AHC	Arab Higher Committee
ANM	Arab Nationalist Movement
BPP	Black Panther Party
CPRS	Center for Palistinian Research and Studies
DFLP	Democratic Front for the Liberation of Palestine
DFPE	Democratic Front for Peace and Equality, popularly called Hadash
ESP	Economic Stabilization Program
DOP	Declaration of Principles
ICO	Islamic Conference Organization
IDF	Israeli Defense Forces
IZL	Irgun militia
JDL	Jewish Defense League
JRP	Jewish Reclamation Project
LHI	Lehi militia
LNL	League of National Liberation
MK	Member of Knesset
NIS	New Israeli Shekel
NRP	National Religious Party
PA	Palestinian Authority. *See* PNA
PASSIA	Palestinian Academic Society for the Study of International Affairs
PCP	Palestine Communist Party
PFA	Palestinian Forces Alliances
PFLP	Popular Front for the Liberation of Palestine
PLA	Palestine Liberation Army
PLF	Palestine Liberation Front
PLO	Palestine Liberation Organization
PNA	Palestinian National Authority. *See* PA
PNC	Palestine National Council
PNF	Palestine National Front
PSF	Palestine Students' Federation

PSS	Preventive Security Service (Palestinian)
SMC	Supreme Muslim Council
TIPH	Temporary International Presence in Hebron
TMF	Temple Mount Faithful
UNEF	United Nations Emergency Force
UNLU	United National Leadership of the Uprising
UNRWA	United Nations Relief and Work Agency
UTJ	United Torah Judaism Party
WZO	World Zionist Organization

Introduction

Israel is exceptional.

You realize this at the start of your journey. At London's Gatwick airport each airline is identified on the electronic indicator by a letter. But not so Monarch, the airline destined for Tel Aviv. Its symbol was *. But nowhere was there a sign leading toward *.

I was supposed to check in three hours before departure. I was already late. Desperate, I buttonholed a young man collecting luggage trolleys. He stared at the monitor, and said: "A" zone. How did he guess? And why didn't the monitor give directions? He pointed the way to the "A" zone. I rushed. Before I could get my bearings I was face to face with a posse of police officers wielding submachine guns. "Tel Aviv?" asked one. I nodded yes. He gestured vaguely toward a blank wall. A seam in the wall opened—to reveal an enormous elevator. The men and women around me chattered in Russian. When the elevator opened, we faced not a series of check-out counters, but a vast, white-painted underground bunker. It looked like the place had been designed to withstand a bomb blast with a minimum of damage.

Israel's uniqueness strikes you again, as you consider its ancient name (Hebrew for Prevailing with God) and remember that it was established only in 1948. It is a young state, and a largely immigrant one, populated by Jews from more than 100 countries.

The mosaic nature of Israel dawned on me one blustery winter afternoon in a café-bakery in south Tel Aviv. Sitting there with my Hebrew interpreter, Rafi, I was overwhelmed not just by the aroma of cakes and pastries, but also by the sheer variety of the desserts along the walls and in the shop window.

"The ones you see there," said Rafi, pointing to a distant tray, "are *rugelech*, from Poland." "Your part of the world," I muttered, clutching my cup of coffee to warm my hands. "My mother's," Rafi said. "You forget that my father was born in Britain." I nodded. "That's *shtrodel* there, from Central Europe. Those are *latkes levivot*, from Eastern Europe." Rafi beckoned the young man at the cash register. He came over and sat down, and turned out to be the owner. Where was he from, I wondered. "Turkey, Izmir," he replied. His name was Yaacov Nouri. What was his favorite cake? "*Uga marokait*," he replied instantly. "Sounds Moroccan," I guessed. "So it is," Rafi said.

"I love it, made with pure honey," Yaacov added, gesturing. He got up and fetched a couple for us. I took a bite, gingerly, at first, then voraciously. So did Rafi. "Different cakes from different Jewish communities in the world," Rafi summed up. "Do they share a common dessert?" I inquired. "Yes," replied Yaacov. "*Ozne haman.*" "The one every Jew eats at the time of the Purim festival," Rafi explained. "It marks the liberation of the Jews from the evil designs of Haman, the Prime Minister of King Ahaseurs of Persia." "In the fifth century BC," added Yaacov.

The state policy of "the ingathering of Jews from the four corners of the world" runs hand in hand with the efforts that are made, in official and private circles, to link the Jewish past with the present. Every year on 9 Av, the day the Second Temple was destroyed by the Roman army of Titus in AD 70, Jews in Israel fast and pray. They shut their eateries, cinemas and theaters. The media devote the day to examining the reasons why the Second Temple fell and the Jews lost their political sovereignty. What lessons can today's Jews draw from that disaster? Are there any parallels between what was and what is? Are contemporary Jews in Israel sliding into the sort of irreconcilable feuding that paved the way for the Jews' defeat and humiliation in the ancient era?

A linkage between the present and the distant past informed and inspired the early Zionists. Their decision to revive Hebrew—long dead as an everyday, spoken language—is a case in point. They viewed Yiddish as the language of the ghetto, which needed to be abandoned. Thus, the revival of Hebrew, a classical language, used for many centuries only in the Jewish liturgy, became closely associated with Zionism. Early on the pioneering Zionists in Palestine set up a Hebrew school. The cementing role of Hebrew among the Zionist settlers of Palestine can hardly be overstated. In a larger context there is a correlation between the rise of Jewish nationalism and the emergence of Hebrew as a living, contemporary language over the past century. During that period Hebrew has flowered as the language of the Jews, first in Palestine, and then in Israel, and now possesses a substantial body of modern literature.

Besides Hebrew, many other aspects of Israeli life today can best be understood in the historical context of Zionism. It started as a religious ideology, and then acquired a political counterpart. While, from the early twentieth century, political Zionism forged ahead, religious Zionism did not disappear. Indeed Zionism evolved as a catch-all ideology with several strands. As its varied adherents journeyed to Palestine and settled there, they put a different spin on it—socialist, nationalist, Messianic and religious fundamentalist.

The metamorphosis of Zionism is neatly captured by the Histadrut (Federation). It was established in Palestine in 1920 as an umbrella organization to encompass all Zionist labor-pioneer groups, with membership limited to Jewish workers, artisans and traders. Within a few decades, Histadrut had been transformed into a multi-faceted body, which combined the seemingly contradictory roles of a trade union federation with the ownership of vast industrial and construction companies and banks, and supplemented it by providing health insurance and social welfare to most Israelis. Today Histadrut's commercial and industrial activities employ one-fifth of the total Israeli workforce.

Initially, in the political Zionist camp socialists were the dominant force. They believed in and practiced social equality and dignity of labor in Palestine. A result was the *kibbutzim* (agricultural communes) movement, which preceded the 1917 Bolshevik Revolution. Today egalitarian socialism has disappeared from the political landscape of Israel. Its citizens exalt private enterprise, and are as addicted to individual gain and consumerism as Americans. Yet Israeli state and society fondly preserve the kibbutzim, which are struggling to survive in radically altered circumstances.

Whatever else has changed in the country, the old drive and enterprise has not. One sees the results of this restless energy in various spheres of Jewish Israeli life—economic, social, military and political.

Traveling by bus on a sunny February morning from Jerusalem to Haifa I witnessed the outcome of the marriage of nature and human enterprise in the coastal strip between the Mediterranean Sea and the inland hills: orchards, fields, and vast, plastic-covered greenhouses. It was as if the coastal plain, 80 miles from north to south and some 15 miles east to west, had been transformed into one gargantuan garden. Yet the area is also home to nearly two-thirds of the Israeli manufacturing industry, which ranges from food processing to fighter aircraft, and furniture-making to silicon chips. Since my last visit in the late 1970s, the Ben Gurion Airport had grown from a medium-sized, passenger-friendly facility to a vast complex of buildings, runways and parks, dotted with multicolor billboards advertising beer, videos and cigarettes. Much else, happily, was still on a human scale. The apartment blocks that filled the towns and cities were seldom higher than four or five stories. Here and there were homes with slanting red tiles, reminders of Britain. But unlike in Britain, everything here was new, clean and smooth. It was closer to traversing a large, rural U.S. county. The feeling of being in small town America was unmistakable. Later, when I looked up the figures on the Israeli economy, I realized that there was more to my feelings than mere impressions. With a per capita income of $16,400, Israel's living standard was more than half that of the United States. It was about 80 percent that of Britain, a country with two and a half centuries of industrial revolution behind it.

In its drive to develop the coastal belt, Israel has not neglected its desert zone, the Negev. Successful research at the Beersheba University, for instance, has led to a technique of growing tomatoes and melons on saline water. It was a research institute at the Sede Boqer Kibbutz in the Negev that perfected the technique for using solar energy to heat domestic water. Today the sun reflectors, installed on roofs almost universally, have made Israeli buildings stand apart in the Mediterranean region.

Like most industrious people, Israelis play as hard as they work. Since the religious injunctions of the Sabbath require the shutdown of all bars, restaurants, cinemas, theaters and nightclubs, and since the Jewish day begins with the sunset, Israeli enjoyment clusters around Friday afternoon and Saturday night. The Ben Yehuda Mall, the pedestrian square in downtown Jerusalem, comes vibrantly alive on Friday afternoons, with pop music blaring out of loudspeakers.

Loitering around the Mall in my shirtsleeves one Friday afternoon in March (spring arrives early in Jerusalem), I felt part of the relaxing, local crowd.

The open-air cafés and restaurants, spread out on the cobbled streets, were doing brisk business. Aproned waitresses with ponytails rushed from table to customer to kitchen and back again, balancing trays as they adroitly threaded their way through. The stores selling clothes, music cassettes, books, electronic gadgetry, mobile phones, take-away pizzas and so on were full. A stubbled old man, in an oversize, camel-color coat, played a violin to no one in particular. Across the street, a big, black-bearded man, beat rhythmically a huge medieval wooden instrument with a well-polished baton. When he stopped, a small, appreciative audience clapped.

Watching the informally dressed people around me, mostly young and white, often tanned, I could be anywhere in a Mediterranean European city on a spring Saturday afternoon. Suddenly an exotic sight pulled me up short. A hefty young man, in a long white prayer shawl, wearing a *kippa* (skullcap)—his left arm circled with a leather strap carrying sacred Jewish prayers on parchment tucked inside a small leather box, his forehead strapped tightly with another talisman-like box bearing prayers—intoned a prayer from a printed sheet, as two bearded men, the proprietors of the religious paraphernalia, watched closely. They were laying the *tefillin* (phylacteries), an integral part of saying the Jewish prayer properly, on the young man. In the midst of a hedonistic Jewish multitude gratifying its material cravings, I witnessed a lax Jew being led into the fold of the pious and the religious. Only in Israel, I concluded, does one encounter scenes such as these, religion creeping up at an odd moment and an odder place.

Though created by Jews and described as the Jewish state in the Declaration of Establishment of the State of Israel (commonly, but wrongly, called the Declaration of Independence) in 1948, Israel is not a religious state. The term "Jewish" in the Declaration is unqualified. So the State of Israel, strictly speaking, is neither religious nor secular. In practice, though, lacking a state religion, it claims to be secular. Yet its state symbol, the menorah, is religious and its flag carries the Star of David, another religious emblem. "The belief of the Jew in his nation is of its essence religious," notes Colin Thubron, a British writer. "To judge it in practical or patriotic terms is to mistake its nature."[1]

The symbiosis between religion and nationalism is aptly captured by the Western (Wailing) Wall in Jerusalem's Old City. In contemporary Israel it is both a holy shrine and a national monument—used for celebrating Jewish holidays as well as patriotic rituals such as the swearing in of military officers. The area around the Western Wall is festooned with Israeli flags at all times. Above all, the Wall appears in the second stanza of the Israeli national anthem, "HaTikva" (The Hope):

> As long as our eyes perceive the beloved Wall
> And tears are shed over the ruins of the Temple
> Our hope is not lost.

On closer inspection, the Declaration of Establishment too inextricably links religion and nationalism. "The State of Israel will be open for Jewish immigration and for the Ingathering of the Exile," it says. This statement was formalized into the Law of Return, 1950. In effect, this law says that Israel is to be open to Jewish immigrants only.[2] It confers on every diaspora Jew an inherent right to become an Israeli citizen.

What about the non-Jews living in Israel ever since its founding? For every five Jews then, there was one Muslim or Christian Arab. Did the State of Israel wish to distinguish between one citizen and the other? Yes. Though citizens of Israel, the Arabs were a threat to the fledgling state, so there had to be a way of telling them apart. And it was institutionalized, innovatively, in the classifications to be recorded in the identity card which every adult Israeli citizen was required to carry. Leum/Quomieh (Hebrew/Arabic: Nation or Nationality): Jew or Arab; Izrahut/Janatieh (Hebrew/Arabic: Citizenship): Israeli. Common citizenship but different nationality. So Jews and Arabs were, and are, treated separately as ethnic groups, not religious groups. (In any case, since a minority of Arabs are Christian, a strictly religious divide would have become complicated.) Having accepted Arabs as a nationality on a par with Jews, Israel found itself adopting two official languages: Hebrew and Arabic. That is the theory. That should mean all road signs must be in both languages. In reality they are not. None the less, on a higher, abstract plane, the thinking behind the concepts of citizenship and nationality is remarkable, and once again innovative.

For those who think of Jews as a race, a trip to Israel can be an eye-opener. Here you have Jews who are white Europeans; Jews who are brown Middle Easterners; and Jews, chiefly from Ethiopia, who are African. At a Jewish settlement on the West Bank I met Ania, the Jewish maid of a leading settler, who was a Mongol, of a Mizo tribe from the Indo-Burmese border area.

Religiously, Jews in Israel are officially divided into Sephardim (from Spain) and Ashkenazim (from Germany), each sect having its own chief rabbi. Since most Jews of European ancestry belong to the Ashkenazi synagogue, the term Ashkenazim denotes both sectarian affiliation and geographic origin. Not so with the Jews from the Middle East and North Africa. They are described as Sephardim in sectarian terms, and Mizrachim (Orientals) in geographical. Today Mizrachim and Ashkenazim are almost equal in population.

The ingathering of these diverse strands of the world Jewry in Israel has been far from smooth. The Zionist movement was almost wholly Ashkenazi. Its pioneers settled in Palestine, and set the foundations first of the Yishuv (Settlement), the pre-state Jewish community, and then of Israel, in the mold of their European background. So when Arabic-speaking Jews from the Middle East and North Africa arrived in large numbers soon after the establishment of Israel, there was much misunderstanding and tension. The only way, Mizrachi/Oriental Jews soon realized, they could find acceptance and integration into Israeli society was by abandoning most of what was "Oriental" about them. They did, reluctantly. They and, more particularly, their children, underwent westernization, imparted to them formally through the educational system and informally through the state-run broadcasting media. In other words, the intermingling of different cultural and artistic mores that occurred due to the arrival of Jews from the West and the East occurred, essentially, on western terms. Today in the cultural sphere, western dominance is most obvious in Hebrew literature and in classical music. But pop is more of a hybrid, with the

Arab/Oriental music having an edge over the European. Only in cuisine have oriental dishes come to hog the mainstream.

Besides the educational system, what helped to acculturate the Mizrachim was conscription into the military, which applied to all Jewish Israelis, male and female. This was a by-product of an innovative system which the founders of the State devised. They combined a small standing army with military training for all Jewish Israelis. Such an approach yielded them the best of both worlds: a low cost of defending the country, and the creation of a universally trained society which could be fully mobilized within a day or two. The shared experience of serving in the Israel Defense Forces (IDF) became the cement that joined Israeli Jewish society across sectarian and ethnic divisions.

Since national security is at the top of the national agenda, the IDF and military service rank high in individual and collective consciousness. The founders of Israel realized merely serving in the IDF is not enough to maintain a highly motivated, mobilized society. They were aware of the need for forging and maintaining a national consensus, with no quarter given to skepticism and doubt, surrounded as the fledgling Jewish state was by hostile Arab neighbors. Consensus was best achieved by reiterating the moral righteousness of Zionism and Israel.

The most effective tool was, and remains, history—the prism through which Jewish Israelis view their self-image. "The Israeli public has been given a one-dimensional version of their own history—beginning with the Jewish colonization of Eretz Israel (Land of Israel)—but especially regarding the events of the [1948] War of Independence and thereafter," writes Yossi Melman, a senior journalist at *HaAretz* (The Land), a much respected Israeli daily, and the author of *The New Israelis*. "Like mainstream American historiography, which has painstakingly avoided the embarrassing truth about the massacring of the Native Americans, Israel's history too has been painted in black and white. Israeli myth has its own good guys and bad guys... [T]he Israeli spin on their own history tells of an unfailingly righteous nation that has always only desired peace. This same legend speaks of how Israel has looked untiringly to open windows of opportunity. But the Arabs, the bad guys, closed the windows and went to war."[3]

Israel's military doctrine, conceived chiefly by David Ben Gurion (1886-1973), the most eminent of the founders of Israel, and backed by the United States, was and remains that the IDF must always maintain qualitative superiority in military hardware and training over the neighboring Arab states. In other words, Israel should be so militarily powerful that its strength should deter the Arabs from attacking it. Even in 1948 the IDF performed so well in its war with the armies from Egypt, Syria, Jordan, Lebanon and Iraq, that it ended up controlling nearly 75 percent of Palestine compared to the 54 percent allocated to the Jews by the United Nations partition plan of November 1947.

During the 1956 Suez War and later, the IDF proved its prowess in conducting tank warfare. And in the June 1967 War, the Israeli air force performed with spectacular brilliance. All in all, Ben Gurion's doctrine was impressively effective for a quarter of a century. The Arab countries did not strike the first blow in 1956 and 1967. Even when Egypt and Syria initiated armed hostilities in 1973 they struck Israel in the Arab territories occupied by it since 1967. That conflict ended in a draw. In contrast, when Israel invaded Lebanon in 1982 its advance was so swift that it reached Beirut within a week. The overall fatalities sum up the picture. In its four major conventional wars with Arabs, from 1948 to 1973, Israel lost a total of 9,520 lives and the Arabs 46,850—a ratio of 1:5.

From humble beginnings, Israel, a country of 5.1 million Jews today, has built up its defenses to the extent that it is currently the ninth most powerful military power on earth. Aside from the five permanent members of the UN Security Council, it is the only state that possesses an arsenal of at least 200 nuclear weapons.

But such massive strength does not make Israel immune from "the enemy within," the title borne by the Palestinians living under the Israeli military in the West Bank and Gaza Strip since 1967. Twenty years later they demonstrated—to the chagrin of Israeli politicians—the impotence of the IDF soldiers to put down a popular civilian uprising, commonly known as the *intifada* (Arabic, shaking off).

The young Israeli conscripts and the older reservists were ill-trained to contain the widespread civil unrest that continued for nearly six years. The IDF was not alone. It worked in conjunction with the police and the security service, called Shin Beth (Hebrew acronym of Sherut Betakhon, Security Service) or Shabak (Hebrew acronym of Sherut Betakhon Klali, General Security Service). Having grasped the vital role played by the Shin Beth's Palestinian agents, the intifada leaders turned their attention to their own "enemy within" during the latter part of the intifada, and initiated a program of assassinating the agents. They succeeded in destroying the Israeli network of 20-25,000 Palestinian agents in the West Bank and Gaza Strip. With this, it became a formidable task for the IDF to re-impose full control over the Occupied Palestinian Territories. As it was, its resort to curfews, firing at the demonstrators, house searches, beatings and torture, and house demolitions in the Occupied Territories to crush the intifada had a deleterious effect on the democratic, law-abiding ethos of Israel. This happened because the IDF is drawn from Israeli society at large. After three years active duty at 18, every Israeli male must serve annually for at least a month until he is 54. Because of the intifada the period of reserve duty was extended, often doubled. Among other things this damaged the economy.

Thus the long-running intifada brought to the surface the contradiction that had existed all along between the realization of the Zionist dream—Jewish settlement of Palestine and the ingathering of world Jewry in Eretz Israel—and its cost to those who lived in Palestine, the Palestinians, in the loss of their homes and their forced exile. Return and construction by one people took place at the expense of expulsion and destruction of the other.

The man who brought this home to me, inadvertently, was an unassuming fisherman in Jaffa, named Muhammad Suri. I met him by chance on a cloudy February afternoon as, accompanied by Rafi, I explored the old Arab Quarter of historic Jaffa. He was standing by himself, sipping beer at the supermarket. Suri was glad to talk—in fluent Hebrew.

Suri invited us to his home, an old, stone building. Over cups of Turkish coffee, he told us that he was born in Acre in 1953 and that his father, a fisherman, migrated to Jaffa when he was five. He was attached to the place, where he had grown up, and to the country, where they had been fishermen for many generations. Referring to the recently arrived Russian immigrants, who were being housed in the Arab Quarter, he alleged official pressures to ease him out of his house. "I was born in this country, and my father and his father and his father were born here," he said, raising his voice. "I'll stay whatever the pressure from the government. I'll never leave." Had anybody mentioned his leaving the country? "No," he replied. "But when you have most of your near and dear ones exiled, you have that fear hovering over you all the time." Where were his blood relations now? He began naming names and where they lived. It started to get too complicated. Suri retreated to his living room, and emerged holding an old pocket diary. It had the names and phone numbers of his uncles, aunts, cousins—all with deep roots in Acre—who, in his words, had been "expelled before and during the 1948 War." The list was long and varied. It showed Suri's blood relations scattered across the continents: Kuwait; Miya Miya refugee camp in Lebanon; Damascus; Jarash, Jordan; Tunis; Gaza City and Khan Yunis in the Gaza Strip; Copenhagen; Nablus in the West Bank; and Charleston, South Carolina.

Mentally recalling the list of the Jewish Israelis I had interviewed recently, I discovered a symmetry in the ingathering in Israel of the Jews from Poland, Russia, Britain, Turkey, Iran, Morocco, India and the U.S. with the dispersion of Muhammad Suri's relatives from Palestine to Kuwait, Jordan, the West Bank and Gaza Strip, Denmark, Lebanon, Syria, Tunisia and America.

Indeed, of the 6.5 million Palestinians today, roughly a half are in the diaspora. Of those who live in the Palestine of the British mandate (1922-48), a quarter are in pre-1967 Israel, classified as "non-Jews" in official documents and carrying identity cards that describe them as Arab Israelis. The rest are in the West Bank, the Gaza Strip and Greater East Jerusalem under overall Israeli control.

Of these, the residents of the Gaza Strip, about a million strong, constitute the bottom of the heap, crammed into an area of about 28 miles by 5 miles—two-fifths of which is under Israeli control and closed to them, because of settlements populated by a mere 4,000 Jewish Israelis. When you cross the military checkpoint from Israel into the Gaza Strip, it is as though you have driven from the affluent suburbs of Los Angeles into the shanty towns of the Bangladeshi capital, Dhaka.

Our taxi drove along a narrow ribbon of road flanked by buildings made of breeze blocks. The ribbon widened, and suddenly the taxi began making waves in a vast pool of brown water, the result of the previous day's downpour. The driver, a veteran of countless trips between the Gaza Strip and Israel, maneuvered like a pilot guiding a ferry across a treacherous river. In Gaza City he had to be equally deft to steer his vehicle through narrow, winding streets, often used as playgrounds by children. The political graffiti reminded the visitor of the turbulent past of the territory.

Nearly a half of Gazans live in refugee camps, a hotchpotch of makeshift houses, dirt tracks, and tall, forbidding watch-towers. The temporary arrangements of 1948, meant to last a few months or a few years, have been turned into permanent, higgledy-piggledy settlements. The inhabitants, young and old alike, make scant distinction between private and public. There are no roads worth mentioning—only dirt tracks and pot-holed streets, which turn into a string of brown puddles after the slightest rain. Open malodorous channels carry domestic sewage. The garbage disposal is accomplished by an army of goats who attack the stinking heaps with unflagging gusto. Donkey carts abound. The overall impression is of desolation: stones, concrete blocks, torn polythene bags, empty bottles. There is a pervasive sense of things left undone, half done—unpaved, unswept streets, rotting piles of garbage, chaotic traffic of men, animals and motorized vehicles on pot-holed roads and dirt streets. All this translates into a per capita income of $930 a year, a measly eight percent of the figure for an Israeli.

While West Bankers were given opportunity, twice, by the Israeli authorities to elect their representatives to run municipal affairs, Gazans were not. The Gaza Strip thus represented the Israeli military occupation in its rawest form. It was only logical that the intifada should erupt there in the winter of 1987. So deep and abiding was the hatred of the Israeli troops among Gazans that when, four winters later after a heavy snow followed by floods, the Israeli Defense Forces (IDF) came to Jabaliya Camp to help evacuate the residents, people pelted them with stones. The IDF retreated.

The intifada stemmed from twenty years of collective and individual frustrations and humiliations that the Palestinians had endured in their dealings with the Jews and the Israeli authorities, military and civilian. Many of the leaders of the intifada—backed by the secular Palestine Liberation Organization as well as the religious Islamic Resistance Movement, known by its Arabic acronym Hamas—were young educated Palestinians, fluent in Hebrew and familiar with Israeli norms, who took over the communal leadership from the pliant, older generation of Arab notables. The intifada caught the imagination and commitment of most Palestinians. In its first four years, it resulted in the arrest of one out of six male Palestinians. And on average one Palestinian died daily, mostly as a result of shooting by the Israeli military or border police.

Ever since the founding of Israel in 1948, and until the intifada, Palestinians had put faith in other Arabs to deliver them from the Israeli occupation, and restore their land to them. This was not to be. Slowly, painfully, they realized that only they could liberate themselves and establish a nation-state, and that they had to rely on themselves.

Before reaching and acting on that conclusion, they went through different phases since the 1948 Arab-Israeli War—what Palestinians call Al Nakba (The Catastrophe). It divided their society into three components: the remnants (inside Israel), the refugees (mostly in neighboring Arab states), and those in the West Bank (under Jordanian jurisdiction) and the Gaza Strip (under Egyptian administration).

The remnants conducted politics in traditional Palestinian ways inside Israel within the limits imposed by the authorities. The exiles participated in the politics of the countries where they lived. Within a decade, however, they as well as those inside Israel turned increasingly radical and adopted rejectionist policies. Their vehement criticism of the Arab states for failing to liberate Palestine led the

Arab League to sponsor the formation in 1964 of the Palestine Liberation Organization.

The June 1967 Arab-Israeli War, which resulted in a swift and humiliating rout of the Arabs, was the turning point. With the West Bank and Gaza Strip lost to the Jewish state, and Israel's Arab neighbors reeling from their defeat, the Palestinians and the PLO emerged as the leading players in their struggle for recovering their land.

They followed a twin-track strategy: attacks on Israeli and Zionist targets; and the building of a network of Palestinian organizations—from trade unions, student associations, and women's groups to doctors' and engineers' syndicates; and from schools and hospitals to veterans' welfare programs. There was a whole set of militias of the various PLO affiliates. Among other things, the PLO set up the Palestine National Fund to meet its financial requirements. It was funded by grants from Arab and other friendly states, and an income tax on the Palestinians living in the diaspora. There were uncanny parallels here with the Zionist movement before the founding of Israel.

The sharper the reality of the PLO and the Palestinians, the greater the resistance of Israeli leaders to acknowledge it. Prime Minister Golda Meir said in 1969 that there were no Palestinians; her aides described them as South Syrians. After her, Prime Minister Yitzhak Rabin graduated to referring to them as "the so-called Palestinians." To Prime Minister Menachem Begin, in the late 1970s, they were "the Arabs of Eretz Israel."

By then the Arab League had recognized the PLO as the sole representative of the Palestinian people, and accorded it full membership; and the United Nations had given the PLO observer status. The PLO, based in Beirut since 1972, had become a "state within a state" within Lebanon, helped by Lebanon's slide into civil war in 1975. The PLO had all the instruments of a state, including foreign missions in scores of countries, but no land of its own.

Israel regarded the PLO's high profile in Lebanon, which it also used as a base for attacks on Israeli targets, as an intolerable challenge. The result was a full-fledged invasion of Lebanon by Israel in 1982, and the expulsion of the PLO from Beirut.

With the PLO now banished to distant Tunis, the Palestinians living in the West Bank and Gaza Strip lost any hope they had of being liberated by an outside power. They were on their own. They met the challenge. In five years they were up in arms against their occupiers, the IDF. They mounted their intifada. It was their struggle and it was headed by local leaders. The PLO backed it. So did Hamas, which was based in the Occupied Territories. The intifada continued, off and on, for several years.

It ended in September 1993 with the signing of an accord between Israel and the PLO in Washington. The agreement was a compromise. The PLO accepted Israel's right to exist in security, and the Jewish state recognized the PLO as the representative of the Palestinian people. Their right to self-rule in the West Bank and Gaza was to be put into practice, in stages.

Which side compromised more and which less remains a point of debate.

What is indisputable, though, is that the overall achievement of Zionism and Israel has been stupendous. In 1897 when the first Congress of the (World) Zionist Organization, meeting in Basle, Switzerland, resolved to "create for the Jewish people a home in Palestine secured by public law," nobody, except possibly the convenor of the assembly, Theodor Herzl, seriously hoped to see this goal achieved. It was only after the collapse of the Ottoman Turkish empire, whose Arab domain included Palestine, in October 1918, coupled with the declaration a year earlier by the British Foreign Secretary, Arthur James Balfour, favoring "the establishment in Palestine of a National Home for the Jewish people," that the situation changed dramatically. Once Britain had been given a mandate over Palestine by the League of Nations in 1922, the pace of systematic Jewish immigration accelerated. By the time Britain handed over the "problem of Palestine" to the United Nations, the successor to the League of Nations, in 1947, the Jews were 30 percent of the population, four times more numerous than three decades before.

"The international achievement of Zionism is in having taken hold of Palestine from within Palestine and, no less important, having made the native Palestinian population seem like the outsider," writes Edward W. Said, an eminent Palestinian intellectual and professor at Columbia University. "Most of the time thereafter, Palestinians have found themselves in the situation of someone outside looking in, and finding that fact of banishment to be the main defining characteristic of [their] existence... We have now become disinherited outsiders."[4]

These words were fresh in my mind when I arrived one cold, sunny morning in March at the Deheisheh refugee camp on the outskirts of Bethlehem along the road to Hebron. Surrounded by a sixteen-foot-high steel-wire fence, the camp was hard to miss. Equally hard to miss was the stench from broken sewage pipes.

Home to over 8,500 Palestinians, Deheisheh is unwieldy, the dwellings of its large, extended families, branching out into rooms and niches held together by cement and rusting steel plates. None had running water. The camp dwellers, displaced from their native homes by the violence of the past, talked fondly of their birth places in Palestine. Muhammad Yusuf Suleiman, a man of 55 with a salt-and-pepper beard, who had lived in the camp since 1954, said: "I come from the village of Deir Aban in Ramle district [now in Israel]. I still have land there. I hope to return before I die." His naivete, without the slightest hint of irony, was touching. In his traditional Arab dress, he seemed a man from the distant past.

Not so Milhem Elian, the owner of an almost empty clothes shop in a narrow, winding street. Brought to the camp in 1949 by his parents when he was just a baby, Elian, a tall well-built man, has known no other place. The experience has hardened him. He claimed to be the first camp resident to be imprisoned by the IDF in 1967 soon after Israel occupied the West Bank. Nevertheless, he has managed to marry and raise a family. "We live in a room not large enough for chickens," he said. "Six people in a room, twenty by seventeen feet. But one Jew and his wife have a whole villa to themselves. You can go and see for yourself—at the Efrat settlement." He pointed, vaguely, southward. "These Jews come from abroad, from Russia, from Argentina and America, take our land and live like lords while we are forced to live like animals."

I took Elian's advice and journeyed a few miles south. On the nearby hills overlooking the highway stood a new settlement—gleaming in the afternoon sun, white stone buildings with red-tiled roofs. This was Efrat. Having arrived from an overcrowded, stench-filled refugee camp, I found the air at Efrat particularly bracing. There were only a few people in the smoothly paved streets. Many of the freshly painted houses were indeed empty.

What had the people claiming an almost continuous political-cultural history in the region, since the advent of Islam in the region—captured graphically in the Dome of the Rock, built in AD 691, crowning Jerusalem—done to find themselves refugees in their own land? The question kept nagging me.

Reading my notes of the visits to the Palestinian refugee camps and the Israeli absorption centers for new immigrants, I was struck by the stark contrast between them. The Jewish Agency and the Israeli Ministry of Immigration and Absorption took meticulous care in preparing the immigrants for their *aliya* (ascent) to Israel, and a systematic follow-up ensued. At the absorption centers at East Talpiyot, Jerusalem, the talk was all about getting a job for the newly-arrived immigrant, fitting it into his/her life, and the pros and cons of certain houses and neighborhoods of Jerusalem. When the focus turned to subjects more social than personal, it was Palestinian terror that got mentioned, and the continuing, frustrating elusiveness of a comprehensive peace with the Arabs.

The priorities were altogether different in the Palestinian refugee camps. The camp dwellers talked of joblessness, survival, making ends meet. They reminisced about their home villages now in Israel. They complained of the indignities suffered at the hands of the IDF or the police. They described their imprisonments and detentions during the intifada, and injuries from IDF shootings. They related how their land had been confiscated by the Israeli authorities, a process which continued unabated, peace accord or not. They described the juggernaut of the Jewish settlements ravaging the West Bank, and the unrelenting Judaization of their places and their everyday life.

So what solution do they have in mind? Repossession of their land and realization of the Palestinian statehood. "An independent and sovereign Palestinian state is required at this stage to fulfill our history as a people during the past century," writes Edward W. Said. "The inventory of what we are and what we have done and what has been done to us can never be completely justified, or even embodied, in a state. The converse of this view—that a state can rectify, defend against, and embody the memory of a past history of suffering—has seemed to Palestinians to account for Israeli theorizing, and for Zionist practice in creating a state apart for Jews."[5]

If such a state comes into being some day—against persistent and heavy odds—it would be less than a quarter of British mandate Palestine, and would cover about half of the area allocated to the Arab Palestinians by the 1947 United Nations partition plan.

1

The Walled Heart of Jerusalem

A Battleground

The Old City, the heart of Jerusalem, sacred to half of all human beings on earth, is bounded by magnificent, crenellated walls. Nothing is more bracing than a march along its ramparts on a spring morning, I was told. The thought of circling the religious core of Jerusalem—where Abraham prepared to sacrifice his sons Isaac and Ishmael (called Ishaq and Ismail by Muslims), where the Jews built their two Temples, where Jesus Christ preached his doctrine and died of crucifixion, and where Prophet Muhammad broke his miraculous night journey from Mecca to Heaven—kept me awake overnight.

Predictably, I began at the Damascus Gate—known among Jews as Shaar Shechem, Gate of Shechem/Nablus, and among Arabs as Bab al Amoud, Gate of the Column—the threshold to the Old City, the undisputed leader of the gates, an emblem of authority. I ambled westward, to the Jaffa Gate, and then the Dung Gate, beyond which the city walls were sealed. Islamic minarets rose above church bell-towers, and Israeli flags fluttered in the air. Despite the television aerials sprouting from the roofs—flat, domed, spiked, slanting—I found the Old City's ambience decidedly medieval. After all, the massive stone walls were erected between 1537 and 1540 by Ottoman Sultan Suleiman the Magnificent, preserving approximately the shape that the settlement had in 1187 when Saladin (Salah al Din al Ayubi) recaptured it from the Crusaders, and began reconstructing it. Malik al Muazzam Isa razed those boundaries in 1219, allowing the town to expand. But its sack by the Mongols in 1244 set the clock back again. It was only under the reign of the Mameluke sultans (1250-1517) that the settlement witnessed sustained reconstruction and expansion. By the time the Ottoman Turks seized the Old City it was furnished with mosques, religious schools, pilgrims' hostels, orphanages and hospitals. All along, it embraced the holiest of holies of the major monotheistic faiths: the Dome of the Rock and Al Aqsa (The Distant) Mosque, the Church of the Holy Sepulchre, and the ancient Western Wall.

Viewing the Western Wall from the Dung Gate along the southern rampart, I saw men and women worshipping stones. Or was I imagining? I hazily remembered reading that some ultra-Orthodox Jews regarded revering the stones of the Wall as a form of idol worship. Later when I mentioned this to Rafi, my Hebrew interpreter, he said dismissively: "Crackpots!"

One cloudless day in March, accompanied by Rafi, I visited the Kotel, the popular term for the Western Wall. A supporting wall, running north to south, and fronted by a vast plaza of bright stone, it is enclosed. Access to it is gained strictly through police checkpoints furnished with metal detectors which—unknown to all save the exceptionally curious—are switched off on the Sabbath.

We approached the monument from the Jewish Quarter, and descended many steps of stone on to a rectangular plaza large enough to hold a congregation of over 100,000; it sloped gently eastward. The warm afternoon sun behind us shone on a wall some 300 feet long and 72 feet high, austere, except for occasional prickly capers between its ashlars, swaying in mild wind. This was the Kotel. It was divided unevenly by movable steel-wire fences, a little over three feet high, laid perpendicular to the monument, with women on one side and men on the other. Another temporary barrier running parallel to the Kotel served as a makeshift gate. Here a plump, spectacled man gave us thin cardboard kippas, or skullcaps. "Throughout the day and night, rain or shine, there is somebody present here, facing the wall in prayer," he said.

"There are more people inside the tunnel," Rafi added, pointing to a vaulted entrance into the wall behind the gatekeeper, "praying at all hours."

I found men, young, old, middle-aged, in black coats and hats at prayer. Some gently pressed the Kotel with their palms, an evocative gesture, whispering all the while. Others, gathered in small groups, chanted their devotions from books, swaying back and forth. Some kissed the smooth, weather-beaten stones. I counted twelve courses of massive, shiny stones—chiselled by the masons of King Herod (r. 37–4 BC) and his son Herod Antipas—topped by many layers of stones of much smaller sizes.

The Jews revere the Kotel as the only surviving fragment of their Second Temple, which was destroyed by the Roman Emperor Titus 74 years after King Herod's death. It is actually a retaining wall built to buttress the windy rock, Mount Moriah, on which the Temple stood.

What is so sacred about the Kotel, and why do the Jews come here? Rafi and I buttonholed the devout as they left.

"This is where Abraham offered to sacrifice his son, Isaac; this is where Jacob was on his way," said Joel Beinin, a tall, graceful, thickly-bearded, black-coated man in his middle age. "This is where Solomon built the First Temple; and this is where it was destroyed after 400 years, and the Jews came back from Babylon and built it again," he continued. "Holiness is never far from here. King David had promised that it would never be ruined, and it has never been [for long]."

There are legends about why the Western Wall survived. One version has it that different sections of the Second Temple were raised by different social classes, with the Western Wall of its courtyard erected by the poor. When Titus went on a rampage in Jerusalem, setting it alight, angels blessed the Western Wall with their wings, declaring: "This work of the poor shall be indestructible." And it was. But exactly when the Kotel became sacred is shrouded in mystery. After the destruction of the Second Temple, Jews were permitted to enter Jerusalem only on the anniversary of the sacking of the Second Temple. Since the pilgrims would go up in silence and descend in tears, the Wall acquired the description "wailing." The purpose of the pilgrimage thus became lamenting the razing of the Temples. (Every so often, I was told, you see a Jew crying quietly, re-enacting the grieving of his ancient forebears.) Now, with open, unhindered access to the Wall, the purpose of the pilgrimage has changed drastically.

"Coming here is like going to the king's palace," said Joel Landover, a tall, 52-year-old accountant in a business suit. "When you go inside [the synagogue] under the vaults you are near the holy of the holies, and nearest to God, so you can add more to your prayer and say what you cannot at home."

Accompanied by Rafi, I entered the synagogue in the wide, vaulted tunnel, which is about 330 yards long and deftly lit to produce eternal sunshine, an element that adds to the congeniality of the place. Groups of worshippers, donning black hats or (sometimes) kippas, gathered around tables stacked with prayer books, invoking the Lord; others facing the Wall, sitting in tubular steel chairs with sky-blue seats, immersed themselves in the scriptures; others offered prayers in front of an ark containing a sacred Torah scroll hidden by a black cloth embellished with golden Hebrew lettering.

"Reading prayers from a book concentrates the mind," Rafi explained. "If the Jews are gathered in a group to pray, then the books become like sheets of music." Facing the ancient monument, lined up against another wall, were shelves of prayer books, some of them tattered through over-use. They were classified "Ashkenazi Version" on one side, and on the other "Sephardi Version." Deeper into the tunnel the worshippers, singing psalms, were lost to the world. Which psalm was the most popular, I asked Rafi. "Offhand, I'd say 137." He recited it:

> By the rivers of Babylon, there we sat down, yea, we wept, when we remembered Zion. We hung our harps upon the willows in the midst thereof.
> For there they that carried us away captive required of us a song; and they that wasted us required of us mirth, saying, Sing us one of the songs of Zion.
> How shall we sing the Lord's song in a strange land?
> If I forget thee, O Jerusalem, let my right hand forget her cunning.
> If I do not remember thee, let my tongue cleave to the roof of my mouth;
> if I prefer not Jerusalem above my chief joy.
> Remember, O Lord, the children of Edom in the day of Jerusalem who said, Rase it, rase it, even to the foundation thereof.
> O daughter of Babylon, who art to be destroyed; happy shall he be, that rewardeth thee as thou has served us.
> Happy shall he be, that taketh and dasheth thy little ones against the stones.[1]

Leaving the cavernous synagogue, I felt a change in the very essence of my existence, as if I had touched solid ground after spinning around in outer space.

Rafi and I resumed our conversation with the faithful.

"I pray for half an hour by myself, and don't participate in communal chanting like others," said Micah Watt, a plump, ruddy-cheeked resident of Jerusalem's ultra-Orthodox neighborhood Mea Shearim. "Also I don't make a request. Real ultra-Orthodox don't address notes to God. There is no such tradition in Judaism."

Watt was referring to the practice of supplicants pressing their scribbled prayers on folded paper between the cracks of the Herodian stones, treating the Kotel as God's mailbox. The practice dates back to the eighteenth century. Now the religious authorities have given it a hi-tech touch. They have installed a fax machine, I was told, for the convenience of those faraway believers, at home and abroad, who are too busy or can't afford to make the pilgrimage and do the deed with their own hands. Every few days the caretakers remove the notes, which have survived wind, rain and dew, and bury them ceremoniously in consecrated ground.

There is much ritual in Judaism, and I witnessed it as a wizened old man in a colorful skullcap noticed the kippa-less thatch of Rafi's wavy hair, an unmistakable sign of secularism, and confronted him with his *tefillin*. Rafi submitted. "The idea behind the *tefillin* is to have the prayer boxes touch your arm, representing force, and your head, representing intellect," Rafi said. "You must say at least three prayers like this daily—on waking up, between nine o'clock and noon, and at sunset."

Rafi then described a ceremony at the Wall he remembered with fondness and pride. It was against the backdrop of the Wall that he had paraded on his graduation in the Israel Defense Forces (IDF) in his late teens. Was it before or after the hand-grenade attack at the Western Wall, I wondered. "Before," he replied grimly. "That was awful. The Islamic Jihad terrorists. It was the graduation ceremony of the Givati Brigade, if I remember it right, on the Feast of the Tabernacles, in [October] 1986. The terrorists threw hand grenades at the parade from the Temple Mount... Enough to cause a carnage. About 70 soldiers were injured. And one man died, a spectator. The outrage was unspeakable. The government caught the perpetrators, though. Three of them, I think. Two were brothers—young Palestinians. After that the government tightened up security all around the Wall."

There was a long pause. "There have been happier times, secularly speaking, at the monument," Rafi continued. "Like when Yehudi Menuhin gave a concert here to celebrate the Israeli-Egyptian Peace Treaty in 1979, and my parents and I came here from Tel Aviv to listen."

In short, the Western Wall today is as much a national monument as religious—as is Yad Vashem, the Museum of Holocaust and Heroism, in West Jerusalem. The many Israeli flags pinned to the Wall flaunt the shrine's national significance. "[F]or centuries this [Wall] was the focal point of their mourning the destruction of the Holy Temple, and the exile and dispersion that followed," write Michael Romann and Alex Weingrod, Jewish Israeli academics. "Since Jerusalem's unification under Israeli sovereignty in 1967, the Kotel represents their triumphant return and control over the entire city."[2]

Rafi and I retreated to the Jewish Quarter to revive ourselves with cappuccino and cakes. We sat in wooden chairs on the cobblestones of HaKaraim Street, not far from Batei Machse Square, beyond which ran the eastern boundary of the Jewish Quarter. The Quarter makes up about an eighth of the Old City. Its chronicle is long and checkered.

Though the Second Temple was razed in AD 70, the Jews were expelled from Jerusalem only after their revolt collapsed in AD 135. They were permitted to return in the fifth century. During the Crusades (1099–1187) they were as much victims of Christian zealotry as were Muslims. Saladin's 1187 defeat of the Crusaders, who had ended the Jewish presence in Jerusalem, brought relief to the Jews. But it was only after Malik Isa demolished the walls in 1219, the Mongols sacked the settlement a quarter of a century later, and the Mamelukes ruled, that the Jews got a chance to establish roots in Jerusalem. In the early fifteenth century they began renting property from Muslim landlords. According to al Obeidiah of Bertinoro, who visited Jerusalem in 1488, there were about 200 Jewish families settled in the town, with their own synagogue named after Rabbi Moshe Ben Nahuman, and known in Hebrew by his acronym RMBN, Ramban, who had visited the town in 1267. The Jews now had two religious monuments: the Wall, separated from the nearest houses by a narrow alley in an area called the Maghrebi Quarter, and the Ramban synagogue. (In contrast Christians possessed 118 buildings related to their religion, and Muslims about 480.)

After the Ottoman conquest of Palestine in late 1516, some of the Sephardic Jews who had settled in Turkey after their 1492 expulsion from Spain moved to Jerusalem. This led to the construction of four Sephardi synagogues in the late sixteenth century. By the early nineteenth century the population of Jerusalem was nearly 8,000, about a quarter of whom were Jews. Following the 1831 rebellion by their Egyptian Governor, Muhammad Ali, the Ottomans imposed direct rule over Jerusalem and its environs. The improved security caused an increase in the local population. The Ottomans granted equal rights to non-Muslims, and appointed them to the local municipal council. The first reliable demographic figures became available after Sir Moses Montefiore of London conducted a census in 1839. It documented 3,000 Jews, with varied backgrounds, among a total of some 10,000 residents. By the mid-nineteenth century there were over a score of synagogues in the Jewish Quarter.

Once houses were built for Jews outside the ramparts in the New Town, from 1860 onward, the number of Jews in the overcrowded, unsanitary Old City declined. A combined census of the Old and New Towns in 1875 showed 10,000 Jews out of a total population of 20,000. Due to the Jewish immigration inspired and encouraged by the Zionist Organization (later World Zionist Organization), an international body founded in 1897, the number of Jews rose sharply. In 1905, two-thirds of the total population of 60,000 was Jewish, with most of the Jews residing outside the historic, walled settlement. When the British captured Jerusalem during World War I, there were 14,000 Jews living inside the Old City. The Western Wall was in the Maghrebi Quarter, which was inhabited by Arabs of North African descent, some of whom had lived there since Saladin's time.

During the British mandate, which began in 1922 and lasted 26 years, relations between Jews and Arabs soured. Arab-Jewish rioting broke out in 1921, 1926 and 1929, resulting from the opposition of the native Arabs to the escalating Jewish immigration under the British auspices. The number of Jews in the Old City shrank to 5,600. It declined further after the eruption of the Arab Revolt in 1936, which continued for three years and led the British to move the Jews out of non-Jewish Quarters for their own safety. The Jews either kept their real estate empty or leased it to Arabs, and moved either to the Old City or to the Jewish neighborhoods of the New Town.

Long before the United Nations General Assembly adopted a resolution partitioning Palestine into Arab and Jewish sectors in November 1947, Jerusalem was virtually split into two parts—the Arab East and the Jewish West—with their inhabitants clashing frequently. By the time the British left in May 1948, there were only 1,700 Jews in the Jewish Quarter of the Old City, and another 300 elsewhere in Arab East Jerusalem.

During the 1948 Arab-Israeli War, fighting erupted in the Old City. The inhabitants of the Jewish Quarter confronted the Jordanian army, and suffered 86 deaths and much damage to private and public property, including synagogues and yeshivas. Finally some 2,000 unarmed Jews gathered at the four Sephardi synagogues to surrender to the Jordanian army, and were later transferred to Israel. (On the other side, some 20,000 Arabs fled Jewish West Jerusalem, which was controlled by Israel.) The Arab residents of the Old City sacked the Jewish Quarter; and the victorious Jordanian army demolished the synagogues and yeshivas based in the area.

The Old City and Arab East Jerusalem came under Jordanian control. Though Jordan's truce agreement with Israel, enforced in April 1949, required it to give Jews access to the Western Wall, it did not do so. Equally, it barred Israeli Arabs, whether Muslim or Christian, from visiting their holy places in the Old City of Jerusalem or Bethlehem.

On the eve of the June 1967 Arab-Israeli war, the population of East Jerusalem was over 60,000. On June 7, the third day of the war, the Israelis captured the Old City. General Moshe Dayan, the Israeli Defense Minister, instantly recognizable by his black eye-patch, was among the first Jews to pray at the Western Wall. After prayers he inserted a petition beseeching God: "Let peace reign in Israel." He then declared: "We have come back to our holiest of holy places, never to be parted from it again."[3]

After sunset on Saturday, June 10, while the war was still in progress, according to Meron Benvensiti, an Israeli historian and former deputy mayor of Jerusalem, the residents of the Maghrebi Quarter were given three hours to evacuate their buildings adjacent to the Western Wall. "Bulldozers... began to topple the one- and two-story houses by floodlight," writes Benvensiti. "By morning... more than one acre had been cleared in front of the Western Wall... It was then decided to demolish the entire Maghrebi Quarter [consisting of 80 houses, shops and a plastic factory, and 619 residents]."[4] The levelled ground was later turned into a plaza.

On June 27, a little over a fortnight after the end of the Six Day War, Israel's parliament, the Knesset, expanded East Jerusalem from 2.5 square miles to more than 28 square miles and extended Israeli laws to it as part of the enlarged municipality of Jerusalem. Due to the flight of about 30 percent of the 60,000 residents of Arab East Jerusalem during and after the war, its population declined to 44,000. But the addition of the huge adjoining area raised the total population of "Greater East Jerusalem" to 71,000, as recorded by an Israeli census in September 1967. According to the new Israeli law, all of the new East Jerusalemites became "permanent residents" of Israel, and received Israeli identity cards, which entitled them to social security and healthcare benefits and voting rights in municipal elections.

It also gave them the option of abandoning their current Jordanian citizenship for an Israeli one. With few exceptions, they ignored the offer.

In April 1968, the government set up a public company to revive and resettle the quarter. Its activities covered an area larger than the old Jewish Quarter, and was, in the words of Amos Elon, "a defiant assertion of a presence even more than a restoration of what had been lost."[5] It meant the expropriation of the land and houses of 5,500 Palestinians.[6]

The new real estate was sold exclusively to Jews. Non-Jews could not buy, or even rent, property in the enlarged Jewish Quarter. Palestinians challenged the official decision in 1968 and again in 1974: first by challenging their eviction from the homes they had occupied in the old Jewish Quarter since 1948, or even earlier; and then by demanding the right to buy property in the new Quarter. Both times the Israeli High Court of Justice ruled against them.

In each instance, it was Muhammad Burqan who brought the case before the court. He had been evicted from his family home in the pre-1948 Jewish Quarter in the mass expulsion of 1968, and lost an appeal then. In 1974, when the government's holding company put Burqan's renovated house up for sale he tried to buy it back. But he was barred. The ban was sustained by the High Court. Advancing a broad politico-historical argument, the court stated that since there had "always" been a distinctive Jewish Quarter in the Old City, there should once again be such a neighborhood. As the "non-Jews" had three other quarters (Armenian, Christian and Muslim) to themselves, it concluded, the government could keep the Jewish Quarter free of non-Jews.[7] The residents of the new Jewish Quarter were so zealous about keeping it pure that when the remains of a twelfth-century church were found in the midst of their district in the mid-1970s, some of them vandalized the plaque on the partially restored site, forcing the authorities to replace the old sign, "St. Mary of the Germans," with "archaeological garden."[8]

It is worth noting that the legal restrictions on non-Jews regarding owning or renting real estate in the Jewish Quarter do not apply to Jews buying or renting property in the non-Jewish quarters either inside the Old City or outside.

The restored Jewish Quarter is starkly different from the others. Its quiet, children-free streets, newly paved and lighted, its arched passageways, and its houses made of new stone, give it an appearance of an expensive, gentrified district, tarted up with art galleries, souvenir shops, studios and craft boutiques. Its public places, dominated by new or restored synagogues and yeshivas of imposing proportions, rob the district of the intimacy, warmth and touch of chaos that are the hallmarks of the rest of the Old City.

The Batei Machse Square, an open space signposted by a Greek column is in the middle of the Jewish Quarter. The sun was setting behind the ramparts of the Old City as the *muezzeins* called the faithful to prayer and a peal of church bells sonorously stirred the calm air. Near the far wall a couple of bearded old Jewish men sat on benches, near an engraving on the wall:

> Thus saith Lord of Hosts; There shall yet old man and old women dwell in the
> streets of Jerusalem, and every man with his staff in his hand for every age.
> And the streets of the city shall be full of boys and girls playing...
> —Zechariah 8:4-5.

Today an estimated 2,000–2,500 Jews live in the Jewish Quarter. Some apartments are owned by Jewish Americans, who only occupy them for part of the year. There are seven yeshivas, some of whose students live in the quarter. Most of the permanent residents are middle-class professionals, almost invariably practicing Orthodox or ultra-Orthodox. At the corner of the Batei Machse Square and HaMekubalim Street, a large leaflet, stuck between notices for flat-sharing, herbal medicine and Indian food, neatly summed up the ambience of the quarter:

The Time for Your Redemption has Arrived!
What is the Messianic Era?
What does "MASHIAIH" mean?
Why is Now an "Era of Miracles"? Consider
* The Unforseen Collapse of the Iron Curtain & its Satellite regimes
* Ingathering of 100s of thousands of suppressed and stricken exiles, converg-
ing in the Holy Land from undreamed of directions
* In the Persian Gulf... lightning-quick victory and the Divine Protection of
Israel.
What can I do?
Listen to the Lubanvitcher Rabbi, Rabbi Menach M. Schneerson, who has
appealed to every individual.

Since there are no legal restrictions on Jews to buy or rent property in the non-Jewish quarters, many live in the Old City outside the Jewish Quarter. Invariably, they are ultra-nationalist, determined to "redeem" all of the Old City from its Christian and Muslim inhabitants. Since 1978, often working in covert collusion with the Israeli government, they have made inroads into the Muslim and Christian Quarters. Their argument is that Jews can, and should, live anywhere in united Jerusalem. But they vehemently oppose giving Muslim or Christian Arabs the same right.

Jewish Penetration of Non-Jewish Quarters

By 1990, five Jewish groups were actively involved in the process of "redemption" of non-Jewish real estate in the Old City: Atara Le Yoshna, a consortium of Jewish property companies closely linked with the Israeli Custodian of Absentee Property and the Israel Land Administration; Atreet Cohanim Yeshiva, initially associated with Atara Le Yoshna; the Ne'emanei Har HaBeit, popularly known as Temple Mount Faithful; Shuvia Banin Yeshiva; and Rabbi Israel Ariel's Temple Institute. Of these Atreet Cohanim emerged as the most active and controversial.

In December 1978, on the eve of the Jewish festival of Hanuchha, eight young Orthodox Jews announced that they had established Atreet Cohanim Yeshiva in the Muslim Quarter to study the ancient priestly texts in anticipation of the imminent coming of the Messiah and the rebuilding of the Second Temple at the original site, on Mount Moriah. They were led by Matityahu HaCohen Dan, a bearded, extrovert Orthodox Jew, who had served in the IDF. This took place only weeks after prime minister Menachem Begin signed the Camp David Accords with Egyptian President Anwar Sadat at the behest of the United States, an event that divided Israel's right-wing, with the ultra-nationalists denouncing it as a sell-out.

The Atreet Cohanim Yeshiva had political ambitions beyond its scholarly work. Allied with Ariel Sharon, the ultra-nationalist Likud leader, Dan aimed to create a Jewish presence around the Haram al Sharif, or Noble Sanctuary, the site of the Dome of the Rock and Al Aqsa Mosque, as a step towards raising Jewish efforts to build the Third Temple where the Dome of the Rock had stood since the late seventh century. "Of course we want to take the place of the Muslims on the [Temple] Mount and clear away their mosque," wrote Menachem Bar Shalom, Atreet Cohanim's public relations director, to a supporter in Sarasota, Florida, in March 1986.[9]

Atreet Cohanim was guided by the ideas of Rabbi Avraham Yitzhak HaCohen Kook, who founded a yeshiva in Jerusalem in 1921 to provide rabbis for the Yishuv (the Jewish immigrant community in Palestine). Kook's ideology rejected both the secular Zionist pioneers' commitment to creating a nation of Jews in Palestine through human endeavor, and the ultra-Orthodox belief in the role of divine intervention in the reestablishing of the Jewish state of Israel. Instead, he asserted the concept of Eretz Israel as an integral part of Judaism along with the cardinal tenets of God, the Torah, and the redemption of the Jews. After his death in 1935, his son reaffirmed the belief that since Eretz Israel was given to the Jews by God they must secure it and defend it by any means necessary.

Dan set up a subsidiary of the Atreet Cohanim, called the Jerusalem Reclamation Project (JRP), in the early 1980s, with the objective of "redeeming" all of the nearly 1,100 properties in the Muslim Quarter, which itself occupies almost half of the Old City.

During the next decade, the JRP acquired 123 properties for an estimated $18 million. The funding was provided by rich Jewish militants living in North America who responded to open appeals from Israel's chief Ashkenazi rabbi, and covert appeals by the Housing Ministry of Israel from at least 1986 onward.[10]

Initially the JRP conducted its dealings in low key. Later they combined force with subterfuge. "Given a foothold in an area or even a courtyard, expansion into adjoining property can begin," wrote Graham McNeill, a British researcher. "The most typical method used is to force an entry to "create facts on the ground" and then to take legal course to prove previous Jewish ownership or occupancy—as was the case with... the Rsass Building in Aqabat Khalidieh, and the Diskin Orphanage and Kindergarten in Aqabat Saraya. Such cases, complicated by confusion over previous tenants, legality of leases and subleases as well as loss of documents, can and do run for years, incurring massive legal costs."[11] Emboldened by its successes, the JRP moved into the Christian Quarter, with the Atreet Cohanim activists occupying St. John's Hospice in the Christian Quarter on the eve of Easter in 1990. This set alarm bells ringing in the Christian circles, worldwide.

By then the JRP's holdings included a museum, several yeshivas and synagogues, dormitories for yeshiva students and more than 50 apartments.

Arab residents, Muslim and Christian, detected a pattern in the acquisitions of the JRP and the Atara Le Yoshna, which concentrated on Al Wad Street—the main artery of the Muslim Quarter, and Chain Gate Street near the Western Wall and leading to Mount Moriah. "Both sides of Al Wad Street are being slowly taken over by the Jews, with the house of Ariel Sharon [guarded at all times by Israeli soldiers] forming a strategic location," said George Hintlian, an Arab Christian resident of the Armenian Quarter.[12]

It was the Sharon affair in October 1987 which alerted the Arab Palestinians inside the Old City and outside. After the JRP announced that it had "rented" its recently acquired large, multi-story house—strategically spanning Al Wad Street—in the Muslim Quarter to Sharon, then Minister of Trade and Industry, Sharon occupied the top floor and held a much-publicized house-warming party, attended by 700 prominent Israelis, including prime minister Yitzhak Shamir. He draped the house with a gigantic Israeli flag, and installed a huge menorah on the roof. The incensed Palestinians rioted, but in vain. The government responded by placing a permanent military guard on the premises. It was one of the factors that stoked the Palestinian anger that would erupt into the intifada two months later.

One sunny afternoon Rafi and I stopped under the archway formed by Sharon's house. Rafi began reading the graffiti written on the stone walls by bored IDF guards: "Let the green beret [the border police under IDF command] in the Old City, Judea and Samaria, and they will fix the intifada" and so on. As Rafi translated the graffiti to me, a couple of IDF soldiers eyed him from a distance, then slowly walked over. Looking very Jewish, with fashionably permed hair, unmistakably Israeli clothing (jeans and a check shirt under a loose, mauve-colored sweater), Rafi chatted with them, and discovered that Sharon only slept there a few nights a month. The cost of this exercise to the Israeli tax-payer, I discovered later, was put at $250,000 to $500,000 a year.

Rafi and I walked down Al Wad Street and faced a sign: "Yeshivath Torah Hagin (founded 1886) Rabbi Isaac Winograd/Igud Lohamey Yeriteh Synagogue"— at the site of an old yeshiva. We entered a battered door, passed a rickety bicycle, and went upstairs. On the first floor were two houses that seemed Arab, and to the left was a closed door which, once opened, led to a stairs and the balcony of the yeshiva. As we reached the top of the steps, I saw a young student packing an Uzi collapsible submachine gun under his clothes as he prepared to go down.

We were soon chatting in fluent English with the principal of the yeshiva, Rabbi Shlomo Haim Aviner across a long, formica table in a makeshift dining hall. A thin-faced man of 52, with a long beard and gray, bespectacled eyes and a cream-colored skullcap, Aviner was born in Lyons, France. He graduated in mathematics and nuclear physics and then studied electronics before coming to Israel in 1966. "After arriving... I felt that moral edification was important," he said. "I needed spiritual science." He worked at a kibbutz, fought in the 1973 Arab-Israeli War, and then enrolled at Rabbi Kook's yeshiva. After graduation he decided to live on a Jewish settlement in the occupied (Syrian) Golan Heights, where he became a rabbi.

An urbane, soft-spoken man, he enchanted me with a simple, humanistic statement: "It takes five years to become a teacher, ten to become a rabbi, fifteen to become a judge, and twenty to become a Jew," he said. "But it takes 25 years to become a human being."

He was well versed on the origins of his yeshiva and the premises it occupied. "The original Torah Hagin Yeshiva was established [in 1886] after the pogroms in Russia. After the pogrom here in 1929 it was closed down. All the Jews were concentrated in the Jewish Quarter by the British mandate authorities in 1936. Following the 1967 War the Jewish presence was recreated in this [Muslim] quarter. At our yeshiva we follow the ideology of Rabbi Zvi Yehuda Kook, who died in 1982." (In 1982, as part of their extra-curricular activities, the students started tunnelling under Mount Moriah, hoping to find a chamber where King Solomon was supposed to have stored several golden vessels used for rituals at the First Temple. They were detected by the Arabs guarding the Mount, who raised the alarm. Rioting followed. The authorities decided to seal the tunnel.)

"After 1967 we only had a synagogue here, and in 1981 we started a yeshiva. When we restarted the yeshiva, there was a negative response from the Arab neighbors. But now we have good relations with them." The image of one of his students packing a submachine gun under his clothes whizzed through my mind.

"All yeshivas were destroyed after the [1948] War of Independence," Aviner continued. "After the War our neighbor was an Arab. He closed down the yeshiva and stored the holy books in a back room. When the Jordanian soldiers ransacked the place, he kept quiet about the scriptures. This Arab became the guardian of our yeshiva. After the 1967 War he took the key of his back room to the military governor of Jerusalem. When they opened it there were 'twenty centimeters' of dust on the books. He saved all the books and no damage was done."

"What was the name of this Arab?" I asked.

Aviner looked puzzled for a moment, then waved his hand, dismissively: "I don't know." He paused. "You can ask his wife downstairs."

I wondered quietly if Aviner would pass his own "human being" test.

After leaving Aviner, Rafi and I knocked on the door of the "good Arab," who, by Aviner's account, lived just a floor below. A plump, middle-aged Palestinian woman invited us in. It transpired that the name of the "good Arab" was Abu Wahid al Bikri al Lakhim, that he had died in 1990, and that his wife, too, had passed away soon after. Our enquiry was over within a few minutes. Yet Aviner, who had crossed the Arab's threshold twice daily for thirteen years, except on the Sabbath and holidays, had never bothered to find out his name, or noticed that his wife, too, had died. (According to David K. Shipler, the Jerusalem bureau chief of *The New York Times* from 1979 to 1984, al Lakhim had stored some 20,000 books, including Hebrew commentaries on the Talmud, published in Warsaw in the 1820s, and the Holy Ark.)[13]

Had I read what Aviner told the writer, Robert Friedman, on an earlier occasion, I would have asked more questions. "In Aviner's view, Palestine was a barren and empty land until the Jews returned," writes Friedman.

"The Arabs are squatters," Aviner told me. "I don't know who gave them authorization to live on Jewish land. All mankind knows this is our land. Most Arabs came here recently... But even if some Arabs have been here for some 2,000 years, is there a statute of limitations that gives a thief the right to his plunder?... We must settle the whole Land of Israel, and over all of it establish our rule," Aviner said. "In the words of Nahumanides [son of Rabbi Moshe Ben Nahuman, who visited Jerusalem in 1267]: 'Do not abandon the land to another nation.' If that is possible by peaceful means, wonderful, and if not, we are commanded to make war to accomplish it."[14]

Friedman also describes Aviner's belief " that a Jewish communal presence in St. John's Hospice... could be the springboard for a more substantial Jewish presence in the Christian Quarter."

After a 1989 court appeal left the Christian Quarter building's title disputed between the Greek Orthodox Church and a former owner, a group of about 150 armed Atreet Cohanim Yeshiva affiliates, calling itself "No'et David," planned to take over the hospice on the eve of the next Passover, which happened to coincide with the Christian Holy Week. Arriving at the premises armed, the Jewish settlers began throwing into the street not only furniture but also the smashed remnants of crucifixes and religious paintings. They then covered the Byzantine cross on the front of the building with a wooden plank and painted a blue Star of David on it. They renamed the hospice No'et David (David's Homestead).

The next day, Thursday, following the tradition of Jesus bathing the feet of the Twelve Disciples, the 78-year-old Greek Orthodox Patriarch, dressed in his official gold robe and crown, washed the feet of his priests, and blessed the faithful by dipping a bouquet of flowers in the dirty water and sprinkling them with it. Then, instead of leading the congregation to the Greek Orthodox monastery, as was the custom, the Patriarch headed for St. John's Hospice, which was guarded by scores of armed Israeli border police who had been seen on the previous day helping the Jewish settlers move in. There the Patriarch and his flock joined the protesting Arabs who were shouting pro-PLO slogans. A young, black-robed Greek Orthodox cleric, raised shoulder-high by the demonstrators, pulled down the plaque bearing the Star of David. Without warning, the police fired tear gas. In the resulting stampede, many clergymen, including the Patriarch, were knocked down and trampled. Within minutes the news flashed across the globe.

Consequently, the protest that ensued was not only local and national but also international. The next day, all churches in Israel and the Occupied Territories shut their doors and protested by ringing funeral peals. It was unprecedented for the Church of the Holy Sepulcher to close down, something its caretakers had never done since the Crusaders' defeat in 1187. John Cardinal O'Connor in New York portrayed the St. John's Hospice take-over as part of a plot to buy up Christian property in the Holy Land. During the controversy that simmered on for several months, David Levy, the Housing Minister, revealed that his ministry had secretly paid $1.8 million to Himnutta Company, a subsidiary of the Jewish National Fund, which owned all land in Israel, for transfer to SBC, a front company, to help it buy the sublease of the hospice for $3.5 million.[15]

Back in court, the Greek Orthodox Church prevailed, and the court decreed that the settlers must leave the hospice. However, it allowed twenty maintenance and security employees to stay on pending further litigation. In reality, they turned out to be none other than the members of the original "No'et David" group affiliated to the Atreet Cohanim Yeshiva. They brought in their families stealthily and settled down.

Nearly five years later I managed to visit the place, which was discreetly guarded from a window on the top story by a small group of young armed men equipped with mobile phones and walkie-talkies. Once the heavily locked door had been opened by the guards from the inside, we went past strollers and bicycles parked on the ground floor, then up the stairs. Two young women were looking after children whose parents had apparently gone to work or study at the local yeshivas. There were cooking facilities. The evidence I saw did not support the official claim that only twenty professional security men and maintenance workers lived there.

Most probably, the residents were in daily touch with the Atreet Cohanim Yeshiva whose registered office in Chain Gate Street was located behind a green, steel-plated door in the modern-looking Ma'aravim Complex of several apartments, a synagogue, and another yeshiva. We were greeted by three young security guards, one wearing a white baseball cap and standing with his back to the door, facing another colleague who was equipped with a mobile phone and an Uzi submachine gun, and a third sitting at a desk turning the pages of a book in Arabic.

"Could we talk to an official of the Atreet Cohanim Yeshiva?" Rafi asked.

"It is part of our security contract that journalists are not to be allowed," replied the guard wearing a baseball cap.

Outside, across the narrow cobblestone Chain Gate Street, was the Yeshiva Shuvia Banin. It belongs to the ultra-Orthodox sect of Bratsilvic, founded in 1815 by Rabbi Nahuman of Bratslav, Ukraine. Unlike other ultra-Orthodox sects its adherents do not have a living chief rabbi. Instead they follow the founder by reading and interpreting his copious volumes.

"We learn our books all the time," said Tsafair Arnon—fat, bearded, black-coated, looking older than his 35 years. "We start our lessons at two A.M." Why? "Because our founder said that midnight is the Holy Hour and early morning is the time we are nearest to God. We get up around midnight. Then we walk through the Muslim Quarter, in groups, not alone, to reach our yeshiva. We are used to it. This is our home even though there is danger."

How did it come to be your home?

"For the last 100 years Jews have lived here in this [Muslim] Quarter. About 60 years ago this was an Orthodox school. Many Jews from Europe helped with money. The students and teachers left after the 1929 riots, but some of them returned. Before 1948 Arabs and Jews lived door to door. But after the 1948 War all the Jews left. But this place [in the Muslim Quarter] was not occupied. In 1967 it was still empty. There were times of tension here like when somebody tried to burn down the Al Aqsa Mosque in 1969. The Jews came to this building in 1981 when it was used by members of the Gush Emunim [Bloc of Faithful]. Some of them slept here.

The whole place was in ruins. We [Bratsilvic] came here in 1982. The Arabs did not want us to move in." Besides the historic animosity between Arabs and Jews, I learned later, the Bratsilvic climbed up to the roof of their yeshiva to sing religious incantations loudly and collectively in the middle of the night.

"We used to come here on foot from Mea Shearim [where 34,000 Bratsilvic families have their central synagogue]," Arnon continued. "Arabs used to kick us, beat us. In 1984 one young yeshiva student, Eli Umedi, was murdered. The situation got tense. Then we took 'revenge action.'" Here he broke into a knowing smile. Did they beat up Arabs with lead pipes and chains? Arnon was non-committal, still smiling. "Anyway, then the Arabs relaxed. Later Sharon set up his house on Al Wad Street, and was given a military guard. That helped."

Actually the violence ceased only after another killing of a Jewish settler, Elhanoun Aron Atalai, a student of Atreet Cohanim Yeshiva, in the Muslim Quarter in 1991 in the midst of the intifada. Israeli authorities followed with the instant confiscation of Muslim property nearby, and severe retaliatory measures against the local Palestinians. Later I saw the memorial to Atalai near a Palestinian cafeteria, inscribed thus:

> Here was murdered
> Elhanoun Aron Atalai
> by the wretched people
> on the night of 14 Adar Tashima (1991)
> "In his blood we will live & Jerusalem we will build
> Remember what the Amaleks [biblical enemy of Israelites] did to you."

Parallel to this reality on the ground exists another—on the roofs of the Muslim Quarter. Jaafar (pseudonym), a plump, middle-aged, well-read Palestinian, introduced me to it one drizzling afternoon. We went up the steps of a wrought-iron staircase at the end of Suq al Huzor/Habad Street. On the flat roofs of the shops and houses were scattered several steel barriers, weather-beaten, stamped POLICE in English and Hebrew. I saw a watch-tower manned by a young guard armed with a machine gun and a mobile phone. A bearded, bespectacled man in a black coat with a mobile phone in hand, and a woman in a blouse and skirt, wearing a beret, walked slowly by. "They have mobile phones and walkie-talkies," Jaafar whispered.

Who are "they"? "The Jewish settlers," came the reply. "There were three fatal stabbings of Jews between 1982 and 1991. But that did not stop the settlers or the government from penetrating the Muslim or Christian Quarters. The question for them was: how to make secure the movement of Jewish settlers in the non-Jewish quarters. The answer: stop using the streets and bazaars to get around." So were there now well-trodden "roofways" being used by the Jews in the non-Jewish quarters? "You see one in front of you. Here. Before a Jew leaves his house he phones and checks with the guard over there, telling him his destination, and the guard checks at the other end. And so on."

Jaafar then took me to a few Palestinian homes where the residents found themselves living cheek by jowl with the newly arrived Jewish settler families. In one place, the Palestinians, sharing a common entrance that opened into a small courtyard, claimed that their upstairs Jewish neighbors pelted them with life-threatening debris. I looked up. The protective steel-wire net they had installed above the courtyard was littered with metal rods, pipes, and heavy stones.

A stickler with words, and fluent in Arabic, Hebrew and English, Jaafar took childlike delight in pointing out the inconsistencies in the names of streets and bazaars. Behind a rainstorm drainpipe by a bakery, he read aloud David Street in Hebrew and English in black letters against a white marble background, and Suq Alloon (Alloon Market) in Arabic. Since David Street is a main shopping artery, popular with Western tourists, it is important to advertise that name in English, leaving its original title intact only in Arabic, a language Israel views as of little consequence to foreign pilgrims and tourists.

In David Street/Suq Alloon we passed a sturdy, middle-aged Palestinian with a hang-dog expression, selling rolls of film. "An informer," Jaafar whispered. We were soon at the Omar ibn al Khattab Square that leads to the Jaffa Gate. To the left was a large, forbidding Ottoman stone structure with incredibly thick walls, now the local headquarters of the Israeli civil and border police. Across its electronically controlled steel-bar barrier there was a restaurant undergoing renovation. "Its owner is an Israeli informer," Jaafar said matter-of-factly.

We retraced our path and continued westward, entering Chain Gate Street. As we proceeded to the Islamic shrine, I recognized the Shuvia Banin Yeshiva, the green steel door of the Ma'aravim Complex, and the Young Israeli Synagogue, written in blue letters in English. Jaafar pointed out that these premises faced the Western Wall Plaza. We reached the end of the street, and faced the twin, green gates standing in a vaulted veranda. Jaafar turned me sideways, and translated a large sign in Hebrew fixed to the mosaic lintel of a distinguished early-fourteenth-century building: "The Western Wall Look-Out of the IDF."

"The building has its own gate opening into the Haram," said Jaafar. "That gives the IDF free access to the whole esplanade. Under the Jordanians it was a school. During the British mandate it was the house of Haajj Muhammad Amin Husseini, head of the Supreme Muslim Council." Now I was able to place the machine-gun-bearing Israeli soldier poised on a roof next to the Western Wall I had noticed on the day I interviewed the pilgrims to the Wall. He had climbed up there from here, a historic Islamic school.

The Noble Sanctuary/Temple Mount

Jaafar and I entered the open courtyard of the Haram al Sharif where the octagonal Dome of the Rock stood, majestic, on a large stone platform, held up by the buttressing Herodian walls. The golden cupola of the Dome of the Rock shone brilliantly in the afternoon sun, as it had for more than thirteen centuries. Surrounded by freestanding archways on all four sides, the Dome of the Rock struck me as a perfectly harmonious blending of shape and color. The glazed Persian tiles covering the outside walls were a sumptuous blend of blue, lapis lazuli, cobalt, emerald, green, ochre and mauve, a feast to the eye, assembled to create abstract, yet wondrous, mosaics. Verses from the Quran in graceful Arabic calligraphy embellished the upper edge of the octagon.

Legend has it that its builder, Caliph Abdul Malik ibn Marwan, wished to raise the newly emerged Islamic faith to the same level as its forerunners, Judaism and Christianity, and outdo the already existing Church of the Holy Sepulcher, then called the Church of Resurrection. Today the Dome is by far the most glaring landmark in Jerusalem, its most insistent and stunning image. Though an indisputably Islamic shrine, it covers the Foundation stone of the Jews, equally revered by Muslims, and is constructed in the Christian-Byzantine style of the late seventh century, most likely on the area where the Second Temple of the Jews had stood. It thus represents a unique synthesis of the major monotheistic creeds.[16]

If the Dome of the Rock is a diamond, sharp, concentrated, and brilliant, then the Al Aqsa Mosque is like a necklace—long, laid-out—built to accommodate more than 5,000 worshippers. Situated to the south of the Dome, on the edge of the vast esplanade, the Al Aqsa looks rather plain, as it faces the Dome from across a medieval fountain, a string of tall, dark green cypresses, and a flight of well-trodden steps to the terrace. Originally constructed in AD 715 by Caliph al Walid ibn Abdul Malik as the mosque for the Haram al Sharif (the Dome of the Rock is a shrine, not a mosque where sermons are preached after the Friday prayer), it has been destroyed and reconstructed several times.

Inside, Al Aqsa is divided by seven lines of columns, pillars of stone and marble, adorned with stylized capitals of various origins, many of them Christian, the legacy of the period when the Crusaders (in the late eleventh century) converted the premises into a church. Compared to the Dome of the Rock, Al Aqsa is spartan, an impression unshaken by its luxurious carpets, glittering chandeliers, gold and blue carved ceiling, and the gold, green, and blue mosaic work of the dome dating back to Saladin in 1189. Saladin's carved wooden pulpit, installed there in October 1187 after his victory over the Crusaders, was burned down on August 21, 1969. The Israeli authorities arrested a young Australian, Michael Dennis Rohan, a member of the Christian fundamentalist Church of God, and he reportedly confessed to the crime. The attack was seen throughout the Arab and Muslim world as a Zionist attempt to destroy the Islamic monuments in Jerusalem as part of a plan to destroy Islam. It led to an international outcry among Muslims. King Faisal of Saudi Arabia convened a meeting of the heads of 29 Muslim-majority countries, which led to the founding of the Islamic Conference Organization (ICO), the first international body of Muslim states.

Pinpricks continue, Jaafar told me. Indeed as we emerged from the Al Aqsa Mosque, we saw a commotion: Israeli police, Arab guards, photographers, and a small group of men being taken away. "Crazy fanatics," said Jaafar. Who? "The men they've arrested. Nutcases, the disciples of Yehuda Etzion, who insist on praying on the Haram al Sharif," came the swift reply. "That's the starting point for reclaiming the Haram for the Jews, and building the Third Temple there." Wasn't the Haram al Sharif forbidden to the Jews, with government notices saying so at the gates to the Mount? Jaafar smiled a cynical smile. "Did you see any notices?" he asked. Nothing in English, but what about Hebrew? "Nothing in Hebrew either, believe me," he replied. There was a strong reason behind the ban, wasn't there? Okay, said Jaafar, here goes: "The inner sanctum of the Jewish Temple is to be entered by the High Priest only, and that also only on Passover. Since nobody knows where exactly that inner sanctum was on the Mount Moriah, Jews are forbidden to walk on it lest they should by mistake walk on that particular spot. Hence all of the Mount is out of bounds to Jews." There was a pause. "That makes all IDF soldiers non-Jews," Jaafar said, still smiling. How? "Because all IDF recruits are brought here as part of their training, to familiarize them with every bit of Israel. And this—" here he stamped the hallowed ground—"is Eretz Israel."

This was exactly the line of Yehuda Etzion who was arrested on the Mount on April 11, 1995, I discovered later. His picture showed him to be a bespectacled, balding, clean-shaven man, dressed in jeans and a flannel shirt. Born in 1951 in Israel, Etzion grew up in an ultra-nationalist household. His father, Abraham Mintz, was a member of Lehi, a militant Zionist organization, which turned to terrorism in the 1940s. After graduating from a yeshiva attached to the Bnei Akiva, the youth section of the National Religious Party (NRP), he became a founder of the Gush Emunim, which led the Jewish settler movement in the Occupied Territories. From Elon Moreh, a Jewish settlement near Nablus, he organized the establishment of Ofra settlement near Al Bireh in 1976, which became the operational headquarters of the Gush Emunim. He was a member of the Gush secretariat until 1978.

The trigger for Etzion, like the Atreet Cohanim Yeshiva, was prime minister Menachem Begin's accord in September 1978 to vacate Egypt's Sinai Peninsula in exchange for a peace treaty with Cairo. They all believed in the Eretz Israel which lay between "Two Rivers [the Nile and the Euphrates]." Rejecting the ideology of the NRP, which accepted the State of Israel as a step towards the final redemption of the Jewish people, Etzion argued that since the leaders of the State of Israel, guided by secular democratic principles, had committed a series of blunders, it was perfectly legitimate to sketch out the full scenario of redemption now. It would include the Kingdom of Israel, a priestly kingdom based on the Temple Mount, and would encompass all the land between the Nile and the Euphrates. It was the duty of true believers to struggle to achieve this aim, he reasoned. In his scenario Etzion assigned a central role to the Temple Mount. The Jews' redemption had stopped because their enemy, the Arabs, possessed the Temple Mount, he argued. Only by retaking the Mount could the Jews restart the stalled process of redemption. As the Israeli government had failed to do so, it was incumbent upon true believers to act.[17]

Soon after the Egyptian-Israeli peace treaty went into effect in March 1979 Etzion met Menachem Livni, an explosives expert, who lived in the Jewish settlement of Kiryat Arba next to Hebron, and was close to the ultra-nationalist Rabbi Moshe Levinger. Livni agreed with the respected ideologue Yeshua Ben Shoshan, that the existence of the "Abomination" (his term for the Dome of the Rock) was "the basis of the hold of Ishmael [the Arabs] in Eretz Israel."[18] Livni believed that the Dome symbolized the powerlessness of the Jews.

In early 1980 Etzion and Livni convened a meeting in Kiryat Arba. Etzion convinced the gathering that demolishing the Islamic monument on the Temple Mount would unfreeze the process of redemption. In more practical terms, he foresaw the demolition of the Dome of the Rock triggering an apocalyptic conflagration between Israel and its Arab enemies which, he confidently forecast, would result in the ignominious defeat of the Arabs, the expulsion of the Palestinian Arabs from Judea and Samaria, and the reconstruction of the Third Temple—a prelude to the rise of the sacred Kingdom of Israel. Others, while committed to reviving the process of redemption, did not share Etzion's overly optimistic scenario regarding the consequent war. In the end the consensus was that work could begin immediately on fleshing out the details of an attack on the Dome of the Rock, with the final decision to be left for later.

Livni planned a ground attack. He spent two years devising a plan. Starting with a detailed layout of the Dome of the Rock and the construction of a working model, Livni organized a theft of large quantities of explosives from an arms factory on the Golan Heights as well as their testing in the Negev Desert. Determined not to endanger Jewish life or property in the adjoining area, Livni meticulously calculated how the Dome of the Rock would break up under the impact of the explosives and how far the shrapnel would descend. Some two dozen bomb-laden participants were trained to scale the walls of the Old City to reach the esplanade of the Temple Mount stealthily. But, in case they were detected by the Arab guards, they were to be armed with tear-gas canisters and Uzi submachine guns fitted with silencers.

Intent on frustrating the Israeli plan to evacuate the last Jewish settlement in the Egyptian Sinai by April 1982, the conspirators wanted to strike before the deadline. Livni wanted a religious go-ahead in the form of approval by a rabbi. Apparently he failed to get it. At the final meeting of the eight activists only Etzion and Ben Shoshan voted in favor of going ahead. So they decided to postpone the project.

The following spring, both Palestinians and Jewish Israelis escalated their terrorist actions, with Hebron emerging as a particular hot spot. In March 1983, Palestinian assailants killed a Jewish yeshiva student in the center of Hebron. In July, six Jewish settlers from Kiryat Arba (with Livni providing logistical support) mounted a daylight machine-gun and grenade attack on the students of the Islamic College in Hebron, killing 4 and wounding 33.

Soon, militants fervently committed to building the Third Temple tried to implement their plan to blow up the Dome of the Rock in the middle of the night. Armed with ladders, ropes and explosives, they scaled the eastern wall of the Old City, and moved quietly to within about 300 feet of the shrine. But an Arab guard noticed them and raised the alarm. In their haste to escape, they left enough clues for police detectives to end up in jail.

Another attempt by Livni and his co-conspirators to blow up the Dome of the Rock got prematurely exposed in the aftermath of an aborted terrorist attack on the Palestinians. On the night of April 26, 1984, a dozen members of the Jewish Underground rigged explosives to the fuel tanks of five buses parked outside the residences of their Palestinian drivers in East Jerusalem, to explode at 4:30 P.M. the next day, Friday, when no Jews were expected to be in the streets. The bombs never exploded. All of the conspirators were picked up by Israel's security service, the Shin Beth, whose agents also arrested 24 other Israelis allegedly involved in terroristic activity. The list included not only relatives of members of Israel's parliament and senior Israeli officials administering the Occupied Territories, but also some high-ranking IDF officers. Shin Beth soon learned of a detailed plan to destroy the Dome of the Rock, led as before by Livni and a team made up largely of experienced IDF men. The court evidence showed that arms and explosives had been procured; some 30 precision bombs had been hidden in scattered places; and trial runs had been conducted. As before, the plotters had acquired tear-gas canisters and silencers for their Uzi submachine guns.

"Had they not been arrested before they had a chance to blow up the shrine, their act would probably have brought a reign of warfare and terrorism upon Israel and Jews everywhere," wrote David K. Shipler of *The New York Times*. "One official in the prime minister's office even estimated that Israel could not have survived the Muslim onslaught that would have come if the Dome had been destroyed."[19]

At the trial , the judge found eighteen of the accused guilty, and sentenced them to prison terms ranging from four months to life, while at the same time commending them for "their pioneering ethos and war records."

On the day he was sentenced to seven years, Yehuda Etzion arrived in court with a picture of the "Third Temple" superimposed on the Dome of the Rock, and the rest of the Temple Mount cleared of all other Islamic monuments. He called on the Israeli government to make "purifying the Temple Mount" its "overriding goal."[20]

This picture is commonly displayed in the yeshivas in Jerusalem, and is sold freely in the Jewish Quarter of the Old City. I bought a copy at the Temple Institute run by Rabbi Israel Ariel. The small museum has a large model of the Third Temple, and displays the vessels and priestly robes to be used there. "We have prepared 60 of the 90 vessels required for the Third Temple," said Efrat Liebowitz, a young, chubby-faced woman in white blouse and long black skirt, who was selling literature at the Institute. "We are also preparing garments for the priests and the High Priest. Work goes on in several yeshivas in the Old City. We have scholars weaving prayer shawls and studying Talmudic texts about restoring sacrificial slaughter in the Temple. We don't know when the Messiah will come, but we should be ready."[21]

I needed to visit the Haram al Sharif to interview Muslim pilgrims. On the morning I spent outside the Al Aqsa Mosque, my find of the day was Ali Salamin, a resident of the Shuafat district of East Jerusalem. A 35-year-old man with a thick black beard, Ali spoke fluent English, having worked for several years with the Arabian-American Oil Company in Saudi Arabia. Well-informed on Islam and its antecedents, he talked about the Haram al Sharif as if it were a grand stage on which prophets and warriors had enacted a historical pageant of monotheism.

Standing in front of a small monument east of the Dome of the Rock, he said, "This is what Caliph Omar ibn al Khattab built after capturing Jerusalem as a scale model for the Dome of the Rock." What is it called? "The Dome of the Chain, *Al Quttab al Silsile*. During Prophet Solomon's rule those who held on to the chain, hanging from the roof of his palace, dropped dead if they told a lie."

Looking up at the Dome of the Rock, Ali began reciting the Quranic verses that embellish the exterior of the walls, the seven verses from Chapter Seventeen, "The Night Journey."

Glory be to Him, who carried His servant by night
from the Holy Mosque to the Distant Mosque
the precincts of which We have blessed
that we might show Him some of Our signs.
He is the All-hearing, the All-seeing.

"In AD 621 God took Prophet Muhammad from the Holy Mosque in Mecca to the Distant (Al Aqsa) Mosque here," Ali explained. "Historically speaking, it remains the first *qibla* (direction for prayer) of Muslims. They faced in its direction while praying. After it had been the first *qibla* for eighteen months, God told Muhammad to make Mecca the first *qibla*. After the Prophet's death in Medina, his burial place became the second holiest shrine in Islam. Then came Al Aqsa."

Ali looked up again, and resumed translating the verses from "The Night Journey."

And We gave Moses the Book, and made it
a guidance to the Children of Israel:
"Take not unto yourself any guardian
apart from Me."

The seed of those We bore with Noah; he was
a thankful servant.

And We decreed for the Children of Israel
in the Book: "You shall do corruption
in the earth twice, and you shall ascend
exceeding[ly] high."

So, when the promise of the first of these
came to pass, We sent against you
servants of Ours, men of great might, and they went
through the habitations, and it was a promise performed.

Then We gave back to you the turn to
prevail over them, and We succored you
with wealth and children, and We made you
a greater host.

If you do good, it is to your own souls
you do good to, and if you do evil,
it is to them likewise. Then, when
the promise of the second came to pass,
We sent against you Our servants
to disconcert you, and to enter the Temple,
as they entered it the first time,
and to destroy utterly that which they ascended to.

"You notice what the Quran says about Beni Israel, Children of Israel, who were later called Jews," Ali remarked. "Our war with the Jews is not religious though—it is political." I nodded. Why the title, "The Night Journey?" "It is the journey Prophet Muhammad made at night on his winged steed, *al Buraq*, Lightning, from Mecca to the Haram al Sharif to Heaven."

Entering the Dome is like stepping inside a cornucopia of color and light, its patterned yellow and red stucco center glowing like the sun, the stained-glass windows filtering in a soft greenish-blue light, the base resplendent with golden mosaics. The columns bore witness to their pre-Islamic origins: remains of the Herodian Temple or the churches destroyed by Persian Emperor Chosroes II in AD 614.

Directly underneath the Dome was the Rock, camel-brown, sunk for the most part like an iceberg into the ground—the Rock of Foundation of the Jewish legend, dating back to the time when the upper world was split from a shard from the pit of Chaos below, the inner sanctum of the Jewish Temple, which the Jews later visited annually (at Passover) to mourn and anoint, which then later served as an altar to Baal and Jupiter, and which Muslims renamed the Rock of Heaven.

An encircling parapet protected the rock from overzealous pilgrims intent on acquiring a bit of its hallowed mass. It was illuminated by soft, subdued light, some of it shining through a gaping hole in its body—the result, I surmised, of the millions of gallons of blood that had flown over the spot from the ritual sacrifices of animals in the Jewish Temple. All things considered, I concluded, the Holy Rock had maintained its legendary status as the Center of the World with admirable integrity, only occasionally surrendering a sharp edge or two.

I followed Ali as he descended to a softly lit chamber with unfissured walls. "The Rock of Heaven is washed twice a week with rosewater," said Ali. "When Prophet Muhammad climbed up the ladder of light to the heaven, guided by the Archangel Gabriel, the Rock rose to follow the Prophet. But Gabriel held it back and left his fingerprints on it." What happened to the winged steed, al Buraq, that brought Prophet Muhammad to the Haram? "The Prophet prayed at the Haram al Sharif, tethered al Buraq by the Western Wall, then walked to the Holy Rock, and ascended to the heaven."

"Under the Rock is a cave with shrines to the prophets Abraham and Khadr (Elijah, to non-Muslims)," continued Ali. Why Abraham? "According to the Quran, the prophet Abraham was the first Muslim." How? "Muslim means the one who submits—to the will of God. And the prophet Abraham was the first to do so and convey His message that there was only One God."

"Beneath it is the Well of Souls (*Bir al Arwah*), where spirits of the past are waiting for the Judgment Day," Ali concluded. So here was the complete history of humankind—from the Creation to the End of Days, I thought.

Next I spoke with Abdul Rabbo, a craggy-faced 80-year-old in a business suit and a black and white checked *keffiyeh* (head dress), a resident of Al Muqabar neighborhood of East Jerusalem. "There is a mosque in Jabal al Muqabar, but I come to Al Aqsa. One prayer here is equal to 500 prayers elsewhere. Here I am nearest to God, and after prayers I feel elevated." His sentiments paralleled the ones I had heard earlier at the Western Wall.

There was another Palestinian from Al Muqabar outside the Al Aqsa Mosque. Abdul Karim Karaki, a small, powerfully built man of 52, was smartly dressed in a black and white tweed jacket and carrying a mobile phone. A guard at the Haram al Sharif, he had held that position for twenty years. Surely I could check with him Jaafar's claim that IDF soldiers came to the Haram regularly. "All the time," Karaki replied instantly. "They come and go as they please. They don't even pay the entrance fee like the others."

Here was also my chance, I thought, to question somebody who was present on the fateful morning of October 8, 1990 in the midst of the crisis created by the Iraqi invasion of Kuwait two months earlier.

The Temple Mount Faithful (TMF), a group of about 1,000 Jews led by Gershon Salomon, committed to reclaiming the Temple Mount/Haram al Sharif in order to build the Third Temple there, had declared that on the Feast of Tabernacles, October 8, they would lay a foundation stone for the Third Temple. In the past, whenever TMF members had tried to enter the courtyard on the Temple Mount in large numbers, the authorities had compromised by letting a few do so through the Israeli controlled Maghrebi Gate under heavy guard to pray for a while and then depart. In mid-September, however, the Israeli High Court banned the TMF from entering the area. But the TMF let it be known that it would defy the court order. Responding to this, in his sermon on the preceding Friday, the preacher of the Al Aqsa Mosque, Shaikh Fadlallah Silwadi, called on his congregation to gather at the Haram on the following Monday morning to frustrate the TMF's plans.

That morning TMF activists, after assembling at Silwan village just outside the walls of the Old City, began marching towards the Mount as planned. Word reached the 3,000 or so Palestinians assembled on the Mount. At around 10:45 A.M. they surged towards the Western Wall and the Israeli police station. They threw stones, which landed in the Western Wall Plaza where Jewish worshippers were gathered. The Israeli security forces fired tear gas shells at thePalestinians.

After the first round of stones and tear gas, one or more of the following incidents triggered a massive burst of fire from the Israeli police and troops: 1) a gun dropped by a fleeing Israeli soldier was picked up by the rioting Palestinians, and this alarmed the soldier's colleagues who started firing; 2) Israeli soldiers from the Mahkame observation post built into the Western Wall shot dead a Palestinian youth waving a Palestinian flag, which enraged the crowd; and 3) a few of the armed Jewish settlers from the Occupied Territories present at the scene began firing their personal weapons.

Whatever the primary cause, by 11:30 A.M., following the Israeli use of tear gas, plastic bullets and live ammunition, 17 Palestinians lay dead, with another 150 wounded. Since most of the Jewish worshippers, having said their prayers (prescribed for the period of 9 A.M. to 12 noon) had left the Western Wall by the time the stone-throwing started, only about 20 of them were hurt. October 8, 1990 became the bloodiest day of the Palestinian intifada, and indeed of the 23 years of Israeli occupation of the West Bank, Gaza Strip and East Jerusalem.

"I was on duty that morning," said Abdul Karim Karaki. "Thousands of people were praying inside and outside the Al Aqsa. There was shooting by the IDF, also by the police. Some Palestinians died near the ablution place [outside the Mosque]. I closed the door of the Al Aqsa [to protect the worshippers]. The whole thing went on from about 10:30 A.M. to evening. The security forces threw 200 gas grenades inside the Al Aqsa and outside. Seventeen people were killed on the Haram, and another four in the demonstrations that broke out in Saladin Street outside the Old City. A policeman fired a shot at my head, but I am short, and there was a tall man behind me. He got hurt."

Karaki pointed out the bullet marks on the walls and gates of the Al Aqsa. Then he took me inside and showed me a large glass container, full of spent gas cartridges, nailed to a pillar. "A souvenir of the Israeli security forces," he said, bitterly. "I feel sad that Al Aqsa was captured by the Jews in 1967. We Muslims feel that our country fell under occupation in 1967. Something terrible happened. Until today I am not reconciled to the fact that my country is occupied. And haven't we suffered? Since 1986 my family has never sat together in full because somebody is always missing, in jail. It was only a few days ago that my son was released after three years in jail, a political prisoner." How often did he pray at Al Aqsa? "At least once a day. And I pray to God daily to send somebody like Saladin to liberate Al Aqsa, the way Saladin did, from the Crusaders."

Karaki directed me to the Islamic Museum to see for myself the Muslim martyrs of October 8, 1990. Near the entrance on the cream-colored wall was a large framed picture. Underneath the Islamic invocation of Allah, on both sides of the image of a powerful fist, emerging out of a tree trunk, holding the barrel of a gun against the background of the Dome of Rock, were seventeen oval-shaped color photographs of the dead, with an inscription describing them as the "Martyrs of Al Aqsa." Save for a woman and a child of indeterminate sex, they were all male, most of them young, teenagers even, a few old, and the rest middle-aged.

Looking at them reminded me of another framed picture on another wall: the color photographs on the front page of the *Yediot Aharonot* (Latest news) on January 23, 1995 of the victims of the double suicide bombing by two Islamic Jihad activists at the Beit Lid bus station near the Mediterranean port of Natanya the day before. The faces in that picture were uniformly young, the faces of IDF conscripts. For the terrorists had struck a well-chosen target: on a Sunday morning at a busy bus station when hundreds of young soldiers were on their way to their bases after the Sabbath.

Both sides, locked in a grim, protracted struggle, had created a long list of martyrs. And they had been conducting their conflict at many levels, with a bewildering variety of weapons: military hardware, suicide bombings, bulldozers, terrorism, stones, subterfuge, knives, tear gas, metal rods, deception, money, diplomacy, courts, and propaganda.

When I traveled to the West Bank and Gaza Strip to visit some Jewish settlements, the parallels between the situation there, and the one existing between the Jewish settlers in the Old City's Muslim Quarter and the Muslim Palestinians, became obvious. The Walled City was a microcosm of what was happening at large in Israel and the Palestinian Territories.

2

Jerusalem

Yerushalayim/Al Quds

Danny Jacobi sounded friendly over the phone, and showed a welcome understanding of how a newly arrived visitor feels in a sprawling city like modern Jerusalem. He simplified the tricky task of entering a government establishment several stories up in a tower block in the Jewish neighborhood of Ramat Eshkol in Greater East Jerusalem. "I'll meet you in the supermarket near the office," he said in fluent English.

I arrived early and walked around the spacious shopping mall. It was well planned, in a central position between residential and office blocks. I detected a whiff of a fortress mentality among the planners, the soft belly of commerce protected by watch-tower structures. Not far was an alien, if not hostile, territory—I was to discover later.

Jacobi was punctual. A pleasant-looking man in his mid-30s, he was every child's image of an ideal schoolteacher. Appropriately enough, I was in the Ministry of Education, the section which produces its own text books, and vets (some would say censors) others before they can be published by private companies.

I spent a useful hour with him during which he plied me with history books in Hebrew. As I prepared to leave I asked him if he would please phone a taxi to pick me up. "Where do you want to go?" he inquired, as he lifted the receiver. The American Colony Hotel. He put the receiver down. "No taxi will take you there," he announced with a finality that baffled me. I expressed surprise. "Well, I have a friend, an archaeologist, at the Rockefeller Museum. He tells me that they really had to shop around to find a Jewish cab company which would accept their calls." But the Rockefeller Museum was only a couple miles from here, and so was my hotel—in Jerusalem, not in the West Bank, I protested. "It's in East Jerusalem," he explained. But Ramat Eshkol, too, was in East Jerusalem. "Ah," he replied, "Ramat Eshkol is a Jewish neighborhood in East Jerusalem." A Jewish neighborhood or Jewish settlement? "Settlements are in the West Bank," he pointed out. "Here we have neighborhoods," he added, straight-faced. The settlements were only in Judea and Samaria, you mean? "We now say 'in the Administered Territories,'" he said. "Or just the Territories." Not always, though.

Before the 1967 war, the land where Ramat Eshkol stood was part of the Palestinian territory under Jordanian control. Soon after, the Labor-led government extended Israeli law over Jordanian East Jerusalem and vast tracts around it, doubling the size of West Jerusalem. New reconstruction included Ramot Eshkol as one of several new parts of the now-expanded city. Even though, legally the Jerusalem Municipality was in charge of the local affairs (land development, housing, etc.) of the unified Jerusalem after June 28, 1967, the central Israeli government decided what was to be done in the expanded city. The overall objective was national: to install an expanding Jewish population in the formerly Palestinian parts of the city so as to destroy any chance of splitting the metropolis again.

The plans to establish Ramat Eshkol, and other new Jerusalem "neighborhoods" such as French Hill and Maalot Dafna followed the pattern of the earlier Israeli blueprints: create self-contained, middle-sized towns with residents serviced by a comprehensive socio-economic infrastructure. Care was taken to ensure that the new settlements were inhabited only by Jews, that the newly created service facilities catered only to them, and that there was absolutely no need for the Jewish residents to have dealings with the surrounding Palestinian population.

Over the next quarter of a century the Israeli government duplicated these plans as it set up more settlements inside the (enlarged) Greater East Jerusalem. It did so against the backdrop of events in the international arena. Responding to the launching of a Middle East Peace Plan by US Secretary of State William Rogers, in December 1969, it decided to fortify the core of Jerusalem by founding Jewish settlements at strategic points overseeing the main roads from the Occupied West Bank into the city. Thus arose Ramat Allon, Neve Yaacov, East Talpiyot and Gilo, virtually surrounding Arab Jerusalem. Israel ignored UN Security Council Resolution 298 in 1971 which declared invalid its actions to alter the status of Jerusalem, including "expropriation of land and properties, transfer of populations and legislation aimed at the incorporation of the occupied section [of the city]."

In 1980, as the Knesset embarked upon consolidating its earlier control of Greater East Jerusalem, culminating in its adoption of a "basic law" which stated that "united Jerusalem is the capital of Israel," the United Nations Security Council reiterated the international position clearly in March 1980 in its Resolution 465, passed unanimously. Referring to its resolutions 237 (1967), 252 (1968), 267 (1969), 271 (1969) and 298 (1971) on the subject, it affirmed once more that "the Geneva Convention Relative to the Protection of Civilian Persons in Time of War, of 12 August 1949, is applicable to the Arab territories occupied by Israel since 1967, including Jerusalem."[1] This Convention forbids the occupying power to change the demography of the territory under its occupation through such means as deportation or transfer of "parts of its own civilian population into the territory it occupies," and discriminatory treatment of the occupied people on the grounds of race, religion, national origin or political affiliation.[2] The Security Council re-stated its earlier position on June 30, 1980 in its Resolution 476, adopted by fourteen votes with one abstention (the United States), specifically expressing "grave concern" at the "legislative steps initiated in the Israeli Knesset with the aim of changing the character and status of the Holy City of Jerusalem." The Likud-led Israeli government responded by setting up a new Jewish settlement at Pisgat Zeev between Neve Yaacov and French Hill, thus fashioning a continuous Jewish residential belt from Mount Scopus to Neve Yaacov with the strategic aim of separating the city's eastern Arab sector from the West Bank.

Israeli governments, whether Labor or Likud, realized these plans by expropriating 30 percent of Greater East Jerusalem, more than four-fifths of which was Palestinian. The authorities classified a further 46 percent of the land as "green zones," thus denying the right of the Palestinian owners to build on their own land, and used up another 6 percent in road building, thus leaving the Palestinians with only 12 percent of the land for development.[3] While the Jewish settlements were established in such a way as to split Palestinian villages and neighborhoods from one another, an elaborate road system was constructed to link the settlements, further isolating Palestinian centers of the population. So, as the Jewish settlements scrambled the old Israeli-Jordanian frontier, they created a host of new, informal borders. "The interface that divides these areas [from its Arab environment] is further dramatized by the massive supporting terraces surrounding the Jewish neighborhoods—they present a kind of 'solid front' facing the adjacent Arab areas," wrote Michael Romann and Alex Weingrod.[4] A quick glance at Mount Scopus from the vicinity of the Old City provides a telling illustration of this statement. From the other side, one has only to stand on the south-western edge of the sprawling Hebrew University on Mount Scopus to realize the strategic advantage the area has over the Old City and the rest of Arab East Jerusalem.

A dramatic weakening of the Arab camp, resulting from the Iraqi invasion of Kuwait in August 1990 and the subsequent Gulf War in early 1991, made little difference to Israel's policy of strengthening its hold over Jerusalem. The Likud-led government responded to the convening of the Middle East Peace Conference in October 1991 by expropriating Palestinian land for two more Jewish settlements in Jerusalem—Har Homa on the southern edge of the city, and Rechis Shuafat next to the Palestinian village of Shuafat.

After almost a quarter century of Jewish colonization of East Jerusalem, more than 38,000 new, government-subsidized housing units had been built for Jews. The corresponding figure for Palestinians was 555. (Despite the finding of a municipal inquiry in 1981 that the Palestinian Arabs needed 18,000 new housing units, the authorities issued permits for only 10,000 housing units during the next dozen years, thus sharpening the more than two-to-one disparity in housing density that already existed between Arabs and Jews.) The Israeli government combined its offer of subsidized housing to Jewish citizens with five-year municipal tax exemption followed by a lower tax rate. Consequently, the Jewish population in Greater East Jerusalem soared from zero in 1967 to 76,000 in 1983, and then doubled during the next decade.

Following the Oslo Accord between Israel and the PLO in September 1993, the climate for further Israeli expropriation of Palestinian land changed. In April 1995, the Likud-led Jerusalem Municipality planned to confiscate 130 acres of Palestinian land in two villages on the city's outskirts. The Labor-led national government soon backed the plan. Palestinian protests failed, and only after the Israeli Arab Members of the Knesset (MKs) threatened to withdraw their support from the Labor-led government and bring it down, did the Rabin government relent.

It was the first time since 1967 that Israel had backed down on land expropriations in the annexed Greater East Jerusalem.

By then the officials had taken to emphasizing that the Jewish population of Greater East Jerusalem now exceeded its Arab counterpart. Unsurprisingly, Palestinian demographers disputed the statistics, claiming that they had been doctored.[5]

These claims became more insistent after Ehud Olmert of Likud defeated Jerusalem's long-time Labor mayor, Teddy Kollek, in November 1993, and the authorities intensified publicity for the fifteen-month-long "Jerusalem 3000" festivities commemorating King David's conquest of the Jesubite stronghold of Jerusalem in 996 BC. The fifteen-member European Union boycotted the celebrations, objecting to the festival's exclusivist theme of Jerusalem as a strictly Jewish and Israeli city. So did the United States: its ambassador to Israel stayed away from the opening ceremony. The Palestinians were not invited. The Hebrew media greeted the launch of the festival—marked by a sound and light and fireworks spectacular—with special radio and television programs and newspaper supplements, while the Arab media said or wrote nothing about it. When questioned on the subject by international news agencies, Faisal Husseini, the best known leader of the Greater East Jerusalem Palestinians, said: "These celebrations not only disclaim Jerusalem's Arab and Islamic identity, they glorify the occupation. Jerusalem was not built 3,000 but 5,000 years ago. The recent occupation is trying to celebrate the old one [by King David]."[6] Husseini's words were lost on Jewish Israelis who supported three "forevers" regarding Jerusalem: "forever Israel's capital," "forever under exclusive Jewish control," and "forever united."

When the Israeli government annexed the Jordanian-controlled Jerusalem and its vast environs in 1967, it planned to absorb its residents in the same way it had the Arabs who stayed behind in Israel in 1948. But this did not work. Unlike the Palestinian Arabs in 1948, East Jerusalemites possessed Jordanian citizenship, and had their own established secular and religious institutions. Almost unanimously they rejected the option of abandoning their Jordanian nationality for an Israeli one. So the Israeli government lowered its sights and decided to absorb them as residents of the city, not the State of Israel, and gave them the right to vote in local elections, not national. East Jerusalemites hardened their non-cooperation with the Israeli authorities by creating additional independent institutions and voluntary organizations of their own and strengthening the existing ones.

But the Israeli innovation of granting local voting rights to Greater East Jerusalem Arabs began to work. The proportion of eligible Arab voters for the mayoral poll rose steadily from 7.3 percent in 1973 to 18.4 percent in late 1983. And there were other encouraging indicators. A survey of high school pupils in 1982 revealed that approximately two-thirds of the Jewish students and just over half of the Arab students had visited both parts of Jerusalem during the past month. But their feelings varied. Whereas only one percent of the Jewish pupils visiting East Jerusalem felt "very uncomfortable," the figure for male Arab students visiting West Jerusalem was 35 percent. Also Arabs were much more interested than Jews in knowing the other side better.[7]

This situation never improved. Indeed, with the eruption of the Palestinian intifada in late 1987, the percentage of the Arabs participating in the mayoral election a year later plummeted to below five percent, and lingered there during the subsequent poll in 1993, the same year as the Oslo Accords.

But even during the period of increasingly peaceful coexistence, marked by rising economic intercourse under Israeli rule in the early 1980s, there was scant mutual comprehension or understanding between Israelis and Palestinians. In 1983, a highly promising year to Israelis, two May events—the Islamic Night Journey and Ascension fell on the Jewish Jerusalem Liberation Day, which was established after the 1967 War—dramatically illustrated the situation. Part of the Jews' celebration took place in the early afternoon in the Old City's Western Wall, where the plaza was festooned with Israeli flags. About the same time, on the esplanade atop the Wall, thousands of Muslim worshippers inside and outside the Al Aqsa Mosque listened to the prayer leader explain the significance of the Holy Rock of Haven from which Prophet Mohammad ascended to paradise. Each side's media totally ignored the other's activity. The events might as well have happened at opposite poles of the earth.

And by all accounts the bitter, protracted Palestinian intifada, which erupted in 1987, reversed the process of reconciliation between the two communities, and stoked alienation and enmity.

Today many conversations and reports in Israel and the Palestinian Territories refer to "before the intifada" and "after the intifada." "Jews once filled East Jerusalem's restaurants and went bargain shopping on Saturdays in the Old City market and on Salah al Din Street, East Jerusalem's main commercial street," noted Yossi Halevi in the *Jerusalem Report* in mid-1993. "Arabs considered it a mark of status to buy clothes in 'Sharia Yafo,' the term they use for all of West Jerusalem. In summer tents were erected near the Damascus Gate, and Jews and Arabs came to eat slices of watermelon and watch kung fu videos... Now the Damascus Gate watermelon stands have been replaced by Route One, Arabs buy their clothes in Ramallah, and Jews shop for bargains and eat in West Jerusalem."[8]

To be sure, the reversal of the process of mutual acceptance and trust came about in stages—in response to violent acts from both camps: individual Palestinian terrorist actions on one side and state violence on the other. A sensational fire-bomb assault on a Jewish driver in the Palestinian district of Wadi Joz in 1988 resulted in the Jews staying away from Arab neighborhoods. The situation worsened sharply in October 1990 after firings by the Israeli police and military on the Temple Mount and Salah al Din Street killed 21 Palestinians. The retaliatory Palestinian actions, often stabbings, resulted in the murders of three Jewish men in Baqaa later that year and four Jewish women in Kiryat HaYovel early the next year. Jewish Israeli vehicles, easily identified by the color of their license plates, became targets of arson attacks, with 450 cars meeting such a fate in 1992, and another 190 during the first half of 1993.

A pattern of mutual, self-reinforcing fear was established. Jews kept away from the Arab sector, apprehensive of terrorism and the occasional antagonistic demonstrations that erupted in the Palestinian areas. It became a common practice among Jews to enter the Old City not through the "Arab" gates on the north and east, but through the gates on the western side of the walled town. Arabs kept away from the Jewish sector, mindful of the constant harassment by the Israeli civil police (blue uniform), and the border police (dark green uniform) under the command of the IDF, who checked their identity papers and searched them humiliatingly. The young, able Palestinian men in their 20s and 30s, the most productive in any society and most mobile, were the most vulnerable to Israeli police and military harassment. Those Palestinians who were obliged to traverse a Jewish neighborhood en route to their place of employment during daytime took to rushing through the area, avoiding eye-contact. Barring emergency, most Jews and Arabs withdrew to their respective neighborhoods after dark, the only Jews in the Palestinian districts being the Israeli border police on patrol.

The decline in tension which followed the signing of the Israeli-PLO accord in September 1993 proved short-lived. Following the killing of 29 Muslim Palestinians at prayer in the Ibrahimi Mosque/Tomb of the Patriarchs in Hebron by a Jewish settler in early 1994, a series of suicide bombings by militant Islamists revived fears among Jews.

This showed in such activities as tourism, as I discovered during a tour of Jerusalem and Bethlehem in early 1995, organized by a company based in Tel Aviv. The tour guide, a dark-haired woman with a bubbling sense of humor, repeatedly warned her charges "never, ever" to go into East Jerusalem, "never, ever" to stray away from her in the Old City outside the Jewish Quarter.

What I witnessed was only one layer of mutual distrust and fear between Jews and Arabs. There are others, often more profound, which are not so apparent, and require inquiry and research. In commerce and industry there is still some ongoing exchange and intercourse between the two sides in Jerusalem, but in other arenas Jews and Arabs remain separated by language, religion and other aspects of life as strongly as before. In the political sphere, too, they remain apart, since Palestinians refuse to participate in local elections and are totally unrepresented at the city hall.

The century-old struggle between Jew and Arab for land continues, with the Jewish Israelis, having gained the upper hand in 1948, continuing to further their position, and the Arab Palestinians trying to resist as hard as they can. More specifically, the two camps, their perceptions shaped by recent history, approach the issue of Jerusalem differently. Jewish Israelis see the city central to their state. "Jerusalem is the heart of the Jewish people, the focus of its yearning, the land of its vision, the cradle of its prayers," said prime minister Yitzhak Rabin, inaugurating the "Jerusalem 3000" festivities in September 1995. Israelis point out that even though from 1948 to 1967 West Jerusalem adjoined the armistice lines with Jordan, and its link with the rest of Israel was precarious, their leaders moved the government and parliament to the city, and saw its population soar from 84,000 in 1948 to 200,000 on the eve of the June 1967 War. Their annexation of a vastly expanded East Jerusalem received almost universal backing among Jewish Israelis. Since then, Jewish citizens have come to consider the Jewish settlements within the newly created Greater East Jerusalem as an integral part of Yerushalayim and Israel, and view them differently from those in the West Bank.

In contrast, Palestinians regard their city, under Jordanian control from 1948 to 1967, as "Al Quds." When the exiled mayor of "their Jerusalem," Rouhi Khatib, aged 80, returned home in May 1993, after a 26-year exile in Jordan, thousands of Palestinians turned out to accord him an enthusiastic welcome. They view all Jewish settlements built outside of their Al Quds but within the (Israeli) Greater East Jerusalem, to be on a par with others established elsewhere in the West Bank. The maps published by Palestinians, whether in Arabic or any other language, are consistent and unambiguous on this point. Consistent with the resolutions adopted repeatedly by the UN Security Council, the Palestinians regard all these Jewish settlements as contravening the 1949 Fourth Geneva Convention, and therefore illegal.

Inadvertently, Israel helped the Palestinians by building a north-south highway cutting through the heart of the city. Though the primary purpose of constructing the six-lane Route One, which runs from Hebron in the south to Nablus in the north, was to connect the Jewish settlements in the north-east with the city center, it has come to symbolize the frontier between the Jewish West and Arab East Jerusalem. Save for a few minor deviations, Route One runs along the pre-1967 armistice lines of Israel and Jordan. Today it has recreated a wall—invisible to visitors but very real to local residents—with the Jewish sector to its west, and the Arab to its east. In a sense Route One formalized what had existed all along not only in terms of international law, as determined by the United Nations, but also the practices of the Israeli government, local and national.

The western countries, including the United States, Britain and France (three of the five permanent members of the UN Security Council), posted parallel consulates in West Jerusalem and East Jerusalem. These consulates functioned independently of their respective embassies in Tel Aviv, and reported directly to the foreign ministry. These and all other members of the United Nations (with the exception of Costa Rica and El Salvador) continued to respect a separate status for Jerusalem as spelled out in Resolution 181 adopted in November 1947, and maintain their embassies in Tel Aviv. The UN resolution called for partition of Palestine, then under British mandate, into a Jewish sector, an Arab sector, and an internationally-administered status for Jerusalem.

Many things about Jerusalem remain in dispute. Even its name: "Yerushalayim" to Jews, meaning "Founded by God," and "Al Quds" to Muslims, meaning "The Holy." It is an apt illustration of the deep divide that exists between the two national groups. The Israeli postal authorities stamp "Arushalayim" in Arabic, a word which does not exist elsewhere, either in writing or speaking. Of the seven gates of the Old City only two carry the same name in Hebrew and Arabic: the New Gate and Herod's Gate, called Flower Gate in both Hebrew and Arabic. The rest have different names in the two languages: St. Stephen's Gate (Shaar HaArayot, or Lions' Gate; Bab Sitna Mariam, or Lady Mary Gate); Damascus Gate (Shaar Shechem, or Nablus Gate; Bab al Amoud, or Gate of the Column); Jaffa Gate (Shaar Yafo, or Jaffa Gate; Bab al Khalil, or Hebron Gate); Zion Gate (Shaar Ziyyon, or Zion Gate; Bal al Nabi Daoud, or The Prophet David Gate); and Dung Gate (Shaar HaAshpot, or The Dung Gate; Bab Harat al Maghribi, or Gate of the Occidental Quarter).

Following its capture of East Jerusalem in 1967, the Israeli authorities changed the name of Port Said Street to HaTsanhanim, or the Paratroopers' Street, to honor those who took East Jerusalem from the Jordanians. But the Palestinians refused to use the name. It was the same when it came to neighborhoods. Palestinians continue to use the traditional Jabal al Muqabar (Mountain of Evil Counsel) for the district just beyond the southern fringe of the former Jordanian Jerusalem, and refuse to use the Israeli title of East Talpiyot.

While it is true that despite their differing ethnic identity, Jews and Arabs apply to the same Israeli administrative agency—be it police or income tax authority—the actual arrangements are almost always segregated. In maintaining law and order there is only one authority: the Israeli police. By taking over wholesale the government machinery of Jordan in East Jerusalem, the Israeli authorities acquired the central police station, situated in the Old City, and absorbed it into its own system. This required Arab policemen to serve under Jewish officers. Their jurisdiction covered the former Jordanian Jerusalem, including all of the Old City. But by the time the renovated Jewish Quarter was occupied by Jews in the mid-1970s, the central police station of West Jerusalem had quietly placed it under its own jurisdiction, thus ensuring that Arab policemen were kept out of intra-Jewish affairs. The converse does not apply. Jewish police and border police regularly patrol Greater East Jerusalem, and carry out such routine tasks as fining Arab motorists or taxi-drivers.

Segregation in the educational system is total, with Arab and Jewish students pursuing different curriculums in separate schools imparting education in Arabic or Hebrew. When, in the immediate aftermath of the annexation of Greater East Jerusalem, Israel replaced the Jordanian system with the Israeli Arab system, most East Jerusalem parents withdrew their children and enrolled them either into private schools or the West Bank municipal school system, which continued more or less as it had before 1967, with the final graduation examination conducted by the Jordanian Education Ministry. This made Israel reverse its policy and revert to the pre-1967 Jordanian curriculum (except for the compulsory teaching of Hebrew), while administering Jerusalem's Palestinian schools under the joint supervision of the municipality and the Ministry of Education. Even then only about half the East Jerusalem students enrolled in the Israeli-supervised system. A marked difference in the educational achievement of Jerusalem's Jewish and Arab students had developed. Over 90 percent of the former finished the final twelfth grade as against 50 percent of the latter.[9]

As in education so in health care. The Israeli system, catering to Jews, stands apart from the Palestinian system, which cares for Muslims and Christians. Health care for Jewish residents is provided by the state-subsidized national health service, largely financed by the Kupath Holim of the Histadrut trade union federation[10] and rendered by local hospitals and clinics. The Palestinian system, inherited from Jordan, which lacked state-sponsored medical care, relies heavily on Muslim and Christian religious charities as well as the United Nations agencies. Even when membership in Histadrut entitles Palestinians to state-sponsored health care, they receive this service in separate clinics staffed with Arabic-speaking employees, which are situated in Palestinian districts of Jerusalem, and cater only to Arabs. Nothing sums up the strict division of the medical care system better than the existence of two ambulance services, the Red Shield of David and the Red Crescent, and two blood banks, one Jewish and the other Arab.

"Generally speaking, Jews are never hospitalized in an Arab institution, even in those urgent or emergency cases where this might appear to be the best option," write Michael Romann and Alex Weingrod. "Should a Jew be injured in the Arab section of the city, a Jewish ambulance will invariably be called in, and it will take him to the nearest Jewish hospital."[11]

While the Israeli authorities merged their own and the Palestinian fire fighting facilities by subordinating the East Jerusalem station to its West Jerusalem counterpart, they left the separate bus transport systems of the two sectors alone— up to a point. They limited the franchise of the Palestinian bus company to the Arab sector while enlarging that of the Jewish bus company to include not only the routes between West Jerusalem and the Jewish settlements in Greater East Jerusalem but also sections of the Arab sector itself, thus undermining the position of the Arab bus company. Overall, Jews may reach any Jewish destination using a Jewish bus. But when Palestinians ride a bus to job sites in West Jerusalem, they cannot choose an Arab vehicle; they must use a Jewish bus before or after crossing Route One.

Yet in the day-to-day affairs that matter most to residents, administrative pragmatism and sensitivity have yet to prevail over popular Jewish prejudice against the Arab minority even when it comes to implementing official policies. The status of Arabic is an apt example. Officially Arabic is on a par with Hebrew, and all Israeli laws are translated into Arabic. But such a basic document as the telephone directory of Jerusalem is issued only in Hebrew, with an option to the subscriber to request a copy in English. There is no official directory in Arabic. Characteristically, when an enterprising Arab businessman printed a directory in Arabic, he included only Arab subscribers.

Palestinians find particularly onerous the absence of Arabic signs even in those administrative centers which the authorities have established exclusively for them. Israeli bureaucrats show scant consideration for Arabic-speaking citizens, and seldom bother to post signs in that language. Even the municipality of "united" Jerusalem, run for more than a quarter of a century by Teddy Kollek, considered a liberal in ethnic matters, failed to treat Arabic consistently on a par with Hebrew, as a state law requires.

In the national context, the authorities lost little time aligning the socio-religious status of Muslim Jerusalemites with that of Muslim Israelis. For Muslim Jerusalemites the question of challenging these official actions did not arise, as their highest religious body, the SMC, refused to acknowledge the authority of the Israeli government, which retaliated in kind, and ignored its existence. The SMC, originally established by the British in Palestine in 1920, dissolved itself when the British departed in May 1948. Following the 1948 Arab-Israeli War, Jordan established a special ministry to fill the gap. When Israel occupied the West Bank and Arab Jerusalem in 1967, the religious personages of the territory revived the SMC, which began supervising Islamic sites and dealing with religious issues in Al Quds and elsewhere in the West Bank. It was financed by Jordan, and Israel made this arrangement official. The SMC maintains its own network of Sharia courts and judges—and so does Israel, where the state president appoints Sharia judges, and the Ministry of Religious Affairs runs Sharia courts whose verdicts are implemented by civil authorities. But the laws and procedures of the two systems are different, and the Israeli government ignores the workings of the courts run by the SMC, based in Jerusalem's Old City. Over the decades the two sides have worked out a modus operandi for routine cases in which Muslim Jerusalemites get approval from Sharia courts, and then register the document with the Israeli bureaucracy.

The continued non-co-operation of the SMC with the Israeli authorities is typical of Palestinian life. A whole range of Palestinian voluntary organizations have maintained this stance from the day of Israeli military occupation. This applies as much to the associations of lawyers, teachers, engineers, pharmacists, businessmen and hoteliers as taxi-drivers. They have all followed a consistent position rebuffing Jewish organizations' moves to merge and form associations covering all of united Jerusalem.

Since the Palestinian rejection of the Israeli rule rests on the international law regarding occupier and occupied, the stance of Arab attorneys towards Israel's legal system is of paramount significance. They continue to boycott Israel's courts, and refuse to apply for membership in the Israeli Bar Council, a sine qua non for practicing law in Israel, and ignore the authorities' gesture of conferring on them the Bar Council membership unilaterally. Consequently, when Palestinians decide to challenge any government action they end up hiring liberal-minded or iconoclastic Jewish lawyers.

What strikes even a casual visitor to the city immediately are the shop signs, either Hebrew or Hebrew/English, or Arabic or Arabic/English. Cafés and restaurants also tell whether it is an Arab or Jewish locality. The almost total absence of women in such a place means it is in an Arab neighborhood. And a mixed gathering, outside the ultra-Orthodox districts of West Jerusalem, unquestionably signals a Jewish environment.

The two communities are separate even in their leisure activities. A weekly supplement in the *Jerusalem Post* and the *Events in Jerusalem* newsletter are full of information about cinema, theater, music, nightclubs, art galleries, museums, cafes and restaurants—all of them in West Jerusalem. Neither carries a word about cultural events in East Jerusalem.

An acquaintance of mine, Peter, a British specialist on the Middle East, had told me that he was staying at the YMCA only a few hundred meters from my hotel. Armed with the phone number of the YMCA from *Events in Jerusalem*, I called. The receptionist said that they had no guest by that name. That surprised me: Peter had planned on staying for a few weeks. It was several days later that I realized that the YMCA I had phoned was in West Jerusalem, not East. So once I had obtained the new telephone number, I found Peter. The receptionist at the YMCA (West) had apparently not even thought to say "Have you tried the YMCA in East Jerusalem?"

The Palestinian intifada widened the cultural gap that has always existed between Arabs and the European Jews who began arriving in the early twentieth century. Respecting the Islamic ban on alcohol, and reflecting the deprivation and suffering resulting from the intifada, most Palestinians voluntarily abstained from drinking in the open. The intifada-driven call for austerity also applied to the cinema, the only popular form of entertainment. As a result the three movie theaters in East Jerusalem closed down, never to reopen. The only public entertainment available to East Jerusalemites were occasional plays performed by two highly political theater companies. In contrast, night-life in West Jerusalem became more lively than before.

Though Greater East Jerusalem has become ethnically mixed due to the Jewish settlements built since 1967, and extensive economic ties have developed between the two communities, there has been no discernible shift or relocation of commercial quarters on either side of Route One. Each of the ethnic groups continues to maintain its own exclusive central business district—the Jaffa Road area in West Jerusalem and the Salah al Din Street area in East Jerusalem.

Once visitors to the city cross Route One between west and east, they immediately notice the change in sights, sounds and smells. The shopping area in West Jerusalem could be anywhere in the European region of the Mediterranean. And the one in East Jerusalem is reminiscent of similar districts in Damascus or Amman: the street-stall holders selling kebabs grilled on red-hot charcoal; the newsstands displaying newspapers and precariously-bound books in Arabic only; the drivers of large, shared taxis merrily shouting their destinations; a young, lithe waiter, fast on his feet, delivering hot beverages in tiny cups or glasses to his scattered customers; an older man lugging a samovar of Turkish coffee: all the Western images of the Orient are here, within shouting distance of Salah al Din Street, just north of the historic Damascus Gate.

How a (European) Jewish Israeli, a journalist, arriving from West Jerusalem sees the scene is well captured by Yossi Halevi in the *Jerusalem Report*. "Walking along Salah al Din a Jew feels disoriented by strangeness," he reported. "The magazine covers at news-stands show pictures of evidently well-known men and women he can't identify; the bookstalls offer almost nothing except Islamic piety and political rage; iced carob juice is dispensed from a large brass samovar on a peddler's back and fava beans floating in vats of steaming water sold as an accompanying snack; groceries stock Shomar-brand mango wafers and lablabs with chilies from the Al Juneidah Dairy—companies and products unknown in West Jerusalem."[12]

Even the small, orderly tourist-oriented Jewish shops in the Old City's Jewish Quarter are far removed from the hustle and bustle of the medieval market of the Arabs with its aromatic spice shops and sacks of musky nuts and dried fruit.

Different days of the Sabbath—Friday for Muslims; and Saturday for Jews—add another dimension to the differences between the two communities. I witnessed the phenomenon one Friday. On my way to Jaffa Road from the American Colony Hotel in the early afternoon, my taxi got caught in a traffic jam. I left the cab and heaved myself up the hill past the New Gate of the Old City, and turned right into West Jerusalem. The small bookshop of Steimatzky, the most extensive chain of its kind in Israel, was crowded. It was hard even to stand up and open a book at the same time. I had scarcely found one volume I was seeking (shop assistants in Israel do anything but assist customers), and begun the search for the next, when an alarm went off, telling us to hurry up and leave. I had planned to get some photocopies done, but that shop had already closed. Within the next half an hour the area became almost deserted as I ambled along to keep an appointment with a Christian Palestinian near the Jaffa Gate. After a few cups of coffee and a long conversation, as we walked toward the Haram al Sharif, we encountered wave after wave of the Muslim faithful who, having finished the afternoon prayers and listened to the sermon at Al Aqsa Mosque, were repairing to their homes watched by young machine-gun-toting Israeli soldiers as well as agents of the Shin Beth. The following afternoon, Saturday, I took a stroll in the usually jammed Jaffa Road area, and counted the number of persons I encountered: only fifteen in as many minutes. In sharp contrast, the business in the Damascus Gate area was brisk, with hundreds of people about. I was struck not only by the contrast in the weekly rhythm of life of Jews and Muslims, but also by the proximity of the two different ways of life.

During my visits to the Old City and its environs, I noticed Arab souvenir shops selling many objects designed to appeal to Jewish pilgrims and tourists, including Stars of David, menorahs, and maps, guides and picture books with overtly Zionist text and images. (At one such store I bought a map of the Old City published by the Jewish Quarter Tourist Administration which showed the Jewish Quarter extending all the way from the western rampart to Via Dolorosa—in the process reducing the Muslim Quarter, in fact the largest of the four neighborhoods, to about the size of the Jewish Quarter, the smallest of the lot.) In stark contrast, West Jerusalem souvenir stores, catering among others for a substantial body of non-Jewish visitors and pilgrims, do not carry any Muslim or Christian religious symbols or objects.

More than religious tolerance or intolerance is involved. This contrasting behavior reflects economic imbalance between the two groups. The financially weak Muslim and Christian Palestinian merchants are not in a position to adhere strictly to their nationalist and religious affiliations by ignoring Jewish customers. The economically strong Jewish traders, on the other hand, can afford to overlook the non-Jewish customers and refrain from stocking Christian and Muslim religious souvenirs.

A similar situation prevails in employment. Israeli Jews are better educated and better off materially than Arabs. They control a very wide range of manufacturing and service industries, and are proportionately underrepresented in manual and semi-skilled jobs. Their business establishments, especially in hotel, catering and construction industries, draw on the Palestinian pool of unskilled and semi-skilled labor. There is no counter-movement: that is, there are no Arab employers engaging Jews in menial and semi-skilled jobs, or even in highly skilled positions. Few Jews, mostly salesmen, suppliers and debt-collectors, need to travel to Arab districts. On the contrary, acute economic necessity forces many Arabs to depend on Jews to earn their livelihood, often in Jewish neighborhoods.

All this takes place within the context of well-defined, deeply entrenched residential segregation, a hallmark of Jerusalem. The 30-year-long "reunification" has not resulted in the emergence of a single ethnically-mixed district. The decision of some liberal-leftist Jewish families to take up residence in East Jerusalem in order to spawn a mixed environment led nowhere. By the early 1980s they had retreated to West Jerusalem.

Persistent attempts by private Jewish capital, especially in the hotel and tourist industry, failed to gain a foothold in the Arab East Jerusalem. (Equally, such was the strength of Jewish opposition that there was no known case of an East Jerusalem Arab enterprise branching out into West Jerusalem or any of the Jewish settlements.) Having experienced the consequences of the sale of their agricultural land to immigrant Zionist Jews since the early 1900s, most Palestinians in Jerusalem resolved to resist the encroachment of Jewish capital into the urban property market. In any case there was no reciprocity. Though there was no administrative or judicial ban on selling or leasing Jewish real estate to Arabs (outside the Jewish Quarter of the Old City), this never happened. Michael Romann and Alex Weingrod note that "Needless to say, under the circumstances of 'United Jerusalem,' Jewish land is never sold or in other ways transferred to Arab ownership."[13]

Urban development in the Jewish neighborhoods of Jerusalem, whether in the West or Greater East, is subject to statutory regulations to ensure standards of construction, occupancy and neighborhood facilities. While the Israeli authorities are fully armed with plans for establishing and developing the Jewish settlements in Greater East Jerusalem, they have never had any planning scheme for the Arab sector of the eastern zone. Israeli bureaucrats routinely reject applications for building in Palestinian neighborhoods. Little wonder that between 1967 and 1984, the most intensive years of a government-financed construction boom in Greater East Jerusalem, nearly 90 percent of non-residential building—industrial plants, businesses and public offices—took place in Jewish neighborhoods.[14] The overall result was a further consolidation of spatial segregation between the two groups.

Due to the tax exemption given residents of Jewish settlements in Greater East Jerusalem, a typical Jewish household there paid less in taxes than its Arab counterpart. The Arabs, about 30 percent of Jerusalem's total population, contributed 26 percent of its tax revenue.[15] But what they got in return in services was only a fraction of their contribution.

This inequity was exposed by Amir Cheshin, a middle aged man who for over ten years was mayoral adviser on Arab Affairs. "Last May [1994] I leaked an unpublished report," he told me. "It compared municipal expenditure in West Jerusalem to that in East Jerusalem [excluding the Jewish settlements]. In East Jerusalem only between two to twelve percent of the total municipal budget items for services are invested in the infrastructure." What were the figures for West Jerusalem? "Two and a half times as high. The report revealed that in half of the Arab neighborhoods in [Greater] East Jerusalem there is no organized sewage system, and in the remaining half the system badly needs repairs. About a half of the water-supply system requires replacing. And drainage problems are severe, I tell you." And the street lighting and road maintenance? "Bad. Why don't you go and look for yourself." Where?

"Try an area which is partly Jewish and partly Arab. Try a couple."[16]

I did: north of the American Colony Hotel I focused on an area that forms the boundary between the Jewish neighborhood of Givat HaMivtar and the Arab village of Isawiya. Trees lined the street at the Jewish end, but as I walked downhill towards Isawiya, the trees disappeared.

Next I studied the southern Jerusalem village of Abu Tur, named after a legendary eleventh-century warrior who attacked the Crusaders from the back of a bull. Abu Tur is spread out along Jerusalem's most spectacular heights. The 1948 Arab-Israeli War split the village, with most of it ending up under Jordanian control, and the rest becoming part of the no-man's land between the armistice lines. It was reunited after the 1967 conflict, and partly rebuilt. Its scenic location attracted middle-class Jews who moved into the apartments constructed along the western edge of Abu Tur. The Jewish population rose steadily, reaching 5,000 in 1983 and nearly 6,000 a decade later, all in the upper section of the village. The Arabs, nearly twice as numerous, were confined downhill in the eastern sector of Abu Tur. While the Jewish zone became progressively posh, the Arab zone became increasingly overcrowded since the residents there were repeatedly denied permits to build new housing. The contrast between the two sides was well captured by the state of Ein Rogel Street, the spatial dividing line. As in the case of Givat HaMivtar-Isawiya, I found the Jewish section of Ein Rogel Street smoothly paved and well maintained, and its Arab section in disrepair.

As for civic services, little had changed since a study of Abu Tur by Michael Romann and Alex Weingrod in 1983. Arab and Jewish pupils attended separate schools, with Arabic and Hebrew as the respective language of instruction. Arab families availed of medical care facilities provided by Arab health clinics and hospitals located in Greater East Jerusalem while Jewish households made use of either the health clinic based in their sector by Histadrut or hospitals situated in West Jerusalem. Though in theory the local community center, run by the municipality and charged with providing entertainment and adult education, was open to both ethnic groups, in reality it catered to local Jewish inhabitants only.

Such studies are of more than academic interest. For they point to the difficulty of achieving a peaceful coexistence between Arabs and Jews, between Palestinians and Israelis, in the city and beyond.

As for Jerusalem, whether united in more than an administrative sense or not, there is another problem besides the Arab-Jew relationship. It concerns intra-Jewish relationships between secular Jews and the modern Orthodox Jews on the one hand, and between secular Jews and the ultra-Orthodox Jews concentrated in the Mea Shearim neighborhood on the other.

3

Mea Shearim

A Fortress of Jewish Ultra-Orthodoxy

I met David Asher in a small, open-fronted café on a narrow street in Mea Shearim in north Jerusalem. Furnished with small tables and black wooden chairs, each table bearing not a menu but an after-meal prayer, elegantly printed on a four-page folder with embroidered borders, the cafe was uncluttered and spotlessly clean. In black trousers and a white shirt, his head covered with a black cap, David exuded the confidence and easy manner that comes with owning and running a successful establishment.

"I was born religious," he began. "In 'Uzda, Morocco. My father was Moroccan, my mother Algerian. They came to Israel in 1948. I grew up in Jerusalem in Baqaa near Talpiyot. Did my army service, then traveled—all over, ended up in New York. I lived in the Village." Doing what? "From 1973 to 1989 I worked with WEVD Radio, the Hebrew language station. I was the producer, and my woman the news-reader, the DJ. We were busy, happy sometimes, not happy other times. But in New York I lost all my Jewish identity. Our Torah says not to do things like eating pork etc. I did all those things and more." What happened after 1989? "Returned home, Jerusalem, my roots. I was single: by then my relationship had ended. Now I am back to being a proper religious Jew. I follow the Torah, and feel healthier, cleaner, clearer." Sitting upright in his chair, he threw a quick glance at his trim body as if to verify his statement. "Some of my friends have become religious [like me]," he continued. "Why? Look around."

He turned to Rafi, my interpreter. "The crime rate in Israel is zooming. Drugs, AIDS. There's no communication between parents and children. Not like when I grew up. We respected our parents even when we didn't agree with them." Is it like that in Mea Shearim now? "Yes," he replied, his dark eyes brightening up. "Mea Shearim is a strong area of Judaism, a strong area. Most of it is full of synagogues and yeshivas." At least it was well demarcated, I remarked. "How do you mean?" he asked. I read aloud the large notices in English I had copied earlier at an entrance to the district:

> DEAR VISITOR, YOU ARE QUITE WELCOME TO MEA SHEARIM BUT
> PLEASE DO NOT ANTAGONIZE OUR RELIGIOUS INHABITANTS BY
> STROLLING THROUGH OUR STREETS IN IMMODEST CLOTHING.
> OUR TORAH REQUIRES THE JEWISH WOMEN TO BE ATTIRED IN

MODEST DRESS. MODEST DRESS: DRESS SLEEVES REACHING UNTIL BELOW THE ELBOWS (SLACKS FORBIDDEN), STOCKINGS, MARRIED WOMEN HAVING THEIR HAIR COVERED ETC., ARE THE VIRTUES OF THE JEWISH WOMAN THROUGHOUT THE AGES. PLEASE DO NOT OFFEND OUR RESIDENTS AND CAUSE YOURSELF ANY UNNECESSARY INCONVENIENCE. WE BEG YOU NOT TO INFRINGE UPON OUR WAY OF LIFE AND HOLY CODE OF LAW. WE BESEECH YOU TO USE DISCRETION BY NOT TRESPASSING OUR STREETS IN AN UNDESIRABLE FASHION. THE MEN ARE REQUESTED NOT TO ENTER BAREHEADED.
Thanking you in advance for complying with our request and wishing you blessings from above for your good deeds.
Committee for guarding modesty—Mea Shearim and Vicinity,
Jerusalem The Holy City.

"See, always so polite," David beamed. "Thanks, please, blessings. It all comes from having a community that is self-supporting, and cares for the weak and needy. There is a stable family life here. Divorce is rare. People live frugally, with lots of books and just a few pieces of furniture. They are not consumerists. We have self-help groups, and they supply anything, from baby clothes to cooking utensils, to poor families." People certainly looked less frantic, I said. "That's because we lead our lives according to the Torah. Everything should be run the way Torah says—at least in Jerusalem. It's a holy place. So only holy people should run it. At the City Hall in Jerusalem they don't read even one sentence from the Torah." That was odd, I remarked, because after the election of Ehud Olmert [in 1993] as mayor, the City Hall had started the Torah culture and Torah education departments. "That's the least Olmert could do, seeing how the ultra-Orthodox, put him there. They're so well organized they'll put Netanyahu in the driving seat when the time comes, you'll see." Then Olmert should take the path of *teshuva* (return, to strict Judaism) himself, I said. "Yes, why not?" replied Asher. "I did. That path is open to all Jews, whether Ashkenazi"—he turned to Rafi—"or Edot Mizrachim (Eastern Peoples) like me. A 'Born Again Jew.'"

The label Haredim/ultra-Orthodox applies to those Jews who adhere to a strict interpretation of the Halacha, Jewish Law. Full observance of the Halacha involves following all 613 religious prohibitions and obligations that regulate Jewish life, from trivial daily bodily functions to the organization of life in society—and separation between Jews and Gentiles. There are two major schools within ultra-Orthodoxy: Hassadim (pious) and Mitnagdim (opponents), and a minor school, Bratslavic, named after the Ukrainian town of Bratslav.

In Mea Shearim the signs of Jewish ultra-Orthodoxy were everywhere. Adult males, bearded to the man, maintained the tradition of donning the garb of the East European ghetto—black trousers, long black coats and wide black hats, their dolefulness relieved by the luster of their heavy-lidded eyes. Their sidelocks, shaped into ringlets, dangled from black hats. The few women about wore long-sleeved dresses, their skirts falling well below the knees and covering the upper part of their heavy stockings, their hair shielded from the gaze of lustful men by a scarf or a wig. "Many of the companies selling products in our neighborhood have to redesign the packaging so that there are no naked women or women dressed immodestly," Rubin Cardova, a tall Romanian Jew, wearing a black kippa over his light-brown hair, explained outside his sweetshop. "Otherwise they will not be able to sell the product here." He offered us a few sweets. "For the same reason television is off limits. You never know when a semi-clad woman will appear—in a commercial or a news item or a play or soap opera. It's the same with most Israeli publications— lots of nudity and lasciviousness."

That explained another social phenomenon in Mea Shearim and other ultra-Orthodox neighborhoods in Jerusalem and elsewhere: wallpapers. At a busy intersection near Cardova's shop, underneath a large sign in Hebrew and English, the stone wall of the two-story building was plastered with posters, fliers and news-sheets. A few bearded men, one of them resting his back against the saddle of his cycle, pored over the contents of the papers.

In the absence of television aerials the burden of modernity was borne by the solar-powered water-heaters clutched to the red-tiled roofs. Other than that Mea Shearim has kept its decrepit charm and character—conspicuously missing from the newer parts of Jerusalem—with dark, weather-worn houses, and rickety balconies laid out on both sides of narrow, crowded streets.

Driven out of the Old City of Jerusalem by overcrowding and poor sanitation, Jews set up a new colony to the north in 1875, naming it Mea Shearim. The settlement, heavily gated to keep the brigands out, was initially open to all Jews. It was only from the early twentieth century that it turned increasingly ultra-Orthodox.

Today, the early history of Mea Shearim is evident. I came across a semicircular sign in Hebrew and English over the entrance to a synagogue at the end of a string of shops, behind rolls of wallpaper and an array of upright brooms:

1898 SYNAGOGUE & FOUNDED 1898
ROTHERS ISSACHAROFF & BABAIOFF

The Hassadim, the leading ultra-Orthodox sect, was established by Israel Baal Shem Tov (1698–1740), a pious Jew, who, rebelling against the literalism of the Talmud attempted to help religious but illiterate Jews relate to Jewish law and doctrine emotionally. He devised a method of total surrender to God through mystical elevation, by singing and dancing. Despite being branded heretic by the Talmudists in 1781, the size of the Hassadi community grew, especially in Poland and Russia. Later, as literacy grew among Jews, the leaders of the sect corrected the initial dramatic lurch towards mysticism and restored a greater respect for the study of the Torah. They studied as industriously as others, but maintained an intimacy in communal life through such practices as congregational singing and dancing. But this balancing act was not enough for these who wanted a total return to the study of the Torah as a means to getting closer to God. They were called Mitnagdim. They thrived in Vilna, Lithuania. To distinguish themselves from the Hassidim, they hid their sidelocks behind their ears. Further division came when the followers of the late Rabbi Nahuman of Bratslav, Ukraine, abandoned the practice of having a living chief rabbi.[1]

At the beginning of the twentieth century a small minority of the Hassidim and the Mitnagdim migrated to Palestine, preferring to live in Jerusalem's Mea Shearim district. Over time, the Hassidim fell victim to hair-splitting factionalism, and broke up into four sub-sects, named after places in Poland: Belz, Gere, Lubavitch (also known as Habad) and Vishnitz. Today the male followers of these sub-sects can be differentiated by subtle differences in the traditional dress and appearance.

Politically, the early ultra-Orthodox in Palestine boycotted the quasi-official organs of the Yishuv, the Jewish community. They did so primarily because the creation of Israel through human endeavor, such as by Zionist pioneers in Palestine, ran counter to their belief that Israel would be redeemed by the Messiah. Secondarily, they were opposed to women's suffrage. They considered Jews as a religious, not ethnic, entity, and believed that the Jewish problems could only be solved by the Torah. When its members in Palestine accepted funds from the Jewish National Fund of the World Zionist Organization to establish kibbutzim and yeshivas, there was a split. The majority opted for co-operation with Zionists on the basis that Zionism could be put to the service of Judaism practised according to the Halacha. The minority, arguing that the Zionist effort to establish the Jewish homeland in Palestine was a "negative event" because it derived from the working of human rather than divine will, formed the Neturei Karta sect. It became the best known of the anti-Zionist sub-sects within the Hassadim.

In return for endorsing the United Nations partition plan for Palestine in 1947, as urged by David Ben Gurion, the foremost socialist Zionist leader, ultra-Orthodox leaders secured from him a written promise that in the future Jewish state laws would be promulgated regarding the Jewish Sabbath and dietary laws, rabbinical courts, and the status of the Chief Rabbinate. Ben Gurion made this decision against the background of the Holocaust after World War II, which had softened the earlier hardline secularism of his socialist Zionist colleagues.

Once Israel was founded in 1948, the ultra-Orthodox party Agudat Israel decided to participate in the state's affairs, including parliamentary elections, thus conferring an ultra-Orthodox recognition on the Zionist state. On the eve of the first general election in 1949 it combined with Mizrahi and several other religious organizations to constitute the United Religious Front (URF). In a parliament of 120, the URF won 16 seats and joined the government headed by David Ben Gurion of Mapai, the Israel Workers Party.

Mizrahi was the vehicle of Orthodox Jews, who were not as strictly committed to following the Jewish law and tradition as the ultra-Orthodox. Formed in 1902 in Vilnius, Lithuania, to counter growing secularization of the education of Jews in Europe, Mizrahi marked the rise of religious Zionism as a distinct faction within the Zionist movement, represented by the World Zionist Organization. The party advocated founding a Jewish national home in Palestine based on the Torah. Its overall thesis was that while "the great redemption" was in the hands of the Messiah, Zionism was helping to realize "a small redemption." In Palestine, Mizrahi ensured that the Chief Rabbinate was organized within the framework of the elected assembly representing the Yishuv, thus laying the foundation for a link between official, secular authority and religion, which was to continue after the establishment of Israel.

Accepted as part of the broad stream of Zionism, the dominant socialist Zionists shared power with Mizrahi. By securing the Ministry of Religious Affairs, the Mizrahi bloc put its stamp on the religious aspect of Israeli state and society during the important formative years. Since then the Mizrahi bloc, renamed the National Religious Party (NRP), shared power in all the coalition governments, whether headed by a left-of-center or right-of-center party. With the NRP in control, the Ministry of Religious Affairs decided how to finance rabbinical councils and rabbinical courts, and influenced the composition and working of the powerful Chief Rabbinate and Rabbinical Council. Over the years Orthodox rabbis, often politically loyal to the NRP, have successfully challenged the legitimacy of non-Orthodox marriages, divorces and conversions in Israel. Despite secular influences, the Sabbath is enforced strictly in Israel. During Sabbath, from Friday sunset to Saturday sunset, there is no public transport and no delivery of telegrams. Newspapers do not appear on Saturday. The Ministry of Religious Affairs is in charge of Jewish shrines such as the Western Wall, so men and women are segregated and rules against working on the Sabbath are strictly enforced at the Wall.

All this goes on in the context of the lack of a constitution in Israel. The statement in the Declaration of the Establishment of Israel in May 1948 that a constitution would be drafted by the following October remains unfulfilled to this day. So the relationship between the state and the synagogue has yet to be constitutionally defined.

Most observers believe that the decision of the Israeli state to make the Halacha binding in such areas of life as marriage, divorce and death (burial without religious rites, and cremation, are forbidden) has general backing among secular Jews. By and large secularists perceive it as an effective way of avoiding conflict between civic and religious centers of power in these personal matters of import.

"Secular Israelis have a need, so it seems, to maintain religious institutions which will keep the faith on their behalf but, at the same time, by the extremist nature of these institutions, make sure that the majority of [Jewish] Israelis have nothing to do with them," writes Rabbi Dow Marmur. "In this way the dominant religion of the Jewish state has become institutionalized vicarious Judaism."[2]

The sharing of authority and responsibility between religious and civil leaderships extends to other important areas such as education. In Palestine each of the three groupings of Zionists—secular socialist Mapai, Orthodox Mizrahi and ultra-Orthodox Agudat—set up its own educational system. After the founding of Israel, the Mapai-dominated government disbanded its network and transformed it into a secular state system, but left intact the Mizrahi- and Agudat-run schools and yeshivas, with the schools to be financed fully, and the yeshivas partly, by public money.

In the Ashkenazi tradition, a yeshiva was a community affair, with the local rabbi acting as its head, and a local student body taught part-time in Yiddish. But in the eighteenth century, yeshivas in Lithuania and Belorussia emerged as regional boarding schools, drawing bright students from a large area. Most of these students, engaged in full-time study and worship, were aged 15 to 24, and unmarried. Later, in 1878, *kollels* (including) emerged as post-yeshiva institutions for brilliant married students who wanted to continue Torah studies. When Orthodox and ultra-Orthodox

Jews from East Europe began migrating to Palestine in the early twentieth century, they transplanted single-sex educational institutions there.

With a dramatic upsurge in Jewish immigration from Arab countries to Israel between 1950–53, the popularity of single-sex schools rose even more, since parents from Arab countries disapproved of their daughters attending mixed-sex schools.

The establishment of Israel as a social welfare state created conditions conducive to the consolidation and expansion of the religious communities, especially the ultra-Orthodox, whose male members are encouraged to spend a lifetime in study and worship. With the safety net of state allowances guaranteeing a minimum living standard, the leaders of the ultra-Orthodox community were able to transform the voluntary ghetto of the past into a formally demarcated territory where they were able to enforce a rigidly Judaistic way of life.

Within a generation of Israel's existence, the self-contained ultra-Orthodox educational system, totally divorced from its secular counterpart, completely socialized the children of the community. Also young people married early, and became parents within a few years. They thus became socially and economically dependent on the community's extended family, which provided mutual assistance and cared for its weaker members. But after fathering half a dozen children, when mature yeshiva graduates tried to find jobs (to supplement the earnings of their wives) they found their choice limited: rabbis or rabbinical judges, or religious functionaries to supervise Jewish dietary laws, etc. Further, as the size of the ultra-Orthodox community, opposed to birth control, increased, the burden of supporting an ever burgeoning body of religious scholars by state and private charity, mainly by the co-sectarians in North America, became unbearable. Agudat's political agenda narrowed to maintaining yeshivas and kollels with public and private funds.

Since the emergence of Israel, the popularity of the religious parties has remained remarkably stable. The influence of the ultra-Orthodox parties increased after the 1981 poll. At that time, they held the balance of power between Labor (47 seats) and Likud (48 seats). To gain their backing, Likud Premier Menachem Begin allocated extra funds to their educational and cultural institutions, exempted ultra-Orthodox women from military service, and made draft deferment for yeshiva students easier.

Besides funding, the subject that has most interested ultra-Orthodox leadership is the exemption from military service for its yeshiva students. The idea was first aired during the 1948 Arab-Israeli War. prime minister David Ben Gurion agreed to exempt them from compulsory draft on the basis that, given the paucity of such students, their deaths in combat could undermine the future of Torah studies. His decision then affected some 500 young men. By the early 1990s the total population of yeshiva students exceeded 100,000 (some 30,000 more than the aggregate student body of the Israeli universities), of which about 20,000 were enrolled in ultra-Orthodox institutions. The ultra-Orthodox claim that intensive, full-time study of Jewish law and tradition is imperative to ensure the spiritual survival of Jews. They point to the Old Testament, which records that Moses exempted the Levis, or priests, from fighting during the 40 years of the Jewish wanderings in the desert.

But the fact is, the ultra-Orthodox leadership fears that exposing its young men and women to two or three years in the secular environment of the military would undermine the continuity and strength of its community by causing defections. Also the very idea of the mixing of young men and women, a common practice in the IDF, is anathema to the ultra-Orthodox. Indeed, in 1953 the ultra-Orthodox frustrated the implementation of a law conscripting women into the armed forces. Its female members threatened to court arrest rather than serve in the military. The government backed down, but insisted that a woman draftee would have to be tested on her religious knowledge. In 1981, Premier Begin discontinued this practice, and gave an option to ultra-Orthodox women to do alternative community service for two years.

All male yeshiva students are deferred from military service so long as the IDF does not need them, though most non-ultra-Orthodox yeshiva students serve in the armed forces.

The overall impression among most Israeli Jews was that the ultra-Orthodox were deliberately avoiding the patriotic duty of military service, an immoral, unethical thing to do. They were also critical of ultra-Orthodox intolerance and zealotry in enforcing strict observance of the Sabbath. This manifested itself publicly and regularly, with the police in Jerusalem closing as many as 130 streets and roads to vehicular traffic on the Sabbath and other Jewish holidays in order to prevent the ultra-Orthodox from stoning passing cars and trucks in "religious self-defense."

The number of such streets in Jerusalem has been on the increase, reflecting the movement of the large ultra-Orthodox families from their increasingly crowded traditional neighborhoods into adjoining areas. A pattern is already discernible. A few ultra-Orthodox families move into a new street, followed by a few more, and start pressuring their neighbors to observe the Sabbath strictly—not to drive or play the radio loudly or work in the back garden. Finally they shut the street down on the Sabbath, thus getting the police involved. With their power increasing at City Hall, the ultra-Orthodox feel increasingly bold.

Mirroring the increase in their size, the ultra-Orthodox have acquired a greater political clout than before. In the quarter century since the 1967 War, the percentage of the ultra-Orthodox among Jerusalem Jews doubled, from 15 to 30. But due to large families, more than half of Jerusalem's Jewish pupils under the age of ten were ultra-Orthodox.

In the November 1993 elections two-thirds of the votes for the winner, Ehud Olmert of the Likud, came from the ultra-Orthodox electors. Overall, the ultra-Orthodox parties secured eight seats in the 30-member municipal council with a total of the religious parties forming the largest single bloc of thirteen—versus the total strength of ten for Labor and the leftist Meretz. Together with seven members of the Likud and the right-wing secular nationalist Tzomet, the rightist-religious alliance controlled two-thirds of the seats in the City Hall. One of the first acts of the new council was to double the budget for the ultra-Orthodox schools.

Nationally, the budget in 1992 raised allocations for ultra-Orthodox educational and cultural institutions to an unprecedented $246 million, a 500-fold increase in less than a decade.

On the eve of this election, at the behest of Rabbi Eliezer Schach, the head of a prestigious yeshiva, a number of Orthodox parties combined to form the United Torah Judaism (UTJ) party. It won six seats. An equal number of seats were secured by another ultra-Orthodox group, Shas. The nucleus of its support was the ultra-Orthodox community within the Mizrachim, the term used for the Jews of Middle Eastern or North African origin.

When Mizrachim arrived in Israel in the early 1950s they were dispersed to development towns in the Negev and Galilee. Some were attracted to ultra-Orthodoxy out of alienation from the dominant European Jewish political-culture in Israel, though the yeshivas were invariably run by Ashkenazim. Over time Mizrachim realized that Ashkenazim were unprepared to regard them as equals academically or socially. They also noticed Ashkenazi reluctance to marry Mizrachim. The resulting disappointment found resonance and a voice in Iraqi-born Ovadia Yosef, the Sephardic Chief Rabbi through much of the 1970s.

Finally, Mizrachi disaffection took a political turn. In the 1982 local election in Jerusalem the Mizrachi ultra-Orthodox, encouraged by Chief Rabbi Yosef, offered their own list of candidates, in competition with the Ashkenazi ultra-Orthodox. The Mizrachi list did surprisingly well.

This led to the formation of Shas in late 1983. It received the blessing of Rabbi Yosef, who visualized it as a vehicle for righting the wrongs being done to Mizrachim by Ashkenazim. He encouraged Arye Deri, a young Moroccan-born ultra-Orthodox rabbi from Bnei Beraq, to join Shas. In the 1984 election Shas, led by Deri, won four seats. It joined the national unity administration, and Deri became a cabinet minister at 29. The government allowed Shas to establish its own educational network, thus raising the total of such systems to four, three of them religious.

In 1988 Shas secured six seats, and became the largest religious group in parliament. Its leading figures, Rabbis Arye Deri and Yitzhak Peretz, became ministers. Though the party's backing came almost exclusively from Mizrachim, its leadership was beholden to the Ashkenazi Chief Rabbi Schach. But when Schach publicly snubbed Yosef, his move terminated the Ashkenazi-Sephardic dual leadership of Shas, with the party now deciding to rely exclusively on Yosef.

During the campaign for the June 1992 election, Rabbi Schach said publicly that "the time has not yet come for Sephardim to take positions of leadership. They need to follow Ashkenazi guidance." Sephardim had not been so blatantly insulted in a long time. This goaded Rabbi Yosef—who had earlier threatened to resign from Shas—to withdraw his threat and to become the top campaigner for the party. Shas improved its overall vote, and retained its six seats. Yosef thus emerged as the most powerful rabbi in the country. In the process he liberated the religious Mizrachim from the domination of their Ashkenazi counterparts.

Born in Baghdad in 1920, Ovadia Yosef was raised in Jerusalem, which has been his base ever since. A brilliant yeshiva student, he became an author at eighteen, and went on to publish nearly 30 more volumes on religious matters. Significantly, he retained the traditional Sephardi rabbinical dress of a gold-embroidered black robe and a blue turban-shaped hat. The medically-prescribed dark glasses he wears also enhance his distinctive appearance.

Throughout his career as a Sephardi rabbi, he suffered slights and insults at the hands of the Ashkenazi religious establishment, which dismissed him as "a donkey bearing books," describing him as more a memorizer of the sacred texts than an original thinker or interpreter. But he sharpened his knowledge and understanding of the Torah, and started to make his mark in the early 1960s, journeying up and down the country, urging his audiences in synagogues and movie theaters to take up study of the Torah. Yet even when he rose to be the Chief Rabbi of Sephardim he was excluded from the Council of Torah Sages, an exclusively Ashkenazi body, the final spiritual and political authority among the ultra-Orthodox Jewry. Among Yosef's memorable rulings, when holding the high office, was the one which declared that the Falashas of Ethiopia were fully Jewish. The other was that Sephardi soldiers should pray separately to preserve their own ritual rather than join the Ashkenazim in a common service. Unlike his hardline Ashkenazi counterpart, Chief Rabbi Shlomo Goren, Yosef has taken a middle position on the thorny issue of Israel and the messianic redemption: "While the restoration of Jewish sovereignty has religious value, it is premature to speculate about its messianic significance." Equally, on making peace with Arab neighbors, he has been dovish. At a conference on Jewish law in August 1989, he declared it religiously permissible to return parts of the Land of Israel if that would "prevent war and save lives."

Having seen his picture on the walls of several shops, cafés and restaurants in different Israeli cities, I was curious to encounter him in the flesh. So I went to the Yasdim synagogue in the Bukharan Quarter of Mea Shearim in Jerusalem one Saturday night. The place was packed, as was the small adjoining room, with admirers glued to the video-screen. Following the custom, the congregation passed around mint and basil branches to taste the sweetness of the just-ended Sabbath. The moment Rabbi Yosef arrived, flanked by aides, pin-drop silence ensued. As he cut through a parting knot of people, the faithful touched his robe and then placed their fingers on their lips, as if he were a Torah scroll. Having seated himself in a chair the size of a throne, he started talking conversationally, as if addressing each of the members of the audience personally.

Emulating his example, other ultra-Orthodox Sephardi rabbis too speak colloquial Hebrew when addressing their congregations. This is in marked contrast to Ashkenazi ultra-Orthodox rabbis who speak literary Hebrew and remain aloof from their audiences. The Sephardi ultra-Orthodox also broke the traditional taboo against television, freely using the medium to give interviews and propagate their views to large audiences, attempting all the time to draw secular Jews back to the religious fold. At well-orchestrated rallies in sports stadiums, in between popular religious music, they lambast the emptiness, corruption and decadence of Israeli secular life and offer to fill the vacuum with a genuine Torah way of life. Their secular critics accuse them of cynically exploiting the gullible among the electorate and point to the charges of corruption and bribery levelled against the party's political leader, Arye Deri.

Nonetheless, it was undeniable that the arrival of Shas on the political stage changed the nature of religious politics. "Mizrachim's drive for [political] self-help resulted in the creation of Shas," said Dr. Meir Buzaglo, a slim, balding,

Moroccan-born Jew with dark tinted glasses, who teaches philosophy at the Hebrew University of Jerusalem. "Shas has its institutions and organization, and it provides good education in its schools. Actually Shas started with education mainly in poor [Mizrachi] neighborhoods. Because of Shas the political stereotype of Mizrachim broke down. Until then, Mizrachi opinions were solicited from taxi-drivers [most of whom are Mizrachim]. Now in the media the Shasnik is one among the few images of the Mizrachi. Several stereotypes are better than one. And with separate elections for parliament and prime minister in the future, more and more Sephardim will split their votes—give one to Likud or Labor for prime minister, and the other to Shas."[3]

4

Mizrachim/Sephardim
Coming of Age

The first thing, when arranging to meet a stranger at a public place, is to ask: How will I recognize you? "I am tall, well-built, balding, Middle Eastern looking, and I'll be wearing a leather jacket," came the reply from my prospective Hebrew interpreter, David Siso. "Middle Eastern looking," I repeated the phrase. He meant he looked like an Arab—that he was an Arab Jew, just as there are European Jews and American Jews. Nobody in Israel says "Arab Jew": it is seen as a contradiction in terms. The words in vogue are Mizrachim and Sephardim. Though used interchangeably, the terms have different meanings. "Sephardim" applies to a religious school within Judaism whereas "Mizrachim" is a geographical term that covers all those Jews not originally from Europe/the West. But the two terms share the same counterpart: Ashkenazim, used in both religious and geographical contexts. Hence the confusion.

I traveled with David Siso by bus from the coastal plain of Haifa to Mount Meron. We began our slow ascent in the mountainous Galilee on our way toward Safed, a center of Jewish mystical tradition, *kabbala*, since the sixteenth century. Each year hundreds of thousands of Jewish Israelis visit the area partly to admire nature, but mostly to visit the shrines of eminent rabbis of the past, revered as *tsadiks*, morally pure men who possessed miraculous powers, in the woods surrounding Safed.

Mount Meron holds the shrine of Rabbi Shimon Bar Yohai, reputed author of second-century Palestine's *Book of Zohar* (Splendor or Enlightenment), the single most influential work of Jewish mysticism. During the springtime Lag Ba'Omer festival, up to 200,000 believers, mainly Mizrachim, gather to pay homage to Rabbi Bar Yohai. Among them were many of Siso's close relatives, all of Iraqi origin, although it was his own first visit. Between the annual festivals, Mizrahi faithful arrive daily by thousands, to pray and call upon Bar Yohai to intercede with the Almighty in moments of crisis. In contrast, among Ashkenazim only the small Hassadi sect members appeal to the *tsadiks* in this way.

We went past the open blue iron gate reserved for males, and entered a courtyard leading to the shrine. Accosted by a bearded man in black, intent on collecting funds, I pumped him for information. "The shrine was built by Rabbi Abraham Galanta 500 years ago," he said. "Rabbi Shimon Bar Yohai was buried here more than 1,800 years ago. The Jews come here to pay respects, mostly those who believe in *kabbala*."

Inside, every room had prayer books stacked against whitewashed walls. The cloths covering the tomb had Hebrew inscriptions embroidered in gold. The one side reserved for women was blocked from view. After praying, his head covered with my tweed cap, Siso glanced at the scribbled entreaties. "Meir Amitel will be undergoing surgery on Thursday. Please pray for him," said one.

How effective are the appeals to Bar Yohai? "I have been married 16 years, and had three daughters," replied Shaul Katchta, who ran the sandwich kiosk. "When my wife was pregnant last time, I prayed at the shrine for a son. We got a son. If you really believe in it, and pray seriously, it works."

To most Ashkenazim this is unfamiliar territory, and their rabbis openly criticize such practices. They blame the influence of Christianity and Islam for Jewish saint worship, which became established in the eighteenth century. The fact that some of the Jewish shrines in the Galilee include Muslim-style domes and carry inscriptions in Arabic lends weight to their reasoning.

The Jews of Morocco have recreated in Israel the legend of a much more recent saint, popularly known as Baba Sali. His grizzled, ascetic face adorns many Mizrachi homes and shops. He was a legend in his life time in Morocco, and was given a posthumous lease of fame and adulation by his son Baruch Abu Hatzeira who re-interred him in Netivot, a largely Moroccan development. Abu Hatzeira declared in the early 1980s that his father's sainthood had reincarnated itself in him, providing an opportunity to Moroccan Jews to continue the tradition. They flock to Netivot in huge numbers on Baba Sali's birthday and, to the disgust of many Ashkenazim and most secularists, turn the occasion into an open-air Arab bazaar, scooping up specially blessed amulets to beat the evil eye. "Were David Ben Gurion to know of this he would turn in his grave," said a Moroccan educator, as he cited the veteran Israeli leader: "'The Moroccan Jew took a lot from the Moroccan Arabs. The culture of Morocco I would not like to have here.'"[1]

Siso and I talked as we ate Katchta's sandwiches. "On arrival in Israel, Mizrachim were sent off to development towns, to the fringes of Israel," said Siso. "They were Europeanized in a rough way. My grandfather, Eliezer, was a rabbi in Baghdad, a highly respected man. He and the whole family were sprayed with DDT before being allowed to disembark from the ship. He never forgave them for that. The Ashkenazi immigration clerks changed our names if they found them unfamiliar or difficult to pronounce. The name of my mother [then eight years old] was Faiwaza. The immigration clerk changed it instantly to Zvi. Her parents did not know what was happening—they did not know Hebrew."

"They arrived wearing local dresses. The Ashkenazi bureaucrats made the Mizrachim discard their traditional clothes, and put them all into western khaki clothes, men and women alike. For Jews like my grandfather it was difficult... Since they did not know the language they had no control over their children, who were being taught in Hebrew; they became helpless."

The migration of Jews from some ten Arab countries occurred in the wake of the Arab defeat in the 1948–9 War, which created anti-Jewish feeling and violence in the Arab world. Mizrachi Jews began arriving in large numbers in Israel in 1949, and a decade later they totaled more than half a million.

They arrived in a Jewish state founded by Ashkenazim in the image of their East European background. Of the 717,000 Jews in Israel in 1948, four-fifths were Ashkenazim, and they dominated every stratum of society, from manual workers to the elite. The long-established small Mizrachi communities in Jerusalem, Safed and Tiberias had nothing to do with Zionism, as they traced their roots to the post-1492 period in Spain when Jews had migrated to other Mediterranean countries, including Palestine. In the process they acquired the name Sephardim, from Sephard, Spain.

"After the establishment of Israel, when Ben Gurion saw about three-quarters of a million Jews, mostly European, versus about twice as many Arab Palestinians, he became quite desperate," said Sami Chetrit, in his mid-30s, with a post-graduate degree in political science from Columbia University, who headed a Mizrachi school in Tel Aviv. "Only the European survivors of the Holocaust came to Israel because they had no other choice. 'We have the state we longed for, but the people we wanted are not here,' Ben Gurion said in 1952. His pleas to American Jews to come to Israel had failed. Their leaders had told him: 'We are not Zionist in your sense of the word. We can be Zionist as American patriots. We'll give you financial support.' All the American Jews who had been to Palestine during the Second World War had returned home, nobody settled here."[2]

And the Israeli reactions? "When the European Jews were faced with us, Arab Jews, in the early 1950s, they panicked," replied Chetrit. "If you read the papers and magazines of that time, everybody was in panic—not only officials and politicians but also journalists, thinkers, academics. They feared that their European culture would be overwhelmed by Arab culture. Dusting Arab Jews with DDT was symbolic."

But Ashkenazi fears were misplaced. The Mizrachim were few, with little formal education, untutored in Hebrew, and without effective leadership. Their political and commercial elite had migrated to the West, not to Israel. Having had almost no grounding in the concept and practice of Zionism, and lacking any previous contacts with the Zionist groups now in power in Israel, they found themselves dumped in temporary housing or shunted to far-off development towns, given poorly paid jobs or assigned to new co-operative farms, *moshavim*, with limited funds. The infusion of this new underclass into Israel allowed the Ashkenazim to move upward socially and economically.

By the mid-1960s, due to higher birth and immigration rates Mizrachim surpassed Ashkenazim in numbers, but they lagged behind in all other aspects of society. In contrast to the cultural autonomy they had enjoyed as Jews in most Arab countries, they were controlled in Israel by leaders tied to political parties, bureaucrats and other organs of the state.

The behavior of the dominant Mapai (later Labor) party toward Mizrachim varied between patronizing and bullying. The Ashkenazi Zionists, like other Europeans, held oriental culture in low esteem, and made no allowance for the common Jewishness they shared with Mizrachim. Mapai/Labor activists, given to glib stereotyping, often described Mizrachim as the "lost generation of the desert" which, by persisting in its old ways, was seriously undermining Israel's European culture.

In the 1950s, the government implemented a system to absorb Arab Jews by modernizing them—that is, Europeanizing them. "Since Mizrachim were excluded from the decision-making process, Ashkenazim decided our fate," said Chetrit. "In the process they destroyed our Arab culture. So what we have today is that half of the Israeli Jewish society has lost its heritage, its culture."

The strategy was effective but the human price was high. "Young people from Morocco or Yemen were encouraged to shed their culture, with their distinctive folklore, and music and dress," notes Stephen Brook, a Jewish British writer. "Everything that had been familiar to these people was taken away from them, and in its place they had to assume the styles and values of an essentially secular Zionism that bore little relation to the way they had been raised... For many Oriental Jews the problems of adaptation proved too great. Slums developed in the new towns and in the old cities. Without a proper job, heads of family lost both their self-respect and the respect of their children, and the entire family structure began to fall apart. Children, unanchored, often turned to crime."[3]

Yet the Ashkenazi establishment remained skeptical. "Maybe in the third generation something will appear from the Oriental Jew that is a little different," Ben Gurion said in the late 1960s. "But I don't see it yet."[4]

To be sure, the newcomers did not always endure the jibes and humiliation silently. But protests did not seem to have much impact on the Ashkenazim. Serious reconsideration of the Mizrachim policy had to await developments in US race relations. Taking their cue from the revival of ethnic pluralism in America, Ashkenazi decision-makers began moderating their stance on the hegemony of European culture. As a result, the Ministry of Education and Culture came up with a program of Mizrachi and Sephardi history, literature and folklore to embellish the secular school curriculum.

By now the authorities were dealing with the second generation of Mizrachi immigrants. Emulating the example and name of the Black Panthers, some of them initiated a protest movement in the late 1960s in Israel. The Black Panther Party (BPP) focused on the discrimination and economic disadvantages, especially in housing, suffered by Mizrachim. By staging large, often violent demonstrations in Jerusalem, embarrassing the governing Ashkenazim-dominated Labor Party, it acquired a high profile. But it failed to win a single seat in the December 1973 election.

In that poll, Menachem Begin's two-month-old right-wing Likud bloc secured 39 seats, partly because of support from Mizrachi voters. Over the years, recoiling from the mistreatment by the Labor establishment, Mizrachim had begun supporting the opposition. Though an Ashkenazi, Begin convinced his Mizrachi audiences that he and his party, treated as a pariah by the elitist Labor leadership since the founding of Israel, stood in the same "excluded" column as they did. Once David Levy, a 32-year-old Moroccan construction worker, became the first Mizrachi elected to parliament on the Herut ticket in 1969, Begin had someone in the party leadership with whom ordinary Mizrachim could instantly identify.

He urged Mizrachim to maintain self-respect, and promised them official treatment on a par with Ashkenazim as Jews and as Israelis. In the 1973 poll Begin went out of his way to boost Levy's importance.

In the May 1977 election Likud emerged as the largest group in parliament mostly because of increased Mizrachi support and the split in Labor. Likud's success was greeted with jubilation by Mizrachim, who taunted Labor leaders, "At last we have paid you back for the DDT." Of the twenty ministers in Begin's cabinet, five were Mizrachi. This was in stark contrast to the total of three Mizrachi ministers appointed during Labor's 29 years in power.

But the Mizrachim's arrival on the national political stage did not end the long-held Ashkenazi prejudices. A year after the swearing-in of the Begin government, the Israeli military chief of staff said: "It will take years and years before Oriental Jews, even those acquiring full education [here], will manage to cope with the mentality of the West."[5]

Having won the support of a majority of Mizrachim, Begin took steps to consolidate and expand it. He exceeded his promise of providing 9,000 civil service jobs to Mizrachim. His police minister, a Mizrachi, opened the doors of the force to fellow-Mizrachim, thus recasting the Mizrachim-hating image of the police.

During the three election campaigns in the 1980s both Labor and Likud wooed Mizrachim. But Likud remained far ahead of its rival.

Just as Labor's 1977 defeat had partly to do with the Mizrachi factor, so too did the Likud failure in 1992. When the Likud candidate list failed to reflect the extent of support the party had among Mizrachim at large, a substantial minority of working-class Mizrachi voters abstained, and many middle-class Mizrachi switched to Labor.

Overall, in the political arena Mizrachim had advanced substantially since becoming a majority in 1965. At lower levels, Mizrachi political power was roughly in line with the community's numerical strength. In the 1992 parliament, one-third of the members were Mizrachi, with the proportion on Labor benches being about 40 percent. By then they had produced a president of the republic, Yitzhak Navon; two deputy prime ministers (including David Levy); an army chief of staff (Moshe Levy); and a secretary-general of Histadrut (Yisrael Kessar).

Furthermore, by then the idea of a Mizrachi political party had emerged. A former Likud parliamentarian, ousted over corruption charges, formed Tami, a Mizrachi party which won three seats and a government ministry in 1981. In 1984, Tami secured only one seat partly because a new Mizrachi party, Shas, also entered the electoral fray. Since then Shas has become a fixture of the Knesset.

But despite all the political progress made by Mizrachim, Shas is the only Mizrachi-led party. Ashkenazim still maintain a monopolistic hold over the government's economic ministries, public sector undertakings, Histadrut's vast industrial complex, and the leading organizations in the private sector.

Equally important, Mizrachim are almost absent from the top echelons of intellectual, opinion-forming and policy-making influence. Halfway through my research in Israel, which included interviewing leading officials, academic specialists, senior journalists, opinion formers and other intellectuals, I realized that, contrary to my intention that half my Jewish interviewees be Mizrachi, I had not encountered a single such person. How was I to fill this gap?

I mentioned my problem to David Eppel, an amiable senior editor of British origin at the Israel Broadcasting Authority in Jerusalem, and asked if there was a Mizrachi journalist in his organization. After saying no, Eppel became pensive, as if he hadn't ever thought of this question. But Avi Gus, an East European senior editor in the Hebrew news section, became tense and defensive. "I speak Arabic and I am an expert on Middle East politics," he said, implying that the only purpose for which a Mizrachi journalist could be employed would be Arabic language broadcasts and/or Middle Eastern events. Then, having assured me that there were no differences between Ashkenazim and Mizrachim, Gus added: "A large number of those in jail are Mizrachim, and a high percentage of criminals are Mizrachim. They have a lower educational level and lower income level."

Why? I asked Professor Sammy Smooha, an Iraqi Jew in the sociology department of the Haifa University. In an office surrounded by books, he began: "For obvious reasons, Mizrachim started out with a severe handicap, social, economic and cultural. Forty years on, there is still a visible socio-economic gap between Mizrachim and Ashkenazim. The Mizrachi per capita income is two-thirds the figure for Ashkenazim. Mizrachim are the dominant majority in the poor and working classes whereas Ashkenazim are predominant in the upper middle and upper classes. It is a vicious circle. Because most Mizrachim live in poor neighborhoods in cities and in development towns, their schooling is poor.... Statistics show that two-thirds of Mizrachi students go to vocational schools whereas two-thirds of Ashkenazi students go to academic schools. You see that clearly in the percentage who matriculate [high school graduation]. For Ashkenazim the figure is 46, and for Mizrachim 25."

And at universities? "Mizrachim are only 20 percent of the student body and Ashkenazim over 70 percent even though the two communities are almost equal in size," continued Smooha. "The additional hurdle for Mizrachim is the university entrance exam. It tests the applicant's general knowledge of western culture, where Mizrachim are at a disadvantage."

What has been the government response? "It recognizes that there are differences in the academic achievement of the two communities," replied Smooha. "But it insists on calling Mizrachim 'culturally disadvantaged,' not 'socially or ethnically disadvantaged.' The Zionist state is in a bind. There is no place for ethnicity within Zionism. Yet, in Israel's predominantly immigrant society, ethnic differences exist. The Ashkenazi establishment tries to close its eyes to it, insisting that even if there is a problem it is receding fast.

"But you have to push the Ashkenazi establishment, as I've done—sting them. Then you get to the second layer, at the truth. You find that Ashkenazim have very deep feelings, prejudices and convictions. You find them full of insecurity, apprehension, and fear that they might lose control, hatred even. They feel that Mizrachim are ungrateful for what has been done for them; they are inferior, overdemanding, overdependent on state [benefits]; they are responsible for their own backwardness because they are not trying hard and expect the authorities to spoon-feed them... and they are always complaining. They nurture unjustified feelings of deprivation instead of working hard, postponing their immediate gratification by investing in further education; and even now middle-class ethics and values elude them."

Smooha's specific argument boiled down thus: "The government's solutions are compensatory education and social welfare. But experience has shown that these steps are just enough to arrest further widening of the gap, but not enough to reduce the gap itself. The government action is well short of a comprehensive social policy. It amounts to tinkering with the problem, not tackling it head on."

My interviews with Mizrachi educators revealed that the "compensatory education" was not the panacea it was made out to be by education ministry officials, and that the problem was deep-rooted, tied as it was to the self-esteem of Mizrachi students, the history books they had to read, and so on.

Instead of carping about the inadequacy of the governmental action, a group of Mizrachi educators and intellectuals set up a non-profit organization, called Kedma (Going East) in 1993.[6] It started two schools for disadvantaged Mizrachi students, in Tel Aviv and in Jerusalem the next year. "At Kedma we respect the student, his parents and culture, which is not the case with the state system," said Dr. Meir Buzaglo. "We want to create self-respect among Mizrachi students, something they have lost in an Ashkenazim-dominated culture. We support our students' identity of themselves, and do not destroy it. The state policy has been to implement the concept of the melting pot under the supremacy of Ashkenazim. This destroyed the identity of all those Jews who came from Arab countries. Later the state policy became 'pluralism/multi-culturalism'—again under the supremacy of Ashkenazim."

What is Kedma's end-purpose? "Ultimately Kedma is about policy, about power structure," replied Buzaglo. "We want the power to decide for ourselves. Our aim is that Mizrachim should take responsibility for their education, be self-reliant and stop being merely critical. We want Mizrachi students to understand their parents, their language, their heritage, where they came from. They should study Moroccan or Yemeni or Iraqi history, and not so much of Russian history which is the case now. In order to do so, at Kedma schools teachers do not use Ministry of Education text books in literature or history, but produce their own material."

What was wrong with standard history texts at school, I asked Sami Chetrit in Tel Aviv. "In history books Mizrachim are marginal," he began. "They appear only in the context of Zionism even though they were not Zionists. These books give only a few pages to their history... to say that they were persecuted. For example in Iraq in 1941. Actually that had to do with the failure of the nationalist coup by [Rashid] Gailani against the Iraqi monarchy which was under the British thumb. But this was a minor affair. There was nothing like what happened in Europe, the Holocaust. But history books state that Arab Jews were miserable etc., and their salvation came through Zionism. As if those Jews had done nothing of any consequence before the arrival of Zionism. Actually, Iraqi Jews were a thriving community. They were one-sixth of the population of Baghdad. As late as in 1949 they opened ten new Jewish schools in Iraq. They were not keen on migrating to Israel. So an underground Zionist group stirred up trouble there, to make them feel insecure."

Dr. Buzaglo had equally strong views on the subject. "History is written often from the viewpoint of the Ashkenazim, who describe the Mizrachi experience," he said. "For instance, when Mizrachim came to Israel, they described their arrival as 'mass immigration'—instead of following the previous practice of calling it an *aliya* [ascent to Israel]. We have to describe things differently, and the textbooks should give a more balanced account. Israeli history is Eurocentric. Mizrachi are only a very small part of it. We Mizrachim know that the current narrative is biased but we do not have a narrative of our own yet."

Another Mizrachi intellectual at Hebrew University took issue with Amos Elon, an eminent Israeli historian and writer. He picked up a copy of Elon's *The Israelis: Founders and Sons*. "Look at the way this man generalizes about Jews and Jewish character," he said. "Page 245. 'It is often said that Jews are congenital worriers... Jews are said to pursue news like others pursue liquor because they are constantly taxed by nervous anxieties.' What Elon writes is valid for Ashkenazim, but how does he know whether Mizrachim feel the same way? The kind of life our forebears led in the Arab countries was certainly not like what Ashkenazim did in Europe. And nobody has bothered yet to find out our Mizrachi characteristics... But even if some studies had been made and results published I doubt if somebody like Elon would have bothered to notice, and alter his view of 'the Jewish character.' Such people never fully absorbed the fact that we Mizrachim were until very recently a majority in Israel."[7]

I asked Buzaglo what sort of narrative should be expected from Mizrachi historians. "Our narrative must take into consideration our Jewish tradition, and so it cannot start from multiculturalism, which cannot help people to establish their identity," Buzaglo replied. "We should start from ethnicity and go to pluralism/ multiculturalism, and not start with pluralism/multiculturalism and then go to ethnicity. We must define who we are before we become part of pluralism. Our identity must start with the Jewish tradition within Arab culture: a symbiosis between Jewish and Islamic cultures."

This is, to put it mildly, heresy in Ashkenazim-dominated Israel today. Not surprisingly, there is much opposition to Kedma schools among academics and Ministry of Education officials. The media are mostly against the project, portraying it as anti-integrationist, planting the seeds of a society segregated between Ashkenazim and Mizrachim.

The debate on the subject impinged on the future of Israel as a society and Israel as a geographical part of the vast Arab world. I raised this subject with many Jewish Israeli interviewees, mainly Ashkenazi. Instead of presenting their individual views, I have produced a compounded ideology, an "established orthodoxy" attributed to an Ashkenazi "spokesperson," ASHK debating his Mizrachi counterpart, MZRH, who represents a compendium of "dissenting heterodoxy" arguments. When necessary, I—as DH—have interjected.

ASHK: Kedma type schools create segregated education.

MZRH: They are part of a multicultural ideology which is official policy now. You are living in the past, in the era of the melting-pot theory.

ASHK: You are living in the past. The differences between Ashkenazim and Mizrachim were there 20-25 years ago. No more. Unless you know the family name you cannot tell the difference by accent any more.

MZRH: That's why you keep telling us we speak in a guttural and Arab-sounding way.

ASHK: You do.

MZRH: You just said there's no difference. Anyway, your Hebrew is influenced by Russian and German—which are not Semitic languages. Hebrew is Semitic, just like Arabic.

ASHK: I know that. I speak Arabic.

MZRH: But not in the right way we do. Do you realize Israel is the only society in the world where the working class speaks the language with the correct accent?

ASHK: For all those years we have been trying to put you right…

MZRH: Trying to remove us from our roots, to convince us that to get along in life, to be accepted by Ashkenazim, we must adopt your incorrect accent.

ASHK: Don't exaggerate. If things were that bad, you wouldn't have so much oriental music on radio. Some people are now complaining that there is too much oriental music on our air waves.

MZRH: That's news to me. Until seven or eight years ago oriental music was taboo on radio. There was demand for it even then, but the Ashkenazi view was: "It's uncivilized music, barbaric."

ASHK: But now new Israeli pop singers are using Hebrew lyrics and Mediterranean motifs.

MZRH: Why don't you use the right term, Arab motifs?

ASHK: Because we are not Arab.

MZRH: We are—Arab Jews.

ASHK: Arab Jews? Don't make me laugh.

MZRH: If you can be a European Jew, or an American Jew, why can't I be an Arab Jew, since my country of origin is Arab?

ASHK: Not so long as they are our enemies.

MZRH: But you can't go on living surrounded by Arabs and Arab Jews, and hope to maintain a dominant position.

ASHK: Militarily, we can maintain that position for a long time, assuming the Americans will back us. Culturally, there are problems. Already, look at our cuisine.

MZRH: More Mizrachi than Ashkenazi. The only facet of life where we have prevailed.

ASHK: An important facet, though. Food—like sex. Nearly a quarter of all Jewish marriages are now mixed.

MZRH: But Ashkenazim are less inclined to marry Mizrachim than the other way around.

DH: What about the children? How are they brought up?

MZRH: They usually follow the father's affiliation.

DH: And that's official.

ASHK: What do you mean?

DH: That this classification of Sephardim and Ashkenazim is recognized officially, by the state.

MZRH: Sure, you can see it even at the Western Wall synagogue—with the prayer books on one side of the shelves marked "Sephardi Version" and on the other "Ashkenazi Version."

ASHK: That's why whenever the subject of legislation on religion comes up in the Knesset, many Ashkenazi MKs [Members of Knesset] say: "Let's do away with this dual system, the Chief Rabbi of Ashkenazim and the Chief Rabbi of Mizrachim."

MZRH: It was the Zionists from Eastern Europe who insisted on having their own chief Ashkenazi rabbi.

DH: Does that mean that before 1922 there was only one chief rabbi and he was Sephardi?

MZRH: Yes.

ASHK: So let's have just one chief rabbi again.

MZRH: No way. This is the one official institution which recognizes our separate identity, where you Ashkenazim cannot dominate us. So we will never let it be abolished.

ASHK: But the differences are getting less and less. More things unite the two communities now than divide them.

MZRH: I'd put it differently. So long as one group stereotypes another, you can say that they are ethnically different. Like in television drama. You see Mizrachi men portrayed with open neck shirts, showing hairy chests, and wearing chains, whereas Ashkenazim are shown cool and better-dressed.

ASHK: That's a flimsy argument.

MZRH: All right. Let's try something heavy. A typical Ashkenazi stereotypes a Mizrachi as backward and irrational; and when he sees that "other" backing Likud—an intransigent party in his view—that confirms his stereotype.

ASHK: What about the typical Mizrachi?

MZRH: He similarly stereotypes an Ashkenazi as a wishy-washy liberal in the Labor party, which shunned and insulted him in the past, and still does not like him to get too close.

ASHK: But we all share the same political culture. We all believe in democracy and freedom of expression and electoral politics.

MZRH: While we share a common political value system we have distinct subcultures.

ASHK: We share common political values today because of the hard decisions the Labor Zionist leaders made in the early days of the Mizrachi mass immigration.

MZRH: The immense price you extracted from us, treating us like dumb cattle!

ASHK: Sometimes you have to be cruel to be kind. There was no way we were going to let your backward, feudal way of life overwhelm our own modern democratic system.

MZRH: That was never a serious possibility. You had all the levers of power. But there are differences. Take religious rites and liturgy. Sephardim are different from Ashkenazim.

ASHK: Only because the diaspora Jews were affected by the music of the communities where they settled. The musical traditions in Europe were different from those in the Arab countries.

MZRH: Also Mizrachim are more pragmatic than Ashkenazim when it comes to religious observation and interpretation. You often find Mizrachim going to the beach or watching television after synagogue on Saturday morning. And only a very small proportion of them are either Orthodox or ultra-Orthodox. And fewer still are truly secular.

ASHK: That's changing.

MZRH: Not really. The vast bulk of Mizrachim still belong to the traditional religious category, *masoreti*. In the family there are differences too. The average Mizrachi family is larger than Ashkenazi.

ASHK: The fertility rates are beginning to equalize. Mizrachi families are getting smaller, and now you have more and more ultra-Orthodox Ashkenazi couples, having ten to twelve children.

MZRH: There's also the traditional role of women in the family and the custom of maintaining strong ties with the extended family.

ASHK: That's a typically oriental way of life. But with an increasing proportion of mixed marriages, this pattern is bound to change.

MZRH: Finally, being predominantly working class or lower middle class, Mizrachim have developed what Professor Smooha calls "proletarian patterns of adaptation." These set them apart from wealthier Ashkenazim.

ASHK: All western societies have a class system.

MZRH: So do Arab societies.

ASHK: Most Arabs are still our enemies. So why keep on harping about the Ashkenazi-Mizrachi problem among Israeli Jews? By talking about differences within us you're weakening the Jewish nation, strengthening misconceptions and providing fuel to the enemies of Israel.

MZRH: That's your way of manipulating us, making us feel we're unpatriotic, even subversive. It's your way of keeping us Mizrachim down, maintaining the status quo—whereby you set the national agenda and make the important decisions, and all we can do is react.

ASHK: You're paranoid.

MZRH: I'm perceptive.

ASHK: Then why can't you see that the government has policies in place, compensatory education and urban renewal? Slowly they're working. And mixed marriages are on the rise. With time the problem will disappear.

MZRH: So you have been saying for nearly a hundred years. Ever since 1897 when the Zionist settlement of Palestine started. Remember the Zionists brought in Yemeni Jews in 1907 for manual work? And housed them on the fringes of the settlements. Segregated housing among Jews!

ASHK: Isn't that stretching it a bit? Our starting point should be the large scale immigration of Mizrachim in the early 1950s. We Zionists maintain that the idea of Jewish ethnicity is a legacy of the diaspora, and we want to do away with that. We don't want to perpetuate these differences.

MZRH: But you cannot abolish reality. If ethnic differences are deep-rooted, you must face up to them.

ASHK: Yes, we always have to start with the past. But we have a design for the future. To create the New Jew, not Ashkenazi or Mizrachi, just the New Jew—the smart, confident Jew—an antithesis to the miserable, persecuted Jew of the ghetto. So official Zionism considers Ashkenazi and Sephardi categorizations as negative characteristics of the diaspora, which must be renounced.

MZRH: Early on the Zionists attacked Yiddish diaspora culture as well as Mizrachi diaspora culture. But then they changed. Look at the Israeli literature in Hebrew. It's all translated from Yiddish. There is no translation of Jewish literature from Arabic or Persian.

ASHK: That's something we should look into. You're more likely to get a positive response from a Labor government than Likud on a subject like that.

MZRH: Since you mention politics, Israeli leaders should worry that the ethnic divide has been strengthened by a political divide. In the 1988 election 80 percent of Mizrachim voted either for Likud or some other right-wing group. And it's the other way around for Ashkenazim with Labor and other leftist groups. As for Likud alone, I'd say about 65 percent of Mizrachim voted for it. Labor ran the government and other institutions when Mizrachim arrived and were badly treated. So they turned to the opposition.

DH: That seems only a partial explanation. You can go for a party as a vehicle of protest that far. But there has to be something more profound which has sealed a solid pact between Mizrachim and Likud for all these decades.

ASHK: Scholarly opinion says that Likud is a modern version of Revisionist Zionism of Vladimir Zeev Jabotinsky with its emphasis on political power, military might, Eretz Israel, Jewish nation and an abiding suspicion of non-Jews. That is one stream, and it established itself in Palestine. Then you have Mizrachim who had grown up in a feudal, authoritarian Arab environment, and brought with them elements of authoritarianism, fanaticism, piety and irrationalism. These two strands came together in Israel at a time when the Ashkenazi pioneers began losing their values of egalitarianism and the dignity of labor, and became venal and corrupt. In 1977 a new compendium of forces assumed power. Over the next quarter century, it has shifted the political center of gravity toward inflexible nationalism and hardline religion at the expense of the humanistic, pragmatic and conciliatory political culture of Israel's first two decades.

MZRH: That is an amalgam of the papers published by Professors Erik Cohen and Shlomo Avineri, both of them blinkered Ashkenazim. Professor Smooha has trashed this thesis so well that I can only summarize his argument laid out in his paper "Jewish Ethnicity in Israel."[8] The basic assumption on which Cohen and Avineri construct their theses is wrong. Mizrachim are not shaping Israeli politics. Ashkenazim continue to dominate politics, and set the agenda and make policy decisions. Almost 40 percent of the Labor MKs are Mizrachi, but look at the Mizrachi Labor cabinet ministers—only three out of thirteen—less than a quarter.

Neither Labor nor Likud examines national issues from a Mizrachi viewpoint. Even Likud does not have a comprehensive policy on Mizrachim.

ASHK: But it has successfully projected a Mizrachi as a top-ranking leader: David Levy.

MZRH: Look at the way the Ashkenazi establishment derides him. Is there any other leader of his rank who is the butt of so many jokes—about his working-class background, his lack of English and so on? There is another misconception popular among Ashkenazim, that Mizrachi political culture is nationalist, extremist and anti-Arab.

ASHK: Isn't it?

MZRH: No, if you look deeply enough. Just as in the religious sphere, in politics Mizrachim are pragmatic. They have always regarded Likud as a vehicle for upward mobility, not as a source of ultra-nationalism.

ASHK: So why are they so solidly opposed to peace with the Palestinians?

MZRH: They are not. Remember how they reacted to Begin's peace treaty with Egypt in 1979? They backed it all the way. And who agreed to the Madrid peace conference in October 1991, which got the whole peace process going? Likud prime minister Yitzhak Shamir.

ASHK: Are you then debunking the thesis of Ben Dror Yemeni, a Mizrachi columnist in the *Ma'ariv* newspaper, that Mizrachim are anti-Palestinian?

MZRH: But on socio-economic grounds—not ideological, as is the case with Likud hawks and religious hard-liners. Mizrachim are against those who compete with them for jobs and those below their socio-economic status—that is, the Palestinians. That keeps them in the Likud camp. So once again their actions stem from direct experience, not some high-faluting ideology. Yemeni's study of Mizrachi university students showed that when Mizrachi enter a university they are almost all Likud. But year by year they change and become liberal. They realize that the conflict with Arabs at home and in the region is at the center of the socio-economic disadvantage they are suffering. They become liberal on the peace issue, and begin to re-examine their own background. University education provides them with tools to examine themselves and their background constructively. And they acquire the self-confidence to appreciate their own culture.

DH: So the situation can change politically only if the educational level of Mizrachim rises, and that is not happening.

ASHK: Since 1989 there has been an influx of ex-Soviet Jews into Israel on a massive scale—adding up to 900,000 by now.

MZRH: We know that has already pushed the Ashkenazi population to 55 percent.

ASHK: There is more.

MZRH: Where?

ASHK: When you examine the global figures. Of the 14 million Jews, only about a fifth are Sephardi.

MZRH: Yet in Israel, the heart of Judaism, we are now more than two-fifths.

ASHK: But for this heart of Judaism to thrive, it must receive sustenance from the Jewish hinterland. And that hinterland is almost totally Ashkenazim.

MZRH: I know. Three out of four Ashkenazim live in the diaspora, whereas only one out of four Sepharadim does so.

ASHK: Then there is the money factor; very important. Ashkenazim in Israel and the diaspora have the money. You don't.

MZRH: Oh, we have some, too. Not as much as you. After all you are four times more numerous than us. But, like you, most of our rich Mizrachim live in the diaspora.

ASHK: Only they haven't been as generous to you as our kith and kin have been to us.

MZRH: That'll change.

ASHK: But that won't put you on top in Israel. You didn't make it even when you had numbers on your side. Now that you're on a downward spiral in numbers, there is no way you can seriously challenge Ashkenazi superiority in Israel's economy and politics.

5

The Secular Center
Pragmatic Politicians

Tucked into a side of a hill, on the western edge of Jerusalem, the Knesset, the powerhouse of Israeli politics, is both a unique building and a unique institution.

A single chamber parliament, it is the supreme authority in Israel. It can, like its British counterpart, pass any law it wishes, which cannot be amended, vetoed or overturned by any other authority, executive or judicial. But, unlike the British parliament, neither the prime minister nor the head of state can dissolve it; only the sitting Knesset can. And only it has the power to order new elections. During the first ten years of Israeli history it functioned with each Knesset deciding its own tenure. Only in 1958 did it fix its term at four years with a proviso for early elections.

Viewed as a tourist site, its multi-story structure of pink stone looks grand— rows of columns majestically holding up the straight roof and forming a line of sentinels around the core. But the face it projects to those who work there, or visit it for business, is altogether different. They enter the building through its vast backyard, part of Kiryat Ben Gurion, a complex of buff-colored stone buildings housing the prime minister's secretariat and the ministries of interior and finance.

One afternoon in February 1995 Rafi and I drove and parked outside the northern gate of the Knesset. The line of visitors to the small office was orderly but long. As we had an appointment with Dr. Yoram Lass, a Labor MK, we went swiftly through security checks. We were soon treading one of several pathways, a long walk in the open to the Knesset proper—an effective precaution against a suicide bomber rushing into the building, I thought. The bunker-like design of the Knesset stemmed, it seemed, from the overriding consideration of withstanding bombing raids. The building was conceived and constructed between 1949 and 1967 when Israeli West Jerusalem hugged the armistice line with Jordan.

At the entrance of the Knesset proper, we faced another set of security guards. They cleared us and directed us to the office of Dr. Yoram Lass. We waited in the cramped office where Rafi chatted amiably with his secretary, whom he had known for some years. Dr. Lass, a tall, elegant man with glasses, arrived, and led us to the cafeteria reserved for MKs and other privileged persons such as journalists and lobbyists. It was a fine establishment, bright and airy, and it buzzed with activity. We planted ourselves by a glass window, and I took up a seat which faced the street.

But Dr. Lass was more interested in watching the television consoles, placed at strategic points inside the cafeteria, flashing the proceedings in the chamber. The house was discussing the role of social workers that afternoon, and Dr. Lass had been scheduled to speak. "Not to worry," he said. "The cafeteria is almost an extension of the chamber." Rafi smiled his rare smile. "That's why people say that more important decisions are made inside the cafeteria rather than in the chamber." Dr. Lass looked away.

Did some of his constituents come to meet him here, I asked Dr. Lass. "No," he replied. "There are no constituents in the way there are in Britain or America. You can say that an MK represents every Israeli voter in general but no one in particular." So the whole country is a single constituency with 120 MKs? "Yes, it's a pure system of proportional representation, where a voter casts his ballot for the party of his choice, and not for an individual candidate. The system goes back to the pre-state days when the Zionist pioneers were anxious to have all viewpoints, no matter how odd, represented in their Elected Assembly," explained Dr. Lass.[1]

Several flaws of the system had become apparent over the decades, I remarked: the leaders of the major parties had often to buy the backing of the small factions to form a coalition government; an MK was not accountable to his or her voters but to his peers in the party, which was not required to follow a legislated system for making up its list of candidates; and there was much temptation for an MK to switch parties for material or political gain. "The Knesset hasn't remained static on the matter," said Dr. Lass. "In 1990 it passed a bill which specified that any MK quitting his party must lose his parliamentary seat. It also raised the electoral threshold from 1 percent to 1.5 percent. That reduced the number of parties in the Knesset from fifteen to ten in the 1992 election."

Which meant less haggling between the leading parties and the small groups, I said. "Haggling nonetheless," interjected Rafi. "In the spring of 1990 it took three months to put together the next cabinet. Shimon Peres failed to do so because of a *diktat* issued to two MKs by a rabbi in Brooklyn." He sipped his coffee. "That's when the idea of a directly elected prime minister was first floated," Dr. Lass said. "Had [prime minister] Yitzhak Shamir not been so resistant to it, we would have had our first popularly elected premier in 1992, instead of 1996."

How did a particular party go about making up its list of 120 candidates for the Knesset? "It used to be a centralized affair, resting solely with the central committee in the case of the Labor Party," came the reply from Dr. Lass. "Then it was shared by the central committee and the district branches of the party. In 1991, when the party was in opposition, its convention adopted the primary system of fixing the Knesset list and electing the party leader. The list was divided into national primaries and regional primaries: the first category for those known nationally, and the second for those known locally. For this each of the 152,000 Labor members had two votes—one to be used for the national list candidates and the other for the regional list." But there had to be some kind of a priori division between the national and regional lists, I remarked. "Yes, in the Knesset list of 120 party representatives, the first 10 were chosen on the national basis. The eleventh was from the Tel Aviv region, the twelfth from the Haifa region, the thirteenth was national and so on—

with the twentieth being an [Israeli] Arab, and the thirtieth being a Druze and so on." (So close are the two foremost secular parties, Labor and Likud, in their organizational structure and the strategic thinking of their respective leaderships, that the right-wing Likud adopted the primaries system when it had to choose its next leader. In that hotly contested election, held in March 1993, Binyamin Netanyahu won—defeating David Levy, a senior Likud figure of Sephardi origin, and Benny Begin, a son of former prime minister, Menachem Begin.)

So at last the voters in the Tel Aviv region knew if one of the party candidates selected from their area was now an MK or not, I remarked. "Yes, but that did not mean they would make a point of approaching him or her with their problem just because they lived in the same region," Dr. Lass insisted. "They would seek out any MK of the party they had voted for, preferring to go for someone they had easy access to. Or sometimes they go for an MK who specializes in a particular area." Like? "I am a doctor and teacher of medicine, and I specialize in public health," he replied. "I did a post-graduate degree in medicine at Harvard University, I was social director at the Medical College of Tel Aviv. Then I was director-general for public health at the Health Ministry. So people approach me mainly in health matters." How did he divide his week? "I spend Monday to Wednesday in Jerusalem because the Knesset meets on these days. But a lot more work gets done in the standing committees of the Knesset. They're like the American Congressional committees. And they work six days a week. Many MKs travel around the country and meet the people. I do. Because we don't have a particular constituency to nurture in order to get re-elected, we try to have a high profile in the public eye." How? "The media. It's extremely important for a sitting MK to be in the news, to be seen and heard in the media."

How strict was party discipline among MKs? "Not as strict as in the British Parliament, but not as loose as in the American Congress," said Dr. Lass. "On minor matters we have freedom of voting in the chamber. But the subject of war and peace, the future of the Palestinian Territories, these are major issues. The party caucus meets once a week, and we discuss all such matters freely. But the final majority vote is binding on all party MKs." The other subjects of weighty import were: absorbing Jewish immigrants from the former Soviet Union, relations between the Israeli state and Judaism, reforming the electoral system, economic liberalization, and the treatment of Israeli Arabs. When an MK defied the majority decision on a major issue, what was the penalty? "In theory he could be thrown out of the party," replied Dr. Lass. "In practice, the issue gets fudged."

Lass's name came up on the television console. The three of us got up. As Dr. Lass rushed to the chamber Rafi and I walked to the press gallery. Here a television camera was locked on the proceedings. At the far end was the fairly full public gallery behind bullet-proof glass. Just to the right of the Speaker's chair was a podium where Dr. Lass was now addressing his audience of six other MKs, including one minister.

Having said his piece, Dr. Lass left the chamber and met us outside. It was time for the "photo opportunity." I suggested a lower floor where the faces of the four founders of Israel beamed at the onlooker. The most familiar image was that of David Ben Gurion dressed in a black suit and tie, his balding head adorned by tousled tufts on the sides, looking appropriately solemn.

Ben Gurion is regarded as the foremost founding father of Israel. During the formative years of the state he made all the important decisions, thus defining the nature of the state and society that were to emerge over the next several decades. He was both the prime minister and the defense minister. He also took charge of foreign affairs, immigration and economic development. Israel has not since then experienced such concentration of power in the hands of a single politician.

Since Ben Gurion's life encapsulated Zionist history in Palestine and the first decade and a half of Israel, it deserves outlining in some detail. Born David Green in Plonsk, Poland, into a lawyer's family, he went to Warsaw University in 1904, and joined the Poale Zion. Two years later he left for Palestine where he became a farm hand and was co-founder of the Poale Zion journal. In 1912 he enrolled at Istanbul University to study Turkish laws and government. The outbreak of World War I brought him back to Palestine. In 1915, following deportation as a troublemaker by the Ottoman authorities, he sailed for New York. There he joined an American battalion of the Jewish Legion being formed as part of the British army. Trained in Canada, he arrived in Egypt as a member of the 40th Royal Fusiliers.

In post-war Palestine the Poale Zion split, with its leftist section leaving in 1919. Its rightist, nationalist section, led among others by Ben Gurion, combined with others to build an umbrella organization to encompass all labor-pioneer Zionist parties: Histadrut. The parties in Histadrut merged, creating the Mapai party in January 1930 under the stewardship of Chaim Arlosoroff. Following the murder of Arlosoroff in 1933, Ben Gurion was elected head of Mapai, a position he held for the next three decades. In 1935 he became the leader of the Jewish Agency for Palestine, then recognized by the British mandate as the official representative of the Jews in Palestine.

Ben Gurion had little time for those Jewish organizations which seceded from the World Zionist Organization. When the extremist Revisionist Zionists, headed by Vladimir Jabotinsky, broke away from the Zionist Organization in 1935, Ben Gurion was among those who argued that the Revisionists had ceased to be Zionists and had turned into fascists.

Differing with other Mapai leaders, Ben Gurion favored the still-born proposal of Britain's 1937 Peel Commission to partition Palestine into a Jewish state, occupying about a quarter of Palestine, and an Arab state attached to adjoining Transjordan. He favored building a Jewish state on whatever land the Zionist pioneers could secure in Palestine.

Like his colleagues Ben Gurion opposed the British White Paper of 1939 which limited Jewish immigration into Palestine. But once World War II erupted he encouraged fellow Jews to join the British Africa Corps. In May 1942, Ben Gurion convened an extraordinary American Zionist Congress at New York's Biltmore Hotel. It coupled its call for unrestricted Jewish immigration to Palestine with a demand that "Palestine be established as a Jewish Commonwealth integrated into the structure of the new democratic world."

After the end of the war in Europe, Ben Gurion began purchasing arms in Europe with Jewish Agency funds. In December 1946 the 22nd World Zionist Organization, meeting in Basle, Switzerland, endorsed the 1942 Biltmore resolution, and appointed Ben Gurion head of the WZO's defense department, bringing Palestine's Jewish militias under a single command. The most important force was the Haganah (Defense). Formed in 1920, the Haganah grew dramatically in the mid-1930s. During the Arab Revolt, when Palestinian Arabs attacked not only British targets but also Jewish settlements, the British fostered and armed the Haganah. When World War II began, the British legalized the Haganah, which instructed its members to join the Jewish units of the British army. More than 40,000 Jews from Palestine, men and women, did so. Once the war ended, however, the Haganah turned against the British, and engaged in the smuggling of illegal Jewish immigrants.

Early in 1947, noticing the convergence of the American and Soviet positions on the partition of Palestine, the national council of the Yishuv, or Jewish community in Palestine, led by Ben Gurion, began formulating plans to consolidate the Jewish sector in Palestine. By the time the United Nations adopted the partition plan in November 1947, the Haganah had become a large professional army supported by 79,000 reserves, armed police and home guards.

With the rejection of the United Nations partition plan by the Palestinians, the scene was set for civil conflict between the Jews and the Arabs. On the Jewish side, besides the Haganah, were the Irgun Zvai Leumi (National Military Organization), founded by the Revisionist Zionists in 1937 and led by Menachem Begin, and its small ultra-radical breakaway faction, Lehi, headed by Yitzhak Shamir and Nathan Yellin-Mor. (Both Begin and Shamir were later prime ministers.) Ben Gurion's repeated attempts to bring the Irgun and Lehi under his control failed. He was particularly concerned about the Irgun, because he regarded Begin as a serious rival. (Nobody could have guessed then that between them, these militia leaders together would govern Israel for 25 years.) When Begin turned out to be the chief planner of the April 1948 attack on the Arab village of Deir Yasin near Jerusalem, which resulted in the massacre of 110 to 254 civilian men, women and children, Ben Gurion used the event to discredit Begin.

The Yishuv leadership, headed by Ben Gurion, and functioning as the provisional government, issued the Declaration of the Establishment of the State of Israel in Tel Aviv on May 14, 1948. Twelve days later it formally set up the Israel Defense Forces (IDF), consisting of 30,000 fully mobilized troops, with Ben Gurion as the defense minister. The IDF was engaged in combat with 26,000 Arab troops, from Egypt, Iraq, Jordan, Lebanon, Syria, and Palestine. The first Arab-Israeli War was on.

The conflict lasted until January 7, 1949. An earlier truce, arranged by the UN on June 11, required the warring parties to cease all military activity including importing weapons. Ten days later, defying the decision of the cabinet, Begin's Irgun began unloading arms and volunteers aboard the freighter *Altalena*, which had reached Tel Aviv from East Europe, to reinforce and re-arm the troops scattered along the beaches between Tel Aviv and Haifa. When the Irgun commanders tried to steer the ship to the shore, Ben Gurion ordered the IDF to shell it. Some 40 Irgun soldiers were killed, with many more injured. The ship sank, and most of the arms and ammunition were destroyed. Though devastated by the event, Begin decided against striking back and starting a civil war. He disbanded the Irgun in September during a lull in the Arab-Israeli fighting.

By acting boldly in the midst of the crisis, Ben Gurion succeeded to secure the Israeli Government's monopoly on armed might, thus strengthening both its power and legitimacy. But the *Altalena* incident intensified the ill-will that had existed all along between him and Begin. They severed all contact, and in later years prime minister Ben Gurion would never address Begin directly in the Knesset, referring him to as "the member sitting to the right/left of so-and-so...."

Under Ben Gurion's command the IDF performed well in the first Arab-Israeli War, securing for Israel an area 21% larger than the 54% of Palestine allocated to the Jews by the United Nations partition plan. The Israeli dead amounted to 6,000 whereas the figure for the opposing side was 18,500, of which 16,000 were Palestinian Arabs. Among other things Ben Gurion ensured that the IDF remained free of party politics, with promotions based exclusively on merit, with no consideration given to the party affiliation of the officer. This tradition has continued and played an important role in maintaining high morale in the IDF.

Following negotiations between the warring parties on the Greek island of Rhodes, Israel concluded armistice agreements with Egypt, Lebanon, Jordan on and Syria. Iraq, which lacked common borders with Israel, signed no such agreement with it.

In the January 1949 election, Mapai emerged as the largest party. Ben Gurion became the prime minister, and formed a coalition government with the help of the religious parties, functioning under the umbrella of the United Religious Front.

As described earlier, the Ben Gurion government passed laws on the observance of the Jewish Sabbath and dietary injunctions, rabbinical courts and the status of the Chief Rabbinate along the lines agreed in principle during the pre-state days.[2] In the Jewish personal laws of marriage, divorce and burial, the administration gave complete power to the Orthodox, ignoring altogether the Conservative and Reform schools.

The relationship between the state and Judaism was of such paramount importance that it needed to be tackled in the constitution, which was supposed to be drafted by October 1949. But this was not to be. Though elections were held in January 1949 for a Constituent Assembly, it adopted only a Transition Law, without a constitution. The Law declared Israel a republic, with a president elected by the Knesset, a single chamber parliament of 120 members, where the leader of the largest party would become the prime minister. The Constituent Assembly then transformed itself into the First Knesset.

The absence of a written constitution provided Ben Gurion with much leeway. While he kept his promise on the religious matters that had been settled during the pre-state period, he was not prepared to yield to the URF in other religious areas. Indeed his disagreement with the URF on the degree of governmental control over religious education in schools caused the downfall of his government in mid-1951.

But the new elections did not change much: the result was another Ben Gurion coalition government including the religious parties.

In the economic field, aware of the non-socialist programs of his partners in the government, the social democratic (rather than socialist) Ben Gurion readily diluted such egalitarian policies of Mapai as income redistribution and economic planning. He became an ardent proponent of a mixed economy.

Above all else, Ben Gurion gave top priority to building up the military strength of Israel. This policy has been the bedrock of the Jewish state ever since. He lost no time in introducing universal conscription for men and women, followed by annual reserve duty for several weeks by men. He visualized the IDF as the chief socializing agent of Israeli adults, an institution without class differences, which would help integrate newly arrived Jewish immigrants.

Ben Gurion decided to double the Jewish population, which stood at 759,000 in late 1948, within a decade. Israel achieved this in only six years. The 1950 Law of Return, guaranteeing every Jew the right to settle in Israel, followed by the 1952 Nationality Law conferring automatic citizenship on those who had arrived under the Law of Return, were effective means to this end. Intent on populating the inhospitable Negev Desert, Ben Gurion set up his home at a new kibbutz there.

The attitude of Ben Gurion to those Palestinian Arabs who remained in Israel was a mixture of disdain and hostility. "He retained the negative view of the Arab personality and character derived from the stereotypes existing not only in the Yishuv but in the West as a whole," writes Professor Don Peretz in *The government and Politics of Israel.* "Although widely read in the classics of several cultures, Ben Gurion never regarded Islamic philosophy or literature as of major significance. He learned Greek and Spanish, but never thought it worthwhile to master Arabic. His attitudes toward Middle Eastern culture were revealed in his evaluation of Oriental Jewish culture and in his policies toward Israeli Arabs. They could not really join the mainstream of life in the Jewish state."[3] In fact, as Defense Minister, Ben Gurion put Israeli Arabs under military administration. His means for dealing with Israeli Arabs was to set up a special department on Arab affairs, headed by an Israeli Jew, in the prime minister's secretariat.

Ben Gurion played a crucial role in deciding the basic orientation of Israel's foreign policy. Though he excluded the 19-member bloc of strongly socialist, pro-Moscow Mapam (United Workers' Party) from his government, he was aware of the goodwill that existed towards the Soviet Union in large segments of the Israeli labor movement. Aside from the Marxist ideology, this had to do with the Soviet actions before the founding of Israel and the 1948 Arab-Israeli War. After backing the partition of Palestine at the United Nations General Assembly in November 1947, Moscow had acted to neutralize western influence in the prospective Jewish state. It arranged arms supplies to the Zionists in Palestine through the branches that (the staunchly anti-British) Lehi had established earlier in Czechoslavakia, Hungary and Romania. The first clandestine shipment of arms from Eastern Europe arrived in Palestine in March 1948. The flow continued for about a year, well after the end of the Arab-Israeli War. On the other hand, Washington was generous to the newly established Jewish state, and provided it with $200 million in credits and grants during its first year of existence.

What turned Ben Gurion firmly pro-West was the most significant underwriting of Israel's continued existence yet in the form of the Tripartite Declaration by the United States, Britain and France on May 25, 1950. The signatories pledged to oppose any attempt to change by force or threat of force the armistice boundaries of Israel set in January 1949. Such a guarantee of its frontiers by the western powers, coupled with a promise to supply it with weapons on the basis of "a balance of forces between it and the Arab states," pleased Ben Gurion greatly. He showed his gratitude to Washington by backing it unconditionally at the United Nations on the issue of the war between North Korea and South Korea which broke out a few weeks later. By signing a treaty of friendship, commerce and navigation with the United States in October 1951, he formalized close ties with Washington, a state of affairs which has continued since then—barring a few periods of strain, especially after the 1956 Suez War, when Ben Gurion refused to withdraw unconditionally from the Sinai as required by the United Nations Security Council.

Taken together, Ben Gurion's actions turned the prime ministry into the most powerful office in the country, far ahead of the presidency of the republic. He was able to do so by channeling all his extraordinary energy and dynamism into the job, seizing opportunities when they arose, and making full use of his control over several networks, domestic and foreign.

In the course of his years as the chief executive of his country, he subsumed his loyalty to Mapai to that toward Israel, and developed his ideology of *mamlachtiut*, or statism. In response, large segments of Israeli society, enchanted by his charisma and vigor, came to regard him as the leading national figure who stood above party politics. Oddly, this popular perception rubbed off on Ben Gurion's party, Mapai, which was regarded informally as *the* national party by all other political groups.

Equally oddly, the actual electoral appeal of Ben Gurion was not widespread. At his best he secured only 38 percent of the popular vote for Mapai. His impact on his colleagues and the party bureaucracy too was limited. His relationship with Mapai's old guard was problematic.

Failing to find rapport with his peers, Ben Gurion turned his attention to younger party activists, some of whom came to share his newly coined ideology of statism. Among his young followers and advisers, whom he promoted in the IDF and the government, were Moshe Dayan and Shimon Peres. Interestingly, most of them came from the military where they had been either officers (Dayan) or high-level technocrats (Peres). Among other things they extended the concept of pioneering, applied initially to agriculture, to such arenas as science and technology, thus terming scientists and technicians too as pioneers. They argued that specialization and efficiency ought to be valued as much as manual labor in agriculture. In retrospect, this was the beginning of the trend whereby Mapai/Labor began moving away from its traditional association with laborers and workers. This trend developed to the point when within a generation of Israeli history, the Labor Party ceased to be the favorite of working-class voters.

Having played a leading role in shaping the basic outline of Israel's internal and external policies, Ben Gurion resigned as prime minister in December 1953, and retired to his private home in the Negev. But not for long. In early 1955 Moshe Sharett, his successor, drafted him to be defense minister when the incumbent, Pinchas Lavon, resigned in the midst of a scandal concerning the exposure and arrest of an Israeli sabotage team recruited from Egypt's Jewish community.

In response to the execution of two ringleaders of the Jewish espionage-sabotage cell in Egypt, Ben Gurion ordered a massive attack on an Egyptian military camp in the Gaza Strip, which resulted in 39 Egyptian deaths. The escalating tension resulted in Ben Gurion replacing Sharett as the prime minister in late 1955.

Within a year Ben Gurion was involved in invading and occupying the Sinai Peninsula in collusion with Britain and France in the Suez War, called the Sinai Campaign by Israelis. He capitalized on the crisis that started with a diplomatic row between Egyptian President Abdul Gamal Nasser and the United States, and then extended to Britain and France.

On July 19, 1956 the United States informed Egypt that it was withdrawing its aid offer for the Aswan High Dam, thus undermining the World Bank loan which was predicated on the US assistance. In response, a week later President Nasser nationalized the Suez Canal, which had been owned jointly by Britain and France. Following a debate on the matter at the United Nations Security Council, Egypt agreed on October 11 to the principles regarding running the Canal, including maintaining its status as an international waterway. This was not enough to satisfy Britain and France, the dominant foreign powers in the Middle East since the collapse of the Ottoman empire in 1918. Determined to cling to their power and influence in the region, they had initiated clandestine talks with the Ben Gurion administration at the highest level to bring about the downfall of Nasser through armed intervention. On October 24 the three governments signed a secret agreement to attack Egypt.

On the night of October 29 Israel invaded the Sinai. On October 30 Britain and France gave a 24-hour ultimatum to Egypt and Israel to cease hostilities and withdraw their troops 16 kilometers from the Suez Canal so as not to jeopardize freedom of shipping. As Israel's forces were some 48 kilometers from the Canal, it accepted the ultimatum. Egypt rejected it. Fighting between the two sides continued. When the deadline ended at 6 P.M. on October 31, Britain and France bombed Egypt's airfields, virtually destroying its air force, and continued attacking Egyptian military facilities for the next 36 hours. Cairo ordered its forces, sent earlier across the Canal into the Sinai, to retreat and thus avoid being encircled by the enemy. They did so by November 2. On that day the United States co-operated with the Soviet Union at the United Nations Security Council to sponsor the Uniting for Peace resolution which condemned aggression against Egypt. The next day, while continuing to consolidate its position in the Sinai, Israel completed its occupation of the Gaza Strip. On November 4 the United Nations General Assembly voted to set up a United Nations Emergency Force (UNEF) to supervise the truce. On November 5 British and French paratroopers landed at both ends of the Canal. Israel, advised by London and Paris, attached unrealistic conditions to accept the United Nations Security Council ceasefire resolution.

Soviet Premier Marshal Nikolai Bulganin addressed a letter to his Israeli counterpart Ben Gurion: "It [the aggression] is sowing a hatred of the state of Israel among the peoples of the East such as cannot but make itself felt with regard to the future of Israel, and which puts in jeopardy the very existence of Israel as a state."[4]

On the night of November 5, British and French forces landed in the Port Said area, and after seizing the town started moving south along the Canal, which had been blocked by the Egyptians with sunken ships. The newly re-elected American President Dwight Eisenhower applied economic pressure on Britain, with the US Federal Reserve Board selling large amounts of British pounds, thus undermining the pound-dollar exchange rate. Yielding to the American-Soviet pressures, the invading governments accepted a ceasefire beginning at midnight on November 6. By then Israel had occupied Gaza and most of the Sinai, including its south-eastern tip, Sharm al Shaikh, at the mouth of the Gulf of Aqaba.

Egypt had lost 1,650 troops and 215 aircraft while Israel's losses were 190 men and 15 warplanes. (At 26 men dead and 5 aircraft lost, the British and French losses were minimal.)

General Moshe Dayan, a protégé of Ben Gurion and the IDF chief of staff since 1953, provided brilliant leadership during the nine-day conflict. Dayan was born in 1915 in the Degania kibbutz near the Sea of Galilee. He joined the Haganah when in his teens. Due to lack of fluency in English he discontinued his studies at the London School of Economics in 1935–6, and returned to Palestine, where he participated in the Haganah operations to counter the Arab Revolt. At the start of World War II, the authorities suppressed the Haganah and sentenced Dayan to five years' imprisonment. After his release in early 1941, he led a British reconnaissance unit into Syria, which was then under the pro-Nazi French regime. He was wounded and lost his left eye. He started wearing a black patch, which later become his universally recognized trademark. During the 1948–9 Arab-Israeli War, after his battalion had captured Ramle and Lod, Dayan was appointed commander of the Jerusalem area. Under the benign guidance of Ben Gurion, Dayan rose rapidly in the military hierarchy.

Following the ceasefire in the Suez War, Dayan fully supported the hardline position that Ben Gurion took regarding evacuating the Sinai. The UN Emergency Force (UNEF) took over the French and British positions. Israel agreed to withdraw much later, after Ben Gurion had secured US commitments to defend Israel's right of passage through the Gulf of Aqaba; prevent attacks from the Gaza Strip; and assist Israel, secretly, in its nuclear research program. On Israel's insistence UNEF troops were posted in the Gulf of Aqaba region, to safeguard Israeli shipping, and in the Gaza Strip exclusively on the Egyptian side. In exchange Egypt was allowed to return to Gaza to administer it.

Whatever the political and diplomatic consequences of the Suez War, it accelerated Israel's policy of shoring up its military, and gave further impetus to its top leaders to acquire nuclear weapons. Both these aims were achieved during the next decade. An official acknowledgment of this came, inadvertently, in the late 1960s in reference to the unprecedentedly harsh way Israel responded to the 1965–6 guerrilla actions by the Palestinians operating from Jordan and Syria.

"The reprisal actions of 1965–6 differed from those which preceded the Sinai campaign," stated *The Paratroopers' Book*, the semi-official history of the IDF's airborne corps. "The operations were no longer acts of vengeance, savage and nervous, of a small state fighting for its independence. Rather, they were blows struck by a state strong and sure of itself, and which did not fear the army it confronted."[5] Though by the mid-1960s Ben Gurion was out of power, and the leader only of the small group Rafi, his doctrine had become a cornerstone of the state's military policy. Also for the next few decades the group of his young protégés such as Moshe Dayan and Shimon Peres continued to dominate Israeli public life.

Lacking the domineering personality and style of Ben Gurion, his successor Levi Eshkol opted for ruling by consensus within his cabinet. Among other things he tried to normalize life in Israel. He liberalized the economy, which had been run on a war footing since 1948. He removed (in December 1965) the travel limitations that had been imposed on Israel's Arab citizens since 1948.

By sponsoring a cabinet decision to bring the remains of Vladimir Jabotinsky from New York to Israel for reburial in Jerusalem, Eshkol lowered tensions between the government and the right-wing opposition led by Begin, a follower of Jabotinsky. This was the first sign of a thaw between the center-left and right of Israeli politics, a definite departure from the Ben Gurion legacy.

It was during Eshkol's premiership that Israel went to war with its Arab neighbors, and won a stunning victory in 1967. The crisis that preceded the conflict brought the traditional, secular left-of-center and right-of-center of Israeli politics together—thus setting a pattern which was to be repeated in peace time in the 1980s. Later the ease with which some leading figures of the (nominally) opposing camps switched sides illustrated the remarkable change that had occurred in Zionist politics within Israel. The sharp lines which in pre-state days divided labor Zionists from ultra-nationalist Zionists became so blurred that crossing from one side to the other aroused no lifting of eyebrows among politicians or the public.

Nothing illustrated this better than the relationship between Yitzhak Rabin, who was to become Labor's prime minister, and Ariel Sharon, an ultra-nationalist hawk, who became Defense Minister. During the 1956 Suez War, as the commander of a brigade, Sharon, then 28, engaged in unauthorized combat and thus destroyed his chances of advancement in the IDF. But soon after Rabin became the IDF chief of staff in 1964, he promoted Sharon to head the IDF's training department, and made him brigadier general in 1967. One of the first decisions Rabin made, after becoming the prime minister in 1974, was to appoint Sharon as his special adviser.

June 1967 War: A Milestone

The third Arab-Israeli War in June 1967 was a milestone for Israel in more ways than one. Internationally, having invaded and occupied 26,370 square miles of Arab territory in Egypt, Syria and the remnants of British mandate Palestine (two and a half times its own area) Israel could no longer portray itself as a small and weak Jewish state surrounded by powerful Arab neighbors bent on extermination. Domestically, it radically altered the Israeli political landscape.

It revived the old debate about the Zionist aims and ways of achieving them, thus opening up avenues for Menachem Begin and his party that had for long been closed. Established political parties now successfully co-opted ethnic and communal leaders of the newly arrived immigrants who now formed a substantial majority of the population. And Israeli Arabs ceased to live under military control.

More specifically, Israel's spectacular victory gave rise to the Moshe Dayan phenomenon, and provided a vehicle later for the political careers of his chief of staff, General Yitzhak Rabin and his chief of operations, Ezer Weizman, who had masterminded Israel's stunning air strategy. All of them happened to be *sabra*, from the Arabic for cactus, meaning prickly on the outside but soft and sweet on the inside, a term used in Israel for the Jews born in Palestine.

The war, though lasting only from June 5 to June 10, 1967, had a long fuse. Taking seriously Israel's threats of overthrowing it, the nine-month-old radical regime of pan-Arabists in Syria, which had been actively aiding Palestinian guerrilla activity against Israel, signed a defense treaty with Egypt in November 1966. Early in April 1967 Israel attempted to cultivate disputed Arab land in the Syrian-Israeli demilitarized zone, thus triggering a confrontation. On April 7, 1967, the IDF escalated the already tense situation by bombing the Syrian Heights, buzzing the outskirts of Damascus, and engaging in dogfights in Syrian airspace. A month later Syria informed Egypt's President Nasser of Israeli troop concentration along its border. On May 16, while promising to aid Syria, Nasser dispatched Egyptian troops to eastern Sinai as a precaution against an Israeli attack.

This signaled the start of an acute crisis. On May 18 Nasser demanded the withdrawal of the United Nations Emergency Force, which had been patrolling the truce lines since the end of the 1956 Suez War on the Egyptian side only. The UNEF withdrew immediately. On May 22, having stationed Egyptian troops in Sharm al Shaikh at the tip of the Tiran Straits, Nasser blockaded the Gulf of Aqaba and the Israeli port of Eilat.

Many Israelis believed their government was behaving timidly. Rather than considering Egypt's closure of the Straits of Tiran an act of war, Eshkol called on the international community to reopen the Straits and the Gulf of Aqaba. The same day his foreign minister, Abba Eban, left for Paris, London and Washington to try to resolve the crisis by diplomatic means. But the diplomacy failed.

As tension rose in the region Premier Eshkol, who also held the defense portfolio, maintained, at least in public, his willingness to continue diplomatic efforts to dissipate the crisis. Other politicians and the public grew impatient. During their consultations with Eshkol, two leading opposition leaders from the contrasting poles of the political spectrum—Menachem Begin, the head of Gahal (the Freedom-Liberal bloc), and Ben Gurion, the leader of Rafi—proposed that he should cede his defense portfolio to Moshe Dayan, a Rafi MK. Despite his reluctance, because of old rivalry with Dayan, Eshkol agreed, and appointed Dayan as Defense Minister in a national unity administration.

On the Arab side, reflecting the popular mood in his country, King Hussein of Jordan, hitherto hostile to Nasser, rushed to Cairo on May 30 to conclude a mutual defense pact, and place his forces under Egyptian command.

Israel had earlier told its superpower ally, the United States, that it would go to war if one or more of the following events occurred: departure of the UNEF, blockading of the Tiran Straits, signing of a Jordanian-Egyptian defense pact, and dispatch of Iraqi forces to Jordan. By the time the national unity government was sworn in on June 1 all but one of these eventualities had come to pass. Three days later Iraqi troops entered Jordan. On June 5 a surprise, pre-emptive attack by Israel on the Egyptian air bases at 7:46 A.M., when all Egyptian pilots were having breakfast, heralded the start of the shortest Arab-Israeli armed conflict.

Israel simultaneously attacked all seventeen Egyptian airfields and destroyed three-fifths of Egypt's warplanes. In the ground fighting in the Sinai, Egypt lost 550 tanks. Later in the day Israel struck at the Jordanian and Syrian air forces on the ground with equally deadly efficiency. It rejected the United Nations Security Council call for an immediate ceasefire on June 6.

On the Egyptian front, Israel captured the Gaza Strip on June 6, the day Egypt decided to withdraw its 80,000 soldiers and 1,000 tanks from the Sinai Peninsula. Having occupied most of the peninsula by June 8, Israel reached the Suez Canal the following day. On the Jordanian front the Israelis captured East Jerusalem as well as Bethlehem, Hebron, Jenin and Nablus by June 7. It then accepted a UN-sponsored ceasefire on this front. The Syrian front witnessed artillery duels on the first four days. Israel violated the UN-sponsored truce on the fifth day, June 9, by launching an offensive to capture the Golan Heights. It achieved this aim by the evening of the sixth day, June 10, when the final ceasefire came into effect. In the naval battle, the Israelis captured Egypt's Sharm al Shaikh on June 7, thus ending the blockade of the Straits of Tiran.

The Arab losses in men and weapons were heavy. The Egyptian dead amounted to 11,500, with a majority dying of thirst in the Sinai, the Jordanian to 2,000, and the Syrian to 700. The Israeli death toll was 778 dead. Arab losses of tanks and aircraft were 930 and 344 respectively; Israel's 100 and 40.

The brilliant Israeli blitzkrieg of June 1967 was a personal triumph for Dayan. He became the most popular and charismatic of the younger generation of Israeli leaders. By joining the newly formed Labor Party in 1968, Dayan returned to the political mainstream. As defense minister Dayan was in charge of administering the Occupied Arab Territories. His power and influence grew. When Premier Eshkol died in February 1969, Dayan was a candidate for prime minister. But to spare the one-year-old Labor Party the trauma of a bitter battle for the top job (between Dayan and his rival Yigal Allon), the party leadership drafted Golda Meir, then in retirement, as premier.

In the Meir cabinet Dayan retained both his defense ministry and the autonomy with which he ran it. In the matters of defense and military administration of the Occupied Arab Territories, his authority was equal to, if not greater than, the prime minister's. He took a hawkish line on the Occupied Territories, and not surprisingly, became the first top-ranking Labor leader to join the cabinet headed by the Likud chief, Begin, without many qualms. Similarly, Rabin remained consistently loyal to the Labor Party during his later political career as defense minister in the national unity governments of the 1980s, but he became well known for establishing a special relationship with prime minister Yitzhak Shamir, the Likud leader.

As for Ezer Weizman, he was the first top-ranking military officer who opted for the right-wing Gahal, led by Begin. Later he acquired the unique distinction of masterminding election campaigns of both Likud (a success) and its rival Labor (a failure). Born in a prominent Jewish family in Palestine, Ezer Weizman was a nephew of Chaim Weizmann, the first president of Israel. He enrolled in the Royal Air Force during World War II and became a pilot, later joining the Irgun. During the 1948-9 Arab-Israeli War, he was one of the first Israeli pilots. After the military conflict he rose to become commander of the air force. Under his command the air force perfected and implemented its plan to destroy the air power of its Arab neighbors during the June 1967 Arab-Israeli War.

The spectacular June victory helped cement the national unity coalition. It was unanimous in its decision to extend Israeli laws to Occupied East Jerusalem. The differences that arose on the future of the rest of the Occupied Arab Territories were contained by postponing the formulation of a coherent policy on the subject. The consensual climate led to the creation of the Israeli Labor Party by combining Mapai with Ahdut HaAvodah-Poale Zion (and Rafi as well). Golda Meir inherited this powerful Knesset bloc when she became the premier in February 1969.

Meir, a Ukrainian Jew who had grown up in the United States, arrived in Palestine in 1917. She was active in Histadrut-Mapai politics. When the British arrested Moshe Sharett, head of the Jewish Agency's foreign affairs section, in 1946, she replaced him. International relations remained her strong card, and she served as Israel's foreign minister from 1956–66. She retired from public life in 1968, only to be redrafted as the prime minister.

The national unity government Meir inherited was undisturbed by the elections of October 1969. The various parties virtually retained their previous strengths in the new Knesset, and the national unity administration that followed had the same composition as the one before. It was not until Meir accepted the peace plan of US Secretary of State William Rogers in July 1970 that Gahal objected and left the government. Now within her Labor-dominated cabinet she had to find a balance between Dayan (defense), Yigal Allon (education, and deputy premier) and Shimon Peres (without portfolio, and then transportation).

On the singularly important issue of the future of the Occupied Arab Territories, Dayan set the pace. He used his office to create Jewish colonies, and in April 1973 he mounted a campaign to annex the West Bank, the Golan Heights and parts of the Sinai. A few months later he unveiled a plan to build a port city of Yamit in the Rafah area, straddling the international border of Egypt and the Gaza Strip. When the moderate finance minister denied him the necessary funding, tensions within Labor rose. A ministerial committee, chaired by Israel Galili, a long-time confidant of Meir, adopted a document that gave a green light for "an urban center" at Yamit and large-scale acquisition of land in the Occupied Arab Territories by the Israeli government and private Jewish organizations. Most Labor moderates saw the Galili Document as a go-ahead for "creeping annexation" of the Occupied Territories. Yet later the party secretariat adopted it as its official platform for the general election due in late October.

Attention of all political parties was focused on the impending parliamentary election, when Israel was attacked by Egypt and Syria on October 6, 1973, on the eve of the Jewish festival of Yom Kippur, the Day of Atonement.

October 1973 War: A Nasty Jolt

Unlike the 1956 and 1967 military conflicts, when Israel had taken the initiative, this time Egypt and Syria mounted pre-planned attacks on Israeli forces, but not inside pre-1967 Israel. They attacked in the Occupied Arab Territories with the aim of regaining the Egyptian and Syrian lands. They took this initiative three years after the Rogers peace plan, which had secured a ceasefire in the 1969–70 War of Attrition, but had failed to pave the way for the recovery of their territories through diplomatic means. The Arab move, which came during the Muslim fasting month of Ramadan, took Israelis completely by surprise. They were about to begin the three-day Yom Kippur holiday, and their military took 72 hours to get fully mobilized instead of the planned 36. The war, which lasted until October 25, became known as the October War, or the Ramadan War (among Arabs) or the Yom Kippur War (among Israelis).

Between October 6 and 8, Egyptian forces crossed the Suez Canal. On the Golan Heights front the Syrians captured Mount Hermon and made gains at Khushniya. The Israelis were unable to check the advance of the Egyptian and Syrian forces. On October 9 the United States began an arms airlift using the planes of the Israeli airline El Al. The Soviet Union began airlifting arms to Egypt and Syria, with the latter getting two-thirds of the shipments. Between October 10 and 12 the Israelis counterattacked on the Golan front, and advanced east of the armistice line, despite an Egyptian offensive meant to relieve the Syrians. The following day Washington started using American aircraft to carry weapons to Israel. On October 15 the Israeli offensive along the Suez Canal, led by General Ariel Sharon, succeeded in creating a wedge between the two Egyptians armies north of the Great Bitter Lake of the Suez, and established a bridgehead on the western bank. That day Soviet prime minister Alexei Kosygin flew into Cairo. Between October 15 and 19, repeated Syrian attempts to regain the Golan Heights were frustrated by the Israelis. On October 16 an oil embargo imposed against the military backers of Israel (principally the United States, Holland and Portugal) by the Organization of Arab Petroleum Exporting Countries went into effect.

Three days later, on October 19, the Israelis pushed southwards to surround the Egyptian Third Army along the eastern bank. On that day Kosygin left Cairo after Egyptian President Anwar Sadat had agreed to let Moscow negotiate for a ceasefire. On October 21 Henry Kissinger, US Secretary of State, arrived in Moscow to negotiate a deal with Soviet leaders. By then America had airlifted 20,000 tons of weapons to Israel, plus 40 F-4 Phantom bombers, 48 A4 Skyhawk ground attack jets, and 12 C-130 transporters. The Soviet weapons shipments to Egypt and Syria totaled 15,000 tons. On October 22 a truce, specified by UN Security Council Resolution 338, went into effect. But soon after the Israelis broke the ceasefire on the Golan front, and regained Mount Hermon.

On October 23–4, violating the truce on the Suez front, the Israelis rushed to Adabiya in the Gulf of Suez to encircle the Egyptian Third Army. But their attempts to seize Port Suez failed. The Israeli breach of the ceasefire angered the Soviet Union. On October 24 Moscow put seven airborne divisions on alert, preparing an airlift to Egypt if the Israelis surrounded the Egyptian Third Army. The following day Washington put its military, worldwide, on "stage three alert," and its 82nd Airborne Division and the nuclear-armed warplanes of the Strategic Air Command on "heightened alert" in anticipation of Moscow's possible direct intervention in the Arab-Israeli War. Israel also placed its nuclear forces on alert. Against this backdrop, UN Security Council Resolution 340, renewing its ceasefire call, went into effect later that day, and marked a formal end of the hostilities.

The war shattered the invincible image of Israel and Dayan. Though the Israeli military performed well later, the label of failure stuck to Dayan. And in fact, the Jewish state's military turn-around had stemmed directly from Washington's massive airlift of arms and ammunition. Israel obtained the crucial American aid by threatening to use its nuclear weapons as a last resort and readying its delivery systems for that purpose.

This and other crucial decisions were made by Meir and her "kitchen cabinet" at an all-night session on October 8–9, 1973 at her Tel Aviv office next to the defense ministry's vast underground headquarters. Besides Meir and Dayan, the participants included General David Elazar, the IDF chief of staff; Yigal Allon, Deputy prime minister; Israel Galili; and Brigadier-General Israel Leor, the prime minister's military aide. The meeting began with an assessment by Dayan. He predicted an imminent collapse of the IDF since its present arms and ammunition stocks were expected to last only about a week, and the sole source of further military supplies was the United States. Therefore the leaders focused on how to get Washington to airlift emergency military supplies. They decided to arm Israel's nuclear arsenal, then estimated to contain more than 23 atomic bombs, to be used against Egyptian and Syrian targets in the eventuality of the IDF's complete collapse. They would inform the United States of this immediately, demanding a prompt airlift of weapons and ammunition to enable Israel to mobilize its collapsing troops for a major counter-offensive and full-scale warfare for an extended period. Urgent orders went out to the regional IDF commander to make operational nuclear missile launchers at a hillside of Kfar Zechariah, situated in the Judean hills south-west of Jerusalem, where nuclear weapons were stored in bunkers, and also to mount the stored atomic bombs on specially adopted F-4 Phantom bombers stationed at the Tel Nof air base. By placing the missile launchers in the open, the Israeli leaders made sure that their presence would be noted by both the American and Soviet spy satellites. The Israeli strategy worked. Following an urgent meeting between Israeli Ambassador Simcha Dinitz and Kissinger at the White House on the morning of October 9, Washington agreed it would immediately make good Israel's arms and ammunition losses.[6]

Besides destroying Dayan's political future, the 1973 war brought about more lasting changes in Israeli society. It erased the line between foreign and defense affairs and domestic politics. It also severely shook Israelis' confidence in their leaders. The radical right, secular and religious, capitalized on popular disappointment with the Labor political establishment, and transformed it into a protest movement and a strong lobby pushing the government to accelerate the colonization of the West Bank.

The IDF's unpreparedness for war, combined with reports that top Israeli officials, including Dayan, had ignored intelligence reports that Egypt and Syria were planning an attack, provided additional ammunition to the opposition Likud in its attack on the ruling Labor alliance. Labor tried to deflect it with a twin-headed strategy. The Meir government appointed an inquiry committee, chaired by Shimon Agranat, head of the Supreme Court. And it presented the Middle East Peace Conference, to be held on December 22, 1973 in Geneva, as a major breakthrough to peace and security. (In fact this meeting achieved nothing. It adjourned after one day due to the impending Israeli general election).

In that poll the Labor-Mapam bloc lost five seats, while Likud gained eight. This encouraged the religious parties to take a hard line in their coalition talks with Meir. An exasperated Meir formed a minority administration with the support of 58 MKs. It did not last long.

The report of the Agranat Commission, published in March 1974, blamed General David Elazar for what went wrong, and cleared Moshe Dayan, the defense minister. When Elazar resigned, however, pressure on Dayan to follow suit mounted. He refused. To get around the problem, in April Meir offered the resignation of her full cabinet.

Unsurprisingly, Dayan did not enter the race for the Labor Party leader, leaving the contest to Yitzhak Rabin and Shimon Peres to be settled by the 600-odd members of the party's central committee. Rabin, backed among others by Meir, defeated Peres.

What particularly favored Rabin was the fact that, as ambassador to the United States, he was not part of the government at the time of the October War, whereas Peres was Transportation Minister. And, as IDF chief of staff during the lightning Israeli victory in the June 1967 War, Rabin was regarded highly as a soldier.

Born into a middle class Russian-Jewish family in Jerusalem in 1922, Rabin graduated from an agricultural college in 1940. The next year he joined Palmach, the strike force of the Haganah, and trained under Yigal Allon. Rabin participated in the successful 1941 Allied campaign in Syria, then under a pro-Nazi French government. In the 1948–9 War, he commanded a brigade on the Jerusalem and Negev fronts.

After the military conflict Rabin headed the IDF's tactical operations branch. Following his graduation from the British Staff College in 1953 and promotion to major-general, Rabin served in a variety of positions including chief of staff. Even while serving as ambassador to the United States, he advised Prime Ministers Eshkol and Meir on important military matters.

Once back home, Rabin joined the Labor Party and was elected to the Knesset in 1973. He was in Meir's cabinet in March 1974, and following her resignation he challenged Peres for party leadership, and won.

Though Rabin gave Peres the important defense portfolio, their relations remained strained. In 1976, despite party policy of forbidding Jewish settlements near Palestinian urban centers on the West Bank, Peres compromised with the ultra-nationalist Gush Emunim movement when they set up a settlement in Kadume near Nablus, an act which Rabin found unforgivable.

Overall Rabin's mind-set was that of a soldier, and it never changed. Though he formally retired from the IDF at the age of 46, he did not really abandon his military uniform. He was more at ease implementing policies and orders than conceiving them. He lacked imagination. In contrast Peres, an intellectual at heart, was known as a man of vision, political and technological.

Born Shimon Persky into the household of a timber merchant in the small town of Vishniva, Poland, Peres was thirteen when his family migrated to Palestine in 1936. After studying at an agricultural school, he joined the Alumot kibbutz. A sensitive youth, fond of reading and of poetry, he was also a good organizer. He served as secretary of the labor Zionist youth group, the Young Worker. Active with the Haganah since 1941, he became its manpower chief in 1947, and later also its weapons procurer. By the time the 1948–9 War ended, he was in charge of the Israeli navy, and became a favorite of Premier Ben Gurion.

Between 1953 and 1959 he served as the Defense Ministry's director-general. He established Israel Aircraft Industries, which went on to manufacture jet aircraft and guided missiles and sophisticated avionics. In 1956, having persuaded France (then colluding with Israel against Egypt) to ship weapons to Israel secretly, he succeeded in getting Paris to sell a nuclear reactor. That deal developed into a much wider co-operation in Israel's development and manufacture of nuclear weapons at Dimona in the Negev Desert. During the visit of the West German Defense Minister, Franz Strauss, to Israel in 1958, Peres also persuaded him to supply weapons clandestinely to the Jewish state. In such dealings, which contravened international embargoes, Peres was involved in forging documents, falsifying the names of the end-users of weapons, and creating fictional purchasing and selling firms.

Peres entered the Knesset in 1959 on a Mapai ticket, and has since then retained a seat. During his tenure as Defense Minister, he first persuaded President John Kennedy to end the US arms embargo and sell Israel defensive weapons such as anti-aircraft missiles, and then prevailed upon President Lyndon Johnson to sell Israel offensive weapons such as tanks and fighter aircraft. Meanwhile, the reprocessing plant to transform uranium into weapons-grade plutonium was completed at Dimona in 1962. The French presence there continued until 1966. In early 1968 the Dimona plant began producing four to five nuclear arms annually.[7]

When Ben Gurion left Mapai in 1965 to set up Rafi, Peres followed him, becoming Rafi's secretary-general. But when the Labor Party was formed in 1968 he left Rafi, and became deputy secretary-general of the new party. The next year he joined Golda Meir's cabinet, eventually as Transportation Minister.

As Defense Minister in the Rabin administration, Peres did much to rebuild the IDF after the traumatic experience of the October War. This helped him to sustain a substantial faction within the Labor Party. Consisting largely of elements who had been Ben Gurion loyalists, it was considered rightist. The faction headed by veteran politician Yigal Allon was leftist. In between these was the largest group, loyal to Rabin, who had been adopted as the favorite son by the old guard Mapai politicians. But Rabin, a newcomer to politics, lacked the experience and confidence to be able to impose his will on more seasoned politicians like Peres and Allon.

During Rabin's premiership as the annual inflation rate soared to 50 percent, and popular discontent grew, his government became less and less secure. 1976 proved to be a year of rising social tensions, and the forerunner of a series of financial scandals. Asher Yadlin, appointed by Rabin as Governor of the Bank of Israel, was indicted on charges of bribery and fraud committed during his directorship of Histadrut's Sick Fund, and later confessed that he had channeled the embezzled funds to the Labor Party's coffers. In May, in a milieu of strikes and worker unrest, policemen were subjected to grenade attacks by the slum dwellers of Tel Aviv. Six months later, following a twenty percent increase in food and transportation charges, workers staged a series of strikes. In December the ruling coalition fell apart, and a new election was announced for May 17, 1977.

Factionalism within Labor on the issue of the Occupied Arab Territories intensified. In January 1977, following a financial scandal, Housing Minister Avraham Ofer (who had conducted Rabin's successful campaign for party leader in 1974) committed suicide. Rabin's inexperience in civil administration, poor communication skills, and continued strained relations with Peres hurt his government's popularity. Yet, in a new challenge by Peres to his leadership in early 1977, Rabin scraped through again.

Then came a revelation that made his position untenable. In March it was revealed that, during his ambassadorship in America, his wife, Leah, had maintained an active account with an American bank in Washington, an illegal act. The next month he resigned as party leader, and party delegates elected Peres his successor. In the May 1977 election the Labor bloc's strength fell to 32. It ceded its traditional leading position in the Knesset to Likud, which won 43 seats. The result became known popularly as a Ma'Hapach (The Upheaval). It signaled the end of an era.

1977 Election: The Unveiling of a New Era

Fifteen of the nineteen seats that Labor lost went to the Democratic Movement for Change (DMC) formed only in October 1976 by Yigal Yadin, an eminent Labor leader, who had become the IDF chief of staff at the age of 32. The DMC campaigned on a platform of reforming the electoral system, improving the lot of Sephardi Jews, and cleansing the administrative and political apparatuses, which had been soiled primarily by the corrupt and nepotistic ways of the Labor establishment.

Summing up the social situation, Eric Marsden, a senior British journalist based in Jerusalem, wrote: "Israel has been governed [for three decades] by interlocking groups of ministers and senior officials, many of them from an elite of about 250 families who rose to prominence in the pioneering days. Along the way many establishment members, and more particularly their sons, have changed direction. There are many instances of fervent egalitarian socialists from kibbutzim whose sons have become capitalist entrepreneurs, technocrats or army leaders, with a right-wing outlook, while still paying lip service to the Labor movement."[8]

So the emergence of Likud as the largest bloc in the Knesset seemed apt in more ways than one. Headed by Menachem Begin, who had by then won the respect even of his opponents as an honest, ascetic patriot and an able leader, Likud had presented itself to voters as an orderly and principled entity. Its election campaign had been masterminded by Ezer Weizman. For his brilliant success, Begin rewarded him with the foreign ministry.

Menachem Wolfovitch Begin was born in Brest-Litovsk in Poland in 1913. He studied at the University of Warsaw, and at sixteen he joined Betar, the youth organization of the Revisionist Zionists, known for its emphasis on iron discipline and militarism. More radical than Vladimir Zeev Jabotinsky, the founder of the Revisionist movement, which combined its ultra-nationalism with conservative socio-economic policies, Begin challenged him in 1938 after becoming Betar commander in Poland. On the eve of the 1939 Nazi invasion of Poland, Begin fled to Soviet-ruled Lithuania. In September 1940 he was sentenced to eight years hard labor in a Siberian camp for engaging in illegal Zionist activities. But, after the Soviet Union had joined the Allies, Begin was released, and drafted into the Free Polish Army. He arrived in Palestine in May 1942 as a soldier of that force, and renewed contacts with the local Betar.

After his demobilization in December 1943, Begin was appointed commander of the Irgun, the militia of the Revisionists. Declaring an armed struggle against the British mandate in January 1944, he went underground, and the Irgun began bombing British installations. Begin repeated his anti-British call in October 1945, five months after the end of the war in Europe. The Irgun's terroristic actions led the British to declare an award of £10,000 (worth $300,000 today) for his arrest. In July 1946 the Irgun bombed the British government offices in the King David Hotel in Jerusalem, killing 91 British, Arab and Jewish officials and staff.

Following this, the Haganah, the main military force of the Jewish community in Palestine, stopped co-operating with the Irgun. A year later the Irgun hanged two British sergeants in retaliation for the execution of three of its members, an act which aroused public anger in Britain. The Irgun participated actively in the conflict which erupted after the UN partition plan in November 1947. The massacre of 110 to 254 Arab men, women and children during a raid by 132 Irgun and Lehi militiamen on April 9–10, 1948 in Deir Yasin village near Jerusalem, planned chiefly by Begin, increased panic among Palestinian Arabs, and turned their mass flight from the prospective areas of the Jewish state into a stampede.

Later, led by Begin, the Irgun ranks refused to be absorbed into the new Israeli Defense Forces formed by Ben Gurion in late May 1948. They continued to participate in the war against the Arab states as a separate entity. This went on until Ben Gurion ordered his forces to destroy the freighter *Altalena*, with its cargo of Irgun volunteers and weapons. While refraining from hitting back at Ben Gurion's forces, Begin did not disband the Irgun until three months later. Soon thereafter former Irgun and other Revisionists re-emerged as the Herut party under Begin's leadership.

In 1949 Begin was elected to the Knesset, where he stayed until 1984. In its first five general elections, his Herut faction won about twelve percent of the vote, which made it the largest opposition group in the parliament. Leading his party as an authoritarian, Begin brooked no challenge. Membership in the Knesset failed to mellow Begin, who stuck to his populist demagoguery and extremist rhetoric of the pre-state period. He was vehemently opposed to the idea of accepting reparations, totaling $2 billion, from West Germany for the brutal atrocities against Jews committed by Nazi Germany, considering it an inadequate step by the Germans. He expressed his opposition by inciting a mob to attack the Knesset. In retaliation, in January 1952, the Knesset suspended him for fifteen months.

This had a chastening effect on Begin. But it took him several more years to fully accept the norms and practices of a democratic system operating through a popularly elected parliament. It was only in the mid-1960s, when he was over 50 years old, that he mellowed enough to compromise his extremism and form an alliance with the Liberals to form Gahal. Winning more than 21 percent of the vote, it secured 26 Knesset seats in the general election of November 1965. An advocate of conservative socio-economic policies, Gahal was opposed to the strong public sector created by Labor. Its other main plank was a commitment to recreating the biblical Eretz Israel.

Given its size, Gahal became the leading choice for partnership in the national unity government that prime minister Levi Eshkol formed on the eve of the June 1967 Arab-Israeli War. Begin was given a cabinet post but no specific portfolio.

Israel's stunning victory in that conflict was perceived by rightists, both religious and secular (such as Gahal supporters), as an event of legendary proportions, tantamount to a divine intervention. More specifically, it lent credence to the grand, ultra-nationalist scenario of recreating the Kingdom of Israel, and gave fresh impetus to militaristic patriotism, the fountain-head of Revisionist Zionism. It made Begin buoyant.

Gahal retained its Knesset seats and its place in the national unity government in 1969. Begin stayed in the cabinet until July 1970 when, protesting the decision to accept an American peace plan which envisaged Israel's withdrawal from Sinai, he resigned, and resumed his opposition role. But Gahal's sharing of power for three years lent it and its leader, Begin, legitimacy and respectability they had lacked before. This would contribute to their electoral victory in 1977.

When the surprise Arab attack on the Israeli forces in October 1973 shook popular confidence and respect for the Labor establishment, Gahal benefited. On the eve of the December 1973 poll, Begin combined Gahal with three smaller parties to form the Likud bloc, an enterprise in which ultra-nationalist Ariel Sharon played a substantial role. The major element uniting these factions was their commitment to incorporate the Occupied Territories of the West Bank and the Gaza Strip into Israel. Ideologically, Likud was an alliance of the conservative, capitalist and ultra-nationalist trends within secular Zionism.

Likud's first performance at the poll showed that the strength of its constituent forces was only 8.5 percent behind the liberal, social democratic forces, represented by the Labor-Mapam alliance. In the subsequent 1977 election, Likud emerged victorious, 7.4 percent ahead of its rival. In a way, this was an aggregate measure of the right wing drift of Israelis, which had begun soon after the founding of

Israel nearly three decades before. Begin was invited to form the government. By coalescing with the religious parties, he secured the backing of 60 MKs, thus bypassing Labor's breakaway Democratic Movement for Change.

Installed in the country's most powerful office, Begin exercised authority in a manner reminiscent of David Ben Gurion, his *bête noire*: highly personal and domineering. But he refrained from making a clean break with the Labor-dominated era. He retained virtually all of the senior civil servants and ambassadors even though most of them had been Labor appointees, but reminded them that the power to make major policy decisions rested with him.

As a firm believer in the recreation of biblical Eretz Israel, Begin was quick to remove the ambiguities and doubts in the previous Labor Governments' stance on the Occupied Arab Territories. He unequivocally rejected the possibility of giving up any territory of British mandate Palestine. His government started publishing maps of Israel without the 1949 armistice lines. Within weeks of taking office Begin journeyed to the controversial Elon Moreh settlement near Nablus. The ultra-nationalist Jewish colonizers, organized under the banner of Gush Emunim, had been allowed to settle there in December 1976 by the previous Labor defense minister, Peres, after their earlier attempts to do so had been foiled by the IDF. During his visit to unveil a synagogue, Begin declared: "There will be many more Elon Morehs." At the same time, Begin refused point blank to recognize Palestinians as a distinct entity in the peace talks Israel wished to have with its adversaries. Aware that his stands on these issues were not much different from Moshe Dayan's, he offered the foreign ministry to Dayan, a Labor MK. Dayan accepted, thus giving the Begin administration a majority of one in the Knesset.

Outside the Bible's Eretz Israel, Begin was willing to trade land for peace with Egypt and Syria. Yet, when Egyptian President Anwar Sadat made his dramatic visit to Jerusalem in November 1977 to declare to the Knesset his acceptance of Israel's existence, Begin's response was tepid. Among those concerned about this were 350 reserve army officers, who addressed a letter to Begin urging him to pursue the path to peace seriously and vigorously. Their action led to the formation of Peace Now, a mass-based lobby for peace, which organized rallies and demonstrations.

The result of the Israeli-Egyptian negotiations that followed was the Camp David Accords, hammered out between Begin and Sadat, with the assistance of US President Jimmy Carter, at the American presidential retreat in Maryland in September 1978. They laid out the framework for a peace treaty between Egypt and Israel, and a resolution of the Palestinian problem.

The highlights were: Egypt would regain the Sinai, in stages, in exchange for an agreement to conclude a peace treaty and establish normal diplomatic and economic relations with Israel. The time-frame for "total peace for total withdrawal" was three years after the signing. Further, over a five-year transition period the West Bank and Gaza Palestinians would gain autonomy and the end of Israeli military rule, while Israel would retain sovereignty over the land and water of these territories and maintain military camps there. During the transition period there would be talks on the final status of these territories between Israel, Egypt, Jordan (if it wished), and the elected representatives of resident Palestinians.

The breakthrough with Egypt won Begin and Sadat the 1978 Nobel Peace Prize. The two leaders signed the Egyptian-Israeli Peace Treaty at the White House in Washington on March 26, 1979. By removing the Arab World's most populous and strategic country from the anti-Israeli camp, Begin thus deprived the Arabs of the military option in their continuing conflict with Israel.

But unlike the case of Egypt, there was no compelling reason for Begin to tackle peacefully the Palestinian problem. He deliberately prevaricated, ignoring the Palestinian autonomy provisions in the Accords until the deadline of May 1980 passed.

Following his electoral success in July 1981, with Likud expanding its base largely among Sephardi Jews, Begin re-appointed the hawkish Shamir as foreign minister and gave Ariel Sharon the defense ministry he had long coveted. With three important ministries run by ultra-nationalists, the Begin administration moved decidedly to the right. It capped its formal annexation of East Jerusalem with the annexation of the Golan Heights in December 1981.

This was followed by a full-scale invasion of Lebanon, which occurred within six weeks of the final Israeli withdrawal from the Sinai in April 1982. The architect of this major military enterprise, which resulted in thousands of mainly civilian fatalities among Lebanese and Palestinians, was Ariel Sharon. Sharon and Begin initiated a war though neither Israel's security nor its existence faced any serious threat. They emerged as strong proponents of the military interventionist policy first adopted by Ben Gurion in 1956, which culminated in the Suez War. That time Israel's attempt at regional hegemony was contained by the unified opposition of the two superpowers, the United States and the Soviet Union. This time the Lebanon War created deep fissures within Israeli society itself. Most Israeli politicians concluded that there were limits to the military and political power of Israel, however determined and well armed, to impose its will on a whole region. Begin and Sharon paid for their flawed action with public censure and loss of influence, if not power. While Begin withdrew from public life altogether within a year after Israel's Lebanon War, Sharon continued his political career—away from the defense ministry.

Born Ariel Shinerman in a Zionist family in Kfar Malal, Palestine in 1928, Sharon joined the Haganah as a youth. After participating in the 1948–9 War, he worked as an intelligence officer. He established Unit 101 to carry out swift cross-border reprisal attacks, and later became a paratrooper commander. During the 1956 Suez War, he exceeded orders and engaged in a battle that caused many casualties, slowing his rise in the military hierarchy. Only when Yitzhak Rabin became chief of staff in 1965 was Sharon promoted to run the IDF's training department, and later elevated to brigadier-general.

During the 1967 War Sharon commanded a division on the southern front, and in 1969 he was put in charge of the southern command. His iron-fist policy toward Palestinian resistance to the Israeli occupation of the West Bank and the Gaza Strip earned the strong condemnation of Palestinians and became a source of controversy among Israelis. In mid-1973 he quit the army to enter politics and was instrumental in the creation of Likud. In the October 1973 War he returned to the military, commanding a division that established a bridgehead over the Suez Canal.

In May 1977 Sharon became Minister of Agriculture in the Likud government, and later became chairman of the cabinet's Settlement Committee. In both capacities he encouraged the Jewish colonization of the West Bank and the Gaza Strip. He believed in territorial maximalism and achieving political ends through military means. He got his chance to put his beliefs into practice dramatically, after the July 1981 elections when Begin named him defense minister.

Soon after Sharon and Begin had withdrawn Israeli troops from the Sinai in April 1982, they finalized plans to attack Lebanon. On June 6 the IDF marched into southern Lebanon with the ostensible aim of clearing the area of the Palestinian commandos and making northern Israel safe from their artillery and rocket fire. But when the United States did not object too much, Sharon and the IDF chief of staff, Raphael Eitan, who was later to join the ultra-nationalist Tahiya (Renaissance) party,[9] implemented a more ambitious plan: to bring about the withdrawal of all foreign forces from Lebanon, then in its seventh year of a civil war, including those of the PLO, and the establishment of a new Lebanese regime under Bashir Gemayel, a right-wing Maronite Christian warlord, which would favor Israel. In short, the game plan of Sharon and Begin was not merely to pacify the northern Israeli frontier—where an unsigned but mutually agreed ceasefire with the PLO had been in place for almost a year—but also to rearrange the regional political landscape and thus establish Israel as the unrivaled power broker in the region.

Commanded by Sharon, on June 13 IDF troops entered Beirut. In collusion with the Maronite Christian Phalange militia, the IDF besieged some 500,000 Lebanese and Palestinians in the three square miles of Muslim (Lebanese and Palestinian) West Beirut. For a month Sharon tried unsuccessfully to secure an unconditional PLO surrender by a combination of artillery fire, air raids, and severing of water, food, fuel and electricity supplies. Following a ten-day truce, the IDF staged an intense bombing of West Beirut for a week, and then subjected it to a more intensified bombardment from the air, land and sea, with Sharon ordering non-stop saturation bombing for eleven and a half hours, using phosphorous shells and concussion and cluster bombs. His actions aroused widespread condemnation in the Arab World and beyond, even angering Washington. It pressured Begin to intervene, and soon after, the 63-day siege ended, and peace returned to the beleaguered city on August 13.

Following US mediation, on August 21 a multinational peacekeeping force of about 1,000 troops from the US, Britain, France and Italy, was deployed in West Beirut to ensure the safe withdrawal of PLO and Syrian troops. On September 1 the last of the Palestinian commandos and 2,700 Syrian troops left West Beirut. The peacekeeping force withdrew soon after.

With 15,700 Lebanese, Palestinians and Syrians dead, of which 13,240 were civilians, versus 350 Israeli military fatalities, the human losses were grossly uneven.[10]

Sharon now set out to become the kingmaker in Lebanese politics, getting Bashir Gemayel elected President later that month. He succeeded, only to see his protégé killed, the result of a huge bomb explosion at Phalange party headquarters on September 14. In retaliation, Sharon allowed his Maronite Christian allies a free hand, which soon led to the murder of some 2,000 Palestinian civilians in the Beirut refugee camps of Sabra and Shatila. This outraged not only many Lebanese, Palestinians and Syrians but also large segments of Israeli society.

In an unprecedented move, responding to a call by Peace Now, some 400,000 Israelis demonstrated in Tel Aviv on September 25, demanding an inquiry into the Sabra and Shatila massacres and a recall of the Israeli troops from Lebanon. The Begin government appointed an inquiry commission chaired by the head of the Supreme Court, Yitzhak Kahan. Yielding to popular pressure, Sharon ordered the withdrawal of IDF troops from Beirut on September 29. The western multinational force re-entered the city.

Following criticism in the Kahan commission's report, Sharon was forced to resign as defense minister in February 1983. But he retained a place in the cabinet as a minister without portfolio. The thousands of IDF troops remaining in Lebanon became targets of ambush, snipers and booby-trapped vehicles, in a growing campaign of armed Lebanese resistance to the Israeli occupation. By spring the steadily rising list of Israeli fatalities had topped 150, pushing the grand total of IDF dead in Lebanon above 500. This turned Israeli public opinion against continued military presence in Lebanon. It demoralized not only the IDF command but also prime minister Begin. Unable to bear responsibility for continued Israeli deaths, he resigned on August 29, 1983, ending his six-year premiership in ignominy.

In the Likud leadership contest that followed, Yitzhak Shamir defeated David Levy. At 68, Shamir was the oldest politician to become prime minister. Born Yitzhak Yzernitzky in a religious family in Poland, Shamir joined the Revisionist Zionist youth movement, Betar. He moved to Palestine when he was 20 and two years later joined the Irgun. When the Irgun split in 1940, with Avraham Stern forming Lehi, Shamir opted for the new group, and with Stern's assassination in 1942, he became one of Lehi's commanders in charge of organization and operations, which included the 1944 assassination of Lord Moyne, Britain's resident minister. Arrested by the British in 1946, Shamir was dispatched to a detention camp in Eritrea. He escaped after four months, and found his way to Paris, where he lived until the founding of Israel in May 1948.

Following his arrival in Israel, Shamir enrolled in the political wing of Lehi, the Fighter's Party. In 1955 he joined Mossad, the Israeli foreign intelligence agency, and served in various senior positions until 1965.

After running a mattress factory for five years, he re-entered politics in the Herut party. He became chairman of the Herut executive; and in the December 1973 election he won a seat in the Knesset. An ultra-nationalist, he opposed the Camp David Accords, yet Begin gave Shamir the foreign ministry in 1980.

As prime minister in 1983 Shamir inherited the results of the Lebanon War: a deleterious involvement in the imbroglio of Lebanese politics, and hyperinflation which had already led to the collapse of several banks. On the positive side, he inherited a US-mediated draft of a Lebanese-Israeli peace treaty, which had been initialed by the two sides in May 1983.

But final signature of the treaty by Lebanon's President Amin Gemayel (brother of the slain Bashir) eluded Shamir, and soon Gemayel annulled it.

Meanwhile, Israeli fatalities in Lebanon rose steadily. At home, hyperinflation was compounded by a chronic balance of payments deficit. The roots of the twin crises lay chiefly in the larger issue of war and peace: the 1973 War, which necessitated massive rearmament during and after the conflict, financed mainly by American credits; the expense of evacuating the Sinai following the Egyptian-Israeli treaty, funded largely by US loans; and the cost of the Lebanon War against the background of rising inflation.

The rise in the military budget from 1974 on had gone hand in hand with increased expenditure on social welfare. The authorities managed this by borrowing heavily at home and abroad, and by curtailing investment. By the early 1980s the problem of huge Israeli loans and balance of payment deficits loomed large. As confidence in the Israeli economy plummeted, capital outflow increased, and the situation grew still worse as the government resorted to ever rising deficit budgeting, expecting to spend itself out of the crisis. Inflation escalated into hyperinflation, running at 400% a year after 1983.

Shamir's inability to resolve the economic crisis or devise a way out of the Lebanese quagmire led to a no-confidence motion against the government, forcing a parliamentary poll a year ahead of schedule. Not surprisingly, Likud lost six seats, and fell behind the Labor-Mapam bloc.

There were two main reasons why Labor overtook Likud. The Democratic Movement for Change, a major factor behind Labor's 1977 defeat, had disintegrated following its controversial decision to join the Begin administration. Its disaffected Labor voters returned to their traditional party whose leaders (confined to the opposition and thus deprived of the chances for corruption and embezzlement of public funds) had improved Labor's popular image. And, shaken by the anti-Labor feelings prevalent among Sephardi voters, the Labor hierarchy went out of its way to open its doors to them. Though this did not impress the largely skeptical Sephardim, it helped to stem the desertion rate.

Still, Peres could not muster a Labor-Mapam majority in the Knesset. Likud's Shamir needed to bargain with seven groups or individual MKs to manage a majority, and found the task daunting. So Peres and Shamir discussed forming a national unity government, an arrangement they justified in light of the looming economic crisis. After several weeks they devised a common set of policies on the economy, the Lebanese War and the peace process, and secured the religious parties' inclusion in the national unity government, with Peres as prime minister for the first half of the term. Shamir became prime minister in 1986. In the 1988 poll, the national unity concord was renewed, and lasted two more years.

National Unity Governments: 1984–90

The two major secular blocs, one right-of-center and the other left-of-center, shared power for six years.

The three governments they formed included the leading figures of both. Likud's Shamir and Sharon became constant features, as did Labor's Peres, Rabin and Weizman. They monopolized the prime ministry as well as the crucial defense, foreign and finance ministries. And they, all of them Ashkenazim, were members of the powerful inner political cabinet.

Peres, with Rabin as defense minister, devised and implemented a three-part withdrawal from Lebanon, ending on June 6, 1985, exactly three years after Israel's invasion. But the withdrawal was not complete. Israel retained a wide security belt inside Lebanon, guarded by 1,000 IDF troops and a 3,000-strong Israeli-run Christian militia, called the South Lebanon Army.

The disentangling of Israel from Lebanon almost coincided with the July launching of the Economic Stabilization Program (ESP), worked out in co-operation with trade unions and employers. It froze prices and wages as well as currency devaluation, and introduced the New Israeli Shekel (equal to 1,000 Old Israeli Shekels). By raising interest rates sharply it introduced a tight money policy. The ESP was so severe that it resulted in a 30 percent fall in real wages in three months. But it held, and it worked. By the end of the year, the annual inflation was down drastically—from 250 percent to about 20 percent. The ESP's success enabled the government to eliminate the budget deficit. Confidence in Israel's economy returned, and with it foreign capital.

On stepping down as prime minister in October 1986, Peres took over the foreign ministry from Shamir, hoping to revive the moribund Middle East peace process. He saw an opportunity in the plan PLO leader Yasser Arafat and King Hussein of Jordan had hammered out in early 1985. It envisaged the Palestinians exercising their right to self-determination within the framework of a confederation of Jordan and Palestine, with a joint Jordanian-Palestinian delegation participating in regional peace talks to be organized under UN auspices. Following his clandestine London meetings with King Hussein, Peres signed a secret memorandum of understanding with him in early 1987. But it was overruled by prime minister Shamir, who stuck to the 1978 Camp David Accords. They stipulated Israel retaining sovereignty over the land and water of the West Bank and Gaza Strip, and did not recognize the Palestinians as a separate entity. In April 1987 the Palestine National Council canceled Arafat's agreement with Jordan. This finally destroyed any prospect of a negotiated solution to the Palestinian problem, and was a crucial factor in the eruption of the intifada in December.

The speed with which the intifada spread from the Gaza Strip to the West Bank, its severity, the overwhelming, enthusiastic backing it won, and the unprecedented unity it engendered among different Palestinian factions, secular and Islamic, puzzled and upset the Shamir administration. The task of crushing the Palestinian uprising fell primarily on Yitzhak Rabin, the defense minister. Emulating his former military adviser, Ariel Sharon, Rabin pursued an iron fist policy to smash the intifada. Besides the conventional means of firings, curfews, harassment, arrests and house searches and demolitions, he called for breaking the bones of Palestinian protesters.

Prime Minister Shamir remained unyielding on the peace process. In early 1988 he rejected the peace proposals of US Secretary of State George Shultz as impractical. The Shultz plan specified a six-month period for talks between Israel and a joint Jordanian-Palestinian delegation to work out a transitional autonomy arrangement for the West Bank and Gaza Strip. This would last three years, during which a final settlement would be negotiated. These talks would run concurrently with an international peace conference, involving the five permanent members of the UN Security Council and all the interested parties, on the basis of the Security Council Resolutions 242 and 338.

But since the Shultz plan lacked any provision for a Palestinian state, the PLO rejected it. When King Hussein finally cut his remaining administrative and legal links with the West Bank in mid-1988, Shamir's strategy of persuading Jordan to join the Camp David process became redundant. It did, though, pave the way for the Palestine National Council to issue a declaration of independence for Palestine "on our Palestinian land" (meaning the West Bank, Gaza and East Jerusalem), renounce violence and terrorism, and accept the existence of Israel at its session in Algiers in November 1988. This had no immediate impact on the Jewish state, but led Washington to establish low-level diplomatic contacts with the PLO.

The general election that November once again produced a stalemate. Peres was not popular. Over the years he had created an image of himself as a victim in a society that craved heroes. Many interpreted his self-control as inability to speak from the heart, and doubted his sincerity. To the bulk of Sephardim, Peres remained the epitome of arrogant Ashkenazi superiority and privilege. They saw him as a suave intellectual, who lacked the common touch and could not be trusted. Peres's hopes that Ezer Weizman, now masterminding Labor's election campaign, would do for Labor what he had accomplished for Likud in 1977, were dashed.

Shamir retained his premiership in the next national unity government, and Rabin his defense portfolio. Rabin and Shamir offered a plan to hold local elections in the West Bank. The Palestinian leadership, determined to continue the uprising, rejected it, reiterating its demand of immediate Israeli withdrawal from the Occupied Territories.

But the PLO was open to talks with any Israeli politician in power genuinely interested in discussing the Palestinian national rights. One was Ezer Weizman, whose dovish views on the subject went back to the late 1970s. He held a clandestine meeting with a PLO official in Geneva in the winter of 1989. Soon after Shamir charged Weizman with violating both Israeli law forbidding contacts with the PLO, and the official policy of boycotting the PLO. Weizman resigned.

Shamir's obduracy on the twin issues of the intifada and the regional peace process led Peres to conspire with Shas, the ultra-Orthodox party, to bring down the national unity government, with a view to forming a Labor-dominated administration with a narrow majority. In March 1990 the Shamir government fell. But, as described earlier,[11] Rabbi Eliezer Schach publicly nullified the Shas-Labor agreement.

Shamir set out to court the secular ultra-nationalist groups—Tehiya, Moledet, and Tzomet, as well as a radicalized National Religious Party. It took him nearly three tortuous months to recruit them to a narrow coalition majority in the Knesset. The result was the most right-wing and ideological government in Israeli history. It enabled Ariel Sharon to fashion an unbeatable alliance of his radical faction within Likud and the secular ultra-nationalists without. As housing minister in Shamir's new cabinet,

Sharon accelerated the building of Jewish settlements on the West Bank. But the pursuit of radical, ultra-nationalist policies in the face of the Palestinian intifada and the moderated stance of the PLO proved counter-productive. Labor returned to power in 1992, an event which, like its counterpart a quarter century before, was popularly called The Upheaval.

But this was not the only dramatic development in the Israel of the 1990s. The country also experienced Jewish immigration on a scale it had not seen for nearly four decades. This time the source was the former Soviet Union, with the second largest Jewish population in the world after the United States. During 1989, the tide of Soviet Jewish immigration rose, increasing Israel's total number of immigrants from 13,300 in 1988 to 199,500 two years later, and creating a new factor in regional politics.

THE DRAMATIC 1990s

Iraq's invasion and occupation of Kuwait on August 2, 1990 benefited the right-wing Shamir government. It diverted the attention of the Bush administration away from pressuring Israel to advance the regional peace process. By claiming a link between Iraq's evacuation of Kuwait and an Israeli withdrawal from the Occupied Arab Territories, Iraqi President Saddam Hussein won the backing not only of Yasser Arafat and the PLO, but also an overwhelming majority of ordinary Palestinians. This in turn undermined the position of Israeli doves and strengthened the ultra-nationalist camp. Bush succeeded in assembling a coalition of 28 countries, including the six Arab Gulf monarchies, Egypt, Morocco and Syria, to militarily confront Iraq on January 16, 1991. Two days later Iraq fired a dozen ground-to-ground missiles at Israel. A couple of these landed in Tel Aviv where the Iraqi target was the defense ministry headquarters. The actual human and property damage done was small, yet thousands of Tel Aviv residents fled. Industry, commerce and education came to a standstill. Those who stayed wore gas masks and stayed in specially sealed rooms during Iraq's bombardment. Though the Israeli defense minister, Moshe Arens, publicly threatened retaliation, the government bowed to American pressure and did nothing. Had Israel intervened in the conflict, most of the Arab and Muslim countries in the anti-Iraqi coalition would have withdrawn, seriously weakening it militarily, diplomatically and morally.

When Iraq hit populated areas of Tel Aviv with three missiles on January 22, Premier Shamir told Israeli television, "It isn't a question of ping-pong: you hit me, I'll hit you."[12] It emerged later that, following the example of Golda Meir in 1973, Shamir had put Israel on full nuclear alert and (according to US satellite pictures) ordered missile launchers in Kfar Zechariah armed with nuclear weapons to be deployed in the open, facing Iraq. The nuclear alert remained until the Gulf War ended on February 27.[13] It was widely conjectured that had Iraqi missiles armed with poison gas hit Israeli targets and caused large-scale deaths, Israel would have retaliated with its atomic weapons.

As it was, Iraq's unprovoked attacks enhanced sympathy for Israel in western capitals. West Germany offered emergency humanitarian aid of $170 million;

a further package, including money to build two submarines, raised the total to $670 million. Washington gave Israel $650 million to cover its Gulf War-related expenditures.

Shamir's public restraint during the Gulf War raised his international status. This was helped further when Shamir agreed to participate in a US-backed Middle East peace conference after the war. But Shamir did so only after all Israeli preconditions had been met: the exclusion of the PLO from the talks; the participation only of non-PLO residents of the Occupied Territories in a joint Jordanian-Palestinian delegation; any settlement to include a transitional period of Palestinian autonomy under the Israelis; and the negotiations to be bilateral, with separate talks between Israel and each Arab interlocutor. In return Israel conceded the principle of land for peace as contained in UN Resolution 242. The peace conference opened in Madrid in late October 1991.

But before that, Shamir joined an extremist enterprise of Ariel Sharon, thereby digging his own political grave. In summer 1991 Sharon announced large-scale plans to colonize the West Bank to emphasize Israel's resolve to hold on to the Occupied Territories (irrespective of the forthcoming peace conference). The plan involved tripling confiscations of Palestinian land, and quadrupling the funds for constructing Jewish settlements, roads and infrastructure. This angered Washington.

So when Shamir requested the Bush administration to become Israel's guarantor for the $10 billion loan it planned to raise to settle the recent Russian immigrants, the White House replied that it would do so only if Israel froze all Jewish settlement activity. Shamir refused to accept the American condition. Relations between Israel and the Unites States became strained.

While Shamir and his ultra-nationalists were busy running the government, Labor leaders, languishing in opposition, pondered their party's inability to improve its electoral appeal. They decided to democratize and decentralize, and at the 1991 convention adopted the primary system for both the party leader and Knesset list. Rabin's replacement of Peres as party leader confirmed the changed image Labor wanted to project. Unlike the visionary Peres, the down-to-earth Rabin inspired trust among Israelis of all classes and ethnic background. His long, distinguished military career, topped by six continuous years as defense minister, had embossed on the national psyche the image of a man totally devoted to the security of Israel—an image Likud and ultra-nationalist politicians found hard to challenge or undermine. Labor won, and formed the government in coalition with the left-wing Meretz (Vitality) and Shas.

The 1992 Upheaval

There was much in common between this Upheaval and that of a quarter century ago. Just as in 1977, it was not the opposition who won but the incumbents who lost. This time, most of the eight seats that Likud lost went to ultra-nationalist secular groups or the radicalized National Religious Party.

Like Labor in 1977, Likud had become tarnished with allegations of corruption and embezzlement of public funds. In March 1992 a report published by the state comptroller charged several Likud luminaries with corruption and misuse of public funds. Shamir's refusal to support electoral reform in the form of direct election of the prime minister made him seem part of that status quo, and hurt his popular standing. His decision to pass up a US loan guarantee for expanding Jewish settlements in the West Bank alienated Russian immigrants, the majority of whom voted Labor. On the other hand, the spending of the vast sums on absorbing the large influx of (Russian) Ashkenazim, at the expense of social welfare, lost Likud some of its normal support among the largely working class Sephardim.

The other major factor alienating Sephardi voters was the rampant factionalism that split Likud between groups led respectively by Shamir, Ariel Sharon and David Levy. On the eve of the central committee's selection of the Knesset list in March, the Shamir and Sharon factions combined to exclude Levy's predominantly Sephardi nominees. Levy protested loudly and publicly, accusing his rivals of turning Likud into "a white elitist party in which Sephardim do not have a chance."[14]

Three years later, in an interview in the Knesset cafeteria, Levy was still critical of his rivals' behavior on the eve of the 1992 poll. A well-built, bespectacled man of 58, capped with a thick mane of gray hair over an unlined, open face, Levy said that "due to the economic liberalization and deregulation, initiated by the Likud government in 1977, many of the economic problems arising from a highly centralized government run by Labor for three decades were solved. Also young leadership came up in Likud, from the Sephardi development towns. But the factionalism of the party's old guard blocked the progress of these young activists."

Levy has a particular rapport with the inhabitants of the Sephardi-dominated development towns. He lived in one, Beit Shean, after arriving in Israel from Morocco in 1957. He made his living as a construction worker, a fact which his detractors constantly refer to. Politically active with Herut, he became mayor of Beit Shean in the mid-1960s, and then an MK in 1969. After the Likud victory in 1977, Premier Begin appointed him Minister of Immigration and Absorption, and them moved him to the housing portfolio. Following the 1981 poll, Begin named him Deputy prime minister, the first Sephardi to achieve this office. But when Levy challenged Shamir for the Likud leadership in 1983, he lost. It took seven years before Shamir, heading a government with a thin majority, included Levy in the cabinet, as foreign minister. His working-class Sephardi background and lack of knowledge of English (he is fluent in French) are the butt of many jokes, undoubtedly concocted by Ashkenazi politicians and journalists.[15]

These unflattering jokes about Levy reached a peak when he challenged Binyamin Netanyahu, his deputy at the foreign ministry, for Likud leadership in March 1993. Netanyahu made his impact on international television channels during the Gulf War. His youthful good looks and facility with sound bites made him an instant television personality. Given Levy's lack of English, Netanyahu was in constant demand to explain Israeli policies during the Gulf conflict.

Born in 1950 in Jerusalem in a right-wing academic family, Netanyahu left for the United States when his father got a teaching job there in 1964. He returned to Israel to do his military service, and became a commander in the Sayeret Matkal (General Staff Reconnaissance), an elite commando force, then returned to the

States to resume his university education at MIT. In 1982, on the recommendation of Israel's ambassador to the United States, Moshe Arens, who himself had an MIT degree in aeronautical engineering, Begin appointed Netanyahu Israel's ambassador to the United Nations. After two years, Netanyahu returned to Israel, and became director of the terrorism research Jonathan Institute, named after his elder brother who had died leading a commando raid to free hostages in Entebbe, Uganda.

Elected to the Knesset on the Likud ticket in 1988, he was Levy's deputy at the foreign ministry. When Shamir made Netanyahu the chief Israeli spokesman at the Madrid peace conference, Levy stayed away from the gathering. Soon after, he got Netanyahu transferred to the prime minister's office. In the Likud leadership contest in March 1993 Netanyahu had the advantage of expertise and funds from his Jewish American friends. 142,000 Likud members favored Netanyahu, and only 27 percent Levy. The deep ill-feeling between the upstart Netanyahu and the veteran Levy persisted.

The Netanyahu-Levy feud had a parallel on the other side of the political spectrum with the Peres-Rabin rivalry. For nearly twenty years these Labor politicians, despite no fundamental differences of policy or ideology, were locked in a personal struggle for power, and engaged in ongoing intrigue and back-stabbing. Labor's June 1992 electoral victory did not lead to immediate reconciliation between the two. Though Rabin gave Peres the foreign ministry, he restricted him to the less important, multilateral talks with the Arab countries concerning refugees, water resources, the economy, environment and regional security and disarmament, which had been initiated by the Madrid conference—and kept him out of the all-important bilateral talks.

After his defeat, Shamir revealed he had planned to drag out the peace talks for the next ten years. But both Rabin and Peres were serious about peacemaking. The Labor-dominated government's lifting of the ban on contacts with the PLO in January 1993 set the scene for secret talks between the two sides, initiated by two Norwegian intermediaries, Terje Rod Larsen and Mona Juul. Though Peres was involved directly through his deputy, Yossi Beilin, the final decisions always rested with Rabin. The resulting Oslo Accord, called the Declaration of Principles (DOP), was based on mutual recognition between Israel and the PLO (as the representative of the Palestinian people), and provided for limited Palestinian autonomy in the Gaza Strip and the West Bank town of Jericho. It was signed at the White House on September 13, 1993 by Shimon Peres and the PLO's Mahmoud Abbas. After the signing, life-long enemies Yasser Arafat and Yitzhak Rabin, prodded by President Clinton, shook hands.

With that most widely seen and televised handshake in history, Rabin and Arafat inaugurated a new chapter in the history of the region.

The Declaration of Principles contained the following timetable:

> By December 13, 1993: The two sides to agree to a protocol on the withdrawal of Israeli forces from the Gaza Strip and Jericho.

> By April 13, 1994: Israel to complete military withdrawal from the Gaza Strip and Jericho, and transfer power to a Palestinian Authority to be nominated by the PLO.

By July 13, 1994: Following an agreement on elections for the Palestinian Council and a Comprehensive Interim Agreement on the structure and powers of the Council, the election will be held after Israeli forces have been redeployed outside West Bank population centers to specified locations. Israel's (military-run) civil administration in the Occupied Territories will be dissolved, with its powers transferred to the Palestinian Authority.

By December 13, 1995: Israel and the Palestinian Authority to start talks on the permanent status issues, including Jerusalem, Palestinian refugees, Jewish settlements, borders and relations with neighbors.

On December 13, 1998: The deadline for the final settlement talks, and the expiration date of the Oslo Accord.

By December 13, 1999: The permanent settlement to take effect.

The Israelis and the PLO transformed the Declaration of Principles into a working document in Cairo on May 4, 1994. The Cairo Accord gave rise to the Palestinian Authority (PA), headed by Arafat. On July 1, he left the PLO's exile headquarters in Tunis to establish the PA in the Gaza Strip and Jericho. Later that month, Peres became the first Israeli foreign minister to visit Jordan openly. His peace efforts culminated in a Jordanian-Israeli Peace Treaty signed in October by Rabin and King Hussein, in the presence of President Clinton. Later Rabin, Peres and Arafat shared the 1994 Nobel Peace Prize.

Opposition to the Israeli-PLO Accord came from both the Israeli right wing, secular and religious, and the radical Palestinian groups, secular and religious. Hamas and Islamic Jihad combined verbal opposition with terror attacks, which escalated after the killing of 29 Muslim worshippers by a Jewish settler at the Ibrahimi Mosque/ Tomb of the Patriarchs in Hebron in February 1994. Rabin responded by sealing off the West Bank and Gaza, thus depriving Palestinians of their livelihood. In October 1994 a Hamas suicide bomber killed himself and 22 Israelis on a bus in Tel Aviv. Three months later, two Islamic Jihad suicide bombers killed themselves and 21 Israeli soldiers at a bus stop at Beit Lid near Natanya.

Meanwhile, anger and apprehension grew among the 120,000 Jewish settlers in the West Bank. In July they adopted a plan to disrupt the redeployment of the IDF in the West Bank, by blocking all highways in the West Bank and erecting "outpost settlements" (with five Jews, a tent and a flag, qualifying as a settlement) overlooking the blocked highways. They would also stage simultaneous demonstrations at main crossroads inside the Green Line (i.e., pre-1967 Israel).

The settlers implemented their plan of occupying strategic hilltops in the West Bank, but success depended on the response of Jewish Israelis inside the Green Line. That in turn depended very much on the terrorism committed by radical Palestinians. After the suicide bombing in January 1995 there was a lull for six months. Then came a suicide attack in Ramat Gan near Tel Aviv on July 24, claiming seven lives. It gave some impetus to the ultra-nationalist settlers' plans, but not enough to win their goals.

While pressing on with arduous negotiations with the Palestinians, Rabin refrained from taking tough action against the Jewish settlers. Except for the IDF's disbanding of 1,000 Jewish ultra-nationalists from the land belonging to the

Palestinian village of Al Khadr on July 31, Rabin ignored the settlers' campaign. So did most of the media. Funeral processions staged by Israeli teenagers protesting the Israeli-PLO accord on its second anniversary failed to capture the popular imagination. Even the suicide bomb-attack by a female Hamas terrorist killing five people, including herself, on a bus in Jerusalem on August 21, failed to generate support for the ultra-nationalist agitation. Instead, overlooked by the media and police, they appeared increasingly ludicrous to most Israelis as they camped on treeless hilltops in scorching summer heat.

Indeed, Arafat and Peres initialed the Comprehensive Interim Agreement on extending the jurisdiction of the Palestinian Authority (PA) to the West Bank and holding elections for the Palestinian Council, on September 14, 1995. It was a complex document of over 300 pages and many detailed maps. Four days later Rabin and Arafat signed the second Israeli-PLO accord, popularly called Oslo II, at the White House with President Clinton.

While criticism from the radical Palestinian side was muted, the reaction from the Israeli right wing was sharp. On October 5 thousands of Israelis demonstrated in Jerusalem against the Oslo II Accord. They burned effigies of Rabin dressed in a Nazi uniform. Later Likud leader Binyamin Netanyahu addressed the demonstrators whose favorite chant was: "Rabin is a traitor." He reiterated his statement that if Likud were elected to power it would scrap the Oslo II Accord.

The tone and content of these speeches, slogans and images had been set earlier, in the wake of the first Oslo Accord. A week after that agreement was initialed, tens of thousands of protesters demonstrated outside Rabin's office. Their most popular banner read: "Wanted for Treason: Yitzhak Rabin and Shimon Peres." Soon caricatures of Rabin in a Nazi officer uniform or Arab dress appeared on walls in Israel and the Jewish settlements in the Occupied Territories[16] and became a common feature at ultra-nationalists' rallies and demonstrations.

Most speakers at these rallies argued that since the Rabin government had the support only of 55 out of 112 Jewish MKs it lacked legitimacy.[17] The anti-Rabin and anti-Peres rhetoric and sloganeering escalated in the summer and fall of 1995 as Jewish settlers in the Occupied Territories and their sympathizers inside Israel whipped up feelings against the government. They routinely labeled Rabin not just a political rival but a traitor to Israel and the Jewish people, a collaborator with rabid Muslim terrorists who agreed to give away parts of Eretz Israel.

Among those who regularly participated in such demonstrations was Yigal Amir, a 27-year-old law student at the Bar Ilan University of Ramat Gan. The discussions of Amir, who had spent five years at the Yavne Yeshiva in Ashdod combining his military service and religious studies, with his colleagues at the university always cited the Torah. He told friends that since Rabin had given away parts of the Eretz Israel to the Arabs it was a *mitzvah* (an obligation) for a pious Jew to kill him. He began stalking Rabin in June 1995.

The rising vociferousness of the right-wing goaded Peace Now to muster its forces in Tel Aviv and plan a rally at the Malkhei Israel Square. And to counter the right-wing assault on his peacemaking, Rabin agreed, unprecedentedly, to address the rally with Peres. The November 4 event attracted some 150,000 people.

Apparently the ambiance of the large assembly so moved Rabin that he joined, again unprecedentedly, in singing the "Song of Peace." It was a routine exercise at Peace Now rallies, but Rabin had to read the unfamiliar words hastily written down for him:

> Let the sun shine, let the morning rise,
> The purest of prayers will not bring us back.
>
> He whose life has been extinguished,
> And has been tucked into the earth,
> Bitter tears will not wake him up,
> Will not bring him back here.
>
> Nobody will bring us back,
> From the deep pit of darkness,
> Nor can the joy of victory,
> Nor songs of glory.
>
> Don't whisper a prayer,
> It is better to sing a song of peace,
> With a great shout.

Ironically, these were to be the last public words of Rabin, a man who never ceased to think or act like a soldier. The song was written after the 1967 War and banned two years later from Israeli radio stations, perceived as undermining the willingness of young Israelis to fight. Soon after its establishment in 1978, the Peace Now group adopted it as its theme song. Its popularity soared after the Israeli invasion of Lebanon in 1982.

At 9:50 P.M. as Rabin walked along a darkened passageway leading to the concourse where his car was parked, Yigal Amir fired two shots and killed Rabin. "I acted alone on God's orders and I have no regrets," Amir told the police. "I had planned to kill Peres and Rabin together, but Peres left alone before Rabin."

The event shocked Israel and the rest of the world. More than a fifth of Israel's population of five million filed past Rabin's body as it lay in state in the Knesset plaza or paid respects to the cortege during its journey from Tel Aviv to Jerusalem. Rabin's funeral on November 6 was attended by some 60 heads of state, including those of Egypt and Jordan.

"Yitzhak Rabin was a son of this rocky soil, of Jerusalem, a first generation son," wrote Aharon Megged, an Israeli novelist. "He was not 'like' anyone [else]. Not Ben Gurion, not Sharett, not Eshkol, not any of the previous leaders of the nation... Not a "man of vision" nor a "man of letters," nor a riveting speaker, and really, neither a diplomat or politician of great sophistication, even when he reluctantly filled all these roles. In everything he did, whether in war or politics—he was determined to carry out the mission he took upon himself [or that was placed upon him] as an outstanding soldier: with all the ability, talent and wisdom with which he had been graced... It wasn't pictures of Spinoza, of Maimonides or of Herzl that adorned the walls of his office, but rather a photograph of his own commander, Yigal Allon... The security of Israel flowed in the veins of Yitzhak Rabin."[18]

Peres as the Premier

As expected, Shimon Peres succeeded Rabin as the premier. Rabin's assassination, and Labor's often repeated argument that the "verbal violence" of Likud and other right-wing groups had created an environment conducive to the tragic murder, put Likud and Netanyahu on the defensive.

A faction within the Peres Government wanted to capitalize electorally on the feelings aroused by Rabin's assassination, by advancing the polls for the Knesset and premiership, not normally due for about a year. Its argument did not prevail. Such a move would have appeared too opportunistic to most voters. Also the electoral campaign would have overlapped the implementation of the Oslo II Accord, due to start in mid-November and culminate in the elections for the Palestinian Council and the PA presidency on January 20.

Once the Oslo-mandated IDF troop redeployment had been carried out, highlighted by the IDF's evacuation of Bethlehem during the Christmas season, most Palestinians as well as Israelis were convinced, at least for the time being, that the peace process was being consolidated.

Then on January 5, 1996 came the news of the assassination (by means of a booby-trapped mobile telephone) of Yahya Ayash, the Palestinian master bomb-maker, who was held responsible for assembling explosives for suicide bombers since October 1994. The Shin Beth's success in recruiting a Palestinian agent, Kamal Hamad, an uncle of the man in whose house Ayash had taken refuge in the Gazan village of Beit Lahiya, and planting a miniature bomb in Ayash's cellular telephone impressed on the public once again that the arm of Israeli intelligence and security agencies was very long indeed. Leaked stories in the Hebrew press had Shin Beth sources claiming responsibility for Ayash's murder, which apparently had been committed partly to restore the agency's reputation, severely tarnished by Rabin's assassination two months earlier. Significantly, having refused to accept the resignation of Shin Beth chief Karmi Gillon after Rabin's assassination in early November, Peres did so on January 8. In his resignation letter, Gillon claimed that "the organization was on the right track."

As expected, the elections to the PA resulted in the victory for Arafat by an overwhelming plurality and for his Fatah movement by a two-thirds majority. Soon after, an early February poll showed 59 percent of Israeli voters backing the Oslo Accords, with only 24 percent opposing, and Peres leading his rival, Netanyahu, by 18 points. The Knesset decided to call the parliamentary and premiership elections on May 29, 1996.

By all accounts, these elections were to be the most significant since the founding of Israel. But, contrary to earlier estimations, they were also to become one of the most unpredictable.

The four suicide bombs between February 25 and March 4 in Jerusalem, Tel Aviv and Ashqelon consumed 59 lives and spoiled the neat calculations of Peres and Labor. The first three attacks were claimed by Hamas, and the last one by the Islamic Jihad. By thus illustrating that Israelis were far from secure, the Islamic extremists undermined Peres's popularity. His lead over Netanyahu in the opinion polls fell, and for the first time he lagged a few points behind his rival.

This happened despite the fact that Peres acted swiftly and forcefully. After the first bombing on February 25, Peres ordered the closure of the West Bank and Gaza Strip, and imposed a naval blockade of the Gaza Strip to prevent Islamic radicals escaping by sea. At a meeting with Arafat at the Erez checkpoint, Israeli chief of staff Amnon Shahak virtually ordered Arafat to arrest fifteen Hamas leaders.

Following the second suicide bombing in downtown Jerusalem on March 3, Peres put Israel on a virtual war footing. He created a special anti-terror command, and ordered a more than mile-wide fence, equipped with electronic surveillance devices and patrolled by motorized IDF units, to be built along the 217 mile border dividing the West Bank and Israel. When Arafat telephoned Peres after the bombing, the latter reportedly shouted, "If you cannot do the job, we will do it—don't tell me you are doing enough. Finish off Hamas! A few arrests here, a few arrests there—that is not enough."[19]

As Defense Minister, Peres ordered the IDF to impose internal closure of the West Bank, with all movement between population centers banned. Further Israeli action followed after the fourth suicide bomb, this time in Tel Aviv, on March 4, the Purim festival day. Following an emergency cabinet session, Peres declared: "Israel will go into any corner where terror has taken root." In an interview with the BBC, Israeli Foreign Minister Ehud Barak, former chief of staff, said: "There is a 50-50 chance of Israel going into the Palestinian Authority areas." By re-entering the Palestinian cities in the West Bank and Gaza with tanks and armored personnel carriers, Israel would have scrapped the Oslo Accords. But the feelings in the Jewish state were running high. "Israelis are now united in their conviction that Arafat cannot deliver the security they long for," wrote Zeev Schiff, a veteran military analyst. "These attacks prove that Israelis must not rely on Arafat for their security. Even when he tells us he is arresting the heads of the terrorist groups, we know that he is not serious."[20]

A measured view was offered by Karmi Gillon, former Shin Beth chief. "Arafat is taking measures against suicide bombers who are en route to carry out attacks in Israel, and he tries to eliminate suicide attacks," he said. "But he is not putting enough pressure on the Hamas leadership."[21] On the other hand, Israeli President Ezer Weizman declared: "If we cannot find the needle we must burn the haystack." Yielding to the mounting pressure, Arafat stated: "I will co-operate fully with Israel to wipe out terrorism." He immediately banned six Palestinian militias, including those of Hamas and Islamic Jihad. By then the IDF—authorized by the Oslo II Accord to maintain overall security in 465 Palestinian villages and refugee camps in the West Bank—had re-entered the West Bank areas it controlled jointly with the PA, conducted mass interrogation, arrested scores of Islamists, and sealed many houses.

There was little doubt that the Qassam Brigade, the military wing of Hamas, wanted to have an impact on the Israeli elections. It figured that wrecking the chances of Peres would also weaken Arafat, and create a political vacuum among Palestinians to be filled by Hamas. Such an estimation seemed logical enough. But when the PA's Preventive Security Service chief, Colonel Jibril Rajoub, tried to propagate the idea that there was a formal collusion between Hamas and Likud, his move backfired.

Soon after arresting Muhammad Abu Wardeh, a student of Ramallah Teachers Training College, for allegedly recruiting two Hamas suicide bombers, Rajoub invited Israel Television to interview him. In that interview, Abu Wardeh "revealed" that the Hamas bombings were "part of a political agenda to help Likud win the next general election." But this did not quite match what Abu Wardeh had said earlier in the day in an interview with the "Voice of Palestine" of the Palestine Broadcasting Authority. "The true reason for the new wave of bombing was to avenge the murder of Ayash," he explained. "The people who did these actions came from the areas under Israeli occupation. You know I have no idea about the people involved in the suicide attacks, but I can say it is all the fault of the Israelis. It started after they killed Yahya Ayash." Little wonder that many Israelis did not take seriously the theory of collusion between Hamas and Likud. "This is a clear attempt by Arafat and Rajoub to save prime minister Shimon Peres from losing the next election," said Tzahi Hanegbi, a Likud MK.

If there was a political collusion of any sort, it was between the Peres Government and Arafat's PA. Though their intelligence services concluded that the order to the Qassam Brigade to mount suicide attacks on Israeli targets inside Israel had come from that section of the Hamas leadership that was based in Damascus, they deliberately played this down. This had to do with Peres's strategy of peace with Syria. Peres unilaterally suspended talks with the Syrians in the United States following the suicide bombings in late February. But he did not wish to further rebuff President Hafez Assad by highlighting anti-Israeli activities in Damascus. Instead Peres escalated his accusations against Iran as the prime instigator of terrorism against Israel.

Arafat joined the Israeli chorus of combating terrorism. In his inaugural address to the Palestinian Council in Gaza city on March 7, he proposed a worldwide campaign against terrorism. The idea caught the imagination of the US President whose staff and Secretary of State, Warren Christopher, organized a "summit of the peacemakers" six days later at the Egyptian port of Sharm al Shaikh, jointly hosted by Presidents Hosni Mubarak and Bill Clinton.

Besides the host countries the summit was attended by the PA and 26 states, including Britain, Canada, France, Germany, Italy, Japan, Russia, Spain and Turkey. Of the 22 Arab League members, 14 attended, the notable absentees being Syria and Lebanon. After a four-hour meeting, the summit communique was read out by Clinton. "The summit had three fundamental objectives: to enhance the peace process; to promote security; and to combat terror," he said. These were to be pursued by "political and economic means," by closer co-operation and by "establishing a working group to seek practical methods for co-ordination."

But diplomatic convention required that the true purpose of the exercise—to bolster Peres's electoral chances—not be mentioned by Clinton or any other leader. Yet by spending 24 hours in Israel, in Peres's company, following the summit—and using it as the occasion to promise Israel an additional $100 million to counter terrorism by purchasing advanced bomb detecting devices, X-ray systems, robots to handle suspected bombs and radar censors—Clinton managed to combine his anti-terrorist mission with an oblique endorsement of Peres in the election campaign.

Thus reassured, Peres terminated the internal closure of the West Bank on March 15. But he continued the closure of the Green Line, thus keeping Palestinian workers out of Israel. Periodic mass arrests, pushing the total of suspected Islamic radicals to 1,000 by the end of March, continued. So too did the blowing up of the houses of suicide bombers, since such acts produced dramatic television footage and impressed Israeli voters.

All this occurred against the background of simmering violence along the Israeli-Lebanese border, where Israel's occupation of Lebanese territory since June 1982 had engendered armed resistance from Hizbollah, or Party of God, a militant Shia Muslim organization formed in late 1982. The conflict between the two sides had waxed and waned.

The formal understanding reached between them in July 1993—that so long as Israel refrained from attacking Lebanese civilians, Hizbollah would not fire rockets at northern Israel—broke down on March 30, 1996. The IDF shelling that day, in response to Hizbollah attacks inside the occupied zone that killed six Israeli soldiers in two weeks, left two Lebanese civilians dead. Hizbollah targeted northern Israel with its Katyusha rockets. When a bomb, purportedly planted by the IDF, killed two Lebanese boys in a village near the occupied zone on April 8, Hizbollah fired more Katyushas. Two days later a Hizbollah suicide bomber killed one Israeli soldier and injured three.

On April 11 Peres responded by ordering a major military operation, code-named Grapes of Wrath. It involved simultaneous Israeli attacks on south Beirut, the Beqaa Valley in the east, and Nabatiya in the south as well as shelling of the United Nations buffer zone, established in southern Lebanon after the Israeli invasion of March 1978. Israel imposed a naval blockade from Tyre to Beirut. Warned by the IDF, some 400,000 Lebanese civilians from the affected area in Lebanon fled. In northern Israel, 20,000 of the 24,000 residents of Kiryat Shimona fled their homes. To damage Lebanon's reconstruction efforts, Israel hit a power station on April 15.

Three days later came a change from the earlier pattern. At 1:55 P.M. in Qana, Hizbollah fighters fired two Katyusha rockets and eight mortars from a cemetery about 380 yards behind a UN post filled with civilian refugees. Eighteen minutes later, with an overhead pilotless drone providing real-time photographs of the ground, Israeli gunners fired six 155 mm shells. They exploded on impact inside the UN compound, and another six burst several yards above the ground, wounding the survivors of the earlier direct hits. Of the 869 refugees sheltering in the large prefabricated conference room, 102 died, and another 200 were injured. The UN commander immediately informed his headquarters at Naqoura, which contacted the Israeli liaison office. But it was not until 2:25 P.M. that the Israeli firing stopped, with 28 more shells falling around the UN perimeter at Qana.

The massacre of over 100 Lebanese civilians shocked the world, and induced active diplomacy by the United States and France to end the violence. A truce took effect April 27 allowing both parties to attack military targets within the occupation zone, but forbidding them to target civilians outside the area. It also set up a ceasefire monitoring group, made up of America, France, Israel, Syria and Lebanon.[22]

Peres claimed that as a consequence of Grapes of Wrath, the Israeli-Lebanese frontier was "calm." But most observers concluded that Israel's attempt to crush Hizbollah left the organization intact. Peres wanted to impress the Israeli voters that he could be tougher than Rabin when it came to punishing Israel's foes. Whereas Rabin's blitz against Hizbollah in July 1993, lasted a week, caused the deaths of 123 civilians and 16 Hizbollah militia, and the displacement of 200,000 people, the Peres operation had lasted sixteen days, and resulted in the killing of 160 civilians and 50 Hizbollah fighters, the homelessness of 400,000 civilians, and damage worth $500 million.

Peres hardened his stance elsewhere as well. On April 1 he declared that he would hold a referendum on any final settlement with the Palestinians. Arafat protested, arguing this was "completely against what had been agreed upon." Peres ignored the criticism, aware that attacks by Arafat were an electoral asset for him.

Yet he needed Arafat's co-operation in getting the Palestine National Council (PNC) to amend its Charter as specified in Arafat's September 9, 1993 letter to Rabin.[23] Arafat concurred with Peres's preference that the PNC should annul the old Charter, with its threats to Israel's existence, rather than deliberate over its wording. So the PNC, meeting in Gaza city, adopted a resolution which called for the Charter to be made consistent with the PNC's November 1988 resolution, which explicitly recognized Israel, the Oslo Accords, and the UN Security Council's resolutions relevant to Palestine, especially 242 and 338, and instructed its legal committee to present a modified version of the Charter within six months. The vote was 504 for and 54 against. "I am very happy to have fulfilled my commitments [to Israel]," said Arafat. The vote took place on April 24, the Day of Establishment of Israel, according to the Jewish calender. Peres said: "It's the most significant ideological change in the Middle East in the last 100 years."[24] In contrast, Netanyahu hammered away his argument that the Oslo Accords had created more Israeli dead, not less, and described Peres's overemphasis on peace as a sign of defeatism, an un-Israeli characteristic.

The prime peace broker, President Clinton, had no doubt about the change in the Charter. He rewarded Arafat with his first White House meeting on May 1, but only after a series of meetings with Peres. On May 13, to bolster Peres's electoral chances, Arafat agreed to let him postpone the IDF evacuation of most of Hebron, originally due by March 28, to mid-June.

Aware of the impact another suicide bomb attack would have on his electoral fate, Peres ordered a complete sealing of Israel from the Palestinian territories 72 hours before the elections. There was no further explosion. Yet he lost.

The 1996 Upheaval

In the prime ministerial contest, Binyamin Netanyahu defeated Shimon Peres by one percent.

The final outcome was decided by two groups, both equal in size (about 11 percent of the voters), inclined to vote en bloc, and existing outside the Israeli mainstream: ultra-Orthodox Jews and Israeli Arabs. Over 90 percent of the ultra-Orthodox, living in tight, urban communities, voted, almost wholly for Netanyahu.

But only 77 percent of the scattered and loosely organized Israeli Arabs did so, almost totally for Peres. Urged by their communal leaders to cast their ballot for Peres "the peacemaker," Israeli Arabs turned out in higher numbers, proportionately, than in the past six general elections; but a significant percentage—7, to be exact—could not bring themselves to vote for Peres, "the perpetrator of the Qana massacre," and deposited blank ballots. With their invalid votes amounting to 31,500—higher than Netanyahu's narrow majority of 29,450—they robbed Peres of victory.

Netanyahu needed to win the ultra-Orthodox in the tight race. He took to wearing a skullcap, something he had not done before, and tried to paint the Labor-Meretz opposition as dominated by atheists. He persuaded most rabbis that Likud's commitment to recreating Eretz Israel was preferable to Labor's territorial compromise. Just 36 hours before the vote, he won the endorsement of Rabbi Yitzhak Kaduri, a 106-year-old ultra-Orthodox patriarch, who placed his frail hands on Netanyahu's head and said: "May God grant that next week you become the prime minister." The flashing of this image on television and newspapers finally tipped the balance for Netanyahu.

Campaign posters proclaimed "Netanyahu is Good for the Jews," implying that Peres was the candidate of the Arabs. Along with this stridency went telegenic Netanyahu's impeccable style on television, a contrast to Peres's stodgy manner. Netanyahu repeated endlessly short, simplistic slogans, concentrating on the emotional issues of the future of Jerusalem and the Jewish settlements. He put Peres on the defensive, charging that the latter would uproot Jewish settlements, divide Jerusalem and allow Palestinian refugees to return, thus endangering the "demographic security" of Israel, and that already he had "sub-contracted" Israeli security to Arafat.

Simultaneously, "Israeli news coverage and attention focused largely, and at times obsessively, on Jewish security—on charges that Mr. Arafat was not extraditing terrorists, on disputes over whether he had actually dropped calls for Israel's destruction from the PLO Covenant," noted Serge Schmemann, the Jerusalem bureau chief of *The New York Times*. "Polls repeatedly showed that most Israelis were convinced that Mr. Arafat was not living up to the agreements, though Israel was at least as culpable by ignoring its contractual obligations to release female prisoners, to make a transit road from Gaza to the West Bank, or to withdraw the military from Hebron. But by failing to counter a one-sided perception of the agreements, Mr. Peres in effect ensured that every terror attack would be perceived as a huge violation and as evidence of government incompetence. Instead of trying to spell out his vision, Mr. Peres was trying to prove that he was tough enough to handle the security risks, taking extraordinary measures against the Palestinians, unleashing a vicious raid into Lebanon, and asserting that Hamas, Islamic Jihad and Hizbollah—three very different organizations—were an amorphous source of anti-Israeli terror backed by Iran, a claim for which the government never produced any strong evidence. The problem was that once Mr. Peres began trying to out-tough Mr. Netanyahu, voters were bound to ask why they should not vote for Mr. Netanyahu."[25]

Since Labor and Likud concentrated heavily on the prime ministerial poll, the small, established parties benefited at their cost, except Meretz, which lost three seats. In the religious spectrum, Shas gained four seats, a symptom of growing political self-confidence among Mizrachim; and the National Religious Party, three. The total of the religious factions came to 23, a record. Equally, by closing their ranks, the non-Zionist Israeli Arabs augmented their strength to eight. Among the new entrants was Yisrael BeAliya, a party of ex-Soviet Jews, with seven MKs, led by Natan Shcharansky. The other was the four-member Third Way, headed by Avigdor Kahalani, who broke away from Labor in protest at the party's agreement to vacate the Golan Heights for peace with Syria. This was part of the reason why Labor's strength fell from 44 to 34. Likud found its size reduced to 22 from 32, with its allies Gesher gaining five, and Tzomet five (down from eight).

The eighteen-member coalition government that Netanyahu formed on June 18 included Likud Gesher, Tzomet, the NRP, Shas, the UTJ, Yisrael BeAliya and the Third Way.[26] It won a vote of confidence by 62 votes to 52.

Netanyahu's cabinet stated its policy guidelines as follows:

1) Retain Israeli sovereignty over the Golan Heights.
2) Strengthen and develop Jewish settlements, and ensure that in the final agreement on Palestinian "self-government," they retain their "affinity" with Israel.
3) Oppose the formation of a Palestinian state.
4) Oppose return of Palestinian refugees to "any part of Eretz Israel west of the Jordan River."
5) Thwart any attempt to undermine the unity of Jerusalem and prevent any action which runs counter to exclusive Israeli sovereignty over it.
6) Ensure that the IDF is authorized to "go anywhere [in Eretz Israel]" to guarantee the security of Jews.[27]

The electoral victory of Netanyahu, albeit by a thin margin, caught by surprise not only the Arab countries but also the United States, whose Secretary of State, Warren Christopher, had visited the Middle East 24 times in three and a half years to advance the peace process. However, President Clinton, who had combined his public warmth toward Peres with an appeal to him to complete "the cycle of comprehensive peace in the region," and cold-shouldered Netanyahu, was quick to accept the result of the "democratic process" in Israel, and congratulate the winner.

But that did not pave the way for a smooth working relationship between the two leaders. At a joint press conference with the US President at the White House after their meeting on July 9, while Clinton remarked that setting up new settlements would "do more harm than good," Netanyahu said: "I cannot preclude new West Bank settlements, but their pattern has yet to be decided."[28] On the Syrian front, in response to Clinton's plea to "re-engage Syria in the peace process," Netanyahu declared: "I rule out further talks with Syria until it ends all support for terrorist organizations based either in Syria or southern Lebanon." Before flying to Washington, he had publicly told the leaders of the 25,000-strong Jewish settler community in the Golan that they could go ahead with ambitious development plans stretching beyond 2000.

Part of the reason for Netanyahu's overconfidence was the imminence of the US presidential election. He knew that a pro-Israeli Democrat President Clinton would not pressure him for fear of alienating the crucial Jewish funding of his election campaign. While in Washington, Netanyahu held a much-publicized meeting with Robert Dole, the Republican candidate for president. Both Dole and Clinton were conscious that between a quarter and a third of contributions to their parties came from Jewish citizens.

Netanyahu showed no sign of resuming talks with the Palestinians or meeting Arafat. On August 2 his government reversed the freezing of the settlement construction which the previous administration had ordered. Aware of Arafat's keenness to meet him, Netanyahu successfully pressured him, through King Hussein, to shut down three East Jerusalem-based institutions of the PA on August 24. But instead of rewarding Arafat, on August 27 the Israeli authorities demolished a Palestinian center for the aged and disabled in the Old City on the basis that it had been built without a license five years before. That day Israel's Defense Minister, Yitzhak Mordechai, authorized the construction of 900 new houses in the Kiryat Sefer settlement near Ramallah. It was only when Egypt's ambassador to Israel, Muhammad Bassiouny, intervened publicly in the peace process that Netanyahu shifted his position. On September 2 he declared that Cairo had given Israel three weeks to start implementing the five previously agreed commitments: Hebron, further redeployments in the West Bank, opening safe passage between Gaza and the West Bank, the freeing of all Palestinian women prisoners, and lifting of the closure of the Palestinian Territories.

Bassiouny's statement came on the eve of a successful conclusion of the clandestine talks between the Palestinians and the Israelis—represented respectively by Mahmoud Abbas and Muhammad Dahlan (acting for Arafat), and Dore Gold and Shimon Shapiro (acting for Netanyahu)—that had been arranged by the Norwegian couple, Terje Larsen and Mona Juul, whose efforts had led to the signing of the Oslo Accords three years earlier. Larsen was now the UN Secretary-General's representative in Gaza, and Juul was the second most important diplomat at the Norwegian embassy in Tel Aviv.[29] On September 3 they signed a document which formalized the resumption of the peace talks. The next day, after a brief handshake in public for the media at the Erez checkpoint, Netanyahu and Arafat held an hour long meeting, and set up a series of committees to conduct negotiations.

This signified that Netanyahu had concluded, however reluctantly, that he needed to confer with Arafat in order to retain the ties the Shin Beth and Aman had formed with the PA's Preventive Security Service (PSS), and that Israel's internal security had become dependent on cooperation from the PA, which had by now demonstrated its ability to suppress Islamic and secular radicals. The evidence of this came from the Damascus-based leader of the Islamic Jihad, Ramadan Abdullah Shallah. Due to the stalemate in the Palestinian-Israeli talks, there was much pressure from the rank and file to resume operations like the ones in February 1996," he told the London-based *Al Hayat* on September 22. "But the Palestinian Authority's intelligence bodies are chasing our activists which makes the execution of attacks against Israeli targets difficult."[30]

But, accepting the PA's indispensable role in maintaining security inside srael did not lead Netanyahu to soften his stance on the core issues of the Israeli-Palestinian conflict: Jerusalem and the Jewish settlements. He made this clear in a dramatic fashion—so dramatic that it triggered a mini-intifada that left 75 people (60 of them Palestinian) dead and over 1,200 (almost all them Palestinian) injured in two days of unprecedented violence.

Some hours after the end of the Yom Kippur at sunset on September 23, ordered by Netanyahu (who soon after undertook a tour of three European capitals), and protected by armed guards, a group of Israeli builders opened up a steel gate on the side of a stone ramp leading to a Palestinian boys' school at the Second Station of the Cross in Via Dolorosa in the Muslim Quarter of the Old City, thus inaugurating a 1,600-foot, 2,200 year old Hasmonean Tunnel which ran north-south beside the Haram al Sharif/Noble Sanctuary compound. In ancient times the Hasmonean kings used the tunnel to channel water from a reservoir into the settlement. Soon after conquering the Old City in June 1967, Israel's Ministry of Religious Affairs pursued the idea of excavating the tunnel. Aware of the sensitivity of the project, it initially allowed ultra-nationalist Jews to do the excavating clandestinely. It was not until 1985 that the job was finished. Eight years later, during the Labor-led administration, the historical site, a blind tunnel, was extended to provide it with an exit into Via Dolorosa, the heart of the Muslim Quarter. But, afraid of provoking violence from the Palestinians, the government refrained from opening the archaeological tunnel to the public. Now, throwing such caution to wind, Netanyahu authorized an opening. Among other things this led to the around-the-clock posting of armed Israeli guards at the exit in the Muslim Quarter.

Palestinians objected vehemently. They viewed the opening of the tunnel as one more ploy to alter the nature of the Muslim Quarter in the Old City, an attempt to take over their Noble Sanctuary from underneath, another example of profanation of Islamic holy sites, and a blow to Arab aspirations in Jerusalem. They remembered how the Israeli authorities had used Ariel Sharon's renting of an apartment in a house on Al Wad Street in 1987 to post a 24-hour armed guard along the main artery of the Muslim Quarter. Describing the Israeli move as "a crime against our sacred places" in his address to the Palestinian Legislative Council on September 24, Arafat called on the Palestinians to protest against "the Judaization of Jerusalem."

The next day, several busloads of students from Bir Ziet University arrived in Ramallah to confront the Israeli checkpoint on the road to Jerusalem. The IDF used tear gas and rubber bullets, and the Palestinian students stones and Molotov cocktails. To disperse the protesters, the Israeli soldiers used live ammunition, and killed nine Palestinians. This enraged some of the PA's armed policemen. They fired back at the Israeli troops. The result was fighting between two armed forces, one Israeli and the other Palestinian—an intifada in which the Palestinians now used small arms. (It later emerged that of some 35,000 armed policeman and security personnel of the PA, only about five percent got involved in the fighting.) The next day, later labeled "the bloody Thursday," violence spread to Bethlehem, Nablus, Hebron and the Gaza Strip. Fighting broke out around the IDF enclave of Rachel's Tomb just outside Bethlehem. In Nablus, after the IDF failed to break into the

Balata refugee camp, Palestinian youths and PA police besieged Joseph's Tomb, another IDF enclave. In the battle six Israeli soldiers and one Palestinian died. In the Gaza Strip the students of Al Azhar University in Gaza City marched on the Kfar Darom and Netzarim settlements where they encountered firing from the Jewish settlers.

Netanyahu cut short his European tour, rushed home and held an emergency cabinet meeting on September 27. He condemned the use of arms by the PA police against the Israelis. He and his aides asserted that the newly opened tunnel posed no threat to the Islamic holy sites, that Arafat had exploited the opening of the historical site to cause a crisis, and that he had orchestrated the Palestinian riots. "If you knew that we were waiting for an opportunity [to riot], why did you supply one?" asked an irate Arafat. "And if he [Netanyahu] knew, then this means he played with fire."[31] Overriding the objections of Washington, the UN Security Council began discussing the violence in the Palestinian Territories on September 27. All the speakers urged Israel to close down the tunnel. The next day the Security Council's Resolution 1073, passed unanimously (with the US abstaining), called for "an immediate cessation of all acts which resulted in the aggravation of the situation."[32]

That day the IDF deployed tanks and helicopter gunships to impose a siege of the urban areas under the PA's control. Israel's military chief of staff declared that in the West Bank his forces had been reinforced to the level of the (1987–93) intifada. The overall result was a "double closure"—internal, barring the Palestinians from leaving their immediate neighborhood; and external, barring them from traveling to Jerusalem, or going abroad.

On September 29 President Clinton summoned Netanyahu, Arafat, King Hussein and President Mubarak for an immediate meeting in Washington to calm the situation and put the Oslo process back on track. Mubarak declined the invitation. The summit was held on October 1-2. It was complemented by bilateral talks between Netanyahu and Arafat. Despite pleas from his interlocutors, Netanyahu refused point blank to close the tunnel. But he welcomed American mediation, in the person of Dennis Ross, to reconcile the differences between the two sides.

By keeping the archaeological tunnel open, Netanyahu demonstrated to his supporters that he was a firm leader. But deep down the unprecedented violence had left him and the Israeli nation shaken. Among other things it upset the business community and slowed down foreign investments, which had risen sharply in the wake of the 1993 Oslo Accord.

This crisis highlighted the strengths and weaknesses of Netanyahu as a politician and an individual. His political ideology was influenced by his ultra-nationalist father, Bentzion Netanyahu, who was close to Vladimir Jabotinsky—the founder of the Revisionist Zionist movement committed to reclaiming the ancient Eretz Israel, stretching along both sides of the Jordan—and who even now believes that "there isn't a Palestinian people," and that "Arab society is by nature unstable... with a strong proclivity toward violence, a society that cannot exist except under rule of tyranny."[33]

Binyamin Netanyahu's political style was influenced by his natural flair for improvisation, salesmanship and his belief in the effectiveness of a slick presentation. As a business executive of a furniture company in Israel, from 1979 to 1982, he had put these skills to a lucrative end. Part of his success as a salesman lay in telling the prospective customer what he/she wanted to hear. This habit was to yield him rich returns in his 1996 election campaign for the prime minister. And it was the same habit which led him to state in Cairo and Amman—and after his first meeting with Arafat—that he would honor the commitments made by the previous government to the Palestinians. Netanyahu had thus emerged as a politician who believed that staging a slick presentation amounted to accomplishing most of the job, and who performed as "a man for all seasons" with surprising ease.

Unlike any other Israeli politician, Netanyahu's political career was shaped by his performance on television. In 1982, as Israel's chief representative at the UN, he had to justify repeatedly his country's invasion of Lebanon on television to the American audience. He did a good job, and began finessing his televisual skills of sticking to simple, emotional points. In his fateful election debate with Peres in May 1996, for instance, he kept repeating how, as a result of the terrorist bombs in Jerusalem and Tel Aviv, Israeli children were afraid to board buses.

Netanyahu's education in the US had invested him with an American accent, a dramatic contrast from the heavily Polish accent of Peres. This and his years in America as a business consultant and a diplomat enabled him to forge friendships with important American Jews, some of them very rich. They successfully funded his highly effective election campaign for the leadership of Likud in 1993. Some of his Jewish American friends were also Israeli nationals; and two of them, Dore Gold and David Bar Illan, were later to become his close aides.

As Israel's ambassador to the UN for two years, Netanyahu claimed to have devised an effective strategy for dealing with the Arabs. The key to success, according to him, was to adopt a hardline and thus drastically reduce Arab expectations, and then yield a little, thereby managing to emerge at the end as a reasonable pragmatist. Little wonder that as the leader of Likud, from March 1993 onward, he attacked the Labor policy on peace as smacking of appeasement based on an inflated assessment of the strength of the Palestinians in particular and the Arab countries in general. After winning high office, he practiced what he had preached. The outcome, to his astonishment and disappointment, was an unparalleled explosion in the Palestinian Territories, and an international isolation of Israel.

Netanyahu became a butt of sharp criticism in the Israeli media, especially when it emerged that he had not consulted the military chief of staff or the head of the military intelligence, Aman, regarding the opening of the Hasmonean Tunnel. This highlighted his primary weakness: lack of experience in government. He had served as Deputy Foreign Minister only for a year, followed by a brief period as an adviser to prime minister Shamir. He was by Israeli standards a political greenhorn. His success in becoming the first directly elected chief executive at 46 did little to temper the dislike and distrust he had aroused in the higher echelons of the military, Shin Beth, civil service and media. This in turn drove Netanyahu to surround himself with a tight coterie of trusted aides—the most prominent being Dore Gold, an economist (who became his chief foreign adviser and later Israel's ambassador to the US), David Bar Illan, a former concert pianist and editor of the *Jerusalem Post* (who became his political planning and communications chief), and Avigdor Lieberman, a Moldavian who had masterminded his campaign for Likud leader (and who was elevated to Director General of the Prime Minister's office). None of them had previous government experience, and all of them owed their positions to their loyalty to Netanyahu.

As Netanyahu's official spokesman, 66-year-old Bar Illan was very much in demand during and shortly after the violence of late September. He made a few controversial statements including the one about disarming the PA's policemen— an idea that, if implemented, would have led to widespread violence. His numerous editorials in the *Jerusalem Post* had established him as an ideological purist, an adherent of Jewish ultra-nationalism, succinctly summed up by Yitzhak Shamir's statement: "The Land of Israel belongs to the people of Israel, for ever, without partners." In his weekly column in the *Jerusalem Post*, Bar Illan unearthed anti-Semitism and anti-Israeli bias in such publications as *The New York Times*. He was quite clear about the Oslo peace process. "The Oslo Accords were mistaken," he said, upon taking up his new job in June 1996. "They were bad. The fact is that we inherited them and we have to get out of the bramble bush."[34]

Extrication from these agreements, however, became difficult when in early October Netanyahu welcomed mediation by Ross, an ardent supporter of the Oslo process. President Clinton, then engaged in his re-election campaign, took much comfort from the fact that Jewish Americans backed the Oslo Accords. An opinion poll, cited in an advertisement inserted by the Israel Peace Forum in major American papers on the eve of the Washington summit on October 1–2, showed that 81 percent of the American Jews supported the Oslo peace process, and that 63 percent approved of the creation of a Palestinian state.[35]

Among European leaders, French President Jacques Chirac, visiting Israel and the Palestinian Territories on October 22–23, publicly backed the idea of an independent State of Palestine, viewing it as helpful, rather then harmful, to Israel's security.

In the Arab world, King Hussein, the only one prepared to give Netanyahu the benefit of the doubt, now warned him that if he did not implement Israel's accords with the Palestinians he would jeopardize its peace treaties with Jordan and Egypt. His declaration of support to the PA became all the more important when Ross, having failed to conciliate the Israeli-Palestinian differences, returned to Washington in late October. The main point of contention was Netanyahu's refusal to make any commitment on what would follow the Hebron Protocol, which would still leave 97 percent of the West Bank under exclusive or joint jurisdiction of Israel. He pressed ahead with his plans to 1) further consolidate Israel's control of Greater East Jerusalem, 2) expand the existing Jewish settlements and 3) set up new ones. A combined example of (1) and (3) was the approval in early December by the Jerusalem District Planning Committee of the construction of 132 housing units for Jews in Ras al-Amoud, a village of 11,000 Palestinians on the outskirts of the Old City. In early December Defense Minister Mordechai approved the construction of 1,200 housing units for the Emanuel settlement in the Nablus area on the 100 acres confiscated from the nearby Palestinian village of Deir Istiya. Later that month, standing on a hilltop in the Ariel settlement, Netanyahu said: "Why shouldn't settlements be developed? Is anyone stopping the development of the Arab villages nearby?" That is, he placed on a par the recently arrived Jewish settlers with native Palestinians living in the area for centuries. His visit to Ariel was significant. The largest Jewish colony in the West Bank, it was near the Green Line, on the outskirts of greater Tel Aviv. By expanding such settlements and increasing the Jewish population, Israel wanted to obliterate the importance of the 1967 armistice line.

For the first time the Clinton administration began to criticize, mildly, the Israeli policy. Alluding to Netanyhau's stance on the settlements, the US State Department spokesperson said: "His statement for an expansion of settlements is certainly not useful and not constructive." James Baker, former US Secretary of State and the architect of the Madrid Middle East Peace Conference, was more robust. "The US policy on settlement should be maintained as it is and it should be frequently articulated, and it should be assertively pursued," he said in early December.

In defiance, on December 13 the Netanyahu Government reinstated subsidies and tax incentives to all the Jewish settlements in the Palestinian Territories by classifying them as "national priority" areas, thus reversing the Labor government's policy. On December 16 at a press conference, when Clinton was asked whether he agreed that the Israeli settlements were "obstacles to peace," he replied: "Absolutely, absolutely."[36] The previous day three former US secretaries of state— James Baker, Cyrus Vance and Lawrence Eagleburger—three past National Security Advisers and two chief Middle East negotiators delivered a letter to Netanyahu. In it they urged him "not to take unilateral actions that would preclude a meaningful settlement and a comprehensive and lasting peace... Such a tragic result will threaten the security of Israel, the Palestinians and friendly Arab countries, and will damage US interests in the Middle East."[37] It was in vain.

Part of the reason for the mildness of Washington's criticism was that Ross was once again engaged in brokering an Israeli-Palestinian deal on Hebron. A meeting between Netanyahu and Arafat on Christmas eve raised hopes which were not realized. The sticking point still was Netanyahu's refusal to commit himself to a timetable for implementing further provisions of the Oslo II Accord—including the IDF withdrawals from rural West Bank, which when fully implemented would get Israel out of all of the West Bank, except Jerusalem "as defined by its municipal boundaries," the Jewish settlements (covering about six percent of the West Bank) and specific Israeli military areas. This, according to the Palestinians, would mean the PA finally controlling exclusively or jointly 85-90 percent of the West Bank.

To torpedo any chance of a deal on Hebron, on January 1 Naom Friedman, a 19-year-old army conscript from a Greater East Jerusalem settlement, emptied his M-16 automatic rifle in the Arab market of Hebron, and wounded seven Palestinians. Luckily, no one was killed. Netanyahu and Arafat cooperated quickly and actively to calm the situation.

But there was no breakthrough in their negotiations, despite President Mubarak's involvement which had led to Netanyahu promising to implement the IDF withdrawals by March 1999 instead of September 1997, as specified by Oslo II. Determined to reject any change in what had been signed and sealed, Arafat rejected Ross's compromise of mid-1998, arguing that he was mediating between enforcement of an accord, witnessed by the US, and a violation of it.

On January 11 as Ross was preparing to return home, and the Egyptian ambassador in Tel Aviv warned that his country's peace treaty with Israel was "close to collapse," King Hussein acted. He flew by helicopter to Gaza City where he persuaded Arafat to accept the compromise IDF withdrawal date of mid-1998. He then flew to Tel Aviv and got Netanyahu's consent the next day.

On January 14 the chief negotiators of the two sides, Saeb Erekat and Dan Shomron, signed the protocol on Hebron. It partitioned Hebron into the H1 (Palestinian) zone, occupying about 80 percent of the city's 5,200 acres, with a population of 100,000, to be patrolled by 400 PA policemen armed with only 100 rifles and 200 pistols, and the H2 (Israeli) zone, which housed some 400 Jewish settlers and about 20,000 Palestinians, and was contiguous with the Jewish settlement of Kiryat Arba. The protocol demarcated a buffer zone between H2 and H1 where the PA police were to carry only pistols. The Palestinian authorities were required to restrict the height of the buildings surrounding H2 in order to prevent sniping at the Jewish targets in H1. The hills overlooking H2 were to be patrolled by joint Israeli-Palestinian units. Finally, and crucially, the Israeli authorities were given the sole authority to control building activity in H2—that is, to expand the Jewish enclaves there, if they so wished.

To the main document were attached the Note for Record, prepared by Ross, and Letters of Assurance by the US Secretary of State, Christopher, addressed to Netanyahu and Arafat. These attachments dealt with the issues covered by the Oslo II Accord. But by introducing new concepts and interpretations, they in effect produced a variant of Oslo II, which strayed sharply away from its parent on crucial issues, and further strengthened the Israeli hand at the expense of the Palestinian.

The Palestinians listed 34 Oslo II arrangements still to be resolved. These included the construction of seaport and airport in the Gaza Strip, safe passage between the West Bank and the Gaza Strip, and the release of women prisoners. Whereas the attachments to the Hebron Protocol required Israel to merely enter into talks about these outstanding issues, it mandated that the Palestinians must act on the following points: reduce the size of the Palestinian police; stop incitement against Israel and Israelis; and complete the process of revising the Palestine National Charter.

Israel made its biggest gain, however, in the single most important issue: the future IDF redeployments in the West Bank covered in Articles X-XI of the Interim Agreement (i.e. Oslo II Accord). Article X, paragraph 2, required that Israeli military forces "redeployed to specified military locations." The subsequent Article read, "The specified military locations referred to in Article X paragraph 2 above will be determined in the further redeployment phase, within the specified time-frame ending not later than 18 months from the date of the inauguration of the [Palestinian]

Legislative Council, and will be negotiated in the permanent status negotiations." Netanyahu succeeded in getting this provision altered substantially. According to *Further Redeployment: The Next Stage of the Israeli-Palestinians Redeployment, Legal Aspects*, published by Israeli's foreign ministry on January 19, 1997, "The further redeployment process will take place in West Bank territory [but not necessarily all West Bank territory], and, in those areas in which it will take place, it will not include settlements, military locations and borders, nor those areas required for the implementation by Israel of its overall responsibility for Israelis and borders. The extent and location of these areas is to be determined by Israel in the light of its security concerns." By managing to add "those areas required for the implementation by Israel of its overall responsibility for Israelis and borders" to the earlier list of settlements, military locations and borders, Netanyahu substantially changed the character of the original Oslo II Accord.

Furthermore, the official Israeli publication pointed out that further IDF redeployments were contingent on the assumption of responsibility for public order and internal security by the Palestinian police. "Only if the Palestinian side proves itself able and willing to comply with its security responsibilities is Israel obliged to transfer additional areas of the West Bank to the Palestinian jurisdiction." Thus Netanyahu formally injected the principle of reciprocity into the agreements, and made Israel's security, as judged exclusively by its government, the sole criterion.

The crucial role played in the marked shift in Israel's favor by the United States was illustrated by Christopher's Letter of Assurance to Netanyahu. In it, Christopher wrote: "I have advised Chairman Arafat of US views on Israel's process of redeploying its forces, designating specific military locations." In other words, Christopher granted Israel the exclusive right to determine the size and nature of the IDF redeployments. Later, Erekat, the chief Palestinian negotiator, wrote a letter to Ross, saying that Christopher's letter "does not oblige" the Palestinians to accept the terms included, or the Israeli definition of "military locations." Ross responded by agreeing to include Erekat's letter in the Minutes of the Hebron Protocol. Whether Erekat's letter had any legal binding remained contentious since the Hebron Protocol was a package deal and the letter was sent after the agreement had been signed.

In return for these concessions to Israel, Christopher in his letter to Arafat assured him that the three further Israeli redeployments in the West Bank would be completed by no later that August 31, 1998 (the first stage by mid-March 1997, and the second by October 30, 1997). Israel agreed to enter into talks on the final status negotiations "within two months of the Hebron redeployment," and commence "immediately" talks on the outstanding issues of the Interim Agreement.

On January 17 the Israeli cabinet began debating the Hebron Protocol and the attached documents. Of the seven dissenting ministers, Benny Begin, son of the former prime minister, was the most vociferous, and the only one to resign. In the course of a marathon meeting Israeli television broadcast a report by its Washington correspondent saying that Israel had given up its exclusive right to define and retain those areas in the West Bank it deemed vital for its security. Instantly, Limor Livnat, the Communications Minister, got an angry phone call from her father, who wanted to know if the television report was true. Netanyahu adjourned the meeting and demanded immediate clarification from the US State Department. After he had received a swift and public reassurance that Israel had the exclusive right to define militarily significant areas in the West Bank, he reconvened the cabinet.[38] The final vote after twelve hours of deliberations was eleven for and seven against.

The debate in the Knesset was less dramatic. Labor, Meretz, Hadash and the United Arab List backed the latest deal. "I truly congratulate the government on the signing of the [Hebron] Protocol based on the Oslo Agreement," said Peres. The vote in the Knesset, was 87 for and 17 against, with one abstention. All the dissenting ministers backed the Hebron Protocol since a minister voting against the government in the Knesset automatically forfeits his post. Excluding the 11 Arab MKs, the vote for the agreement was 76 out of 109 Jewish MKs, or 70 percent. This tallied with the *Yediot Aharonot* poll which showed 67 percent of Jewish Israelis backing the latest deal and 25 percent opposing. The IDF began withdrawing immediately from the H1 zone of Hebron.

Opinion was divided on the meaning of the Hebron Protocol. Some analysts perceived it as signaling Likud's acceptance of the Oslo process it had maligned before, signifying its shift to the political center. Labor functionaries were relieved that the ultranationalist Jewish claim to all of Hebron—the city of the Jews' biblical ancestors—was waived by a Likud leader, a son of a Revisionist Zionist. The Jewish settlers were angry. "We were the racehorse for Netanyahu before the elections," said one of their leaders in Hebron. "But once he passed the winning post, he consigned his racehorse to the abattoir."[39]

Netanyahu rebutted the charge. "Anyone who tells you that we are leaving Hebron is telling you a lie," he said to a group of visiting Jewish American students. "We are there and we are there to stay for all time... We are redeploying in Hebron [not from Hebron]."[40] What he apparently meant was that Israel had the exclusive control of the Tomb of the Patriarchs/Ibrahimi Mosque, and that it would not cede the site or share it with the Muslim Palestinians. In all the tortuous, time-consuming haggling over Hebron, this had been the core issue, and by agreeing to partition the city, with its most prized religious site under continued Israeli control, Arafat had made a big concession to Rabin in order to close the Oslo II deal.

In Israel, Netanyahu's tactical compromise—partly due to the intolerable pressures, external and internal, and partly due to lack of an alternative plan on Hebron—enabled Peres to launch seriously the idea of a national unity government of Likud and Labor. For this to happen there had to be a common platform. It materialized on January 22 in the form of a National Agreement Regarding the Negotiations on the Permanent Settlement with the Palestinians, based on the principle, among other things, of precluding the dismantling of the Jewish settlements in the "Western Land of Israel," and signed by Yossi Beilin (Labor) and Michael Eitan (Likud).

On borders, the Beilin-Eitan Document stated that the majority of settlers will live on their settlements under Israeli sovereignty "in order to preserve territorial continuity between the settlements and Israel," and that those living outside the annexed Palestinian area will receive "special" treatment regarding their Israeli citizenship and their ties with Israel, and that "their right of free and safe passage" to the annexed areas will be guaranteed. The Jordan Valley will either be put under Israeli sovereignty or treated as "a special security zone," with IDF units posted along the Jordan.

The Beilin-Eitan Document treated Israeli security and Palestinian self-determination as inter-related subjects. It required that the Palestinian entity have no army and remain demilitarized, and that it must accept the Jordan Valley as "the security border" of Israel. It was to be barred from stationing a foreign army inside its boundaries, and its security forces were to be legally required to cooperate with its Israeli counterparts to foil terrorism. The enhanced powers of the Palestinian entity could be described as constituting "Enlarged Autonomy" or "a State."

According to this Document, Jerusalem, the capital of Israel, with its existing municipal borders, was to be "a single united city within sovereign Israel," where Muslim and Christian holy places would be granted "special status."

The Document wanted Israel to have the right "to prevent the entry of the Palestinian refugees into its sovereign territory" and the right to impose limits on "the entry of refugees into the Palestinian entity" as decided "within the larger discussion of Israel's security issues."

It urged "special effort" to conclude talks on the final status, and "especially to finalize the borders between Israel and the Palestinian entity before the intended date for further redeployment," and added that if "the borders are not finalized before the third redeployment [by August 1998] Israel will redeploy so that up to 50 percent of the West Bank will be designated as territories A and B."

Significantly, Netanyahu too began mentioning vacating only 45–50 percent of the West Bank, something he would officially confirm two months later during the Har Homa controversy. This was about half of the Palestinian expectations.

On the eve of his departure for the United States in mid-February, Netanyahu declared "I will tell President Clinton, 'You must make it clear to [President] Assad that he must think of other options, as the option of total withdrawal from the Golan does not exist from our point of view.'"

Yet his tough talk on Syria failed to assuage the seven hardline ministers who had voted against any withdrawal from Hebron. They acted while he was in Washington, where he had a long meeting with Clinton. They were instrumental in forming the 17-member Eretz Israel Front in the Knesset. Besides them the group consisted of Ehud Olmert (a Likud MK and Mayor of Jerusalem) and Michael Kleiner (a Gesher MK), the Front's secretary. The Front accused Netanyahu of loosening Israel's hold over Jerusalem by refusing to build at Har Homa. He denied that he had given an assurance to Clinton not to build there.

The 450 acre site, a pine-covered long, steep hill, known as Jabal Abu Ghneim (Abu Ghneim Mountain) and situated near the Palestinian town of Beit Sahour between Jerusalem and Bethlehem, was categorized as a green area after its incorporation into East Jerusalem by Israel following the June 1967 War. But the Yitzhak Shamir government responded to the holding of the Madrid Peace Conference in October 1991 by expropriating the Palestinian land at Har Homa.[41]

In the first phase 6,500 housing units to accommodate 30,000 Jews were to be built, with the second phase raising the total of the settlers to 70,000, thus making it the largest project of its kind since 1980. But the Labor administration that followed in 1992 froze the plan. In early 1997 Netanyahu confirmed the status quo. But when the Eretz Israel Front criticized his decision, he backtracked immediately. And by unfreeezing the Har Homa project he froze the Oslo peace process.

On February 26 the Israeli government approved the Har Homa housing plan despite a warning from the Shin Beth chief, Admiral Ami Ayalon, that the Palestinians would react violently. Many in the cabinet reckoned that since Arafat was scheduled to leave for the United States on March 2, he would make sure to control any Palestinian protest that might arise.

Har Homa was meant to be a wedge on Jerusalem's southern boundary into the centers of Palestinian population inside and outside the city. By surrounding the Palestinian territory with these settlements, the Israelis wanted to pre-empt any chance of ceding a single square centimeter of Jerusalem to the Palestinians in their final status talks.

Well-practiced in dissimulation, Netanyahu kept shifting his ground during the lengthy Har Homa controversy. At a press conference in early March in Cairo he said the building of this settlement had to do with housing shortage in Jerusalem. By the end of the month, however, he had imbued it with unparalleled significance. "The real struggle that is aimed at us is not about Har Homa but about our sovereignty in Jerusalem, and, in the end, about our sovereignty in Jaffa and Ramat Aviv."[42] He did so while being at odds with popular opinion among Jewish Israelis. A poll published on March 19 in the Ma'ariv showed that while 60 percent supported construction at Har Homa "in principle" (with 26 percent opposing), 40 percent backed construction "right now" (with 47 percent opposing), and only 28 percent were for construction despite international isolation and a conflict with the Palestinians (with 57 percent opposing).

Netanyahu's action elicited adverse reaction not only from the Palestinian leadership but also Clinton. On March 3 he personally criticized the Israeli action on Har Homa But Netanyahu was defiant. "There was nothing new in what he [Clinton] said," Netanyahu told the IDF Radio.

But what his negotiators presented to the Palestinians on March 9 concerning Israel's first redeployment plan was new—and surprising. It covered only nine percent of the West Bank, with a mere two percent of the area changing its status from C (exclusive Israeli control) to A (exclusive Palestinian control). This shocked the Palestinians, who had been expecting 30 percent. Well aware that the Hebron Protocol allowed Israel to determine unilaterally the extent of its pullbacks from the West Bank, Peres said: "It is crucial to consult the Palestinians as confidence building measures are a vital plank of the peace process."[43]

Two days later Arafat instructed his officials to sever all contacts with Israel in protest at its actions. When the Palestinian leaders warned repeatedly of large scale violence if the Har Homa project went ahead, Israeli Justice Minister, Tzahi Hanegbi, a confidante of Netanyahu, retorted on March 16, "Whoever launches violence could quickly find himself packing a suitcase and traveling backwards and forwards from Tunis to Baghdad as he [Arafat] did for many years." He threatened that if violence erupted again, the IDF might re-occupy the PA-controlled areas and drive Arafat into exile. He also hinted that Mossad agents could assassinate Arafat.[44]

Ignoring two written appeals by President Clinton, Netanyahu gave his final consent to the Har Homa project on March 18. Three days later, on the Jewish Purim festival, the situation changed abruptly. A six-pound bomb, carried in a bag by Musa Ghnemiat, 28, exploded in a cafe in Tel Aviv, killing the bomb-carrier and three Israelis, and hurting 62. Unlike previous suicide bombers, however, who were single and often unemployed, Ghnemiat turned out to be a father of four with a permit to work in Israel. A resident of the Israeli-controlled village of Surif, six miles southwest of Bethlehem, he had a regular job at a restaurant in Rishon LeZion near Tel Aviv.

Netanyahu gave no quarter to the argument that the Tel Aviv bomb was a result of his persistence with the Har Homa project, thus violating the seminal Oslo Accord, which had listed Jerusalem and the settlements as the issues to be settled in the final status talks, implying thereby that neither party could take steps to prejudge the ultimate outcome. In contrast to Netanyahu's stance, according to a poll published in *Ma'ariv* on March 28, 62 percent of Jewish Israelis saw a connection between the Har Homa construction and the Tel Aviv bomb, nearly twice the number who did not. Actually, what had happened now had a ring of familiarity to those who had watched the Arab-Jewish conflict over the past decades. "It's the same old story—the Israelis provoke the Arabs by some flagrant violation of the peace, the Palestinians react violently and then the Americans line up behind the Israelis in condemning 'terror,'" said a veteran Egyptian journalist.[45] However, this time around even some top US officials began wondering if Netanyahu was following a policy of humiliating the Palestinians with *fait accomplis* like Har Homa, even at the risk of goading them into terrorist actions, with a view to blaming them for the collapse of the Oslo process he had opposed from the start. They inferred that he did not mind being pressured by his hardline cabinet colleagues: they provided him with an expedient foil. If he had wanted, he could have called their bluff by preparing seriously to form a national unity government on the basis of the Yossi Beilin-Michael Eitan Document. They had nowhere else to go, and were unwilling to face a fresh Knesset poll, fearing that they would not do as well as they had done before.

Instead, he prepared to confront the Palestinians and let it be known that the IDF had finalized plans to re-occupy the PA-controlled areas if need be. Anticipating major rioting by the Palestinians on March 30, the Day of the Land, the IDF stationed tanks and snipers close to the PA enclaves. But the day passed relatively peacefully.

While constantly exhorting Arafat to repress Hamas, Netanyahu showed little stomach for doing the same himself. The case of the Jordan-based Dr. Musa Abu Mazruk, head of Hamas's political bureau, was illustrative. After he had been arrested in the US for violating immigration laws in October 1995, Israel filed a 900-page extradition petition, alleging his involvement in murder, conspiracy and other crimes. But on April 3, for reasons of "security and prevention of terrorism,"

Israel dropped its extradition request.[46] Apparently Netanyahu was wary of inflaming Hamas supporters by trying Mazruk in Israel.

Yet on the eve of his meeting with President Clinton in Washington on April 8, Netanyahu, addressing the American-Israeli Public Affairs Committee (AIPAC), complained that he was being asked to make concessions "in return for a real crackdown by the PA on the terrorist organizations," and added, "This will be pure and simple surrender to terrorism."

A sign of his success in Washington came even before his talks with Clinton. At a press conference before the meeting, Clinton spoke about curbing terrorism, but said nothing about "a temporary halt to the construction at Har Homa"—a proposition mentioned in the official press briefings. After their two hour long session, a dejected-looking American President, accompanied by a beaming Netanyahu, described his talk as "long and candid," and departed, leaving the visitor to address the press conference.

The submission of the position papers by a high level Palestinian delegation in mid-April to Albright made little difference. Since Netanyahu refused to stop work on the Har Homa settlement, there was no prospect of a thaw in the frozen peace process.

In the past the several crises that had developed during the Labor-led governments were resolved because first Rabin and then Peres were sincere in their commitment to achieving peace. They accepted the basic premise that the core intent of the May 1994 Oslo I Accord was to help create a mutually acceptable balance of power between Israelis and Palestinians over five years so that the two peoples could co-exist peacefully. The degree of mutual trust that had been built up was aptly illustrated by the fact (revealed by Arafat in March 1997) that there existed a hot line first between Arafat and Rabin, and then between Arafat and Peres, along with the use of back channels of communication. That ended when Netanyahu assumed office. He severed the hot line and discontinued back channels.

The immense disparity of power—political, military, economic and intelligence—between the two sides has been obvious all along. Israel has 80 percent of the cards and the Palestinians only 20. (This was aptly captured by President Clinton spending half an hour with Arafat at the White House and two hours with Netanyahu.) Unlike Rabin and Peres, Netanyahu resorted to using all his cards combatively, humiliating not only the Palestinians but also King Hussein.

Netanyahu seemed unable or unwilling to realize that his hardline stance was strengthening Hamas and the Islamic Jihad, and that there would be less peace for Jewish Israelis if he returned less land to the Palestinians. Nor had he thought through the prospect of destroying Arafat, politically or physically, which would lead to anarchy.

Netanyahu's intransigence was at odds with the popular sentiment prevalent among both Israelis and Palestinians. An opinion survey of Jewish Israelis by Tel Aviv University in late March showed that 60 percent wanted the peace process with the Palestinians to continue. And a poll conducted by the Nablus-based Center for Palestine Research and Studies (CPRS) in late April revealed that 60 percent of the Palestinians backed the peace process. On the issues of Jerusalem and self-determination for the Palestinians, there was much greater flexibility among Jewish Israelis than Netanyahu would have the world believe. A survey of Jewish Israelis, published by *Ma'ariv* on March 28, showed that 50 percent thought that the Palestinians deserved a state (with 45 percent disagreeing), and 44 percent supported the founding of a Palestinian state alongside Israel (with 50 percent opposing). Even on the issue of Jerusalem, the Tel Aviv University poll showed that 43 percent of Jewish Israelis were prepared to yield part of Jerusalem to the Palestinian autonomous entity. If Arab Israelis were included in the above opinion surveys, there would be a majority among Israelis both for sharing Jerusalem with Palestinians and the founding of the State of Palestine. These findings provided a firm ground for a directly elected Israeli chief executive to pursue policies that would secure peace in exchange for land. But Netanyahu's year in office showed clearly that he was not that kind of leader. The chance of his being sacked by a motion of no-confidence by 81 MKs was minimal.

The only other way he could have lost power was to have been found guilty of fraud and breach of public trust in the Bar On Affair by the Supreme Court. But the court upheld the attorney-general's ruling by a majority vote on June 16, 1997.

The Bar On Affair dated back to the previous December when Michael Ben Yair, the then attorney general, sensing that Netanyahu wanted him out, resigned. Following their search for a pliable successor to Ben Yair, Leiberman, director general of the prime minister's office, and Hanegbi, Justice Minister, proposed Roni Bar On for the job. On January 10, 1997 Netanyahu added a last-minute change to the cabinet agenda and won a small majority for Bar On's appointment. This happened at a time when two Shas ministers were publicly wavering about their stand on the Hebron Protocol. With seven ministers in a cabinet of eighteen already opposed to the accord, Netanyahu was keen to avoid an embarrassing tie by gaining the support of the Shas ministers. But Bar On, a Likud member, was just an obscure criminal lawyer in Jerusalem. The outcry in the legal establishment at his elevation was so loud that he resigned after one day in office.

On January 22 Ayala Hasson, an Israeli TV journalist, alleged that Arye Deri, leader of the Shas party, who had been on trial for corruption for some years,[47] had threatened to deprive Netanyahu of a cabinet majority for the Hebron Protocol unless Bar On got the job of attorney general. In turn Bar On was expected to allow a plea-bargain to Deri, whose long trial was on the verge of ending.

A police inquiry followed. Within a month it became apparent that Deri and others close to the government were involved in Bar On's appointment. Deri's lawyer, Dan Avi Yitzhak, resigned, and denounced his erstwhile client. It transpired later that Yitzhak was the favorite for attorney general. But his acceptance of the job would have required him to step down as Deri's defense counsel. To forestall this, Deri threatened to deny Netanyahu two crucial Shas cabinet votes on the Hebron Protocol.

Inevitably, the police investigation extended to Netanyahu. During a four hour interview—in which Netanyahu repeatedly said, "I don't know" and "I don't recall"—the police interrogators warned him that he might face criminal charges, the main one being that by replacing the previous attorney general with someone more malleable, he expected to gain politically. His lawyer, Yaacov Weinroth, said that his client should not be blamed, as "he was misled about the acceptability of Bar On by Tzahi Hanegbi, the Justice Minister."[48]

On April 16 the Interior Minister, Avigdor Kahalani, announced that in its 995 page report the police had recommended that Netanyahu be charged with "fraud and breach of trust." The final decision, however, rested with the attorney general, Eliakim Rubinstein, Bar On's successor. On April 20, his 80-page report recommended that Netanyahu and Hanegbi not be indicted, and that Deri should be charged with fraud, extortion and obstructing justice. The fate of Leiberman was left undecided.

Though Rubinstein repeatedly said, "There are grounds for suspicion over Netanyahu's part in the appointment of Bar On but insufficient evidence [based solely on the testimony of one witness, Dan Avi Yitzhak] to bring him to trial," Netanyahu put a different gloss on his statement. "The bottom line is that I did not commit any crime, and the attorney general confirmed that," he said in a national broadcast.[49]

Thus, in a year in office, Netanyahu survived three severe crises, including the ones centered around the cabinet approval of the Hebron Protocol, and the opening of the Hasmonean Tunnel in the Muslim Quarter of Jerusalem"s Old City. This reinforced his vainglorious perception of himself, and reaffirmed his views not only about the Palestinians but also about the role of Israel in the region—as expressed in his book, *A Place Among the Nations: Israel and the World*. His concept of the "Fortress Israel," was at variance with the vision of Peres and Rabin of Israel of progressively expanding the peace process with the Arab world, starting with the immediate neighbors, and then going on to include not only Iraq and Saudi Arabia, but also Iran. In his views Netanyahu was out of line even with the hawkish Yitzhak Shamir, the head of the earlier Likud-led government. Shamir had reluctantly concluded that Israel's doctrine of total self-reliance in security was virtually unattainable, and that it needed the co-operation of Arab neighbors to feel truly secure, and this led him to participate in the Madrid Middle East Peace Conference in 1991.

Any attempt to revert to the doctrine of 100 percent self-reliance in defense and security for Israel would mean further bolstering the military and Shin Beth. As it was, the Israel Defense Forces had been the single most important feature of the state and society since the founding of Israel.

6

The Israel Defense Forces
The Sword and Social Cement

On just one stretch of a Jerusalem road, one finds the signs of the long, checkered history of the city. At one end, a mansion built by the Ottoman sultan in the mid-nineteenth century to house his governor of Jerusalem is now the American Colony Hotel. At the other end, past the walled US Consulate, a mini-fortress complete with an electronically-controlled steel gate, stands an Israeli war memorial. At the apex of a triangular platform of stone, two tablets record the date of the battle, the name of the combat unit, and the names of the Zahal[1] soldiers who fell.

This is one of over 900 war memorials erected all over Israel. Altogether they commemorate the deaths of over 15,000 Israeli soldiers who died during or shortly after the seven wars since Israel's founding in 1948. That gives Israel one war memorial for every 17 dead. The figure for the United States is one memorial for 15,000 killed, and for Europe 10,000. Little wonder that Remembrance Day in Israel is an important event.

Remembrance Day falls on the eve of the anniversary of the establishment of the state. Since May 14, 1948 fell on Iyar 5, 5708 in the Jewish calendar, the actual date varies from year to year. The rationale for the Israeli government's decision to declare Iyar 4 as the Remembrance Day was simple: to draw the causal connection between those who died fighting for the founding of the Jewish state and its continued existence.

Sirens signal the start of Remembrance Day, then a two-minute silence, followed by the lighting of the remembrance torch at the main town squares, a few speeches and the communal singing of the national anthem, HaTikva (The Hope). The celebrations follow the same pattern in Israel as in western countries.

But a week before Remembrance Day is Ho caust Day, commemorating the six million Jews killed by the Nazis, an occasion of special significance to schools. "The overall purpose of the Holocaust Day is to inculcate the feeling among students that they are descendants of the Holocaust," explained Michael Yaron, an inspector at the Ministry of Education and Culture in Jerusalem. A son of a Jewish couple who had arrived in Palestine from Germany in the mid-1930s, he had been a history teacher for 28 years. "What we try to do is to make schoolchildren feel psychosis, feel that they are the descendants of the victims, an integral part of the people who actually suffered the Holocaust. Jewish students absorb this view and feeling through education and through visits to Yad Vashem [the Holocaust museum in Jerusalem].

They do so through other means as well: television documentaries, movies, radio programs. On the Holocaust Day the children read poems etc. They also try to find a Holocaust survivor and invite him to address them. And the official choice of the date was made to link the Holocaust with the Independence and Remembrance Days that follow soon after."

There is yet another anniversary that is unique to Israel. Each of the country's cities and major towns adopts a specific unit of the IDF, and then celebrates its birthday. Tel Aviv adopted the armored corps. On its October birthday, armored personnel carriers and tanks fill the city's main square, and their crews happily welcome visitors to inspect their machines and chat with them. The adults arrive with their children, who are the prime target of the IDF. The purpose of the exercise is to put the IDF on display for the youngsters in a civilian, almost carnival-like atmosphere, and motivate them to see military service not as an unavoidable chore, but as a thrilling, patriotic rite of passage.

"For its first three decades, Israel's education was primarily designed to indoctrinate and encourage the country's youth into volunteering for the elite and commando units," notes Yossi Melman. "These special forces make a big point of emphasizing their unique abilities. Their soldiers receive special decorations, medals, wings and different uniforms. Schoolchildren, from early on, are fed on heroic stories, and they learn to worship these elite units."[2]

Military draft, introduced under the 1949 Compulsory Service Law, was part of Ben Gurion's statist ideology, which held that a highly centralized government was the best way Israel could overcome the centrifugal tendencies of a society composed predominantly of recent immigrants. Along with military conscription went a uniform system of education, health care and trade union services, all provided by centralized national agencies.

Creating and strengthening the public agencies to absorb the large influx of immigrants and impart to them the still evolving Israeli identity, fell to the nearly 760,000 Jews who were there at the founding of Israel. Between 1948 and 1954, they had to cope with the daunting job of absorbing an almost equal number of new Jewish immigrants. The adult arrivals could not be socialized in schools, so that task fell largely to the IDF, which has continued as a vital agency of socialization and social development.

Indeed the IDF has imparted certain national characteristics: directness, a no-nonsense approach to life, informality and a certain distaste for luxury. Many Israelis consider social niceties a waste of time. The roots of this behavior lie in the IDF. "When I reported at the base on my first day in the IDF, the reception clerk gave me a form to fill in," recalled Rafi Singer. "'Thank you,' I said. 'Never say thank you in the army,' said the clerk curtly."

There are still other implications of the universal draft. In most western societies youth in their late teens tend to challenge traditional values and the establishment. In Israel they join the IDF, and find themselves having to shoulder life and death responsibilities. By being absorbed early into the established order Israeli youths tend to grow up conservative.

And Israeli Jews arrive at universities more mature than in any other country, something evident at Hebrew University in Jerusalem. Its main campus on Mount Scopus is an architectural odditity. The campus gardens lie next to cavernous rooms bored into a hillside at different levels. Like a snake in the snake-and-ladders game, every so often the campus turns on itself, leaving the visitor baffled. But, like the Knesset, Hebrew University boasts a fine, spacious cafeteria. Its round tables and black plastic chairs spill out into a large, cobblestoned courtyard.

It was here that I had a long conversation with a group of students about the IDF. Male and female, all in their mid-20s, they all had honorable IDF records and an extraordinary grasp of English.

"Since your childhood you are brought up to serve your country in the army," said Ana, a middle-class resident of Natanya. "The IDF service is a rite of passage toward a full Israeli citizenship. The main point to remember is that the IDF is a popular, living institution. It is everywhere, and it's very Israeli."

"The first thing that strikes a visitor to Israel is the ubiquitousness of gun-carrying soldiers, male and female," I said. "You see them everywhere, in the street, at bus stations, especially on Sundays."

"Getting back to their bases after the Sabbath," explained Ana. "You don't have to be a foreigner to notice soldiers in the street. As a child and a teenager you see them all the time, and you know that when you are eighteen you'll put on the military uniform whether you like it or not."

"There are other ways in which the IDF predominates but which we don't see every day," said Eli, who wore a small ring in his ear. "About a third of Israel's beaches are closed to civilians, because they are for exclusive IDF use. And large parts of the Negev are closed to the public because they are used for military exercises."

"I grew up on closed bases as my father is a career military officer," said Esther. "When you are drafted you are asked to state your preference for a closed or open base. In my case [my preference] was granted. All the time I was on a closed base. I was an officer—very tricky to be friendly with your troops and at the same time issue orders. In the army you learn to take responsibility, and mature early."

"At closed bases there are opportunities for women to take officer courses," said Ana. "I became an officer within a year. Then they transferred me to an open base which I did not like. There was none of the camaraderie and dedication you find on the closed bases. People there were not interested [in their jobs]. They were the Unit 805." Everybody smiled, except me. I looked at Ana inquiringly.

"8 A.M. arrive; zero, do nothing; 5 P.M. finish," she explained. "The clock watchers, the ones who did not take the IDF home."

"You could say I was like that," said Sarah. "I was on an open base near my home town, five minutes by bus. I did clerical jobs. I was secretary to a lieutenant-colonel. For me it was just a job. The only difference was that I was in uniform and that I earned only $100 a month, which was very cheap to the IDF. But then as an IDF soldier you get concessions in travel, theater tickets, etc. Also the IDF organized day trips to Jerusalem, visits to the theater, concerts and so on, and organized discos. There was social life attached to the IDF."

"An opportunity to meet the opposite sex?" I asked.

"One out of five serious romances starts in the IDF," Eli said.

"If I had to get involved with a guy from the IDF he'd better be from an elite unit," said Ana.

"It's hard to get into elite units unless you come from a kibbutz," said Micah. Slow in speech, he had a fine record in the air force. "Also it depends on what you mean by elite. The air force thinks it is elite. But not everybody in the air force is a pilot, you know."

"What does carrying a gun do to you?" I asked.

"A gun gives you power, power to kill," said Ana. "The initial impact is strong. But the effect wears off."

"As an IDF reserve officer in the air force, I am allowed to carry a pistol," said Micah. "But I don't. Some of the reserve officers do, though. It all depends on your personality."

Despite a constant flow of coffee I detected a certain flagging of energy. But I could not let them go until they had addressed an important issue.

"Is the IDF an equalizing institution?" I asked. "Does it expose the conscript to those sections of society he or she is unlikely to meet in unregulated, civilian life?"

"On a base there are different groups," replied Esther. "In my department we were all Ashkenazim, middle class, with good academic backgrounds. We did not mix with others, like Sephardim."

"On an open base, you are out of the premises come 5 P.M., and you go your own way," said Eli. "But on the closed bases you have comradeship, a tight life spent together with others, and there you meet different sections of society and learn more about them."

"The IDF exposes the draftee to experiences he would not normally have," said Sarah. "There is mixing in so far as in the IDF you come across people who have not done their matriculation [high school graduation]. Outside the army you don't come across such people, but in the army you do. However, there can be proper mixing only between middle class and high class, but none between lower class and middle class."

"How important was the IDF to you in strictly personal terms?" I inquired.

"The IDF is important for jobs," said Micah. "Certain jobs are given only to those who have served in the IDF. Also if you haven't served in the IDF you are not entitled to certain social security and mortgage benefits."

"You could say there is a clear dividing line between those who have done the IDF service and those who have not," said Eli. "IDF personnel enjoy social esteem, whereas the non-IDF are marginalized."

"For a young person the social aspect of life is important," said Esther.

"The prestige and advantage of the IDF service depends on where the conscript serves—in a combat unit, intelligence unit, non-combat unit, desk job, kitchen, storekeeping, etc.," explained Micah. "The combat unit has the highest rating, and the competition to get in is tough. You can have ten applicants for each place. The kids from the kibbutzim are strong here. They have a background of communal life, and they adjust easily to the IDF life."

"What about the reserve duty?" was my last question.

"We have none," said Sarah.

"For men it goes on until they are 51," said Micah with a sigh. "Nobody likes the reserve duty. It is such a chore. It became more of a chore during the intifada, which went on and on. It turned the IDF into a police force, charged with restoring law and order. Which is not the IDF's job, really."

"Also the length of the reserve duty went up," said Eli. "Too many complications and unforeseen situations came up at all levels—in the field and at the high command level. A new set of problems arose, disciplinary, moral-ethical, ending up in military trials."

During the six years the intifada lasted, 250,000 IDF troops were posted in the West Bank and the Gaza Strip.[3] That amounted to one in three of all male Jewish Israelis, aged 18 to 50.

The severity and pervasiveness of the Palestinian intifada in December 1987 caught the IDF command by surprise. Its initial reaction was to treat the phenomenon as if it were only short-term rioting, limited mainly to the Palestinian refugee camps and their surroundings, and led by a rag-tag collection of malcontent youths throwing stones and gasoline bombs. As in the past, it dispatched conscript troops with a mandate to restore "normal conditions."

This response had partly to do with the IDF's experience in 1970 of tackling increased acts of violence by the Palestinians in the Gaza Strip, the territory which was the first to erupt into the intifada seventeen years later. As the head of the southern command from 1969 to 1973, Ariel Sharon was in charge of the Gaza Strip, which was placed under emergency regulations about a year after its capture by the IDF in June 1967. Sharon used harsh methods to repress the Palestinian resistance, and got the situation under control by 1972.

The major difference between the events of 1970-72 and the intifada, however, was that this time the Palestinian resistance was home-grown: it was not directed by or dependent on Palestinian organizations operating abroad. But it was still intolerable for Israel. In January 1988 Defense Minister Yitzhak Rabin ordered the IDF to "strike the intifada off the agenda."[4] That soon proved impossible.

Often lacking riot control equipment and police training, the IDF soldiers and their officers frequently over-reacted. This led to charges of excessive force, and gross violation of the rules of engagement they were supposed to follow. But soon the Palestinians lost much of their fear of the IDF, and the Israeli public lost its faith in the military's ability to quickly restore the status quo. "For an army and society long accustomed to military campaigns which were for the most part short and often glamorous, the protracted failure to carry out those instructions [of Rabin] was a sobering experience," noted Professor Stuart Cohen of Bar Ilan University.[5]

The intifada had combined rioting with large scale non-violent resistance in the form of strikes, boycotts of Israeli goods and taxes, and mass resignations from government jobs. By the end of the Gulf War in early March 1991 the uprising had forced the issue of Palestinian self-determination to the fore, and the Israeli military leadership publicly concluded that it faced a unique challenge.

This was one of the several problems facing the IDF command. It was having to devote a disproportionate amount of time and expertise to tackling the intifada, at the expense of its core concerns of defending the country against external aggression. Posting conscripts and reserves in the West Bank and Gaza took them away from their training and exercises. Tackling civil disturbances, a psychologically demanding undertaking, began to demoralize the ranks and their field commanders. Also, the very concept of deploying soldiers in small units to quash a civilian insurgency ran counter to Israel's military doctrine of operating in large units equipped with high-technology weaponry.

In response, the IDF command cooperated with the Shin Beth to increase surveillance of suspected Palestinian activists, and bolstered the heavily Druze border guard police under its command.[6] It also established a separate elite unit to locate Palestinians suspected of violent crimes, and to execute them. Consisting of conscript volunteers, this unit became the police, judge, jury and executioner. Over the months the trigger-happy operations of these death squads terrified Palestinians, while creating unease among some MKs and members of the government who demanded their dissolution.

The unsatisfactory state of affairs was summarized in the spring of 1992 by Zeev Schiff, the country's foremost military commentator, thus: "One cannot help feeling that confrontation with citizens, and with a people subject to Israeli conquest, has generated a distortion in the IDF. Our elite forces, the flower of our youth, should not be focusing their attention on the slaying of wanted suspects—even if they are murderers. Their eyes should be on other targets and on different enemies."[7]

Changes in Military Doctrine and Perceptions to History

In a sense, Israel's military was running parallel to its political history. Just as in politics, old military certainties were gone, opening the way to replace old doctrines of outright defeat or decimation, with new ideas such as containment of the enemy. And in military as well as political history, June 1967 was a watershed, as was the surprise of the October 1973 Arab attack.

From the late 1940s, Israel's military-political hierarchy adopted the doctrine of precipitate action against its enemies, both as reprisal and as pre-emptive strike, and did so in the widest possible context.

Israel used reprisal successfully in the mid-1950s, reacting to the Palestinian guerrilla attacks mounted from the Egyptian-administered Gaza Strip. In contrast, Israel's 1956 invasion and occupation of Sinai was an example of a successful pre-emptive strike, in collaboration with Britain and France. About a decade later came another instance of retaliatory action to counter Palestinian commando actions launched from Syria. And Israel's performance in the June 1967 War was the most spectacular example of its adherence to the concept of determined, precipitate action in its pre-emptive version.

It was applied once more, in its retaliatory version, to counter the persistent Palestinian guerrilla threat from south Lebanon, which reached a peak in early 1978. It materialized as an Israeli blitzkrieg in south Lebanon in March 1978. The military action succeeded in emptying the border area of armed Palestinian activity, and provided the IDF with a rationale to carve out a self-declared security zone inside Lebanon, to be patrolled by its troops and an Israeli-trained and financed Lebanese force, called the South Lebanon Army.

Israel's next dramatic military move by was pre-emptive—the June 1981 clandestine bombing of the Iraqi nuclear reactor being assembled near Baghdad. This proved to be Israel's last successful use of precipitate armed action with specific military aims.

Had Israeli Defense Minister Ariel Sharon stuck to this tried and tested doctrine in his 1982 invasion of Lebanon, he would likely have vacated Beirut after the last PLO fighter and Syrian soldier left the city. But he did not. He went on instead to play king-maker in the Byzantine politics of Lebanon, and landed the IDF and Israel in a mess.

The military events in Lebanon had a profound effect on the state and society in Israel. "Israeli over-confidence of 1967 was shattered partially in the 1973 War and then more fully in the 1982 Lebanese invasion," said Benny Morris, a Jewish Israeli historian. A bespectacled man in his mid-40s, Morris is a fellow at the Hebrew University's Truman Institute, and the author of *The Birth of the Palestinian Refugee Problem, 1947–1949.* "The 1973 and 1982 Wars together shattered the invincible image the IDF had acquired in 1967. Due to this, ordinary people, journalists and academics began to question the IDF and the generals. Serious questioning of Israeli policies and popular history began in the mid-1980s."

The mid-1980s also marked the end of the era of heroes in Israel. The heroic period was remarkable for the ease with which successive Israeli governments presented the periodic regional hostilities as wars of survival for the Jewish state. Along with this presentation ran the official line, which highlighted Israel's right to make itself secure behind internationally accepted borders while striving hard to seek peaceful coexistence with its Arab neighbors. The Israeli authorities' continued success in convincing the public of the state's righteousness required a wide consensus at home. They attained it with a combination of tools, both short-term, such as news management, and long term, such as education and the IDF.

Those in charge of education in Israel were aware of the significance of historical myths and heroes in the national culture. "The Zionist movement from the very beginning felt an urgent need to develop a new set of Jewish heroes who would compensate for 2,000 years of passive behavior in the diaspora," said Dr. Reuven Gal, director of the Israeli Institute for Military Studies, who had served as the chief psychologist of the IDF for many years. "There was a stress laid on military valor and prowess, ranging from pre-diaspora Jewish historical figures like the Maccabees and the defenders of the Masada, up to modern warriors like Trumpeldor and beyond. They form an important part of the army's educational process, in which new recruits are taken to places like Tel Hai [Trumpeldor's burial place] and Masada to give them positive examples of behavior in combat."[8]

Yosef Trumpeldor (1880-1920) is the most celebrated hero in the Zionist annals in Palestine. After his death in 1920, the labor battalions of immigrants from southern Russia were named after him, as was the youth organization of Revisionist Zionists—Betar, the acronym of Berit Trumpeldor (the Covenant of Trumpeldor).

Born in southern Russia, Trumpeldor became the first Jewish commissioned officer in Russia. In 1912 he migrated to Palestine and worked on a kibbutz. He fought with the British during World War I, and after the 1917 Revolution returned to Russia to organize Jewish youth emigration to Palestine. He returned to Palestine, where in January 1920 the Jewish settlements in the upper Galilee, then part of French-ruled Syria, became embroiled in the anti-French campaign by local Arabs. Trumpeldor and his followers traveled to Tel Hai, near present-day Kfar Giladi, to assist its Jewish settlers. In the subsequent bloodshed, Trumpeldor became one of eight Jewish fighters killed. His reported last words, "It is good to die for our country," are engraved on the pedestal of a roaring stone lion that stands where they fell. Trumpeldor became the archetypal Jewish settler who ploughed during the day and guarded the settlement at night. On his death anniversary thousands of schoolchildren visit Tel Hai for a commemorative service.

One of the most famous incidents in Jewish military history took place in AD 73 at the fortified castle of Masada, which the Roman King Herod the Great had built on a rock overlooking the Dead Sea. Following the Jewish revolt in Palestine in AD 66, Jewish zealots captured the Masada fortress. Having crushed the uprising in Jerusalem in AD 70, the Romans besieged the Masada, but the zealots refused to surrender. Finally, when the Romans broke through and seized the castle, they found that all but 7 of the 960 Jews had killed themselves, preferring death to surrender. Over the centuries the event has aroused mixed feelings among Jews since Judaism disapproves of self-annihilation and requires that suicides be buried outside the fence of a cemetery.

But as Jewish immigration to Palestine accelerated after World War I, the intellectuals among the Zionist pioneers began re-examining the mass suicide at Masada. They gave it a different spin: fighting to the end was preferable to surrendering and losing independence. An eminent Zionist poet, Yaacov Lamdan, coined the line in 1927: "Never again will Masada fall!" This became a rallying cry of the Zionists in Palestine, and Masada a leading symbol of Jewish heroism in pursuit of attaining independent statehood. Since the establishment of Israel, a visit to Masada is mandatory for the youth movements of all Zionist political parties, and IDF recruits take their oaths of allegiance there.

The IDF, successor to the pre-statehood Haganah, began performing well from its birth on June 4, 1948, three weeks after the outbreak of the first Arab-Israeli War. It captured enough land to reduce the Arab-ruled area to a mere 22 percent of Palestine, about half of what the UN partition plan had allocated the Palestinians. This provided much grist for the heroism mill. "Due to the Holocaust the Jews and the Zionists lacked confidence," said Benny Morris. "They created myths about the 1948 War and the events surrounding it partly to bolster their own egos."

The Israelis call that war the War of Independence. But if it was a war of independence, when exactly was it declared, by whom and against whom? This was the question I posed to several Jewish Israelis: old and new historians, journalists and university students.[9]

Amos Elon is a doyen of traditional Israeli historians, with a biography of Theodor Herzl and the translation of Herzl's copious diaries to his credit.

A tall, slim, bespectacled man in his late 60s, Elon's book-lined Jerusalem apartment is filled with pictures of him with President Anwar Sadat of Egypt, Prince Hassan of Jordan, and Yasser Arafat.

ELON: The War of Independence started with the United Nations partition plan in November 1947. After the partition plan, Arabs stopped everything, began attacking the Jews. The lines were drawn. That was the beginning.

DH: That was a civil war, wouldn't you say?

ELON: Yes.

DH: By their very nature civil wars just break out, they are not declared. But a war of independence must be declared.

ELON: Calling it the War of Independence was a retroactive action. This name was put on it later.

DH: If this war was declared by the Zionists against the British, the foreign rulers of Palestine, then it finished on May 14, 1948 when the British left.

ELON: No need for this line of inquiry. Actually the term was borrowed later to appeal to the American people. It was a public relations job.

At Hebrew University, Taniya Alfersey, a pretty history student with blonde hair and dangling earrings, summed up the prevalent view thus: "It started as the War of Independence from the British. Then it became the War of Independence from the seven Arab armies which attacked Israel in May 1948." (The Arab League, which declared war against Israel, had seven members then; but two of them, Saudi Arabia and North Yemen, did not participate.)

"There are three terms in use: War of Independence, War of Liberation, and War of Establishment," said Benny Morris. "The War of Establishment is the most accurate. But because it is neutral, it is not very appealing. The War of Independence is the most satisfying psychologically. Every [Jewish] Israeli can identify with the War of Independence. Americans had a War of Independence."

On the floor above Morris's office, I put the question to Professor Moshe Ma'oz, a specialist on Middle Eastern history. Ma'oz, in his early 60s, was wearing an open neck shirt, sandals and dark glasses. "The War of Independence was never declared," he said. "It was post factum. It never was for independence from a foreign power. It was a defensive war against the Arab invasion. But the terms used were Milhemet HaAtzmaut (independence) or HaShihrur (liberation)." I pursued the matter. "If it was a war of liberation or independence, it could not be against the Arabs because the Arabs were not the rulers of Palestine," I argued. "It is a mess," said Ma'oz. "That is why I use a neutral term, the War of 1948."

In Haifa I raised the matter with Ilan Pappe, a "new historian" at Haifa University, and the author of *The Making of the Arab-Israeli Conflict, 1947-51*.[10] A muscular man in his thirties, Pappe radiates boundless energy, both physical and intellectual. "There are four terms in use: War of Independence, War of Liberation, War of Establishment, and War of Post-Mandate Palestine," he explained. "And there are two phases of the war. The first phase began in early 1946 when the conflict was between the Jewish Agency and the British mandate. You could stretch it, and call it a war of independence.

But because of the Arab involvement, it was more a civil war than a conventional war. The second phase began after May 14, 1948. The Arab League did not declare war against Israel until after it had been established. So you could not call it the War of Independence, because Israel was independent when a conventional war started on May 15, 1948." His views were at odds with the entry on "The War of Independence" in the quasi-official *Political Dictionary of the State of Israel*, which divides the conflict into five phases, two of them preceding the founding of Israel.[11]

By most accounts, the conventional war went through four phases: 1) May 14 to June 10, 1948, followed by a 28-day UN truce; 2) July 9–18, 1948, followed by another UN truce; 3) October 15 to November 6, 1948, followed by a UN truce in the south on November 6, and in the north and center on November 30; and 4) November 21, 1948 to January 7, 1949, when the warring parties accepted the UN Security Council armistice resolution.

According to the popular and official Israeli version of the events, on May 15, 1948, a day after Israel's establishment, the armies of five Arab countries—Egypt, Transjordan, Iraq, Syria and Lebanon—invaded the newborn state. The Egyptian army was only about 22 miles from Tel Aviv when, according to the *The Political Dictionary of the State of Israel*, it was stopped by "a hastily mobilized blocking force, assisted by the first fighter planes which had arrived from Czechoslovakia." Basically, it was touch and go for a fledgling republic of three-quarter million Jews, invaded by five enemy states with an aggregate population of 40 million. If Israel survived, and succeeded in concluding armistice agreements with these countries, it was a miracle—a repetition of the Old Testament confrontation between diminutive David and giant Goliath.

The prevalent view is well reflected in Amos Elon's *The Israelis: Founders and Sons*. "The invading Egyptian force comprised a number of infantry brigades, roughly totaling 10,000 men," Elon writes. "Their infantry was supported by a small air force, heavy artillery, tank and armored units. The fledgling Jewish state, barely a few days old, was as yet unequipped with anything but the most primitive weapons. The total strength of the invading Arab armies has been estimated at 23,500. They were amply equipped with British and French-made tanks, airplanes, heavy artillery, spare parts, and ammunition. Their four-pronged invasion was uncoordinated but simultaneous. The Israelis at this stage had some 3,000 'irregulars' under arms and 14,000 inadequately trained recruits, only 10,000 rifles with 50 rounds of ammunition each, four ancient cannons smuggled in from Mexico, [and] 3,600 submachine guns." Elon also cites Abdul Rahman Azzam Pasha, an Egyptian diplomat and secretary-general of the Arab League, the collective of seven independent Arab states formed in 1945, threatening "the Jews of Palestine with a bloodbath in the manner of Genghis Khan and Tamerlane."[12] Whatever the rhetoric used by the Arab leaders inside and outside Palestine, the final decision to attack the Zionist state collectively came on May 12 (after Jordan and Egypt had been persuaded to join the plan), only three days before the actual fighting. Though King Abdullah of Jordan was nominally the supreme commander of all the Arab forces, there was no central command.

In recent years three important, scholarly works by a group of young Jewish Israeli historians have appeared. Besides the books of Benny Morris and Ilan Pappe, there is *Collusion Across the Jordan* (1988) by Avi Shlaim. In it Shlaim deals at length with the tortuous clandestine talks between the Zionist leaders in Palestine and Emir Abdullah of Transjordan (later Jordan's King Abdullah).

These scholars took advantage of the declassification of archival material chiefly in Britain and Israel, where a 30-year moratorium on state secrets prevails. In the case of military matters Israel imposes a 50-year moratorium. But due to frequent overlap between the foreign and defense ministries, previously unavailable military information became available from 1978 onward. Also material from the Arab side, often in the form of diaries, letters and memoranda, began appearing from the late 1970s. Lastly, several Palestinian documentation centers in Lebanon, mostly in Beirut, and the West Bank made their documents available to researchers. "Considering the richness and originality of the material," noted Ilan Pappe, "it is obvious why the historiographical portrait of the war required drastic change."[13]

According to Pappe, on May 15, the five Arab League members added 23,500 troops to some 12,000 irregular Arab forces, most of them Palestinian, already engaged in the fighting with the Zionists, which had erupted in January 1948. Pappe's grand total of 35,500 on the Arab side is slightly higher than the figure of 30,280 provided by Morris. On the Zionist/Israeli side, Morris concludes that on the eve of the war in May 1948, Haganah had "mobilized and deployed in standing military formations" 35,780 troops.[14] It is noteworthy that this figure is considerably higher than 27,400 "first line troops" of Israel suggested by Walid Khalidi, editor of *From Haven to Conquest: Readings in Zionism and the Palestinian Problem until 1948*, published by The Institute of Palestine Studies, Beirut, in 1971.[15]

Khalidi's figures for the weapons possessed by the Zionists in April 1947 tie up neatly with Morris' statistics pertaining to September 1947. Morris adds that between October 1947 and July 1948, the Haganah's arms factories produced 16,000 submachine guns, 210 three-inch mortars, 3,000,000 9 mm bullets, and 150,000 grenades. Also, thousands more weapons were purchased, or stolen from the withdrawing British, during the first months of the war."[16]

Official Israeli historians point out that at the start of the war the Haganah did not possess tanks or artillery. According to Khalidi, the Arab side altogether had 102 artillery pieces while the Israelis had 4. But whereas the Arabs had only 40 three-inch mortars, the Israelis had 803 two-inch, three-inch and six-inch mortars. In the hilly terrain of Palestine, a mortar is a better "artillery" weapon than a cannon. As for armor, the Arabs' light tanks and armored cars were vulnerable to the Israelis' anti-tank rifles.[17]

On the crucial point of air power, Khalidi quotes chapter and verse to show that the Zionists/Israelis received 10 Messerschmitt ME 190 fighters from the Czech government, by May 20. Indeed, *The Political Dictionary*, as cited earlier, refers to the deployment of air power by Israel in the early days of the war. Going by Khalidi's material, the Arabs and Israelis were evenly matched in the air.[18]

As for the armies themselves, only Jordan's Arab Legion, commanded by

British General John Glubb, was professionally led. The Lebanese and Syrian troops were former territorial militiamen. The Egyptian and Iraqi troops were badly led, and were equipped with poor British-supplied arms. Little wonder that the Arab offensive lost momentum by early June. As a result, a UN-brokered truce followed for four weeks. By now, whereas the strength of the regular Arab troops reached 35,000, the Israel Defense Forces numbered 65,000.

The ceasefire favored the Israelis more than the Arabs. Britain abided by the UN embargo on arms sales to the warring parties, thus depriving Egypt, Iraq and Jordan of their sole source of weapons and ammunition; but Czechoslovakia and other East European states, encouraged by the Soviet Union, successfully ignored the ban, and continued supplying military hardware to Israel.[19] Within Israel, Ben Gurion, while clandestinely receiving weapons for the Haganah/IDF, forced Irgun not to take delivery of the arms from East Europe, partly to show that he was enforcing the UN embargo. Equally important, unlike Israel, none of the Arab countries had arms manufacturing facilities of its own.

No wonder that in the ten-day fighting that erupted on July 8 the Israelis did well. The Arabs accepted a ceasefire of unspecified length to allow UN mediation efforts, led by Count Folke Bernadotte, a member of the Swedish royal family, to succeed. The IDF was now 90,000 strong. In early September, Bernadotte produced a comprehensive peace plan identifying the IDF-controlled Negev as Arab territory. Israel was not pleased. Bernadotte was assassinated on September 17 by three activists of the Zionist Lehi, popularly known as the Stern Gang. In mid-October the IDF unleashed a series of offensives, followed by short-lived ceasefires. The final truce was signed on January 7, 1949. "In these offensives, the IDF beat the Transjordanian and Egyptian armies and the ALA [Arab Liberation Army] in the Galilee, and conquered large parts of the territory earmarked in 1947 by the United Nations for a Palestinian Arab state," writes Benny Morris.[20]

Undoubtedly, the IDF's overall performance was brilliant. Yet, as Prussian General Karl von Clausewitz stated, war is diplomacy by other means. So in the final analysis, the IDF gains resulted from the non-military achievements of the Zionists in Palestine and elsewhere. Conversely, the Arabs inside and outside Palestine came out worse in the war because of what had preceded the hostilities. "[T]he fate of Palestine, and hence that of the Palestinians, had been determined in the session rooms and corridors of the UN, in the meetings of various international inquiry committees and inside the discussion halls of the Arab League long before even one shot had been fired," concludes Pappe. "It was the Jewish success first in building the infrastructure for a state and then in winning the diplomatic campaign that decided the battle long before it started; as it was the inadequacy of the Palestinian leadership and the meandering politics of the Arab League that helped explain the consequences of this war."[21]

Nonetheless, the events of the first Arab-Israeli War showed Ben Gurion that it was possible for Israel to create and maintain "qualitative superiority" in military hardware, training, mobilization and motivation over the combined strength of its neighboring Arab enemies. Out of this experience emerged Ben Gurion's military doctrine of "qualitative superiority" over the Arabs. Once he introduced Israel's nuclear weapons factor into the equation, with French assistance from 1957, he laid an unshakable foundation for the continued implementation of his military doctrine. The generosity of the United States has ensured that the doctrine remains as valid today as it was when first conceived by Ben Gurion.

Indeed, Ben Gurion's thesis was twin-headed, devised to meet the Arab threat both abroad and at home. His solution for the Palestinian Arabs who refused to leave Israel was to ensure that they were concentrated in certain areas, and that these were administered by the IDF, the same agency charged with safeguarding the external security of the Jewish state.

7

The Double Marginals
Israeli Arabs

After my attempts over the telephone had failed to locate Dr. Adel Manna at the Truman Institute of Hebrew University, I drafted Rafi, my Hebrew interpreter who studied international relations at the university, to help my search.

When I mentioned the name, Adel Manna, Rafi immediately said, "But he is an Arab." I was dumbstruck—or I would have asked Rafi, "Isn't an Israeli Arab allowed on the teaching or research staff of Hebrew University?" "In theory, yes," he would have replied. "But in practice…"

The facts came from Dr. Manna when I finally tracked him down, and he came for tea at the American Colony Hotel. "Though 1,200 of the 25,000 students at Hebrew University are Arab, there are only two Arab professors, both of them in the medical faculty," he told me. "As a researcher at the Truman Institute, I'm the only other Arab on the university's teaching-research staff. Nationally, of some 6,000 professors, only twelve are Arab—that is 0.2 percent—most of them at Haifa University."

A light-skinned, balding man wearing thin-framed glasses, Dr. Manna has a quintessentially professorial appearance. He studied Middle Eastern history at Haifa University and Hebrew University. (A June 1993 *Jerusalem Report* article mentioned Manna's Hebrew University diploma "prominently displayed" at home, and that Hebrew books, "including an 11-volume series on Israeli history," lined his shelves.) Manna later won a scholarship to Oxford. He has since then taught history at Haifa and Hebrew Universities in Israel as well as at the West Bank universities of Birzeit and Al Najah.

History has placed Manna and some 950,000 other Israeli Arabs at the margins of two societies: Israeli and Palestinian. "Israeli Arabs are double marginals: marginal to Palestinians and marginal to Israeli Jews," he said. "Yet they are the most open-minded people because of what they are. They are Palestinian by nationality, and they are also Israeli citizens. They know the Jewish society well, their language, culture, day-to-day life. That makes them an ideal bridge between Israeli Jews and Palestinian Arabs."[1]

The fate of a double marginal, especially one as perceptive and well-read as Manna, is unenviable. The conflict of being simultaneously a Palestinian Arab and an Israeli citizen starts to nag early on. "I was born in late 1947 in the village of

Majd al Kurum in western Galilee," Manna said. "My father had land there. During the 1948–9 War our village surrendered. Still, the Israelis decided to expel lots of people from our village to Wadi Ara and to the East and West Banks [of the Jordan River]. The Israelis put young men over sixteen and young couples under thirty, including my parents, in buses [to get rid of child-bearing couples], and said to them: 'Go to [Jordanian King] Abdullah.' My family stayed in Nablus, then moved to Amman, then to Syria and finally Lebanon. We lived in Beirut, then moved to Ein Hilwa refugee camp, near Sidon. We lived there until early 1951. Then my father and fifteen others and their families hired a boat from Sidon port. We landed at a point north of Acre. Since my father had papers pertaining to the November 1948 Israeli census, he was allowed to stay in Israel. But half of our village, including my uncle, is still in the Ein Hilwa refugee camp."

For every three Arabs who were registered during the first Israeli census, one was left out because he/she lacked a "permanent dwelling." This claim was made to me by Emile Shukri Habibi. A Christian Arab born in Haifa, Habibi was an eminent public figure who successfully combined politics with literature and journalism. A bear-like figure with a sad, mustached face, he chain-smoked. His office at Arabesque Publishing House in Haifa, was sparse. "My father was the *mukhtar* (leader) of his community in Haifa," Habibi said. "We were nine brothers and sisters. Nobody remained in Israel [in 1948] except me and my sister. Others were forced to leave—for Lebanon, Syria and Jordan. One becomes accustomed to such separation. Yet the dream of reunion never dies. It's one of the main elements of the collective consciousness of Israeli Arabs. The other element of this consciousness is that we consider this to be our homeland. We have become a minority in our homeland because of Israel, and because of the expulsion of most Arabs from the land. Unlike the Palestinians who became refugees, we stayed put. We were prepared to die in our homeland instead of going into the diaspora. Today we are protected by the knowledge and confidence of being the original inhabitants of this country. We never feel like foreigners even when we are discriminated against. They, the Israeli Jews, are the foreigners, we say."[2]

Having worked as a news reader in the Palestine Broadcasting Station, Habibi resigned in 1943 to work full-time for the Palestine Communist Party (PCP). In 1945 he was one of the co-founders of the League of National Liberation (LNL), a leftist Arab group. Four years later he played a leading role in the creation of Maki, the Israeli Communist Party, out of the merger of the PCP and the remnants of the LNL. Maki recognized the State of Israel without accepting the Zionist doctrine guaranteeing all Jews the right to settle in Israel, and backed the right of the Palestinian Arab refugees to return home, and the founding of the Palestinian state in the territory allotted to the Arabs in the United Nations partition plan of November 1947. Habibi became an MK in 1951 and maintained a seat in the Knesset for more than 20 years.

"Israeli Arabs had to fight for their rights in their homeland," Habibi continued. "The Jewish state treated us as *mekhots la garder*, outcasts. Until 1954 the Israeli government actively encouraged Arabs either to leave or convert to Judaism. It wanted a Jewish state clear of all Arabs. For those Arabs who remained, the state policy was not to recognize them as a national group, but to fracture them into religious minorities: Muslim [75 percent], Christian [15 percent], Druze. Even among Muslims the Israelis tried to separate the bedouin from the rest. In 1956 the Druze were allowed to join the IDF. They are Arabic speakers, but they have been so brainwashed that they feel more Israeli than the Jews. Until 1966 Israeli Arabs were under military rule when they could not travel without the military governor's travel pass, just like Africans in [apartheid] South Africa. Most of our fertile land was confiscated 'for security reasons.' We could not depend on aid from the Arab world. Maki helped us to be practical and to depend on ourselves. We did. Maki was the only political organization which opposed military administration of the Arab-inhabited areas and discrimination against Arab citizens. Along with the progressive forces in the Jewish population we fought back vigorously for Arab rights, and secured an end to the military rule and land confiscations in 1966 [actually December 1965]. The fact of our persistence is tantamount to a miracle. We paid dearly for our struggle. We never had the illusion that someone on a white horse will come and deliver us, and learned early on to rely on ourselves, exclusively."

Why did the Israeli government end the military administration of the Arabs in 1966? Was it the comparatively liberal policy of prime minister Levi Eshkol? Was there a greater sense of security among Jewish Israelis? Or a combination of both?

"Until 1966 Israeli Arabs' movements were restricted in order to control our labor so that we could not go and sell our services in Haifa, for example," explained Atallah Mansour. A tall, bespectacled man of 61 and a Hebrew-language journalist since 1954, Mansour was born in Nazareth in a Christian family. He joined the Arab auxiliary of Mapam, a left-wing Zionist party, and its kibbutz fifteen miles from Nazareth. He published his first book, a novel based on his experiences at the kibbutz, in Hebrew. His latest volume, *Subtenants*, examines Israeli policy towards Arab citizens. "In the mid-1960s the Jewish immigration dropped; in fact there was more outflow than inflow," Mansour continued. "That's when the government lifted the military administration of us, so that we could fill the labor shortage caused by the outflow. We got this information from the horse's mouth as they say. The government opened some archives in the late 1980s on the Israeli Arabs. Towards the end of 1990 we held a seminar here [in Nazareth], and invited top Israeli officials on Arab affairs. They argued, and we got the facts from their discussion. For example, on the eve of the [first] general election in 1949, the Israeli leaders debated 'Should Arabs be allowed to vote?' 'No,' said many. 'They are not part of the Jewish state.' Others said, 'The world would think that we were following a divide and rule policy towards the local Arabs.' And so on. As the discussion was in progress somebody entered the room, and announced that Mapam and Maki [the Communists] had already included Arabs in their electoral lists. Too late, if Mapam, a Zionist party, has Arabs on its [auxiliary] list then other [Zionist] parties cannot keep them out of their lists. So we cannot deny them voting rights. That was the consensus that emerged. That's how we came to possess the basic right of voting."[3]

While military administration was the overt face of the Israeli rule, education was the subtle, long-term tool employed by the state to socialize the Arab minority in the way it wanted. From the start the central government acquired exclusive control over education in Israel. Its Ministry of Education and Culture set up separate departments for Hebrew and Arabic schools. At the university level instruction was exclusively Hebrew.

Dr. Majid Al Haj, a senior lecturer in sociology at Haifa University is a strongly built man in his early 40s. "The Arab education system in Israel is a system for controlling the Arab population," he said. "The Arabic language schools are controlled by the Ministry of Education—the curriculum, textbooks, budget, appointment of principals and teachers, everything. In the Arabic system there are the state and private sectors. But the Arabic private sector is controlled by the government even though it is financed by private sources, whereas the Hebrew private sector is not controlled by the government even though it gets public funds. In the Hebrew system there are the state secular, the state religious, and the private religious sectors. About 25 percent of the Hebrew schools are in the private sector. Even though they get public funding they are autonomous. For example, the policy of teaching Arabic as a compulsory subject from the seventh to the ninth grade, introduced in 1994, does not apply to the private sector in the Hebrew schools."[4]

The tight control over the Arabic language schools resulted in engendering a generation of schizophrenic Arabs. Among them was Dr. Manna. "As kids we had to celebrate the Feast of Independence, decorate the school and so on," he said. "The Day of Independence, based on the Jewish calendar, varies from year to year. We had to sing songs on that day, including the national anthem HaTikva, The Hope. It goes:

> As long as still within our breasts,
> The Jewish heart beats true.
> As long as there is hope in the heart,
> As long as the soul is longing for Zion. After 2,000 years of exile,
> This hope can materialize in the land of our fathers.'

This is what Arab children were required to sing, a Zionist hymn. At school we had this, and at home my father would tell me: 'On this day the Jews expelled us from our own homes, our own land.' For us it was a personal trauma. But I had to sing songs which boiled down to: the Jews came and liberated us! But liberated us from whom, from ourselves? I'd ask. The Arab teachers would not say anything. They could not, for fear of losing their jobs. And my father would say: 'This is politics. We are a minority here. We cannot say much. The Palestinians who resisted are refugees now. My own brother is a refugee in the Ein Hilwa camp.'"

The subject of Palestinian Arabs and what happened to them before and after the 1948 War kept coming up. "I studied Middle East history at Haifa University, from 1969 to 1972," said Dr. Manna. "'The Palestinians were expelled,' I'd say in a discussion in a history class. 'No, we wanted the Palestinians to stay,' the Jewish students would say, 'but their leaders told them to leave, and the Arab countries promised that they'd bring them back when the Zionists had been defeated.'

I would tell them my personal experience. 'I'm not making an abstract historical point,' I'd say. But it was no use."

A pioneering study of the Palestinian refugees was made by Benny Morris and published in 1987. His research was based on archival material released mainly by the Israeli and the British governments. Morris set out the competing claims thus: "The general Arab claim, that the Jews expelled Palestine's Arabs, with premeditation and preplanning, as part of a grand political-military design, has served to underline the Arab portrayal of Israel as a vicious, immoral robber state. The Israeli official version, that the Arabs fled voluntarily and/or that they were asked/ordered to do so by their leaders, helped leave intact the new state's untarnished image as the haven of a much-persecuted people, a body politic more just, moral and deserving of the West's sympathy and help than the surrounding sea of reactionary, semi-feudal, dictatorial Arab societies."[5]

Morris divided the period under study—December 1947 to July 1949—into two parts: up to June 1948, when some 400,000 Palestinians became refugees; and after, when about 300,000 Palestinians became refugees.

"To what extent was the Arab exodus up to June [1948] a product of the Yishuv [Jewish community in Palestine] or Arab policy?" Morris asks. "The answer is as complex as was the situation on the ground. Up to the beginning of April 1948, there was no Yishuv policy or plan to expel the Arab inhabitants of Palestine, either from the area destined for Jewish statehood or those lying outside it... The prospect and need to prepare for the invasion gave birth to Plan D, prepared in early March. It gave the Haganah brigade and battalion-level commanders *carte blanche* to completely clear vital areas; it allowed the expulsion of hostile or potentially hostile Arab villages... The matter was never discussed in the supreme, political, decision-making bodies, but it was understood by all that, militarily, in the struggle to survive, the fewer Arabs remaining behind and along the front lines, the better, and, politically, the fewer Arabs remaining in the Jewish state, the better."[6]

What about the Arab side? "The records are incomplete, but they show overwhelming confusion and disparate purpose [among Arab leaders inside and outside Palestine], with 'policy' changing from week to week and area to area," Morris concludes. "No guiding hand or central control is evident." As to April 1948 and the start of the main exodus, he adds, "I have found no evidence to show that the [Palestinian] AHC [Arab Higher Committee] issued blanket instructions, by radio or otherwise, to Palestine's Arabs to flee... There were a spate of appeals in early May by Transjordan, the AHC and various Arab leaders to the Arabs of Palestine to stay put, or if already in exile, to return to their homes. But the appeals, given the war conditions along the fronts, had little effect... Besides, in most areas the Haganah physically barred return."[7]

As for the period after June 1948, which involved fighting between Israel and Arab forces, Morris concludes: "From July onward there was a growing tendency in the IDF units to expel... just as the pressures on the remaining Arabs by leaders inside and outside Palestine to stay put grew and just as their motivation to stay put increased... Ben Gurion clearly wanted as few Arabs as possible to remain in the Jewish state.

He hoped to see them flee. He said as much to his colleagues and aides in meetings in August, September and October. But... Ben Gurion always refrained from issuing clear or written expulsion orders; he preferred that his generals 'understand' what he wanted done."[8]

Morris caps his conclusions thus: "In general, in most cases the final and decisive precipitant to flight was Haganah, IZL [Irgun], LHI [Lehi] and IDF attack or the inhabitants' fear of such attack."[9]

His book has been widely acclaimed as a refreshingly objective piece of well-documented history, and he is regarded as an important member of the rising group of new historians. "But," he told me in early 1995, "old historiography is quite strong. Most school and college textbooks follow the traditional view. My book was translated into Hebrew and published only in 1991, four years after the English edition. During the first year [of the Hebrew edition] people kept saying, 'The Palestinians left because their leaders told them to et cetera, but now nobody challenges what I've said in my book. However, I agree that the trickle-down is slow. It will only happen through universities. Today's students are tomorrow's teachers. And my book is being used at universities."

Ultimately, the purpose of Israel's state educational system, according to State Education Law of 1953, is, for both Jews and non-Jews, "to base elementary education... on the values of Jewish culture and the achievements of science, on love of the homeland and loyalty to the state and the Jewish people."[10]

One result of this doctrine is inordinate distortion of history in textbooks. The lopsidedness was pointed out to me by Said Barghouti, the inspector for history education in Arabic high schools in Israel. "In the Arabic schools twenty percent of history texts are about Jews whereas in the Hebrew schools only two percent of history concerns Arabs," he said. Barghouti talked with me in his unheated Nazareth office on a cold evening.

While referring to the Jewish immigration to Palestine under the Ottomans and the British, history books in Hebrew invariably say: "The Jews immigrating to Eretz Israel, Land of Israel." In fact no such entity existed, and what came into being on May 14, 1948 is Medinat Israel (State of Israel), not Eretz Israel.

"I went through an educational system where the term Palestinian or Palestine was not used in a textbook or by a teacher, only the term Eretz Israel was used," continued Barghouti, a graduate of Haifa University who obtained an MA in history from Hebrew University.

The system thus created a generation of Israeli Arabs who were culturally shipwrecked. "I grew up knowing a lot about Zionist culture and literature but nothing about Palestinian history, culture etc.," recalled Manna. "On the other side, in the Hebrew schools Jewish students study Jewish history, Zionist-Arab conflict etc.; they learn very little about Palestine and Palestinians. In the Arabic system, history textbooks in secondary schools give the history of Palestine under the Ottomans until World War I, then the history of the Zionists. They ignore the history of Palestine and the Palestinian identity. They educate the Arab students for Israeli citizenship, and so the students know nothing about their own cultural and historical identity... But when your textbooks and education prove inadequate to explain everyday reality and the evolving political-military situation, you lose confidence in the educational system."

Undoubtedly, the wars of 1967 and 1973 and the intifada impinged strongly on the communal consciousness of Israeli Arabs. "After the 1967 War the brunt of discrimination shifted to the Palestinians in the West Bank and Gaza," said Habibi. "The Israelis could not rule by force all of the Palestinians, inside and outside Israel, together. At the same time contacts between the Palestinians across the Green Line [the pre-1967 border] increased."

The intifada accelerated politicization of Israeli Arabs, who had long felt leaderless. With the traditional upper- and middle-class leadership gone into exile in 1948, the remnant of the Palestinian Arab community, now confined almost wholly to rural areas in the Galilee, found itself in a weak position. Except for Maki, a non-Zionist, fringe group, it was barred from national Israeli politics. Until 1958 even the left-wing Mapam allowed Arabs to enroll only in its auxiliary Arab organization rather than the main body. "On the Israeli Arab side, there was fear of being involved in politics," explained Manna. "The general perception was that if you became too involved in politics then calamity would strike you as happened in 1948. Therefore Israeli Arabs kept low political profiles. They realized that they were second-class citizens, and that this was a Jewish state and an ethnic democracy. They learned this the hard way. Between 1948 and 1966, any Arab who did not vote for a Zionist party was considered anti-Israeli."

Given the secrecy of the ballot, how would anybody know the pattern of voting, I asked. "Most of us live in wholly or predominantly Arab villages and towns," Manna said. "So anybody can judge from the results of individual polling stations as to how the electors had voted. The Zionist parties can see whether or not the Arabs had voted for their affiliated Arab list—a practice which continued into the early 1980s. And they know that by controlling individual *mukhtars* and heads of *hamulas* (extended families), they secure votes en bloc. Generally speaking, Arabs voted for the Zionist party which controlled either the Ministry of Education [for jobs as teachers] or police [for travel permits and security clearance]. If an Arab did not vote for a Zionist party he could not get a job [as a teacher] and a permit to travel to work, and could end up in jail. He knew that he had to have good relations with the police and Shin Beth, and the civil service. So during the 1950s and 1960s more than two-thirds of Arabs voted for the Zionist parties. They even voted for the [ultra-nationalist] National Religious Party because it controlled the police, interior and education ministries. If you wanted to be a teacher, the only white-collar job available, you needed [security] clearance from the police and Shin Beth. So, all told, the first and second generations of Israeli Arabs were subdued." It was only in the mid-1970s that the situation changed. Labor permitted Arabs to join the main party in 1971, initially accepting only Arabs who had an IDF background (i.e., Druzes) or were bedouin. Labor and Mapam continued to run separate Arab lists in the Knesset elections.

Israel's performance in the October 1973 War made the local Arabs realize that the Zionist state was not invincible. This encouraged them to increase their support for Rakah, New Communist List, particularly when it was the only party in the December 1973 poll to demand an unconditional Israeli withdrawal from the Occupied Territories, and the recognition of the national rights of the Palestinians. With 37 percent of the Israeli Arabs backing it, Rakah's strength in the Knesset rose to four.

The other factors which impinged on the communal psyche of Israeli Arabs were the growing nationalist movement in the occupied West Bank and Gaza Strip, and the rising prestige and international recognition of the Palestine Liberation Organization (PLO), culminating in its being given an observer status at the UN in late 1974.

In that year the elected representatives of Israeli Arabs formed the National Committee for Heads of Arab Local Authorities. The central administration hoped it would become a rival to Rakah. But by spearheading the protest against the government's takeover of 2,000 acres of Arab land in the Galilee, through the "Day of the Land" strike on March 30, 1976, Rakah increased its popularity, and frustrated the official plan. With the aggregate loss of some 90 percent of their land through government confiscations since 1948, feelings among Israeli Arabs were running high. Their demonstrations on the Day of the Land were violently broken up by the police, resulting in the deaths of six Arabs and injuries to 70. This radicalized the National Committee, which decided to adopt a joint program for Arab civil rights and Palestinian self-determination.

As a result, the total Arab vote for the Zionist parties fell to 37 percent (only 11 percent for Labor), whereas it rose to 50 percent for the (Marxist) Democratic Front for Peace and Equality (DFPE), popularly called Hadash, formed by the alliance of Rakah and the Black Panther (Sephardic Jewish) Party, which won five Knesset seats.[11] Only after this electoral setback did Labor properly open its doors to Arab citizens. But its policy of maintaining a separate Arab affairs department, often headed by an Ashkenazi Jew, continued until late 1994.

Rakah leaders actively promoted the national rights of the Palestinians. One of them, Emile Touma, was secretary of the Arab People's Conference in Support of the Palestine Revolution. In mid-1980, after there had been no progress on the Palestinian front as agreed by Israel in the 1978 Camp David Accords, the Arab People's Conference sponsored a manifesto which combined its twin-headed demand for equality for Arab citizens and an Israeli-Palestinian peace based on self-determination for Israelis and Palestinians, with a call on the Israeli government to negotiate with the PLO on the subject of a Palestinian state. The manifesto was signed by thousands of Israeli Arabs, and this worried Begin's Likud government. It banned the congress of the Arab People's Conference on the eve of its assembly in December 1980 called to endorse the manifesto.

Israeli Arabs were deeply antipathetic toward Likud. At the next general election in 1981 as many as 29 percent of them backed Labor in order to keep Likud out. Labor's gain was at the expense of Hadash, whose vote stabilized around a third of the Arab total.

The 1987 intifada, and the iron fist policy toward it adopted by Yitzhak Rabin, Labor Defense Minister in the national unity government, alienated many Arab members of the party. Israeli Arabs showed their support for the intifada with a general strike on December 21. Among those who issued the call for the strike was Abdul Wahab Darawshe, a Labor MK. He left Labor, and formed his own Arab Democratic Party (ADP), the first group of its kind. It called for the withdrawal of Israel from all Arab territories occupied in 1967, and the convening of an international conference on the Middle East attended by all concerned parties, including the PLO, as the sole representative of the Palestinian people, on an equal footing. In the 1988 poll, when 58 percent of the Arabs voted for non-Zionist groups, the ADP secured one seat.

1987 also witnessed the expansion of the National Committee into the Supreme Surveillance Committee of Arab Affairs, with the addition of Arab representatives of all political groups, including the Zionist parties. The Supreme Surveillance Committee called demonstrations and strikes to further the rights of the Arab citizens. In addition to the already established Day of the Land, it declared Days of Equality (June 24, 1987), Peace (December 21, 1987) and Housing (November 15, 1988).

The daily diet of news on the intifada raised the nationalist consciousness of Israeli Arabs. They underwent a process described as "Palestinianization." "We began to say 'We are Palestinian,'" recalled Atallah Mansour. "Though our identity document says *leum*, nationality, Arab, we insisted that our nationality was Palestinian, and our citizenship Israeli. This put us in a bind as Israel and the PLO were at war then."

With no let-up in the intifada, the Israeli Arab interest in the fate of the Palestinians remained high. Through voluntary charity organizations they provided monetary and other assistance to the Palestinian victims of Israeli policies and actions. When in December 1992 Premier Yitzhak Rabin expelled over 400 Hamas and Islamic Jihad men to south Lebanon, Israeli Arab leaders called a one-day strike. It got the almost unanimous support of the community.

"The intifada proved to be a real, live political educator of Israeli Arabs," said Dr. Majid Al Haj. "They did not need schooling to come to grips with their identity. They now learned their history from other sources: political parties, parents, books at home, the street and the media. In this regard Arabic schools are lagging behind society at large."

Books on Palestine became commonplace. Given the frequency with which the current Palestinian intifada was being compared to the 1936–9 Arab uprising in Palestine, such titles as *The Arab Resistance in Palestine, 1917–1948* by Naji Alwash, published in Beirut, were popular. In a 30-page chapter, before dealing with the Arab Revolt proper, Alwash sets the scene, and gives central place to Izz al Din Qassam (1881-1935), the first Arab leader in Palestine to preach and practice the doctrine of armed resistance to the British mandate and Zionist immigration in Palestine, a struggle in which he lost his life. "Qassam was a religious man, a preacher, eloquent, with a rich vocabulary, a man of knowledge in many areas," Alwash wrote. "He placed his skills and knowledge at the disposal of his religious center in Haifa. He began to inspire his audience to revolt against repression and against foreign rule... He decided to establish a revolutionary and principled movement based on the Islamic faith and a secret organization of its own. He took to holding clandestine meetings. His movement was based on the following principles:

resistance should be based on Islamic precepts as well as practical and political principles, which should be applied to raise the members' political consciousness and national identity as well as their understanding of the cultural aspects of Islam; Britain was the root cause of the oppression of the Palestinian Muslims as Zionism was linked with British imperialism, and so the focus should be on the anti-mandate struggle with the objective of stopping the Zionist movement from colonizing any more land in Palestine; and an armed revolution will be able to end the British mandate, and that such a revolution requires the setting up of a secret organization, training fighters in military warfare, and encouraging popular participation in the resistance."

The fact that Hamas and the Islamic Jihad, the Islamic groups active within the intifada movement, had now named their armed wings after Qassam, made such laudatory biographical information about him topical, relevant, and politically contentious in Israel. The easy availability inside Israel of such fiery material, in stark conflict with the official chronicle, which either ignored Qassam or made a cursory reference to him, began to worry liberal-minded Jewish Israeli educators and policy-makers. Something needed to be done, they concluded. The initiative to update the curriculum at Arabic schools as well as history textbooks in light of the dramatic change that had occurred outside schools came from the fellows of the Truman Institute at Hebrew University in 1991. Important Arab officials of the Ministry of Education, which controlled 437 Arabic schools with some 200,000 students, were invited to participate. But the textbook project really got going only after the Labor victory in the general election of June 1992. In the new cabinet the Ministry of Education went to Shulamit Aloni, a member of the left-wing Meretz, and then to her party colleague, Amnon Rubinstein. They backed the idea of changes in the curriculum and textbooks for the Arabic sector.

Both Dr. Adel Manna and Said Barghouti were commissioned to write history books. "It was agreed at the outset that the official curriculum should familiarize the [Arab] student with 'What is a Palestinian Arab?'" said Barghouti. "It is a daunting task in several ways. We, Arabs in Israel, are still grappling with our identity. Arabs have lived here, in this land, as Arabs for 3,000 years—since the rule of King Solomon. And as Muslim Arabs we have an almost continuous history here of more than 1,300 years. Our collective problem stems from the rise of Israel, the national state of the Jewish people, in 1948. And my problem as the author is how to narrate a national history of Arabs which is part of the State of Israel, which is the state of Jews. We, Arab educators, are wrestling with this intractable problem. We can find some space within the dichotomy that Israel is a Jewish national state, but it is also a democratic state. As Arab educators we use the democratic charter of Israel to build our curriculum, to help sharpen our communal identity."

As the author of a book on history, Barghouti had to work within the long-established rules of the Education Ministry and its department charged with writing and supervising textbooks. First, the editorial committee of the ministry publishes a limited edition of a book, and circulates it among educators and specialists for their comments. Once these are received and discussed, the text is finalized, and a commercial edition appears.

Barghouti, an employee of the Education Ministry since 1972, encountered opposition to the way he handled the chapter, "The Palestinian Problem" in *Social-cultural Changes in the Middle East, Vol. III*, in its initial, limited edition version. To do justice to the 1917 Balfour Declaration which, by all accounts, is the seed that grew into the plant called Israel 31 years later, Barghouti devoted five pages to the subject. His editorial committee cut his text down to a single page. "All my references to Arab land expropriations by Israel were excised," he said. "I was told, 'If you write about land expropriations this will create hostility against the Jews at the present time.'"

While working on *History of the Middle East, Vol. II*, Barghouti ran into trouble on his definition of Zionism. "Zionism is a belief that Jews constitute a nation which has its own identity and that they have the right to be a free nation like others and that they have the right to return to the land they consider as the land of their ancestors, which they call the Land of Israel," he wrote. The editorial committee at the ministry rejected this, regarding it as too qualified. So the final version read: "Zionism is a movement which had been created in order to achieve the historical right of the Jews to return to their own land and build their own state."[12]

On the other hand, said Barghouti, "We state that Arabs in Israel are an integral part of the Palestinian nation. It is the first [official] textbook to say so."

Life became much easier for Israeli Arabs when Yasser Arafat and Yitzhak Rabin shook hands at the White House in Washington after the signing of the Israeli-PLO Accord in September 1993. They no longer had to try to maintain conflicting loyalties to two warring parties.

"Today we are the most enthusiastic supporters of the Israeli-PLO Accord of September 1993," said Emile Habibi. "We, the Israeli Arabs, forming one-sixth of the national population, are a strong force for coexistence between Palestinians and Israeli Jews. We also know that we will benefit from the peace process more than any other section of the Palestinian people."

But a pact between Israel and the PLO has created a different set of choices for Israeli Arabs. "Now there is the Palestinian Authority and a Palestinian flag, and there will be a Palestinian state one day," said Atallah Mansour. "But we are in Israel and not in Palestine. We are not going to migrate to the future State of Palestine. So we ought to integrate with the Israeli mainstream."

The ongoing debate among Israeli Arabs revolves around the question whether they should back mainstream Zionist parties or non-Zionist groups like the Democratic Front for Peace and Equality and the Arab Democratic Party. The result of the 1992 Knesset poll showed the community to be evenly divided on the subject. Though Rabin managed to form a government without including the DFPE and the ADP, his administration lost its majority when he compelled the Shas leader, Rabbi Arye Deri, to resign his ministerial post following renewed police charges of corruption. The fact that Rabin did not then invite the DFPE or ADP to join his coalition, while enjoying their support, strengthened the hands of those Israeli Arabs who favored Zionist parties. Their argument was that so long as Israeli Arabs supported non-Zionist groups they would be confined to the margins of Israel's national politics.

Deep division within the community adversely affects its overall strength in the Knesset. Of the 2,657,000 Israelis who voted in the 1992 election, 282,700 were Arab, which translated into a ratio of 1:9, which should have resulted in 12 Arab MKs. Instead they won only eight seats, including a Druze member of Likud.[13]

On the other hand, the legitimization and empowerment of the PLO opened new vistas for the DFPE and the ADP, and certain individual Israeli Arabs. Dr. Ahmad Tibi, a gynecologist from the Arab town of Taiba east of Natanya, became a close adviser to Arafat. This has caused much adverse comment in the Jewish Israeli media. "Israel does not want Israeli Arabs to be too involved in the peace process because they know the Jews better than any other Arabs: their strengths, weaknesses, tricks, real interests, operating methods etc.," said Dr. Adel Manna. "That is why most Israelis are upset at the high-profile involvement of Ahmad Tibi as Arafat's adviser."

Nonetheless, at crucial moments Israeli Arab politicians have played a central role in Palestinian politics since the Israeli-PLO Accord. For instance, when tension between the PLO and Hamas rose dangerously high in the Gaza Strip in November 1994, following the fatal shooting of a dozen Palestinians by the PA police, the Israeli Arab MKs intervened, successfully, to lower the temperature.

Six months later these MKs dramatically intervened on behalf of the Palestinians, in the Knesset itself. In late April 1995 the Israeli government had unveiled plans to confiscate 130 acres of Palestinian land in Greater East Jerusalem to build housing for Jews. Protest by the PA and others got nowhere. On May 17, when fourteen of the fifteen United Nations Security Council members backed a resolution criticizing the Israeli move, the United States, determined to aid Israel, exercised its veto for the first time since the end of the Cold War in 1991. The Rabin administration was all set to go ahead with its confiscation plans when the DFPE and ADP MKs tabled a no-confidence motion in the Knesset on May 22. As the government had the backing only of 58 MKs in a house of 120, its downfall was assured. Fearing this, Premier Rabin climbed down, and the government "suspended" its land confiscation plans.

Outside the Knesset, the Supreme Surveillance Committee, commonly regarded as the parliament of the Arabs in Israel, remains committed to its two major aims: 1) peace and the furtherance of Palestinian national rights; and 2) closing the economic gap between Arabs and Jews in Israel.

Since September 1993 there has been discernible progress on the first goal. But the socio-economic chasm between the two communities in Israel remains wide. Figures for 1991 revealed that whereas the monthly income of a four-member Jewish family was $1,419, that of an Arab family was $815. While nearly 50 percent of the Arab families lived below the official poverty line, the corresponding figure for the Jews was only 10 percent. The twenty percent unemployment among Arabs was twice the rate for Jews. A similar ratio prevailed in infant mortality. The difference in the level of local public services could be gauged by the per capita local government budget: Arab $42; Jew $133. Whereas the gap between the two ethnic groups finishing secondary education was not much, Arabs 45 percent and Jews 65 percent, at the university level Arabs lagged behind Jews by 3 to 1.[14]

"At five to six percent of the university enrollment, the Arabs are only at about a third of their demographic proportion," said Dr. Adel Manna. Yet over 40 percent of Arab university graduates were either jobless or employed in semi-skilled work. The situation is unlikely to change since large swathes of industry, science and research, tied to the vast military establishment, remain closed to Israeli Arabs because of their lack of service in the IDF. In theory, they can volunteer for the military on an individual basis. But it is common knowledge that the IDF leadership is opposed to having large Arab contingents in the army (Druze males, who are drafted, are only five percent of the overall Arab population), and the Arabs do not want to expose themselves to a situation which requires them to fight fellow Palestinians or other Arabs. Only when there is a comprehensive peace between Israel and its Arab neighbors can one realistically expect Arab citizens of Israel to serve in the IDF like their Jewish counterparts.

Meanwhile continued unemployment and under-employment among Arab university graduates is providing fertile ground for the rise of Muslim fundamentalism, which is represented in Israel by the Islamic Movement. Its roots go back to the mid-1930s when the Egyptian-based Muslim Brotherhood established branches in Palestine. Dormant for three decades after the emergence of Israel, the religio-political movement revived as a result of renewed interest in Islam among those Israeli Arabs who joined Islamic colleges on the West Bank after 1967. Some 100 members of an Israeli Arab organization, called the *Usrat al Jihad*, Family of the Jihad, led by Shaikh Abdullah Nimr Darwish, were arrested in 1981 on charges of possessing illegal arms. Darwish was a resident of the village of Kfar Qassim, the site of a massacre of 47 unarmed Arab men and women by the IDF on the eve of the Suez War on October 30, 1956. After their release from jail in the mid-1980s the followers of Darwish formed the Islamic Movement with the objective of returning society to the pristine precepts of Islam. It set up grass roots organizations such as community centers, libraries and clothing workshops. It recognized the State of Israel *de facto* but not *de jure*, and called on its supporters to boycott the Knesset election in 1988. But it participated in the 1989 local elections, and with 20 percent of the popular vote, it won control of six local councils, including Umm al Fahm, the second largest Arab town after Nazareth.

Islamic Movement members were as interested in the fate of the Palestinians in the Occupied Territories as were the secular Israeli Arabs. Both sections of the community were horrified by the massacre in Hebron of Muslim Palestinians at the Tomb of the Patriarchs/Ibrahimi Mosque by Baruch Goldstein, a resident of the adjoining Kiryat Arba settlement, in late February 1994. They responded with almost the same vigor as did the Palestinians. In Arab towns like Nazareth, Jaffa and Rahat (in Negev), three-day protests turned violent. In Rahat one Arab was killed by police firing. The mourners at his funeral chanted, "In blood, in spirit, we'll redeem you, O martyr!"—a chant which had not been heard inside pre-1967 Israel before. This aroused fear in many Jewish Israelis that an Arab intifada from within the Israeli borders was in the making. Such fears proved ill-founded, but the events following the Hebron massacre made many on both sides of the ethnic divide reassess their long-term relationship.

Summing up the overall Israeli Arab scene, Atallah Mansour, a veteran journalist with 35 years of service with the prestigious *HaAretz* daily, said: "While most Israeli Arabs want reconciliation and coexistence, there are small groups like the Islamic Movement which say, 'We'll get all of [British mandate] Palestine.'"

In a sense the supporters of the Islamic Movement in Israel are mirror-images of the members of those ultra-nationalist Jewish groups who wanted all of British mandate Palestine as their Land of Israel. Acting on this belief, some 350,000 Jews, religious and secular, have settled in the areas beyond the pre-1967 borders of Israel, with about half of them in Greater East Jerusalem, and the rest in the West Bank.

8

New Frontiersmen
Zealots on the Hills

I employed the foot-in-the-door technique when it came to interviewing Rabbi Moshe Levinger in Hebron in March 1995. Rafi and I broke away from the group of visitors from Tel Aviv, who were being given a guided tour of the Jewish Quarter by Naom Arnon, the spokesman for the Kiryat Arba settlement but a resident of the nearby Beit Hadassah Jewish enclave. Levinger's two-story stone house was easy to find. Standing next to the rebuilt synagogue, it lay in the path of a pedestrian approaching the Jewish enclave from a lane of shuttered, squalid Arab shops, some of them carrying the graffiti in Hebrew, "Mavet la Aravim (Kill the Arabs)" and a military command post bristling with gun-carrying soldiers.

A young daughter of Moshe Levinger answered the door bell, and Rafi explained the purpose of our call. She disappeared long enough for me to read the tablet on a wall nearby declaring that the new complex had been completed by the Ministry of Housing in 1989 (when a Labor-Likud unity government was in power). At strategic points in and around the enclave were troops armed with submachine guns. Every time I looked up I saw a young soldier with a gun on a rooftop, alert as a hawk. Levinger's daughter returned. Yes, he would see us, but he needed a while to get ready.

Three of the eleven children of Moshe Levinger, aged 59, and his wife, Miriam, 57, were home. We waited in a large open plan hall, harboring a kitchen on the far side and a library of books, all of them in Hebrew, in a near corner. Born in Jerusalem, of a professor father of German origins, Levinger had grown up surrounded by books.

Moshe Levinger is bald, with a long white beard. He was wearing a black skullcap and black-framed glasses. "Hebron has a special place in Judaism," he began. "In the Bible we see that God permits three patriarchs to settle in Hebron. These men led our world. Of the eighteen Jewish prayers, the first prayer is about the patriarchs. Therefore it is our duty to rebuild villages and towns here, because they belong to us, Jews. All this is in the territories which are the heart of the Land of Israel, which God promised to the Jewish people. We pray and resolve to return to our Holy Country, Israel. We say in our prayers Eretz Israel as our country. If the Jewish congregation is in Holland or Egypt, outside our Holy Country, they all say the same thing: they feel outside of their homeland, hoping and praying it will become our home.

There is no period in our history when we said that our connection with Tel Aviv or Herzliya or Natanya or Haifa was stronger than our connection with Beit El, Hebron, Nablus, Beit Lehem [Bethlehem], Tekoa. These holy cities are the heart of Eretz Israel. They formed our first congregation during the First Temple and the Second Temple periods. We had connections [with the people] over the mountains, who were sometimes Philistine. But the Jews lived in Judea and Samaria. Therefore we think that it is a mistake to think that this is an occupied territory. It is the heart of our country. Abraham came to this place under the command of God. God instructed him— first to Shechem [Nablus], then Beit El where a tabernacle was built. Another tabernacle was at a place which is now modern Ramallah. To say Nablus is an Arab city is a lie. Nablus is more Jewish than Tel Aviv. Our connection with Hebron is stronger than with Tel Aviv."

For Levinger these were not just mere words. He is the leading pioneer of Jewish settlement in the West Bank, having begun the process within a year of the Israeli capture of the territory from Jordan in June 1967. "At the time of the Passover in 5728 [April 1968] we came here, about four families, all together 50 people, to Park Hotel. It was a hotel only in name, it was empty. We rented the whole place. We paid for it, four shekels per bed. The hotel had 40 beds in all. Later people said that I was a poor trader, that I should have bargained and got the rate down to three shekels a bed. If I had been a better trader I'd have brought it down to three shekels. Anyway, in spring 1968 four Jewish families, led by me, came to Hebron. Today 1,000 families live in Hebron and Kiryat Arba. We did not know at the beginning how much time it would take to settle here. But we are a people of 3,000 years ago. We have a long perspective. In another 30 years the Jewish community here will be bigger than it is now."

According to a booklet, *Hebron Massacre 1929*, edited by Rachavam Zeevi, a leader of the ultra-right wing Moledet group—given to me by Arnon, the tour guide— the history of Hebron's Jewish community could be summarized as follows. For about 500 years it lived in peace with its Arab neighbors. This changed in 1929 when the community was 900 strong. "In [August] 1929 burning, murdering etc. happened, Arabs slaughtered us," Arnon told his visiting Jewish audience. "The Jewish Quarter was totally destroyed, and 67 Jews were murdered. The British mandate did not do anything. Actually, the British police evacuated the Jewish community from Hebron. The Jewish houses were given to Arabs." (The fact that the Jews in Hebron had rejected the offer of the Haganah militia for protection went unmentioned. Also, according to Eliakam Haetzini, a leader of the Jewish settlers in Kiryat Arba, some of the Jews who had been evacuated in 1929 returned, and remained until 1937, the first phase of the 1936-9 Arab Revolt.) "After the 1967 war the Israeli government should have returned Jewish families to Hebron," said the booklet. "Unfortunately this did not happen. In the spring of 1968 Jews rented the Park Hotel... Later on the Labor government built Kiryat Arba in 1971. Further construction took place in 1975-76 [under Labor] and again in 1979-80 [under Likud]." Arnon provided the update. "This was the old Jewish Quarter," he said. "In 1979 one Kiryat Arba mother, Sarah, went to bury her son Abraham in the Jewish cemetery in Hebron, but was barred. This angered the Jews in Kiryat Arba.

In protest several Jewish women of Kiryat Arba, led by Miriam Levinger, barricaded themselves inside Beit Hadassah [then an abandoned building]. They demanded a renewed Jewish presence in the city. The government of Menachem Begin besieged the building." prime minister Begin apparently reckoned that such a move would exacerbate the already tense relations between Arabs and Jews in Hebron and its surroundings. "But the government changed its mind after Palestinian terrorists machine-gunned six Kiryat Arba Jews just outside the Beit Hadassah in May 1980," continued Arnon. "It allowed the Jews to move into downtown Hebron. Today about 50 Jewish families live in the town, plus 120 yeshiva students."

The Bnei Akiva youth movement of the National Religious Party, and Jerusalem's Merkaz HaRav Kook Yeshiva, run by Rabbi Zvi Yehuda Kook, the leading ideologue of the Orthodox NRP, were the main forces behind the Jewish colonization of the West Bank, before they together formally set up the Gush Emunim in early 1974. Kook's father, Rabbi Abraham Yitzhak HaCohen Kook, who became the first Ashkenazi chief rabbi of Palestine in 1922, was renowned for deviating from the official Orthodoxy, which held that redemption of Jews and Israel would come only through divine intervention, and not human endeavor, and rejected Zionism as a Jewish version of secular nationalism, an offspring of the eighteenth-century Enlightenment and the 1789 French Revolution. Instead, Abraham Kook offered a synthesis of "the divine concept" and "national sentiment" which, he stressed, could underline the evolving institutions of the Yishuv, the Jewish community in Palestine. His son, Zvi, the leading interpreter of his ideology, argued that secular Zionists, despite their irreligiosity, were the inadvertent bearers of a messianic redemption, and that the State of Israel was an unwitting instrument of divine will. "Zionism will wither away if you cut it from its mystical-messianic roots," said Rabbi Moshe Levinger, a former yeshiva student of Rabbi Zvi Kook. "Zionism is a movement that does not think in rational terms, in terms of power politics, international relations, world opinion, demography, social dynamics, but in terms of divine commandments. What matters only is God's promise to Abraham as recorded in the Book of Genesis."[1]

It was therefore not surprising that Rabbi Zvi Kook's definition of Eretz Israel coincided with the Revisionist Zionists', and included parts of present-day Jordan and Lebanon. A few weeks before the 1967 War, Kook lamented the truncated nature of the State of Israel. "Where is our Hebron?" he asked. "And where are our Shechem [Nablus] and our Jericho? Where are they? Can we ever forsake them? All of Jordan, it is ours. Every single inch, every square foot... belongs to Eretz Israel. Do we have the right to give up even one millimeter?"[2]

Kook attributed Israel's spectacular victory to divine intervention. His followers called 1967 Year One of the Era of Redemption. One of his star students, Moshe Levinger, was among the group of Kook's acolytes who met in the Kfar Etzion settlement in 1974 and established the Gush Emunim. Founded as a Zionist settlement in 1927, Kfar Etzion fell into the hands of the Jordanian army in 1948, and was then retaken by Israel in 1967. The message of the newly formed Gush Emunim was simple: Kfar Etzion was not negotiable, nor was the rest of Judea and Samaria, its names for the West Bank.

Gush activists emulated the tactics that Levinger and his colleagues had successfully deployed in Hebron and Kiryat Arba, to establish Jewish settlements in the West Bank. They combined their colonizing endeavor— centered around a strategy of intermittent confrontation and bargaining with the government— with building up an organizational infrastructure. They opened numerous branches throughout Israel, and infiltrated local parents-teachers' associations and synagogue management committees, in order to gain followers and prospective settlers.

All along the new Jewish colonizers included a substantial body of secular Jews. Prominent among the early settlers was Eliakam Haetzini, one of the Jews who joined Levinger in establishing the first Hebron settlement. Haetzini's parents came to Palestine from Germany in 1938 when he was twelve. He trained as a lawyer, and ran a successful practice before moving to Kiryat Arba. Now his house in Givat Mamre adjoining Kiryat Arba provided a panoramic view of the surroundings and contained an eclectic library. Haetzini is a leader of Tehiya, a secular right-wing party. Formed in October 1979 by Galia Cohen and Moshe Shamir, after they had left Likud to protest the Israeli-Egyptian Peace Treaty of March 1979, which involved uprooting the Jewish colonies in the occupied Sinai, Tehiya wanted Israel to annex the West Bank and Gaza. Its share of Knesset seats in the 1980s varied between three and five. But it failed to win a single seat in 1992.

"I was one of the 20–30 people who rented rooms at Nahar al Khalil [hotel] owned by Fayez Qawasmeh, in Hebron," Haetzini began. "Hebron is a special place for Jews, the place of Abraham and King David. Anyway, after the Passover I returned to my villa in Ramat Gan. After a clash [at the hotel] the Jewish party was allowed to remain at the [nearby] military camp, in caravans. First the government was taken aback. Then the government said in October 1969 that it would build something for the settlers in a suburb near Hebron. Kiryat Arba means four towns, referring to the four hamlets that existed near Hebron in biblical times. The construction of houses began in 1971. I was among the 150 pioneers who took up residence in Kiryat Arba. I rented out my villa in Ramat Gan, and gave up my lucrative legal practice." He turned to his wife, who was hovering in the background. "She was not sure because of the children's education. But they had a truly Zionist education here in body and soul. We are here because this is the heart of the Land of Israel where the Bible really took place: Judea and Samaria, Beit El and Hebron, where our prophets and kings were born and bred; not in Tel Aviv. The coastal plain was on the margin. Historically it was in Philistine hands. King David came from Beit Lehem (Bethlehem), a Hebrew name. Daily more and more Jews are realizing this. That is why today Kiryat Arba has 6,500 Jews, about a third of them non-observant, like me. It started with 400 *dunums* [about 100 acres] in 1971, now it has 4,000 *dunums* [1,000 acres]." His wife brought coffee and cakes.

"Mind you," Haetzini continued, "there have been ups and downs. In the village of Rojeib near Elon Moreh [near Nablus], the government took over private Arab land for security purposes. The Arabs went to the High Court, arguing that this was only a pretext, and that the government will settle civilians. General Chaim Bar Lev gave an affidavit in which he agreed with the Arabs. So the court ruled in favor of them in early 1980. Unlike many others in Kiryat Arba, I was pleased.

I told them that taking over Arab land for security reasons means that once the military leaves, the civilians must leave with it, so says the Hague Convention. But in Kiryat Arba we did not come for military purposes but as part of the process of the return of the Jews. So we are here for good, come what may. Still fifteen of us went on hunger strike for 45 days, and only then did the authorities agree to give us land not taken over for security reasons."

On the whole though, Menachem Begin's goverment supported the Jewish settlers. Indeed, by 1980 the Gush Emunim had established twenty colonies on the West Bank. Begin's Likud government had, in most analysts' view, inherited Labor's "equivocal" policy—the end result of which was that during the decade the Labor-led administrations occupied the West Bank and Gaza, 34 Jewish settlements had sprung up. Less than half were in the Jordan Valley, which the IDF claimed was needed for Israel's military security. While proclaiming that it was holding the Palestinian territories merely as leverage to obtain peace treaties from its Arab neighbors, Labor began colonizing the West Bank.

This had partly to do with domestic politics. Intense rivalry between Defense Minister Moshe Dayan, the hero of the 1967 conflict and Yigal Allon, Deputy prime minister, translated into competition over who was more hawkish on the Occupied Territories. In the tussle that ensued between the Jewish settlers in Hebron and Dayan's IDF, Allon helped the settlers, paving the way for the official establishment of Kiryat Arba following the cabinet's decision in October 1969.

Allon's plan for the Occupied Territories, unveiled the next year, was designed to ensure Israel's security (by making the Jordan Valley its international border) while minimizing the increase in the Arab population within the enlarged Israel. The plan proposed Israel annexing a wide strip of land along the Jordanian border north of Jerusalem, two-thirds of the area of the West Bank south of Jerusalem, and the southern half of the tiny Gaza Strip, and ceding the rest of the Palestinian territory to Jordan, with no role for the Palestinians at all. Not to be outdone, Dayan initiated his own program of colonizing the West Bank.[3] The existence of a national unity government, which included the Gahal/Likud until August 1970, helped the hawkish faction within Labor. Later, since the National Religious Party, committed to annexing the Occupied Territories, was still in the cabinet, it ensured that unauthorized Jewish settlements were treated lightly.

Once Likud became the leading partner in the administration, in which the NRP held important ministerial posts, the pace of colonization accelerated. A small, but highly significant, indicator of the change was Begin's routine use of the term "Eretz Israel", instead of the official "Medinat Israel." The settlement drive really got going after the Israeli-Egyptian peace treaty of March 1979. By neutralizing the Arab world's most populous and powerful state, this treaty removed the threat of war against Israel. The next five years witnessed the most intense construction activity in the West Bank and Gaza. Then there was a slowdown because of the economic crisis and the Lebanon quagmire. But the official commitment to building and expanding settlements remained. Even when Shimon Peres was the prime minister during 1984-6, five new settlements went up. Little wonder that continuing growth in the size of the Jewish settler community showed no sign of decline. In 1977, when Labor lost to Likud, there were 5,000 Jewish settlers in the Occupied Territories; a decade later the figure had reached nearly 60,000. The settlements, administered by elected councils, were grouped in regional councils, which were then brought together under the umbrella of the Council of the Jewish Communities in Judea, Samaria and Gaza.

Meanwhile, Israel's strategy of confiscating Palestinian land and acquiring ownership of water resources in the Occupied Territories continued. The Israeli government and private Jewish bodies possessed only one percent of the land in the West Bank in mid-1967 following Israel's annexation of Greater East Jerusalem. Nearly a quarter of a century later, in the autumn of 1991, the situation was summed up by Yossi Halevi of the *Jerusalem Report* thus: "Of the West Bank's roughly 5 million *dunums* [nearly 2,000 square miles], some 1.5 million *dunums* [600 square miles] are government-owned for either military or civilian use. Ownership of an additional million *dunums* [400 square miles] is being contested between the [Israeli] government and local Arabs, according to Uri Ariel, secretary-general of the Council of the Jewish Communities in Judea, Samaria and Gaza. The rest of the land [50 percent] is privately owned by Arabs."[4]

At that time Israel was ruled by a Likud-dominated right-wing administration headed by Premier Yitzhak Shamir, who was committed to the Jewish settlement of the West Bank and Gaza. As mentioned earlier,[5] he backed the large-scale colonizing plans of his housing minister, Ariel Sharon, unveiled in the summer of 1991, which annoyed the Bush administration. Washington translated its feelings into action by threatening to deny its guarantee of the $10 billion loan the Israeli government wanted to raise in the international financial markets to absorb the large intake of Soviet Jews. The underwriting would have cost US taxpayers $800 million. Shamir, standing by his commitment to settlement, chose to put his loan effort on hold. Colonizing of the West Bank and Gaza went on. While this reassured the ultra-nationalists, the government's failure to secure international loans had a negative impact on the Soviet/Russian immigrants. This was one of the factors that led to the defeat of Likud in 1992.

Meanwhile, the Jewish settler community in the West Bank and Gaza continued to grow. During the Gulf War in early 1991 the settler council claimed that it represented 92,000 settlers. Since public expenditure on the Jewish settlements was undertaken by different ministries— housing and construction, agriculture, energy, education and culture, immigration and absorption, and transport— it was easy for the government to bury the figures in the general budget of each ministry. So no official statistic on the total amount spent on Jewish settlements was available. But, according to Meron Benvenisti, who has maintained a database on the West Bank for many years, the total government expenditure on Jewish settlements during 1967-92 amounted to $5 billion, or about $50,000 per settler. Between 1990 and 1991 the figure jumped from $530 million to $830 million, amounting to 2.8 percent of the national budget.[6] The official settler population statistic for 1993 was 116,400. The signing of the Oslo Accord by Israel and the PLO in September of that year made scant difference to the growth. By agreeing not to challenge the Israeli occupation during the interim agreement, the PLO let Israel continue creating "facts on the ground" in the Occupied Territories. As a result, by early 1995 Israel had confiscated a further 6,778 hectares (about 22 square miles) of Palestinian land, and allotted about six square miles to stone quarries, and close to five square miles for "nature reserves" which, going by the past record, were widely expected to be used for future Jewish settlements.[7] The Jewish construction activity had used up three square miles of Palestinian land.

In the larger political context, Israel's recognition of the PLO as the representative of the Palestinians (who had until then been officially represented by the non-PLO Palestinian delegates within the joint Jordanian-Palestinian delegation to the Madrid peace conference) opened a new chapter in the historical conflict between Zionist Jews and Palestinian Arabs. Since it tilted the existing balance moderately towards the latter, it buoyed the mood of the Palestinians. Conversely it depressed the Jewish settlers in the West Bank and Gaza.

This change manifested itself on the ground, especially in Hebron, a historical flashpoint. Ever since 1967 the settlers have held the right to pray inside the Tomb of the Patriarchs, known as the Ibrahimi (derivative of Abraham) Mosque to the Palestinians. The city's Palestinians had deeply resented the re-establishment of the Jewish enclaves in their midst in 1979-80. And the decision of Rabbi Meir Kahane to take up residence in 1980 at the adjacent Kiryat Arba settlement, already the base of Rabbi Moshe Levinger, heightened tension.

Born Martin David Kahane in 1932 to the family of a rabbi in Brooklyn, New York, Meir Kahane joined the Betar, the youth movement of the Revisionist Zionists, as a teenager. He obtained a law degree from New York University, and was ordained as an Orthodox rabbi. His increasingly militant views led him to establish in the mid-1960s the Jewish Defense League (JDL) which resorted to such violent acts as bombings in the cause of "defending Jews." He coupled this with harassing the Soviet missions in New York to highlight Moscow's ill-treatment of Jews. Declaring that the only way a Jew could escape gentile values was to live in Israel, he migrated there in 1971. After the 1973 War, he became virulently anti-Arab. In 1976 he set up his own political party, Kach, which became known widely by its symbol of a clenched fist. Kahane opposed Jewish social or sexual intercourse with non-Jews, and insisted that only Jews had the right to live in the biblical Land of Israel. He therefore advocated expulsion of Arabs from the West Bank and the Gaza Strip as well as Israel. "Our final aim is to expel all Arabs from the Land of Israel," Kahane said in June 1980. "We want the [Israeli] government to make the Arabs feel as miserable as possible by cutting off social benefits . . . [If that fails] we're calling on the government to organize a Jewish terrorist group that would throw bombs and grenades and kill Arabs."[8] Kahane and his Kach activists did not wait around for official action. They took to beating up Arabs in their homes, smashing cars and shop windows in Arab towns, insulting, harassing and threatening them. Such activities brought Kahane 62 arrests until mid-1980, but only two convictions.

Among his followers was a fellow-resident at Kiryat Arba, Dr. Baruch Goldstein. Born in 1957 in Brooklyn, Goldstein was educated and got a medical degree in New York. In 1983 he migrated to Israel, where he chose to live in Kiryat Arba, and served in the IDF. He became a close colleague of Meir Kahane. Unlike the Jewish settlers elsewhere, who avoided contact with Palestinians, the residents of both Kiryat Arba and the Jewish settlements in Hebron went out of their way to impress their presence on the Arabs of Hebron. As Yisrael Medad, one of the settlers, recalled, "On Sabbath we used to demonstratively stroll in prayer shawls through the Arab market."[9] This was partly to browbeat the local population, and partly to underline the point that the Jews, expelled in 1929, had returned.

In the rising Arab-Jewish tension in the Occupied Territories, starting in spring 1983, Hebron again emerged as a hot spot.[10] In March 1983 Palestinian assailants fatally stabbed a Jewish yeshiva student in downtown Hebron. In retaliation half a dozen Jewish settlers from Kiryat Arba killed four students of Hebron Islamic College. A climax came in April 1984 with the arrest of Jewish extremists who had plotted to blow up the Dome of the Rock in Jerusalem. It was against this background that Kahane was elected to the Knesset on the Kach ticket in July 1984. His supporters included Goldstein and Yona Khaykin, an American Jewish settler living in Hebron's Jewish Quarter. "We came to Hebron out of a sense of adventure and outrage," said Khaykin. "The adventure is building a Jewish kingdom. The outrage is that Arabs are still here."[11]

His Knesset seat gave new respectability to Kahane and his ideology. Israel's fiasco in Lebanon following its 1982 invasion, and the economic crisis of the mid-1980s, created despair, especially among young Israelis, which Kahane channeled into his anti-Arab campaign. A poll of young Jews aged 15–18, taken in April 1985, showed 42 percent backing the idea of expelling Arabs from Israel, the West Bank and Gaza. A survey of Israeli voters in October revealed 9 percent support for Kahane, an eight-fold increase in a year—enough to give his Kach group eleven seats in the Knesset.[12] This worried the major parties in the national unity administration. At their behest the Knesset passed a law barring a political party preaching racism from running for election. On the eve of the November 1988 parliamentary poll, the government ruled that Kach was racist and could not participate in the forthcoming election. When Kahane challenged this in the Supreme Court, he lost. Had Kach been allowed to enter the race, it would have won six Knesset seats. In October 1990 Kahane was assassinated in New York.[13]

Among those shattered by this news was Baruch Goldstein. He now joined the Kahane Chai (Kahane Lives) group, headed by the deceased leader's son, Baruch Kahane. Goldstein was elected to the local council of Kiryat Arba on the Kahane Chai ticket, the only candidate of its kind. But such was the popularity of Kahane's ideas in Kiryat Arba that, to the delight of Goldstein, the local council decided to name the settlement's principal square after him. A memorial tablet read: "In memory of Rabbi Meir Kahane, a lover of Israel, a giant in Torah, heroic in deeds, murdered in sanctification of the Divine Name."

As a doctor and a local councilor, Goldstein was popular among Kiryat Arba residents, many of whom worked in Jerusalem, and traveled by bus. After dark the drive along a partly narrow, winding road, flanked by terraced hills, running through Palestinian villages, towns and refugee camps, was hazardous. The easily identifiable Israeli buses were targets of Palestinian attacks by rocks and gasoline bombs, an activity which escalated during the intifada.[14] Those Kiryat Arbans injured in these instances of violence were treated by Goldstein.

Like other Jewish settlements, Kiryat Arba was strongly opposed to the Israel-PLO Accord of September 1993. It saw this as a betrayal of the concept of "redeeming" the land of all of biblical Israel. On the other side, radical Palestinians perceived the agreement as a betrayal of the historic rights of the Palestinian people to all of Palestine under British mandate, and vowed to continue the intifada. Tension escalated.

The pattern of the past repeated itself. A typical example was the fatal stabbing of Chaim Mizrahi, a resident of the Beit El Jewish settlement by a Palestinian in late October 1993. Its chief rabbi, Zalman Melamed, invoked the doctrine of *pikuach nefesh*, or preservation of soul, which states that saving (Jewish) life overrides all aspects of the Halacha, Jewish law. (This doctrine is open to different interpretations, depending on whether a religious authority decides to interpret all human life or narrows it to Jewish life.) The Beit El residents took the cue and went on a rampage, smashing the cars of Palestinians living near the settlement, hoping thus to deter future attacks on Jews. And so it went: a stray armed assault on a vulnerable individual Jew by young Palestinians; then a communal response by the Jews, who damaged Palestinian cars and property, overturned vegetable and fruit stalls in Arab markets, and blocked major West Bank roads with burning tires; and an escalation by Palestinians in the form of hurling rocks and gasoline bombs at Jewish buses and cars.

Sometimes the pattern varied. In mid-December 1993 Jewish settlers killed three Palestinians returning home from work outside the village of Tarqumiya near Hebron. A month later a group of Palestinians engaged in a gunbattle with IDF soldiers in Hebron, and lost four men. Tension rose as the Muslim fasting month of Ramadan started on February 11. Two days later a group of Hamas activists, posing as Israeli collaborators, lured a Shin Beth agent to a rendezvous in Ramallah, and killed him. To most Kiryat Arbans, including Goldstein, this was a new and menacing development. They were not reassured when on February 16 IDF soldiers shot dead a wanted Palestinian radical in the village of Halhoul near Hebron—an event that triggered serious Palestinian rioting in the village.

Midway through Ramadan, on February 25, was Purim, a Jewish festival that celebrates the Israelites' victory over the Amaleks, a Syrian tribe whose destruction was enjoined by the Old Testament. On the eve of Purim, Goldstein went to Hebron's Tomb of the Patriarchs/Ibrahimi Mosque to hear the Purim story that Haman, the Persian King Ahaseurs' prime minister, who wanted to annihilate the Jews, was a descendant of an Amalek king. As a follower of Kahane, he believed that the Amaleks were not just a specific ancient tribe, but an ongoing anti-Jewish entity which perpetuated itself in different forms in different generations. Having appeared as Nazis in Germany before 1945, the Amaleks had taken on the form of the Arabs, especially Palestinian Arabs. It was a religious duty of pious Jews to confront and annihilate present-day Amaleks, Kahane had stressed, thus destroying evil, and paving the way for the coming of the Messiah.

Early the next morning at about 5 A.M., on Purim, Goldstein returned to the Tomb of the Patriarchs/Ibrahimi Mosque clad in his reserve-duty army uniform, which now concealed his Galil assault rifle and several rounds of ammunition.

To the soldiers on duty he was a familiar figure, and they let him pass without search. Inside, hundreds of Muslim Palestinians were offering their dawn Ramadan prayer. Goldstein walked into the prayer hall, and standing behind a pillar fired 111 bullets from his assault rifle. 29 people died and another 67 were injured. He was beaten to death by the outraged Palestinians.

The massacre sent shock waves at home and abroad. The PLO suspended its talks with Israel on the implementation of the Declaration of Principles it had signed five months earlier. The Israeli government of Yitzhak Rabin, deeply embarrassed, was quick to condemn the killings. President Ezer Weizman called the Hebron slaughter "the worst thing that has happened in the history of Zionism." Numerous private and official Israeli and Jewish organizations expressed sorrow, and denounced the slaughter and its perpetrator. Many of the condemnations, however, apportioned equal blame to Goldstein and the Israeli authorities which, they said, had abandoned the Jewish settlers.

A similar division existed among the residents of Kiryat Arba. Several of them, acolytes of Kahane, publicly argued that the people Goldstein killed were not innocent men at prayer in a place of worship, but modern day Amaleks, the followers of Adolf Hitler and Yasser Arafat; and by avenging the Amaleks, he had sanctified God's name, *Kiddush Hashem* a central mission of the Jews.[15] Among those who adopted this stand were the leaders of Kahane Chai and other banned ultra-nationalist groups who, having gone underground, gave interviews to radio stations in Israel from undisclosed locations. The central thrust of the mainstream Israeli press commentary condemned the Hebron massacre as the crazed work of a psychopath rather than a politically motivated outrage.

Admiration for Goldstein did not cease with public eulogies at his funeral which, despite heavy rain, was attended by more than 1,000 Kiryat Arbans. The secular elementary school's management instructed teachers to limit remarks about the Hebron massacre to Goldstein's "saintly nature" and his self-sacrificing devotion to his medical practice. At Hebron's Talmud Torah elementary school, children were regularly bussed to Goldstein's grave to recite Psalms in his memory. A local poll revealed that 63 percent of Kiryat Arbans wanted the government to recognize Goldstein's widow, Miriam, as a "war widow," since he was killed by Arabs.[16]

In contrast, my Hebrew interpreter, Rafi, felt too embarrassed to translate the inscription engraved on Goldstein's grave, and needed persuading to do so:

> Here is buried
> The Saint Dr. Rabbi Baruch Kapal Goldstein
> May the Lord avenge his death
> He is the son of Rabbi Israel
> Who is still alive
> (May he live long)
> He is the seventh generation of
> Rabbi Shneor Zalman Goldstein
> He gave his life for the sake of
> The People of Israel, their Torah and Community
> His hands were clean
> And his heart pure

He was born on 5 Teveth 1947 [5707 AM] (TafshenYad Zion)
He was murdered for sanctification of the Lord on 14 Adar 1994
[5754 AM]

A young couple, speaking Russian, arrived. The man, wearing a skullcap, placed a small stone on the grave and kissed it. Five months earlier an unknown admirer of Goldstein had left a leaflet behind, declaring, "According to the Halacha, Yitzhak Rabin deserved the death penalty for treason." This was soon after the authorities had arrested about a dozen Kiryat Arbans, including Lt. Oren Edri and Rabbi Ido Alba, on suspicion of forming a terrorist group to kill Arabs for attacking Jews. Citing the Gemara, Jewish oral law, Rabbi Ido Alba said in an interview with the *Jerusalem Post* on January 18, 1995: "[I]t decrees that one must wage war against gentiles who attack Jews, or who even try to harm the Jewish community. My only 'crime' is that I believe that one must carry out what is written . . . According to the Torah, we are in a situation of *pikuach nefesh* in time of war, and in such a situation one may kill any gentile. According to the Halacha, there is no such thing as innocent. No gentile on the side that is at war against us is innocent."

After these arrests signs appeared in the settlement naming suspected informers of the Shin Beth. Planting informers in Kiryat Arba was comparatively easy. Unlike at other Jewish settlements, the local council there did not screen its prospective residents. This had to do with the biblical tradition, which maintained that Hebron was a "town of refuge," where even a Jewish murderer, pursued by the avenging family of the victim, could take sanctuary. As it was, Kiryat Arba's current residents included Menachem Livni, the mastermind behind the 1984 plan to blow up the Dome of the Rock.[17] Following a presidential pardon after he had served only seven years of a life sentence for murder, Livni was now head of the settlement's "science think-tank."

Rafi and I had arrived at Goldstein's grave after meeting Naom Arnon at Kiryat Arba's public relations office. The ante-room of Arnon's office had a black and white print of Rabbi Avraham Yitzhak HaCohen Kook. In the lobby a Jewish history of Hebron was on display on a wall. "Genesis 23 has all the [historical] details," Arnon told us in his modest office. "According to Judges 3, twelve spies were sent by Moses to Canaan to evaluate the Promised Land. Ten of them said 'We don't have the power to occupy the Promised Land.' But Kaleb and Joshua disagreed. They encouraged the Israelites to conquer the Promised Land, and succeeded. See how history repeats itself." Arnon paused. "One of the pictures on the wall you saw explains that Aviner, a general of King Saul, was buried in Hebron. King David had his capital in Hebron for seven and a half years before moving it to Jerusalem."

Walking around Kiryat Arba, I felt I was in one of the posher Jewish suburbs of Greater East Jerusalem: street after street of four-story apartment blocks of cream-colored stone, interspersed with playgrounds and grassy slopes. Among other things I now understood how and why the Jewish settlers, as only five percent of the overall population of the West Bank and Gaza, were consuming 40 percent of the water.[18]

Visiting Kiryat Arba, established during the Labor rule, complemented my earlier trip to Elon Moreh settlement, which too had been established when Labor was in power. Here Rafi and I had placed ourselves into the hands of Pinchas Fuchs.

Fuchs was a small man of 53 with a luxuriant white beard. A leading member of the Elon Moreh settlement, home to 1,500 people from a score of countries, he took foreign visitors around the settlement. Over time, he had perfected a system of conducting a tour as thorough as it was economical in time and effort. Fuchs held a Ph.D. in chemical engineering from the City University of New York, and worked from home for a computer firm. An urban man to his fingertips, born and raised in New Jersey and New York, how did Fuchs and his family end up on top of a desolate mountain near Nablus in the West Bank?

In 1976 he and his family joined some 5,000 other American Jews who moved to Israel that year. He started working as a chemical engineer in Rehovot, near Tel Aviv. He and his family would have continued to live in Rehovot, a pleasant place reminiscent of small-town America, had he not visited an old friend, Avi Yoram, at the army camp of Kadume near Nablus. Yoram was one of the pioneers who had struggled to set up a Jewish settlement near Nablus—Shechem of biblical times—after Israel's West Bank victory in 1967. After repeated attempts, the Labor government allowed the agitators to live in caravans inside Kadume army compound. In early 1977 it permitted them to establish a settlement at Elon Moreh. The inside story of Labor's shift revealed Peres helping the Gush Emunim agitators, overtly and covertly, in order to undermine Rabin, who had earlier defeated him in a leadership contest. This was a re-run of the bitter rivalry a decade earlier between Yigal Allon and Moshe Dayan, which had shaped the decision to establish the Hebron and Kiryat Arba settlements. The net losers in both cases were the Palestinians.

A few months later, Labor lost the parliamentary elections to Begin's right-wing Likud, setting the seal on Elon Moreh. And early the next year Begin gave permission for another Jewish settlement in the area, near the Palestinian village of Rojeib, about three miles from Nablus. Fuchs joined fourteen other Jews and their families to resettle the Promised Land at Rojeib. Instead of pitching tents they parked trailers on the site. The Palestinians protested. They appealed to the High Court—and won. The court ruled against the state confiscation of the Palestinian land, arguing that the government had failed to establish the security ground for its action. (Had it confiscated land on the basis of "public purpose," instead of "security purpose," it would have probably won.) "So the IDF threw me out of my own house in Israel!" said Fuchs, still scandalized.

Having lost the new site in early 1980, the trailer-owning families moved to the much larger Elon Moreh. Three years later there were buildings ready for occupation. Thus solidified, Elon Moreh expanded steadily, and today is a well-run community, with an impressive infrastructure: schools, local authority offices, regional council offices, an infirmary, three synagogues and well-stocked shops. It is home to a spice mill and a meat processing plant which provide livelihoods to a high proportion of the settlers.

Unusual among the Jewish settlements on the West Bank and Gaza Strip, Elon Moreh has no perimeter fence. "If we put up a fence then the Arabs will plant olive trees two inches from it, even though olive trees are not native to this area," Fuchs explained. "Moreover, once you erect a fence you define the boundaries, like a prison. All of Eretz Israel is ours."

But a barrier at the entrance was a dramatic reminder of the settlers' concern for security. "At night a spotlight is focused on the valley," said Fuchs. "There is a beltway around the settlement, and it's patrolled by an army Jeep with a soldier sitting in the open-ended back, with his machine gun pointed outwards. There is an army post, with walkie-talkies, in constant contact with the defense ministry in Tel Aviv."

Security, local and national, was very much on the mind of Fuchs. He pointed to the Mount Ebal summit, the highest in the northern West Bank. "See the antenna?" he asked. "It picks up as soon as a Jordanian aircraft takes off in Jordan. The flight time between Amman and Tel Aviv is 2.5 minutes, exactly. Without that antenna there'd be no warning to the IDF. None whatsoever... You can see into the Jordan Valley, also Mount Hermon, though they're shrouded in fog this morning." I looked, and saw an Israeli army base in the valley.

Having finished his geography lesson Fuchs turned to history. "After crossing the Jordan Valley our patriarchs would take this road to Shechem, the main artery connecting it with Jerusalem and Hebron," he said confidently. "Abraham had taken the same road [pause] probably. Jacob took the same road. And several centuries later Joshua trod the same road to return to the Promised Land." Later, in the cozy kitchen of his two-story home, he could not read a passage from the Old Testament without relating it to the present. While reading Genesis 23:15—"And Abraham weighed to Ephron... 400 shekels of silver" [to pay for the Machpela cave to bury Sarah] he looked at me, and said: "See, Abraham paid for the land, it says here in black and white. Can the Arabs today show that they paid for the land they claim to be theirs? Can they?"

The Jewish settlement in Beit El, only about twelve miles from central Jerusalem, established near the twin Palestinian towns of Ramallah and El Bireh, was founded the same year Fuchs joined the settlers' movement: 1978. But, a strictly religious settlement, it took only Orthodox Jews often affiliated with the National Religious Party. The initial population of 30 families had mushroomed to 600, a total of 4,000 people. Since Beit El is considered by the Israeli government as part of the Jewish belt designed to surround Jerusalem, it belongs to a different official category than Kiryat Arba and Elon Moreh.

Here our guide was Zeev Libinskin. At 40, he sported a dense, black beard, and like Rabbi Moshe Levinger and Rabbi Shlomo Aviner, a resident of Beit El and the head of the Yeshiva Torah Chaim in the Muslim Quarter of Jerusalem's Old City, was a graduate of the Merkaz HaRav Kook Yeshiva. "Its policy is to encourage its students to spread out in Judea and Samaria, and set up settlements there," Libinskin told us.

The Rabin administration came in for criticism from Libinskin. "This government says that our presence here is an impediment to peace," Libinskin averred in his monotonous voice. "We say that only our presence here can ensure peace." He halted in an area full of finished houses. "There are 40 newly built empty houses here," he began. "The government does not want us to sell these. But we are putting pressure, and it is likely to bend."

Libinskin's optimism was well founded. The Labor-led administration was equivocal on the Jewish settlements. Four months after Rabin's cabinet assumed office in July 1992, it declared a halt to all publicly funded construction in the West Bank and Gaza, thus removing the hurdle holding up the US administration's guarantee of Israel's $10 billion loan. But it allowed privately financed construction in the Occupied Territories, requiring only approval from a Special Cases Committee whose chairman was well known for pro-settlement views. And the official policy of allowing the "thickening" of settlements along the Green Line continued.

"Special case permits" were issued liberally. And the hawkish Housing Minister, Binyamin Ben Eliezer, was only too willing to provide the infrastructure of roads, electricity, water and sewerage facilities. "Even where [Jewish] settlers broke into completed houses that the government had deliberately left unsold, Ben Eliezer has supplied the infrastructure," revealed Leslie Susser, an Israeli journalist, in early 1995. "Despite the 'freeze,' enough houses have been built for the Jewish population in the territories to grow by more than ten percent to over 140,000 (a figure based on households paying municipal taxes)—since the September 1993 signing of the Declaration of Principles with the Palestinians."[19]

A survey undertaken by the *Jerusalem Report* in February 1995 revealed that ongoing Jewish settlement activity was in progress almost everywhere in the West Bank, particularly near Jerusalem, in the Kfar Etzion bloc near Bethlehem, and north-east of Tel Aviv. Outside of these areas, construction was either in progress or in the offing at fourteen other settlements. House prices in the settlements near Jerusalem and Greater Tel Aviv had risen by 40 percent over the previous six months.[20]

These developments reflected Rabin's both short-term (tied to the September 1993 Accord with the PLO) and long-term aims (to be secured through the final status agreement with the PLO). Rabin was still wedded to the 1970 Allon Plan: to treat the Jordan Valley as the security perimeter of Israel and to gain control of as much of the land and water of the West Bank as possible while avoiding the thankless task of administering hostile West Bankers and Gazans. Since then, Israel has obtained control of most of the West Bank's land and water. It has implanted some however, 170,000 Jews in the territory, plus another 180,000 in Greater East Jerusalem. Having conceded the principle of self-rule for Palestinians, to be administered by the PLO, Rabin seemingly realized the potential of using the 128 Jewish settlements in the West Bank for two distinct purposes: 1) ensuring Israel's security along the Allon lines, and 2) a rationale to annex parts of the West Bank adjoining Israel.

Ministerial studies had concluded that fourteen Jewish settlements in the Jordan Valley and another group of two dozen around Jerusalem, including the Kfar Etzion bloc, would be enough to underwrite the security of the Jewish state and its capital. As for 2), a study by an Israeli think-tank had concluded that by annexing about one-tenth of the West Bank along the Green Line, Israel could reclaim some 70 percent of its Jewish citizens now settled in the Palestinian territory. To align plans 1) and 2), the Jordan Valley's Jewish settlements would have to have a status midway between being an integral part of Israel and an integral part of the Palestinian entity.

For the period of the interim agreement, which ends in May 1999, Rabin decided against moving any settlers. Despite repeated calls from various quarters to remove the 400-odd Jewish settlers from downtown Hebron in the wake of the Ibrahimi Mosque massacre in early 1994, he stuck to his position. Indeed he went on to combine increased Israeli military presence in the West Bank with an accelerated program of road building to interconnect the Jewish settlements into integrated blocs, and to provide them with roads bypassing Palestinian population areas. The official purpose was to prevent scattered Jewish communities from turning into besieged outposts. But clearly the roads would have military value as well. Rabin continued quietly issuing "special permits" to private companies to construct more houses in the settlements, and entitling many settlers to tax concessions.

At the same time, the Israeli government managed to divide hundreds of Palestinian enclaves, making the prospect of a viable Palestinian state in the future a virtual impossibility.

But Labor and Meretz supporters argued that the PLO's only alternative would be worse—to negotiate with a future Likud-led administration. Likud's interpretation of UN Resolution 242, the foundation of the 1991 Middle East peace conference, was that, having given up the Sinai, 88 percent of the Arab territories conquered in 1967, Israel need not withdraw from the rest. Summarized by Ariel Sharon, Likud hawks said: "Peace for peace; Israel should not offer Arabs more than what they are offering Israel—an end to hostilities."

After the May 1996 elections, the new Likud government tried hard to replace Labor's "territory for peace" call with Likud's "peace for peace."

This signaled a firm setback for the Palestinians and their territorial aspirations.

9

The West Bank

A Diminishing Heritage of Palestinians

It is rare to find an individual whose life roughly mirrors the chronicle of his/her country. But I was lucky. I found Badran Bader Jaber in Hebron.

I met him in February 1995 at the University Graduates Association building. Two contrasting images dominated the hall: a large painting in black with touches of red, portraying the massacre at the Ibrahimi Mosque/Tomb of the Patriarchs a year earlier, and another, a pleasing pastoral scene in green and golden yellow. Badran Jaber arrived, carrying a walking stick curled at the top. A veteran of a score of hunger strikes in jail, he looked older than his 47 years. He had spent ten in prison, and another four under "town arrest," his current status.

"I was born in Hebron, and am a graduate of Jordan University, Amman, 1969," Jaber began. "That year my elder brother, Fathi, was arrested by the Israelis, and sentenced to 25 years in jail. But he was released in 1985 in a prisoner exchange. In between, I was jailed four times."

"My first arrest came in 1972," Jaber continued. "I spent four months under interrogation. Then I served six months under administrative detention. This is the measure introduced by the British mandate during emergency. You are detained for up to six months at a time without any charges being pressed against you. I was released in 1973."

1973: In August the Palestine National Front (PNF), consisting of Palestinians of all political hues was formed clandestinely as an autonomous West Bank and Gaza affiliate of the banned PLO. Between the 1973 War and April 1976, the PNF staged demonstrations and strikes, which paralyzed the Occupied Territories periodically. The Israeli government responded with army fire (which took a toll of 30 Palestinian lives in the first half of 1976), long curfews, arrests and administrative detentions, deportations and house demolitions.

"My next arrest came in 1975," Jaber went on. "One day, returning home from my country cottage, I saw some *fedayeen* (commandos) outside Hebron. They arrested me because they said that I did not report the presence of *fedayeen* to the IDF. I served three and a half years behind bars."

1976: prime minister Rabin called elections in 24 West Bank municipalities, expecting that the PNF would boycott the election, thus enabling "co-operating Palestinians" to assume local power. But the PNF contested the election, and won 18 of the 24 municipalities, including almost all major towns and cities.

1978: Following the signing in September of the Israel-Egypt Camp David Accords, which included limited autonomy provisions for the Palestinians, nationalist West Bankers publicly formed the National Guidance Committee. It was headed by 22 local mayors and leaders of trade unions and professional syndicates. Among other things it resisted the Israeli-sponsored Palestinian armed militia, called Village Councils. The military regime reacted with draconian press censorship, widespread arrests and deportations.

"I was hardly out for two years when I was picked up again by the IDF in 1980," Jaber said. "The interrogation in prison went on for three months."

1980: By then the Israeli military regime had dissolved most of the PNF-controlled local councils. In May 1980 it deported the mayors of Hebron (Fahd Qawasmeh) and nearby Halhoul (Muhammad Milhem) as punishment for a Palestinian terrorist attack in Hebron, which had resulted in six Jewish deaths. Early the next month bomb attacks by Jewish terrorists on the mayors of Nablus and Ramallah, Bassam Shakaa and Karim Khalaf, maimed them.

1981: On November 8, 1981 the Likud government set up the Civil Administration in Judea and Samaria, whose head was appointed by the Area Military Commander. The first head was Menachem Milson, professor of Arabic literature at Hebrew University. West Bankers responded with strikes and demonstrations, quelled by the IDF. In spring 1982 protest revived, led by schools and universities. The Israeli government again responded with gunfire, large scale arrests and beatings, and house demolitions. In May 1982 it banned the National Guidance Committee. The Occupied Territories were quiescent when Israel invaded Lebanon in June—a change from the norm established in previous years. During 1977-82 Palestinians mounted 500 protests annually. The total fatalities caused by the inter-communal conflict during 1968-83 were 92 Palestinians and 36 Israelis, 22 of them soldiers.[1]

"My next imprisonment started in May 1985," Jaber went on. "I was accused of working as a member of a political organization. They said that someone told them that I had a leaflet by the Popular Front for the Liberation of Palestine, and that I gave it to a man in 1980. And they arrested me in 1985![2] I spent time in Ramallah and Hebron jails, and in Jneid near Nablus. In Jneid we went on hunger strike for 23 days to get back our rights. After the Minister of Police had a meeting with us in jail, they granted us all our rights in 1987, even our copy books. But they refused to let us transfer anything to the outside. For security reasons. I had made a copy book out of a dictionary of English to French and made it into an Arabic-French dictionary. I spent about 12 months working on it 14 hours a day. They confiscated it. More than once I have dreamed that I had it and that I took it to my colleagues at the school where I teach [sociology and geography] and said to them, 'This is what I did in jail.'"

1984–7: As the Israeli government found itself unable to extricate itself from the quagmire of Lebanon, Palestinians stepped up their protest. From late 1984 on there were random assaults on IDF soldiers and Jewish settlers. Israeli mobs took to lynching individual Palestinians. In early August 1985 Defense Minister Yitzhak Rabin officially unveiled an "iron fist" policy. The result was widespread arrests and administrative detentions, frequent closure of schools and universities, and demolition of the houses of Palestinian suspects. In response West Bankers and Gazans mounted large demonstrations in the winter of 1986–7 and the following spring. During 1982-6, the number of annual protests varied between 3,000 and 4,400, a manifold increase over the 500 or so annually 1977–82.[3] The intifada began in December 1987.

"I was arrested again in February 1988, the same administrative detention exercise," said Jaber wearily. "I was sent to the Ansar III detention camp south of Beersheba, because all the jails in the West Bank and Israel were full.[4] There were tents everywhere at the Ansar III. We were in a military security zone, near a base. You could hear planes landing and taking off. There were some 5,000 prisoners and detainees. They elected me their leader. When Rabin visited Ansar III they told him about me. So when my maximum six month period [of adminstrative detention] expired, they immediately slapped another one on me. This thing went on until November 1990."

1988-90: This was the most virulent period of the intifada.[5]

"Since November 1990 I have been carrying this green ID instead of the normal orange ID," Jaber concluded, flashing his card. "I can't leave Hebron. And this entitles an Israeli policeman or soldier to interrogate me and detain me for up to 96 hours without charge."

I returned to Hebron about a month later, and interviewed Badran Jaber specifically to get his version of how the Jewish settlement in and around Hebron had come into existence. He drew a sketch on a piece of paper and made a key. Here is his account (see map on p *x*):

A: "During the 1967 Six Day War, on June 9, the IDF entered the Ibrahimi Mosque using armed force," Jaber began. "In early 1968 they set up an IDF base east of Hebron, for army purposes and maneuvers. They closed the area of the Wadi (Valley) al Hussein. Moshe Dayan came here, and called the local leaders. He told them that the area would be closed, not confiscated, for military purposes... We tried to return to our lands and farms, but were barred.

B: "After the Battle of Karameh in Jordan[6] there was danger of the *fedayeen* striking in the West Bank. In April 1968 there was an incident at Fayaz Qawasmeh's hotel with the Jewish settlers. That is why the IDF moved the settlers from his hotel to the military base. The IDF had two pre-fabricated buildings for the settlers. It was the IDF's solution for Qawasmeh's hotel incident. Later three *dunums* [three-quarters of an acre] of our family land was confiscated. They did it for establishing Kiryat Arba. In mid-1969 Moshe Dayan had a meeting with the local leaders. He told them: 'This is the city of our patriarchs. We are sons of Abraham, we have a place inside Hebron and near the tombs of the Patriarchs.' Later the IDF moved the settlers from its base and took them to Kiryat Arba, which carried the sign: 'Here will be built soon a big settlement.' We tried to protest. But it was no use.[7] In 1970 they confiscated the industrial area, and joined it with Kiryat Arba. 400 *dunums* [100 acres]. They closed off a new area east of Kiryat Arba. The [1970] Black September events depressed the general Palestinian mood.[8]

C: "In 1970-71 the Israelis began using the IDF field for military training. They took over 1,000 *dunums* [250 acres]. They bulldozed trees, fences, summer cottages, everything, including my summer cottage, for military purposes. In 1971 they began to build sections A and B of this sketch—houses for settlers. In 1972 came the infrastructure: water, electricity, sewerage, streets, shops, clinics, police station, schools, kindergarten, telephones etc. There was much protest by Hebron people, but it was unsuccessful. The Black September events had so destroyed our morale that the Palestinian activists could not guide the people forcefully.

D: "In 1971–2 they confiscated the highest hill in the Hebron sector, Jalas Mountain, for a transmission tower. The area belonged to my relative, Abdul Hamid Jaber [then aged over 80], who owned more than 300 *dunums* [75 acres]. He was approached by the IDF, but he refused even to rent the plot... Of the cultivated land confiscated by the IDF were 17 *dunums* [four acres] belonging to the family of my wife Hamida.

E: "Within four years, by 1976 [under Labor rule], they completed the infrastructure, and brought in about 2,500 people. In 1977-8 [under Likud] the Israelis took over more than 3,000 *dunums* [741 acres] north-west of Kiryat Arba. They called the settlement Givat HaSinai after the Sinai which Israel evacuated following the Egyptian-Israeli Peace Treaty. In 1982 they brought many settlers from Yamit settlement in Sinai after it had been dismantled.

F: "In late 1983 the Israelis took over 3000 *dunums* [741 acres] at Tsagrat al Abid. The IDF confiscated the area between Hebron and Saeer village, which is 11 kilometers [about seven miles] from the center of Hebron. The IDF had confiscated uncultivated land and not bothered to even inform the owners. They call it 'Closed Military Area.'

"By now the Kiryat Arba complex plus Givat HaSinai plus the closed IDF areas totaled 14,000 *dunums* [3,460 acres]. In 1968 the total had been 1,400 *dunums* [356 acres]. Israelis start with a small stone and build it up into a mountain.

"But there is no end. On March 9 [1995] the IDF confiscated 700 *dunums* [153 acres] of agricultural land in Wadi al Ghurous and Wadi al Hussein along with the vineyards opposite Tel Avot, to expand Tel Avot, a settlement with red-tiled houses you can see from Hebron."

"So far 65 percent of the cultivated land of the Palestinians in the area has been confiscated by the IDF," said Jaber, summing up. "The trees in these lands include olives, grapes, figs, almonds, apricots, pistachios. It was like a part of heaven, with different colors of the trees blossoming. When I was in my early teens [under the Jordanians], I'd steal ripe fruit at night. Those were the days of my boyhood!

There was a swimming pool. There was a natural spring. We would play and swim. Girls would pass and we would whistle. Those were the days!"[9] For the first time a smile flickered past his face.

Suddenly, what Rafi and I had seen on our trek from Eliakam Haetzini's house in Givat Mamre to Kiryat Arba proper, became comprehensible. We went past a paratrooper base, consisting of some 30 large khaki tents. On the opposite side of the main road, behind a stone embankment, were old Arab houses. As we plodded uphill along a curve, we went past a vineyard. I saw an Arab working the soil with a donkey-driven plough. The original Kiryat Arba settlement had expanded so much from its initial modest beginning, I realized, that it had now circumscribed Palestinian houses and fields. This also explained why the sprawling Kiryat Arba and its suburbs were not fenced all around. The fencing was unbroken where the settlement faced Hebron, but disappeared from its ever-expanding rear.

This intersection of the Muslim Arab and the Jew reaches its apotheosis at the Tomb of the Patriarchs/Ibrahimi Mosque in downtown Hebron, a derivative either of the Hebrew root *hbr*, meaning friend, or the Arabic word *haber*, meaning granary. The first seems more apt: Muslim Arabs call the town Al Khalil al Rahman, The (Beloved) Friend of (God) the Merciful, or Al Khalil for short, a reference to the prophet Abraham/Ibrahim, whom the Prophet Muhammad called the First Muslim, since he was the first to preach monotheism. The Tomb of the Patriarchs, containing the graves of Abraham/Ibrahim and Sarah, Isaac/Yitzhak/Ishaq and Rebecca, and Jacob/Yaacov (later called Israel) and Leah, is the second holiest site of the Jews, after the Western Wall. The site, known officially among Muslims as Al Haram al Khalil, the Sanctuary of the Friend, and popularly as the Ibrahimi Mosque, is the fourth holiest shrine in orthodox Islam, after Mecca, the birthplace of Prophet Muhammad; Medina, the deathplace of Muhammad; and Jerusalem, the site of the Al Aqsa Mosque. Muslim tradition has it that Prophet Muhammad visited the Al Haram al Khalil on his night flight from Mecca to Jerusalem.

Situated at the entrance to the fertile northern highlands from the arid southern region, Hebron was a strategic settlement, and a thriving town, when Abraham's wife Sarah died there in about 1800 BC. Genesis 23:7–14 describes Abraham's purchase of the Cave of Machpela to bury Sarah.

Around 1250 BC, Moses led the Israelites from Sinai to the Hebron region. His successor, Joshua, conquered Hebron and other Canaanite areas in c. 1200 BC. His capture and destruction of Hebron is described in Joshua 10:36–7. But Hebron revived. After King Saul, David chose Hebron as the capital of Judah, and was anointed there as king of all of Israel. He moved his capital to Jerusalem in about 1002 BC. The first Hasmonean king John Hyrcanus captured Hebron in 134 BC. Written references to the burial places dating back to about 200 BC, suggest that by the time King Hyrcanus arrived in Hebron, there was a structure built around them. To protect them properly, Roman King Herod the Great constructed a rectangular perimeter of sturdy stone walls, which remains intact. Over the centuries Byzantine, Crusader and Mameluke structures were built to create the complex that still exists today.

The site appears at first glance to be a massive fortress, especially because of the heavy presence of armed Israeli soldiers. The waxing and waning powers of Jews, Christians and Muslims have left their marks on this oldest revered site of monotheism. Following the failed Jewish revolt, the city was destroyed in AD 70, and Jews were banished. But as before Hebron came to life again and thrived. The Byzantinian basilica with four rows of columns was completed in AD 570. After Hebron fell to Caliph Omar ibn al-Khattab in AD 637 he converted the church into a mosque. He allowed the Jews not only to return but also to build a small synagogue within the Herodian precinct.

After expelling the Jews from Hebron, the Crusaders converted the mosque and adjoining synagogue into a church and a monastery. Written records show that the monks found a circular chamber containing bones, believed to be those of Abraham and Isaac, and another chamber holding the bones of Jacob along with fifteen jars containing the bones of his sons.

In 1187 Saladin captured Hebron. In 1191 he furnished the Great Mosque with a magnificent wooden pulpit. He allowed the Jews to return to Hebron. During the Mameluke period (1250-1517) the monument became an exclusively Muslim shrine. In 1267 Mameluke Sultan Baybar banned entry of non-Muslims into the Cave of Machpela. However, he let Jews pray through a window in the wall erected at the entrance of the cavern. In 1318 the Mameluke sultan built the adjoining Jawliye Mosque. He also added a small mosque containing, according to Muslims, the cenotaph of Joseph, and another small mosque for women in the south-eastern corner of the complex. In a corner is a shrine that holds a stone bearing a footprint, which, according to Muslim tradition, is one Adam left on his way to the garden of Eden. In the 1330s aboveground cenotaphs of marble were constructed over the ones that lay subterraneanly. Once the aboveground cenotaphs were ready and decorated with embroidered shrouds, the Mameluke sultan sealed the passage leading to the subterranean chambers. He then permitted the Jews to go no higher than the seventh step of the outer staircase and pray there. Following the expulsion of the Jews from Spain in 1492, some came, via Turkey, to live in Hebron, then part of the Ottoman empire. The number of resident Jews increased steadily. At the beginning of the British mandate in 1922, they were about 800 strong in a town of 50,000 people, rising to 900 at the time of the 1929 Arab-Jewish riots, which led to their exodus. Those few who returned in 1931 finally left in 1937 when violence recurred. Three decades later the Israeli military took charge of the Tomb of the Patriarchs/Haram al Khalil, which had been under the management of the *waqfs* (religious trusts) department of the Jordanian government since 1948. The IDF implemented the Jewish demand to pray inside the precincts.

Gradually, the IDF institutionalized the initial tentative arrangements, and established separate entrances for Muslims and Jews under heavy Israeli military presence. Once the Kiryat Arba settlement was founded in the early 1970s, followed by the Jewish enclaves in downtown Hebron a decade later, the Jewish settlers repeatedly announced their intention to evict the Muslims from the Tomb of the Patriarchs altogether. The Israeli government used major violent incidents in Hebron, whether against Jews or Arabs, to expand the rights of Jews at the Tomb of the

Patriarchs at the expense of Muslims. By installing the ark, containing Torah scrolls, it converted the interconnecting rooms between the cenotaphs of Abraham and Sarah, and Jacob and Leah, into synagogues. It kept the Cave of Machpela shut, but assumed control over a small area in Isaac's Mosque to make an opening so that written prayers by Jews could be dropped into the Cave of Machpela—a practice similar to the one at the Western Wall in Jerusalem. Following the massacre of Palestinians in February 1994, the site was closed. When it reopened in November, Muslims, who had been the victims of premeditated violence, discovered that their access to the cenotaphs and their right to pray anywhere within the precinct had been curtailed further. Earlier, on June 26, the official inquiry commission had concluded that Baruch Goldstein had acted alone, and that "We cannot accuse anyone of negligence."

Visiting the sacred site from the Jewish and Muslim sides on different occasions gave me a particular understanding. In mid-February 1995 I took a local taxi for a general run of the city, ending with a visit to the Haram al Khalil.

At the Muslim entrance of the Haram al Khalil, my taxi driver Khadam and I went past a heavy entrance barrier and metal detector, followed by a search of my camera bag by young armed IDF soldiers. We went up many steps along the Mameluke stairway, to be met at the top by more soldiers with Uzi submachine guns. Another metal-detector check. We followed a man in a black and white *keffiyeh* to whose inquiry, "Are you a Muslim?" I replied, "No." Past a passageway, we entered the Jawliye Mosque—a prayer hall furnished with overlapping carpets under a vaulted, whitewashed roof with hanging lights. Through the grilled partition separating it from the main building, I had a glimpse of the shrine of Leah. As the time for the afternoon prayer approached I, a non-Muslim, had to leave.

Intent on visiting the remaining cenotaphs, I asked Khadam to try the Jewish side. I was equipped with a press card issued by the government Press Office. Unlike the cramped feeling one gets on the Muslim side, the Jewish approach was altogether spacious and pleasant, taking the visitor first to a vast, gently rising courtyard. At the outer checkpoint one of the three soldiers looked at my press card and let both of us proceed to the inner checkpoint. Here the three soldiers were standing against the background of rooms marked "Armory" and "Weapon Loading." A discussion ensued in Hebrew, with Khadam explaining to the soldier with a mobile phone that he needed to take me around to explain in English what was what. The serviceman asked Khadam if he was a Muslim. Yes, he replied. The soldier contacted his superior on his mobile phone, saying something like a Muslim wanted to enter from the Jewish side. "Lo, lo (No, No)!"

A few weeks later I was back, this time in the company of Rafi and Naom Arnon, the spokesman for Kiryat Arba. It was as if we were visiting long-lost friends. Arnon was a familiar figure to the soldiers, and Rafi's embroidered shoulder-bag, bought in India, became a subject of friendly inquiries. Arnon acted as our guide briefly before leaving us to join an after-wedding party gathered in a special room in the complex. We entered the room connecting the halls over the cenotaphs of Abraham and Sarah. Though now a synagogue, with a Torah ark in a corner, the ambiance of the place was palpably Islamic. There were Quranic verses in Arabic on the tiles along the plinth in the room. Behind a walled grille I saw a cenotaph covered with an embroidered shroud carrying an inscription in Arabic: "This is the tomb of the Prophet Abraham/May peace be upon him."

When Israel set up an inquiry commission after the massacre by Baruch Goldstein, the local Muslim religious trust boycotted it. Instead it co-operated with the committee appointed by the PLO Chairman, Yasser Arafat, and headed by the local mayor, Mustafa Abdul Nabi Natsche.

"Our conclusions were different from those of the Israeli inquiry conducted by the Shinkar Committee," he told me. "We found that many of the IDF soldiers did not report for guard duty that morning. There were only a few present when the shooting happened. Later, IDF men were involved in the shooting inside the Ibrahimi Mosque. We sent the report to Chairman Arafat. He did not publish it." Natsche spoke the last sentence in a neutral tone.

"After the massacre by Goldstein the Israelis put a partition in the Ibrahimi Mosque," Natsche continued. "They are committing a violation of our mosque. They have limited the number of Muslims who can pray." But that was not all, I discovered. "The Israelis closed the wholesale vegetable market for security reasons, because it is adjacent to the Jewish settlers in the city center. There are 1,500 soldiers in the city mainly to protect some 400 settlers. That is, four soldiers for every Jewish man, woman or child. The Palestinians are not allowed to travel in their cars in the city center. They are harassed by soldiers and settlers. Palestinian youths are stopped at random, made to raise their hands against the wall, and beaten by soldiers. This has severely hurt the economy of the city. All this for the security of some 50 Jewish families and 120 yeshiva students." He got up and faced the wall-map of Hebron. "All the local streets leading to the main road to Kiryat Arba have been blocked with concrete drums so that the Jewish settlers can move freely," he said, pointing out the streets. "The Palestinians living there have to leave their cars some distance away and walk to and from their homes."

Later, leaving the building, I took a good look at the decrepit building carrying a sign "Municipality." The town hall was typical of the run-down state of the city itself: the pot-holed roads, the leaning electric poles, a general air of shabbiness. This state of affairs in turn was reflective of the decline in the economy, and the dependence, political and economic, on Israel.

"There is no industry in Hebron, aside from the traditional crafts of pottery, glass and leather-tanning, so people live on agriculture," explained Natsche. "Most people here depend on work in Israel, mainly construction. But due to the closure [ban on entry into Israel] since January 22 [1995], following a suicide bomb explosion, there is a lot of unemployment here." He was appointed mayor by the Israeli authorities in late 1985, not elected. But he had been a deputy to the popularly elected mayor, Fahd Qawasmeh, from April 1976 to May 1980, when they were both sacked following the killing of six Jewish settlers in downtown Hebron.

Fahd's wealthy relative, Fayez, was the owner of Nahar al Khalil Hotel which, for mysterious reasons, turned into the Park Hotel in the Israeli media. "I built the hotel in April 1965 with twenty rooms," Fayez, an alert man of 61, began. "After the June 1967 War, when the Israelis came, it was practically empty, there was no business.

Everything was depressed in the West Bank." He lit his second cigarette. We sipped delicious cardamom coffee in his elegant stone villa.

"In April 1968 Moshe Levinger and some other persons came to my hotel, and said that they worked at Kiryat Gan [near Tel Aviv] and wanted to spend their Passover in Hebron," Qawasmeh went on. "I didn't ask why; maybe it was hot and humid in Kiryat Gan and the weather was nice in Hebron. They took six rooms with two beds each for one week at 5 liras per room. They had arrived with small pieces of luggage and appeared like travelers. On the second day they said that another group was coming. They took four more rooms. Then another group came, and they took six more rooms. I had very few guests, and the rooms had been empty. They spent three days like that. On the fourth day they put up a sign in Hebrew and English, 'Hebron Settlers.' I threw out the banner. The moment they said they were settlers I started quarreling with them. Then they said they wanted to cook. Until then they had been bringing food from outside. I refused them permission. Then they wanted to remove chairs from the hall of the hotel and use it as a school for their kids. I refused. They wanted to put up an Israeli flag. We began disputing and quarreling. After eight days of this we went to the military governor, and told him 'If you don't take them out of my hotel there will be trouble.' After two days the military governor came and took them to the military base. Then the IDF put it about that the owner of this hotel was a Fatah supporter, which was a criminal offense. After a month or two Levinger and company approached us to rent some space in the hotel to open a restaurant. We refused to discuss anything with them. I've closed the hotel since then, and it has remained shut. On March 14, 1969 I was arrested and put under administrative detention which lasted nine months."[10]

There has been an organic link between Jerusalem and Hebron since ancient times, with water-rich Hebron quenching the thirst of dry Jerusalem. And both have attracted the monotheistic pious. With the advent of Islam, Hebron emerged as a deeply religious and conservative city. In the twentieth century, for instance, it never succumbed to the lure of cinema, perceived by its residents as a corrupting medium. Today it boasts 40 mosques, one for every 300 Muslims, and also harbors the only Islamic university in the West Bank.

This institution, recognizable from a distance by an entrance gate capped by a dome of white stone, decorated with a Quranic verse, is an example of self-help. Unlike Birzeit and Al Najah Universities, which were founded by rich local families, it was set up by numerous small donors in 1971. They established a college of the Sharia (Islamic Law) and religion, with 50 students. Now there are more than 1,400 students, and the university also provides courses in Arab history, education and psychology. Since the Student Council was established, it has been controlled by the Islamic Bloc, except in 1986 when the secular Fatah triumphed. The Islamic influence is apparent in a series of powerful murals, including images of a Palestinian peasant woman holding up a model of a vast Islamic monument, and a large banner, inscribed "In the name of God the Merciful: Read in the name of God, who created you" in Arabic unfolding over a book.

In the small, threadbare cafeteria, I conversed with a group of female students—Amani Jaabari, Nabila Isnaineh, Sabiha Ahmad and Khadija Hafiz assisted by Saida, my Arabic interpreter. Clad in jeans and shirts underneath white scarves, they were soft-spoken, but far from shy.

On the Ibrahimi Mosque: "The prayer space for Muslims has been reduced to take only 300 instead of the 1,500 before the massacre," said Sabiha Ahmad. "Sometimes Muslims are forced to pray in the street. And the place for Jews has been expanded." None of them had been to the Ibrahimi Mosque in the year since the slaughter. Nabila Isnaineh said, "I am afraid to go there to pray because I think the massacre will happen again."

On the Jewish settlers in the city center: "When the fancy takes them they rampage through the fruit and vegetables and upturn stalls," said Khadija Hafiz. "They go about the town with submachine guns. At night they deliberately play loud music and make the situation difficult for the Arab neighbors to drive them away. The same happens in the neighborhood of the Ibrahimi Mosque, where the IDF joins in. The Arabs in the area cannot sleep and are late for work. These settlers in Hebron's center are a provocation and a source of conflict. They must leave."

On the Jewish settlers in Kiryat Arba: Amani Jaabari, a student of Arab history, lived in the village of Al Shuab, which is circumscribed by this complex. "To get to my own home in Al Shuab I have to go past an IDF checkpoint," she said. "It is like living in one country and studying in another."

In the registration hall, buzzing with activity, and in the Student Council office, I interviewed Bassam Mutaweija, the secretary-general of the Council. With the impatient energy of a 20-year-old, he began. "Our university has contributed many martyrs to the struggle. In July 1983 Zionist terrorists attacked our university with assault rifles and hand grenades, and martyred four Muslims. In 1987 as soon as the intifada erupted, the Israelis closed our university. It stayed shut until 1991. Lots of our students were arrested, including seven of the nine Student Council members. One hundred and twenty students belonging to the Islamic Bloc were imprisoned, and a minority of them are still inside. And some students were martyred." Can you give me names? "Yes, Amjad Momeini and Amjad Abu Khalif."

Were any university students killed in the Ibrahimi Mosque massacre in February 1994? "Yes, some, I don't know the exact number. After that massacre we had three days of mourning at the university. We utterly reject the new arrangements the IDF has made at the Ibrahimi Mosque. This is an Islamic mosque, and Jews have no right to be there. The Israelis have taken the first step to controlling our mosque completely. They have limited the number of Muslim worshippers. They have turned our mosque into an Israeli military base." What have you done in protest? "As we are under military occupation, we cannot protest properly," he replied. "All we can do is to send letters to the UN and other international organizations. But they achieve nothing, because the UN treats Israel as its spoiled baby. Look, who controls the UN Security Council? America, the godmother of Israel. Our main weakness is that we are not an armed people like the Jews [of Israel]."

Some days later at an exhibition organized by the Islamic Bloc at the Al Najah National University in Nablus, I saw sets of enlarged color pictures of Palestinians, always young and bearded, displaying machine guns, loading and unloading them, posturing bravely. The pictures were at once a symbol and a reality, an act of defiance, but also an attempt to assert a right which their occupier, the IDF, conferred automatically on Jewish youth, male or female, the day they turned eighteen. Young Palestinians, encountering daily the Israeli Jews of the same age, carrying submachine guns like businessmen carry briefcases, eyed them with envy. Next to these images of daring lay pictures of martyrs, those who had sacrificed their lives in the struggle for the liberation of their homeland. Nearby an assortment of hand-crafted items made by the "Islamic prisoners of Israel" were for sale.

Saida and I had arrived at the university on March 11, the beginning of the spring semester, the day the Islamic Bloc unveiled its book exhibition. The walls of the hall were draped with flowing green banners, inscribed with Islamic prayers in Arabic. On long tables, thousands of books, many of them with gold-embossed covers, were neatly laid out. Omar Mahmoud (a pseudonym), told me that he and his comrades had worked four days and nights around the clock to organize the display. "For every copy sold the Islamic Bloc will get a certain percentage," he said. The money would strengthen the Bloc, which had won elections to the Student Council for three years running in the early 1990s (the university had been closed by the Israelis from 1988-91). The administration of Al Najah University, I was told, played to the tune of the Palestinian Authority. When it discovered the book exhibition by the Islamic Bloc on the day the university reopened for registration, it objected, but instead of escalating tension by attempting to shut down the display, it closed the whole institution for a day.

In the late 1970s Al Najah had 750 students and 75 teachers, and now with a student body of 5,000 students and a teaching staff of 400, it was the largest university in the West Bank. Both the students and staff had a reputation for Palestinian nationalism, which had been long nurtured in Nablus. With a population of 200,000, Nablus is now the largest city of the West Bank, even including the Palestinian East Jerusalem, and the unofficial capital of the northern sector of the territory.

Like Hebron, its southern counterpart, Nablus is a strategic place. Established by Roman Emperor Flavia Vespasian in AD 72, it thrived as an east-west gateway because it was endowed with an abundant water supply from springs. Nablus is a twin of the nearby Shechem, an Old Testament settlement, where Abraham and his family, having left their native Ur in Iraq, arrived on their first entry into the land of Canaan. Captured in AD 637 by Muslim Arabs, it remained under Muslim rule until 1967, except between 1099 and 1187 when it was ruled by the Crusaders. A severe earthquake destroyed much of Nablus in 1927. In the 1930s it was a leading center of Arab resistance to the Jewish immigration into Palestine, and the birthplace in 1936 of the Arab Higher Committee (AHC), which led the Arab Revolt of 1936-9. Following the 1948-9 Arab-Israeli War, it became part of Jordan, and later a center of Palestinian guerrilla activities against Israel, initially directed by Yasser Arafat from the Casbah, the Old City.

A maze of narrow lanes and byways, arched bridges, tunnels and cul-de-sacs, buzzing with the ceaseless activity of a thriving bazaar, the Nablus Casbah was an ideal place for the hide-and-seek of clandestine activities, and a nightmare for IDF and Shin Beth personnel, especially after their informer network collapsed during the intifada. In the one-room sawmill we met a middle-aged printer, Khalid Nabulsi. He gave us a calendar he had printed, a pictorial catalogue of the 54 young men and teenaged Palestinians killed during the first three years of the intifada. The aging walls of the Casbah were plastered with fliers displaying a picture of Imad Nasser, a tousle-haired youth with intense eyes, and announcing the fifth anniversary of his death. Killed by the IDF in December 1989 in a raid on a local barber shop, Nasser was the founder in 1988 of the Ninjas of the Casbah, an armed group which concentrated on assassinating suspected Palestinian collaborators.

In the square outside the Casbah, the Saturday fruit and vegetable trade was in full swing. As in Hebron, the local industry has not progressed beyond the traditional making of soap and olive oil. A match factory closed down in the face of tariff-free Israeli imports. In the absence of an emerging industrial bourgeoisie, the city's leading families continue to dominate the region's wheat and olive-based agricultural economy, control wholesale trade, and own much real estate. Among them is the Shakaa clan, whose senior member is Bassam Shakaa. Born in 1930 and elected mayor at 46, in 1980 he made news headlines worldwide, as a victim of a Jewish terrorists bomb explosion, in which he lost both his legs.

The attack on him was a reprisal for a terrorist operation against the settlers in Hebron, which in turn was retaliation for the creation of the Hebron settlement allowed by the Israeli government after Miriam Levinger and other Kiryat Arba women occupied the old Beit Hadassah building in April 1979. Following the establishment of the Beit Hadassah enclave, Kiryat Arba settlers had taken to praying at the Tomb of the Patriarchs on Friday evenings and then visiting the well-guarded Beit Hadassah for a communal meal. On the first Friday in May 1980, Palestinian gunmen fired their automatic rifles and threw hand grenades at the party of Jews, some of them armed, as they approached Beit Hadassah. Six Jews lay dead, and another sixteen were injured. The attackers made a quick getaway. The military governor of the area imposed an indefinite curfew, and deported not only the elected mayor of the city, Fahd Qawasmeh, but also the head of the Muslim religious trust, responsible for the management of the Ibrahimi Mosque/Tomb of the Patriarchs, Shaikh Rajab Tamimi—to Lebanon. "The first day the Israeli army came to Hebron [in June 1967] they flew the Israeli flag over the Ibrahimi Mosque, and they have continued Judaizing the Haram until it is virtually a synagogue now," said Shaikh Tamimi. "They come into the Haram... in their boots and shoes. Twice they brought a dog with them as a provocation for they know Muslims consider dogs to be unclean. They tore up the Quran there."[11] Once the 30-day period of mourning for the Jewish dead had ended, a group of Jewish terrorists struck at three important leaders of the (Palestinian) National Guidance Committee, among them Bassam Shakaa.

"After that explosion in my car, I spent five months in Stanmore Hospital in the London suburb to recover," Shakaa said. He was a surprisingly cheerful-looking man, with a ruddy face and a graying mustache. "The welcoming procession [for me] took three hours to cover one kilometer from the mayor's office to the Nablus Library." He turned to a large black-and-white photograph hanging from the wall behind his wheelchair, of the marchers carrying him on their shoulders under a fluttering Palestinian flag. His eyes brightened as a smile spread over his face. "In those days my house was in the valley near Elam Ridge by Rafidiya Hospital," he continued. "We moved to this house in 1986, five years after I was sacked as mayor by the Israelis." (When prime minister Shimon Peres decided to nominate a mayor in late 1985 his choice fell on Ghassan Shakaa, a junior member of the same family.)

Unlike a fellow patrician, Fayez Qawasmeh, Shakaa was resolutely opposed to the 1993 Oslo Accord. "The division among Arab countries shown during the Gulf War, the weak situation of Arabs due to the collapse of the Soviet Union; all that helped the United States impose the Oslo Accord on the Palestinians," Shakaa explained. "The Accord is a framework which will not lead to a Palestinian state and independence. It will lead to a more complex clash in the future because it has complicated the ongoing conflict between Zionism and Palestinians. The bottom line is that Palestinians cannot forget themselves, cannot cancel themselves. Israel already controls 55 percent of the land in the West Bank. Its confiscation of more Palestinian land continues. The Israelis do not have the right to be here. They are an occupation force. They have changed our laws, demography, geography and established Jewish settlements against the international law. Since their actions are illegal, they must face the consequences at some point." Why does the PLO not take Israel to the International Court of Justice? "Ours is not only legal but also a political and humanitarian struggle. Due to the force used by Israel, backed by the US, we have suffered. If you go to the [Israeli] High Court, the IDF blows up your house. Due to this, we have not gone to courts. The international legal institutions failed to stop Israel to establish more and more Jewish settlements. When it comes to the crunch at the UN Security Council, America uses its veto in favor of Israel. And Yasser Arafat failed to get Israel to stop activities against the international law."

Leaving Shakaa's vast stone mansion, I surveyed the scene on that fine sunny morning in March. Covered with a green carpet speckled with wild flowers, the surrounding biblical mountains were a stunning sight.

A strong sense of history permeated the discussion I had during my next trip to Nablus with a few academics in the courtyard of Al Najah University. I posed the question: Why did Israel come about? "A Christian-Zionist alliance supported the Jews in their idea of a homeland in Palestine," said Dr. Mansour Abu Ali, head of the geography department. Dark and clean-shaven, Dr. Abu Ali, in his early 40s, carried blue plastic worry beads. "The roots of this alliance can be traced to the nineteenth century. During the Ottoman period [1517–1917] there was no conflict between Jews and Muslims. The Jewish idea of a homeland was supported and developed in Europe. Without western support Israel would not have come into existence."

"The conflict is not between Israel and Palestinians or Jews and Arabs since its roots go beyond modern times, into pre-Christian times," stated Jamal Joudeh, professor of political science in his early 50s. "You cannot overstate the strategic importance of this part of the eastern Mediterranean. The commercial routes of the area became apparent when the Greeks occupied the land. Look at the effort Alexander the Great made to capture Tyre [in south Lebanon]. Later Palestine became the center of leading religions. Then in AD 637 Islam came and took over the region, and got rid of the European occupation. Then the Crusaders. Salah al Din finally got rid of the Europeans. Then renaissance and industrial revolution in Europe, and the emergence of nationalism there. Britain carried 'civilization' to 'barbaric' countries around the globe. Palestine became more important than before. Jews were encouraged to think of their ancient homeland because it suited western interests. The emergence of the Zionist theory can be understood only in that context. Zionists had a European way of thinking. They used it to convince fellow Europeans of the value of setting up a Zionist state in Palestine, and how it was in western interests to do so. Israel was established here in 1948 as a representative of the West. It remains a representative and protector of the West in this region. Israel became all the more important once Britain and France had lost direct control over the region after World War II. Palestine is the center from where you can control the whole region: Lebanon, Syria, Jordan and Egypt. The coast of Palestine is strategic since it leads to Sinai as well as Lebanon and Syria and Jordan. The strength of the Jews in the West forms a supporting element in this nexus. The Zionist lobby in Europe and America is strong. Initially the West had tried to control Palestine directly and on its own; now Israel is an additional power for the West in the region. The awareness by the Arab leaders of this western political strategy at that time was very low or non-existent."

"The leadership of Palestinians and Arabs failed to understand the full political implications of the establishment of Israel in 1948," said Dr. Iyad Barghouti, a social scientist. "Due to their social and political background the Arab leaders failed to deal with the problem. They too were linked with the West. And Israel stood for the West. The present situation is that the Arab leadership does not represent the people; that is, it lacks democratic credentials. The West trusts Israel partly because it practices democracy."

"There is the importance of Israel as a spiritual, religious state to the Jews," Dr. Abu Ali said. "Secondly there is the political and strategic importance of Palestine. Israel is the front of the West into the East. The third dimension is economic. The Third World is a vast consuming block of the world. The West wants to keep markets open for the western manufacturing industries and needs a foothold in the countries like Palestine and Egypt. Fourthly, there is a confrontation now between Islam and the West. Islamic fundamentalism is the leading enemy of the West and Christianity. People in the West don't trust Muslims. This is not surprising because there has all along been conflict between western culture and oriental religions like Islam. Finally, Israel is the silk glove of the West. Through Israel the West wants to exert influence over the Arab world. As US Defense Secretary, Dick Cheney, said on the eve of the Gulf War, there are two American aims: protect Israel; and preserve the West's oil supplies."

After studying the capitals of the northern and southern zones of the West Bank, it was essential to pick a place in the central sector, preferably a refugee camp, home to one West Banker out of nine.[12] My choice fell on the Jalazoun refugee camp, near Ramallah, where 8,000 Palestinians lived. Set up in 1950 under the Jordanian rule, it held 7,000 residents on the eve of the 1967 War, which pushed a substantial minority across the Jordan River into the East Bank (of Jordan).

The immediate and overall impression that Jalazoun conveys to a visitor is of a transient place, where exiled people rested, temporarily, expecting to return to their native abodes in the near future. That was why the UN Relief and Works Agency for Palestinian Refugees (UNRWA) was established by the United Nations following the December 1949 General Assembly resolution to care for Palestinians who lost their homes and livelihood during the 1948-9 Arab-Israeli War. Initially UNRWA erected two-room shelters for each family. But as months turned into years, and years into decades, and families multiplied, with no prospect of a return home, the camp dwellers took to adding rooms and porches and building upwards. The local UNRWA director, himself a refugee and a camp resident, turned a blind eye. Streets and roads emerged, unplanned, pot-holed, without pavements, kept under constant surveillance by the IDF base established on top of an overlooking hill.

Most dwellings are low, single or double-story, built of breeze blocks or stone. All were covered with graffiti in the colors of the Palestinian flag, red, black, green and white. Many of the slogans acclaimed Fatah, others Hamas, and still others smaller groups such as the Popular Front for the Liberation of Palestine. There were occasional leaflets on the walls bearing the sad-looking face of Shaikh Ahmad Yasin, the Hamas leader. The first hint of rain, I was told, and streets turn into mud lanes, and sewers overflow.

Luckily for Saida and me, it was a dry crisp morning in February. We called on Habib Shaheen, the director of the camp. His office, built on a raised platform near the entrance gate, was a small structure with doors painted sky-blue, the UN color. Behind a large steel desk Shaheen sat, tapping his cigarette in an Air France ashtray. Acting as the middle man between the UNRWA and the refugees, he looked after the UNRWA property, supervised the services provided by the agency, decided who should live in his camp, and distributed food and welfare benefits.

Soon his office chairs were occupied by Walid al Bayed, lightly bearded, small and slim; the mustached Riyad al Safi holding blue worry beads, and Abu Jamil al Safi, Riyad's 50-year-old father. Presently Nasr Mahmoud Zubaidi arrived. He was a sinewy man, clean-shaven, and followed by Hamad Mahmoud Adaibe, with a receding hairline and looking older than his 39 years.

Despite the difference in their ages they had two things in common: smoking and imprisonment. Soon a cigarette-smoke cloud filled the office.

Though only 22, Walid had been arrested three times, and had served 26 months behind bars. "I participated in a Day of the Land demonstration on March 30, 1986," he began. "But they arrested me in December for that. Two months, in a jail near Jenin. The second time was in January 1988, soon after the intifada, for throwing a Molotov cocktail. Eighteen months, spent in Darie detention camp near Hebron.

The third time was administrative detention in July 1990. Spent six months in Ansar III detention camp in the Negev. On my release I was given a green ID, which meant that I could not leave the Jalazoun camp. Three years like that. Only after the Oslo Accord was I given the regular orange ID. I am now a first-year student at Birzeit University. I am doing history and political science, and enroll for a course when I've earned enough [as a construction worker]."

Twenty-four-year-old Riyad was a veteran of five imprisonments and detentions. "The first time was in October 1984 when I was thirteen," he said. "A Shabak [Hebrew acronym for General Security Service] man in civilian clothes arrived with an IDF unit at about 10 P.M. They broke into our house. I was in bed. A soldier pulled my hair, and asked me my name, and then ordered me to wear my clothes. My parents tried to stop him, and they hit my father who had himself served a jail sentence. They handcuffed and blindfolded me and put me in a Jeep. They drove around for a while. Then they took me to the Ramallah jail, actually a tent outside the jail. They abused me and threw me around like a piece of luggage. Then six soldiers came and beat me. I was in prison for ten months. The next time was in November 1986, for two months. The third time was in 1988, for eight months. In May 1990 there was a demonstration in our camp after the murder of seven Palestinians in Rishon LeZion [near Tel Aviv]. They imposed a curfew. But people were throwing stones. Shabak men shot at the demonstrators. A bullet hit me in the stomach. I was in the hospital for twenty days. One week after I had left hospital an IDF death squad wearing masks broke into my home. They made me run from my home to a gathering area for prisoners. I fell down, and they caught up with me, five of them. They deliberately hit me on the stomach. It hurt badly. They removed their masks, and I could see them clearly, the Israelis. In July 1990 I was arrested along with six others, all of us under administrative detention. Each of us was interrogated by the Shabak man, Captain Maher. 'I didn't mean to shoot you in the stomach,' he told me. 'I meant to shoot you in the neck, to see you die.' So I replied: 'It is in the hands of God. If he wishes, then I'll die; if not, then not.'"

Riyad lit a cigarette, and offered me one. A non-smoker, I made an exception, and accepted it. "I was out after the six month detention ended," he continued. "But they arrested me again under administrative detention in November 1991. Another six months." What had he been doing since his release? "Work as a laborer and study. I enrolled at Birzeit University to study political science and social sciences. I take courses when I have saved enough." Abu Jamil, Riyad's father, who was incarcerated for two years in 1969 for his membership of Fatah, looked visibly proud of his son.

Hamad Adaibe had three stints in jail, starting in 1977, when he was 23. "The first time was for three and a half years; then in 1983 for two weeks, for interrogation. The last time was in December 1990 for 20 months."

Nasr Zubaida, now 34 and employed as a sanitary worker by UNRWA, had his first imprisonment when he was half that age. "For throwing stones and Molotov cocktails," he said. "Two years in Beersheba prison. Then in 1982 I was jailed for eight years for threatening local collaborators, and for throwing a Molotov cocktail which injured an Israeli soldier. I spent most of the time in Jneid jail near Nablus.

Soon after I got out I married, in April 1990."

I noticed tittering and nervous laughter as my interviewees described their experiences of arrest, jail, beatings and shootings. They had, it seemed, developed a sardonic sense of humor as part of their survival kit.

How were the conditions in prison? "In 1977, quite awful; no mattress, no radio," Nasr replied. "If you talked politics you were punished, including solitary confinement. Everything was oppressive. We struggled. We went on hunger strikes, first for eight days, then 12 days, and finally 23 days. Drank only water. This was just to get a mattress and a pillow. First I was at Beersheba jail. Two of my colleagues in Beersheba, Jaafari and Rahman, died during a hunger strike in 1980."

What was the daily routine? "Wake up, exercise, breakfast," replied Riyad. "While eating we always talked politics. We are a political people, inside prison and outside. All our experience is politics. Then different political factions had discussions among themselves. We gained this privilege through struggle. Then exercise for half an hour. From 2 to 4 P.M. read books, read and write; from 4 to 6 P.M. a general meeting of all prisoners, political analysis. But the routine during my administrative detention in the Negev was different. There were 30 prisoners in each tent. We played cards, chess. At the end of my detention we got radio and TV. Dinner was at 6.30 P.M., and bed at 11 P.M."

Had imprisonment weakened or strengthened their convictions? "I'm the same, before and after," came the reply from Nasr. "I'd do it again what I did." I turned to the younger men. "The living conditions in a prison are such that they harden you, make you strong," said Walid. His friend, Riyad, nodded in agreement. "Even if I were to be imprisoned 50 times I would not give up the struggle for the Palestinian national rights," replied Riyad. "Jail has a great effect on your personality when you are young. It made me stronger."

If one were to think of the PLO as a regular army, the men in the room would be counted as its combatants. They were not atypical. Indeed, as Shaheen, the director, pointed out: "At the height of the intifada in August 1990 there were 480 males [aged 15 to 50] in prison. Now [in March 1995] 70 are still in jail." This meant that at least one out of every three Palestinian males in the camp (aged 15 to 50) had endured imprisonment. At least they had survived the long intifada. Eight camp dwellers had perished in the struggle, victims of numerous army firings. Nasr recited their names: Amin Raja, Amjad Badawi (aged 19), Awad Tabsin, Mustafa Sharaka (aged 17), Tahrir Arayshe, Ahmad Shankl, Hussein Musaaid and Marouf al Safi. There was an eight-sided memorial pillar in their honor, decked by a Palestinian flag and lights at the center of the main square of this indigent settlement of refugees.

Once again the Jalazoun camp was typical. Indeed it was less militant than Deheisheh near Bethlehem, with over 8,500 residents. "During the intifada," its director, himself a Palestinian refugee, told me, "Sixteen people were killed, seven were deported, four houses were demolished and two were sealed." For a people who have been thrown out of their native land, losing a house is a particularly traumatic experience.

Like deprived people elsewhere in the world, these refugees and their progeny had long memories. Nasr said that his family was originally from Lod, now the site of Israel's sprawling international airport. Walid's family was from Dawayma village near Hebron. "The IDF entered the village in July 1948 and killed some people," he said. "The rest fled out of fear. My family fled to Jericho, then Taiba village near Ramallah, and finally ended up in the Jalazoun camp."

What were the reasons for the Palestinian defeat in 1948? "No Arab country helped the Palestinians," explained Riyad. "This happened because the Arab leaders could not make decisions on their own: they were under the control of Britain and France. Israel was superior militarily. The Arabs did not have good weapons. Israel had much better weapons. Also Britain was a superpower in those days; and its policy was to keep the Arab governments weak. The Iraqi and Egyptian soldiers fought well on the battlefield, but their leaders were the pawns of Britain. So when they captured some areas, as in Jenin, their army generals got orders to withdraw." His father, Abu Jamil, agreed, and added: "The Jews did not have the power on their own to occupy Palestine. Without the British help they would not have been able to do what they did."

Why did Israel come about? "It was in the mutual interest of the Jews and the European governments to enable the Jews to come here and occupy us to fulfill their aim in this part of the world," replied Walid. "Helped by Britain, the Zionist movement found a rationale, and built up world opinion that the Jews should have their homeland here. What happened to them in World War II also helped them. But the Arabs had nothing to do with what happened to the Jews in Europe. Yet we have been forced to pay the price for the crimes of the Germans."

Why were the Arabs defeated again in 1967? The reasons given could be summarized as follows. There was a lack of military supplies and weapons in the Arab camp. Israel attacked the Egyptian air force on the ground and destroyed it. Israel was determined to take the Old City in Jerusalem which was important to the Jews. The Jordanian military was under King Hussein who was under the British influence. The Jordanian army had been rough on the Palestinians in Jordan during 1948–67. The Palestinian revolution had just started (after the establishment of the PLO in 1964). Yet the Palestinian commandos fought well in the West Bank and Gaza.

Would they accept the pre-1967 borders as a permanent solution? "I would accept that the West Bank, Gaza and East Jerusalem are enough for us," said Riyad. "But there must be complete Israeli withdrawal from there." All the eight Jalazoun residents present endorsed Riyad's position, except Hamad Adaibe, a member of the Islamic Jihad. "We claim sovereignty over the whole of the British mandate Palestine," he said. "This is our land. The Jews took our land, our assets. We have to struggle to recover what is ours. Each phase of the struggle has its own methods. We do not know how long the struggle will go on. But I know that the Muslims throughout the world will support us. I used to be a member of Fatah, but I left in 1980."

There was vigorous disagreement with Hamad's views from the rest of the assembly. Why? "Islam would exclude other religious groups like Christians and Druzes from participating in the Palestinian nationalist struggle," was one reason offered; "The anti-Israeli struggle is about Palestinian nationalism, a subject which the Islamic Jihad ideology does not address," was another; "The Islamic Jihad wants to internationalize the struggle, but we want to keep it as our struggle limited to Palestine," was still another; and finally, "Under secularism everybody speaks up, Muslim or not, and gives vent to his opinion, but not so under a religious ideology."

What they were unanimous about was that there had been no economic improvement from the 1993 Oslo Accord. Indeed with frequent sealing of the Israeli borders to West Bankers and Gazans, heavily dependent for their livelihood on work in Israel, the economic situation had deteriorated.

Within the Jalazoun camp the UNRWA was the chief employer, providing such public services as garbage collection, road maintenance, sanitation, health clinics and education (which is compulsory up to age fifteen). In the private sector, jobs were available in metal workshops, groceries and garages. These activities provided employment to about a third of the job-seekers. The rest were dependent on work inside Israel, mostly in construction, sometimes as manual laborers in factories. The average wage was NIS (New Israeli Shekel) 60 or $20 a day, about half of what a Jewish laborer earned, they said. In other words, when the Israeli border was closed to West Bankers and Gazans, the jobless rate in Jalazoun shot up to 65–70 percent. Again Jalazoun was typical. At the Deheisheh camp unemployment, normally at 40 percent, doubled when the Green Line was sealed off.

The inequality in the living standards of Israelis and Palestinians is stark. At $2,067, the per capita GNP of West Bankers (in 1992) was one-sixth that of Israelis; and at $1,622, the per capita GNP for West Bankers and Gazans together was only one-seventh.[13] Since then the disparity has grown.

This state of affairs is the end result of the policies Israel has followed in the Occupied Territories regarding land confiscation, land use and planning, water resources, agriculture, industry, commerce, employment, taxation and financial services.

Ever since its occupation of the Palestinian territories, Israel has pursued a dual land strategy. Large scale confiscation of Palestinian land has not only advanced the Israeli policy of "redeeming" the soil of Eretz Israel, but has also severely weakened the close link that Palestinians have traditionally maintained with agriculture and land, thus undermining their nationalist feelings. The success of this policy is illustrated by the fact that between 1967 and 1985 the percentage of West Bankers engaged in agriculture declined from 46 to 27. (The corresponding figures in the Gaza Strip were 32 and 18.)[14] The displaced Palestinian labor had to find alternative means of livelihood. With the non-agricultural sectors of the economy in the Occupied Territories rigidly controlled by the Israeli military regime, Palestinian workers had no choice but to seek employment at below market rates as unskilled or semi-skilled workers in Israel in its agriculture, construction, and catering industries. Not surprisingly, by 1985, as much as 54 percent of West Bank wage laborers were employed in Israel. (In Gaza it was 67 percent.) That explained why half the workforce in the Israeli construction industry was Palestinian.[15]

Within a year of its occupation of the Palestinian territories in 1967, Israel had consolidated its economic stranglehold over the West Bank and Gaza Strip.

It was the source of 75 percent of the Palestinian imports, and the destination of 40 percent of the Palestinian exports. By the end of the 1980s these statistics had risen respectively to 90 percent and 66 percent.[16] The trade imbalance was equally striking. In 1986 Israel's exports to Occupied Territories amounted to $780 million, and its imports to $289 million, giving it an annual trade surplus of $491 million.[17]

By issuing some 200 military orders, Israel so mutilated the inherited Jordanian taxation law that a Palestinian living in the West Bank ended up paying more in taxes than a person with the same income resident in Israel, a country known for its high taxation. And, despite their dramatically lower living standards, West Bankers found themselves subsidizing Israelis. According to Meron Benvensiti, the Israeli director of the West Bank Data Project, in 1987 more than $80 million collected from the Palestinians in the Occupied Territories was channeled into the Israeli public treasury.[18] And the flow continued.

Following its capture of the West Bank and Gaza in June 1967, Israel immediately closed all Palestinian as well as other Arab and non-Arab banks, and froze their assets and liabilities. While it allowed the Jordanian dinar as joint legal tender with Israeli currency, it specified exclusive control by the Bank of Israel in all banking activities. Because of Israel's insistence on this condition for the reopening of the closed banks, and because of Jordan's insistence that the West Bank-based banks must function under the supervision of the Jordanian Central Bank, West Bankers were for all purposes deprived of normal banking facilities until September 1986, when the military permitted the opening of the Cairo-Amman Bank in the territory. Dependence on private, expensive banking and credit arrangements for two decades damaged the West Bank economy badly.

The cumulative effect of stagnant output, high taxation, restrictions on import of foreign currencies, and the long absence of proper banking and credit facilities was to reduce funds for investment in industry and other capital projects. The industrial backwardness of the Occupied Territories could be judged by the fact that in 1987 the value of the annual industrial output in the territories was a mere $85 million, equal to the production of one medium-sized Israeli company.[19]

"The Israeli government's policies are designed to increase the structural integration of the Palestinian economy into that of Israel at the expense of all indigenous economic development initiatives so as to prevent the possibility of any economic competition," state the authors of *Israeli Obstacles to Economic Development in the Occupied Palestinian Territories*. "The occupied Palestinian territories are thus captive repository markets for Israeli goods against which they have no protection. Israeli restrictions are designed to work for the benefit of the Jewish Israeli state and to exclude the Palestinian economy from world markets. The majority of Palestinian workers are dependent on external demand for their cheap, flexible labor; and Palestinian industrialists and manufacturers are restricted to local markets and demand lest they compete with their Israeli counterparts."[20]

The overall situation was much worse in the tiny Gaza Strip, which is home to almost half of the Palestinians in the Occupied Territories.

10

Gaza

The End of the Line

"We had to do guard duty in the observation post overlooking the refugee camp in Gaza," said an Israeli soldier, a reservist in a highly decorated unit, in an interview with *Kol Halr*, a Hebrew weekly in mid-1992. "Every day... children would come and start shouting for us to throw some food. At first, we thought this was a game. Later, we saw that they would jump on everything we threw, even if the bread was full of sand." Once, he continued, he had witnessed a group of Palestinian teenagers kill a pigeon with a slingshot. After grabbing it, "They... started arguing who would get what piece. They ate it raw."[1] Earlier, in an interview with the *Jerusalem Report*, Yossi (a pseudonym), a member of Israel's Golani Brigade, a combat unit, had remarked: "Gaza is the end of the world, and Rafah is the pit at the end of the world."[2]

Nothing has changed since then in Gaza. Rafah, the name borne both by a town and a refugee camp, is home to 120,000 Gazans. For me, a photograph of a back alley of low breeze-block dwellings with roofs of corrugated sheet, bisected by an open sewer of stagnant liquid in the foreground, with a tattered Palestinian flag, limp on its pole, aptly captured the squalor of Rafah. Having emerged from a filthy maze of alleyways, Abdul Hakim al Samra, my Gazan interpreter, and I found ourselves stomping on a wide sandy road, lacerated once again by open sewers, strewn with cinderblocks, plastic bottles, broken bricks, and pieces of cement. Single-story shelters, screened by a wall of uneven, rusting metal sheets, demarcated both sides of the sandy road. Relief came when we chanced upon a soccer match, with smartly dressed players, and young and enthusiastic spectators erupting in cries and shouts of support or denigration.

Not far away, shouts of another kind filled the desert air. Many men and women, standing close to a high metal-wire fence, were conversing loudly across a no-person's land over 50 yards wide. The people on the other side, the sovereign soil of Egypt, too were clawing the fence as they shouted. An IDF Jeep, mounted with guns, went past slowly. The Gazans and Egyptians continued talking loudly, uninterrupted.

Rafah, a town along the Egyptian-Palestinian border, had expanded before and after the 1948-9 Arab-Israeli War, when Gaza became an Egyptian-administered territory. The situation changed in June 1967 when the Strip was occupied by Israel.

The new Egyptian-Israeli boundary following the 1978 Camp David Accords left Rafah sliced into two parts, one Egyptian, the other Gazan. The partition, however, did not respect family connections, which continue across the international fences. The talk, Abdul Hakim told me, was as much about family matters as property left behind. A freelance journalist, Abdul Hakim al Samra had brought many foreign reporters and authors to this site, a Middle Eastern version of the Berlin Wall. In his mid-30s, he was a graduate of the American University in Cairo, and at ease with the English language.

The Rafah salient that juts into Egypt leads to the port of Al Arish, which connects overland with Port Said at the northern end of the Suez Canal, across which lies mainland Egypt. As a gateway between west Asia and north-east Africa, Gaza has had a long and turbulent chronicle. The repeated conquests and pillages by foreigners made the native people all the more determined to resist alien rule. Having subdued them in 332 BC, Alexander the Great punished them by selling into slavery some 10,000 Gazans. (History repeated itself when, following their occupation by Israel in 1967, Gazans struggled against the Israelis vigorously, and were severely repressed.) When their Roman masters adopted Christianity in AD 313, the pagan Gazans fought the Christians long and hard, but yielded in the end. Like the rest of the region, Gaza fell to Muslim Arabs in AD 635. It changed hands during the Crusades, which ended with the rise of the Mamelukes. In 1517 it was incorporated into the Ottoman empire, and mostly stayed there.

During World War I, the 1915 Ottoman offensive mounted from Gaza to capture the Sinai and the Suez Canal, showed the British the strategic importance of the Palestinian region as a buffer to safeguard Egypt and the Suez Canal, Britain's lifeline to its empire in India. The British resolved to acquire control over Palestine after victory in the war, and General Edmund Allenby succeeded in expelling the Ottomans from the region in late 1917. The vicious fighting and heavy British bombardment left Gaza devastated. Indeed, Gaza City was so badly damaged that nothing of historical value survived.

Traveling from Jerusalem nearly 80 years later, I mused over the long chronicle of strife in Gaza. Little did I know that I was heading for a battle frontline, at least in appearance. As our shared taxi with white Gaza license plates neared the military checkpoint at Erez, I saw a whole battery of concrete barriers on both sides of the road. Young soldiers with machine guns abounded. We stopped behind a monstrous-looking IDF truck.

Each of us, five male and two female passengers, was thoroughly checked, with the young IDF soldier looking carefully at each document and each passenger: an unflinching eye-to-eye contact. It was the first time since my arrival in Israel ten weeks earlier that I had encountered such treatment. The soldier asked a passenger, a bearded man in his early 30s, to get off the vehicle, and pass through a metal-detector. He detained a young Palestinian. Past the IDF checkpoint, we reached a set of barriers manned by a joint force of Israelis and Palestinians, then finally a checkpoint which was (nominally) fully Palestinian. Here an older policeman in khaki trousers and a khaki sweater was standing leisurely between two vertical cement concrete barriers with tea glasses on top. He waved us through, the way I remember the IDF soldier doing when I had returned to Jerusalem in the car of a Jewish settler from Beit El.

The five mile ride to the center of Gaza City was along a narrow road. Donkey carts were a common sight. Our vehicle approached Palestine Square, the hub of the capital, filled with the lively chaos of an Arab city exacerbated by rain and mud.

Struggling to safeguard my bag from the splashing cars, I allowed myself to be dragooned inside a rickety car by its driver, a young, chirpy Palestinian in his early 20s. It was clear from his expression that he had never heard of the Cliff Hotel, but passers-by gave him a clue. I could sense that we were heading toward the sea. The face of the city improved. The buildings became steadily higher and newer. Finally, the newly built Cliff Hotel, its restaurant lapped by sea waves, lifted my sagging spirits.

The next day Abdul Hakim proved quite methodical. "From head to toe the Gaza Strip is 46 kilometers [29 miles]," he said. "The total area is 360 square kilometers [139 square miles]. There are sixteen Jewish settlements. Then there are the closed IDF areas. Finally, there is the security perimeter running along the border between the Gaza Strip and Israel. All told Israel and its 3,000 Jewish settlers control some 40 percent of the Gaza Strip." That gave a population density of 54 per square mile for the Jewish settlers and 13,012 per square mile for the Palestinians, a ratio of 1:241.

The population explosion had started in 1948 due to the Arab-Israeli War, when 180,000 refugees from the rest of Palestine joined 160,000 native Gazans. The crowding showed up in Jabaliya camp, north-east of Gaza City. Here 77,000 people were crammed into an area of just under one square mile. The adjacent village, roughly the same area, was home to a mere 10,000 Palestinians.

The refugee camp is situated in a sandy depression less than a mile from the coastline. One of its landmarks is Suleiman's Pool, filled with raw sewage, near an elementary school, a watery grave for several of the pupils. Abdul Hakim drove me to the site of the first demonstration of the intifada, on December 9, 1987: an open sandy ground littered with the usual debris, cinderblock dwellings with a couple of cars parked outside, a few men lounging and many children loitering—an eminently forgettable place, except that it was near the school from where students had emerged in their hundreds shouting slogans on their march to the local IDF base. The demonstration had ended with the loss of four lives, victims to army bullets.

The immediate trigger for the protest was an accident on December 8 at a gasoline station near the Erez checkpoint, in which an IDF truck hit two Palestinian vehicles transporting Gaza workers from the Jabaliya camp, killing four and injuring more. When the news reached the camp its dwellers perceived the accident as a deliberate act, a revenge for the stabbing of a Jewish trader, Shlomo Sakal, in Gaza City's Palestine Square the day before, with the rumors describing the IDF truck-driver as a close relative of the dead man.

There were of course deeper causes for the eruption of the intifada. Its roots could be traced to the "iron fist" policy toward the Palestinians announced by Defense Minister Yitzhak Rabin in August 1985. This policy resulted, in the words of Ziad Abu Amr, a soft-spoken professor of political science at Birzeit University, in "loss of life [115 shot by the IDF in three years], imprisonment, detention, house or town arrest, demolition of dwellings, deportation, fines, interrogation, travel restrictions, curfews, closure of educational institutions, unjust taxes, economic hardships, and the like."[3] The figures for the West Bank, collected by Meron Benvenisti, showed that between April 1986 and May 1987 there was a weekly average of 56 violent demonstrations, involving stone-throwing, raising the banned Palestinian flag, distributing leaflets, and painting walls with nationalist graffiti. There was also an average of four incidents a week involving the use of firearms, knives, explosives and gasoline bombs. And each week 81 West Bankers were arrested for participating in a demonstration or engaging in terrorist activity.[4]

Tension began rising steadily from mid-1987, especially in the Gaza Strip. In the early summer six members of the Islamic Jihad escaped from Gaza's central jail. Soon after they assassinated Captain Ron Tal, head of the IDF military police in Gaza. In the early autumn there was an armed confrontation between the Jihad activists and Israeli security forces in which four Jihad militants and one Shin Beth officer were killed.

On November 25, the news that an armed member of the Popular Front for the Liberation of Palestine-General Command, had landed at the Gibor army camp in northern Israel by flying a hand-glider from south Lebanon, and killed six Israeli soldiers, electrified the Palestinians. It made them realize that despite its overwhelming military might and tight security measures, Israel was still vulnerable. This feeling was bolstered when, following the fatal stabbing of Shlomo Sakal on December 7, Foreign Minister Shimon Peres said that the government should seriously consider demilitarizing Gaza. Just before these events, the 14th Arab League summit, which met in Amman from November 8–11, had focused on the Iran-Iraq War, and paid scant attention to the Palestinian problem. This made West Bankers and Gazans resolve to take their fate into their own hands.

The intifada, which lasted nearly six years, went through the following phases: December 1987 to early August 1990 (ending with the Iraqi occupation of Kuwait); August 1990 to February 1991 (the end of the Gulf War); March to October 1991 (convening of the Middle East peace conference); November 1991 to June 1992 (Labor's electoral victory in Israel); and July 1992 to September 1993 (signing of the Israeli-PLO Accord).

"The intifada started small, became more violent, and then settled down to a pattern of big or small demonstrations," said Dr. Adel Manna, an Israeli Arab academic. "It became a state of mind for Palestinians. Once they realized that they could not get liberation through intifada they started a war of attrition from 1990-91 onward which went on until the Oslo Accord."[5]

Dr. Mahdi Abdul Hadi of the Palestinian Academic Society for the Study of International Affairs (PASSIA), based in East Jerusalem, described the opening year of the intifada as the "Palestinian Year," when the inhabitants of the Occupied Territories, acting on their own, put their problem back on the international agenda, and rid themselves of the remnants of Jordanian control. During this period the local intifada leadership devised such innovative tactics as refusal to pay taxes to the Israeli authorities or accept identity documents. Then came the "PLO Year," when the PLO, representing both Palestinian communities, inside and outside the Occupied Territories, and headquartered in Tunisia, took the center-stage, and imposed strict control over the local leadership in the West Bank and Gaza. This period culminated with the 1988 Palestine National Council (PNC) declaring a Palestinian state, thus preparing the ground for a diplomatic solution. The third year, ending in December 1990, was to have been the "Israeli Year," with bridges to be constructed between the two camps.[6] But it got sidetracked when Labor quit the national unity government (March 1990), the PLO-US contacts were suspended following the failed raid on Israeli beaches by the Palestine Liberation Front in retaliation for the earlier killing of Palestinians in Rishon LeZion (May 1990), and Iraq's invasion of Kuwait (August 1990).

Within ten days of the massive demonstration in the Jabaliya camp on December 9, 1987, the intifada had spread to all parts of the Gaza Strip, the West Bank and East Jerusalem, with predominantly young protesters attacking the Israeli security forces with stones and gasoline bombs, and the latter responding with tear gas and live ammunition. On December 19 East Jerusalem experienced the worst violence since the June 1967 war. By the end of the month, after the Israeli forces had shot dead 24 Palestinians, both the PLO and the Islamic Center, the front organization of the Muslim Brotherhood, had given the spontaneous uprising their support.

On January 8, 1988, the day the PLO-sponsored United National Leadership of the Uprising (UNLU) issued its first communiqué, Israel shut down all universities and schools in the Occupied Territories. The UNLU communiqués were printed and distributed clandestinely, and were then broadcast by the Al Quds Palestinian Arab Radio, based in Damascus, and the Voice of the PLO Radio, operating in Baghdad.

Communiqué Number One called for "a general and comprehensive strike until Wednesday evening, January 13, 1988," and included specific instructions to "Brother workers," "Brother businessmen and grocers," "Brother owners of taxi companies," and "Brother doctors and pharmacists." Containing a "General warning" that "Walking in the streets will not be safe in view of the measures that will be taken to make the comprehensive strike a success... [T]he strike groups will be deployed throughout the Occupied Homeland," it ended with the slogan of the strike: "Down with the occupation; long live Palestine as a free and Arab country." (Later, unable to stop or intercept this highly effective means of communication, Israel's Shin Beth resorted to issuing its own forged communiqués in order to sow dissension in the Palestinian ranks. An example of this was Communiqué 38 put out in late October 1988 on the eve of the Palestine National Council session in Algiers. The genuine communiqué and excerpts from the Shin Beth version are reprinted in *Intifada,* edited by Zachary Lockman and Joel Beinin.[7] At about the same time Hamas issued its own communiqué. In order to maintain the intifada's popular character, both the PLO and Hamas advised use of "popular weapons" by the Palestinians, such as stones and gasoline bombs (later knives, axes and stone cutters), and not firearms or explosives.

In response, Yitzhak Rabin declared on January 19 that the "first priority" of the IDF was to "use force, might and blows" to quash the rioting. The result was a series of "aberrations" (according to the IDF), "atrocities" (according to the Palestinians) by Israeli soldiers, including the live burial of four Palestinians who were saved from death by asphyxiation in the nick of time. Two days after Israeli chief of staff, General Dan Shomron, declared on February 23 that the soldiers were allowed to resort to beating as a device for dispersing the rioters, and not as punishment, CBS television showed Israeli soldiers beating bound Palestinians in order to break their bones. Responding to the international criticism, the IDF unveiled a specially designed device for dispersing crowds: a mechanized stone thrower, equipped with a machine to break a large rock and spit hundreds of medium-sized stones at high velocity at demonstrators through its revolving turret. When the intifada showed no sign of subsiding, the government tried to protect Israelis from its effects by sealing off the Occupied Territories. It did so on March 28, 1988 after nearly 21 years of occupation and eleven years of issuing a map of Israel without the 1949 Green Line armistice lines.

Believing that the "evil genius" of the PLO's military chief Abu Jihad (Father of Struggle), Khalil Wazir, was responsible for the continuing uprising, the Israeli government decided to eliminate him. Israel's death squad commandos assassinated Wazir at home in Tunis in the early hours of April 16, 1988. Shocked Palestinians protested violently, and sixteen lost their lives, victims to IDF shootings. And to the consternation of the Israeli authorities, the loss of Abu Jihad made little difference to the intensity of the intifada. In any case, Hamas, functioning outside the PLO, had become a major, independent player, and had been so recognized by UNLU.

Furthermore, the intifada had captured the Palestinian teenagers. "No child, no teenager is immune from the politics of the intifada," noted Helen Winternitz, an American researcher, based in the West Bank. "Throwing a stone, and thereby joining the makeshift army of the intifada, is a rite of passage into manhood. Every boy knows this dictate. To do less is to be a weakling; to do more is to be a hero."[8] Along with stone throwing went two other major protest activities: raising the Palestinian flag, and spraying the walls with political graffiti, often in one of the four colors of the Palestinian standard. The flag's red signified the blood of martyrs; green, the fertility of the Palestinian plains; white, peace; and black, the oppression of occupation (to be removed when Palestine had been liberated).[9] "Bits of green, black and red cloth, the PLO colors, hang from telephone lines, like torn laundry," noted Yossi Halevi, a journalist, serving his reserve duty in the Gaza Strip. "Walls on the main streets are scarred with white streaks of paint blocking out political slogans; sometimes several layers of black- or green-lettered slogans alternate with whitewash. But on the alley walls the slogans and fantasy images of the intifada have not been erased."[10]

The graffiti expressed nationalist, anti-Israeli sentiment, and conveyed information about forthcoming strikes or demonstrations, commemoration of martyrs and nationalist days, boycott of Israeli products, and campaigns to assist specific groups of Palestinians (such as calls to employ those under town arrest). The youthful ranks of the PLO and Hamas spray-painted or stenciled their graffiti at strategic locations for maximum exposure. "Yes, yes to the blessed Intifada;

Yes to the United National Leadership of the Intifada" read the wall near the coffee shop in the main square of the Jalazoun camp. "Revolution, revolution against the occupier." "No to the Zionist entity." "O Jews, leave our land." The map of mandate Palestine, the Palestinian flag and a gun frequently accompanied the slogans. Also the combined image of an eagle and a picture of Arafat embracing (the assassinated) Abu Jihad. No great artistry was needed to spray garbage bins of all sizes with "Israel" or "Shamir's Office." Shamir was consistently drawn as a donkey, Rabin as a monkey, and Ariel Sharon as an elephant. Other popular anti-Israeli images were: a machinegun firing bullets at an Israeli flag, and a sword slashing the Star of David. Explaining the details of a graffiti operation, Adil, a young Palestinian activist, told Paul Lalor, a British researcher, "If there was an order to put up a certain slogan in Manara [downtown Ramallah] there would be three or four people involved—some to do it, others to keep watch. It was usually done at night, and sometimes we would barricade the road to give us time to get away in case an army patrol came."[11] When the graffiti artists failed to escape on time, they sometimes paid a heavy price. During the first two and a half years of the intifada, seven Palestinian graffiti writers were shot dead by IDF patrols. The IDF combined this tactic with a policy of fining the person who failed to remove graffiti from his property.

As for the leading figures, many of those involved in the intifada were young educated Palestinians, fluent in Hebrew, who took over the communal leadership from the older generation of Arab notables. Both UNLU and Hamas urged the Palestinians to resign from all posts of the government, stop using public services, withdraw money from Israeli banks, boycott Israeli products, cease paying taxes, and join the strikes they called periodically. UNLU and Hamas committees issued circulars containing instructions in these matters, and urged all Palestinians to share the sacrifices required by the intifada. The Palestinians used charity funds, religious and secular, to support the large number of families where husbands or brothers were jailed. Actions by the Israeli security forces, involving firings, curfews, harassment, beatings, arrests and house searches and demolitions severely disrupted all Palestinians' lives.

By the time the intifada entered its second year in December 1988, Palestinians could claim substantial achievements. In July King Hussein of Jordan relinquished the last vestiges of legal and administrative ties between Jordan and the West Bank, thus laying to rest any prospect of Israel exercising its "Jordanian option" to resolve the Palestinian problem. On November 15 the Palestine National Council, meeting in Algiers, proclaimed the independent State of Palestine, and accepted UN Resolutions 242 and 338. Addressing a session of the UN General Assembly on December 14, held specially in Geneva following the US administration's refusal to grant Arafat a visa, the Palestinian leader renounced all forms of violence, and recognized Israel's right to exist in peace, thus paving the way for official dialogue between the PLO and the United States.

According to the head of the IDF's budget office, the intifada cost the IDF more than $750 million during the first year. And, according to the Bank of Israel, the Israeli economy suffered a loss of $500 million due to a decline in tourism, construction and exports to the West Bank and Gaza.[12] In mid-May 1989, prime minister Shamir proposed elections to choose Palestinians to negotiate with Israel. Both UNLU and Hamas leaders rejected the offer, seeing it as a ploy to defuse the intifada.

But the continued defiance and protest by Palestinians took its toll on the community. For instance, in 1989 the residents of the Jabaliya camp had to endure 156 days of curfew, cooped up in their homes day after day with only brief releases to do essential shopping. The cumulative effect of army shootings, beatings and long curfews, eventually manifested in the rise of clinical depression and schizophrenia, up from 189 cases to 226 between April 1989 and February 1990, according to Dr. Muhammad Abu Sweieh, the head of the camp's health clinic.[13]

The vital importance of the curfew in the military's counter-intifada strategy was highlighted by an account of his 11 P.M. IDF reserve duty in Gaza's Nuseirat camp by Yossi Halevi of the *Jerusalem Report.*

> The unpaved, sandy streets are dark and totally still. Like the rest of Gaza, Nuseirat is under nightly curfew, from 9 P.M. to 3 A.M. We park in the central square... lit by the sporadic streetlamps that illumine only scattered patches, like spotlights... Rows of political slogans have been painted on to a concrete wall, and our job is to find someone to erase them. We come at night because the curfew allows us to operate freely, without the crowds of stone throwers that follow us by day... Alon [the unit commander], a university student, chooses a house at random. He bangs on the door and the whole sleeping camp seems to reverberate. "*Iftah, jeish* (Open, army)!" he shouts. Our few Arabic phrases are all imperative... Alon shows them [Ahmad, the head of the household, and his two sons] the wall, then sends them home for paint and brushes.[14]

The Israeli politicians' fear that the intifada would spread among the Arabs of Israel was fulfilled in May 1990. Early morning on May 20 Ami Popper, a young Jewish resident of Rishon LeZion, near Tel Aviv, took his elder brother's rifle and drove to an intersection where Palestinians from Gaza gathered daily as casual laborers to be hired by Israeli contractors. Brandishing his weapon, he forced the Palestinians to squat on the ground in three rows. He then began firing at them. As the Palestinians ran helter-skelter, he reloaded his rifle, and fired again. He then jumped into his car and sped away. His carnage left seven dead and eleven injured. The news of the murders caused outrage not only among West Bankers and Gazans but also among Israeli Arabs, and resulted in rioting in which fifteen more Palestinians lost their lives.

The retaliatory action by the pro-Iraqi Palestine Liberation Front (PLF) had far more serious consequences. During the early hours of May 30, the Jewish holiday of Shavuot, the PLF's sixteen commandos, tried to land in two groups on the Nitzanim and Gaash beaches of Tel Aviv, with a plan to attack a military officers' camp. But one team was intercepted on the high seas by the Israeli navy, and the other on land by the border police. Together the Israeli forces killed four guerrillas, and captured the rest. When Yasser Arafat refused either to dismiss the PLF leader, Abu al Abbas (Muhammad Abbas Zaidan), from the PLO's executive committee (something he was not authorized to do) or condemn the planned PLF's operation, arguing that the PLO's agreement with the United States exempted attacks on military targets inside Israel, Washington suspended dialogue with the PLO.

Several weeks later a far more shattering event shook the region. On August 2 Iraq invaded and occupied Kuwait. Ten days later the Iraqi president, Saddam Hussein, made a linkage between Iraq's evacuation of Kuwait and Israel's evacuation of occupied Arab territories. This made him a hero among Palestinians. By integrating the Palestinian national demand into the wider regional conflict, Saddam Hussein lifted the intifada from its recent doldrums and infused new life into it.

"[During the first heady year] a festive violence lit the streets of Palestinian neighborhoods and villages with burning tires whose acrid black smoke tasted of success," noted Helen Winternitz. "When the IDF, border police and Shin Beth countered with bullets and truncheons, tear gas, tax raids and mass arrests, the violence was checked superficially, but smoldered underground like coals... And when Saddam Hussein rose against the established order in the Middle East, the winds from Iraq blew an ideological oxygen that inspired Palestinians. The coals were rekindled into pro-Saddam flames."[15]

Saddam Hussein's proposal was rejected summarily by US President George Bush, who took the lead in rallying the international community against Iraq. During the ensuing crisis, the Palestinian problem caught world attention on October 8, when Israeli border police shot dead seventeen Palestinians and injured another 150 during rioting at the Haram al Sharif/Temple Mount in Jerusalem, triggered by the plans of the Temple Mount Faithful to lay a foundation for the Third Jewish Temple on the mount. The rioting that followed in the commercial district of East Jerusalem led to three more deaths, making it the highest single day of Palestinian fatalities since the start of the intifada. Iraq ordered three days of mourning. The UN Security Council unanimously adopted a resolution which expressed alarm at the violence, called on Israel to abide by the Fourth Geneva Convention, and instructed UN Secretary-General Javier Perez de Cuellar to dispatch a mission to the region and submit a report by October 30.

But Israel refused to receive the UN mission. On October 24 the Security Council unanimously called on Israel to reconsider its decision. Shamir's government in Israel remained obdurate. Perez de Cuellar recommended that a special session of all 164 UN members be called to discuss measures to make Israel comply with the Fourth Geneva Convention. Following the release of Perez de Cuellar's report on November 2, Gaza erupted in riots, and the IDF caused injuries to 300 people in three days and imposed an indefinite curfew. But nothing happened at the Security Council. In its next communiqué, Number 65, issued in December, UNLU urged Palestinians to use "all means" in their anti-Israeli struggle, thus going beyond its policy of limiting protest action to stone throwing.

By the time the intifada completed its third year in December 1990, the Palestinian death toll was put at 930 to 1,104, including 76 to 161 children under sixteen-years old. Of these 307 to 310 were suspected Palestinian collaborators murdered by Palestinians. The number of Israelis killed, military and civilian, was 21 to 23. More than 119,000 Palestinians, a sixth of them children, were seriously wounded. 2,050 Palestinian houses were demolished or sealed. At any given moment Israeli prisons and military detention camps held some 14,000 Palestinians, about four percent of the total male population of the West Bank and Gaza Strip aged above fourteen. "Almost every Palestinian family has paid a price for the intifada, be it a relative dead, a house demolished, a friend crippled, a job lost, a sentence endured, an education interrupted, a business ruined," reported Helen Winternitz.[16]

Some Palestinian households suffered more than others. The Abu Namous family, originally from Beersheba and now living in Gaza City, was an example. Abdul Hakim and I ran into the taciturn, 24-year old son of the family, Jamal, by accident in Gaza City. His mother, Baraaka Abu Namous, was an articulate woman of 41, who had delivered her first child, Ahmad, when she was 15, and had since then borne nine more, five male and four female. The youngest, a boy, was three and a half. Ahmad and the next son, Nidal, were married, with children, and lived with their parents. Altogether an extended family of twenty, they occupied three rooms, with a small courtyard in the back. A glance at the main room, used as a bedroom at night, revealed no furniture, only rolls of striped woolen rugs stacked in a corner. On the fading, sky-blue wall facing the tiny window by the alley, there was a picture of the Dome of the Rock next to a framed verse from the Quran, its gold letters meekly reflecting the sun.

Baraaka's husband, Muhammad Harb, had been too ill to work. Of the four grown sons only one, Ahmad, a father of four, had a job. He was with the Palestinian Authority police, and earned $263 a month. The second son, Jamal, arrested for throwing a gasoline bomb at an IDF patrol in 1988, had spent nearly seven years in Israeli prisons. It was hard to imagine such a shy-looking man doing such a daring thing as lobbing a Molotov cocktail at soldiers. "Ansar III was the worst," he said. "I was there for three years. We went on a hunger strike there. We got some rights. But there is no Israeli promise that you can trust. In jail it was just eating and sleeping. They gave us just enough food to keep us alive. They treated me like a monkey. They would throw food at me as if I were an animal."

The third son, Ziad Muhammad, a serious-looking man of 22, had also suffered in the intifada. He was injured in a leg by an IDF bullet three years earlier. His younger brother, Imad, aged 18, was shot twice by the IDF: once in an arm when he was only 12 years old, and then again in a leg when he was 15. "I still have a bullet inside my leg," he told me matter-of-factly. Dressed in black trousers with red and green patches and a flashing smile, Imad seemed more suited for a career as a pop singer than a stone-throwing subversive in the ranks of the PLO. The remaining two brothers were too young to challenge the Israeli occupation.

But the mother, Baraaka, too had suffered. "I remember the first time the soldiers came, in the middle of the night," she recalled. "I opened the door. They put a gun against my breast. I was so frightened I went dumb. Couldn't speak, couldn't even cry. Terrible. The next time was in 1991. Again in the middle of the night. This time I would not open the door. So they jumped over the front wall. They had torches which they flashed. Then they switched on the lights. Suddenly in the middle of the night we had Israeli soldiers with guns all over the house. I protested. They hit me and kicked me. I was pregnant, and lost my baby. I traveled to Amman for hospital treatment. The PLO paid for it. Bless them!"

Her description of the night raid by the IDF, and my view of the room used for sleeping at night, reminded me of a passage in *The Yellow Wind* by David Grossman, an Israeli journalist and writer.

Whoever has served in the army in the "territories" knows how such rooms look from the inside during the night. Whoever has taken part in searches, in imposing curfews, in capturing a suspect at night, remembers. The violent entry into rooms like this one [in the Deheisheh camp near Bethlehem], where several people sleep, crowded, in unaired stench, three or four together under scratchy wool blankets, wearing their work clothes still in their sleep, as if ready at any moment to get up and go wherever they are told. They wake in confusion, squinting from the flashlight, children wail, sometimes a couple is making love, soldiers surround the house, some of them, shoes full of mud after tramping through the paths of the camp, walking over the sleep-warm blankets, some pounding on the tin roof above.[17]

Despite all the suffering and trauma the Abu Namous family had endured, they showed no self-pity. They all seemed to have been steeled by the experience, not demoralized. With her head held high, Baraaka had lost none of the high spiritedness that I imagined her possessing when she was younger. Nor was there any sign that she or other Gazans were prepared to accept anything less than a fully-fledged sovereign state of Palestine.

Equally remarkable was the fact that by the end of 1990 the intifada had equaled in its longevity the 1936-39 Arab Revolt. There was as yet no sign that the intifada was faltering.

The Israeli assessment of the intifada was mixed. There was satisfaction among civilian commentators that earlier IDF tactics of shootings and beatings had given way to a systematic escalation of response—tear gas, gravel throwing by machine, rubber and plastic bullets, capped finally by live ammunition—in order to reduce Palestinian fatalities. But feelings in the IDF were turning increasingly sour. "Going to the Territories just stinks," said Yossi, a 21-year-old soldier. "You dislike the Arabs. You don't believe in what you're doing... Patrolling the streets of Rafah, nervous to take each step, knowing that a gasoline bomb or bullet can come at you from any direction. You're worried that you're going to get it in the face." Another draftee described an early-morning foot patrol in Gaza's Bureij camp: "We walk slowly through back alleys that curl around main streets, listening for distant whistles and howls that alert the camp to our presence. We scan the rooftops for falling cinderblocks, intersections for flying stones. On main streets we eye passing cars, to make sure no one tries to run us down."[18]

Summing up the general mood prevalent among the young conscripts, David Horovitz of the *Jerusalem Report* wrote: "The initial excitement at getting 'some real action after all the training' has long since paled into a mixture of revulsion for the Palestinians, a sense of humiliation at having to carry out regulations that leave him [the Israeli soldier] impotent in the face of stone throwers, and frustration with the government for failing to initiate a political solution that could free the army from the West Bank and Gaza."[19]

In the political arena, the rightists, whether in the government or outside, became more convinced that Israel must keep the West Bank at all costs, and based their argument on military and security grounds rather than ideology. The leftists took a contrary view. According to Zeev Schiff, a leading military commentator, and Ehud Ya'ari, "Many [Israelis] by now understand that security is not just about territory and strategic depth. It also has to do with this increasingly embittered population that interacts with Jewish society."[20] The failure of the Israeli government, in the eyes of the liberal left, was that it had been dealing with the symptoms rather than the causes of the intifada.

Helen Winternitz summarized the mood in West Bank villages: "In the most hidden place of all, in the mind of many Palestinians, the intifada has wrought irrevocable change. Although many are desperately depressed about its lack of concrete results, they still believe there is no alternative to their struggle for statehood... To one carpenter in a village north of Jerusalem, the intifada is like climbing a ladder whose rungs are burning beneath your feet. You cannot go back down."[21]

Little wonder that most Palestinians came to see Saddam Hussein as their liberator. They were behind Yasser Arafat when he embraced the Iraqi leader, physically and ideologically. When the Gulf War started on January 16, 1991 they waited to see whether Saddam Hussein would hit Israel. And, when two days later twelve Iraqi Scud missiles landed in or near Tel Aviv and Haifa, their trust in the Iraqi President rose. "The Occupied Territories were under curfew during the 44 days of the Gulf War," said George Hintlian, a Christian Palestinian intellectual. "So people would go up at night to their terraces despite the wintry weather, and watch the skies. Every time they saw a Scud in the sky, they would start dancing and shouting 'Allahu Akbar!' (God is Great!). This made the Israeli soldiers mad. They didn't know what to do. So in desperation they would just fire in the air."[22] In mid-February 1991 Arafat had a meeting with Saddam Hussein in a Baghdad bunker. Later, in an interview on Jordanian state television, he said, "By Allah, by Allah, I tell you that the day when I and my brothers Abu Uday [father of Uday, Saddam Hussein] and Abu Abdullah [father of Abdullah, King Hussein] will pray at Al Aqsa is very soon."[23]

When on February 28, having already evacuated Kuwait, Baghdad accepted the ceasefire conditions of President Bush, including the unconditional acceptance of all twelve Security Council resolutions on the subject, many Palestinians wept openly. But a few weeks later, they realized that the situation in the region would never be the same again. "We made absolutely no mistake by supporting Saddam, because we will soon begin to reap the fruits," said Faizeh Jayousi, a Palestinian teacher in Tulkarm. "Now the entire world knows that the core of the Middle East crisis is the Palestinian issue, and that without solving it there will be no stability in the region."[24]

The fourth year of the intifada, ending in December 1991, added a further 368 Palestinians to the growing list of the dead, a large majority of them killed by the IDF. The proportion, however, of suspected collaborators murdered by Palestinian militants began to rise from the previous 30 percent of the total Palestinian fatalities. This was due to three main reasons. First, intifada leaders increasingly realized that unless the Shin Beth's 20,000-strong intelligence network, which underpinned the Israeli military regime, was totally demolished, the IDF would succeed in reimposing its control. Second, Palestinians were being squeezed economically as a result of the expulsion of the more than 400,000 Palestinians who lived and worked in the Gulf monarchies. Finally, the Palestinian community had begun turning inward the anger and frustration it felt at the defeat of Saddam Hussein.

Another result was that confrontations between the young protesters and the IDF acquired a ritualistic air. "Except for an occasional hand grenade or Molotov cocktail, the intifada has become a sport, a mutual hunt with well-defined rules," noted Yossi Halevi of the *Jerusalem Report* in his diary, published in October 1991. "Our patrols are stalked, then hit with stones and bottles. When we get angry enough, we chase stone throwers and exchange roles with them, becoming hunters instead of prey. Each side has its advantage: We wear helmets, they outrun us and know the terrain. We have guns, but everyone knows that [that] only seems to be an advantage: We are forbidden to shoot stone throwers. One day some teenagers break the rules of the hunt. Instead of running for cover after throwing stones, they stand in the middle of the street, taunting us with their fearlessness. A soldier aims their gun at them, hoping they'll flee. One of the teenagers extends his arms as though holding a gun, and mimics the soldier's pose. Our job is to 'demonstrate a presence' in the army phrase, and prevent the masked terrorists from taking over the camps. The stone-throwers' job is similar: To prove that we don't rule the streets. As we mount our trucks after a foot patrol and drive away, they follow at a safe distance as though they are expelling us, throwing rocks and shouting taunts about our mothers' promiscuity. We have demonstrated our presence, they have proved their audacity."[25] Another interpretation of this well-worn exercise came from Yossi, a member of an IDF combat unit, with long experience in Gaza. "It's their victory when we shoot them dead; the families get money, there's world attention," he said. "And it's our victory when we allow ourselves to be humiliated."[26]

On the Palestinian side, the Madrid peace conference in October 1991 split UNLU and Hamas, which opposed participation in it in any form. Within the PLO the radical Popular Front for the Liberation of Palestine (PFLP) and the Democratic Front for the Liberation of Palestine (DFLP) hardened their opposition as Arafat's Fatah actively backed the conference. Soon Arafat punctured the Shamir government's claim that it was not dealing with the PLO since many of the Palestinian delegates (officially within the Jordanian delegation) openly declared that they were taking their orders from the PLO.

Labor won the June 1992 parliamentary election. But this had no impact on the intra-Palestinian politics. Tension between Fatah and Hamas escalated into serious street fighting in Gaza in early July. But, following successful mediation by neutral Palestinians, the two sides pondered the proposal to revive the intifada.

In September, soon after Israeli officials claimed that the intifada was finished, the armed Fatah Hawks in the Rafah refugee camp had a five-hour gun battle with the IDF, in which two Palestinians were killed. Demonstrations, and sometimes gunfights with the IDF, throughout the Occupied Territories followed successive rounds of the post-Madrid Israeli-Palestinian talks, resulting in deaths of more Palestinians.

In December the government responded by imposing an indefinite curfew and sealing off Gaza. Two days later the West Bank and Gaza commemorated the fifth anniversary of the intifada—the last year increasing the total death toll by 136—with a general strike. A depressed Rabin told a visiting American Jewish delegation: "I wish Gaza would detach itself from Israel and sink into the sea."[27] Hamas militants ambushed and killed two soldiers, this time in Hebron, on December 12, and topped their operations the next day by kidnapping an Israeli border guard officer, Nissim Toledano, in the Israeli town of Lod, and demanding the release of their leader, Shaikh Ahmad Yasin. The government responded by imposing an indefinite curfew in Gaza, the hotbed of Hamas. When Toledano was found dead on December 15, Rabin ordered the arrest of 1,200 Palestinians suspected of membership of Hamas or Islamic Jihad, and expelled 413 of them to the no-man's land in south Lebanon on December 18.

When the indefinite curfew in the Gaza Strip was lifted the next day, there was severe rioting in Khan Yunis, the second largest city. The IDF shot dead six Palestinians, and over the next three days killed five more. The Israeli debate on the future of the Gaza Strip, initiated by a petition by 36 army reservists urging withdrawal from the territory, intensified. An increasingly popular view blamed Gaza-based Hamas as chiefly responsible for terrorist activities against Jews; therefore, severing Gaza from Israel would lead to a dramatic decline in terrorism. Among those who advocated evacuation from the territory was (former) Brigadier Yitzhak Pundak who, as the military governor of Gaza in 1970–72, had played a leading role in repressing the Palestinian resistance. "I see no alternative to a unilateral Israeli disengagement from Gaza's rebellious population," he now declared. "The gravity of events in Gaza does not stem from the [Palestinian] resort to firearms, rather from thousands of children who take a hand in throwing stones and burning tires."[28]

With Hamas emerging as the main threat, the Rabin administration decided to confer respectability on the PLO. Acting on its initiative, the Knesset lifted the long-established ban on contacts with the PLO on January 19, 1993.

Meanwhile, Rabin, now premier and defense minister, continued his iron fist policy. The only difference was that he was doing so as the 400-plus Hamas and Islamic Jihad leaders who had been banished to makeshift camps in south Lebanon mounted an effective public relations campaign against Israel. And Hamas activists inside the Occupied Territories showing no sign of laying down their arms.

"With the deportation issue dragging on, unresolved, and despair taking root among Palestinians in the face of mounting Israeli repression, there has been a sharp increase in the cycle of violence between Palestinians and Israelis," noted Daoud Kuttab, a Palestinian journalist, in mid-March 1993. "The shootings of Palestinians correspond with a marked increase in the number of Palestinian assaults on Israelis... It is hard to pinpoint how the latest escalation of violence began and where it is going... The most convincing explanation is that there is little hope for a peaceful solution in the near future. In fact Palestinians are more skeptical today with a Labor government in Israel than they were during the days of Likud."[29]

The situation became so critical in the Gaza Strip in mid-March that Rabin, then visiting the United States to meet the newly elected President Bill Clinton, cut short his trip. In repeated clashes between the protesters and the IDF during March 20–23, sixteen Palestinians lost their lives. In an unprecedented move, Rabin ordered checkpoints along the Green Line, the pre-1967 border of Israel, and at the entrances to Jerusalem, denying West Bankers and Gazans access to Jerusalem unless they had special permits. He basically redrew the 1949 armistice line (except in the case of Greater East Jerusalem), which Israel under the Begin administration had officially removed sixteen years before.

Gazans and West Bankers showed their disapproval of the peace negotiations with a general strike on April 27 on the eve of the ninth round of talks. The continuing violence pushed the number of Palestinians killed by the IDF and Jewish settlers in May to 34, a figure reminiscent of the early, intense days of the intifada. In an unprecedented action, the IDF fired an anti-tank missile at a residential block in Gaza City in June, killing two residents. The periodic murdering of suspected Palestinian terrorists by the IDF's Samson Unit death squads continued.[30]

There was no formal end to the intifada, just as there had been no official launching of it. However, once PLO Chairman Yasser Arafat's had in his letter of September 9, 1993 letter to Rabin renounced the use of violence against Israel and assumed responsibility over "all PLO elements and personnel in order to assume their compliance, prevent violations and discipline violators," the PLO-UNLU wrote itself out of the intifada.

But Rabin's reply to Arafat made no mention of a cessation of his government's violent methods. So the undercover assassinations by the IDF's Samson Unit continued, including its dramatic killing in broad daylight of six Fatah militants on March 28, 1994. While I was photographing their memorial in Gaza City, a dark, bespectacled man approached Abdul Hakim to inquire about the purpose of my activity. Once reassured, Mufeed Abu Aied who worked for UNRWA, told us the tale. "The six Fatah activists were in a car, and were distributing leaflets," Mufeed said. "They stopped at this intersection to get gasoline. They were surprised by Israeli undercover agents dressed like Palestinians. Sixteen of them came in three cars from three directions. They used Uzi submachine guns to kill the Fatah men. They killed them instantly, but one of them, Nahiz Muhammad Oudieh, was still alive. So the undercover agents repeated the shooting. My brother, Jibril, saw this with his eyes. Since then he has gone crazy. He is still in trauma and is unable to get a job. The Israeli agents did not allow ambulances to come through. So a woman bystander who was injured was denied immediate medical treatment."

Mufeed Abu Aied was the first English-speaking Gazan I had interviewed during my stay, a member of the local middle class who, by Abdul Hakim's reckoning, formed about 30 percent of the population. Abdul Hakim himself was well-qualified to be included in my sample of interviewees.

Born in the village of Beit Lahiya in northern Gaza, in a well-to-do family, he was sent to the American University in Cairo. "It was not our first choice," he told me. "Lebanon was closed and there were no places at Jordan University in Amman. In Egypt all local universities were closed to Palestinian students after Sadat's peace treaty with Israel. The AUC was mighty expensive. It cost $300 a month for nine months a year for three years. I got a degree in computer programming in 1983. When I returned to Gaza after graduation, I was picked up by the IDF at the [Rafah] checkpoint. They threw me in jail, and interrogated me for two months. I was surprised by how much they knew of my political activity in Cairo. They said you met so and so on such and such a day etc. How did they know all this?"

Following the peace treaty, Israel set up an embassy in Cairo, I said matter-of-factly. Abdul Hakim paused, took in my words and nodded. "I denied everything," he continued. "Back in Gaza and Israel, I applied for a job. NCR [National Cash Register] in Tel Aviv selected me for a job. When they saw that I lived in Gaza they said, 'Get a clearance letter from the interior ministry.' Forget it, I said to myself, with two months in an Israeli jail my chances were zero."

"Then I got into the restaurant business in Tel Aviv mainly because I liked Italian food. I was employed by an Israeli who lived in Europe and had a chain of Italian restaurants in Israel. His Tel Aviv restaurant was near the US embassy. The chef was Palestinian, also all the waiters. It was hard work, running the restaurant until late in the evening, rushing back home, a ride of 75 minutes by car, and up early in the morning. So we rented an apartment in Tel Aviv, broke the law about the Palestinians not staying in Israel overnight. Somebody reported. So we were all arrested, then released after two months. I was re-employed by the same Israeli. Soon after the intifada started, I was arrested under administrative detention. Served six months in jail. My Israeli boss, who lived abroad, didn't care. He re-employed me, and appointed me manager of a new restaurant he opened in Haifa. I had seven people working under me. This went on until I was arrested [for the third time] in late 1990 for being a leader of Fatah in my village. Spent four months in prison. So all-told three political arrests, and one for staying overnight in Israel. Now there is simply no question of having a proper job in Israel. At most I could expect to be employed as a casual worker on a daily basis."

He took me to his village of Beit Lahiya, a little over a mile south-west of the Erez checkpoint. After the overcrowded refugee camps and Gaza City, Beit Lahiya felt like a half-abandoned habitation. Responding to my wish to meet more of the territory's middle class, Abdul Hakim introduced me to Abdul Qadir Ealin, the owner of a store selling groceries, soft drinks and hurricane lanterns. An avuncular man of 66, he wore a white *keffiyeh* held down by a black *igal* (rope).

"Under the Israeli occupation the situation was very bad," he said in fluent English. "Much better now under the Palestinian Authority. But we have no freedom of movement, and the economic situation is worse. One million Gazans live in an area of 45 by 8 kilometers [28 by 5 miles] almost half of which is still occupied by the Israelis. Because agricultural produce is cheap, Gazans working on land do not make enough money, and so they, too, seek work for wages. And that sort of work is available mostly in Israel. In the past 60,000 Gazans used to work in Israel, now only 5,000 are allowed in. The unemployment is high. Because people have no jobs they have no cash. Ninety percent of my sales are on credit. In the past our vegetables and fruit used to go to Saudi Arabia, Jordan and Kuwait through Israel, but now that is closed [because the Israeli authorities discovered that the Islamic groups were using these trucks to smuggle explosives]." What was the solution? "Israel must leave the Jewish settlements in Gaza and the West Bank," replied Abdul Qadir. "Donor countries should provide funds for factories to create jobs. Palestinians should be re-employed in the Gulf states. Loss of their jobs there has caused a problem here."

As I brought Abdul Qadir, standing against the half-empty shelves of his wares, into the view-finder of my camera, I noticed a framed photograph of a younger man, crouching on the soil of a garden, above a line of hurricane lanterns. Who was he? "My son, Hassan, assassinated by the Shin Beth," said Abdul Qadir. "In 1978 he was sentenced to 20 years in jail as a leader of the Popular Front in Gaza. He was released in 1985 in the prisoner exchange. In September 1986 he got a telephone call, and the caller told him to go and pick up something, a package, in the back garden of his house. When he did, he got blown up by an explosive. He was gone!" Abdul Qadir sat down. He struggled to hold back tears. The murder had occurred nearly nine years ago, but so severe was the blow to his psyche of the sudden, dramatic loss—the body of his beloved son blown to pieces—that he still found it wrenching to recall.[31] "After murdering my son, they arrested me!" Abdul Qadir continued, having regained his composure. "I was so distraught that I couldn't eat. 'How can I eat when my son has just been killed?' I'd say to my jailers. So they put me in solitary confinement for three weeks." Yet, like his son, Abdul Qadir remains loyal to the Popular Front for the Liberation of Palestine (PFLP), of which he is the acknowledged leader in the village.

What explained the strength of the PFLP in the Gaza Strip? Its roots lay in the Arab Nationalist Movement (ANM), which came into being in 1952 as a result of the merger of two groups, composed chiefly of the students and staff of the American University in Beirut. Its main slogan was: "Unity, Liberation, Revenge." It had placed much hope in the coup by nationalist military officers in Egypt in July 1952, especially as a vehicle to effect Arab unity. Since Gaza was administered by Egypt, during the rule of radical President Gamal Abdul Nasser, the Gaza branch of the ANM found itself in a congenial environment. Acting in conjunction with the Egyptian army, it participated in guerrilla attacks on Israel. After the Palestine Liberation Organization was formed in 1964, Nasser allowed it to post its military wing, the Palestine Liberation Army, in Gaza, where male secondary school students were given compulsory military training.

When the Egyptian military departed from the Gaza Strip during the June 1967 War, it left behind its arms and ammunition depots as well as its underground bunkers. These were inherited by Palestinian militants. Those belonging to the ANM, which transformed itself into the Popular Front for the Liberation of Palestine in December 1967, became particularly active against the Israeli occupation. By 1969 the Palestinian guerrillas held sway in the refugee camps at night and harassed the Israeli army during the day. Later that year when General Ariel Sharon became commander of the Southern Command, he decided to tackle the problem systematically.

By appointing a local scion, known for his moderate, pro-Jordanian views, Rashid Shawwa, as mayor of Gaza City in 1970, Sharon tried to divide the Gazan community.

In mid-1971 he began to implement the military part of his counter-insurgency plan with a ruthless resolve. To improve IDF patrolling he had the densely populated refugee camps criss-crossed with wide roads. To facilitate access for IDF armored vehicles he had entire sectors of refugee camps bulldozed. He punished stone throwers with deportation to Jordan. He banished the families of suspected guerrillas to the IDF detention camps in the Sinai. He ordered the IDF to carry out house-to-house searches while he placed whole towns and camps under long curfews, and resorted frequently to blowing up the houses of suspected terrorists. By February 1972, the IDF had killed 104 Palestinians and arrested 742 more. This weakened the Palestinian resistance but did not destroy it. The riots that erupted in the Shaati (beach) camp, adjacent to Gaza City, in September spread throughout the Strip, and continued for two months. Sharon quelled them with an iron hand. In the process he lost Rashid Shawwa who, responding to the popular outcry, resigned. During the following summer Sharon left the IDF to enter politics. But before then he had implemented another part of his plan in the Gaza Strip.

He secured the approval of the Labor-led government, headed by Golda Meir, to establish five military-agricultural settlements in Gaza in order to split the Palestinian communities and prevent the emergence of a large contiguous swathe of Palestinians. Thus in 1972 Erez, Netzarim, Nahal Qatif D, Kfar Darom and Morag came into being. The land confiscation by Israel that started the colonization process continued relentlessly for more than two decades. By the time the Israeli-PLO Accord was signed in September 1993, over one-third of the Gaza Strip had been seized by Israel, and the number of the original colonies had more than trebled. The settlements were safeguarded by high barbed-wired fences, land mines and IDF troops. The size of the ultra-nationalist settler community reached a peak of 4,500 when the Oslo Accord was concluded, and then began to decline steadily.

As Abdul Hakim and I drove southward along Gaza's main north-south highway we traveled a short distance buttressed by the Jewish settlements—Gush Qatif on the Mediterranean side and Kfar Daroma on the opposite—green fields, separated from the road by a razor-wire fence, decked with skull and cross-bones signs in red, and guarded by soldiers in watch-towers, their machine-guns pointing outward. Abdul Hakim described how each settlement was accessible directly from various Israeli crossing points. The principle of the Jewish settlements having direct road access to Israel was later to be applied to all of the 128 Jewish colonies in the West Bank before the IDF troops were redeployed in January 1996.

The Gush Qatif settlement bloc remains a world unto itself, a Garden of Eden in the hell-hole of the Gaza Strip. It includes the HaShalim Beach (for the exclusive use of the settlers and Jewish Israelis), a tourist village and a beach hotel with a restaurant offering a panoramic view of the Mediterranean Sea. Here Jewish settlers live in the midst of water-sprinkled lawns, fragrant trees, orange groves and greenhouses. A resort hotel built for $9 million and catering epecially to Orthodox Jews, however, was forced to close in 1989 as a direct consequence of the Palestinian intifada.

The insularity of the settlers, physical and psychological, was well captured by Robert Friedman, a Jewish American journalist, in his account of a visit in the midst of the intifada to the head office of the Gaza Regional Council in the Neve

Dekalim settlement of the Gush Qatif, and an interview with the elected head of the Council, Zvi Hendel, a 41-year-old Romanian Jew, "with a knitted yarmulke and an easy smile." Like all other settlements in the Gaza Strip, Neve Dekalim was surrounded by "barbed wire, watch-towers and heavily armed Israeli soldiers." Across the road was the Khan Yunis refugee camp with 50,000 Palestinians crammed into an area of less than one square mile, living in grinding poverty. "We have two reasons for being here," Hendel explained to Friedman. "First, it's our land. Secondly, our presence enhances Israel's security. We're the eyes and ears of the army." On the intifada, Hendel's analysis was simple. "Our good Jewish hearts have exacerbated the intifada," he said. "If we had killed 200 Arabs at the beginning of the intifada, it would be over. If we expel 7,000 troublemakers now, everything would be okay." Hendel told Friedman that before the outbreak of the intifada, "The settlers tried to build a 'harmonious' life with the Arabs," and added: "But even during the intifada, I have maintained friendships [with the Arabs]. I'm sorry I can't take you with me to visit my Arab friends... but they are afraid." He went on to claim: "'99 percent' of the Arabs oppose the intifada, but they are terrorized into rebelling against Israeli rule by a small number of Palestinian activists." But this did not square up with what Friedman discovered at the nearby Atzmona settlement. When he saw a group of Ethiopian Jews loading sacks of potatoes on to a truck there, he requested an interview with them, but this was brusquely rejected by the Jewish American settler who was supervising the loading. "Before the intifada, the settlements in the Gaza Strip had employed Palestinian refugees to do most of the manual work," wrote Friedman. "No longer. The settlers are afraid to allow Palestinians into the settlements, despite Hendel's claims of good fellowship."[32]

Following the implementation of the 1993 Israeli-PLO Accord in July 1994, when the Palestinian Authority took charge of administering limited self-rule in the Gaza Strip—with the Jewish settlements remaining under the exclusive control of Israel—the significance of the Netzarim settlement rose sharply. Situated on the fringe of Gaza City's southern suburb, it overlooked the capital, and its location allowed the IDF to slice the Gaza Strip into two. It was described variously as "a bone stuck in our throat" (the Palestinian Authority) and "an obstacle to peace" (the left-wing ministers of the Israeli government). Housing a mere 30 Orthodox Jewish families, it became, in the words of a reporter of the *Jerusalem Post Magazine*, "perhaps the most heavily protected spot in the Middle East."[33] This came about after the junction of the settler access road and the Palestinians' north-south highway attracted the attention of Gaza's bombers, who wanted the settlement closed. In November 1994 a Palestinian suicide bomber blew himself up and killed three IDF officers, and another Palestinian gunned down an Israeli army officer.

But the tenacity to hold on was not limited to the settlers, it extended to the government as well. Why were the Israeli authorities so keen to keep the Jewish settlements in the miserable Gaza Strip, I asked Abdul Hakim. "To bargain about the cost of giving them up just as they did in the case of Sinai with the Egyptians," he replied. "For the present the rumor is that the settlers are pumping out water from Gaza to Israel. So they need these settlements to carry out this theft."

11

The Palestine Liberation Organization

Armed Resistance to
Red-Carpet Respectability

There is no mistaking where you are in the Gaza Strip village of Beit Lahiya when you see a line of short steel poles in a dusty road painted red and white: the colors of Fatah, the leading constituent of the Palestine Liberation Organization. It is Fatah's local branch office. Inside, near a large logo of Fatah, two crossed machine-guns protecting the Palestine of the British mandate era, I met Muhammad Talouli. At 27, he was a member of Fatah's central committee of the northern district. He epitomized the up-and-coming image of the ruling party of the future in the Palestinian territories.

Talouli was a native Gazan: his parents came from the village of Dimra near the IDF's Erez checkpoint. During the 1948 War they set up home in the Jabaliya refugee camp, and Muhammad was born there a year after the 1967 War. "I became a member of Fatah when I was fourteen," he told me in hesitant English. "I was put in jail in 1985 because I threw a gasoline bomb at an IDF patrol. Six years. I spent much of my time studying in the prison. I was released in 1991. I applied for a place in the Al Azhar University [in Gaza City] and was accepted. I am now in my final year, doing education."

The northern district had "something like 30,000, or about 40,000 families," he told me, "with the average family having seven members. During the intifada, more than 10,000 Fatah members were jailed in our northern district." Taking into account other political groups participating in the intifada, would he reckon that every other family had a male member in prison? "Yes, definitely. And all parties tried to help the families of those who were jailed or wounded or martyred. Fatah used to pay an outright sum to the family of a martyr. But then we had a financial crisis. Now the party is recovering slowly. Recently we gave $100 each to the families of the martyrs."

Fatah and other secular groups were particularly strong in the refugee camps, I discovered. Since Fatah's philosophy was simple—resistance to Israel, with no official position about what would follow once the Israeli occupation ended—it was popular.

Indeed Gaza's Al Bureij camp had provided two of the three co-founders of Fatah: Salah Khalaf, known as Abu Iyad, and Khalil Wazir, or Abu Jihad. The third, Yasser Arafat, also known by his *nom de guerre* of Abu Ammar,

200

belonged to the al Husseini clan from Gaza. His father died there in 1953 while Arafat was at university in Cairo.

Gaza's emergence as the seedbed of Palestinian nationalism lay in the divergent policies of Jordan, which politically annexed the West Bank after the 1948 War, and Egypt, which merely administered the Gaza Strip. Whereas the king tried to inculcate a Jordanian identity among West Bankers as well as the Palestinian refugees in Jordan, the regimes in Cairo kept the flame of Palestinian identity flickering in Gaza.

Hundreds of Gazan students attended Egyptian universities. Among them was Salah Khalaf, an obstreperous young man of nineteen, who enrolled in a teacher training college in Cairo in 1951. Born in 1932 into a middle-class household in Jaffa, Khalaf and his family had fled in 1948. He met Yasser Arafat, then in his second year of civil engineering at Cairo University. In 1952 they won election to the executive committee of the Palestine Students' Federation (PSF). Arafat became its chairman.

Muhammad Abdul Raouf Arafat al Qudwa, nicknamed Yasser, was born in Cairo, though his merchant father was originally from Khan Yunis in the Gaza Strip. When his mother died in 1933, his father sent him to live with relatives in the Old City of Jerusalem. He later attended Cairo University (then called King Fuad University), where he had compulsory military training.

After graduating from college, Salah Khalaf worked as a teacher in the Gaza Strip, maintaining his position with the PSF. In August 1956 he and Arafat traveled to Prague to attend the International Student Congress, which accepted the PSF as a member. By then Arafat had met another Palestinian refugee, Khalil Wazir, a 20-year-old, with an intense gaze and a sharp mind. The trio became life-long personal and political friends. There was a particular chemistry between Arafat and Wazir, the former being hot-tempered and impetuous, given to acting before thinking, and the latter cool, rational and given to deliberating before acting.

Born in a middle class household in Ramle, Palestine, Wazir and his family fled the IDF in mid-July 1948. He grew up in the Al Bureij refugee camp in Gaza. In 1954 the Egyptian military selected him for commando training and military instruction. He met Yasser Arafat in Cairo at a Palestinian student demonstration. Wazir was later commissioned as a lieutenant in the Gazan brigade of the Egyptian army.

During the 1956 Suez War, Arafat was called up as a reserve officer in the Egyptian army, and assigned to a bomb disposal unit. With the Gaza Strip and the Sinai falling to the Israelis, Wazir's Gazan unit retreated to Cairo. Before the fall of the Strip, Khalaf left for the Egyptian capital, and then Europe. He enrolled as a student in Stuttgart, Germany, and so did Wazir.

Graduating as a civil engineer in 1956, Arafat worked for the Egyptian Cement Company, and after two years for Kuwait's public works department. Wazir joined him there, and they floated the idea of setting up a Palestinian organization committed to liberating Palestine. They produced a journal, *Falastinuna: Nida al Hayat*, or Our Palestine: The Call of Life. Khalaf joined in when he arrived in Kuwait in March 1959. They decided that Fatah, the reverse acronym of *Harkat al Tahrir al Falastini*, or Movement for the Liberation of Palestine, should be a movement, not a party.

Later that year, they began to publish the journal in Beirut, and distribute it throughout the Middle East. This helped the establishment of secret cells of Fatah not only in Kuwait but also in the Palestinian refugee camps in Jordan, Syria and Lebanon. By then the basic Fatah ideology and tactics had crystallized: revolutionary violence, practiced by the masses, was the only way to liberate Palestine and liquidate all forms of Zionism. In short, Fatah believed in a people's war.

Wazir returned to Stuttgart to organize Palestinian students in West Germany. He also established contacts with the National Liberation Front of Algeria which defeated French rule in July 1962. Wazir and other Fatah leaders traveled to Algiers in December and secured official recognition for their movement. Fatah opened its bureau in Algiers in 1963, headed by Wazir. He set up a network of contacts with other radical states and liberation movements. The following March he and Arafat visited Peking and then Hanoi, North Vietnam. In the summer he helped organize a military training camp for some 100 Fatah recruits in Algeria.

In January 1964 the first summit of the Arab League directed Ahmad Shuqairi, a Palestinian lawyer who had served as under-secretary for political affairs at the Arab League headquarters in Cairo during most of the 1950s, to consult fellow Palestinians and present a plan for a body to enable Palestinians to play their part in liberating Palestine and determining their own future.

Shuqairi had trained as a lawyer, and served on the Arab Higher Committee during 1946. After the 1948 War he moved to Damascus, and was a member of Syria's UN delegation in 1949-50, and then worked for the Arab League. From 1957, he served as Saudi Arabia's Minister of State of UN affairs and UN ambassador in 1957-62.

Within a few months of the summit, he produced a document entitled the Palestine National Charter, demanding the founding of a democratic and secular state in Palestine as constituted under the British mandate. It was adopted by the delegates, chosen by Palestinians from several Arab countries, who assembled in East Jerusalem, in late May 1964. The event was inaugurated by Jordan's King Hussein, and attended by Palestinian luminaries scattered across the Middle East and elsewhere. Wazir and a few other activists of Fatah, now past its clandestine phase, attended the assembly, but insisted on remaining independent. Their argument for unleashing a people's war on the Zionist entity fell on deaf ears.

The conference established the Palestine Liberation Organization as an umbrella body. It included a 350-member Palestine National Council,[1] which elected a central council and an executive committee chaired by Shuqairi. Egypt's President Nasser provided full backing.

Also in 1964 the Syrian regime of the radical, pan-Arabist Baath Socialist Party, decided to assist Fatah in guerrilla actions against Israel. Aware of the earlier Arab summit resolution on Israel's theft of Jordan River water, Fatah's Al Assifa (The Storm) militia, headed by Wazir, launched an attack on the Israeli Water Carrier in the Galilee on January 1, 1965 from Ein al-Hilwa refugee camp in south Lebanon. The plan to blow up the water pipes was far from successful. Nonetheless January 1 remains an important commemorative date in the official Palestinian calendar.

The use of *noms de guerre* by Fatah leaders can be traced to this event. Arafat, Wazir and Khalaf were jailed by the Lebanese authorities for two months after the attack. In prison Arafat chose Abu Ammar, Father of Construction, signifying his profession as a civil engineer, and Wazir, Abu Jihad, Father of Struggle.

Arafat and Wazir moved to Damascus, where the Syrian government continued to provide military training facilities. They traveled to the West Bank, Jordanian, and Gazan refugee camps to recruit for Fatah.

By mid-1966 Fatah's guerrilla actions against Israel had become an element in regional politics. Syrian forces bore the brunt of Israel's fierce retaliatory response, but Jordan was not spared. Indeed in late 1966 Israel struck heavily on the West Bank village of Samu. These skirmishes proved to be the preamble to the June 1967 Arab-Israeli War.

The Arabs' humiliating defeat in the 1967 war was a political-military earthquake in the Middle Eastern region. Among its principal Palestinian losers was Shuqairi. On the eve of the war, he indulged in hyperbolic rhetoric on his radio station, out of all proportion to his small militia. He was compelled to resign his chairmanship of the PLO in December 1967.

But the Six Day War had its silver lining even for the defeated Palestinians. So said Albert Aghazarian, a pipe-smoking, Armenian native of Jerusalem's Old City and lecturer on Middle Eastern history at the Birzeit University on the West Bank. "The positive aspect of the 1967 War was that it gave birth to Palestinian nationalism," he told me. "I should know because I went through a phase when I was indoctrinated to believe that I was Jordanian."[2]

Arafat reached the same conclusion in the heat of the moment. Unlike most of his colleagues, who were paralyzed by Israel's crushing defeat of the Arab states, Arafat saw a welcome opportunity for Palestinians to become self-reliant and initiate their own armed liberation struggle against Israel. After an acrimonious executive committee meeting, Arafat, given to the doctrine of "doing something," crossed the Jordan River with his aide, Abu Ali Shaheen, and disappeared behind the Israeli lines. Basing themselves in a village near Jenin, they set up the infrastructure to launch a guerrilla campaign. Arafat then secured Fatah's consent for an attack on an Israeli target in September 1967, hoping it would trigger an escalating series of armed assaults. To Arafat's disappointment, though, it was not enough to shake the Israeli military. Drawing on information from captured Jordanian files, the IDF repressed the Palestinian resistance, killing over 60 guerrillas and arresting 320 by the end of the year. Among the prisoners was Abu Ali Shaheen.

But Arafat, endowed, it is said, "with nine lives," escaped. He made his getaway from the back window of his Al Bireh hideout wearing women's clothing—so the story runs—as Israeli soldiers entered the front door.[3]

Within three months Arafat achieved a military success that firmly established Fatah as the prime force among Palestinians. This was the military confrontation between the IDF and Fatah guerrillas at the Jordanian border town of al-Karameh on March 21, 1968. The Israeli-Jordanian frontier was buzzing with guerrilla activity, with Palestinian commandos crossing the Jordan River at night, placing land-mines or throwing hand grenades, and then returning to base.

On March 18 a land-mine exploded under an Israeli schoolbus, and killed two. In the early hours of the morning of March 21 an IDF armored column, along with some 7,000 infantry, advanced into Jordan to destroy the guerrilla infrastructure. The Israelis, who had expected the Palestinians to flee, instead faced stiff resistance from the 400 commandos backed by Jordanian army artillery fire. When the battle ended at sunset, 28 Israelis were dead and 34 of their tanks damaged against the death of 98 Palestinian guerrillas. Such an IDF loss was unprecedented.

Since a Jordanian claim of involvement would have invited punishing Israeli retaliation, Fatah and Arafat took most of the credit, with the smaller Popular Front for the Liberation of Palestine garnering the rest. Overnight thousands of Palestinians volunteered to join Fatah. The organization soon abandoned its collective image to project the image of a single personality—that of Arafat.

Little wonder that in the Palestinian territories, March 21 remains an important day. I got a whiff of this while interviewing the headmaster of the oldest high school in the middle-class Al Rimal district of Gaza City on March 20. Festooned in a sea of Palestinian flags and portraits of Arafat and Wazir, the school was festive. A middle-aged teacher told a highly embroidered story about Force 17, Arafat's elite security unit. "During the Battle of al-Karameh," he began with a twinkle in his eyes, "seventeen *fedayeen* (commandos) took up positions in the trenches along the Jordan River, armed with RPGs [rocket-propelled grenades]. As the Israelis crossed over they stayed put. They fired their weapons at point-blank range and made a hash of the Israelis. In the end all of them were killed, except one. But they will live as long as there is Force 17!"

As it was, for the next two and a half years the Palestinian resistance rode an unprecedented wave of popularity at both public and official levels. "From March 1968 to September 1970, the Palestinians appeared to have seized the moral leadership and attained enormous influence over almost the entire Arab world—despite the fact that they still lacked a secure territorial base and possessed only a minuscule fighting force (not more than 15,000 guerrillas) and a rudimentary political infrastructure," noted Professor Michael C. Hudson, an American specialist on the Middle East. "Syria provided sanctuary; Egypt provided diplomatic support; Algeria supplied [military] training and material; Saudi Arabia and the Gulf states provided money; Jordan and Lebanon almost provided a state."[4]

The role of Egypt, the single most important Arab state, and its president, Nasser, who remained popular even after the 1967 defeat, was crucial in the rise of Fatah and Arafat. Nasser received Arafat in April 1968, saying "I would be more than glad if you could represent the Palestinian people and the Palestinian will to resist [Israel], politically by your presence and militarily by your actions." He then advised Arafat to preserve Fatah's independence from Arab regimes, but to co-ordinate with them in the same way that Jewish guerrilla groups did with the mainstream Zionist movement before the founding of Israel.[5] Nasser gave a pledge to arm and train Fatah recruits. Fatah emerged as the Palestinians' mainstream party the way Mapai did among Zionist pioneers in Palestine, with Arafat as a latter-day Ben Gurion. Nasser, the towering leader of the Arab world, had anointed Arafat as Mr. Palestine, a label which, despite the sharp vicissitudes of the Middle Eastern politics, stuck firmly.

The Rise of the Radical PLO

At the fourth session of the Palestine National Council in July 1968, Fatah and other smaller guerrilla groups affiliated to the PLO considerably stiffened the National Charter. The modified Charter declared: "Armed struggle is the only way to liberate Palestine."(Article 9) Of the 33 articles in the rewritten Charter the other important ones were: "Palestine, with the boundaries under the British mandate, is the homeland of Palestinian Arabs, and is indivisible" (Articles 1 and 2); "The Jews who lived in Palestine before the Zionist immigration are considered Palestinian" (Article 6); "The partition of Palestine and the founding of Israel are illegal since they violated the will of Palestinians and the principle of self-determination included in the United Nations Charter" (Article 19); "The Balfour Declaration and the British mandate for Palestine are null and void" (Article 20); "The Palestinians reject all solutions which are substitutes for total liberation of Palestine" (Article 21); and "Zionism, associated with international imperialism, is racist, expansionist and colonial, and Israel is the instrument of the Zionist movement" (Article 22). The PNC rejected the UN Security Council Resolution 242 since it made no specific mention of Palestinians.

The next PNC congress, convened in February 1969 in Cairo under the red and white logo of Fatah, reflected the overwhelming strength of the guerrilla groups, with Fatah's claimed force of 15,000 commandos at the head. The PNC, at Nasser's behest, elected Arafat Chairman of the PLO's executive committee, which included three more Fatah figures, including Wazir and Khalaf. But Arafat ensured that the leaders of all other commando groups, irrespective of their political views, were included as well. Taking his cue from the Elected Assembly of the Jewish community in Palestine, which represented all hues of Zionism, Arafat was keen to have all those who believed in Palestinian nationalism affiliate to the PLO. Also, aware of how Palestinian rivalries during the 1936-9 Arab Revolt had undermined the uprising, he wanted to gather every Palestinian faction under the PLO umbrella.

Among the smaller parties the Popular Front for the Liberation of Palestine (PFLP), led by George Habash, was the most important. Born in 1925 into a Christian family in Lydda (later Lod), Palestine, Habash's family moved to Amman during the 1948 War. A brilliant student, and extraordinarily eloquent, he graduated in medicine from the American University in Beirut. In 1952 he co-founded the Arab Nationalist Movement. Under his leadership the ANM's Palestinian members formed a "Preparatory Committee for Unified Palestinian Action" in early 1966. Overall, though, Habash put his faith in Egyptian President Nasser to liberate Palestine through a conventional war with Israel. But the Arab defeat in the June 1967 War destroyed this possibility. In December Habash merged the Palestinian section of the ANM with the Syria-based Palestine Liberation Front led by Ahmad Jibril, to form the Popular Front for the Liberation of Palestine. It immediately undertook guerrilla operations against Israel, and participated in the much-celebrated Battle of al-Karameh in March 1968.

Arafat inherited the infrastructure of the PLO, which included not only the organizational and financial bureaucracy, but also the Palestine Liberation Army, trained by Egypt and stationed in the Gaza Strip, and popular organizations—

the unions of artists, doctors, engineers, farmers, journalists and writers, lawyers, students, teachers, women and workers—founded by diaspora Palestinians in the Arab countries. He took over the Palestine National Fund, set up by the PLO to fund its work. The contributions came from Arab and other friendly countries, a Palestine tax collected by certain Arab states, an income tax on Palestinians living elsewhere in the diaspora, and donations from affluent Palestinians. Arafat relied on his own business contacts and skills, and appealed successfully to fellow Arab leaders, especially the oil-rich rulers, for substantial contributions to the PLO.

With Jordan providing a home to almost half of the Palestinian refugees from 1948, the ten refugee camps there emerged as important centers of Palestinian commando presence. The presence of a large body of trained armed men posed a threat to the regime of King Hussein. When he imposed restrictions in February 1969 the commandos protested violently. The subsequent compromise between the king and Arafat proved fragile. While the monarch quietly prepared for an armed showdown with the guerrillas, the PFLP and its breakaway, the Democratic Front for the Liberation of Palestine, headed by Nayif Hawatmeh, adopted increasingly radical policies.

As Habash graduated from radical Palestinian nationalism to an internationally-oriented Marxism-Leninism wedded to bringing about global revolution, he identified international Zionism, world imperialism and Arab reaction as the enemies. "Arab reaction" included the monarchical regime of King Hussein. Equally, Hawatmeh, born in 1934 in the Jordanian city of Salt into a Christian family, perceived the liberation of Palestine and Jordan as inseparable. Habash believed that hijacking an airliner would be more effective in drawing world attention to the plight of Palestinians than killing Israelis. His first target was an Israeli plane at the Athens airport in December 1968; the hijacking resulted in the release of sixteen Palestinian prisoners.

Periodic clashes between armed Palestinians and the 55,000-strong Jordanian army started in the spring of 1970. Fatah, then based in Amman, had 20,000 armed men in its Al Assifa militia. The party leadership was evenly divided between right and left, with Arafat often acting as a mediator between Salah Khalaf and Farouq Qaddumi, a former member of the Baath Socialist Party, on the left, and Khalil al Wazir and Khalid Hassan, close to the conservative Saudi royal family, on the right.

The truce between the Palestinian commandos and Jordan, brokered by the Arab League in June 1970, frayed in early August when King Hussein accepted the US regional peace plan aimed initially at securing a truce between Egypt and Israel in the War of Attrition, started by Cairo in 1969. Since Hussein's action contradicted the Palestinian position as well as the stance adopted by the latest Arab League summit (held three years earlier), relations between him and the PLO soured. Tension heightened following the PFLP's hijacking of three western airliners (American, British and Swiss) on September 12. The emptied planes were moved to Dawsons Field, an abandoned airstrip in the Jordanian desert, and blown up once Israel refused the demand to free Palestinian prisoners.

Though Arafat and other Fatah leaders were divided over confronting King Hussein, they were swept into the maelstrom that followed the destruction of the airliners. Fighting erupted between the Palestinians joined by radical Jordanians, and the Jordanian army on September 15. Four days later, the Syrian-based Palestine Liberation Army crossed with tanks into northern Jordan and captured Irbid. Assured of US and Israeli backing, Hussein deployed his air force against the Palestinians in Irbid. The Palestinian armored units withdrew to Syria and an Arab League-mediated ceasefire began September 25. Since Palestinian militia units were often based inside refugee camps, there was much fighting in the overcrowded camps. The casualties included about 4,000 dead. The Palestinians called the event "Black September."

The net gainer was Israel. The number of Palestinian guerrilla actions against it fell steeply, from a monthly total of 300 to about 50.

The truce was solemnized on September 27 by an Arafat-Hussein handshake, with Nasser observing. But chances of a lasting reconciliation faded when the Egyptian President died of heart failure three days later. Slowly, the Jordanian forces began to tighten the noose around the Palestinian commandos, isolating some 4,000 of them in the hilly areas in the north-western corner of the country. Arafat, hiding in the hills with his men, tried but failed to seek a rapprochement with Hussein in late April 1971, and then escaped to Syria. His fighters were decimated by the Jordanian military in July, finally ending the PLO's armed presence in Jordan.

King Hussein tried to make amends for the iron fist he had wielded against the PLO by proposing a United Arab Kingdom, with the federated provinces of Jordan and Palestine, after Israel withdrew from the West Bank. But the tenth PNC, meeting in April 1972, rejected his proposal.

Having lost its Jordanian base, the PLO had to relocate. Syria, with ten Palestinian refugee camps, was one choice; Lebanon, with thirteen camps, was another. But Syria, under the iron hand of President Hafiz Assad, was hardly likely to give the PLO freedom of action to mount guerrilla assaults against Israel. So the choice fell to Lebanon, the least centralized state in the region. Already the hilly terrain of southern Lebanon had proved ideal for Palestinian commandos to mount periodic attacks on Israel.

A State Within A State

The PLO gradually relocated to west Beirut in 1972. Lebanon's comparatively free atmosphere allowed the PLO the diplomatic impact it had not made before. During the decade it functioned from the Lebanese capital, the PLO emerged as a state-within-a-state.

The October 1973 Arab-Israeli War altered the regional balance of forces in favor of the Arabs. Besides restoring Arab unity, it underlined the immense power of an economic weapon, oil, which the petroleum-producing Arab states had hardly used during the 1967 conflict. This diminished the PLO's post-Black September desperation which had led it increasingly to mount dramatic terrorist actions such as the killing of eleven Israeli athletes in September 1972 at the Munich Olympics.

Israel's retaliatory air strikes on the Palestinians in Lebanon and Syria killed 200 to 500 people, most of them civilian.[6] In December 1973 the PFLP suspended actions against Israeli targets abroad. Fatah followed its lead two months later. Israeli targets inside the Jewish state and the Occupied Territories, however, were still regarded as legitimate.

A renewed confidence made Palestinian leaders edge toward realism and moderation. The initiative came from Nayif Hawatmeh, a Marxist intellectual who maintained good relations with the Communist Party of the Soviet Union. He was instrumental in persuading the Kremlin, after the October 1973 War, to recognize the PLO as "the sole legitimate authority, representing the Palestinian people," and to invite Arafat, Habash and himself to Moscow in mid-November. In early 1974, Hawatmeh proposed the idea of setting up a national authority in the West Bank and Gaza as the first step toward the liberation of all of Palestine. Participating in the ongoing public debate, Salah Khalaf (Abu Iyad), an eminent Fatah leader, said: "The question we must ask ourselves is whether, by refusing to accept anything less than the full liberation of all Palestine, we are prepared to abandon a portion of our patrimony to a third party." He pointed out that the Zionists had obtained their state of Israel in the late 1940s by accepting only a portion of the land they claimed whereas the Palestinians, by consistently saying no, had ended up with nothing.[7]

Echoing these sentiments, the twelfth Palestine National Council, meeting in June 1974, called for the establishment of "the independent combatant national authority for the people over every part of the Palestinian territory that is liberated... Once it is established, the Palestinian national authority will strive to achieve a union of the [Arab] confrontation countries, with the aim of completing the liberation of all Palestinian territory."[8] The PLO was ready to accept the mini-state of the West Bank and Gaza, if only as a (theoretically) transient stage, a stance rejected by the PFLP's Habash, who could muster only about a quarter of some 250 PNC members present. Speaking in favor of the resolution, a delegate said: "Remember, remember what Ben Gurion told the 22nd Zionist Congress at Basle in 1946: that the Zionists would accept a state within a reasonable part of Palestine without forgoing their historic rights to it all."[9]

The PNC resolution provided Arafat with a means to win broader diplomatic recognition. The first sign of success came in mid-October when the United Nations General Assembly decided by 115 votes to 4 to hold a special discussion on the question of Palestine, something it had not done for the past 22 years, and to invite the PLO "as representative of the Palestinian people" to participate in the debate.

In late October the seventh Arab League summit declared the PLO to be "the sole and legitimate representative of the Palestinian people" with "the right to establish the independent State of Palestine on any liberated territory," and conferred full membership on it. (Arafat had attended the 1969 and 1973 summits on an ad hoc basis.) It was with great reluctance that King Hussein of Jordan, who had claimed special interest in the West Bank, accepted this resolution, which meant diplomatic recognition for the PLO. At the conference's closing session on November 2, Arafat declared: "Today is the turning point in the history of the Palestinian people and the Arab nation.

I vow to continue the struggle until we meet together in Jerusalem with the same smiling faces as we see here tonight."[10]

On November 13, 1974 Arafat arrived in New York surrounded by the most stringent security the city had witnessed. Just before noon Arafat entered UN headquarters in the glass and steel skyscraper on the bank of the East River. He wore his usual fatigues, topped by his trademark checkered *keffiyeh*. He received a standing ovation as he entered the General Assembly hall. Everybody joined, except the American delegates. Two sets of seats were empty, those of Israel and South Africa. As Arafat raised his arms in a revolutionary salute, he inadvertently exposed a holster at his side which, UN officials insisted later, was empty of its normal content, a Beretta pistol.

In his 100-minute speech, he dwelled on the past (drawing parallels between western imperialism and the Zionist colonization of Palestine); described the present (the anti-colonial nature of the PLO's struggle and the Palestinians' suffering under Israeli occupation); and portrayed the future of his dreams (that "I may return with my people out of exile, there in Palestine to live... in a democratic state where Christians, Jews and Muslims live in justice, equality, fraternity and progress"). He ended his address thus: "Today I have come bearing an olive branch and a freedom fighter's gun. Do not let the olive branch fall from my hand. I repeat: do not let the olive branch fall from my hand." It would be another fourteen years before Arafat would be invited again to address the General Assembly, convened especially in Geneva due to US refusal to grant him a visa.

Israel vehemently denounced the PLO's diplomatic victory. Its UN ambassador railed against Arafat's "band of murderers and cut-throats" who had plunged the UN into a "Sodom and Gomorrah of ideals and values," and went on to attack the international community which, during its "days of degradation and disgrace, of surrender and humiliation," had allowed such an event.[11]

On November 22, at the end of a nine-day debate, the UN General Assembly adopted Resolution 3236, describing the PLO as "the representative of the Palestinian people," and reaffirming the Palestinian right to self-determination and national independence, and the right of the Palestinian refugees to return to their homes and property. The vote was 89–8 with 37 abstentions. Another resolution, which passed 95–17 with 19 abstentions, gave official UN observer status to the PLO.

In December, Zehdi Terzi, the PLO's representative to the UN, was invited to participate in the Security Council debate on the Palestinian issue. On January 22, 1975, the Council endorsed the General Assembly stand affirming the Palestinian right to establish an independent state. But the resolution was vetoed by the US administration of President Gerald Ford.

The PLO scored another diplomatic victory on November 10, 1975, when the General Assembly passed Resolution 3379, defining Zionism as "a form of racism and racial discrimination." The vote was 72–35, with 32 abstentions.[12]

The enhanced status of the PLO abroad rubbed off on its internal affairs. Khalil Wazir became more active, ordering numerous guerrilla operations against Israel. He emerged as the right-hand man of Arafat, who was Chairman of both Fatah and the PLO, which besides Fatah now included the Arab Liberation Front (pro-Iraq),

Democratic Front for the Liberation of Palestine, Palestine Communist Party, Popular Front for the Liberation of Palestine, Palestine Front for the Liberation of Palestine-General Command, Palestine Struggle Front, and Saiqa (pro-Syria). Wazir assisted Arafat in trying to impose PLO discipline and a centralized military command on the various constituent organizations without alienating any of them. Arafat applied his powers of mediation and consensus-building to keep together diverse groups—some Marxist-Leninist, others pan-Arabist, still others funded by such Arab states as Iraq, Syria and Libya. Inside the West Bank, the PLO-sponsored Palestine National Front won most of the mayoral posts in the local elections that Israel held there in 1976.

Civil war erupted in April 1975 between left-leaning Lebanese Muslims, headed by Kamal Jumblat, and rightist, mainly Maronite Catholic, Lebanese Christians, led by Camille Chamoun. Expectedly, the PLO allied with the Lebanese National Movement (LNM) headed by Jumblat. They set up a joint military command against the rival Lebanese Front, which insisted on the expulsion of the armed Palestinians from Lebanon as a precondition for discussing political and constitutional reform in Lebanon. By early April 1976 the LNM-PLO alliance controlled two-thirds of the country. In desperation the Lebanese Front turned to Syria through (Maronite) President Suleiman Franjieh, who had friendly relations with his Syrian counterpart, Hafiz Assad. The latter was afraid that by giving the PLO a venue for its armed struggle against Israel, a radical Lebanese regime would provoke the Jewish state into an all-out invasion of Lebanon, which would draw Syria into the conflict at an inopportune time. He decided in June to aid the Lebanese Front. In July, after Syria and the Lebanese Front had gained the upper hand, there was a ceasefire, except in south Lebanon, where the PLO's anti-Israeli activities were being hampered by an Israeli-backed Christian militia. In late October the eighth Arab League summit decided to authorize a 30,000-strong Arab Deterrent Force, consisting mainly of Syrian troops, to maintain peace in Lebanon.

The May 1977 Israeli electoral victory of Likud, led by hardliner Menachem Begin, introduced a new factor into the regional politics. An equally dramatic event occurred later that year on November 19 when Egyptian President Anwar Sadat addressed the Israeli Knesset in pursuit of peace. When he signed the Camp David Accords in September 1978, Arafat and the PLO were shattered. By agreeing to a unilateral peace with Israel, Sadat broke the Arab commitment to a multilateral peace under UN auspices, and deprived the Arab League of the option of war with Israel to settle the Palestinian problem. The Accords laid out the framework for a peace treaty between Egypt and Israel, and a resolution of the Palestinian problem based on Palestinian autonomy in the West Bank and Gaza for an interim period of five years. But the autonomy was to be granted only to the people, not to the land, which was to remain under permanent Israeli sovereignty.

Arab leaders responded swiftly and unanimously. Condemning the Camp David Accords at the November 1978 Arab League summit in Baghdad, they decided that pan-Arab sanctions against Egypt, including suspension of its League membership and severance of diplomatic relations, should go into effect if and when it signed a peace treaty with Israel. It did, in March 1979, and the League moved its headquarters from Cairo to Tunis, while the PLO shifted the Palestine National Council from Cairo to Damascus.

The Baghdad summit also addressed the funding of the PLO. The oil-rich Gulf states promised it $250 million annually for the next 10 years. Together with another $100 million from Iraq, Libya and Algeria, the total formed about 70 percent of the PLO's $500 million annual budget. More came from taxes that Arab states collected from Palestinians working there. Other revenue came from the Samed Foundation, the commercial-industrial arm of Fatah. During the PLO's stay in Lebanon, Samed mushroomed to encompass manufacturing plants in Lebanon, farms and factories in other Arab states, and trading in equities and commodities in international markets. That financial base, plus the unifying experience of fighting Israel's 1978 invasion, enabled the PLO to consolidate and strengthen its fighting forces. Its military arm, functioning under Wazir, now consisted of 23,000 armed commandos, and 8–10,000 troops of the Palestine Liberation Army. The virtual break-up of the Lebanese military in early 1976 enabled the PLO to build up an arms arsenal that now included tanks. Indeed, equipped with new Soviet weapons, some 3,500 Palestinian commandos resisted the invading IDF in south Lebanon in 1978.

All this was of grave concern to the Begin administration. After reelection in July 1981, it set out to cut the PLO and Arafat to size. The hawkish new Defense Minister, Ariel Sharon, moved after the full implementation of the peace treaty with Egypt in late April 1982.

The pretext came on June 3. A member of the Palestinian group led by Abu Nidal tried unsuccessfully to assassinate Shlomo Argov, Israel's ambassador to Britain. Abu Nidal had been expelled from the PLO in 1974, and sentenced to death in absentia by a Palestinian court for trying to murder a PLO leader, Mahmoud Abbas. Nevertheless, Israel used the unsuccessful assassination attempt on Argov to justify a full-fledged invasion of Lebanon on June 6.

Though Arafat and his security and intelligence chief, Salah Khalaf, did not expect the Israelis to advance to Beirut, they had made contingency plans. The PLO stood its ground under siege in Beirut for two months, from June 13 to August 13.

Begin traveled to the United States from June 20 onward, while Sharon unleashed intensive bombardment against West Beirut. His intention was not only to secure an unconditional surrender of the PLO but also to liquidate Arafat. He failed on both counts. The only way he could defeat the PLO was by deploying his soldiers in the streets and alleys of West Beirut to wage guerrilla war, thus incurring high casualties, a politically unacceptable option. On July 3 he cut off all food, water and fuel into West Beirut, and subjected it to intense artillery bombardment. But he had to reverse his decision four days later under pressure from US President Ronald Reagan.

The spirit of PLO fighters was high. On July 9 they attacked IDF units. Sharon responded with intense artillery fire and bombardment for three days. Then came a brief truce which lasted until July 21. That day the PLO took the audacious step of attacking the IDF behind its lines. Sharon staged more intense bombing of West Beirut. Yet the morale of PLO commandos remained high, with Arafat, surrounded by journalists, freely traveling around West Beirut. By refusing to surrender unconditionally, Arafat demonstrated that the PLO was capable of withstanding savage pounding by the enemy.

Finally, from August 1–12, Sharon subjected West Beirut to unprecedentedly intense bombing from air, land and sea. Since the Israeli siege imposed in mid-June, nearly half of West Beirut's half a million residents had departed. The IDF attempted to seize the PLO headquarters in the Fakhani district, but failed due to strong resistance by the Palestinian commandos. The attackers lost many of their men; and the failed attempt brought home to Sharon the cost Israel would have to bear if it engaged in house-to-house fighting.

In the meantime, the evacuation of the PLO and its commandos was being negotiated in talks overseen by US envoy Philip Habib.

On August 12, later to be called Black Thursday, Sharon ordered saturation bombing on the scale of the Allied attacks on Dresden during World War II. From dawn parts of West Beirut were subjected to non-stop air, artillery and naval bombardment for nearly twelve hours, as the Israelis also cut off water supplies and let the city burn. When the onslaught, which caused the deaths of at least 500 civilians, finally ceased, the IDF set roadblocks, making sure that no food or fuel entered West Beirut. Sharon's action sent shock waves not only through the Arab world and beyond, but also through the Israeli government itself. The fierce attack ended on August 13. Six days later Israel accepted the PLO's evacuation plan.

Summing up the long ordeal West Beirutis had endured, Sandra Mackey, a resident American journalist, wrote: "For 70 days, the Israelis pounded Beirut with bombs and mortar rounds. Shelling came from the north, from the hills, and from the sea. Night after night, the skyline exploded in flashes of orange and yellow by ascending spirals of white smoke from exploding munitions. Israeli gunners, known for their precision, landed rounds on hospitals marked with red crosses and crescents as well as on the headquarters of the International Committee of the Red Cross."[13]

Sharon wanted not only to destroy West Beirut but to eliminate Arafat. That plan never quite succeeded, but caused hundreds of deaths. Eight buildings, including apartment blocks, were razed to the ground in the IDF's repeated attempts to kill him. Arafat himself, working with Khalaf, resorted to operating from, and even sleeping in, his moving car. Arafat also limited his radio phone conversations, aware that the Israeli radio-direction finders took less than fifteen minutes to locate his position.[14]

Arafat left Beirut for Tunis on August 30, escorted by a Greek warship and under an air umbrella furnished by the US Sixth Fleet.

Pushed to the Margin

Arafat's situation on arrival in Tunis in September 1982 was distinctly bleak. Both the PLO and Fatah had been yanked out of the core of the Middle East and thrown to a peripheral Arab capital, 1,490 miles from Israel. The 8,000 PLO commandos were scattered to camps in Syria, Iraq, North Yemen, Libya, Tunisia and Algeria.

A chink of light soon came from Amman. With a view to reviving the old idea of confederation between Jordan and a future Palestine, King Hussein began courting Arafat. He allowed Wazir to establish an office in Amman. From here Wazir set out to renew his contacts with PLO activists in the West Bank who had successfully penetrated Palestinian institutions including student and trade unions, chambers of commerce, women's organizations and the press.

Unlike Fatah, most of the radical constituents of the PLO, including the PFLP and the DFLP, moved to Damascus. The Syrian capital also emerged as the hotbed of Fatah militants—led by an artillery officer, Muhammad Said Musa Margha, known as Abu Musa—who were dissatisfied with Arafat's leadership, saying he rewarded loyalty rather than performance, and had spawned a bloated bureaucracy. They rebelled and took over a PLO base in eastern Lebanon in May 1983. Seeing the hand of the Syrian leader Hafiz Assad behind this, Arafat flew to Damascus to meet him, but their talks yielded little. Fighting between Arafat loyalists and opponents erupted in eastern Lebanon in June. When Arafat sought the assistance of Rifaat Assad, the influential younger brother of Hafiz, to curb the power of Fatah rebels, the Syrian leader was enraged, and ordered a summary expulsion of the PLO chief in June. Hafiz Assad's move angered the Palestinians in the Occupied Territories. The *mufti* (religious leader) of Jerusalem issued a *fatwa* (religious decree): "It is the duty of every Muslim to assassinate the Syrian President for the crimes he has committed against the Palestinian people."[15]

Apparently, by backing Abu Musa the Syrian President wished to topple Arafat and take control of Fatah, and thus the PLO. Arafat, committed to maintaining the independence of the PLO at all costs, was determined to resist Assad. The bad blood between Arafat and Assad continued, and the power game between the two leaders had yet to be played out.

The IDF's early September withdrawal to the Awali River in south Lebanon opened up opportunities for the Palestinian fighters to play a role in the unfinished Lebanese civil war. In mid-September Arafat resurfaced in the port city of Tripoli, and set up bases in the nearby Palestinian refugee camps. Soon he and his 4,000 commandos were besieged by Fatah rebels and Syrian troops, with IDF naval gunboats blocking their exit by sea. Once expelled from their Beddawi camp bastion on November 17, their fate seemed doomed. "Already crippled by Israel, Yasser Arafat has [now] been finished off by Syria," stated *The New York Times* in its editorial on November 18. "Such is the bizarre ending of a movement that, for all its daring, never found a political vision." But like the rumored death of Mark Twain, such comments about Arafat and the PLO proved premature.

This time, the Saudis came to Arafat's rescue, arranging a plan that combined an orderly evacuation of Arafat and his militia, with a Syrian promise not to try replacing Arafat as the PLO head. But it took a month to arrange it. Meanwhile, Ariel Sharon, now a minister without portfolio, bayed for Arafat's blood, declaring that "he should not be allowed to leave Tripoli alive." So while the pro-Damascus forces observed a truce, IDF gunboats began raining shells, hoping to kill the PLO chief. US intervention silenced the Israeli guns, and allowed five Greek merchant ships, under UN flag and escorted by a French warship, to take on board Arafat and his loyal troops.

Leaving Lebanon again, on Christmas Eve 1983, aboard the *Odysseus Elytis*, a defiant Arafat said: "The struggle is not over. We will continue until we reach Jerusalem, the capital of our Palestinian state."[16]

But despite the brave words, from December 1983 to December 1987 Arafat floundered in the same way that the Palestinians in the Occupied Territories did.

Having failed to make any tangible gains with an essentially left-of-center line, Arafat now leaned rightward, for reconciliation with the pro-western leaders like King Hussein and President Hosni Mubarak of Egypt, hoping thus to win the recognition of Washington. He appeared unaware of the secret written commitment the United States had made to Israel in September 1975, as part of the Egyptian-Israeli Sinai II Agreement, not to recognize or negotiate with the PLO until it abandoned terrorism against Israel and recognized its right to exist.[17]

In November 1984 Arafat convened the Palestine National Council in Amman. It was boycotted by all the Damascus- or Baghdad-based radical Palestinian groups, and was thus dominated by moderates. By threatening to resign as PLO Chairman, Arafat consolidated his position. Among other things the assembly decided to move the PNC headquarters from Damascus to Amman.

Arafat went on to sign a five-point accord with King Hussein in February 1985, meant to ease the PLO's way into an international conference on Middle Eastern peace. "Palestinians will exercise their inalienable right of self-determination when they and Jordanians will be able to do so within the context of the formation of the proposed confederated Arab states of Jordan and Palestine," stated the operative Article 2. This raised more questions than it answered since the State of Palestine had not graduated beyond an idea and a hope.

Equally seriously, Jordan and the PLO later began arguing about the PLO's position on the crucial UN Security Council Resolution 242, which implies recognition of Israel within secure borders. Jordan said that the PLO had accepted it whereas the PLO executive committee insisted that it had not. When top US officials, using King Hussein as intermediary, urged Arafat to accept Resolution 242, the PLO Chairman agreed provided Washington said in writing that it endorsed self-determination for Palestinians. But President Reagan was not prepared to go beyond "Palestinian self-rule." This led to friction between Hussein and Arafat. In February 1986 Hussein announced annulment of the year-old Jordan-PLO accord. He then closed down all PLO offices in Jordan and expelled many PLO functionaries, including its military chief, Wazir.

Israel was unimpressed by Arafat's professed drift toward pragmatism. Its intelligence reports showed that, having lost their capacity to mount attacks on Israel from the soil of Lebanon, Arafat and Wazir had devised a maritime strategy to hit Israeli targets. In this the southern Cypriot port of Larnaca played a key role. It had become a hotbed of international spies specializing in monitoring maritime and air traffic. Inevitably Israelis and Palestinians were part of the motley crowd, interested as much in watching ships and airplanes as one another. A three-member hit team of the PLO, belonging to Arafat's Force 17, attacked an Israeli yacht moored at Larnaca's marina on September 25, 1985 killing three people, claiming they were Mossad operators doing more than just monitoring Mediterranean traffic.

Outraged, Peres's national unity government, known to be conferring clandestinely with King Hussein, vowed retaliation.

It came on October 1. Six Israeli F-15 fighter-bombers flattened three PLO offices, including Arafat's, twelve miles south-east of Tunis, on the Gulf of Hammamet. (The PLO then moved its offices to villas scattered across the middle class district of Al Manzeh in Tunis.) The raid occurred around 10 A.M. when the administrative offices were buzzing with activity, and took a heavy human toll: 56 Palestinians and 17 Tunisians. But by pure chance it missed its prized target. Returning from abroad the previous night, Arafat dallied over a late-night dinner at the seafront villa of the PLO's envoy to Tunisia, Abdul Hakam Balawi, and fell behind schedule the next morning. So he was not in his office when the Israelis staged their air raid.[18] The UN Security Council's 14–0 condemnation of Israel (the US abstained) was a poor consolation to Arafat. He interpreted Israel's action, authorized by Peres, as counter to the Israeli premier's declarations of seeking peace. Among other things this reconciled Arafat with radicals Habash and Hawatmeh, from whom he had been estranged for a couple of years.

This reconciliation was consolidated in April 1987 when the 426-strong Palestine National Council, meeting in the Club des Pins conference hall near Algiers, finally buried the PLO-Jordan accord of 1985. Amid much show of renewed solidarity between Arafat and his radical rivals, the PNC decided to form multi-party co-ordinating committees for the occupied homeland.

That PNC session fitted well the general pattern of Palestinian and Arab politics. "I don't believe that Arab history has ever known a final estrangement," remarked Khalid Hassan, the former foreign minister of the PLO, in a radio interview. "Our Arab history is full of agreements and differences. When we differ and then grow tired of differing, we agree. When we grow tired of agreeing we differ, and so on. After every agreement or difference we pass through a time that changes things... [T]his is the Arab nature."[19]

Time was about to change the situation radically in the Occupied Palestinian Territories.

Intifada: A Kiss of Life

The eruption of the intifada, a grass roots movement, in the Occupied Territories on December 9, 1987 ended the debilitating post-Beirut phase of PLO politics.

Always keen to exercise power and initiative, Arafat gave currency to the term *intifada* (uprising) in his address on the Voice of the PLO Radio on December 10. But he felt uneasy in early January when the leaders inside the Occupied Territories decided on their own to form the United National Leadership of the Uprising (UNLU), consisting chiefly of Fatah, the PFLP, the DFLP and the Palestine Communist Party.

The intifada's power affected the Palestinian leadership in the diaspora, making the fractious leaders of several PLO affiliates sink their differences. This trend was accelerated by the assassination of Wazir who had worked for many years with the PLO's Occupied Homeland Directorate to create a PLO infrastructure in the West Bank.

To show that the Fatah leadership in Tunis was doing more than merely applauding the intifada, Wazir dispatched three Fatah commandos to Israel's Negev desert to attack the Israeli nuclear weapons plant at Dimona. On March 7, 1988 they hijacked a bus carrying the nuclear facility's employees from Beersheba to Dimona. Halting the bus at a roadblock, and luring the hijackers into negotiations, Israeli police conducted a surprise assault that left six people dead, including all the hijackers. Arafat claimed the event a victory since, in his words, it had drawn attention to the clandestine Israeli atomic bomb factory, "the most dangerous military target in the Middle East." (However, the Dimona plant had earlier been exposed in the (London) *Sunday Times* of October 5, 1986 with a detailed report and photographs by Mordechai Vanunu, a former nuclear technician there.) Unsurprisingly, the audacious attempt by Palestinian guerrillas angered Israel, particularly Defense Minister Yitzhak Rabin, and its inner cabinet decided to liquidate Wazir.

"Removing a senior commander from enemy ranks would not settle the Arab-Israeli conflict, but the Israelis badly needed some sort of victory four months into the intifada," explained Dan Raviv, an American reporter, and Yossi Melman, an Israeli journalist, in a book on Israel's intelligence agencies. "In addition, the experience of the 1970s had taught Mossad that assassinating top terrorist leaders caused severe disruptions in the PLO and its splinter groups. It made them fear the Israelis; it made them hesitate in planning their violence; and it forced them into making mistakes. Perhaps even more than the Israelis needed a triumph, they believed that the Palestinian resistance movement was overdue for a setback."[20] In fact, the operation proved politically counter-productive for Israel.

The Israelis did a professional job, involving the IDF's elite Sayeret Matkal commandos as well as frogmen, agents of Aman, or military intelligence, and operators of Mossad. On April 12, 1988 three Mossad operatives arrived in Tunis as Lebanese tourists, speaking Arabic with a Lebanese accent, assigned to rent two minibuses and a station wagon. On the night of April 15–16 they waited at the beach to pick up 30 Sayaret Matkal members brought ashore in rubber dinghies from an IDF missile boat anchored offshore. Just before 1 A.M. they drove the Israeli commandos to the nearby Sidi Bou Said suburb of Tunis. They stopped a block away from Wazir's villa, where he lived with his wife, Intissar, a Fatah activist, and their fourteen-year-old daughter and two-year-old son. 22 commandos stayed put, in case things went wrong. A Mossad agent led the commando leader to the telephone junction for the area, where he short-circuited the system. The Mossad operative then drove the eight-strong unit to Wazir's villa.

Just after 1:30 A.M. the commandos, armed with submachine guns and pistols, smashed into Wazir's house, shooting dead three men—Wazir's driver, a Palestinian guard and a Tunisian guard—who came between them and their target. They had done several practice runs on a model of the house during their training in Israel. Now they headed for the main bedroom upstairs. Khalil Wazir was still up, as was his wife. He was in the midst of composing a clandestine message to the intifada leadership. Alarmed by the noise downstairs, he picked up his pistol, and moved to the bedroom door, with Intissar trailing behind. He opened the door and, finding hooded men coming upstairs, fired a shot. That was his last act. He fell in a hailstorm of 67 bullets that poured from the guns of his Israeli assassins. Intissar watched aghast, expecting to be murdered. But she was not.[21]

Arafat, on a tour of the Gulf states, hurried back to Tunis. He was shattered by the news of the murder of his closest ally, his confidant for three decades. A Mossad report described Wazir as "a highly intelligent man, a good organizer with a precise, analytical mind and great reserves of strength."[22] His other major leadership asset, making him a marked man in Israel's political establishment, was his valued ability to conciliate disputatious factions within the unwieldy PLO. Though Arafat later told his biographers, Andrew Gowers and Tony Walker, "We were one spirit in two bodies," in fact they were complementary: the cool, calculating Wazir balanced Arafat's emotionalism and volatility. Yet Arafat's declaration in the wake of Wazir's violent death came to pass. "Those who think the assassination of Abu Jihad will smother the Palestinian uprising are deluding themselves," he told the *Financial Times*. "His death will give new life to this heroic revolt." And it did. Arafat found an echo in the words of Ezer Weizman, then a member of Israel's inner cabinet, who had opposed al Wazir's assassination. "It does not contribute to the fight against terrorism," he told reporters. "It distances the peace process and will bring greater hostility [toward Israel]."[23]

Instantly the martyr Abu Jihad became a unifying symbol, a legendary figure, revered equally by all PLO factions. His portraits appeared in as much profusion as those of Arafat. Even today this trend continues, with the mustached, chubby face of Abu Jihad alongside Arafat's, staring at visitors in Palestinian Authority offices.

Another unexpected development encouraged the unprecedented PLO unity that Abu Jihad's murder created. It came from King Hussein who, too, felt the power of the intifada. "Since there is a general conviction that the struggle to liberate the occupied Palestinian land could be enhanced by dismantling the legal and administrative links between the two banks [of River Jordan], we have to do our duty, and do what is required of us," he said in an official communique on July 31, 1988. "Jordan is not Palestine. And the independent Palestinian state will be established on the occupied land after its liberation, God willing." Hussein's statement finally laid to rest the "Jordanian Option" that Peres and, to a lesser extent, Rabin had been bandying about since the early 1970s. In human terms it meant the loss of jobs of 21,000 Palestinian civil servants and others who had been on Jordan's payroll.

Before finalizing plans for an emergency Palestine National Council on the intifada, Arafat secured a promise from all non-Fatah leaders that there would be no walk-outs. Keenly aware that the policy of the United States, "the godmother of Israel," toward the PLO now mattered most, he called the PNC's nineteenth session on November 13, 1988, five days after the US presidential election. Again the venue was the Club des Pins conference hall near Algiers. It attracted 380 of the 450 PNC members.

On November 15 the PNC unanimously adopted the political communique which, while upholding the "glorious intifada" of the Palestinian people, referred to the favorable language of UN General Assembly Resolution 21L/43/1 of April 11, 1988, on the intifada.

On the more controversial resolution to establish the State of Palestine, Arafat deployed his deputy, Salah Khalaf (Abu Iyad), to successfully clinch the argument. By a large majority the PNC adopted the Proclamation of the Independent State of Palestine. "The Palestine National Council, in the name of God, and in the name of the Palestinian Arab people, hereby proclaims the establishment of the State of Palestine on our Palestinian territory with its capital Al Quds al Sharif (Holy Jerusalem)," declared Arafat after he had been elected President of the new state and the Palestinian flag had been hoisted inside the marble-floored conference hall. "The State of Palestine is the state of Palestinians wherever they may be." The tautology was deliberate, its purpose being to leave undefined the boundaries of the State of Palestine—something the Israeli parliament, at Ben Gurion's behest, had done 40 years before.

The PNC's acceptance of two states in mandate Palestine was buried in an earlier paragraph: "Despite the historical injustice inflicted on the Palestinian Arab people, resulting in their dispersion and depriving them of their right to self-determination, following upon UN General Assembly Resolution 181 (1947), which partitioned Palestine into two states, one Arab, one Jewish, yet it is this resolution that still provides those conditions of international legitimacy that ensure the right of the Palestinian Arab people to sovereignty and national independence."[24] By accepting the UN partition plan of 1947, the PNC paved the way for acceptance of the subsequent UN Security Council Resolutions 242 (1967) and 338 (1973), a development which deeply interested the current UN General Assembly.

And so November 15 became another memorable date in the Palestinian calendar, on a par with January 1 (the start of the armed struggle against Israel) and March 24 (the decision to confront the IDF at al-Karameh, Jordan).

Following the PNC's action, 70 of the 103 countries which had already recognized the PLO accorded it full diplomatic status. But the country that mattered most, the United States, was not impressed. Indeed its Secretary of State, George Shultz, described Arafat as an "accessory to terrorism" and therefore "a threat to US national security," and denied him a visa to address the UN General Assembly. The UN hit back by resolving 154–2 (with the US and Israel dissenting) to hold a special session at its European headquarters in Geneva on December 13 to hear Arafat.

On December 7 Arafat met in Stockholm with American Jewish leaders bearing Shultz's letter setting out what Arafat should say in his UN speech in order to get official US recognition. Unable to decide on his own, Arafat signed a "secret" statement, subject to the approval of the PLO's executive committee. It read: "1) That it [the executive committee] is prepared to negotiate with Israel within the framework of the international conference a comprehensive peace settlement of the Arab-Israeli conflict on the basis of UNSC Resolutions 242 and 338. 2) That it undertakes to live in peace with Israel and other neighbors and respect their right to exist in peace within secure and internationally recognized borders as will the democratic Palestinian state which it seeks to establish in the Palestinian Occupied Territories since 1967. 3) That it condemns individual and state terrorism in all its forms and will not resort to it."[25] This statement amounted to a unilateral PLO concession. The PLO had hitherto insisted on formally recognizing Israel (as opposed to the implicit recognition built into Resolution 242) only in return for Israel's acceptance of the right of the Palestinian people to a sovereign state. Little wonder that Arafat failed to get an unequivocal endorsement of the secret statement from the PLO executive committee when it met in Tunis.

The Swiss provided unprecedentedly tight security to Arafat at the old League of Nations headquarters in the Palais de Nations on the banks of Lake Geneva. Fourteen years older than when he had last addressed the General Assembly, and graying, Arafat appeared in the hall dressed in pressed battle-green military fatigues, and his trademark *keffiyeh*. In a long speech, he described peaceful coexistence with Israel, and rephrased Shultz's precise points. But since he did not specifically renounce violence and recognize Israel, the US response was negative. To make Shultz change his mind, Arafat called a press conference the next day. "Between Algiers and Geneva we have made our position crystal clear," he said, reading a prepared statement in English. "We accept the right of all parties in the Middle East conflict to exist in peace and security. I repeat for the record that we totally and absolutely renounce all forms of terrorism."[26]

Within a few hours Shultz said that the United States was "prepared" to open "a substantive dialogue with PLO representatives." This meant middle level talks between the PLO and the American embassy in Tunis. A week later Yitzhak Shamir, heading a new national unity government in Israel, responded. He denied Peres, "the peacenik," the coveted foreign ministry, which he allocated to a Likud hardliner, Moshe Arens.

When Peres brought about the downfall of the government in March 1990 and then failed to form a Labor-led coalition, thus allowing Shamir to rule as the head of the most right-wing administration in Israeli history, Arafat's hopes of successful negotiations with Israel through Washington faded. Further, he found Israel welcoming a rising tide of Jewish immigration from the Soviet Union, with immigrants jumping from 13,300 in 1988 to 199,500 just two years later.

This became a matter of concern throughout the Arab world, and dominated the seventeenth Arab League summit held in May 1990 in Baghdad, hosted by President Saddam Hussein. Its resolution described the emigration of Soviet and other Jews to Palestine and other Occupied Arab Territories as "a new aggression against the rights of the Palestinian people and a serious danger to the Arab nation as well as a gross violation of human rights, the principles of international law and the Fourth Geneva Convention of 1949." It called on the UN Security Council to prohibit settlement of Jewish immigrants in the Occupied Territories. By stating that Jewish immigration was a threat to the "Arab national interest," the summit strengthened the hands of Jordan and the PLO, laying the foundation of an incipient alliance between them and Iraq, whose president played a leading role in the debate.[27]

Saddam Hussein endeared himself to Palestinians by announcing emergency aid of $25 million to the intifada. Relations between Iraq and the PLO had been cordial ever since Baathist military officers seized power in Baghdad in July 1968. Among other things they allowed the Voice of the PLO radio station to be set up in Baghdad. When pressured by the Tunisian government to relocate its military department, after the 1985 Israeli air raid on PLO headquarters, the PLO shifted it to Baghdad in early 1987.

Arafat became a frequent visitor to the Iraqi capital. Voice of the PLO radio played a pivotal role in sustaining the intifada. Part of the reason Arafat refused to discipline Abu al Abbas for the failed 1990 terrorist action on an Israeli beach was that his group, the Palestine Liberation Front, was backed by Iraq.

Whatever reservations Arafat had about Saddam Hussein's invasion and occupation of Kuwait on August 2, 1990 evaporated on August 12, when the Iraqi leader offered a peace plan, including "preparations" of the withdrawal of "Israel from the Occupied Arab Territories in Palestine, Syria and Lebanon; Syria's withdrawal from Lebanon; a withdrawal between Iraq and Iran; and the formulation of arrangements for the situation in Kuwait" in line with earlier Security Council resolutions.[28] This multi-faceted idea became popularized as a direct linkage between the issues of occupied Kuwait and the occupied Palestinian territories, to be settled simultaneously. Many Palestinians came to believe that Saddam Hussein's strong stand in the Kuwait crisis would force the United States and Israel to agree to the linkage he proposed. This perception prevailed not only in the West Bank and Gaza but also among the Palestinians in Jordan, an important factor that contributed to King Hussein's refusing to adopt an anti-Iraq stance during the Kuwait crisis and the subsequent Gulf War.

Saddam Hussein's popularity among Palestinians remained high. On the eve of the Gulf War in mid-January 1991, Arafat declared: "Palestinians will stand alongside Iraqis in the trenches."[29] This complemented his warm bear-hug of Saddam Hussein, an image screened repeatedly on western television screens. Arafat's prediction that Israel would respond to Iraqi missiles with its own attacks, thus joining the US-led anti-Iraq coalition uninvited and causing the departure of the coalition's Arab members—the Gulf states, Egypt, Syria and Morocco—proved wrong. When some of Arafat's aides questioned the wisdom of his deepening involvement with the Iraqi leader, he replied: "This is the will of my people."[30] Given the fevered environment created by the gathering clouds of a major war—culminating in the assembling of 750,000 troops in the Gulf region and an unprecedented arsenal of weapons, including some 700 nuclear arms—the Palestinian people had expressed their will unequivocally and dramatically.

At the same time Arafat tried to sell the PLO's plan to settle the Kuwait crisis peacefully. But, with the Arab world deeply divided, he got nowhere. Then, on the eve of the Gulf War, Arafat learned that his remaining long-term colleague, Salah Khalaf, the PLO's security and intelligence chief, was gunned down. It was in the house of Hayil Abdul Hamid (Abu al Hol), head of the PLO's internal security, in a suburb of Tunis, on January 14 around 11 P.M. Salah Khalaf, his deputy Fakhri Omari, and Abdul Hamid were all killed by Hamza Abu Zaid, a bodyguard of Abdul Hamid. The young assassin turned out to be a member of the Abu Nidal group, who had infiltrated supposedly the most secure organ of the PLO: its internal security department. It was the same Abu Nidal group whose members were arrested by the British police in June 1982 for the failed assassination of Israeli ambassador, Shlomo Argov, which was used by Israel as a rationale to invade Lebanon.

Arafat, who heard the news in Baghdad, rushed back to Tunis, where he broke down at Khalaf's wake. Both his long-time friends and confidants, Wazir and Khalaf, were now dead, leaving him to tackle the monumental tasks of the present and the future all on his own, an unnerving prospect even for a man who had been playing a leadership role for a generation.

During the early period of the Gulf War, which started on January 16 (January 17 Baghdad time), Arafat was confident that Iraq would withstand the onslaught by the US-led Coalition of 29 nations for a long time. But after an unparalleled non-stop coalition air campaign, including 106,000 air sorties against Iraq and occupied Kuwait, followed by a four-day ground campaign, Iraq completed its unconditional withdrawal from Kuwait by February 28 and accepted a temporary ceasefire. Throughout the conflict the Palestinians in the Occupied Territories were immobilized by an indefinite curfew imposed by Israel, receiving food and other necessities at home from the UN Relief and Works Agency.

Arafat was down but not out. Even in the midst of the devastating air campaign against Iraq, he managed to retain a historical perspective. "There is something here that the West seems incapable of understanding or absorbing: that the dynamism of our people is not a passing phase," he told the London-based *Mideast Mirror*, in mid-February 1991. "The dynamism of our people is deeply rooted in history. Ours is an epic people. It has been struggling since 1917, from the Balfour Declaration until today... That is 73 or 74 years, three generations."[31]

This time what seriously threatened the future of the PLO was the loss of grants from a bankrupt Iraq and the alienated oil-rich Gulf states, which had so far provided a substantial part the PLO's budget. Arafat ordered belt-tightening, which curtailed not only the high living of many senior PLO bureaucrats and diplomats but also expenditures on schools, hospitals and social welfare. Since the 1967 War, the PLO's Steadfastness Fund had channeled an average of $20 million annually into the West Bank and Gaza. Its welfare department, based in Amman, supported families of "martyred" (a single payment of $1,500), wounded, arrested ($120 a month stipend), or deported. This meant welfare payments to over 90,000 Palestinian families, a fifth of whom had sacrificed a member to the nationalist cause.[32]

Once President Bush had, in his March 6 address to the US Congress, reiterated the need for "a comprehensive peace [which] must be grounded in the UN Security Council Resolutions 242 and 338 and the principle of territory for peace," his Secretary of State, James Baker, actively tried to convene an international peace conference on the Middle East. In mid-July, President Assad made a dramatic concession on Syria's terms for attending; on August 1, Israel agreed to come. Baker's chances of success improved sharply.

But the Shamir government had extracted a heavy price. "If Israel has said yes to the conference, it is because all the conditions that it has set have been accepted by the US administration," Arafat complained in an interview to French television on August 3. "No to the presence of the PLO, no to an independent Palestinian state, no to [Palestinian] representatives from Jerusalem, and no to the resolution of the status of Jerusalem."

As the United States had suspended its contacts with the PLO since June 1990, Baker initiated talks with Faisal Husseini, living in East Jerusalem, and Hanan Ashrawi, based in Ramallah, prominent Palestinians officially unconnected with the PLO. His queries were: "Will the Palestinians come to the talks as part of a joint Jordanian-Palestinian team; will the PLO forgo a public role in the talks; will the Palestinians forgo a representative of the diaspora in the delegation; and will the Palestinians forgo a representative from East Jerusalem."

The answers came in the fourth paragraph of the political resolution adopted by the twentieth PNC assembly on September 28. "The PLO, as the sole legitimate representative of the Palestinian people, reserves the right to make up the Palestinian delegation from the people inside and outside the homeland, including Jerusalem, and to define the form of its participation in the peace process on the basis of equality," it read. The resolution was carried by 256 votes to 68.

Again Arafat called the PNC session near Algiers. Of the 456 members more than 350 attended. Of these 313 voted for the resolution, which set guidelines for the Palestinian representatives—both a mandate and the limits that were not to be crossed—with only 18 opposing. Equally significantly, the PNC replaced the controversial Abu al Abbas on the executive committee with his deputy, Abu Ismail. It expanded the executive committee from fourteen members to seventeen, with the additional seats going to moderates.

Later, the PLO's 99-member central council, a standing body bridging the PNC and the executive committee, approved the fourteen non-PLO Palestinians (eight of whom had either been jailed by Israel, put under house arrest or subjected to a travel ban) to join the Jordanian-Palestinian delegation, and appointed a steering committee to guide the Palestinian negotiators according to the PNC's principles. Headed by Faisal Husseini, the committee included Hanan Ashrawi, a Christian, and lecturer in English literature at Birzeit University.

The Middle East peace conference opened on October 30, 1991 in Madrid, in the Royal Palace's grand Hall of Columns, under the joint chairmanship of President Bush and Soviet President Mikhail Gorbachev. Though kept out of the official proceedings, the PLO's steering committee, represented by Husseini and Ashrawi, made a palpable impact on the international media, represented by nearly 4,700 journalists.

Faisal Husseini, balding and clean-shaven, came from the illustrious family of the al Husseinis who had arrived in Jerusalem from Mecca in the thirteenth century. In recent times the family had had the distinction of providing, from 1922 to 1937, the local mayor and the mufti of Jerusalem, Haajj Muhammad Amin Husseini, an uncle of Faisal. Born in 1940 in Baghdad, where his family had taken refuge, Faisal grew up in Cairo. His father, Abdul Qadir, was the field commander during the Arab Revolt. Following the UN partition plan of November 1947 Abdul Qadir Husseini took up arms against the Zionist forces, and died in the Battle of Kastel near Jerusalem in 1948, and was buried on the Haram al Sharif, an honor of the highest degree. Among the visitors to the Husseini household in Cairo in the 1950s was Yasser Arafat. After his university education in Cairo, Faisal returned to his family home in East Jerusalem, then under Jordanian control.

He worked in the Jerusalem office of the PLO after its founding in 1964, and then enrolled at the military academy in Homs, Syria, for an officer's course for the Palestine Liberation Army. After the June 1967 War he returned to Jerusalem, where he was contacted by Arafat during the latter's sojourn in the West Bank to set up a guerrilla infrastructure. After Arafat's escape from Al Bireh, the IDF arrested Faisal Husseini, and sentenced him to a year in jail for concealing two of Arafat's guns. He remained politically active, and in 1979 opened the Arab Studies Center, a research organization, which Israel believed was a front for co-ordinating PLO activities in the Occupied Territories. The Israeli authorities soon closed down the Center and put him under administrative detention. After his release he was placed under city arrest, which lasted for five years. In the spring of 1989 came another spell of administrative detention. Though he was not a formal member of Fatah, he was widely considered to be close to it and to Arafat.

A highly intelligent and likable man, moderate in behavior and pragmatic in his views, Husseini emerged as an ideal bridge between Baker and Arafat. At the Madrid conference, even though Dr. Haidar Abdul Shafi was the official head of the Palestinian section of the Jordanian-Palestinian delegation, the insiders knew that it was Husseini who was the real leader of the Palestinians.

The Palestinian case was brilliantly presented in English by Hanan Ashrawi, the official spokesperson for the PLO's steering committee. An eloquent woman with short black hair, self-assured and lucid—at ease with English and explaining the complexities with an occasional shaft of wry humor—she was a dramatic contrast to Arafat, with his stubbled face and *keffiyeh*, his halting English, and his tendency to speak in slogans and catchphrases in television interviews. In the minds of television viewers, the supplanting of Arafat with Ashrawi encapsulated the PLO's transition from armed resistance to respectability. The insatiable demand of the US media for Ashrawi showed that at last the Palestinian cause was getting a hearing before the American public. She had honed her persuasive skills in the periodic briefings her colleagues at Birzeit University began giving to foreign journalists at her home in Ramallah after Israel closed down their university in early 1988 due to the intifada. (It remained shut until early 1992).

Born Hanan Mikhail in 1946 into a well-to-do Christian doctor's family in Nablus, she was at the American University of Beirut studying English literature in 1967, when Israel occupied the West Bank. She pursued post-graduate studies at the University of Virginia, where she took an active interest in Palestinian politics. Upon returning to the West Bank in 1973, she began teaching at Birzeit University. She married Emile Ashrawi, a photographer and a former rock musician, and a resident of East Jerusalem.

Having thus infiltrated the Middle East peace conference through Ashrawi and Husseini, Arafat expanded his area of maneuver. This, he concluded, could best be done by undermining Shamir's repeated claims that he was not dealing with the "terrorist" PLO; and by establishing contacts with opposition Labor leadership with a view to improving its chances of success at the 1992 parliamentary poll.

As for Shamir, having conceded separate talks between the Israeli delegation and the Palestinian section of the joint Jordanian-Palestinian delegation, he pursued his (as yet) unpublicized strategy, which he summarized only after his defeat in 1992: drag out the talks with the Arabs for the next ten years while ensuring that the Jewish settlement of Judea and Samaria went ahead at full speed.[33] As a result, the Israeli delegates consistently limited their negotiations with the Palestinians to the structure and legislative powers of the Palestinian Authority during the interim period, and refused to discuss the weighty subject of transition from the interim accord to the final agreement or the application of the principle of land for peace embodied by UNSC Resolution 242.

During this stalemate came the dramatic news of the April 8, 1992 crash of Arafat's private airplane—a Soviet An-26, in the Sahara desert near the Sudanese-Libyan border—caused by a severe sandstorm during a flight from Khartoum to Tunis. The fate of the PLO chief remained unknown for several hours. But the old survivor emerged alive from the crash while the pilot and co-pilot perished. To the joy of his supporters, the incident reconfirmed not only his personal indestructibility but also that of the Palestinian people and their nationalist aspirations.

Arafat had not, however, emerged unharmed by the accident. He realized later that he needed brain surgery for a blood clot, and underwent an emergency operation at the Hussein Medical Center, Amman, on June 1. On June 19, he invited Haidar Abdul Shafi, Faisal Husseini and Hanan Ashrawi to Amman for a much publicized meeting. In the presence of journalists and television cameras the three Palestinian representatives congratulated Arafat on his speedy recovery. The objective of the stage-managed exercise was to give a lie to the repeated assertions by Shamir that his delegation was dealing with representatives of the West Bank and Gaza who had no direct ties with Arafat's terrorist PLO. When Shamir's rival, Yitzhak Rabin, declared his intention to negotiate with the West Bank and Gaza Palestinians irrespective of who they in turn consulted, he was charged with devising a secret plan to deal with the terrorist PLO if he won power. In return, the Labor Party's communique baldly stated: "Despite the Likud declarations and despite the fact that it is sticking its head in the sand, this government has ongoing direct negotiations with the PLO." With Shafi, Husseini and Ashrawi hugging and kissing Arafat in public on their television screens, Israeli electors knew who to believe. Labor won on June 23.

The 1994 memoirs of Mahmoud Abbas (Abu Mazen), the PLO's second top official, entitled *The Road to Oslo*, provides details of the clandestine contacts between the two leading Israeli political parties and the then outlawed PLO. In his chapter "Indirect Contacts with the Labor Party," he stated that Labor leaders, including Yitzhak Rabin and Ephraim Sneh, discussed what strategy the PLO should pursue in its (indirect) negotiations with Shamir's Likud-led government. They advised the PLO to slow down progress in the peace talks, and also to strive to mobilize the Israeli Arab voters for Labor and leftist groups. Abbas also said that PLO officials and Likud politicians met in Europe in December 1991, but nothing came of this.[34] In a February 1993 article in *Hadashot*, staff reporter Yehoshua Meiri described how, while having coffee at the Hilton Ramses Hotel in Cairo on January 19, 1992, he had seen Yossi Beilin, a close aide of Shimon Peres, enter a nearby room, guarded by an Egyptian security guard, followed several minutes later by Nabil Shaath, a long-time aide of Arafat. Meiri reported the outcome of that encounter, as summarized by a PLO official, thus: "Beilin promised that if Labor won the election, it would stop [Jewish] settlements, lift the ban on meetings with the PLO, and agree to [Palestinian] autonomy on the basis of the UN Security Council Resolutions 242 and 338." When Labor came back in July 1992 and Premier Rabin dragged his feet on lifting the ban on PLO contacts, a PLO official leaked a story about a clandestine meeting between the PLO leadership and a "senior Labor Party personality" in late October.[35] But the ploy did not work. It was only after Arafat had conducted talks with the long exiled leaders of Hamas in the wake of Rabin's expulsion of over 400 Islamists to southern Lebanon, and set up a joint PLO-Hamas committee on the deportations, that the Israeli premier acted.

Ironically, the single most important thing that unbanning the PLO legitimized, was the clandestine dialogue between the hitherto terrorist organization and the Israeli government.

Secret Diplomacy and the Handshake of Reconciliation

Once the Knesset legalized the PLO on January 19, 1993, the unofficial, clandestine talks between Professors Yair Hirschfeld and Ron Pundak, and Ahmad Qrei (Abu Alaa), arranged earlier by Norwegian mediators Terje Rod Larsen and Mona Juul, became official. As the only PLO official who besides Arafat knew almost all about the finances of Fatah and the PLO, Qrei had proved beyond any shadow of doubt that he could keep a secret. Also, Qrei was the author of a policy document reasoning that economic integration of the West Bank and Gaza and Israel should underpin any peace settlement between Palestinians and Israelis. This paper, presented by Larsen to Yossi Beilin, later deputy foreign minister under Peres, met with Peres' approval. He dispatched Hirschfeld in December 1992 to meet Qrei for exploratory talks. On his side Qrei worked under the supervision of Mahmoud Abbas, who reported directly to Arafat.

Against the background of a worsening crisis in the Gaza Strip, and lack of progress in the Madrid-formula talks, Peres added his ministry's director-general, Uri Savir, to the Israeli team on May 20. Then came the addition of Joel Singer, the ministry's legal adviser. Singer was a hardliner who had participated in the talks culminating in the 1978 Camp David Accords. As legal adviser to Rabin's defense ministry for five years, he had Rabin's confidence, and shared his obsession with Israeli security. Singer and Savir bargained hard, and had their way on most of the contentious issues.

They stuck firmly to the time frame of five years for the interim period, as first specified by Begin in 1978. The PLO had publicly insisted on one year, expecting to compromise on three years. Now its secret negotiators gave in fully to the Israeli demand. Having conceded that the highly disputatious subjects of the right to return of the Palestinian refugees, the final borders of Israel and the Palestinian territories, and the status of Jerusalem be postponed to the final phase, the PLO representatives yielded completely on the running sore of the Jewish settlements. They seemed satisfied with the Israeli reminder that only after their government had stated, in August 1992, there would be no more "public funding" for the settlements that Washington had reversed its previous stance and agreed to guarantee Israel's $10 billion international loans. The result was the absence of any mention of the Jewish settlements in the draft accord. The Palestinians' failure to see the loopholes, especially regarding "public funding," that the Israeli declaration implied, only became clear after the Oslo Accord had been implemented. It illustrated dramatically how poorly they had bargained. In return for such vital concessions, all Qrei got was Israel's recognition of the PLO as "the representative" (not "the sole representative" as Arafat wanted) of the Palestinian people. Once Rabin officially conceded this in late July, the deal was virtually done.

The final draft, after fourteen clandestine meetings, entitled "Declaration of Principles on Interim Self-government Arrangements," was initialed secretly in Oslo on August 19 by Peres and Qrei, followed by a public announcement 11 days later. Then came an exchange of Arafat-Rabin letters on September 9–10, with Arafat recognizing "the right of the State of Israel to exist in peace and security" and accepting "the United Nations Security Council Resolutions 242 and 338," and Rabin stating that "the government of Israel has decided to recognize the PLO as the representative of the Palestinian people and commence negotiations with the PLO within the Middle East peace process."

The signing of the document by Peres and Mahmoud Abbas, the second seniormost official of the PLO, on the sunlit lawns of the White House on September 13 came after a dramatic intervention by Arafat only hours before the ceremony. He proposed that since Rabin in his letter of September 10 had recognized the PLO as the representative of the Palestinian people this fact should be reflected in the Declaration of Principles (DOP). Accordingly, Arafat insisted that the first sentence of the document reading "The government of the State of Israel and the Palestinian team (the Jordanian-Palestinian delegation to the Middle East peace conference), representing the Palestinian people, agree that..." be modified to read: "The government of the State of Israel and the PLO team... agree..." Rabin was hesitant, but Peres persuaded him to comply.

The dramatic difference in the treatment afforded to Arafat by the United States—a red carpet instead of a denied visa—neatly encapsulated the metamorphic change that the PLO chief had undergone, from guerrilla leader to world statesman. Yet he retained his military fatigues and his checkered *keffiyeh* when he appeared at the signing ceremony at the White House; and he delivered his speech in Arabic (whereas Rabin addressed the gathering in English). His offering of the hand of friendship to Rabin to solemnize the Declaration just signed by their designated deputies, and Rabin's grasping his hand after some hesitation, thrilled not only the over 3,000 American and other dignitaries assembled on the White House lawn but also the hundreds of millions of television viewers worldwide. Despite all the aura of spontaneity, which assured the Handshake a place in the list of Historic Moments of a Generation, the exercise had been pre-arranged by President Clinton, who had escorted the two leaders from the White House reception hall to the table where the accord was to be signed.[36]

Each side had its own reasons to clinch the deal. The Labor government realized that if it did not negotiate with the PLO it would be forced to talk to Hamas and the Islamic Jihad. "The rising strength of the Iranian-backed fundamentalist movement in the territories administered by Israel, and in the Middle East as a whole, influenced the Israeli leaders to explore the possibilities of a deal with the PLO," wrote Chaim Herzog, President of Israel from May 1983 to April 1993. "It became clear that apart from Mr. Arafat, there was no other valid interlocutor and that without him, the peace talks might collapse."[37]

At home, Rabin was more down to earth. "I prefer the Palestinians to cope with the problem of enforcing order in the Gaza Strip," he told the mass circulation *Yediot Aharonot* on September 7. "The Palestinians will be better at it than we were because they will allow no appeals to the Supreme Court and will prevent the Israeli Association of Civil Rights from criticizing the conditions there by denying it access to the area. They will rule by their own methods, freeing—and this is most important—the Israeli army soldiers from having to do what they will do."

Israel also realized it would get a better deal from the aging leadership of the PLO, weary after nearly two generations in exile, than from the much younger and more dynamic leadership, both secular and religious, in the West Bank and Gaza. Having grown up under Israeli occupation, and grasping not only Hebrew but also the fault lines of Israeli society and politics, these Palestinian leaders knew how to put them to advantageous use.

For now, however, the Israelis exploited several advantages over the Palestinians. First, they chose the mode of clandestine talks, and maneuvered the top Palestinian leadership into it. Historically, both Israel and the Zionists in Palestine had preferred secret diplomacy to public negotiations. They had struck a clandestine deal with King Abdullah of Jordan before the 1948 Arab-Israeli War. In 1991, by making its Arab adversaries agree to bilateral talks outside the UN umbrella, Israel gained twice. It could play individual Arab parties against one another. Most importantly, since the contents of an agreement reflect the balance of power—military, economic, diplomatic—between the bargaining parties, Israel, unmatched by any separate Arab party, stood to benefit.

Along with this diplomatic strategy went operational tactics, which focused on intelligence-gathering. In all its dealings with the Palestinians, Israel had laid great stress on recruiting agents and spies. Its success could be judged by the accuracy with which its bombers flattened PLO headquarters in October 1985, and the chilling efficiency with which its operators carried out the assassination of Khalil Wazir in April 1988. But the Israeli intelligence apparatus constantly strived higher. In 1990 Mossad had a great success, recruiting Adnan Yasin during one of his trips to Paris for his wife's cancer treatment. Its research had shown that 44-year-old Yasin, fond of drink, was a high spender, and his wife's treatment was eating rapidly into his modest savings. He was deputy to Abdul Hakkam Balawi, who was both the PLO's ambassador to Tunisia and the head of the PLO's internal security. Since Balawi and Yasin had been posted in Tunis before the PLO's expulsion from Beirut in September 1982, they played a leading role in smoothing the way of the PLO into Tunisia. In the process they acquired open access, day or night, to the top leadership and offices of the PLO. Obviously, by recruiting someone like Yasin, who traveled frequently to Europe, Mossad stood to reap a rich harvest of information.

Its officials approached Yasin posing as businessmen from a West European country—a "false flag" operation. They paid Yasin handsomely, and declared their true identity only after they had so compromised him that he could not quit. They now made bigger demands on him, eventually making Yasin place bugging devices in the offices of top PLO officials, including Mahmoud Abbas and Ahmad Qrei, who were both involved in the ultra-secret talks with the Israelis, and possibly Yasser Arafat. The signals from Yasin's transmitters were picked up in Israel's embassies in Paris and Rome, and from there passed to Mossad headquarters in Tel Aviv.[38] This damaging breach of security went undetected until November 1993, three months after the crucial Declaration of Principles had been settled. So Israel struck that most important accord with the PLO armed with the highly secret details of the strategy and tactics of Arafat and Abbas.

Among the important factors that drove the PLO to reach an agreement with Israel was its poor financial state and a crisis of confidence in the top leadership. In mid-July 1993, after the tenth round of Madrid formula talks with the Israelis had proved as sterile as the preceding nine, Haidar Abdul Shafi, head of the Palestinian delegation, publicly called for a radical reform of the Palestinian hierarchy and decision-making. Three weeks later, disgruntled at how Arafat was directing the negotiations, Husseini and Ashrawi, official members of the Palestinian delegation since April, arrived in Tunis with their resignations in hand. Arafat pacified them by promising an emergency meeting of the executive committee to discuss his leadership and the PLO's acute financial straits.

By now the PLO's cash crisis had deepened to the point that employees of its schools, clinics, hospitals and newspapers had gone unpaid for up to six months. The PLO's welfare fund for the families suffering under the Israeli occupation had shrunk from $8 million a year to $2 million. On top of this came an Israeli move that hurt the fragile Palestinian economy badly. In March 1993 Rabin ordered Israel's closure from the Occupied Territories, depriving tens of thousands of Palestinians, dependent on work in Israel, of their livelihood.

These factors produced an environment in which unprecedented criticism of Arafat came to the fore. His detractors openly accused him of paranoia, autocratic behavior, egotism, sheer love of power, refusal to delegate authority, and rewarding personal loyalty rather than competence. On policy issues they were critical of his chronic overreaction, his swinging between extremes: to the right after the expulsions from Lebanon, flirting with King Hussein and Mubarak; and then to the left, warmly embracing Saddam Hussein. They condemned the corruption at the upper echelons of the PLO, although they never accused Arafat of being personally corrupt. Arafat himself continued to live frugally, neither drinking nor smoking, happy to be sharing meals with his bodyguards. His admirers highlighted Arafat's capacity to inspire devotion, his manic dedication to the cause, indefatigability, and exemplary personal courage in mortal danger or emergency. Most significantly, they pointed out that against heavy odds, Arafat had held together the PLO, and that he had maintained the PLO's independence, frustrating attempts by the leading Arab powers to co-opt it. By any standards, they argued, these were outstanding achievements.

The debate on Arafat's leadership had hardly started when news broke of the secret deal between Israel and the PLO. The initial popular reaction to the DOP was positive. Those who marched with Palestinian flags in the streets of the Occupied Territories felt that liberation was near. But once they studied the document carefully they realized, depressingly, that all it contained was a road map to peace and a mere possibility of liberation, if that, nothing more. Modeled on the September 1978 Camp David Accords, it offered only limited autonomy, the first one applying to the Gaza Strip and a small West Bank town (Jericho), and the second to the West Bank minus Greater East Jerusalem. The interim agreement was to last five years after the modalities of the first stage had been implemented.

Of the eighteen PLO executive members, seven either resigned in protest or refused to attend the meeting to discuss the DOP. Of those present only eight voted for it. The opposition included Farouq Qaddumi, a Fatah stalwart and the PLO's foreign minister who, as counterpart to Peres, should ordinarily have signed the DOP in Washington. And of the ten groups affiliated to the PLO, only Fatah, the Democratic Palestinian Union, Palestine People's Party, and Palestine Struggle Front accepted the accord. Prominent among those who opposed it was George Habash of the PFLP. He referred to his ties with Arafat before the 1991 Madrid conference. "Our friendship was based on the condition that we work according to our PLO National Charter program: (a) the right to return [for Palestinian refugees], (b) self-determination for the Palestinians, and (c) the right to an independent state," he said on October 8, 1993. "The Oslo agreement makes no rules on these subjects. On the contrary, it does not include an Israeli withdrawal and the Jewish settlements will remain where they are."[39] The most telling criticism of the DOP was that there was no mention of Israel as the occupying power, which meant that the indisputably Occupied Territories had in effect been turned into the Disputed Territories.

Condemning the DOP on these grounds, Hamas rejected the Oslo Accord.

At the PLO central council meeting on November 12, among those having second thoughts was none other than Mahmoud Abbas, who had signed the DOP in Washington. "This agreement carries in its bowels either an independent state or the consecration of the [Israeli] occupation," he warned. "It all depends on our mentality as we deal with it, on our instruments and on our preparations."[40]

Part of the reason for the unease of Abbas was the discovery that Adnan Yasin was an Israeli mole.

Abbas's suspicion was aroused when he realized how knowledgeable Peres was about the tactics he had discussed only in a secret session with Arafat. On his return to Tunis, Abbas contacted Arafat, who recalled how Dennis Ross, the US State Department official dealing with the peace process, had insisted on meeting him not in the PLO office but at his hotel in Tunis. Arafat ordered a sweep of all PLO premises while the internal security chief, Balawi, conferred with his Tunisian counterpart. The discovery of bugging devices in the offices of Abbas and Qrei confirmed the worst fears. But they had no clue who the culprit could be.

Their break came from the Tunisian intelligence. Tipped off by their counterparts in Paris where Yasin's signals were received (and apparently monitored by French intelligence), the Tunisians intensified their investigation. The radio transmissions emanating from Yasin's house led them to their quarry, on November 2. They handed him over to the PLO's justice department. Arafat confiscated the passports of all PLO employees to ensure that none of them fled. He also imposed a news blackout on the investigation of the two alleged moles, the other being a radio operator at the PLO's telecommunication center.

A doctored report of the PLO's investigation published later was an exercise in damage limitation. Its conclusion was that the bugged desk, chair and lamp in Abbas's office, supplied by a "French businessman," had been placed there only on October 10 after they had been picked up in Marseilles by Adnan Yasin's son, Hani (who was found not to be implicated).[41]

Most likely Mossad officials, urged by their boss Rabin, then engaged in the most delicate and important clandestine talks with the PLO leader, had pressed Yasin hard to plant bugging devices and use other means to let them into the counsels of the five PLO leaders who masterminded the negotiations in Tunis: Arafat, Abbas, Qrei, Yasser Abd Rabbo and Hassan Asfour (of the Palestine People's Party).

Asfour's party and Rabbo's Democratic Palestinian Union were vocal in their support for the Oslo Accord. So were Fatah and the Palestine Struggle Front. An opinion survey showed that roughly half of the Palestinians polled accepted the Oslo Accord, while about a quarter, backing either Hamas or secular radical groups, rejected it, with the rest undecided.

On the Israeli side, 63.6 percent supported the Accord, with up to 30 percent against. In the Knesset, the accord won a comfortable majority, with three defecting Likud MKs (out of 32) voting for it. Opposing the agreement, Likud leader Binyamin Netanyahu spelled out five principles on which peace should be based: preventing the creation of a Palestinian state; preserving the unity of Jerusalem; maintaining the IDF's responsibility for security in the Palestinian territories; offering guarantees for the Jewish settlements in the Territories; and a ban on the return of Palestinian refugees. He volunteered to form a national unity government with Labor to advance peace "in the way the majority of Israelis would like to see it go," but Rabin rejected his offer.[42]

A majority of Israelis backed the Oslo Accord primarily because it promised an end to the bloody strife they associated with the Palestinian intifada. Almost half of Palestinians supported the agreement because they felt that it would result in the Israeli military relaxing its grip over the Occupied Territories, and among other things ease draconian travel restrictions on them.

In the immediate aftermath of the Accord, both sides were disappointed. There was no change in the hardline behavior of the Israeli soldiers on patrol and at roadblocks. Twenty Palestinians were killed in the first two months of the Accord. Equally, a rising number of Israelis became skeptical about Arafat's call to his followers to abjure violence. Their doubts were confirmed when on November 13 the Israeli government announced that the five Palestinians suspected of killing a Jewish settler belonged to Fatah. They were unimpressed by the sight of Arafat sharing that year's Nobel Peace Prize in December with Rabin and Peres in Oslo.

The situation changed when Baruch Goldstein massacred the Palestinians at prayer in the Ibrahimi Mosque/Tomb of the Patriarchs in late February 1994. The PLO suspended its talks with the Israelis and demanded an armed UN presence to protect Palestinian civilians in the Occupied Territories from the Jewish settlers and Israeli soldiers. But due to the strong opposition of Israel and the United States, it did not get very far. America's foot-dragging at the Security Council delayed until March 18 the Council's passage of Resolution 904, which condemned the Hebron massacre and called for measures to guarantee the safety of civilians in the Occupied Territories, including a Temporary International Presence in Hebron (TIPH), not part of the UN operations.

The PLO returned to the negotiating table on March 30. As a result, Mustafa Natsche, dismissed as mayor by the IDF in 1983 for "incitement" against Israel, was reinstated in the Town Hall. On taking office, he declared that "the precedent of allowing foreign observers to be stationed in the Occupied Territories signaled a qualitative change in long held Israeli policies and practices vis-a-vis the Palestinians."[43] This proved to be a highly unrealistic view. It was not until May 8 that a contingent of 135 lightly armed observers from Denmark, Italy and Norway— forming the TIPH—arrived in the city on a renewable three-month mandate to "provide adequate protection" to the local Palestinians. The IDF billeted them in a northern suburb of Hebron, far away from the tense city center. During their stay there were clashes between the Palestinians and the Jewish settlers, but the TIPH was unable to intervene. The IDF soon declared the area "a closed military zone" and barred the entry of the TIPH. And when the IDF imposed a curfew it applied not only to the Palestinians but also to the TIPH. As a result the TIPH aroused more sympathy among Palestinians than respect, especially when it failed to get the Ibrahimi Mosque reopened by the time it left on August 8, the end of the initial period of its mandate.

By then, however, the DOP had been transformed, slowly, into a working document signed by both parties in Cairo on May 4, 1994. Among other things it gave rise to the Palestinian Authority (PA)—Al Sultah al Falastiniya in Arabic, and HaRashut HaFalastinit in Hebrew—an executive and legislative body.

12

The Palestinian Authority
An Embryo

"Mansion House."Abdul Hakim al Samra said the words in passing as he drove slowly by an impressive complex a few blocks from the beach in Gaza City one cloudy morning in March 1995. The name sounded familiar to me, a Londoner. The Mansion House is the official residence of the mayor of the City of London. Built in 1752, it has a long history. Not so with its Gaza City namesake. It was constructed by the British during their mandate in Palestine for the regional administrator of Gaza, and their stamp was obvious in the red-tiled slanting roofs of the sprawling structure. Now 80 years old, this Mansion House had witnessed a succession of powers in Gaza: the British, the Egyptians, then briefly (in 1956–7) the Israelis, reverting back to the Egyptians, and since 1967 the Israelis again.

"It was the residence of the IDF governor," said Abdul Hakim. "During the intifada he set up the Ansar I [detention] camp in tents here, in the compound, when the central jail got too full. Now the Palestinian military uses it as a training camp." I looked out of the car, and saw smartly dressed Palestinian recruits lined up for a drill.

"I was here on May 18th last year," Abdul Hakim said, "the last day of the IDF in the Gaza Strip." Not all of the Strip? "No, of course not," he said wearily. "The Mansion House was the last facility the IDF vacated according to the Cairo Agreement [of May 4]. A historic moment, as they say." He smiled his rare smile. "Worth witnessing. It was like the hot days of the intifada. The Israelis were scared shit that they would be buried in stones. So they tossed tear-gas canisters in the air as they fled, chased by us. But there was one difference, one big difference... Among their chasers were Palestinian policemen in uniform, with machine-guns. In fact they were running ahead of us all. Quite a sight, I tell you. And the moment they entered the Mansion House they went wild, firing their machineguns in the air. We had never heard such a racket before, and never will." His face was wreathed in smiles.

For a few weeks, these 3,000 policemen operated in a judicial vacuum. It was not until May 21 that Arafat, still in Tunis, instructed civil and religious courts in the Gaza Strip and Jericho to begin operating according to the laws operating before the 1967 Israeli conquest. These included Ottoman, British, Egyptian and Jordanian (in the case of Jericho) laws. The Israeli foreign ministry was swift to call Arafat's move "meaningless and invalid," stating that the more than 2,000 military laws and orders issued by the IDF since June remained in force and were binding on "all of the parties." Its legal adviser, Joel Singer, who had participated in the clandestine talks culminating in the Oslo Accord, said: "Neither Arafat nor the Palestinian Authority is able unilaterally to abrogate Israeli military obligations." He was right. Clause 9 of Article VII of the Cairo Agreement stated: "Laws and military orders in effect in the Gaza Strip or the Jericho Area prior to the signing of this Agreement shall remain in force, unless amended or abrogated in accordance with this Agreement." More ominously for Palestinians, Major-General Matan Vilnai, commander of the IDF's southern command, added that if the peace process did not work Israel would consider all its options. "In the extreme sense that means Israel returning to Gaza."[1] There was no mincing of words on the part of Israel, which knew exactly what sort of accords it had signed in Oslo and Cairo, and how limited were the powers it had agreed to vest in the Palestinian Authority (PA).

By mid-June, Arafat had appointed twenty members of the Palestinian Authority executive that he headed, providing a judicious mix of West Bankers and Gazans, including Faisal Husseini, Mustafa Natsche, Munib Masri and Zakaria al Agha, and outsiders, including Ahmad Qrei, Intissar Wazir, Nabil Shaath and Nasser Yusuf. Yet he showed no sign of moving to the self-rule Palestinian territories. Involved in raising foreign money to fund the PA, expected to run up a huge deficit, on his own terms, he tried to pressure the donors by postponing his departure from Tunis. There was an equal measure of uncertainty about whether he would set up the PA headquarters in Jericho (because it was situated in the larger Palestinian territory of the West Bank) or Gaza (because it contained 98% of all the Palestinians being granted limited self-rule).

Arafat chose Gaza, and on July 1 he arrived in the capital of the Gaza Strip for a surprisingly subdued reception. True to form, Arafat was late arriving. A welcoming assembly of over 1,000 local dignitaries, waiting since morning in the fiercely hot desert sun, got no more than a quick wave of arms by the PLO Chairman and soon to be leader of the new Palestinian Authority.

Among those present for the occasion was Harb Abu Namous, a grandfatherly figure sporting a white beard, a traditional black cloak and white headdress kept in place by two rounds of black rope, of the extended Abu Namous family in Gaza City. He was downbeat. "To be frank, I should have listened to my family, stayed home and watched Abu Ammar [Arafat's *nom de guerre*] on television," he said. "Once Abu Ammar had marched past the soldiers' guard of honor, he was immediately surrounded by a sea of bodyguards, like whirling sand in a sandstorm. All we could see from a long way off was a black-and-white checkered *keffiyeh* bobbing up and down in the midst of soldiers. I had the vision of hugging and kissing the President of Palestine on our soil, welcoming him properly." Harb heaved a deep sigh. "It was a dream, a silly dream. Then the bodyguards just bundled Abu Ammar into an open-top limousine, and he was off to the highway to Khan Yunis, his family town." Did Harb then retire to his television set? "Yes. What else?"

The recently established Palestine Broadcasting Authority meticulously recorded the activities of Arafat for the next few days in the Gaza Strip and Jericho.

He made the right moves to present himself as the national leader, above party politics. At a public rally in Gaza City, attended by 70,000, near the Mansion House, he embraced Dr. Haidar Abdul Shafi, aged 75, the grand old politician of Gaza, a man with a long history of unswerving commitment to the Palestinian cause who would later emerge as a leader of the independent Palestinian opposition. Addressing Shaikh Ahmad Yasin, the imprisoned leader of Hamas, Arafat said: "You are the shaikh of us all. We will not rest until you are here by our side." This was received with thunderous applause by the crowd.

At the press conference in the evening at the beachside Palestine Hotel, his temporary abode, he was more reflective. "The most important challenge for us is to build the new Palestinian Authority which will lead to an independent Palestinian state, our democratic state, a state for free persons, a state for democracy, equality and non-discrimination," he declared. "The road from Gaza leads through Bethlehem and Nablus to Jerusalem." But it was only on the following day that, in the dilapidated environment of the Jabaliya camp, the birthplace of the intifada, Arafat publicly addressed the pros and cons of the Oslo Accord, a subject of much import to ordinary Palestinians. "Many of you think the Oslo [Accord] is a bad agreement," he said. "It is a bad agreement, but it is the best deal we could get in the worst situation."[2]

In the coming weeks and months these statements would come to haunt Arafat. The first and foremost concern of Arafat as well as Premier Yitzhak Rabin was security. It was significant that soon after naming the last member of the Palestinian Authority cabinet, Arafat, both the president of the PA and its interior minister, appointed a Higher Security Council.

Rabin and Arafat were concerned that in the period following the conclusion of the Oslo Accord, its popularity among Israelis had declined steadily. Among Palestinians, it was bitterly opposed by Islamists and by radical secular groups. This state of affairs was well mirrored in the death tolls on the opposite sides of the national divide. In the eight months since the White House signing ceremony, 150 Palestinians had been killed by the IDF or its undercover agents, and 45 Jews by Palestinians.

Both the Israeli government and the Palestinian Authority were anxious to see that no security vacuum resulted from the hand-over of power. Israel turned a blind eye when the PA exceeded the limit of 9,000 policemen specified by the Cairo, or Oslo I, Agreement, or set up organizations not authorized by the Agreement. According to Annex I, Article 3 the PA was allowed one security force with four operational divisions: civil policing; public order maintenance; emergency services; and internal intelligence service, popularly called *mukhabarat,* information-gathering organization.

But so intent was Rabin on safeguarding Israeli security by co-opting the emerging PA to destroy the Palestinian Islamist forces that he authorized a clandestine meeting in Rome with the chief of Shin Beth, Yaacov Perry, and the IDF's deputy chief of staff, General Amnon Shahak, with Colonel Jibril Rajoub, a top official in the PLO's military department, and Muhammad Dahlan, a leading official in its Occupied Homeland directorate, five months before the Cairo Agreement.

Arafat later named Dahlan and Rajoub as the Gaza and Jericho heads of the Preventive Security Service (PSS), an agency with an essentially political mandate, to work directly under him.

In Rome these officials cut a deal. The PSS would pass on to Israeli intelligence information about the Palestinian groups opposed to Oslo, particularly Hamas and the Islamic Jihad, and Israel would give *carte blanche* to the PSS in the Palestinian areas even outside of the Cairo Agreement, to curb any opposition to the Accord.[3] How the PSS was to operate was revealed by Ehud Ya'ari, a senior Israeli columnist. "Fatah-armed bands whose members were [until recently] wanted by the Israeli security services, like the Hawks, will have special tasks," he stated in the *Jerusalem Report* of January 13, 1994. "They will be charged with putting down any sign of opposition; the intent is for them to administer show punishments at the earliest possible stage, aimed at creating proper regard for the new regime." Ten months later, in November, something approaching this scenario came to pass in the Gaza Strip, bringing the territory to the brink of a civil war.

By then Arafat, President/Chairman of the Palestinian Authority, had set up the following uniformed and plain-clothes security organizations in the Gaza Strip and Jericho:

Uniformed: presidential body guard; Force 17 (originally set up in March 1968 after the Battle of al-Karameh to protect Fatah leaders and later to collect information on Israel and carry out certain operations against Israeli targets); and police.

Plain clothes: internal/domestic intelligence or *mukhabarat*; Preventive Security Service; military intelligence; and Force 18, the special task security force, which dealt, among other things, with Israeli collaborators. When asked why he required so many cloak-and-dagger organizations, Arafat replied: "The Syrians have fourteen, the Egyptians have twelve. I only have six to help me."[4]

The uniformed forces, wearing either blue or camouflage, were largely drawn from the PLO's Palestine Liberation Army, which had been scattered in half a dozen Arab countries since 1982. The remainder were recruited locally, chiefly from former members of Fatah's Hawks or its *shabiba* youth group. In both cases what counted most was faithfulness to Fatah and its leader Arafat. The PLA personnel were retrained for civil police duty in Egypt or Jordan. But, judging by their later actions, it was doubtful if they really learned to give priority to the rule of law over their unquestioning loyalty to Arafat. When the PLA units arrived at the Gaza frontier at Rafah from Egypt or at the Allenby Bridge from Jordan, they registered their names and serial numbers with the IDF. As expected, these soldiers-turned-policemen moved into the camps just evacuated by the IDF. By spring 1995 their numbers soared to twice the ceiling of 9,000. Less than a million Gazans were now policed by a force of 18,000; in comparison, over seven million New Yorkers are policed by 38,000 cops.

Though the uniformed men were the visible segment of security in the PA territories, an equally or more important function was performed by the plain-clothes agents of the Preventive Security Service. The word "Preventive" could be interpreted in one of two ways: prevent actions damaging to security; or prevent any expression of opposition to the peace process. They used surveillance, harassment and elimination of opponents of the Oslo and Cairo Agreements, often in conjunction with the IDF and Shin Beth. The 4,000-strong force, divided evenly between Gaza and the West Bank, consisted mostly of young Fatah activists and former political prisoners from inside the territories.

At 30, Muhammad Dahlan, a dapper, clean-shaven man, became perhaps the world's youngest chief of a security organization. A native Gazan, he was a political activist and a natural leader. "I headed the *shabiba* movement in the Gaza Strip, and I have struggled along with my brethren against the occupation," he told the Jerusalem-based *Al Quds* newspaper. "I was expelled to Jordan, and arrested. I then left for Cairo where also I was arrested. I went to Iraq where I had the opportunity to work with Abu Jihad [Khalil Wazir], God bless his soul. I learned a lot politically and socially from him, and from President Arafat himself... I have a good relationship with President Arafat developed through my work in Tunis where I was responsible for the military operations in the Gaza Strip during the intifada."[5]

In contrast to the neat figure of Dahlan, 41-year-old Jibril Rajoub looked roly-poly, despite his military uniform. He operated from a large, tastefully furnished office near Jericho. Born in Hebron, he became embroiled with Fatah and its armed struggle against Israel in his mid-teens, was arrested in 1970 and sentenced to twenty years in prison. In jail he taught himself Hebrew and English, "the languages of the enemy," and became chairman of the Fatah prison committee. Freed in a May 1985 prisoner exchange, Rajoub immediately plunged into political activity, becoming chief of the outlawed Fatah in the West Bank. Soon after the intifada began, Israel expelled him to Lebanon. From there he went to Tunis, where Arafat appointed him an assistant to Abu Jihad. When the PLO signed the Oslo Accord, Arafat appointed Rajoub as one of two heads of the new PSS, and he arrived in Jericho in June 1994.

Besides establishing the West Bank headquarters of the PSS near the small, deserted Palestinian refugee camp of Aqabat Jabr south of Jericho, Rajoub started a PSS academy there, to put 200 cadets through a two-year course. They would learn techniques of gathering and transmitting information as well as the complexities of civil law, human rights, legal procedures and the gathering of evidence. He accepted only West Bankers as Academy cadets or as PSS agents because, "they know the towns, villages and alleyways of the West Bank like the back of their hands."

Even in the IDF-controlled West Bank (all except tiny Jericho), the PSS operated as a long arm of Fatah. And since the PSS was not established by Arafat as the PA chief but as the PLO leader, it functioned outside the reach of judicial scrutiny. "When you are talking of the PSS, you're talking about Fatah," Rajoub told the *Jerusalem Report*. "And they are everywhere, in every camp, town and village."[6]

Equally controversially, the PSS went about strengthening the peace process through means which were at best questionable and at worst illegal. It set about disciplining the press, and those persisting in their foolhardy views were persecuted. In March 1995 the Jerusalem offices of the PFLP weekly *Al Umma* were burned down after it had ignored warnings from the PSS about "coverage hostile to the Palestinian Authority." Even the pro-Fatah *Al Quds* felt the wrath of the PSS and

Arafat when it showed any sign of independence. In August the daily was banned from the Gaza Strip and Jericho to discourage it from carrying a statement by the dissident PLO leader Farouq Qaddumi describing the Oslo Accord as "a surrender of Palestinian rights."

But what caught international attention was the PSS detention and interrogation of *Al Quds* editor Maher Alami after Christmas. His "crime" was that he did not splash on the front page the complimentary Christmas sermon of the Greek Orthodox Patriarch in Bethlehem, comparing Arafat and Caliph Omar ibn al-Khattab regarding their favorable treatment of Christians. He only published it on page eight. Alami's ordeal ended after six days only because of the interest the international press took in his fate.[7]

Since Hamas and the Islamic Jihad had rejected the peace accords, and since the IDF and Jewish settlers still controlled two-fifths of the Gaza Strip, the bitter conflict between them and Israel was still on. The IDF and its hit squads targeted Islamist militants no matter where they were, and the latter continued to strike at Israeli Jewish targets.

The Rabin government expected the PLO would join forces to squash the Islamists. But there was a line that the PA and Arafat could not cross: an open armed alliance with Israel against Hamas, which enjoyed substantial grass roots support, especially in Gaza, would escalate into a civil war, to the detriment of all Palestinians.

But Israel continued its efforts to eliminate radical Islamists. On August 12, 1994 Israeli undercover agents killed two Hamas activists in East Jerusalem. Two days later the military wing of Hamas, the Qassam Brigade, attacked near the Gush Qatif settlement in the Gaza Strip, killing one settler and injuring five. The PA police chief, Nasser Yusuf, arrested twenty Hamas activists. On August 27 Qassam Brigade members killed two Jewish builders in the Israeli town of Ramle, angering Rabin. "The entire agreement with the PLO is predicated on the understanding that the PLO must combat terrorism and its perpetrators," he said. "If Yasser Arafat is unable to fulfill his part, why should Israel continue implementing agreements when there is no certainty that he could later comply with them."[8]

Besides responding to Israel's actions against its members, the Qassam Brigade persued its own agenda. At the top of it was the release of Hamas prisoners, especially Shaikh Ahmad Yasin, from Israeli jails. On October 11 it kidnapped an IDF soldier, Nachshon Waxman, and offered to exchange him for 200 Hamas prisoners including Yasin. When Rabin confidently announced that Waxman was being held in Gaza, the Israeli media offered Arafat a stark option: choose peace with Israel, or peace with Hamas. Arafat made his choice clear when the PA police rounded up some 400 Hamas loyalists without charges, set up roadblocks, conducted identity checks and shut down the pro-Hamas Islamic University—the kind of actions associated with the IDF to most Gazans.

Through back channels the PSS supplied intelligence to the Israeli government, based on which Rabin ordered a rescue operation on October 14 in Bir Nabala village where Waxman was being held. The operation went wrong. Waxman and his three captors were killed. The next day the Gaza Strip closed down to mourn "the martyrs of Bir Nabala." To avenge their deaths, on October 19 a Hamas suicide bomber blew himself up in a bus in downtown Tel Aviv, killing 22 Israelis and sending a shock wave through Israeli society. The government arrested 1,350 Islamists in Israel and the West Bank, and reaffirmed its resolve to strike at terrorists no matter where they were.

On the morning of November 2, when Hani Abid, the 27-year-old co-editor of the Gaza-based Islamic Jihad weekly, *Al Istiqlal*, opened the door of his car, an explosion killed him instantly. The assassination had the hallmarks of an Israeli undercover operation. Nine days later, Hisham Hamad, a young Jihad activist riding a bicycle, detonated himself outside the Netzarim settlement, killing three IDF soldiers. The PA police arrested 120 Islamic Jihad members. But this was not enough to pacify Rabin. He held a crisis meeting with Arafat in Madrid. There the Israeli premier warned the Palestinian leader that if there was more violence against IDF personnel in the territory under his control, the Israeli army would re-enter the PA areas, and take out the terrorists "regardless of the autonomy and the Palestinian police."[9] Had Rabin translated his threat into action, he would have been very much within his rights. For Clause 1 of Article VIII of the Cairo Agreement stated: "Israel shall continue to carry... the responsibility for overall security of Israelis and [Jewish] settlements [in the areas under Palestinian Authority control], for the purpose of safeguarding their internal security and public order, and will have the powers to take the steps necessary to meet this responsibility."[10]

Chastened, Arafat accepted the advice of his hardline PA police commander in the Gaza Strip, Major-General Nasser Yusuf: crush Hamas.

On November 18, following their Friday prayer and sermon in Gaza City's elegant, newly-built Palestine Mosque, a stronghold of Hamas, about 1,000 Gazans prepared to march to the central jail to demand the release of the Hamas members being held there without charges. They found their path blocked by some 200 uniformed Palestinian police and plain-clothes PSS agents. As they tried to force their way through the police lines, a mêlée ensued. Shots were fired. Soon three men lay dead. The word spread fast. In streets all over the city, police and protesters fought pitched battles. By sunset, thirteen men were killed, and over 200 injured.

Arafat did what Ehud Ya'ari, an eminent Israeli commentator, had predicted, mobilizing not only Fatah but also its supposedly disarmed and disbanded armed wing.[11] The Fatah Hawks mounted an armed demonstration on November 21 which ended with a rally of 10,000 addressed by a belligerent Arafat. The rapidly escalating intra-Palestinian tension thrilled most Jewish Israelis. "The clashes signal that Arafat will no longer tolerate the Islamist opposition," Yossi Sarid, a Meretz minister known as a peacenik, declared approvingly. "He now understands that it's either him or them."[12] The next day a Palestinian policeman was killed. And on November 24 shots were fired outside the residences of two eminent Hamas figures. While most Jewish Israelis waited for a Palestinian civil war, the Israeli Arab MKs joined Dr. Haidar Abdul Shafi to cool the situation. Arafat allowed Hamas to hold a public meeting on November 26, provided there was no display of arms. In return, Hamas secured a promise from him that there would be no presence of (uniformed) police at the gathering.

Palestinians and Arab Israelis heaved a sigh of relief while most Jewish Israelis felt disappointed. The old equation still held though, with Israel and militant Islamists engaged in a deadly battle, and the Palestinian Authority wishing to see total peace prevail but unprepared to confront Muslim radicals all the way for fear of triggering a disastrous civil conflict. In any case, relations with Israel were still tenuous.

In the early hours of January 2, 1995 an IDF patrol shot dead four Palestinian policemen, injured one and arrested another in a gun battle near Beit Hanoun village in northern Gaza. The IDF claimed it was mistaken identity; Palestinians saw the incident as a cold-blooded murder of their policemen by the IDF. The PA and the Israeli government blamed poor co-ordination, and pledged to improve communication. But, in retaliation, on January 22, two Islamic Jihad suicide bombers killed themselves, twenty IDF soldiers and one civilian at a bus stop in Beit Lid near Natanya. Outraged Israelis reacted with anger and grief. The Rabin government imprisoned a further 200 Islamists, bringing the total since the Tel Aviv bombing to over 2,000.

The score of violent deaths since the September 1993 Oslo Accord was: Palestinian 235, Israeli 110.

At the initiative of Egyptian President Hosni Mubarak, whose regime also faced violence from extremist Islamists, there was a mini-summit of the Egyptian, Israeli, Jordanian and Palestinian leaders in Cairo on February 2. Rabin pressed Arafat to get tough with the Islamic terrorists. "After Beit Lid you arrested only seven members of the Islamic Jihad," he said to Arafat. "We arrested 200. We arrested 1,350 after the Dizengoff [Tel Aviv] bombing in October." Arafat replied, "We arrested many others in the past, but they were acquitted."[13] The PA police had either pressed no charges or produced insufficient evidence to secure conviction in court.

President Mubarak, who had established military courts in Egypt to try suspected Islamic radicals, advised Arafat to circumvent the normal judicial system. On February 7 Arafat resurrected an Egyptian law of 1962 (when Gaza was administered by Cairo), and set up a State Security Court. Presided over by three judges, it was authorized to try cases referred to it, either by the PA's attorney-general or its chairman/president, outside of the civil law. When Raji Sourani, a prominent lawyer and head of the Gaza Center for Rights and Law, said that such courts undermined "the independence of the judiciary," and marked "the beginning of a trend toward militarization of Palestinian society," he was arrested on February 14.

Rabin remained firmly committed to his efforts to eradicate Muslim terrorists by all means. His pressure on Arafat to do likewise was paying off, and co-operation between the PSS and Israel's Shin Beth and IDF was increasing. One result was a thunderous explosion in an apartment in the Shaikh Radwan suburb of Gaza City on April 2, leaving four people dead. Among them was Kamal Kheil, a member of the Qassam Brigade, wanted by both Israelis and the PA. The PA said the explosion was an accident in a terrorist bomb factory, but refused to turn the bodies over to families.

Reprisal came on April 9, the anniversary of the Deir Yasin massacre by Zionist extremists in 1948. Near the Kfar Darom settlement in the Gaza Strip, a Palestinian car packed with explosives hit an Israeli bus, and another crashed into an IDF convoy; eight soldiers and settlers died. The attacks were claimed by both Hamas and Islamic Jihad, and subsequent PA arrests landed 170 in jail.

Efforts by Haidar Abdul Shafi and Abdullah Hourani, a member of the PLO executive committee, to bring about a Palestinian rapprochement, stalled. Their common platform demanded full withdrawal of Israel from the Gaza Strip, dismantling of the Jewish settlements, and the release of all political prisoners held by Israel and the PA. When this document, the National Reconciliation Agreement, was ready for signing in May, Arafat refused to do so, stating that the agreement did not contain commitments by Hamas and the Islamic Jihad to cease attacks against Israel from inside the Gaza Strip. Critics argued that Arafat's refusal showed he had succumbed to the pressure by Rabin opposed to Arafat-Islamist reconciliation.

Arafat realized that the PA's economic survival was now heavily dependent on grants from western states, which wanted transparent and accountable institutions in place before they fulfilled their financial promises. They channeled their grants, in equal measure, through the World Bank and the United Nations. The World Bank paid wages to 15,000 public sector employees, and the UN provided salaries and the running cost of the 9,000-strong police force as well as public works and other projects.[14] UN Secretary-General Boutros Boutros-Ghali appointed Terje Larsen, 47, a Norwegian social scientist who had arranged the secret Israeli-PLO talks, as UN Special Co-ordinator in the Occupied Territories. Larsen established UNSCO headquarters in Gaza, and set up a UN Local Aid Co-ordination Committee to meet the donors' transparency and accountability requirement, chiefly by auditing randomly the receipts of the funds spent.

Even during the first year, July 1993–June 1994, the PA faced a deficit of $150 million. Taxes were low due to high unemployment, which itself reflected Israel's deep cuts in the number of Palestinians it allowed to work in Israel, and the frequent closure of the Green Line that followed terrorist bombs. By January 1995, Israel had reduced the Palestinian total from 120,000 to 45,000, and made up the shortfall by importing 70,000 Romanian and Thai workers.[15] After the suicide-bomb attack on January 22, Israel barred all unmarried Palestinian workers under 30, reducing the total Palestinian workers to a mere 20,000. Little wonder that from July 1994 to June 1995, Gaza's already low living standards dropped 25 percent.

As Abdul Hani, a small, bearded grocer in Khan Yunis put it in March 1995: "Things are worse economically than before. Last year at the time of the Eid al Fitr in February, I bought 250 pieces of cheese and sold them all. This year I ordered only 35 and sold only 15." He caressed his scanty beard gloomily. "You can see the sweets I bought for the Eid," he continued, pointing out his wares on display under an awning. "Two weeks after the Eid so many are still unsold."

The only area where there were overt signs of progress was in some public works, especially sewage, electricity and telephones, and some increase in health services.

Private sector construction was booming partly to meet office and housing demands by the Palestinian Authority, and partly to accommodate affluent Palestinians returning from the diaspora. From the beachfront in Gaza City one could see high-rise apartment and office blocks going up. The PA had also cleaned up the beach, and overall Gaza had been sprucing itself up with liberal coats of whitewash, in the process wiping out the graffiti of the intifada. With the end of the nine P.M. to four A.M. curfew, a permanent feature under Israeli occupation, the general atmosphere was now relaxed.

There were many overt signs of a people slowly but surely emerging as a nation and a state: the Palestinian flag flying, the arrival of the Palestine Broadcasting Authority on radio and television. Even the many who disapproved of the PBA's tedious coverage of Arafat's doings could not help feeling proud that it existed.

The Palestinians' rising self-confidence transcended politics and economics, to the socio-cultural sphere. In religious affairs, they successfully challenged King Hussein's authority to act as the custodian of the Islamic shrines in Jerusalem by ignoring his appointment of 66-year-old Shaikh Abdul Qadir Abidin as the mufti of Jerusalem. Arafat was quick to respond, appointing a Jerusalemite, Shaikh Ekrima Said Sabri, as mufti of Jerusalem and the Holy Land. A bespectacled, bearded man of 55, Sabri sat in his office near the Dome of the Rock, behind a vast pinewood desk. The numerous volumes on the shelves added an air of scholarly authority to his Ph.D. in Islamic law from the oldest university in the world, Cairo's Al Azhar.

"Before taking up this position, I was for many years the director of preaching and guidance at the Islamic Waqf [Trust]," Sabri told me in mid-January 1995. Sipping the aromatic Turkish coffee, I wondered aloud about the title of Sabri. "Just as the Greek Orthodox Patriarch Diodoros I is the patriarch of Jerusalem as well as Israel, the Palestinian Territories, Jordan, Kuwait and the United Arab Emirates, I am the grand mufti of all of Jerusalem and the Holy Land of Palestine," he explained. "And just as the religious pronouncements of Patriarch Diodoros apply to the Greek Orthodox in all these countries, my *fatwas* [religious decrees] apply to all Muslims living in my area."

I asked about Shaikh Abidin, whom King Hussein had appointed to the same post a few days before Sabri. "Once the Palestinian National Authority was established, whatever residual powers had been vested in King Hussein passed to the PNA," came the reply.

Soon after came a test to prove whose *fatwa* Muslim Palestinians were going to follow. In the Islamic calendar, Ramadan, the holy month of fasting, begins with the sighting of the new moon. Since the sighting depends on the condition of the sky, cloudy or clear, Ramadan begins on different days in the Muslim world. At least it did in 1995. On Monday January 30 at about 7 P.M., Sabri announced before a gathering of the religious leaders, that the moon had been spotted and that the first day of Ramadan had begun. At about the same time in Gaza City, Arafat issued a statement. "For the first time in the history of the Palestinian nation, we announce to the Arab and Islamic world the witnessing of the new Ramadan moon from the Al Aqsa Mosque under the Palestinian National Authority," he declared.[16] Sabri's rival, Abidin, waited for a signal from Amman, which came 24 hours later.

But by then all Palestinian Muslims had already finished their first day of fasting.

This was an easy win for Arafat and his nominee. But when it came to Arafat and his supporters confronting Israel on the issue of the Jewish settlements on the West Bank, it was a different story.

I witnessed one such instance on January 17, 1995. It was a breezy, cool morning when young men in jeans and windbreakers began gathering near the imposing new mosque on the outskirts of Al Bireh. Their leader carried a large Palestinian flag with "Fatah Movement" inscribed. They began shouting slogans: "No Peace with Settlements"; and *"Biladi, biladi"* (my land or my homeland). Older men arrived, including the mufti of Jerusalem, then a group of women, among them Hanan Ashrawi.

The demonstrators planned to march along a zigzag route to the top of a hill, the site of the Psagot settlement with some 115 families, protesting both the expansion of this colony and the seizure of Palestinian land to construct an access road that would enable the Jewish settlers to bypass Al Bireh on their way to Jerusalem and beyond. They marched along a road whose surface declined from asphalt to stone to freshly leveled soil, with construction machinery busily shaping the gently rising hill on both sides of the prized ribbon. Across a U in the road, the demonstrators haphazardly crossed a trickling stream, and headed uphill to a plateau. IDF soldiers, armed with machine guns, were waiting, standing next to Jeeps and armored personnel carriers. The protesters stopped, and formed a well-behaved crowd. Speeches followed, including those of four PA ministers. The audience consisted of some 300 Palestinians of assorted ages and dress, from the jeans, windbreakers and sneakers of young men to traditional, embroidered ankle-length dresses of middle-aged matrons—plus another 75 media people. I looked hard, but did not see the settlement. It stood above the steep embankment cut to make the access road, and was invisible from where I stood. While we listened to speeches, a large band of youths climbed to the heavily guarded gate of the fenced settlement.

Suddenly we heard a volley of shots. We turned tail. A bullet fell by my side. I picked it up, and started running downhill. Others did the same, men, women, youths. I was soon running beside two Palestinian women dressed in skirts and high-heel shoes. One of them stopped, took off her shoes, and resumed her downhill flight faster than before. The Israeli soldiers started chasing us. "We are safe now," I mumbled to myself as we reached the threadbare stream. Not really. By now the young soldiers were in hot pursuit of their quarry—the Palestinian youths—and were running and firing in the air. I had thought the firing outside the settlement was to disperse the crowd, and once that was achieved, the troops would stay put. But no, the rules of the game were different here.

I was now on a level asphalt road, walking briskly, not running. Ahead of me were three Palestinian matrons, in long embroidered dresses and shawls, mumbling angrily in Arabic. Three young Israeli soldiers, in their late teens, went past the women. One, with a crew cut, stopped. Slowly, he raised his machine gun aimed at one of the women, now standing still, and lowered the muzzle. The soldier pointed his gun at the second woman, then raised it a few inches above her head, and fired. Only a few yards away, I watched, petrified.

The woman stood straight, unflinching. The young soldier turned, broke into a trot, and joined his comrades, all of them now chasing Palestinian youths.

Later I saw the battle continuing near the mosque, the starting place. When one soldier caught up with a stone-thrower, another shouted: "Give him to me. I want to kill him." (The words, in Hebrew, were translated by a local journalist who had also returned to the assembly point.) "It is like *West Side Story*, a street gang warfare," I said to my interlocutor. "Except that one side has machine guns, and the other stones," he said. "It's an unequal fight." It was hard to disagree.

And in the final analysis, the Al Bireh demonstration was a futile act. Within a year of the protest, the Psagot settlement expanded from 115 to 140 families.[17] Arafat tried in vain to recover what he had conceded in the Oslo Accord, which contained not a word about the Jewish settlements in the West Bank and Gaza.

More disappointingly for Palestinians, Arafat did not seem to learn from his past mistakes, or alter his methods from those necessary to run a guerrilla organization to those required to run a democratic state. His secretiveness, deviousness and skillful manipulation, assets in maintaining the unity of the PLO, now became liabilities. Arafat had maintained his leadership of the PLO by showing repeatedly that he was indispensable, and that he possessed an uncanny sense of survival. Part of his success in emerging as the first among equals lay in his skill in engendering controlled tensions between different PLO factions and even among his Fatah colleagues, and then intervening as a mediator. Equally importantly, his exclusive control of PLO and Fatah funds was a powerful bargaining tool. But for a democratic state to emerge, there had to be less secretiveness, a sharing of power, and much more delegation of authority.

Continuing the old pattern in a new environment, when fighting Israel had given way to talking, Arafat resorted to nominating negotiators at the eleventh hour, and providing them with insufficient guidelines. When the inevitable stalemate ensued, he would emerge to bargain directly with Rabin and reach agreements, thus boosting not only his ego and his indispensability, but also his public image as a statesman actively pursuing the "peace of the brave."

Arafat obfuscated his failures in the talks, releasing piecemeal the details of the agreements. Even Fatah stalwarts like Abdul Hakim al Samara turned critical of Arafat. "When Rabin reaches an agreement he immediately gives the Hebrew translation to all MKs in parliament," he said. "As for Arafat, even PA ministers do not fully know what has been signed. So then you find in the Arabic press the PA spokesman says so and so. And then the Israelis say, 'Read the agreement.' And always the Israelis are right. Every day we find more and more 'secret' parts of the agreements." Arafat also made a poor choice of negotiators. "The Palestinians he appointed to negotiate the implementation of the Oslo Accord were no match to Haidar Abdul Shafi, Hanan Ashrawi and Faisal Husseini [the Madrid negotiating team]," Abdul Hakim added. "To put a novice like Nabil Shaath, a man trained in business administration, against Amnon Shahak, an experienced general and deputy chief of staff of the IDF, to negotiate security was a disaster. No wonder the full details of the Cairo Agreement came out in the Arabic press only in bits and pieces."[18]

As months passed, realization of the grave flaws in the Oslo process seemingly led Arafat to alter his approach in subsequent talks involving IDF redeployment and elections to the Legislative Council and the presidency of the PA. It was only on September 22, after thousands of hours of tortuous talks between the Arafat- and Peres-led teams, that the final draft was initialed in the Egyptian resort of Taba. The formal signing took place at the White House six days later, hosted by President Clinton.

The Taba Agreement, popularly called Oslo II, with 31 Articles, 7 Annexes and 9 maps, was 314 pages long. It divided the West Bank into A, B and C Areas; and provided for elections and responsibilities for the Legislative Council and the PA presidency; a phased release of Palestinian prisoners; and a timetable for implementation.

Palestinian jurisdiction would begin after the elections. In Area A, the PA was to exercise full control over civil affairs and security; in Area B, the PA was to exercise control over civil affairs and public order, with Israel taking charge of overall security; and in Area C, Israel was to exercise full control—including security, territorial jurisdiction and Jewish settlers.

Area A consisted of seven Palestinian cities—Jenin, Nablus, Tulkarm, Qalqilya, Ramallah, Bethlehem and Hebron—and covered two percent of the West Bank. Even there, PA control over civil affairs and security was not unqualified. It was required to guarantee freedom of movement to Israeli civilians and settlers through these urban centers, and provide joint Palestinian-Israeli escorts for their vehicles. Area B included 465 villages, 24 percent of the territory and 63 percent of the population. Here the IDF had the power to intervene at its own discretion to maintain overall security. The rest of the West Bank, taking up 73 percent of the land, was labeled Area C. Finally, Oslo II spelled out the powers of the PA presidency and Legislative Council, both subject to review and final approval by Israel.

Full IDF evacuation of the Area A cities, except Hebron, was scheduled for the end of 1995, followed partial withdrawal from Hebron by March 28, 1996. And in line with the Declaration of Principles, talks on final settlement would start no later than May 4, 1996, and the five-year interim agreement was scheduled to expire on May 3, 1999.

The IDF's evacuation of the West Bank cities, starting with Jenin on November 13, reached a climax with its withdrawal from Bethlehem on December 21, leading to a four-day open-air party there, combining the celebration of Palestinian nationalism with Christmas.

Thus, the run-up to the Palestinian elections started in a mood of euphoria generated by the IDF withdrawal from six of the seven West Bank cities. The 88 members of the Palestinian Council (with seven from Greater East Jerusalem) were to be elected from sixteen multi-seat constituencies by 1.45 million voters. Six seats were reserved for Christians and one for Samaritans.

Arafat had allowed Fatah activists to choose candidates for the Council primaries, but canceled the results because the "insiders" known for participation in the intifada emerged strong at the expense of the Tunis-based "outsiders." He issued his own list which included such Fatah outsiders as Ahmad Qrei,

Nabil Shaath, Abdul Hakkam Balawi and Intissar Wazir. Oslo II required that four-fifths of the cabinet be chosen from the Legislative Council, so Arafat wanted his former cabinet colleagues to get elected.[19] And his chosen insider candidates emphasized wealthy members of traditionally powerful families over leaders of the refugee camps. Therefore, many of the rejected Fatah activists decided to run as independents.

Both the Islamist and secular opposition boycotted the election. Yet 644 men and 28 women entered the Council race. Arafat's rival for the presidency was Samiha Khalil, a 73-year-old leader of the Fatah-led Palestine Women's Movement, from Ramallah. A veteran of social reform, she voiced vague opposition to the Oslo Accords, but her statements were buried inside Palestinian publications while Arafat regularly dominated the front page.[20] The PA-run television continued to report slavishly the minutiae of Arafat's daily activities. Its task was made easier by the location of its studios next door to Arafat's office on Al Rashid Street along the Gaza beach front. The PA-run television openly favored the Fatah candidates. It was left to the less effective PA radio to give access to non-Fatah candidates.

Fatah hopefuls put a rosy gloss on the Oslo process, arguing that it was leading to an independent Palestinian state. Their opposition rivals highlighted the many flaws of the agreements with Israel. Such independent stalwarts as Haidar Abdul Shafi also demanded that the Palestinian Authority executive be made accountable to the Palestinian Council, which should also have a say in reaching the final settlement with Israel.

Many of the complaints by non-Fatah contestants about intimidation, including beatings, by Preventive Security Service agents went unchecked or overlooked by the Israeli authorities, or by the teams of international observers monitoring the poll. This was a measure of the goodwill that the Palestinian Authority enjoyed with the international community.

An outstanding instance of that goodwill came on January 9. The 30 donor countries, meeting in Paris, announced a further aid package of $865 million for 1996-7. When added to $460 million pledged earlier but not yet disbursed, the total came to $1.32 billion, or 46 percent of the Palestinian per capita GNP. The Paris meeting was timed to boost the electoral chances of Arafat and his party. And, as expected, the PA-run radio and television milked the story.

Oslo II allowed the Palestinians living in Greater East Jerusalem to participate in the Council elections but with strict limitations. Half the Jerusalem electoral district lay outside Jerusalem, in the West Bank proper. The Jerusalem-based Palestinians were considered "absentee electors" entitled to vote by mail from a post office. Since the local post offices were unable to handle all the voters, a vast majority of the 55,000 registered Palestinians had to use post offices outside the city as polling stations. The Israeli government outlawed public meetings for electioneering, or public display of any electoral material, and swiftly arrested those who broke the bans. To further discourage the Palestinians from voting, the Jerusalem municipality under the mayorship of Likud's Ehud Olmert plastered the walls of Greater East Jerusalem with posters warning that Palestinians voting for a "foreign government" would lose their residency status in Jerusalem, and with it, their health care and social welfare benefits. Only two days before the election, the foreign ministry finally stated that voting would not affect the right of the Palestinians to live, work and have health insurance in Jerusalem. The end-purpose of this Israeli strategy was to depress the Palestinian voter turn-out, and prove that Greater East Jerusalem Palestinians did not want to share the Palestinian Authority rule along with West Bankers and Gazans.

To intimidate the Palestinians on election day, the Israeli government deployed an extra 4,000 soldiers, chiefly around the post offices in East Jerusalem where only 5,000 Palestinians were allowed to vote, and officials videotaped Palestinians casting their ballots.

Little wonder that the voter turn-out in the Jerusalem district was only 40 percent versus 68 percent in the West Bank and 86 percent in Gaza. The overall 68 percent was quite impressive for a people largely untutored in balloting for political and demographic reasons. Indeed, everyone voting in the Gaza Strip was doing so for the first time.

Arafat won by 87 percent to 12 percent for Khalil. In the Council, Fatah and its allies secured 57 seats, and the opposition 31 (21 of them independents, including 4 pro-Islamists, and 10 Fatah dissidents). Among the independents were Haidar Abdul Shafi, who obtained the highest votes by any candidate, and Hanan Ashrawi, one of the six Christian members.

The overall assessment of the poll by international monitors was summed up by James Zogby, an Arab-American member of the U.S. team. "Having observed elections in the US over the last 30 years, I can honestly say that I saw nothing in Gaza that I had not seen in Philadelphia, Chicago, New York or Detroit," he said. "This is not to excuse such behavior, but rather to put the irregularities in context. Overall, the Palestinian elections were free and fair."[21]

Undoubtedly, the January 20, 1996 poll was a landmark in Palestinian history. It conferred legitimacy on the Palestinian Authority and Arafat, and Peres described it as "a positive endorsement of the peace process," while Arafat perceived it as "a foundation for a Palestinian state." In the words of Ashrawi: "It was a commitment by the Palestinian people to the democratic process, a vote for the democratic state and the rule of law." A grander and highly optimistic view was taken by a senior Fatah leader. "This is the end of Greater Israel or Greater Jordan," he said. "This is the most important result of the election. It is not possible now for Israel to absorb or expel the Palestinians, or return them to Jordan."[22]

On February 12, Arafat took the oath of office as President of the Palestinian National Authority, *Rais al Sultah al Wataniyeh al Falastiniya* (as the Authority is inaccurately called by Palestinians at official and popular levels) on the Quran before Salim al Zaadoun, the acting chairman of the Palestine National Council, and Qusai al Abadleh, the chief justice of the Palestinian Authority. Among those present at the Mansion House ceremony were the religious and civic leaders of the West Bank and Gaza, and the newly elected members of the Legislative Council.[23]

Arafat intended to have some influence in the Israeli election scheduled for May 29, hoping to help encourage a Peres-Labor victory. But this time around there was another Palestinian faction that also wanted to have an impact on the Israeli poll:

the Qassam Brigade of Hamas. Deeply opposed to the Oslo Accord, which it regarded as unjust, it wanted to hurt Peres's chances by showing that Israelis were still vulnerable to random acts of violence. It carried out three suicide-bomb attacks in Jerusalem and Ashqelon in a week, two on February 25, and the third on March 3. The next one on March 4, the day of the Purim festival, in Tel Aviv was claimed by both Qassam Brigade and the Islamic Jihad. Following this carnage, which resulted in 59 instant deaths, Israel imposed the most stringent siege of the West Bank and Gaza since the Gulf War in early 1991. This meant that West Bankers could not travel even within the territory.

As a result, 51 Palestinian Legislative Council members, trying to reach Gaza for the opening of the Council, were held overnight at IDF checkpoints on March 6–7, and then taken to the Strip under IDF escort. This was hardly a propitious inauguration of the world's youngest parliament.

Its opening session was held at the spacious auditorium of the Shawwa Cultural Center, a bland, modern building, in downtown Gaza City. Here the members had to make do with chairs without desks, and improvise. Once they had been sworn in, they elected the Speaker. The Fatah candidate, Ahmad Qrei (known as Abu Allaa) defeated his independent rival, Haidar Abdul Shafi, by 57 votes to 31. Since Oslo II specifies that in the case of death, incapacitation or resignation of the PA president, the council speaker becomes the acting PA president, Qrei now assumed the second highest office in the Palestinian Territories. In contrast to the often disheveled appearance of Arafat, the bald, clean-shaven Qrei, dressed in a well-cut dark business suit with a matching tie, looked decidedly professional. Born in 1941 into a well-to-do household in Abu Dis near Jerusalem, Ahmad Qrei and his family fled as a result of the 1967 Arab-Israeli War. An economics graduate, he became a banker in Beirut. When the PLO moved its headquarters to Beirut he grew close to Arafat. On Qrei's advice, Arafat reorganized Fatah's economic wing (designed to provide jobs for martyrs' families) as the Samed Foundation, and put Qrei in charge. Under his directorship, Samed expanded its manufacturing in Lebanon. Qrei invested Samed funds into international stock markets as well as industry and agriculture elsewhere in the Middle East and North Africa. When the PLO was expelled from Beirut to Tunis in 1982 he moved there, and was appointed economic adviser to Arafat. He was elected to the central committee of Fatah in 1989, and was a member of the Palestine National Council. When the economic condition of the Occupied Territories deteriorated sharply due to the Kuwait crisis and the Gulf War, he produced a plan to revive the Territories' economy. Not surprisingly, following the 1993 Oslo Accord, he was appointed Secretary-General of the Palestinian Economic Council for Development and Reconstruction by the World Bank.

In his inaugural speech to the Legislative Council, Arafat combined his condemnation of the terrorist actions perpetrated by "the enemies of peace" with his criticism of Israel for sealing the Palestinian Territories which, he said, "was decimating our economy and undermining our achievements."

The closure was becoming a depressing way of life, at least for Gazans. In the 669 days that had passed since the Cairo Agreement in early May 1994, the Gaza Strip had been shut off from Israel for 295 days—almost half.

The daily loss to the economy of the Strip amounted to $4 to $5 million. This time Israel had compounded the ban on goods and workers out of Gaza with an additional ban on the imports of materials from Israel into Gaza, thus creating severe shortages of basic necessities, such as food and medicine, as well as much needed building materials.

By so doing, Peres meant to impress upon the Israeli electorate that he could be extraordinarily tough with the Palestinians when the situation so demanded. Yet he lost.

Netanyahu as Premier

The greatest loser in the region was Arafat, who had prepared no contingency plan to deal with Peres's defeat. As in past crises, he conferred with the leaders of Egypt and Jordan. Alarmed by Netanyahu's repeated assertions that Israel would not vacate the Golan Heights, President Assad too sought regional support. At his behest, the Arab League convened a summit in Cairo, the first such gathering in nearly six years.

The Cairo summit's communiqué on June 23, 1996 confirmed the Arabs' commitment to the Madrid-initiated peace process, and reiterated the Arab positions: total Israeli withdrawal from the occupied Arab lands for total peace, based on UN Security Council Resolutions 242 and 338; an end to Jewish settlements on Arab soil; and a sovereign state for the Palestinians with its capital in Jerusalem. "If Israel abandons basic principles like return of occupied land for peace, or reneges on existing agreements," continued the communiqué, "the resultant setback to the negotiations would oblige all Arab states to reconsider the steps they have taken toward Israel in the context of the [regional] peace process."

In response, Netanyahu said, "Preconditions that hinder security for Israel are incompatible with peace negotiations."[24] Describing the Arab call for Israel's re-commitment to the concept of swapping occupied land for peace as "an unacceptable precondition," he asserted that this principle was nothing more than "a general guideline."

This was not so. In his seminal statement to the US Congress on March 6, 1991, a week after the end of the Gulf War, President George Bush stressed the need for "a comprehensive peace [which] must be grounded in the United Nations Security Council Resolutions 242 and 338 and the principle of territory for peace." [25] This was the seed which seven months later yielded the Middle East peace conference in Madrid.

While opposing conditions by the Arabs, Netanyahu reaffirmed his own: No to the withdrawal from the Golan Heights; No to a Palestinian state; No to the Palestinian capital in East Jerusalem; No to the return of Palestinian refugees (as that would constitute a threat to the "demographic security" of Israel); and No to freezing the Jewish settlements.

On the Palestinian front, he complemented his uncompromising stands on the subjects to be settled during the final round of negotiations—the status of Jerusalem and the Jewish settlements, and the return of Palestinian refugees—with hardline statements on current issues: the evacuation of Hebron and the easing of the closures of the West Bank and Gaza. "I'll let Palestinian workers back into Israel only if the Palestinian Authority sustains its crackdown on Hamas, the Islamic Jihad and other militant organizations operating from its territory," he stated. Apparently, the continued incarceration of nearly 1,200 Islamists in PA jails, most of them without charge or trial, was insufficient to convince him of the PA's tough stance on the issue.

On evacuating four-fifths of Hebron, agreed by Premier Peres, Netanyahu said: "I'll fulfill the agreement to withdraw the IDF from Hebron only if I am assured of the security of the Jewish settlers in the city." But certainly his predecessor, working with top military and intelligence officers, had made adequate provisions for the settlers' security, and fixed March 28 as the deadline for evacuation, which he later unilaterally suspended in the run-up to the Israeli elections. Arafat protested: "We cannot agree to retreat from what has been already attained and agreed upon, as this would mean a return to the unknown whose results cannot be foreseen by anybody."[26]

While Netanyahu could afford to turn a deaf ear to Arafat's protestations, he could not ignore Egypt. He visited Cairo on July 18, and reportedly told President Mubarak that he accepted "the Madrid formula." In practice, though, his government reversed its predecessor's official policy of a freeze on settlement construction. By mid-August Arafat, in despair, addressed a letter to Israeli President Weizman, complaining that his standing among Palestinians was being undermined by Netanyahu's policies, and warned that he could lose control if matters continued along present lines. Responding positively, Weizman proposed a meeting.[27]

Desperate to meet Netanyahu, if only to reassure his followers that the Oslo process was alive, on August 24 Arafat closed down three East Jerusalem-based institutions of the PA—the Statistical Office, the Geographical Center and the Youth and Sport Department—as demanded by the Israeli leader. What he got in return was the razing of a Palestinian center for the aged and disabled in the Old City.

"Israel has declared war on us," said Arafat in his address to the Legislative Council. He called for a general strike on August 29, Thursday, followed by mass protest prayers at the Al Aqsa Mosque on Friday and at the Church of Holy Sepulcher on Sunday. When IDF troops stopped thousands of Muslim Palestinians from reaching the Al Aqsa, Arafat said: "We are the ones who waged the longest uprising in the twentieth century, and murder, imprisonment and expulsion did not terrorize us. I don't have a magic wand, but I have the children of the intifada."[28]

But it was only after the Egyptian ambassador to Israel waded into the controversy publicly in early September, that Netanyahu finally instructed his aides to sign a document with Arafat's envoys to formalize the resumption of peace negotiations. The first Netanyahu-Arafat meeting on September 4 created a glimmer of hope.

Any chance of a breakthrough for peace, however, vanished on September 23 when Netanyahu's decision to allow the re-opening of the ancient Hasmonean Tunnel in the Old City's Muslim Quarter led to unprecedented violence, involving the PA's armed policemen and the IDF.[29] At the subsequent summit in Washington with Clinton, Netanyahu agreed to mediation between Israel and the Palestinians by Dennis Ross, a senior US envoy.

In the short run, Netanyahu's intransigence, instead of weakening Arafat and lowering his expectations, ended up strengthening him both at home and abroad. By issuing a call to protest Israel's actions following the re-opening of the ancient tunnel, Arafat created a united front, which encompassed both the governing Fatah and the Islamist opposition. He thus reclaimed the ground he had lost due to the growing impoverishment of the Palestinians (whose living standards had fallen by 20 percent over the past year) and the draconian steps he had taken against Islamists. The fact that Hamas leaders decided during and after the September 1996 events to suspend bomb attacks against Israeli targets implied that they did not wish to damage the unity that had arisen in the Palestinian ranks.

On the specific issue of the Hasmonean Tunnel, the Arafat camp was soon able to claim a *quid pro quo* when it announced on October 9 that it had built, with the semi-clandestine assistance of Israeli Arabs, a subterranean mosque for 7,000 worshippers under the platform of the Noble Sanctuary in an area known as Solomon's Stables, once used by the Crusaders for their horses, which provided the underground support for the south end of the Noble Sanctuary/Temple Mount. [30]

By so doing, the Palestinians claimed, they had pre-empted any future attempts by militant ultranationalist Jews to penetrate the Noble Sanctuary subterraneanly. Abroad, besides the favorable UN Security Council resolution on the Tunnel, Arafat scored a success at the European Union. Following his meeting with EU foreign ministers on October 1, the EU urged Israel to shut the Tunnel and implement its commitments under the Oslo Accords. Recognizing that "the recent incidents were precipitated by frustration and exasperation at the absence of any real progress in the peace process," the EU statement reaffirmed that "Israel has no right to take actions which prejudge the outcome of the future negotiations on the final status of Jerusalem" and that the Palestinians of East Jerusalem should enjoy the human rights afforded them as "inhabitants of Occupied Territories under the Fourth Geneva Convention."

Three weeks later came a visit to the region by French President Jacques Chirac. In line with the French (and EU) policy, which does not recognize Israel's sovereignty over East Jerusalem, Chirac refused a tour of the Old City in the company of Jerusalem's mayor, Ehud Olmert. Addressing the Palestinian Legislative Council, Chirac said, "A Palestinian state is not in any way a danger to the security of anyone. On the contrary, a Palestinian state and a comprehensive and just peace guarantee security for all."[31] Later, prodded by his argument that since the EU provided 85 percent of the foreign aid to the PA it was entitled to a seat at the negotiating table, the EU appointed its own representative to the peace talks—the Spanish ambassador to Israel, Miguel Angel Moratinos—with a brief to maintain contacts with the negotiating parties.

When Netanyahu pressed ahead with his plans to further consolidate Israel's grip over Greater East Jerusalem, and expand the existing Jewish settlements and set up new ones, the Palestinians in particular and the Arab League in general reacted to the Israeli moves predictably. On November 22 a joint meeting of the PA cabinet and the PLO executive committee combined its call to the Palestinians to reclaim their confiscated land with a pledge to support any Palestinian resistance politically and financially. "Israel insists on ripping apart the West Bank in order to prevent the creation of a Palestinian state, but we are determined to defend our lands by all possible means against racist settlement plans," stated the communiqué of the meeting of Arab League foreign ministers in Cairo on December 1, 1996. It called on Israel to stop building Jewish settlements on the West Bank and the Gaza Strip, and cease expanding the Golan settlements.

But Netanyahu was adamant. He topped his defiant statement on November 27 with a letter to President Mubarak on December 1 in which he said: "I made clear [during my recent meeting with you] that our policy, our right to settle and build upon existing settlements, accords with peace." Following the Israeli cabinet's December 13 decision to reinstate subsidies and tax incentives to all the Jewish settlements in the Palestinian Territories, Arafat, in an interview with *Yediot Aharonot*, warned that "Netanyahu knows that this [decision by his government] is a time bomb."[32] What he meant was that by injecting a growing number of ultranationalist Jewish settlers into the Palestinian community of the West Bank, Netanyahu was pushing two hostile groups into close proximity in a small area, thus planting the seed of a bloody conflict in the future. His only solace this time came from Washington where Clinton described the Israeli settlements as "obstacles to peace."

Due to Mubarak's intervention there was some progress regarding implementation of Oslo II. Netanyahu agreed to implement the stipulated IDF withdrawals by March 1999, eighteen months later than the original date. Refusing to be a party to the rewriting of the previously agreed provisions, Arafat rejected Dennis Ross's compromise of mid-1998.

The only major player who had not intervened in the Israeli-Palestinian talks so far was King Hussein. Aware that more than half of his subjects were of Palestinian origin, and that the only way to consolidate Jordan's peace treaty with Israel was to ensure that the Israeli-Palestinian track of the peace process did not collapse, he acted. He flew to Gaza City where he reportedly told Arafat, "If you are too firm, Netanyahu will win, and there won't be a Hebron withdrawal. Even if you don't trust him, it's better to commit Netanyahu to a particular date for further redeployment. And if he does not fulfill his commitment, you'll be able to raise an international hue and cry."[33] He thus persuaded Arafat to accept the Israeli deadline of mid-1998, and then got Netanyahu's agreement.

The Hebron Protocol signed on January 14 partitioned the city into H1 (Palestinian) and H2 (Israeli) zones. In a letter attached to the main document, US Secretary of State Christopher assured Arafat that the three further Israeli redeployments in the West Bank would be completed by no later that August 31, 1998. Israel agreed to negotiate "immediately" on such outstanding interim issues as the safe passages between the West Bank and Gaza, the building of (sea and air) ports in the Gaza Strip, and further prisoner releases. In return the PA pledged to fight terror and prevent violence, confiscate illegal arms, and complete the process of revising the Palestine National Charter . As a result there was much support for the Hebron Protocol in the PA cabinet and the Legislative Council. But unlike on the Israeli side, the debate was inhibited, if only for a practical reason.

As Rafiq Natsche, a Council member from Hebron and a Fatah leader, revealed, only a few copies of the Protocol were available in the chamber, and none in Arabic.

As a result the major concessions that Arafat had made to secure the Hebron Protocol, and which were to be published in *Further Redeployment: The Next Stage of the Israeli-Palestinian Redeployment, Legal Aspects*, released by Israel's foreign ministry, went largely unnoticed. In his defense, Arafat could argue that, assisted by Mubarak, he had succeeded in transforming the US from a co-sponsor of the Oslo process to the guarantor of the implementation of Oslo II. But this was a misreading on his part. When it came to a crunch Washington failed to deliver.

In any event, Arafat did not have to wait long after the Israeli redeployment in Hebron to realize that Netanyahu was an unreliable partner for peace. Israel's approval of a Jewish settlement of Har Homa at Jabal Abu Ghneim on the eve of his departure for a week-long visit to the United States on March 2 proved the point dramatically.

Alluding to Har Homa, Saeb Erekat said, "We are not talking about another settlement here or there. We are actually witnessing the tearing up of the West Bank into shreds; and that amounts to destroying our future on this land as a distinctive national entity."[34] Arafat agreed: "This is a big breaching to what had been agreed, and it is against the United Nations resolutions, and also against the American letter of guarantees [which accompanied the Hebron Protocol], and against all the agreements that had been signed." He convened a meeting of the PA cabinet and the Fatah executive committee to discuss the matter. And the Legislative Council called a general strike on March 1.

For once the Palestinians found the US on their side. On March 3 after a White House meeting with Arafat, Clinton said: "The important thing is for these people on both sides to be building confidence and working together, and so I would have preferred the decision [to construct Har Homa] not to have been made because I don't think it builds confidence. I think it builds mistrust and I wish it had not been made." In contrast to Netanyahu's claims to all of Jerusalem, Arafat limited himself to a part of the city. "Part of Jerusalem was Arab, is Arab and will remain Arab, and eventually will become capital of Palestine," he said.[35]

During his first extended state visit to the United States, Arafat covered a lot of ground. After two days of talks with officials and politicians in Washington, he went to New York. There, besides breakfasting with the presidents of major Jewish organizations, he had a meeting with the editors and journalists of *The New York Times*. He also briefed the UN Security Council, which was then debating the Jabal Abu Ghneim/Har Homa project. The rest of his itinerary took Arafat to Plains, Georgia—where he met former President Jimmy Carter, who reminded the press that his administration (1973–77) had declared the Jewish settlements illegal— and Houston, Texas, to meet George Bush and James Baker, the architects of the Madrid peace conference.

When Arafat returned to Gaza on March 8, he had another shock awaiting him. The next day Israel presented its first redeployment plan. It covered only nine percent of the West Bank, containing merely 50 villages and 20,000 people, to be turned into A category (exclusive Palestinian control), with seven percent coming from the existing B category, where the PA exercised joint control with Israel. This was less than a third of what the Palestinians had expected. They saw Netanyahu's meager offer as an ominous sign that Israel would deny them enough land for a viable state, their final aim. Therefore Arafat's decision on March 11 to suspend all contacts with Israel had the unanimous backing of the Palestinians.

On March 18 Netanyahu gave the final go-ahead for the Har Homa project. The next day there was a minor disturbance in Bethlehem, followed by a major one on March 21 in Hebron, when one Palestinian was killed and 100 injured by Israeli firings. On that day, when the Jews were celebrating the Purim festival, a Palestinian bomber in a Tel Aviv café killed four people, including himself. Arafat was quick to condemn the explosion, the first in more than a year. But that did not stop Netanyahu from claiming that he had "hard intelligence" that Arafat had given "the green light" to Hamas to commit "fresh acts of violence." Arafat denied the charge. US intelligence sources supported his denial, and so did US Secretary of State Albright.[36] Israeli officials then began referring to Arafat giving the "green light" in a roundabout way, and finally alluded to the "body language" he had used.

Though the Palestinian protest continued, chiefly in Hebron, for another week, it was by and large restrained. The total human toll claimed by the Har Homa project, was nine Palestinians and three Israelis dead, and over 800 (mostly) Palestinians wounded.

While sticking to his boycott of the Israeli authorities, Arafat did not rule out co- operation on specific points. For instance, at the CIA's intercession, a meeting took place on April 8 between Israeli security chiefs and their Palestinian counterparts in Gaza City, in the presence of Arafat. The Israelis provided the names of two suspects involved in the Tel Aviv bomb who, they claimed, were living in the PA enclaves. The next day the PA's Preventive Security Service arrested them, including the head of the cell, Ahmad Ghneimat, 25. He led them to the grave of Sergeant Sharon Edri, who had gone missing in central Israel while on his way home from an army base in September. It emerged that this six-member Qassam Brigade cell was established in Surif in late 1995, and consisted of members of the Ghneimat clan. The light skinned Ghneimats looked more like Israelis than Palestinians, worked in Israel and were fluent in Hebrew. Since they owned a car with yellow Israeli license plates they could travel freely within Israel. Besides the Tel Aviv bomb and Edri's murder, their cell was held responsible for killing five Israelis in the Gefen Tirosh area and two soldiers along the Hebron-Jerusalem road (these murders had earlier been attributed to the Halhoul cell of the Popular Front). It was also established that Musa Ghneimat had committed suicide in the Tel Aviv cafe, and that his bomb had exploded prematurely.[37] If nothing else, these revelations contradicted Netanyahu's assertion about Arafat's "green light" to the terrorists in the wake of the Har Homa.

Faced with the most serious crisis yet in the peace process, Arafat tried to rally support at home and abroad—at the Arab League, Islamic Conference Organization, Non-Aligned Movement, and UN. On March 31, 1997 the Arab League foreign ministers adopted a resolution that the League members, except Egypt and Jordan, should freeze their relations with Israel, end the multilateral talks with it, and restore the secondary and tertiary trade boycott of it. Over the next several months this led to the collapse of the multilateral track of the Madrid peace process.

At the behest of Arab League members and the PLO's observer at the UN, the world body debated the Har Homa/Jabal Abu Ghneim issue four times between early March and late April. On March 7, a UN Security Council resolution calling on Israel to stop the Jabal Abu Ghneim and other settlement activity, was backed by fourteen out of fifteen members, but vetoed by the United States. Washington specifically objected to the mention of the illegality of the settlement activity in the resolution. More importantly, it did not want the UN to intervene in a process that, in its view, was bilateral. President Clinton said later, however, that the US veto should not be interpreted as supporting the settlements.

On March 13 the UN General Assembly adopted a resolution demanding the stoppage of the Har Homa and other Jewish settlements, by 130 votes to 2 (Israel and United States). Since the Assembly resolution was non-binding, the Arabs then introduced a milder resolution at the Security Council. On March 21 it was backed by thirteen members, with one abstention, and but was once again vetoed by the US. "I am disappointed that my government saw fit to veto the Security Council resolution after standing up and saying it opposed settlement activity," said James Baker, former US Secretary of State.[38]

The Arabs persisted. They returned to the General Assembly, and using the special "Uniting for Peace" procedure (whereby members are asked individually if they want an emergency debate on a particular subject), succeeded in having an emergency session to debate the issue. It was only the tenth time in 52 years that the Assembly had made such a decision.[39] On April 25 the General Assembly adopted a comprehensive resolution by 134–3 (Israel, United States and Micronesia). It condemned the construction by Israel, "the Occupying Power," of a new settlement at Jabal Abu Ghneim, demanded "immediate and full cessation of the construction and of all other Israeli settlement activities," reiterated that the Fourth Geneva Convention applies to the Israeli-Occupied Territories, and called for "the cessation of all forms of assistance and support by member States for illegal Israeli activities in the Occupied Territories." Furthermore, the resolution required the Secretary-General to report to the Assembly on its implementation within two months, and kept open the option of another emergency session.

At home, taking his cue from the Yossi Beilin-Michael Eitan document of January 22—signifying a united platform of the leading Israeli political parties on the final settlement—Arafat decided to forge a united Palestinian front on the eve of the final status talks. He received a positive response from those Palestinian factions that had hitherto opposed the Oslo process. On February 27 ten Palestinian groups met in Nablus to participate in the Comprehensive Palestinian National Dialogue Conference, and formed a 33-member secretariat for the purpose. Among those attending were not only the secular Popular Front for the Liberation of Palestine and the Democratic Front for the Liberation of Palestine but also Hamas.

Netanyahu's decision regarding Har Homa hardened attitudes among all Palestinian factions. By early March the reality on the ground was such that Arafat could not dismiss as fanciful the Hamas view that Israel had no intention of vacating the Palestinian Territories, and had merely reorganized the arrangement of occupation by inserting the PA between the occupier and the occupied. So on March 10, when Hamas and Popular Front leaders in their meeting with him asked him to release the remaining of their colleagues, Arafat agreed. By so doing he opened himself to criticism by Netanyahu of failing to curb terrorism on an ongoing basis, thus violating the principle of reciprocity. But by his unilateral decisions on Har Homa and further IDF redeployment in the West Bank, Netanyahu had so undermined Arafat's credibility among his constituents that the latter was in danger of being publicly pilloried. There was no prospect of Arafat wringing political and economic benefits for Palestinians from the Oslo process, so he could no longer prove to his constituents that negotiating with the Israelis was preferable to confronting them.

Soon after another long, sterile meeting between Netanyahu and Clinton in Washington, a Palestinian delegation headed by Saeb Erekat and Mahmoud Abbas met Albright and other US officials on April 11–12. In their position paper, they demanded 1) cessation of all Israeli unilateral steps, including a halt to all settlement activity in the West Bank and Gaza, and particularly East Jerusalem; 2) implementation of the pending items in Oslo II, especially the completion of the Israeli troop redeployments in the West Bank; 3) start of the final status talks, provided they were held in parallel to 2); and 4) the final status negotiations to lead to the implementation of UN Security Council Resolutions 242 and 338, as stated in Article I of the Oslo Accord.[40]

None of this had any impact on Netanyahu, who persisted in his refusal to stop work on the Har Homa settlement, thus keeping the peace process frozen. He had taken to playing his very strong cards aggressively against Arafat, whose only effective card was withholding cooperation with Israel on security. Arafat had the option of inciting insurrection, but knew that he would be unable to control it. Such a step would therefore have ended up undermining his authority and strengthening the hands of the Islamist opposition.

13

Islamist Opposition
Hamas and Islamic Jihad

The sleek, well-varnished desks in the neat classroom reflected the sunshine that filtered through the semi-opaque glass of the eastern window. In one corner, a glass-fronted print of a life-size skeleton captured squares of sunlight through the windows, an unintended X-ray. The chalkboard announced the school's religious-political affiliation: "Bismillah al Rahman al Rahim" (In the name of God, the Merciful, the Compassionate). I was at the Islamic University in Gaza City, waiting to meet Dr. Mahmoud Zahar, a surgeon with a degree from the Ain Shams University of Cairo, who taught nursing students.

Dr. Zahar's office was in one of the several low, buff-colored stone buildings scattered around the campus. This building held a vast sign in bronze "The Islamic University Gaza 1978–1398"[1] written in Arabic and English over its entrance. Inside his neat office, Zahar rose to shake my hand. An energetic, eloquent man, his deliberate movements invested him with the gravitas appropriate for the official spokesman of Hamas.

"The Oslo Accord has made things worse for us," Zahar said. "With its control of 40 percent of the Gaza Strip, Israel continues its illegal occupation. And this has been accepted by the international community, which thinks that peace has been achieved. It thinks that the Israelis have given us our freedom, which is untrue."

What alternative did Hamas offer? "Our action plan stems from our analysis," he began. "This land is our land. Israel is here as a new kind of imperialist. We propose to neutralize this imperialism. That can be accomplished through an ongoing struggle by the believers both inside and outside Palestine, which is holy land to every Muslim in the world. Once an Islamic state comes into being [in the region] Israel will be demolished. God's Second Promise will be implemented." Zahar opened a drawer, took out his copy of the Quran, and opened the page. "Chapter 17, the Night Journey, verse 7," he replied. "If you do good... and to destroy utterly that which they ascended to."[2] Looking up from the Quran, Zahar added, "The Temple equals Jerusalem. The First Promise was kept by God: the Jewish state fell, due to corruption and deviation from the true path. So the First Temple was destroyed. If Jews again fall into corruption then God will fulfill His promise through the hands of His Servants, those who are true to Islam. That is, true Muslims from outside and inside Palestine will demolish the existence of the

Jewish state and establish a new situation. Signs of corruption and deviation from the true path among Jews are manifest: killing of innocent people, spreading robbery and expropriation, illegal confiscations, drugs, illegal affairs, bribes etc. The Jews are actively preventing the establishment of an Islamic regime in this region. The manifestations of injustice against Muslims by Israelis can be seen in every walk of life."

How long would it be before "The Promise of the Second" came to pass, I asked. "Nobody can tell exactly how long it will be for the prophecy to come true. Nobody before the intifada knew that it would happen. But it did. Likewise the Second Promise will be shared by the people under occupation, and they will establish a Palestinian state and expand the borders of Islam." I asked for a photocopy of the Quranic verse, and Zahar was quick to oblige. But before giving the copy to me, he picked up a pair of scissors and cut the Xerox sheet where it had picked up part of the facing page of the Quranic verse I had asked for. Instead of throwing the strip printed with the Quranic text in the dustbin, he caressed it, and gently deposited it in his desk drawer.

Zahar's optimism about the rise of an Islamic Palestine stemmed from the rapid advance that Hamas had made since its founding by Shaikh Ahmad Yasin and six other leaders of the Islamic Center soon after the outbreak of the intifada in December 1987.[3] The Center was the religious charity that the IDF allowed the Muslim Brotherhood to operate. The Brotherhood was led by Yasin. Born in 1936 in a land-owning household in Jora village, near the northern border of the Gaza Strip, Ahmad Yasin joined the clandestine Muslim Brotherhood in the mid-1950s, a few years after suffering crippling injuries in a sporting accident, which left him permanently wheelchair-bound. He worked as a schoolteacher in Gaza, then studied English in Cairo. With the repression of the Brotherhood in Egypt and Gaza in 1966, he was imprisoned, and released after the Israeli occupation of Gaza. He resumed teaching, as well as leading the reorganized Muslim Brotherhood.

A pan-Islamist party originating in Egypt in 1928 under the leadership of Hassan al Banna, the Muslim Brotherhood started as a moral-social reform movement, and then acquired political overtones in 1939. It set up branches in British mandate Palestine between 1942 and 1945. The doctrine of the Brotherhood was that Islam was a comprehensive, self-evolving system, applicable to all times and places. Under al Banna's leadership, besides being a political-religious body, the Brotherhood also included athletic, cultural, and economic activities. After 1948, the Brotherhood in Gaza became intertwined with its Egyptian counterpart, and in the West Bank with its Jordanian counterpart. Following Egypt's 1954 ban, the Brotherhood in Gaza went underground. This gave a chance to such newly established, secular political parties as Fatah and the Arab Nationalist Movement to grow. These groups drew most of their support from the Palestinian refugee camps where political consciousness and anti-Israeli sentiment were high. In contrast, native Gazans, many of them possessing arable land or real estate, were less militant in their feelings against Israel. Socially conservative, they were able to maintain their traditions, having been spared displacement from their native villages and towns. So they were more likely to back the Muslim Brotherhood than the secular ANM or Fatah.

The situation changed with the Israeli occupation in 1967. The upsurge in guerrilla activities by the secular Palestinian groups brought severe repression by General Ariel Sharon from 1970 onward. Shaikh Yasin urged his followers to purge society of social-moral ills and lead pious lives, arguing that the Islamization of society was a precondition for the establishment of an Islamic state in a liberated Palestine, thus skirting the contentious issue of resistance to Israeli occupation. After Sharon retired from the IDF in 1973, the Israeli government allowed Gazans some limited freedom of association. It issued a license to Yasin in the autumn of 1973 to establish the Islamic Center as a charity to run social, religious and welfare institutions such as schools, clinics and mosques, authorizing it to receive *zakat*, or a religious tax, amounting to 2.5 percent of income, from the believers. The Israeli move was in line with its general policy of favoring traditional, conservative Arab institutions and leaders under its rule, hoping they would undermine the secular nationalist forces.

With the PLO becoming the dominant force in the Occupied Territories from the mid-1970s, Israel encouraged the growth of the Islamic Center. Brigadier-General Yitzhak Segev, then military governor of the Gaza Strip, told David Shipler, the Jerusalem bureau chief of *The New York Times*, that he had financed the Islamic movement as a counter-weight to the PLO and the Communists: "The Israeli government gave me a budget and the military government gives to the mosques."[4] The mosques to which Brigadier-General Segev channeled the government cash were the ones run by the Islamic Center. In 1980, when the Muslim fundamentalists burned down the pro-PLO Red Crescent Society in Gaza City run by Dr. Haidar Abdul Shafi, the IDF looked the other way. The IDF-Shin Beth complicity with the Islamic Center was confirmed by Moshe Arens, defense minister from February 1983 to September 1984. "There is no doubt that during a certain period the Israeli governments perceived it [Islamic fundamentalism] as a healthy phenomenon that could counter the PLO," he said. "There even was a certain attempt by the army and Shabak [Shin Beth] to encourage the Islamic fundamentalists against the PLO."[5] Toward the end of Arens' tenure as Defense Minister, the Israeli government began altering its policy, partly because another, newer fundamentalist organization, the Islamic Jihad, was following a militantly anti-Israeli stance.

In April 1984 the Israeli authorities arrested Yasin, now confined to a wheelchair, for illegal possession of arms, and sentenced him to thirteen years in jail. But in May 1985 he was freed as part of a prisoner exchange. Upon his release, Yasin resumed his social work from the Islamic Center in the poor Jawrat al Shams district of Gaza City, focusing on turning Palestinians away from secularism. But when the intifada erupted in late 1987, Yasin and his colleagues in the Islamic Center leadership could no longer resist pressure from their grassroots to engage in a political struggle against the Israeli occupiers. The result was the founding of Hamas as the activist arm of the Islamic Center/ Muslim Brotherhood.

In August 1988 the Hamas leadership issued a Charter, setting out its ideology and basic policies. (At about the same time it set up its clandestine armed wing, the Izz al Din al Qassam Brigade.) Describing Hamas as part of the Muslim Brotherhood, an international body, the Charter stated that "it is a distinctly Palestinian movement that gives allegiance to God, regards Islam as a way of life, and works to raise the banner of God over every inch of Palestine." The Charter reaffirmed Hamas's allegiance to the Muslim Brotherhood credo: "God is the goal; the Prophet is the model; the Quran is the constitution; the *jihad* is the path; and death in *jihad* is our most sublime aspiration." More specifically, it stated: "The Land of Palestine is an Islamic *waqf* (trust) for Muslim generations until the Day of Judgment. It is inadmissible to abandon whole or part of it, or to concede it wholly or partly... No organization, whether Palestinian or Arab, has the right to concede Palestine wholly or partly." Indeed, the Charter added: "Abandoning any part of Palestine is an abandonment of a part of religion. The patriotism of Hamas is part of its religion. Only a *jihad* can solve the Palestinian issue."

In the liberation of Palestine, it stated, each of the three factors—Palestinian, Arab and Islamic—had a role to play. It described the PLO "as a father, brother, relative or friend" of Hamas," but distanced Hamas from its secularism: "Secular thought is incompatible with religious thought, completely incompatible... [W]e cannot abandon the present and future Islamism of Palestine in order to endorse secular thought." The Charter looked internationally too. "The Arab states surrounding Israel should open their borders to the *mujahedin* (those conducting the *jihad*) of the Arab and Muslim peoples so that they play their role and add their effort to the effort of their brothers, the Muslim Brotherhood in Palestine," read the Charter. "As for other Arab and Islamic nations, they should facilitate the *mujahedin* movement."[6]

These abstract statements had practical implications. For example, the Muslim Brotherhood in Jordan came to play a pivotal role in the life of Hamas. The Jordanian Brotherhood, bolstered by Egyptian exiles, supported King Hussein. In return, Hussein's ban on political parties in 1957 exempted the Brotherhood on the grounds that it had been registered as a religious charity. Its freedom of action facilitated support of the Muslim Brotherhood/Islamic Center in the West Bank and Gaza. Since then the Jordanian and Palestinian sections of the Muslim Brotherhood have worked together closely even when their assessments of the Palestinian situation have been far from identical.

In short, the Hamas Charter called for the reversal of Israel's occupation of the West Bank, Gaza and Arab Jerusalem, and the founding of an Islamic state there, and finally, the establishing of an Islamic state in all of Palestine. Thus there was a parallel here with the June 1974 resolution of the Palestine National Council which accepted the idea of a mini-state in the West Bank and Gaza, albeit as a transient entity, to be used to liberate all of mandate Palestine.

When it came to participating in the intifada, Hamas used the same methods for mobilizing its supporters—leaflets, communiqués, graffiti, demonstrations and strikes—as the PLO's United National Leadership of the Uprising (UNLU). But unlike their PLO counterparts, Hamas communiqués started with the Islamic invocation of "In the Name of God, the Merciful, the Compassionate," and contained Quranic verses, and Hamas graffiti, often written in green, were different from those of the PLO. They concentrated on three major themes:

Islam and Palestine, Jews and Israel, and responses to events and/or calls for action. The most popular slogans included "Our land is Islamic, this is the identity," "Revolution, revolution against the occupier; there is no solution except the Quran," "No to the Zionist entity," and "O Jews, leave our land."[7]

What further distinguished Hamas from the PLO was its use of the mosque, an ubiquitous institution. In the Gaza Strip there were some 600 mosques: one for every 1,600 Muslim Palestinians. The proportionate number of mosques for the West Bank was half as many. Many, especially in Gaza, became known as strongholds of Hamas or the Islamic Jihad, who turned these venues of prayer and religious learning into centers of political activity and assembling points for marches and demonstrations. Also Hamas often combined street protest with religious anniversaries or events in Islamic history. Furthermore, as a religio-spiritual movement, Hamas provided a balm for the confused, agitated minds of Palestinian youths. "Since June 1988, scores of people from all walks of life (religious and non-religious, poor, well-to-do, educated and non-educated, merchants, businessmen, and even some Christians) visited the home of Shaikh Ahmad Yasin, seeking his good offices, on a daily basis," noted Professor Ziad Abu Amr. "During the intifada, most of the Israeli-controlled government institutions, including courts, were practically shut down. The secrecy of the [banned] PLO factions and the fact that they do not enjoy spiritual authority increased the demand for the arbitration of the Hamas leaders. While resort to Hamas undermined the authority of the Israeli occupation, it also undermined the authority of the PLO and nationalist institutions."[8] Also the influence of young Hamas activists in the Islamic hierarchy began rising at the expense of the old, traditional leaders who in the West Bank depended on Jordan for their salaries. Alarmed at this, Israel formally banned Hamas in May 1989.

A year earlier, Israeli Defense Minister Yitzhak Rabin had met with Dr. Mahmoud Zahar, who proposed a three-stage solution to the Palestinian problem: 1) Israel to declare its intention to evacuate the Occupied Territories and restore Palestinian rights, with the withdrawal to be completed within a few months, and the Palestinian Territories to be transferred either to the United Nations, European Community or Arab League; 2) Palestinians to choose their representatives by means to be decided to the satisfaction of all parties, with no input by Israel; and 3) the final settlement to be negotiated by the Palestinian representatives and Israel.[9]

In early April 1989, Premier Yitzhak Shamir, with Rabin, offered elections, but without any mention of Israel's intention to withdraw from the Occupied Territories, followed by a handover to an international or regional body, as Zahar had proposed. Therefore Hamas's Communiqué No. 40, dated April 17, 1989, stated: "Our enemy will not concede anything to us except by force. We call on our sons to be fully on guard against anything our crafty enemy proposes. Let our slogan be 'No!' to the initiatives of Rabin and Shamir, and 'No!' to elections until the occupation is banished."[10]

Hamas combined its opposition to Israel with a critical stance towards the PLO. When the PNC proclaimed the founding of the State of Palestine in Algiers in November 1988, Yasin regarded the declaration premature. "We have not liberated any part of our country upon which we could found our state," he said in an interview with *Al Islam wa Falastin* magazine. "We must have land upon which we can stand in freedom and establish our state without prior conditions and without concessions."[11]

With the intifada intensifying, and Hamas acquiring a solid constituency of its own, the Israeli authorities decided to act against this fast-emerging Islamist force. In mid-May 1989 they arrested more than 250 Hamas activists, including Yasin. He was charged with conspiring to abduct and murder two IDF soldiers, and attack Israel's Palestinian collaborators. Replying to the charges in the Gaza military court, Yasin reasoned that the Palestinian people preferred non-violent means to achieve their liberation, and that they resorted to violence in self-defense and only after having concluded that their Israeli occupiers understood nothing but force and violence. As a people under occupation, Palestinians had no choice but to resort to any and every means, violent or peaceful, to resist and participate in the intifada with the aim of ending oppression and corruption, and instituting justice. He cited chapter 57, entitled Iron, verses 25–7 of the Quran:

> Indeed, We sent Our Messengers with clear signs,
> and We sent down with them the Book and the Balance
> so that men might uphold justice.
> And We sent down iron, wherein is great might,
> and many uses for men,
> and so that God might know who helps Him and His Messengers,
> in the Unseen.

Since Islam required the believer to struggle for justice, and fight those who perpetrated oppression with weapons, no matter what their faith or belief, Yasin continued, he and other members of Hamas had no choice but to resort to arms. Yasin was convicted and sentenced to fifteen years imprisonment, which only raised his prestige among his followers. The image of 53-year-old Yasin, a sad-eyed figure with a sparse salt-and-pepper beard and a round white-cloth cap became a frequent feature of Hamas leaflets and wall graffiti.

The presidency of Hamas passed to Dr. Abdul Aziz Rantisi, a pediatrician, whose bearded, bespectacled face would become a familiar image on the international newscasts in late 1992 and early 1993, when he became spokesman for the 400-plus Islamists deported by Israel to Marj al Zuhur in south Lebanon. Born in the village of Javne near Jaffa in 1947, his family took shelter in the Khan Yunis refugee camp during the 1948 War. He studied at Alexandria University in Egypt before and after the Strip fell into Israeli hands in 1967, and came under the influence of the (banned) Muslim Brotherhood in Egypt. After his return home, he practiced at the Khan Yunis Hospital, and was also involved with the Islamic Center's health care programs. He was close to Shaikh Yasin, and spent three years behind bars himself. After dismissal from his job at the Khan Yunis Hospital for encouraging fellow doctors not to pay taxes to the Israeli military government in 1984, he opened a private clinic, and became head of the medical department of Gaza's Islamic University, in 1986. During the intifada he served two periods of administrative detention before his expulsion to Lebanon.

Rantisi continued close co-operation with the Muslim Brotherhood in Jordan, which, like most West Bank and Gaza Palestinians, supported Iraqi President Saddam Hussein. This also lessened tensions between Hamas and the PLO, and Hamas expressed interest in joining the Palestine National Council. But Arafat regarded Hamas's demand of 40 percent of the PNC seats as excessive, so nothing came of it.

Hamas, however, was second only to Fatah in numbers of prisoners and detainees in Israeli jails. "With Hamas in the forefront, the Brotherhood could achieve, in less than four years, the kind of credibility, popularity and legitimacy the PLO had earned over two decades," wrote Professor Ziad Abu Amr.[12] Though Hamas constantly reiterated its religious ideology, what swelled its ranks had more to do with its radicalism than its Islamism. Shaikh Yasin was more of a political figure than a religious luminary.

Once the PNC in late September 1991 had sanctioned Palestinian participation in the international Madrid peace conference, the scene was set for a confrontation between Fatah and Hamas. It came in mid-1992 in the Gaza Strip with bloody clashes between the two parties. Mediation by local leaders and Arab Israeli MKs helped to cool tempers. But the basic contradictions remained, with Hamas now identified as more radical than any secular faction.

Hamas used the period around the fifth anniversary of the intifada, December 9, 1992, observed by a general strike by Palestinians, to escalate the uprising. Between December 7 and 13, the members of its Qassam Brigade attacked IDF patrols in Gaza and Hebron. As mentioned before, after killing four soldiers, they kidnapped the border police officer, Nissim Toledano, and offered to exchange him for their leader, Shaikh Yasin. When Premier Rabin refused, they killed Toledano. Most of the 1,200 Islamists Rabin arrested and the 413 he deported to southern Lebanon were professionals—doctors, engineers, teachers, journalists, lawyers and professors. The UN Security Council condemned the action and demanded the immediate return of the Palestinians to their homes, while reaffirming the applicability of the Fourth Geneva Convention to the Palestinian territories occupied by Israel since 1967. As it had done many times before, the Israeli government ignored the unanimous resolution. Later, however, Rabin and his colleagues came to regret the deportations which, unwittingly, did more to swell the ranks of the Islamist organization than any of their own recruiting drives.

Among the expellees was Shaikh Bassam Jarrar, from Al Bireh in the West Bank. In his mid-40s, he sported a dense black beard, which, oddly, enhanced his movie star looks. But Jarrar was more bookish than artistic. An impressive collection of leather-bound volumes in his drawing room testified to his scholarship. Son of a shopkeeper in Ramallah, he grew up as a brilliant student, with an avid interest in religion. He pursued his inclination at Damascus University, where he graduated in Islamic studies in 1973. Upon his return home, he taught religious studies, eventually at Ramallah Teachers' Training College. He was intensely political, and started out backing the PLO when the Israeli authorities considered it as their foremost enemy. But once the PLO was expelled from Beirut to Tunis in 1982, his loyalty began to wane, and he turned increasingly to the then-legal Islamic Center/Muslim Brotherhood.

His tentative backing solidified into a commitment once the intifada erupted in late 1987 and Islamic Center leaders founded Hamas.

For Jarrar, the intifada meant five periods of administrative detention. "The last time was in April 1994, and I was freed four months later," he told me. "My deportation to south Lebanon along with 400 others lasted a year. With administrative detention you know you'll be released after six months. But deportation is a leap in the dark. When you are deported you know that you'll be away from your country and your family for several years, or even forever. It is only because our deportation caught international attention, and the western media followed our fate, that the Israelis relented. They let us back home."

"We were in the Lebanese mountains in the middle of winter, and in difficult physical conditions, facing the prospect of never returning home. But the overall experience was enriching to us. We felt like we were in the middle of a war, war of the media. In it we achieved a lot. The media gave us a chance to express our thoughts to the whole world. We told the world what was going on in the Israeli Occupied Territories. That way we got in touch with the Lebanese people, with the Arab people and other peoples. More than 1,100 foreign delegations came to see us near Marj al Zuhur in one year of our detention—that is three every day. This gave a boost to the Islamic movement throughout the Arab world and the Muslim world. Overall, Israel's attempts to portray Palestinians as hardline fundamentalists failed miserably."

Indeed later, General Danny Rothschild, the military governor of the Occupied Territories, admitted publicly that the expulsion of the Muslim fundamentalists was meant to help the PLO, and that it was a total failure.

Instead, the Israeli action brought the PLO and Hamas together. Hamas leaders based in Jordan, Syria, and Iran, as well as the leading figures of the secular radical Palestinian groups based in Damascus, flew to Tunis for a meeting with Yasser Arafat. Together they formed committees to deal with the fate of the Islamist expellees, and intra-Palestinian relations inside and outside the Occupied Territories. The Hamas team then flew to Khartoum to discuss the possibility of Hamas joining the Palestine National Council. But the Hamas demand for two-fifths of the total seats was once again judged unreasonable.

Israel's lifting of the ban on the PLO in January 1993 made Hamas, still outlawed, a distinctly radical organization. Its appeal increased as the Gaza Strip slid deeper into violence in March. Opposed to post-Madrid talks between the Palestinian and Israeli delegations, it actively supported a general strike call on the eve of the ninth round of negotiations in late April. Israel intensified its repression of Hamas, and in early August Hamas' military wing killed three IDF soldiers in attacks near Jerusalem and Tulkarm.

After the Oslo Accord

Expectedly, Hamas rejected the Oslo Accord, which also resulted in the virtual break-up of the PLO, with six of its ten constituent organizations opposing the agreement. These secular factions, most of them based in Damascus, decided to ally with Hamas under the umbrella of the Palestinian Forces Alliance.

At the same time a determined effort was made to avert intra-Palestinian violence. The initiative came from Hamas and Fatah prisoners who issued a statement against the resort to violence between those with different views of the Oslo Accord. The initiative was backed by Dr. Rantisi, the Hamas leader, from his mountainside exile in south Lebanon.

After this agreement with the PLO, the IDF intensified efforts to kill Hamas and Islamic Jihad militants, and even Fatah Hawks. On November 24 the IDF's undercover Samson Unit killed Imad Aql, a 24-year-old from Jabaliya camp, in a Gaza City suburb. Regarded as the commander of the Qassam Brigade in the Gaza Strip, he had been accused of killing a dozen Israeli soldiers and four Palestinian collaborators. Premier Rabin publicly praised his assassination. But the Samson Unit did not stop at eradicating radical Islamists. It went on to settle scores with Fatah Hawks, even though, in accordance with the Oslo Accord, they had been turning over weapons to the IDF under an amnesty plan, a policy which had revived friction between them and the Qassam Brigade

But the massacre of Muslims at Hebron's Ibrahimi Mosque by the extremist settler Dr. Baruch Goldstein on February 25, 1994 reversed the divisive trend in the Fatah-Hamas relationship. The Hebron event made all Palestinian factions close ranks. Due to the constraints of Oslo, Fatah Hawks could not publicly threaten vengeance. But Hamas was under no such restraint. It promised to avenge the Hebron killings by carrying out five operations against Israeli targets.

Its first attack came on April 6. A Qassam Brigade member, with explosives strapped to his waist, blew himself up in a bus in Afula, leaving seven Israelis dead. The second suicide bombing occurred a week later at the Hadera bus station killing five. According to the Israeli intelligence, both these bombs had the imprint of Yahya Ayash. Born in 1966 in the village of Rafat near Ramallah, Yahya was a son of a well-to-do farmer. He had studied electrical engineering and chemistry at Birzeit University, a combination which turned him into an innovative bomb-maker, and earned him the nickname "The Engineer" for his skill in detonating unusual cocktails of chemicals. He became active in the intifada in 1990–91, and went underground in 1992. Pursued relentlessly by the IDF's West Bank undercover unit, code-named "Cherry," since 1993, he escaped death or arrest several times. After the Cairo Agreement of May 1994, he slipped into the Gaza Strip, thus putting himself, technically, out of the reach of Israel. But since his parents and his two brothers, as well as his wife and two sons, continued to live in Israeli-controlled Rafat, the security and intelligence agencies kept them and their farmhouse under constant watch. Once when an IDF unit searched the house in the middle of the night, but failed to find Ayash, it smashed all the furniture. The Israeli interception of the family members' telephone conversations and 24-hour surveillance continued, an exercise which in the coming months was to prove fruitful.

The Gaza Strip in which Ayash found a niche was a place where, chastened by the Hebron killings and the assassination of six of their comrades by the IDF's Samson Unit in March 1994,[13] the Fatah Hawks had signed an amity pact with the Qassam Brigade.

But more importantly, once the PLO established the Palestinian Authority in Gaza in July 1994, Hamas had to define a new relationship with the PA which, as a creation of Oslo, was committed to "a peaceful resolution of conflict between the two sides." From then on, Palestinian-Israeli relations were determined not merely by what the PA and Israel did, but also by what Hamas did.

Indeed, by kidnapping IDF soldier Nachshon Waxman, and exploding a suicide bomb on a bus in downtown Tel Aviv, in October 1994, Hamas acquired the initiative it did not possess before. The Tel Aviv bombing was the most violent attack in Israel in sixteen years. Whereas Jewish Israelis condemned the terroristic outrage unanimously and unequivocally, Palestinians were divided in their opinion. PA officials expressed sorrow and condemnation, but the prevalent view among young Palestinians was altogether different. "The Hamas gunmen are wildly popular, particularly among the young who see the underground guerrillas as role models," reported Said Ghazali of the Associated Press. "The Israeli occupation for 27 years has left deep scars, and many Palestinians still remember humiliations at the hands of the Jewish soldiers. The Izz al Din al Qassam Brigade's guerrillas are seen as heroes who stand up to the hated occupiers and right past wrongs." Faraj Dababesh, a 20-year-old student, told Ghazali: "The children here are taught the songs of the Qassam Brigade. Don't forget people here learn the tactics of Hamas in the mosques." And two-fifths of the mosques in the Gaza Strip were under Hamas influence.

With the internal security of Gaza now in the hands of the PA, Israel intensified its anti-Islamist efforts in the West Bank and Greater East Jerusalem. As described earlier, the tit-for-tat between the Qassam Brigade and the Israeli administration turned into a violent confrontation between Hamas and the PA in mid-November.[14] But as before, Hamas and the PA pulled back from the abyss of a civil war. In the complex relationship that had developed between the PA, Hamas, and Israel, the PA faced a grave dilemma. "We made peace with our enemy of 47 years, not to make enemies of our own brothers," said Nabil Shaath, Minister of Planning and International Co-operation in the PA cabinet, and a senior aide to Arafat. "Once we really resist them [the Islamic radicals] on the street, they're willing to kill us too... If we arrest them, we look like human rights violators, Uncle Toms and lackeys of the Israelis."[15]

While the PA and Fatah had to grapple with this intractable problem, Hamas consolidated its position as the leading constituent of the ten-member Palestinian Forces Alliance based on the rejection of the Oslo Accord. In late December 1994 its representatives attended the PFA meeting in Damascus. They concurred with the decision not to participate in the election for the Palestinian Legislative Council to be established under Oslo. But they found the decision for no talks with PA Chairman Arafat, puzzling. Indeed, the headquarters of the Popular Front for the Liberation of Palestine and the Democratic Front for the Liberation of Palestine had already dispatched many of their personnel to the Gaza Strip, who had contacted Arafat. But popular backing for these secular, rejectionist groups was minimal. Hamas was by far the leading opponent of Oslo.

Islamic Jihad impressed itself strongly on the popular psyche on January 22, 1995 when two of its young Gazan activists, Anwar Sakura and Salah Shaker, blew themselves up at a bus stop at Beit Lid near Natanya, killing 21 Israeli soldiers.[16] The bombers and their planners had chosen their target and timing carefully. On Sunday mornings, all over Israel, thousands of young IDF personnel use buses to return to their bases after spending the Sabbath at home.

"The Islamic Jihad only aims at Israeli military targets," stated Fathi Abdul Aziz Shikaki, the exiled Jihad leader based in Damascus. "We are freedom fighters resisting Israeli occupation." Responding to the carnage caused by the Beit Lid bombs, he said, "We want Israelis to share our pain."[17] In the view of Shikaki as well as other militant Palestinian leaders, terrorism was an effective tool of the oppressed because it leveled the oppressor's superiority. In the Shajaiye neighborhood mosque, Shaikh Abdullah Shami, an Islamic Jihad leader, who had known Anwar Sakura for several years, said: "The Israelis have caused immeasurable suffering to the Palestinians, and deserve to be attacked until all the [Palestinian] refugees have returned to their homes in Palestine." With his thick black beard, thin-framed glasses, and skullcap, the 40-year-old Shami might be mistaken for a Jewish zealot. In his interview with the *Jerusalem Post* after the Beit Lid bombings, he was surprisingly candid. When asked why Islamic Jihad attacks had become more violent while the suffering imposed on Palestinians had declined from what it had been during the intifada, Shami replied: "First we had knives, then we got guns, then bombs, now car bombs."[18]

The Lebanese Muslim militants had been the first in the region to resort to suicide bombing in the course of the 1975–90 civil war in Lebanon in which the United States, France, Britain and Italy had all intervened. On April 18, 1983 they used suicide truck-bombing against the US embassy in West Beirut, killing 63 people, including 17 Americans. On October 23 the truck-bombing of the US and French military headquarters in West Beirut left 300 dead. The person who killed him/herself in the process was regarded by radical Islamists as a martyr in the path of God, described in the Quran (Chapter 3 "The House of Imran" verse 164) thus:

Count not those who were slain in God's way as dead,
but rather living with their Lord, by Him provided,
rejoicing in the bounty that God has given them,
and joyful in those who remain behind and have not joined them,
because no fear shall be on them, neither shall they sorrow,
joyful in blessing and bounty from God,
and that God leaves not to waste the wage of the believers.

The method of being killed in "God's way" varied. Since suicide, committed by explosives strapped to the body of a person or carried in a vehicle, was a recent phenomenon it had caused debate in religious circles. "A Reading in the Islamic Law of Martyrdom" in a Cyprus-based Arabic weekly, *Al Islam wa Falastin*, in mid-1988, gave one exposition of the subject. "Perhaps it is a blessing of God bestowed upon one *mujahid* or two *mujahideen*, enabling him or them to charge against the enemy's position, or against a concentration of enemy military forces on a martyrdom mission, assaulting with explosives, smashing down everything around them, inflicting the heaviest losses, breaking down the enemy's morale and determination in the face of this Islamic spirit of martyrdom which cannot be resisted," wrote the anonymous author. "At the same time it increases fear of Muslims after a long period of weakness and humiliation, and it increases the volunteers for martyrdom who seek *jihad* in the way of God."[19]

Since the suicide bombers had come from the Gaza Strip, the fledgling PA in Gaza had to respond to this terroristic action. Its police picked up many Islamic Jihad activists in the Gaza Strip, including Ala Siftawi, the editor-proprietor of *Al Istiqlal* weekly, and banned the magazine. Siftawi spent six weeks in jail, and the magazine remained closed for nearly two months.

In Gaza City I picked up the March 17 *Al Istiqlal*, the first issue after it had been "unbanned." "'No' for killing words and breaking the pen," read the defiant headline of its front page editorial. I met Siftawi at his modest, ground floor office on a busy thoroughfare. Above his desk, a large black-and-white photograph of a dashing, young man stared at me. He was Shaheed (Martyr) Hani Abid, the Islamic Jihad activist killed by the Shin Beth four months before, who still was listed as the *rais al-tahrir* (managing editor) of *Al Istiqlal*. It was hard to believe that Siftawi, mild-mannered and bearded, had, along with five other Islamic Jihad activists, planned a successful jailbreak from the Gaza central jail six years before—which had turned him and the others into overnight heroes. He escaped to Damascus where he became a journalist, slipping back into the Gaza Strip soon after the PA was installed there. His Islamic orientation was a divergence from the politics of his father, a co-founder of Fatah and the PLO in the Gaza Strip, and a contemporary and friend of Arafat. Ala had come under the influence of Dr. Fathi Abdul Aziz Shikaki, a co-founder of the Islamic Jihad in the early 1980s.

As it was, Dr. Shikaki, a bear of a man, started out as a pan-Arab nationalist, with Nasser as his hero, but became disillusioned with him after the 1967 Arab defeat, and joined the Muslim Brotherhood. Born in 1942 into a poor family in Zarnuqa village near Ramle in Palestine, his parents fled to the Gaza Strip in 1948, and lived in Rafah refugee camp. He worked as a teacher, and in the mid-1970s went to Egypt to study medicine. He came under the influence of Shaikh Sayyid Qutb, a radical Egyptian Islamic thinker, and author of *Signposts Along the Road*, who argued that there was an irreconcilable contradiction between "the rule of God and the rule of man," and that the existence of one required the destruction of the other. He believed that only a "believing elite," a new generation imbued with Quranic teachings, was capable of leading "the society of belief" against "the society of unbelief."[20] As someone who strongly believed in action, Shikaki admired Ayatollah Ruhollah Khomeini, who led Iran's 1979 Islamic revolution against the Shah's secular, pro-western regime. Later that year, Shikaki published *Khomeini: The Islamic Solution and Alternative*, and was soon jailed. After spending two brief stints in jail, and securing a medical degree from Zigazig University, he returned home. His co-founding of the Islamic Jihad was truly secret. When Shikaki was arrested and sentenced to a year in jail in 1983, it was for incitement against the Israeli occupation and not also for belonging to an illegal organization.

The organization did not claim responsibility for its first guerrilla operation against Israel. But the 1986 grenade attack by three Jihad activists at the IDF graduation ceremony at the Western Wall was so sensational that the group could no longer remain anonymous. Shikaki was sentenced to nine years' imprisonment on charges of smuggling weapons into Gaza and belonging to the unlawful Islamic Jihad. While he was in jail, Jihad activists killed Captain Ron Tal, commander of the IDF military police, in August 1987. And in early October they engaged in a gunbattle with an IDF patrol in Gaza City's Shajaiye district, leaving one IDF officer and three Jihad militants dead. Later Islamic Jihad leaders would claim that their dare-devil actions in the summer and autumn of 1987 created the conditions for the eruption of the intifada. In any event, once the intifada was underway, and the jailed Jihad activists had taken to using prisons and detention centers as recruiting grounds, Israel deported Shikaki to Lebanon in August 1988. From there he moved to Damascus.

By then the Islamic Jihad, a small, cohesive group, had become known for its organizational skills, ideological clarity, tight discipline and strict secrecy. It was beholden to Iran, a source of its foreign funds.

In his book on Ayatollah Khomeini, Shikaki quoted approvingly the Ayatollah's call to all Muslims "to eliminate the core of corruption, Israel," and declared it to be their religious duty to do so. Tawfiq al Tayib, a Palestinain Islamic ideologue, argued in his pamphlet, *After the Two Catastrophes*, that the 1948 and 1967 Arab defeats by Israel were defeats respectively of liberal Arab thought and socialist-revolutionary Arab ideology. "The natural reaction to the [Zionist] challenge lies in the Islamic trend which constitutes the defense line," he wrote. "It has played a historic role in the restoration of the psychological balance of both the Islamic community and the educated Muslim."[21] Like al Tayib, Shikaki and other Jihad theoreticians perceived the implanting of the Zionist entity in the Arab Muslim world as a deliberate western attempt to split the Islamic *umma* (community) and westernize it with a view to subjugating it materially and spiritually, paralyzing its will. A story splashed on page seven of the *Al Istiqlal* I had with me fitted the above Islamist thesis: "Israeli travelers in Jordan: Dancing in Jordanian hotels."

Just across the road, up a few flights of stairs, in the company of Abdul Hakim al Samra, I was in the offices of *Al Watan*, the Hamas mouthpiece, established in December 1994. At sixteen pages an issue and a circulation of 10,000, it was more popular than *Al Istiqlal*. Behind the publisher's large desk hung a map of Palestine, identical to the standard-issue Israeli tourist ministry map, but with the Dome of the Rock and other Islamic shrines floating in the Mediterranean, and the Palestinian flag aloft in the left-hand corner. Imad Faluji himself turned out to have a more colorful background than Siftawi.

"After my secondary education I went to the Soviet Union, to Kharkov, Ukraine, to study civil engineering," the young publisher began. "It was cheaper to study there than anywhere else. I was there from 1981 to 1987. Spent a year learning Russian. Toward the end I began setting up Islamic groups among foreign Muslims and Soviet Muslims. I traveled through seven Soviet republics during holidays, trying to set up Islamic groups. The authorities did not like what I was doing.

So in 1987 they put me on a plane to Prague. It was later in that year that the intifada started here. I was close to Shaikh Yasin. After his arrest in 1989 I became more involved with Hamas. I was arrested in 1991 and sentenced to six years' imprisonment. In the course of the prisoner release program that followed the Oslo Accord, I was freed in June 1994." Did that moderate his opposition to the Oslo Accord? "No. The Hamas policy is clear. It wants Israeli withdrawal, not military redeployment, from the occupied West Bank, Gaza and East Jerusalem and from the Jewish settlements, as a prelude to the founding of a Palestinian state in the West Bank and Gaza, with East Jerusalem as its capital. That is the minimum position of Hamas. Actually, nothing more radical than the Fahd Plan adopted by the Arab League in September 1982."

And the Palestinian Authority? "The PA is Palestinian, and we cannot be against a Palestinian organization. I went to meet Arafat when he arrived in Gaza last July. I went as a Hamas leader. The permission to establish our weekly magazine, *Al Watan*, was given by Arafat himself, as a paper of the Palestinian opposition."

But when *Al Watan* took seriously its role as an opposition organ, Arafat hit back hard. In mid-May it printed a story stating that the PA had tortured and unduly detained Nidal Dababesh, a Hamas activist injured in a mysterious explosion in Gaza City, in order to prevent him from contradicting the PA version of the event. (It was widely believed that the Palestinian and Israeli intelligence services had colluded to cause the explosion in order to kill suspected bomb-makers.) As Interior Minister, Arafat ordered *Al Watan's* closure for three months. The PA attorney-general, Khalid Kidre, accused it of publishing "seditious material and libeling the PA and its security apparatus." Its managing editor, Sayyid Abu Musammeh, was arrested, tried and convicted by the State Security Court within 24 hours, the midnight trial barely lasting a few minutes. He was sentenced to three years' imprisonment. "Trials in this Court are grossly unfair, violating minimum requirements of international law," concluded Amnesty International in August 1995. "State Security Court trials have been held secretly in the middle of the night. Many started around midnight, some reportedly lasted only minutes. Those presiding are security officers who have never before served as judges."[22] Defendants were not permitted to select their own attorneys, and the court-appointed attorneys were invariably employees of the PA's security forces.

The charges of torture by the PA were borne out by the report published by BeTselem, an Israeli human rights group, in September 1995. It concluded that from July 1994 to August 1995 in the Gaza Strip six Palestinians in custody had died of torture, which included beatings, sleep deprivation, lack of medical attention, tying-up and hooding. "Veterans of Israeli jails make up the rank and file of the PSS [Preventive Security Service]," reported Shyam Bhatia in the (London) *Observer*. "Palestinians say it is no coincidence that the interrogation methods used by PSS agents mirror the tactics employed by Israel's secret police, the Shabak. Hooding, or covering the victim's head with a sack as he is beaten or questioned, is a trademark of the Shabak. In Arabic this form of torture is known as *shabah*, a word also used for ghosts or ghouls."[23]

This uncanny parallel between the behavior of the security forces of Israel and the PA was a symptom of their growing co-operation and co-ordination. "It is clear to us that the Palestinian Authority is a weak tool in the hands of Israel," said Faluji. "So the more Israel puts pressure on the Authority, and in turn on Hamas, the more pressure Hamas will put on Israel. Our rifles can never be trained on the Palestinian Authority. Israel will pay the price for anything the Authority does to us… Our *jihad* is against the Israeli occupation."[24]

In that *jihad*, suicide bombs had come to play a central part. It was not accidental that the *Al Watan* of March 9, 1995 carried a glowing report on the legendary Yahya "The Engineer" Ayash. Israel's most wanted terrorist had become the most elusive. Always one step ahead of the Israeli intelligence and security agencies, he was reported to have successfully passed himself off as an ultra-Orthodox Jew driving a car pasted with ultra-nationalist stickers. Before disguising himself as a woman, it was said, he had mastered a female gait.

The suicide bomb on July 24 on a bus in Ramat Gan, near Tel Aviv, which killed seven Israelis, was attributed to Ayash. The Shin Beth was unable to decide conclusively whether the next attack, by a female Hamas activist on a Jerusalem bus on August 21, was orchestrated by Ayash or one of his star pupils, Muhyi al Din Esharif, a 29-year-old resident of East Jerusalem who, like Ayash, was an electrical engineering graduate.

Since Arafat was anxious not to jeopardize a successful outcome to his talks with Israel on IDF redeployment and PA elections, he negotiated a deal with Hamas leaders, encouraging them to cease their violent campaign against Israel. They reached an unannounced understanding in September that Hamas would suspend armed acts against Israel while debating their stance on the elections. The signing of Oslo II with Israel in late September strengthened Arafat's hand. He could convincingly argue that Israel was serious about extending self-rule to the West Bank. On October 10 he released such prominent Hamas figures as Mahmoud Zahar and Ahmad Bahar, whom he had jailed in late June. To facilitate the reconciliation process, Israel permitted a Hamas team to leave for Khartoum for consultations with the exiled Hamas leaders who gathered there. Hamas branches had sprung up among Palestinians in Jordan, Syria and Lebanon. And because of its Islamist ideology it was allowed to open offices in Iran and Sudan, where Islamic fundamentalist regimes were in power. The meeting in Khartoum ended with a decision to explore the details of an agreement with the PA.

On October 29 Israeli intelligence sources released the news that three days earlier Islamic Jihad leader, Dr. Fathi Shikaki, was assassinated by five bullets in his back, outside a hotel on the Mediterranean island of Malta. The two hitmen had escaped on a motorcycle. Shikaki was returning to Damascus via Malta after a visit to Libya. The gleeful hints by Rabin and Peres, attending a regional economic conference in Amman, of the Mossad's involvement were schizophrenic. While keen to impress Israeli citizens that their campaign against terrorism was succeeding, they did not wish to confirm official involvement in a murder committed in a foreign country. (Rabin himself would fall victim to an assassin's bullets within a week of this event.) The Israeli government's action reminded Hamas of the relentless energy with which it pursued them. Hamas negotiators regarded this a bad omen, but continued their talks with Arafat.

In their consultations with the exiled leadership, the Hamas team seriously considered the idea of Hamas establishing an electoral wing to participate in the forthcoming PA election. As Israel began implementing its military withdrawal from West Bank cities from mid-November onward, the climate for a PA-Hamas accord improved. Yet at the meetings held between the two parties in Cairo, away from local pressures, a stalemate ensued. In return for acceptance of all the agreements the PLO had signed with Israel, and ceasing its armed attacks against Israel, its negotiators demanded that Hamas be treated on a par with the PLO, and retain the right to revive its military struggle should a radically altered situation in the future so demand.

Furthermore, they wanted an iron-clad guarantee that Israel would not pursue the Hamas fugitives it held responsible for past guerrilla operations. Arafat was not in a position to give such an understanding on his own nor did he expect to receive such a promise from Israel. As a result, any chance of Hamas participating in the PA elections evaporated. As for the Islamic Jihad, with its exclusive commitment to armed struggle against the Israeli occupiers, there was no question of participating in any poll in which there was even the faintest involvement of Israel.

Hamas's position on the PA elections, scheduled for January 20, 1996, remained as Zahar had described it to me in March 1995. "We say yes, when it comes to electing our representatives at the local and non-governmental levels among Palestinians, living inside and outside Palestine, without any preconditions. As for national elections, if the Israelis are aiming for autonomy for Palestinians under their aegis, then we will not participate. Because we reject the whole idea of autonomy contained in the Oslo Accord. We want national independence. Also because in any such elections 'outsider' Palestinians will not be able to participate. If the national level elections are for independence, and not autonomy, and are held by an international body like the United Nations, then we will participate."

Any lingering hope that Hamas would soften its stance disappeared on January 5, 1996. At about nine A.M. that day there was a call for Yahya Ayash on a mobile phone in Gaza. His host, a friend from university days, Osama Hamad, picked up the phone, and gave it to Ayash, because the call was from his father in Rafat. Hamad left the room. Five minutes later when he returned, he found Ayash lying in a pool of blood, his head blown off.

When Ayash had first approached Osama Hamad in June 1995 for refuge in his house in Beit Lahiya village, the latter was then employed by his 43-year-old uncle, Kamal, an affluent building contractor in Gaza City. Osama Hamad reportedly warned Ayash that his uncle was not "clean"—that is, he had contacts with the Shin Beth. Yet, inexplicably, Ayash not only ignored the warning but, contrary to the usual practice by fugitives, stayed on in the same house for a long time. After Osama had finished working for his uncle, the latter gave him a mobile phone to keep in touch. On January 4, Osama Hamad was to recall later, his uncle asked for the phone, which he later returned the same day. It was during this period that the

Shin Beth agent(s) either planted a miniature bomb inside the old telephone, or replaced it with a rigged phone. The bomb was detonated, while Ayash conversed with his father, by a signal broadcast to it over the mobile telephone network. The cellular phone networks in both Gaza and the West Bank were owned and operated by Israeli companies. The disappearance of Kamal Hamad, who left behind his luxurious Mercedes-Benz and cream-colored stone house, confirmed his involvement as an Israeli collaborator. Reports in the Hebrew press mentioned a fee of $1 million for his services and a forged passport with a United States visa. Many Palestinians were shocked to discover that the Islamic movement had been so deeply penetrated by the Shin Beth.

As soon as the news of Ayash's murder broke, shops and businesses in the Gaza Strip and West Bank closed down in mourning. The two-story farmhouse of his parents in Rafat was draped with a green Hamas flag. It was a Friday, the holy day of Islam. Soon the air was filled with readings of the Quran broadcast over the loudspeakers attached to the minarets of the mosques. The preachers delivering their sermons after the Friday noon prayers focused on Ayash's life, portraying him as a hero of resistance against the oppressive Zionist occupiers. By introducing the suicide bomb, a weapon of fiendish power against which there seemed no protection, into the Palestinian struggle and proving himself also to be an adept bomb-maker and a recruiter of martyrs, he had helped change the power equation in which hitherto the Palestinians had been almost powerless, they told their grieving congregations. In short, Palestinians regarded Ayash as a folk hero because he frightened the mighty Israeli state and society. Later that day Arafat called on Mahmoud Zahar, and told him: "We came here to share your loss." In his later statements he condemned Israel for violating the PLO-Israeli peace deal which had put internal security of the Gaza Strip into the PA's hands, adding that the killing of Ayash ran counter to "the spirit of reconciliation."[25]

To Jewish Israelis, Ayash was evil incarnate, a demon responsible for the deaths of 68 human beings.[26] They viewed him as a psychopathic mass murderer, who dispatched his own acolytes to certain death alongside their victims. They felt angry and scandalized at the behavior of Arafat, whose popular standing among them had all along been very low. For his part, citing his attendance at the Eastern Orthodox Christmas ceremonies in Bethlehem, Arafat excused himself from joining the funeral procession of Ayash.

On that day the Gaza Strip witnessed an unprecedented outpouring of grief and homage to Ayash. An estimated 300,000 people joined the funeral procession from the Hamas-run Palestine Mosque in Al Rimal district of Gaza City to the Martyrs Cemetery on the outskirts of the city. "Peres, prepare your coffin; Ayash's ghost will appear before you," chanted the mourners. "We want buses [to be blown up]! We want cars!" Those selling Ayash posters did a roaring business. The image of a handsome young man with a luxurious thatch of black hair and an intense gaze, was everywhere. Within days, it was to be found all over the Palestinian refugee camps of Jordan, Syria and Lebanon. A later rally in his honor in Nablus drew 100,000 people, half of the city's population.

"Ayash is a link in the chain of the holy *jihad*," declared the Hamas leaflet. "Let the occupying invaders and their stooges await the response to the Zionist crime." It did not spare the PA, calling it "the Trojan horse of the Zionists," and accusing it of "failure to protect its own people against Israel."

During this emotional period two persons were to prove prescient. One was Yahya Ayash's mother, Ayisha, a sturdy, outspoken woman of 53; the other was an unnamed Israeli security official. "Yahya taught his students, you know, so he will be avenged," predicted the mother confidently. "We may have got even with 'the Engineer,' but his legacy will claim a lot of blood," warned the Israeli expert.[27]

The acolytes of Ayash struck back on February 25, 1996, the second anniversary of the massacre of Muslim Palestinians in Hebron by Dr. Goldstein. Early that morning, Majid Abu Wardeh, a 20-year-old college student from Al Fawwar camp near Hebron, disguised as a uniformed Ashkenazi IDF soldier, his hair dyed blond and his ears pierced with rings, stepped on to bus number 18 on Jaffa Road in downtown Jerusalem. He detonated 33 pounds of explosives, mixed with nails and ball bearings, strapped to his waist, instantly killing 24 people, three of them Palestinian, and injuring 80. The bomb wrecked the bus, reducing it to a blackened skeleton, the roof blown sky-high. About half an hour later, 26-year-old Ibrahim Hussein Sarahneh, a thin-eyed, tousle-haired resident of Al Fawwar camp, also disguised as an IDF soldier, joined a crowd of conscripts waiting for rides at a road junction outside the coastal city of Ashqelon, and blew himself up, instantly killing one soldier.

The communiqué by the Qassam Brigade referred to the Students of Yahya Ayash which, in the estimation of Palestinian and Israeli sources, consisted of 70 to 80 ultra-militants within the Qassam Brigade. It was established later that they received their orders from the Hamas leadership in Damascus. "If Israel is serious about peace then it should release Hamas prisoners and stop hunting down Hamas *mujahideen*," it said. "If this were done then Hamas would worry about every drop of bloodshed." It gave Israel one week to consider its offer of a cease-fire on these conditions.

This was in line with the statements made earlier by the supreme leader of Hamas, Shaikh Ahmad Yasin, and Imad Faluji. In his interview with *Ma'ariv* in June 1995, Yasin had repeated his "earlier offer" of a truce with Israel that "could last ten to fifteen years." And in July 1995 Faluji told the *Jerusalem Report*: "We haven't recognized Israel yet. But we are ready to accept a ceasefire, through a third party, for a set period of time that would be renewable."[28] Yet there were persistent reports of a split in Hamas. It centered around the tactic of using suicide bombers to kill innocent civilians, an act which many religious figures, including some in the Hamas movement, considered unIslamic.

Obviously, there was a lack of centralized control within the movement; and there were differences on tactics which, in the view of insiders, stemmed primarily from varied perceptions due to the fractured nature of the Palestinian community. "In Palestine we are living in different situations militarily, politically and socially," said an official close to the Hamas high command. "There is a big difference between the West Bank and Gaza Strip. There is no split, but you could say there are different tactics."[29] Apparently the population in the Gaza Strip, the birth place and nerve-center of Hamas, was more radical than in the West Bank, and this was mirrored in the thinking of the local leadership. Equally, the perceptions of the insider Hamas leaders and the outsiders did not coincide. Mahmoud Zahar alluded to this, albeit indirectly. "The assessment of those of us who are living here is different from the people outside," he said. "The people outside receive their information from television reports or telephone calls. We live the fine details and our assessment is much more realistic."[30] The subtext of this statement indicated that the insider Hamas leaders wanted accommodation with the PA and suspension of attacks on Israeli targets while the outsiders wanted to continue the military struggle.

Though the outside elements were weak on a realistic analysis of the situation, they were strong on providing funds. Given the penury of the Palestinians in the partially Occupied Territories, particularly Gaza, Hamas was heavily dependent on funds from abroad to run its kindergartens, schools, health clinics, mosques and social welfare agencies, the socio-cultural infrastructure which was the bedrock of its popular support. Among those who had conceded this was none less than Shaikh Ahmad Yasin. When asked by *Ma'ariv* in mid-1995 about foreign funding of Hamas, he denied that Hamas received money from any Arab or Muslim government, and added: "Financing comes mainly from the Palestinian donors around the world."[31] Most of these contributors were resident in Jordan, Lebanon, Syria and the oil-rich Gulf states. But there were also many among some 500,000 Palestinians settled in Europe and North America who made donations to Hamas through the Muslim religious charities set up in such western countries as Britain, Canada and Germany.

Despite the differences between pragmatists and militants within the Hamas movement, the Qassam Brigade ensured that the suicide bombers came from West Bank villages or refugee camps under the overall control of the IDF so as not to violate the understanding Hamas's political leaders had reached with Arafat not to embarrass the PA by launching attacks on Israelis from the PA-controlled self-rule areas. (This understanding did not extend to the Islamic Jihad, which showed scant interest in devising a *modus vivendi* with the PA.)

Given the acute despair and deprivation, material and spiritual, that prevailed in the West Bank refugee camps, there was no dearth of volunteers for suicide missions. A Shin Beth investigation in Al Fawwar camp, housing less than 1,000 families, including those of Majid Abu Wardeh and Ibrahim Sarahneh, the bombers of February 25, revealed that 30–40 youths were willing to carry out suicide attacks.[32] Now the homes of their parents were spray-painted with the Qassam Brigade's newest slogan: "More Jewish blood will be spilled until Palestine is freed from its occupiers."

This became more likely when the Israeli government did not take the Qassam Brigade's offer of a conditional truce seriously. The Brigade had struck partly to demonstrate to Israel that killing Ayash did not damage its capacity to strike. There was an unintended parallel here with the assassination of the PLO's Khalid Wazir, or Abu Jihad, in 1988 when Israel hoped that eliminating him would end the newly started intifada. It didn't work. When its deadline of a week passed without any response from the Peres administration, the Brigade struck again—on the same day,

Sunday, the same bus (number 18), the same city (Jerusalem), and about the same time and place. The suicide bomber this time was Riad Karim Sharnoubi, 24, a sad-looking, mustached student of the Ramallah Teachers' Training College. Of the eighteen people he killed instantly, two were Palestinian and six were Romanian contractual workers. Unlike Abu Wardeh and Sarahneh, Sharnoubi came from a village, Burqah, in the northern West Bank under the overall security control of the IDF. That he had accomplished his mission despite the closure of the West Bank from Israel, constant helicopter surveillance of Jerusalem, and the provision of a uniformed guard on every bus, showed that Israel's security measures were far from foolproof. Indeed, it was fairly easy to walk into Israel from the West Bank if a person did not use a car.[33] Since a suicide bomber, once equipped with explosives attached to his/her waist, needed no further expertise, assistance or backup, his/her bomb became the most lethal weapon in the arsenal of terrorism so far.

The Qassam Brigade's political strategy was to raise the popularity of Hamas at the expense of the PLO and the PA. They believed the best way to achieve this was to discredit Arafat, by showing that he could gain nothing further from the Israeli administration, which would be the case if Likud and its leader, Binyamin Netanyahu, won the forthcoming elections. The most effective tactic to boost the electoral chances of Likud was to demonstrate that the Peres government was incapable of providing security to its citizens. The sharp drop in Peres's fifteen to twenty percent lead in opinion surveys showed that the Qassam Brigade plan was working. Hamas militants also hoped their attacks would outrage Jewish settlers in the West Bank so as to trigger similar actions by the settlers, thus setting the scene for a bloody confrontation between settlers and Palestinians, and the derailing of the Israeli-PLO peace process.

But the attribution of the next bomb, on March 4, which killed 12 persons and wounded 100, was problematic. Both the Qassam Brigade of Hamas and the Qassam militia of Islamic Jihad claimed responsibility. The carnage occurred on the Jewish festival of Purim, the second anniversary of Goldstein's massacre of Muslims in Hebron. Since the Islamic Jihad had a score to settle with the Israeli government for the assassination of Fathi Shikaki, it had the motive to commit this act of terror. Also, unlike the previous three occasions, this suicide bomber, later identified as Ramez Obeid, a 23-year-old university art student from a refugee camp in the Gaza Strip, did not strap explosives to his waist but carried them in a bag, the major reason why he was denied entry into the Dizengoff Square shopping mall, full of children in Purim costumes. His bag contained land-mines filled with TNT, bottles of benzene and nails. It was discovered later that he had been smuggled out of the Gaza Strip by an Israeli Arab driver, carrying scrap metal from the Strip to Israel, for a fee of $1,100. The driver had dropped him off in Tel Aviv at the Dizengoff Square shopping mall a minute before the blast.

Israel's emergency measures on March 3 included internal closure of the West Bank, banning travel between population centers, and ending the employment of Palestinians not only in Israel but also outside of their own village or town. "No one goes in, no one comes out," declared Major-General Ilan Biran, the IDF commander of the West Bank. The total ban on cross-border traffic meant severance of food and cooking-gas supplies to the West Bank and Gaza Strip.

"It is the tightest closure and sealing of borders Israel has imposed on Palestinians since 1967," said Abdul Hakim al Samra. "The worst thing to do is to seal the borders like this, or to impose a long-term curfew, when people cannot work. Lack of work leads to acute frustration and anger, which turns ultimately into violence. When people work, they have to get up early and return home late and go to sleep. So they have no time or energy for planning [violent] actions, or doing anything against the authorities." What was the feeling in the Gaza Strip? "We feel like we are inside a jail while the Jewish settlers are allowed to come and go as they please. We are not permitted to go to Israel or the West Bank, or go sailing over the waters of the Mediterranean, or fly into the sky. We used to be controlled by one authority, the Israelis; now we are controlled by two, Palestinian and Israeli. It is worse, much worse."

The feelings of Gazans and West Bankers did not figure in Peres's plan of action. Following the second explosion in Jerusalem on March 3, he angrily urged Arafat to act. The latter immediately banned six Palestinian militias, including those of Hamas and Islamic Jihad. With another bomb going off in Tel Aviv on March 4, the pressure on Arafat from Israel and the United States mounted. "I will co-operate fully with Israel to wipe out terrorism," he declared. That night he convened an emergency meeting of PA officials and Hamas's political leaders in Gaza City. He told the Hamas representatives bluntly: "Either you assert control over the military wing or I will ban Hamas as a political organization." The next day, the Hamas political leadership called on "our brothers in the Izz al Din al Qassam Brigade to halt their military operations... to fortify national unity." They responded positively and swiftly. "We will stop our armed activities for three months [until after the Israeli elections] to give the Israeli government and the Hamas political leadership... a chance to reach a ceasefire," said their communiqué issued late on March 5. "But should Israel hurt Hamas fugitives in the West Bank and Gaza, the ceasefire will be violated."

But by the night of March 5–6 the die had already been cast. The PA and Israel had agreed to carry out co-ordinated action against the Hamas movement. "There is no dialogue either with Hamas's political or military wing," said Mahmoud Abbas, a top PLO official, in Gaza on March 6. "We will go after Izz al Din al Qassam [Brigade], root out every bit of its infrastructure and demolish its vicious organization."[34]

Starting in the early morning of March 6, the PA police raided Gaza's Islamic University and 30 other Islamist institutions. "All mosques in the Gaza Strip are under the control of the PNA," declared Khalid Kidre, the PA's attorney-general. In the West Bank towns under its control, the PA acted likewise. Tipped off by the Israeli intelligence, it raided the Ramallah Teachers' Training College, and arrested 21 students, including Muhammad Abu Wardeh, who allegedly recruited Majid Abu Wardeh and Ibrahim Sarahneh to become human bombs. A serious-looking man of 22, Abu Wardeh was tried immediately, found guilty and sentenced to life imprisonment. In the joint-control areas on the West Bank, where Israel was in charge of security, the IDF shut down all schools, colleges, clinics and charitable bodies functioning under the Hamas aegis. It re-entered the villages it had vacated in December while, in the words of an Israeli liaison officer, "the PA police stepped out of the way," and arrested 170 Islamists. To break completely links between the West Bank and Gaza, the IDF ordered that some 1,200 Gaza students studying in the West Bank must return home forthwith.

The next day, March 7, addressing the inaugural session of the Palestinian Council in Gaza City, Arafat called for an international campaign to combat terrorism, an idea originally aired by President Hosni Mubarak of Egypt. The White House took the suggestion, and organized a Summit of the Peacemakers in Sharm al Shaikh, Egypt, within a week.

Both the PA and Israel widened their nets to catch Islamists. Widespread arrests of Islamists in the PA areas on charges of "incitement against the PA"—amounted to 600 in the Gaza Strip alone by March 9, and included all of Hamas's political leaders and some of the Qassam Brigade's officers. The arrests won Arafat public praise from Peres and US Secretary of State Warren Christopher, but the Qassam Brigade issued a new communiqué. Blaming the Israeli and PA crackdown for its decision, it "has decided to resume its martyrdom attacks against the Zionists... The Palestinian National Authority's arrest of Hamas fugitives will completely destroy any understanding or future agreement between Hamas and the PLO."

Meanwhile, ordinary Palestinians suffered. It was the hope of the Peres government that they would blame Hamas and the Islamic Jihad for their current woes, and turn against these organizations. But Palestinians, who had suffered immeasurably under the 27-year-long Israeli occupation—which continued, albeit in a reduced and disguised form—showed scant signs of holding the Islamist factions solely responsible for the current situation. "I blame both the Islamic groups and Israel," said Abdul Hani, a shopkeeper in the main square of Khan Yunis. "The Islamic guys for not realizing that border closure hurts Palestinians, and the Israelis for doing nothing. The Israelis hold the key to solving the Palestinian problem, but they are not sincere. See how they are co-operating with Jordan after the peace treaty. But for Palestinians they are always putting impediments. They ruined our economy, and made us dependent on jobs in Israel. Now they have shut us out of their labor market. What is more, they are not even allowing flour into the Gaza Strip. How can I run my grocery without bread?"

Abdul Hani was one of the Palestinians in Gaza City who demonstrated against the sealing off of the Gaza and West Bank on March 17, a strictly controlled protest, flaunting the officially sanctioned slogan: "Yes to peace, No to the siege." Addressing them, Arafat accused "Iran and some Arab countries" of the recent explosions in Israel in order to make Palestinians despair about the peace process. By naming Iran directly and publicly, Arafat obliged Peres, who had for some years been leading a campaign against Iran as a terrorist state. The next day Peres allowed flour into the Gaza Strip. Earlier, on March 15, he had ended the unparalleled internal closure of the West Bank. But on the eve of the end of the one-month-long closure of the Israeli border, March 24, he extended it by another month. The only concession he made was to let West Bankers work in the West Bank's Jewish settlements.

With the unemployment rate in the Palestinian Territories running at an unprecedented 60 percent, there was growing alarm in PA headquarters,

Peres's office, and President Bill Clinton's White House that an economic collapse would ensue unless urgent remedying action was taken. As a result, many UN-supervised emergency labor-intensive projects, lasting until June (past the Israeli elections) and costing $100 million, were initiated.

The relief was widely welcomed, but was not enough to dispel the despair that had descended particularly on the Gaza Strip. "People ask, 'What are we left with?'" said Abdul Hakim al Samra. "They can suffer for a long time. They have much capacity for suffering. Then they reach a breaking point. Then nobody knows what will happen. This is what happened with intifada in 1987. And it lasted six years."

In March 1996, before being arrested for the third time by the 21-month-old Palestinian Authority for "incitement against the PA," Dr. Mahmoud Zahar said: "If this [repressive] policy continues, I fear it will only drive people underground."

Three months later, after Netanyahu's election as premier, Zahar was one of the 1,200 Islamist radicals in PA jails, held without charge or trial. Yet this was not enough to satisfy Netanyahu, who demanded that Arafat sustain his drive against Hamas and the Islamic Jihad.

At the same time Netanyahu's own policies were unwittingly aiding the Hamas cause. His decision in September to open the ancient Hasmonean Tunnel in the Old City, resulting in widespread violence between the security forces of Israel and the PA, eased tensions between the PA and Hamas and engendered national unity among Palestinians of all political hues. The fact that the Qassam Brigade leaders decided during and after these events not to carry out bomb attacks against Israeli targets implied that they did not wish to damage the unity that had arisen in the Palestinian ranks.

Netanyahu's continued obduracy, combined with his humiliation of the PA and Arafat, helped Hamas to win supporters for its view that Israel only understood force and violence, and that the Israeli leader was interested only in manipulating the Oslo Accord to turn the PA into his agent to accomplish what his country had failed to achieve as the sole occupying power of the Palestinian Territories: crush radical Islamists.

Hamas leaders did not approve of the Hebron Protocol of January 1997, but they told Arafat that they would express their opposition in a democratic fashion. In response Arafat invited them to participate in the Comprehensive Palestinian National Dialogue Conference in late February. They accepted the invitation.

Relations between Hamas and the PA improved further when Netanyahu persisted with his plans to establish the Har Homa settlement at Jabal Abu Ghneim in early March. On March 10, when Hamas and Popular Front leaders asked Arafat to release the remaining of their colleagues, Arafat agreed.

But unlike in the previous September, the Qassam Brigade of Hamas did not refrain from terrorism in its retaliation against Israel on the Har Homa issue. The detonation of a bomb by a Qassam Brigade activist on March 21 in Tel Aviv put Arafat in a quandary. He tried to ward it off by claiming that the bomber had come from Lebanon and was a member of the Lebanese Hizbollah, a pro-Iranian group. But once the Israelis had come up with specific names of the those involved, who, according to their intelligence, were living in a PA-controlled area, it was hard for Arafat to withhold his cooperation—for that specific case. The PA's arrest of the six members of the Surif cell, active since late 1995[3,5] satisfied Israel and the CIA, but angered Hamas leaders.

Overall the relationship between Hamas and the PA remained problematic. Arafat did not want to repress Hamas and the Islamic Jihad to the extent of causing civil war, thus playing into the hands of Israel. At the same time he knew that terrorist acts by Islamist radicals were undermining the peace process, which had after all spawned the PA.

Arafat was aware, too, that despite the repression it had suffered at the PA's hands, Hamas continued to be the main rival of Fatah. A Hamas rally in Khan Yunis to commemorate Yahya Ayash's assassination in early January 1997 drew 40,000 people; and the turnout for a similar demonstration in Nablus was equally large. By early April, the Islamic Bloc, affiliated to Hamas, had gained control of the student bodies in all seven institutions of higher education, except the Al Azhar University in Gaza City.

Driving such an organization underground through relentless repression was not the best of options. Its members drew their inspiration from the Islamic scriptures, especially the Quran, the Word of God. Such people could sustain their faith and belief in their righteousness for a long time. Indeed, they could point to the tenacity with which Zionist Jews, religious and secular, had stuck to their beliefs and succeeded in their mission. There was, in fact, much in common between religious fundamentalists of Islam and Judaism. And they did not fade away merely because they were described as cranks, fanatics, zealots or religious fascists by those who regarded themselves as rational and secular. In the case of Muslim Palestinians and Jewish Israelis, they both made their case on the ground of divine promises. No matter how arcane such an argument may seem to secular westerners, it is very real in the lives and thoughts of hundreds of thousands of ordinary Jews and Muslims living in Israel and the Palestinian Territories today.

14

Divine Promises
The Disputing Inheritors

Just as post-1967 Israel, with its rule extended to the West Bank and Gaza Strip, provided an environment in which ultra-nationalist Zionism, religious and secular, flourished, so the Palestinian entity, stemming from the 1993–95 Oslo Accords, is set to create, willy-nilly, conditions in which the proponents, religious and secular, of the liberation of all of mandate Palestine will thrive. Since the radical Palestinian secularists—inspired initially by their antagonism to the nexus of American imperialism, Zionism and Arab reaction—subscribe to a waning ideology, and since they have little grassroots support, the task of retrieving all of Palestine has fallen almost wholly on Islamic fundamentalists.

Besides the beards and skullcaps that Jewish and Muslim fundamentalists often share, there are more significant points where the two intersect. "As Muslims we believe in the Torah," said Shaikh Bassam Jarrar. "We believe in Ibrahim [Abraham], Ishaq [Isaac] and Yacoub [Jacob], later called Israel, as prophets. But the Torah was written 900 years after Moses had died, peace be upon him, and so it deviated from the original." The Quran, on the other hand, was compiled "within twelve years of the death of Prophet Muhammad, peace be upon him. We believe that the Torah is partly true and partly not. But I am prepared to take the Torah as it stands."

That seemed a common enough ground for a debate between Islamic and Jewish fundamentalists. But this was a non-starter. So, instead of reporting their arguments separately, I will present them as a dialogue between the Jewish "Amnon" and the Muslim "Zaki."

AMNON: The starting point is Genesis 12:1 and 2. "Now the Lord had said unto Abram, 'Get thee out of thy country, and from thy kindred, and from thy father's house, unto a land that I will show thee. And I will make of thee a great nation, and I will bless thee, and make thy name great; and thou shalt be a blessing.'" Then you have Genesis 12:6 and 7: "And Abram passed through the land unto the place of Shechem unto the plain of Moreh. And the Lord appeared unto Abram, and said, 'Unto thy seed will I give this land'."
ZAKI: We Arabs are his descendants through his son, Ishmael (Ismail).
AMNON: Look up Genesis 12:8. Abram moved to a place between Beit El and Hai, where he built an altar to the Lord. Then in Genesis 12:13 you have Abram

and his wife Sarai returning from Egypt with a lot of cattle, gold and silver to this same earlier place. Abram now lived in the Land of Canaan. In Genesis 12:15 you have the Lord saying unto Abram, "For all the land which thou seest, to thee will I give it, and to thy seed for ever."

ZAKI: Once again, since we Arabs are descendants of Abram, we have as much historical claim to this land as anybody else.

AMNON: But the covenant that the Lord made with Abram covered a much larger area. See Genesis 12:18 to 21: "In the same day the Lord made a covenant with Abram, saying, 'Unto thy seed have I given this land, from the river of Egypt unto the great river, the river Euphrates. The Kenites, the Kenizzites and the Kadmonites. And the Hittites and the Perizzites and the Rephaims. And the Amorites and the Canaanites and the Girgashites and the Jebusites.'"

ZAKI: That's roughly the region where the Arabs are living today. The phrase 'Abram's seed' was meaningless until he had a son. And that is what Genesis Chapter 16 is all about. After Abram and Sarai had lived in Canaan for ten years, and Sarai had borne no children, you have 16:3 where Sarai "took Hagar her maid the Egyptian, and gave her to her husband Abram to be his wife." Then you have 16:15: "And Hagar bore Abram a son, and Abram called his son's name, which Hagar bore, Ishmael." Abram was then 86 years old.

AMNON: But Sarai took care of the relationship between Abram and Ishmael in Genesis 21:10 to 12: "[Sarai] said to Abraham, Cast out this bondwoman [Hagar] and her son [Ishmael]: for the son of this bondwoman shall not be heir with my son, Isaac. And the thing was very grievous in Abraham's sight because of his son. And God said unto Abraham, "Let it not be grievous in thy sight because of the lad, and because of thy bondwoman: in all that Sarai hath said unto thee, harken unto her voice: for in Isaac shall thy seed be called." That settles it.

ZAKI: Except that God's speech continues... Genesis 21:13: "And also of the son of the bondswoman will I make a nation, because he is thy seed." This ties in perfectly with what is described in Genesis 17:4."The Lord said unto Abram: 'Behold, my covenant is with thee, and thou shalt be a father of many nations.'" Please note "many nations."

AMNON: You are ignoring Genesis 15:13 and 14: "And the Lord said unto Abram, 'Know of a surety that thy seed shall be a stranger in a land that is not theirs, and shall serve them; and they shall afflict them 400 years. And also that nation, whom they shall serve, will I judge. And afterward shall they come out with great substance.'" Isn't that about the Jews, in servitude in Egypt?

ZAKI: Let us return to the basic points: the seed of Abram and the land offered to it by the Lord. Genesis 17 is the key. The Lord reveals himself as "the Almighty God," renames Abram and Sarai as Abraham and Sarah, amplifies his covenant with Abram, and prescribes circumcision for the male progeny of Abram "as a token of covenant betwixt me and you." In 5 to 8 the Lord said unto Abram, "Thy name shall be Abraham; for a father of many nations have I made thee. And I will make thee exceeding fruitful, and I will make nations of thee, and kings shall come out of thee. And I will establish my covenant between me and thee and thy seed in their generations for an everlasting covenant, to be a God unto thee and to thy seed after thee. And I will give unto thee, and to thy seed after thee, the land wherein thou art a stranger, all the Land of Canaan, for an everlasting possession; and I will be their God." And 24 and 25 read: "And Abraham was ninety years old and nine, when he was circumcised in the flesh of his foreskin. And Ishmael his son was thirteen years old, when he was circumcised in the flesh of his foreskin." Remember that when the covenant of circumcision was made with Abraham, and the Land of Canaan was promised "as an everlasting possession," it was the thirteen-year-old Ishmael who was circumcised along with Abraham. Isaac was not born yet.

AMNON: Maybe so. But in the same Genesis 17 God made a clear distinction between Ishmael and Isaac, who was yet to be born, and between Sarah and Hagar. Genesis 17:16 says: "God said unto Abraham, 'I will bless Sarah, and give thee a son also of her... She shall be a mother of nations; kings of people shall be of her.'" But God said nothing of the sort about Hagar. And God's covenant was explicit. Genesis 17:21: "And God said, 'But my covenant will I establish with Isaac, which Sarah shall bear unto thee at this set time in the next year.'"

ZAKI: You're skipping the earlier verse, Genesis 17:20. "God said, 'As for Ishmael, I have heard thee. Behold, I have blessed him, and will make him fruitful, and will multiply him exceedingly; twelve princes shall he beget, and I will make him a great nation.'" And when Abraham died it was both Ishmael and Isaac who buried him. That's Genesis 25:9. Anybody with even the tiniest shred of objectivity would agree that the descendants of Ishmael have every right to consider themselves of the seed of Abraham.

AMNON: They may say what they like, but there is no divine sanction behind it. The basic question is: Did God treat Isaac and Ishmael on a par? No. Here is Genesis 26:2 to 4. "And God appeared to Isaac, and said, 'Sojourn in this land [of Gera], and I will be with thee and bless thee; for unto thee, and unto thy seed, I will give all these countries, and I will perform the oath which I swore unto Abraham thy father. And I will make thy seed multiply as the stars of heaven, and will give unto thy seed all these countries.'"

ZAKI: Why do you stop? God's speech doesn't end there. It continues: "and in thy seed shall all the nations on the earth be blessed."

AMNON: What does that mean?

ZAKI: You tell me.

AMNON: Whatever I say about that can only be speculation. What is sure is what God said to Jacob. Genesis 28:13 and 14: "And, behold, the Lord stood above it [the ladder between the earth and the heaven], and said, 'I am the Lord God of Abraham thy father, and the God of Isaac: the land whereon thou liest, to thee I will give it, and to thy seed. And thy seed shall be as the dust of the earth, and thou shalt spread abroad to the west, and to the east, and to the north, and to the south; and in thee and in thy seed shall all the families of the earth be blessed.'"

ZAKI: Again there is a reference to the blessing of "all the families of the earth." Think of Esau, Jacob's elder brother. He was deprived of his status as successor to Isaac by Jacob's trickery.

AMNON: But God sanctified Jacob's position however he got there..Why else would God change Jacob's name in the way He had done with Abram? Look up Genesis: 9 to 13—God appeared to Jacob again, and said, "Thy name shall not be called any more Jacob, but Israel shall be thy name." And God said unto him, "I am Almighty God. Be fruitful and multiply; a nation and company of nations shall be of thee, and kings shall come out of thy loins. And the land which I gave Abraham and Isaac, to thee I will give it, and to thy seed after thee will I give the land."

ZAKI: Once again a reference to "company of nations."

AMNON: Only this time Jacob had twelve sons: Reuben, Simeon, Levi, Judah, Zebulin, Issachar, Dan, Gad, Asher, Naphtali, Joseph and Binyamin.

ZAKI: Mind you, four of these were by maidservants: Gad and Asher by Zilpah, the maidservant to Leah; and Dan and Naphtali by Bilheh, the maidservant to Rachel.

AMNON: A common practice in those days, it seems. Anyway, there you have the Twelve Tribes, or Nations, if you like.

ZAKI: We call them and their descendants Beni Israel, Children of Israel.

AMNON: Or the Israelites—as in the Old Testament.

ZAKI: So even if we accept your argument that present-day Palestine was promised by God to Abraham and his descendants, you must limit yourselves to Beni Israel, Children of Israel.

AMNON: Fair enough.

ZAKI: Then are all the Jews in Israel today Beni Israel?

AMNON: What do you mean?

ZAKI: How is it possible that Falashas, Ethiopian Jews, have the same ancestry as Arab Jews born in the Middle East and North Africa, and European Jews, many of them with blond hair?

AMNON: Intermarriage.

ZAKI: Impossible to get pure Africans like Falashas through intermarriage.

AMNON: So what's your theory?

ZAKI: I have no theory. Only God's promise. His promise applies to a certain family, the family of Israel and not to Jews as a religious group. There was no such group as Jews in those days.

AMNON: Were there Muslims then?

ZAKI: No, not in the way we use the term today. After Solomon's death in 930 BC the United Kingdom of Israel broke up into two. Ten of the twelve tribes lived in the north, then called Israel, and two in the south, Judah. Israel lasted until 722 BC when it fell into the hands of the Assyrians. Judah continued to exist, but from 605 BC its people, called Jews, were taken into exile by the Babylonians. Today's Jews acknowledge that the ten Israelite tribes were lost.

AMNON: Come to the point.

ZAKI: In 586 BC Nebuchadnezzar of Babylonia defeated the ruler of Judah, populated by two Israelite tribes. He enslaved some of the Israelites and took them to Babylonia. Some of those returned to Palestine. Among them some became Christian. Later, when Islam came to Greater Syria and Iraq in the seventh century, a large majority of these Israelite tribes converted to Islam. The process continued into the sixteenth century, under the Ottomans in Palestine.

AMNON: That's the most distorted view of Jewish history I've ever heard.

ZAKI: Most of the Beni Israel adopted Islam or Christianity. But many pagans embraced Judaism. Reading history you see that certain nations, which were not Beni Israel, adopted Judaism. Some of them were Arab, like the Kinda tribe. There was a Jewish kingdom in Yemen. During Prophet Muhammad's time in the seventh century in Arabia some tribes were Beni Israel and others had adopted Judaism. Then there was the Kingdom of Khazar, a Jewish kingdom, not Beni Israel, near the Caspian Sea in the tenth century.

AMNON: Yes, the Kingdom of Khazaria. Its Jewishness went back to AD 740 when Bulan, the military king of Khazaria, converted to Judaism.

ZAKI: So he was not a Beni Israel.

AMNON: You talk as if Jews and Beni Israel are different groups.

ZAKI: They are. Every Beni Israel is a Jew, but not every Jew is a Beni Israel.

AMNON: What are the proportions?

ZAKI: Experts estimate that about one-tenth of today's 14 million Jews are Beni Israel. And God's promise applies only to them. Not to the nine-tenths of today's Jews who are converts, and have nothing to do with the lineage of Jacob/Israel.

AMNON: So nine-tenths of the Jews in Israel today have no right to return?

ZAKI: It depends. Most of the Mizrachim or Sephardim living in Israel today probably are Beni Israel. But worldwide Sephardim are only one-fifth of the Jewish population.

AMNON: What about me, an Ashkenazi?

ZAKI: Most of you are not Beni Israel; you are converts to Judaism.

AMNON: So I can't claim Eretz Israel as my Promised Land?

ZAKI: You said it. But what's your definition of Eretz Israel? What are its boundaries?

AMNON: Those of the Hebrew kingdom under King David and King Solomon.

ZAKI: David and Solomon are more than kings. To us they are prophets like Abraham, Isaac, Jacob and Moses. We don't separate our belief in them from that of Prophet Muhammad. So the holiness of Palestine to us comes from our belief in all these prophets before Muhammad, who lived here, preached here and ruled here. The most mentioned name in the Quran is Prophet Moses. He appears in the Quran 136 times.

AMNON: That many. Well, he was our law giver. He gave definition to Judaism.

ZAKI: To monotheism; that's why we have a prayer niche for him in our Al Aqsa Mosque.

AMNON: The first proper monotheistic kingdom was under David and Solomon, Eretz Israel. Yet in modern times the British banned the settlement of Jews in Transjordan even though it was part of Eretz Israel. In fact half of Eretz Israel lay to the east of River Jordan.

ZAKI: But then you didn't have the Negev desert. Now you do.

AMNON: We're entitled to something in return for the land lost east of River Jordan; aren't we?

ZAKI: I question the very basis of your right to return. To start with, the Divine Promise was not unconditional. The Beni Israel were required to obey the Lord and his commandments and laws individually and collectively.

AMNON: And if they did not, then God's wrath would be upon them. The Fifth Book of the Torah, Deuteronomy—the addresses of Moses to the Israelites before entering Canaan—chapter 28, verses 63 to 66. "And it shall come to pass, that as the Lord rejoiced over you to do you good, and to multiply you; so the Lord will rejoice over you to destroy you, and to bring you to nought; and you shall be plucked from off the land wither thou goest to possess it. And the Lord shall scatter thee among all people, from the one end of the earth even unto the other; and there thou shalt serve other gods, which neither you nor thy fathers have known, even wood and stone. And among these nations shalt thou find no ease, neither shall the sole of thy foot have rest; but the Lord shall give thee a trembling heart, and failing of eyes, and sorrow of mind. And thy life shall hang in doubt before thee; and thou shall fear day and night, and shalt have none assurance of thy life." Haven't we been through this? Haven't we suffered?

ZAKI: Yes, in ancient times too. Because the Beni Israel committed collective apostasy, they were punished. The population of Israel was captured and removed by the Assyrians, and the people of Judah by the Babylonians.

AMNON: But the prophets told the Israelites that a section of the exiles would return.

ZAKI: They did. And they built the Second Temple, in 515 BC. Finally, they enjoyed a period of political independence under the Maccabees, from 166 to 63 BC.

AMNON: That's all we have tried to recreate ever since, most recently with the founding of the Zionist Congress in Basle in 1897.

ZAKI: But that has nothing to do with the prophecies in the Torah. There is no prophecy of another return after the one from the Babylonian exile. In any case the last of the prophets passed away long before the devastation of Jerusalem in AD 70.

AMNON: The prophecies mentioned not only restoring the temple and religious life of the Israelites but also heralding a golden era when the lion would lie down with the lamb, and the desert would blossom, and swords would be changed into ploughshares.

ZAKI: The second part hasn't come to pass yet.

AMNON: That won't happen unless the first part materializes, as the precondition for the second. The return of the Jews to their Promised Land and the re-establishment of a religious Jewish state is a precondition for the arrival of the Messiah and the beginning of a golden age.

ZAKI: You must get the facts right about the Promised Land. Since Ishmael was the progenitor of Arabs, God's promise to Abraham applies to Arabs as well. We can't accept your elimination of all the children of Abraham except Isaac. We Arabs have as much right to Palestine as our Promised Land as you have.

AMNON: Two peoples claiming the same inheritance. Who settles the conflicting claims?

ZAKI: Time will tell. But one thing is certain: you can't have it all.

AMNON: That's the way it appears—for now.

ZAKI: That sounds like a temporary acceptance.

AMNON: Nothing is forever.

ZAKI: Except divine promise.

15

Summing up the Past, Surmising the Future

An extraordinary combination of geography, geopolitics and history has made part of the hinterland of the eastern Mediterranean a unique place on earth. As the region where much of the chronicle described in the Old Testament and the New Testament occurred, the Holy Land/Palestine/Israel is by far the most widely discussed subject—politically, culturally and religiously—in the western world.

At the heart of the Holy Land lies Jerusalem. Much time and space have been devoted in western literature, religious and secular, to this remarkable city. The Talmud (Learning)—the multi-volume compilation of the Jewish oral law, codified around AD 200, and the successive commentaries—cites a medieval sage thus:

> Ten measures of beauty alighted upon earth; nine were possessed by Jerusalem,
> and the tenth was shared by the rest of the world;
> Ten measures of sorrow alighted upon earth; nine were possessed by Jerusalem,
> and the tenth was shared by the rest of the world.

Overall, there has been more sorrow in Jerusalem, with a recorded history dating back to about 1900 BC, than beauty, more agony than ecstasy. It has been captured and lost by 40 different armies. In the twentieth century alone it has witnessed battles by the Ottomans, British, Jordanians and Israelis. Strife, hatred, bloodshed and holiness have gone hand in hand here, as have religion and politics. "Our city has always suffered for its holiness," said 77-year-old Arif al Arif, a former mayor of (Jordanian-controlled) Jerusalem, in the late 1960s. "Holiness is its tragedy. Perhaps that is why our people... can remember nothing but struggles. Blood. They have been harmed by this sanctity more than they have benefited."[1]

In the late nineteenth century, a new, secular dimension was added to the continuing historical, religious argument among Jews and other monotheists: nationalism. (The ongoing debate whether Jews are a religious or an ethnic group can be traced back to this development of a century ago.) Among the Jews of Europe, nationalism manifested itself as political Zionism—a term coined by Nathan Birnbaum in 1893, and applied to the Jewish nationalist movement that aimed to create a Jewish state or national center in Ottoman Palestine, the historic homeland of the forebears of Jews. Until then the aspiration to return to Zion—the Canaanite name of the hill on which Jerusalem stood—to recreate it as a spiritual-religious center of Jews, had been couched in religious terms and expressed in the liturgy, with the ideology underlying this yearning called "religious Zionism." Political Zionism emerged formally as the Zionist Organization (later renamed World Zionist Organization), which the first Zionist Congress, held in Basle in 1897, established, and which defined Zionism thus: "Zionism strives to create for the Jewish people a home in Palestine secured by public law."

Between then and 1948, the birthdate of the State of Israel, a series of events, coupled with ceaseless lobbying by European and American Jewish leaders, contributed toward the realization of the Zionist aim. The principal events were: the failed Ottoman offensive from Gaza in 1915 against the Allied Powers during World War I, the 1917 Balfour Declaration, the League of Nations mandate to Britain in 1922, the discovery of oil in Iraq in 1927, and the genocide of some six million European Jews by Nazi Germany during World War II. Interlinked with these crucial events were instances of convergence of interests of leading world powers: Britain and the United States in 1916–17; Britain and France in 1920 at the League of Nations (which the United States did not join); and the United States and the Soviet Union in 1947 at the United Nations, the successor to the League of Nations.

At the beginning, in 1897, when the Ottoman empire extended over most of the Arab Middle East, there was no administrative-political unit called Palestine. The term had gained currency among the western travelers to the Holy Land in the nineteenth century, and was used, vaguely, to mean the geographical area roughly between the eastern Mediterranean Sea and the desert. In the Ottoman empire, this territory was scattered over the *sanjak* (Turkish, district or county) of Jerusalem and the *vilayat* (Turkish, province) of Beirut, with Jerusalem and suburbs ruled directly from Istanbul.

As it happened, this place was, and remains, the most strategic territory in the Middle East—the meeting point of Africa, Eurasia and the Mediterranean—providing access not only to Egypt via the Sinai Peninsula but also Jordan, Syria and Lebanon. In the Middle East, the Red Sea and the Mediterranean Sea are set apart only by the narrow isthmus of the Suez. And the distance between Gaza, the most south-eastern point of the Mediterranean Sea, and Aqaba, at the head of the Gulf of Aqaba on the Red Sea, is not very much longer than the Suez isthmus. The land between the Mediterranean Sea and the head of the Persian Gulf too can be seen as an isthmus. While longer than the isthmus of Suez or Gaza-Aqaba, ancient traders found it short enough to develop it as a thriving trading route between East and West. Among the early conquerors who realized the potential of the region as a commercial crossroads was Alexander the Great. His occupation of Palestine in 333 BC underlined the economic importance of the area. During his occupation of Egypt from 1798 to 1801, the French general Napoleon Bonaparte chose the Palestinian path, unsuccessfully, to advance toward India.

Once the Mediterranean Sea and the Red Sea were connected directly by the Suez Canal in 1869, the Middle East regained its position as the foremost intercontinental highway. By occupying Egypt in 1882, Britain ensured control of the Suez Canal, now its lifeline to its empire in India.

The outbreak of World War I between the Allied Powers (Belgium, Britain, France, Italy, Japan, Montenegro, Russia and Serbia) and the Central Powers (Austria-Hungary, Bulgaria, Germany and the Ottoman empire) opened up unprecedented opportunities for Zionist dignitaries, who had been lobbying their cause in the leading European capitals and in Washington. They reasoned that the colonization of Palestine by European Jews would create a western outpost in the Middle East which would be immensely beneficial to the West. This was a convincing enough argument, as the Balfour Declaration would show.

The Balfour Declaration arose out of the convergence of Zionist aspirations with Britain's imperial aims, which came to the fore during World War I. The January 1915 Ottoman offensive against the Suez Canal across the Sinai Peninsula, which was repelled by the British, made London realize anew the strategic importance of Palestine in defending the Suez Canal, its lifeline to India, and caused it to resolve to control Palestine after winning the war. In a memorandum to the Cabinet in March 1915, Sir Herbert Samuel, a senior civil servant of Zionist persuasion (later appointed British High Commissioner for Palestine), proposed establishing a Jewish homeland in Palestine as a cornerstone of British policy in the Middle East. Until then world Jewry, concentrated in Germany, Austria-Hungary, Russia and America, had by and large remained neutral in the war. With the United States joining the conflict in April 1917 on the Allied side, the role of American Jewry became important. In order to gain its active co-operation, the pro-Zionists in the British government, led by Premier David Lloyd George and Foreign Minister Arthur James (later Lord) Balfour, proposed backing the Zionist cause in September 1917, but failed to win cabinet approval. They then sought the advice of US President Woodrow Wilson, known to be a pro-Zionist. Wilson replied that the time was inopportune for anything more than a statement of general sympathy for the Zionists. But next month, responding to Zionist pleas and rumors of Germany wooing the Zionist movement, Lloyd George and Balfour broached the subject again with Wilson. After some hesitation, he approved a draft statement which, following minor editing, was issued by Arthur James Balfour on November 2, 1917 in the form of a letter to Lord Rothschild, a British Zionist leader.[2]

Endorsed by the chief Allied Powers, the Balfour Declaration was included in the San Remo Agreement of 1920—the title given to the decisions on the Middle East made by the Supreme Council of the League of Nations. According to the Agreement, Britain and France were authorized to decide the nature of the League of Nations mandates for the region and submit them to the League for debate and voting. The Balfour Declaration was incorporated into the British mandate over Palestine authorized by the League of Nations in July 1922. The freshly demarcated, sword-like Palestine disrupted the geographical continuity of the Arabic-speaking world extending from Mauritania along the Atlantic to the Persian Gulf. Among those who noted the geopolitical importance of this development was Soviet leader Joseph Stalin. Instructed by him, in 1924–5, the national delimitation commission dealing with the Caucasian region, allocated the Zangezur strip, inhabited by Azeri Turks, to the Republic of Armenia, thus dividing the Nakhichevan region bordering Turkey, from mainland Azerbaijan, the land of Azeri Turks.

Stalin thus broke the territorial continuity of Turkic lands, from the Balkans to China, and eliminated a potential bridgehead for a regional enemy.[3]

The second prong of the British strategy in the Middle East was the Emirate of Transjordan, its protectorate. Its ruler, Emir Abdullah al Hashem, nurtured ambitions to annex the whole or part of Palestine.

Britain thus created enough tensions and contradictions in the region to assure itself an ongoing lead role as the occupying power as well as the protector and the sole arbitrator, with a large area for maneuver and manipulation between the competing interests of Palestinian Arabs, the immigrating Jews from Europe and Transjordanian Arabs.

The discovery of commercial quantities of oil in Iraq in 1927 increased the strategic and economic value of Palestine since it provided a gateway to the Iraqi oilfields through Transjordan. Following the decision of the British navy, which underpinned Britain's superpower status, to switch from coal to oil in 1913, the military-strategic importance of petroleum rose sharply. With the Iraqi oilfield in Mosul turning out to be the world's largest, the prospect of the British quitting Palestine after assisting its people to become self-governing—as was its plan in Iraq, its other mandate territory—evaporated.

As it was, in 1922, the familiar argument of an occupying or imperialist power that it must stay to maintain peace between local hostile groups was unconvincing in the case of Palestine. At eight percent of the population, Jews were hardly in a position to initiate or sustain civil strife. By introducing an external element— European Jews—into Palestine, Britain meant to make the Jewish community a viable opponent of the Arabs by letting it expand dramatically. That is what the British actively encouraged, leading to the Jews becoming eighteen percent of the population in 1931, enough to withstand a sustained assault by the local Arabs. Once their proportion reached a third of the total population, as it did in the spring of 1939, the Jewish community was large enough to sustain a civil war; and this provided the British with a convincing rationale to stay on as the mandate power "to keep the peace between hostile communities." It is worth noting that in the Hindu-majority Indian empire of Britain, Muslims, the largest religious minority, were a quarter of the total population, and succeeded in thwarting Indian progress toward independence unless the sub-continent was partitioned into India and Pakistan, which happened in August 1947. In Cyprus, another British colony, a *de facto* partition came about after independence in 1960, primarily because the minority, (Muslim) Turks, at about one-fifth of the island's population, could not be made to accept the dominance of the majority (Christian) Greeks.

After World War II, fearing expulsion from the Suez Canal zone by Egypt, the British moved their troops and weapons to Al Arish in the Sinai. This showed they were determined to hold on to Palestine as a gateway to the crucial Iraqi oilfields. It was only after the fear of a forced withdrawal from Suez had passed that London finally decided that Palestine had become ungovernable, and referred the problem to the United Nations.

In the region, though, Britain was intent on maintaining the hegemony it had enjoyed for over three generations. And Stalin, the leader of the emerging Soviet bloc, was equally intent on expelling British imperial power from the strategic Middle East. He reckoned that the best way to achieve this was by depriving London of any rationale to stay on in Palestine, if only to contain the murderous conflict between Arabs and Jews. This meant having to back the UN partition plan. He did. And, but for the eight-strong Soviet bloc vote, the Palestine partition plan, needing two-thirds majority, would not have been passed, by 33 votes to 13, at the General Assembly on November 29, 1947.

Almost half a century later, my conversations with several post-graduate Jewish students of history and international relations at Hebrew University revealed that none of them was aware of the vital role performed by the Soviet Union in the creation of Israel. Nor were they aware of the crucial part played by the supply of arms, including fighter aircraft, sent from Czechoslovakia, under the orders of Moscow, to the Zionists in Palestine, beginning in March 1948, two months before the establishment of Israel.

In any case, by 1948 the center of Zionist activity in the diaspora had shifted from Britain to the United States, which had emerged as the uncontested leader of the West. The discovery of the unprecedented scale and horror of the Holocaust that European Jews suffered at the hands of Nazi Germany produced a groundswell of sympathy for Jews and Israel in the United States and elsewhere in the West.

Once Israel had materialized, its links with America strengthened rapidly. These became all the more important as the Suez War of 1956 sounded the death-knell of British and French imperialism in the region.

Over the next decade, American commitment to the survival and strengthening of Israel became so strong that by the time of the spring 1967 crisis in the Middle East, US intelligence efforts in Egypt had been tailored to Israeli needs. The Jewish state's total alignment with the United States in the international arena had its parallel in domestic politics: the center of gravity of Israeli politics moved steadily to the right. A milestone was reached in mid-1967 when ultra-nationalist groups, including Menachem Begin's Gahal—hitherto considered untouchable by the Labor establishment—were invited to join a national unity government.

The stunning victory that the Jewish state scored in the June 1967 War with the Arabs left such a strong imprint on state and society that neither Israel's stand-off in the October 1973 armed conflict nor its ignominious withdrawal from most of Lebanon three years after attacking it in 1982 wiped it off. "For the new generation of Israeli Jews, born after the 1967 War... the West Bank belongs to Israel," said Professor Moshe Ma'oz of the Truman Institute at Hebrew University. "It does not see any difference between Jaffa and Hebron."[4] So thorough has been the success of the Israeli state, aided by the mass media, in this case that even the map printed in *In the Land of Israel* by Amos Oz, an eminent liberal-leftist writer and journalist, active with the Peace Now group, labels the West Bank and the Gaza Strip as territories "held by Israel since 1967," rather than "occupied by Israel since 1967."

The endeavor, official and unofficial, to give an ultra-nationalist spin to contemporary history continues hand in hand with a sustained effort to do the same with distant chronicles, both at popular and intellectual levels. "Historian Yaacov Shavit has produced a series of academic books, including

History of Palestine, Volumes VI-VII," said Ilan Pappe, a Jewish Israeli historian at Haifa University. "In Palestine the Jews were only one percent of the population from the eleventh to the late nineteenth century. There were small Jewish communities in Jerusalem, Hebron, Tiberias and Safed. They were all Ottoman subjects until the collapse of the Ottoman empire in 1918. But reading Shavit's books, you would think they were the only people living in Palestine. This is typical of the official literature and other literature in Israel. It is the traditional Israeli view: Palestine was an empty, arid land where nomads attacked the settled population."[5] This may seem a clear-eyed, objective view to most non-Israelis, but in mainstream Jewish Israel, academics such as Pappe are often dismissed as anti-Zionist, self-hating Jews.

Israeli authorities are used to implementing their decisions with such thoroughness that sometimes they end up as victims of their own success. After the 1967 occupation of the West Bank and Gaza, they damaged the economies of these territories so effectively that they made a very substantial proportion of the Palestinians dependent on casual work in the Jewish state. By so doing, they created a host of problems, not least of which was weakening the security of Israel. For some 30 years the Israeli media and government invariably described the PLO as a terrorist outfit, and Yasser Arafat a bloodthirsty, terrorist leader, not even a guerrilla leader, much less the chairman of a national liberation organization. Then, one day in September 1993, the Israeli public found its prime minister, Yitzhak Rabin, shaking the hand of the arch terrorist of all times, Arafat, before a world audience. Part of the reason why Labor leaders today find it an uphill task to swing a convincing majority of Jewish Israelis in favor of peace and reconciliation with the PLO—and maintain that position for any meaningful length of time—is that month after month, year after year, they and other politicians presented the PLO as evil incarnate, devoid of any saving grace.

Just as in Northern Ireland, so in Israel and the Palestinian Territories, perceptions on terrorism vary. On the Jewish Israeli side today there is an unqualified condemnation of terrorism as a political weapon, despite the fact that during the decade leading to the founding of Israel in 1948, first the Irgun and then both Irgun and Lehi used terrorism quite effectively against Palestinian Arabs and the British: undeniably, it played a significant role in the emergence of the Jewish state. The existence of an impressive museum in Tel Aviv dedicated exclusively to Irgun, and the naming of an important thoroughfare in that city after Lehi, are just two of the numerous examples of the official recognition conferred on the Jewish terroristic organizations of the recent past. It is worth noting, too, that the respective leaders of Irgun and Lehi—Menachem Begin and Yitzhak Shamir—went on to become prime ministers of Israel, and together held that office for as many years as did David Ben Gurion, the towering Labor leader and the prime founder of Israel.

A slight stretching of one's historical perspective should make plain the fact that today most Palestinians and Israeli Arabs are equivocal about the role of terrorism in politics in the same way that most Jews in Palestine were before the founding of Israel.

"Today Israelis have official terrorism," said Dr. Adel Manna, an Israeli Arab historian. "They terrorize with laws. They demolish houses, they arrest you arbitrarily, they humiliate you at random, they parade you in handcuffs at your workplace. They deport you. They send death squads. They have laws of occupation, the Law of the Dominant Party. Whatever Israel does is 'official.' The Palestinians have only the weapon of resistance which they use as much as they can. Each day they see more and more of their land confiscated and turned into Jewish settlements, despite the Oslo Accords. They feel desperate. They choose the only effective weapon they have, suicide bombing."[6]

On the Israeli side, most politicians take a narrow view of security, focusing almost exclusively on its military and law and order aspects, and sidelining the larger political context. Military security of a state is best assured within the framework of political security; and in the case of Israel and the Palestinians, that means a peace settlement that is seen by a vast majority of the Palestinians, by far the weaker party in the conflict, as just and equitable. UN Security Council Resolution 242 of November 22, 1967, on which the current Middle East peace process is founded, refers to "a just and lasting peace" in the region.

The Israeli state and media have reared two generations of citizens on the promise of creating an environment that is absolutely free of any threat of Arab terrorism, an unrealistic aim in the present-day world. The reality, deplorable though it is, remains that today no government, not even that of the United States—which witnessed an explosion in Oklahoma City in April 1995 that killed 168 people—can offer 100 percent protection to its citizens from random bombs and bullets. The examples of Britain and Spain, both western nations, are pertinent. The violence stemming from the conflict between Protestant and Catholic Christians in Northern Ireland—rooted in the antagonism of the Catholic natives to the Protestant settlers brought in from Scotland during the rule of Oliver Cromwell (1599-1658)—has since 1969 made London, universally regarded as a peaceful metropolis, a bomb-prone city. In Spain, the violence linked to the nationalist aspirations of the Basque minority continues to be expressed in bombs and assassinations. No Briton or Spaniard realistically expects its government to put a definite and final end to such random violence, which mainly maims and kills innocent civilians.

While diligently and rightly pursuing those Palestinians who perpetrate terrorism against its citizens, the Israeli administration has not been evenhanded in meting out justice to proven terrorists per se, irrespective of their ethnicity. Among others, BeTeslem, the Israeli human rights organization, pointed out that following the massacre of Muslim Palestinians by Dr. Baruch Goldstein in early 1994, his house in Kiryat Arba was not demolished by the IDF, a punishment that is invariably meted out to the family of a Palestinian terrorist. The life sentence of Menachem Livni, involved in the plot to blow up the Dome of the Rock and in the killings of Palestinian students at Hebron's Islamic University, was commuted to seven years in jail. After the assassination of Premier Yitzhak Rabin in November 1995, it was revealed by official sources that the intelligence agencies had concentrated so much on the scenario of an extremist Palestinian murdering Rabin and other Israeli leaders that they had neglected to take seriously the proposition that Labor politicians might be targeted by Jewish zealots.

"Not even the Sabra [Palestine-born Jews] establishment—of which Rabin was a founding member—can escape blame for the murder [of Rabin]," wrote Zeev Chafets in the *Jerusalem Report*. "The Shin Beth (the quintessential Sabra security force), which was under Rabin's own command, failed to protect him from the gunman. But that failure was the last link in the chain. None of the country's agencies of law and order, including the army, the police and the courts, have been willing or able to effectively stand up to the [Jewish] zealots. Instead, they indulged them. They allowed the leaders of Kach and Kahane Chai movements to roam the country giving interviews with impunity... They stood by while settlers flaunted court orders, and rabbis incited to sedition and murder. Partly, this was the result of political calculation by the Labor Party (yes, and Rabin himself) who didn't want to alienate potential Orthodox support. But more profoundly, it was a lack of will, a show of weakness and irresolution by a liberal, secular Zionist establishment that seems to have lost faith in itself and its ideals... Yitzhak Rabin paid for that failure with his life."[7]

It was the self-same political opportunism that led the Israeli government to support the rise of the Muslim Brotherhood/Islamic Center, especially in the Gaza Strip. So intense was its hostility towards the PLO, a secular, nationalist body, that it encouraged the rise of a rival religio-political movement from 1973-84 on the expeditious principle that any group that reduced the PLO's influence among Palestinians was a positive development for the Jewish state. This short-sighted policy was seen to prove extremely harmful to Israel. As if to live down that self-damaging record, in recent years Israeli politicians have taken to crusading against Islamic radicals among Palestinians and other Arabs with a zeal that can only be counter-productive.

It is understandable that, having lost a long-standing ideological foe in the form of the Soviet Union and leftist Arabs, following the collapse of the USSR in late 1991, Israel felt a need to fill the resulting vacuum, and found Islamic fundamentalism a credible and viable ideology to target.

But at the popular level, distrust and hatred of Israel in the Arab world remain so entrenched that any railing against a Muslim group or country (such as Iran) by Israeli leaders induces the response which can be summarized thus: if Jewish Israelis are rabidly against something, then there must be something beneficial for Muslims and Arabs in it.

It needs to be noted that Israel's unrelenting pressure on the Occupied Territories increasingly made Palestinians turn to religion for succor. The number of mosques rose sharply, and the influence of preachers and prayer-leaders grew. The example of the Deheisheh refugee camp was typical. Before the intifada it had only one *jami* (major) mosque. During the intifada the residents constructed another such mosque with their own meager resources. And a third *jami* mosque went up soon after the intifada. So, while the indigent refugees built two impressive, new mosques with voluntary contributions, a hospital, funded by outside sources, remained unfinished because the money ran out.

The rising interest in Islam provided one key to understanding the growing popularity of Hamas. The other key lay in the analysis that once the PLO had compromised heavily on its basic tenets contained in the Palestine National Charter in its Oslo Accord with Israel, an alternative organization was bound to arise if only to fill the political vacuum created by the PLO's retreat. So even if six-year-old Hamas had not existed in 1993, some such party would have emerged in the aftermath of Oslo.

Shorn of its references to Islam, the 1988 Charter of Hamas was not much different from the one the PLO had adopted in 1968. In any event, the idea of Zionism as imperialism is not the monopoly of the likes of Dr. Mahmoud Zahar of Hamas but is shared by a Christian intellectual such as Albert Aghazarian, a resident of the Old City of Jerusalem. "An imperialist power always likes monopoly," he said. "The Zionists and Israel take a monolithic view of history, not pluralistic. They constantly stress only four key elements—the First and Second Temples in ancient times, and kibbutzim and the 1967 War in recent times—and ignore all others. This applies as much to the excavations carried out by the Israelis. There are many layers there, many successive empires have called the shots here. The Jewish layer pertains to only 120 years when they had their own *leum*, peoplehood; and before that were the Israelites, for about 450 years. Applying all its power, determination and stamina, the State of Israel is demolishing all other mirrors at the expense of its own. The mounting of the Jerusalem 3000 festival in September [1995] is a perfect example of that monopolistic policy."[8]

Such perceptions are not limited to Palestinians, and are to be encountered widely among Israeli Arab intellectuals. "Like other imperialists, Israelis look down upon the local people as retarded," said Dr. Manna. "They know what's good for the natives. We will make progress, economic development, in their land, and show them. Even when Zionists were a tiny minority [in Palestine] their attitude was not to recognize natives as people, to deal with them directly. Instead they tried to make deals with Arab 'leaders'—to make peace with the Hashemites in Transjordan, the Egyptian regime, and so on. They wanted this country without the people. This was the end objective. This land belongs to the Jews. You know the Jewish National Fund does not buy land here, it 'redeems' land; the same with the IDF when it confiscates Palestinian land. It is all 'redemption.' This is how they teach history in Israeli schools."

Yet not every Jewish Israeli ends up parroting the conventional, mainstream views. There are notable exceptions. Historian Ilan Pappe is one such. "The [pioneering] Zionists thought of Arabs as they thought of swamps, mosquitoes, stones and other negatives of nature around them, never as human beings with their own rights and own dignity," he said.

Misconceptions and myth-making are not, however, the monopoly of one side. In the Palestinian camp the tendency to indulge in hyperbole and rose-colored analyses, however comforting in the short term, ultimately proved damaging. "In the 1948 War, because the Jews did not capture East Jerusalem, it allowed the Palestinians to create myths about their fighting prowess," said Aghazarian. "Those fighting at the Jaffa Gate, Old City, would say: 'We put sewer pipes in the barrels of our guns, and the Zionists thought we had cannons.' Then we had the inane statements like 'If every Arab spat on Israel it would drown in spit,' and 'If every Arab threw an orange at Israel it would drown in oranges,' and so on. This enabled the Israelis to manufacture the myth of facing the colossal power of five Arab countries." But the Arab propensity for exaggeration persisted. Even a slight chink in the armor of Israel was perceived as bearing a potential for the ultimate demise of the Jewish state. "Before the 1967 War the thinking among Arabs was that contradictions between Ashkenazim and Sephardim would be able to destroy Israel from within," said Emile Habibi, the veteran Israeli Arab writer-politician. "This was mere fiction. But the bogey of extermination which was developed by Israel, using the sensationalist Arab slogans, helped in bringing together Ashkenazim and Sephardim, especially under the threat of war in 1967."[9]

Sometimes myths are created instantly. Palestinians today invariably use the term *Al Sultah al Wataniye al Falastiniye*, the Palestinian National Authority, which is not the term mentioned in the Cairo Agreement that the PLO signed with Israel. The official term mentioned in the Agreement is the Palestinian Authority; and the title the Palestinian *National* Authority has more to do with the term used in the main Palestine National Council resolution passed in 1974 than what happened between the PLO and Israel nearly twenty years later.

In a different, but more profound, context, Israeli textbooks state that the Zionist Jews migrated to Eretz Israel, which did not exist—and not to Ottoman Palestine, which did exist.

In the everyday lexicon the almost universal Jewish Israeli habit of using the terms "terror" and "terrorism/terrorists" endlessly—without lacing them with such variants as "guerrilla operation," "violent action," "bloody explosion" etc.—has the inadvertent effect of robbing the word "terror" and its derivatives of the shock value they contain. As if in retaliation to this Jewish Israeli norm, Palestinians often say "the Sunday event" or "the event on Monday," instead of even uttering such words as "the killings on Sunday" or "the massacre on Monday."

Then there is the sociological fact of Jewish Israelis being news-junkies, and reacting instantly to the latest development, behaving in a mercurial fashion. "[Jewish] Israelis are obsessive listeners to the radio news," writes Amos Elon, an eminent Israeli historian and commentator. "It is almost a druglike addiction. Few try to kick the habit; even fewer succeed... Israeli buses are often equipped with radio sets... The loudspeaker, attached above the luggage racks, emits mostly pop music, lost in the general commotion. But every hour on the hour comes the NEWS. It blares out over the noise of the traffic, and the entire bus falls silent... No people in the entire world tunes in to the news as often, as regularly, and with such fervor. Seven or eight times a day, at the sound of the news beep, most Israelis pause at whatever they are doing, to hear whether there has been another air battle or artillery exchange across the Suez Canal or some new act of sabotage by Arab terrorists. Not infrequently the names of the latest casualties are read out. (My God, isn't that so and so's son?) Modern Israelis turn to their radios like their ancestors once turned to prayers." But there is more to this Jewish Israeli ritual today—which oddly parallels the prayer calls to Muslims five times a day—than merely keeping abreast of what is going on. "The habit of following the news so often and so closely partly explains the sudden shifts in the public mood, which can be as sharp as they are frequent," continues Elon. "Israelis easily fall from heights of exhilaration to dark abysses of gloom; from glowing hope for imminent peace to bleak depression that the war will never end and that they may be crushed by it."[10]

"Crush, or be crushed": that has been the leitmotif of the politics of Palestine/Israel for the past many decades, the two nations locked in an intimate embrace, unable to disengage, unable to devise a means of coexistence, even a tentative one—until 1993. "Palestinians were the first to understand that solving the national conflict through one people's annihilation of the other is not possible in our time," said Habibi. "But the scenario of getting rid of Palestinians is still persistent in the Israeli public opinion much more than the idea of getting rid of Jews is amidst the Palestinian public opinion. That is the main hindrance to real peace. We Palestinians dared to drink our bitter cup and come to the conclusion that there is no other way but reconciliation with Israel. But we say to [Jewish] Israelis, 'You have not drunk your bitter cup. Hence the recurrent crises in the peace process. You cannot run away from drinking your bitter cup. Without your leaders telling you this, you will not comprehend the scope of the price extracted from Palestinians to have your State of Israel.'"

To a non-partisan outsider, the price seems plain enough: three-quarters of the British mandate Palestine. But most Jewish Israelis do not see it that way, nor do their leaders.

Yet the past must be addressed, and a reasonably objective balance sheet drawn. For, in the words of Dr. Manna, "The past, present and future are interlinked; and unless you change your attitude to the past you cannot connect correctly with the present and the future." Specifically, he would like Israeli textbooks to address two central questions, something they now omit: Why did Palestinians resist Jewish immigration? And what caused the Arab Revolt of 1936-9?

As for Israelis drinking their bitter cup, Habibi did not bring out and address the question: why does a community drink "a bitter cup"? The short answer is: only when it finds itself in dire straits. That is what happened to Palestinians, or at least to the PLO. After the 1991 Gulf War, it found itself beset with a host of crises—ranging from loss of funds from the oil-rich Gulf states and, equally damagingly, depletion in popular support as more and more Palestinians turned to Hamas. In contrast, Israel and Israelis today are hardly in dire straits. Certainly, IDF soldiers got weary of controlling the Palestinian intifada, especially in the Gaza Strip. But there are four other vital dimensions to the Jewish state—the rate of Jewish immigration, the economy, Israel's links with the diaspora Jews, and its ties with the United States—which show no sign of slackening or fatigue. A steady inflow of Jews from the former Soviet Union at about 70,000 annually is assured beyond the turn of the century. Israel's economy remains buoyant, helped partly by the surge in its diplomatic recognition following the Oslo Accord, and the new trade opportunities that have ensued. Thirdly, Israel continues to pay top priority in tapping into the tremendous goodwill it enjoys among diaspora Jews. Its highly-developed and effective programs in this field ensure that many diaspora Jews get the opportunity to visit Israel at least once before they reach their mid-20s. For instance, all Israeli universities have well-tailored programs for diaspora Jewish students which run from three weeks to six months. The thinking behind all this is simple: even if the diaspora Jew decides not to emigrate to Israel, he/she must have a first-hand knowledge and experience of the Jewish state, since that would enhance the chance of a financial contribution to Israel through the Jewish National Fund, which owns 93 percent of all land in Israel. Finally, Washington's unqualified support for Israel—military, economic, diplomatic—remains firm. This has strong bi-partisan backing not only in the US Congress but also public opinion. As the US is the sole superpower today, its stance on Israel carries immense weight, regionally and globally.

In sum, Israel remains powerful economically, militarily and diplomatically. It therefore negotiates with both the Syrians and the Palestinians from a position of strength.

This has been the case all the more since Benyamin Netanyahu became prime minister. He has exercised Israeli power to the full not only in his dealings with the Palestinians but also with the US administration whenever he has seen fit. Having succeeded in lowering the Palestinians' expectations regarding the 1995 Oslo II Accord, through unilateral steps, brow-beating and procrastination, and having established himself as an obstructionist negotiator, he does not inspire much hope about a successful conclusion of the final settlement with the PLO—especially when he has put the hawkish Ariel Sharon, his foreign minister, in charge of conducting these negotiations. Aware of the complexities of the exercise, the 1993 Oslo Accord allowed a period of up to three years for these talks, starting with the second anniversary of the 1994 Oslo I Accord—early May 1996. Indeed, on that day the two delegations met, but only as a symbolic gesture, since the Israelis were in the midst of their elections. Later the path to the final status negotiations remained blocked so long as Netanyahu stonewalled on the implementation of the January 1997 Hebron Protocol, which required him to carry out three redeployments in the West Bank by August 1998. It was not until late October 1998 that he signed the Wye River Memorandum to carry out the combined first-and-second withdrawals by late January 1999 in exchange for strict Palestinian implementation of the steps to guarantee Israeli security.

Since, at the Wye Plantation, Arafat refused to consider extending the life of the seminal Oslo Accord—due to end five years after the signing of Oslo I on 4 May 1994—the final settlement must be reached by May 3, 1999. It seems most unlikely that this deadline will be met due to the highly controversial, emotion-laden subjects to be tackled: 1) Palestinian refugees, 2) Jewish settlements, 3) final borders, 4) status of the Palestinian entity, and 5) Jerusalem. By now the Israeli positions on these issues are widely known. They are well summarized in the bipartisan National Agreement Regarding the Negotiations on the Permanent Settlement with the Palestinians signed by Yossi Beilin (Labor) and Michael Eitan (Likud) in early 1997. [11]

Palestinian Refugees

Since the Madrid peace process is based on the UN Security Council Resolution 242, which pertains to the June 1967 War, at best Israel will limit the discussion only to those Palestinians who became refugees as a result of that conflict even though the Resolution refers generally to "achieving a just settlement of the refugee problem"—an issue that has been with the UN since the 1948–49 Arab-Israeli War, and on which the UN has repeatedly called for the return of the Palestinian refugees to their homes and livelihood. But the chances are that when the Palestinian delegation raises the subject of the three-quarter million Palestinians who lost their homes in the 1948–49 War, and who now number over 2.5 million, it will get short shrift from the Israelis. It is highly unlikely that Israel will pay heed to the argument of the PLO—which, unlike the PA, represents both the home-based and the diaspora Palestinians—that it is morally wrong for Jews to exercise their right to Return, based on ancient history, while denying the same right to the recently uprooted Palestinians. As a compromise, Israel may discuss the possibility of a token number of post-June 1967 Palestinian refugees returning—but only to the territory controlled by the PA. Deeply concerned about the demographic trend in the area of British mandate Palestine, which is running against Israel despite the upsurge in Jewish immigration from the former Soviet Union since 1989, the Jewish state wants to minimize the number of Palestinians returning home.

An agreement which denies some 40 percent of the overall Palestinian population of over 6.5 million the right to return home, will plant seeds of discontent which will, going by past history, sprout in the future.

Jewish Settlements

The break-neck speed with which the Labor-led government spent $100 million on twenty bypass roads during the run-up to the phased implementation of Oslo II in early 1996, and the same unseemly haste with which the Likud-led administration embarked upon building a further twelve bypass roads in the immediate aftermath of the Wye River Memorandum was remarkable. The official reason given in both cases—to minimize contact between the Jewish settlers and the Palestinians to help the PA to assume greater control over the territory to be handed over to it—was deceptive. The true, unexpressed objective in both cases was to do to the West Bank what Israel had done to the Gaza Strip in the early 1970s[13]: to establish a road network which severs the Palestinian urban centers and inhibits their natural growth while linking the Jewish settlements with one another and with Israel. The end purpose is to ensure that in case of an armed conflict between Israel and a future Palestinian entity, Palestinian civilians and soldiers are trapped into enclaves which the IDF can easily surround and overpower. The Netanyahu government has made the bypass roads "safe" by banning Palestinian construction inside a wide belt along both sides of the roads.

Regarding the Jewish settlers, who at the time of the Wye Memorandum numbered 175,000 outside of Greater East Jerusalem, it has been calculated that some 70 percent are concentrated in 10 percent of the West Bank which is contiguous with Israel, and covers the Jewish state at its narrowest point, less than nine miles wide. If the Israelis insist on annexing 10 percent of the West Bank, then the Palestinians are likely to demand in exchange an area equal or larger than the one they cede to Israel elsewhere—say, in the Negev adjacent to the Gaza Strip. As for the 30 percent of the Jewish settlers living outside the annexed West Bank territory, Israel will insist that they retain their Israeli citizenship and protection as well as the right to "strengthen" the settlements.

With Netanyahu as premier, and Ariel Sharon first as infrastructure minister and then foreign minister, the Jewish settlers have played an important role in the forging of Israeli policy on settlements. Netanyahu's election victory in 1996 conferred respectability to the ultra-nationalist credo, summed up by Eliakim Haetzni, a settlers' leader, thus: "Judaism's central pillar is the Return [to Zion] and Eretz Israel, which includes the Land of the Patriarchs, where I am based now [in Givat Mamre, Kiryat Arba]. If you don't believe in this, then you're not a Jew."[14] Echoing this view, Netanyahu told *The Times* in December 1997, "The West Bank is part of Israel proper."[15]

Final Borders

The subject of final borders is linked with Israeli security and Jewish settlements. Security concerns remain paramount among top Israeli decision-makers. According to the military doctrine first enunciated by Yigal Allon in 1970, and then adopted by one of his lieutenants, Yitzhak Rabin, the eastern security border of Israel lies along the Jordan Valley. After Rabin's assassination, there was no indication that Shimon Peres had disavowed his doctrine. Netanyahu has repeatedly mentioned annexing the Jordan Valley to safeguard Israel. The second salient Israeli security concern remains the narrow neck of the pre-1967 Israel. Ten miles north of Tel Aviv, it is particularly vulnerable to artillery and rocket attacks by hostile forces from the West Bank. Both these issues will have to be resolved. If the past is any guide, they will be—at the cost of the weaker party, the Palestinians.

On the other hand, the erection of a border fence equipped with surveillance equipment, that is constantly patrolled by the IDF, must go a long way to satisfy Israel's security needs, and lessen pressure on the Palestinians to concede territory to Israel.

PLO leaders are aware of the different Israeli plans for ceding to the Palestinians no more than 45-50 percent of the West Bank. They regard the debate on the subject among Jewish Israelis as "an internal" matter with no particular relevance to them. They are only too aware that the UN General Assembly Resolution 181 of November 1947 allocated 45.4 percent of the British mandate Palestine to the Arabs, and that the present West Bank, Gaza and East Jerusalem together constitute about a half of that figure. As far as they are concerned they made their one-time "historic compromise" in the Oslo Accord of 1993 by accepting Israel's right to exist in peace in exchange for its return of the Occupied Palestinian Territories to the PLO, according to the UN Security Council Resolution 242. It is hard to see the Palestinian leadership giving up half of its already halved territory.

Status of the Palestinian Entity

It is noteworthy that the Beilin-Eitan document treats Israeli security and Palestinian self-determination as inter-related subjects. It stipulates that the Palestinian entity should have no army and must remain demilitarized, and that it must accept the Jordan Valley as "the security border" of Israel. It also requires that the Palestinian entity be barred from stationing a foreign army inside its boundaries, and that its security forces be legally bound to cooperate with its Israeli counterparts to foil terrorism. The enhanced powers of the Palestinian entity may be described as constituting "Enlarged Autonomy" or "a State," says the document.

As for Netanyahu, his position on the subject was summarized broadly by Leslie Susser, a senior writer with the *Jerusalem Report*. "Netanyahu would want to give no more than 50 percent of the West Bank, probably less, to the Palestinians. He would like to keep the Palestinians in enclaves. He would demand total control over the water resources of the West Bank, and ensure that there is no cut-off of water supplies to Israel. He would insist on full Israeli control over the Jordan Valley, and demilitarization of the West Bank. He would bar the Palestinian entity from forging a military alliance with any state."[16]

The PLO will strongly resist each of these points. Its strong card is its threat to declare an independent State of Palestine as soon as the Oslo Accords expire on May 3, 1999. When the Palestine National Council proclaimed the (symbolic) establishment of the State of Palestine in November 1988, 70 of the 103 countries which then recognized the PLO accorded it full diplomatic status. Today 77 countries recognize the passports issued by the Palestinian Authority, which has several trappings of the government of a sovereign state, including its own airline.

Overall, therefore, reaching an agreement on this subject will be a Herculean task.

Jerusalem

The position of Netanyahu on Jerusalem is inflexible: it is the eternal, undivided capital of Israel. The Beilin-Eitan document too takes the same position, describing Jerusalem, with its existing municipal borders, as "a single united city within sovereign Israel" and its capital, where Muslim and Christian holy places would enjoy special status. But it allows for the possibility of the Palestinian entity setting up its capital in one of the nearby towns like Abu Dis.

The PLO is not proposing to return to the pre-1967 situation of a divided city. It wants the Holy City to remain united, and become the joint capital of Israel and Palestine. But the Israeli position on Jerusalem has been so uncompromising, and the issue so emotionally charged, that negotiations on it will be particularly tough and acrimonious. Among the points to be settled will be establishing final borders of Jerusalem that are acceptable to both sides.

While, strictly speaking, Jerusalem is a subject that concerns only Israelis and Palestinians, it has much wider implications. It was the arson attack on the Al Aqsa Mosque in 1969 that acted as a trigger for the creation of the Islamic Conference Organization (ICO), the first official pan-Islamic institution of inter-governmental co-operation, at the initiative of King Faisal of Saudi Arabia. By establishing a committee on Jerusalem under the chairmanship of King Hassan of Morocco, the ICO signaled that the fate of the Holy City concerned all Muslim states. This position remains unaltered.

Though the final Palestinian-Israeli talks are to be conducted independently of what has been agreed in Oslo I and Oslo II, the earlier agreements have created certain precedents in procedures and institutions that would be hard to ignore. Under the current accords Israel has the right to "retake control" of the areas run by the PA. Netanyahu reiterated this by stressing that the IDF would protect Jews no matter where they lived in "Eretz Israel."

But the Oslo Accords are fixed-time agreements. They will all expire on May 3, 1999 unless they are extended by mutual consent, an idea which Arafat rejected at the Wye Plantation in October 1998. So after that date each of the two parties will be free to take any unilateral step it wants to, and face the consequences. Whether or not Arafat declares a sovereign State of Palestine will depend largely on the response he gets from the rulers of Egypt and Jordan, the states bordering the Gaza Strip and the West Bank respectively.

Since Egypt is for all practical purposes the leader of the Arab League, Mubarak's view will count more than King Abdallah's (Jordan's new king). Mubarak is likely to back the idea. He has shown himself to be more independent-minded than the Jordanian monarch. When, following the Hasmonean Tunnel violence in September 1996, Clinton invited the Israeli, Palestinian, Egyptian and Jordanian leaders to Washington for a meeting, Mubarak declined the invitation. He has come to dislike and distrust Netanyahu, rebuffing the latter's overtures for a meeting, and has repeatedly advised Arafat against making too many concessions to Israel. Responding to the Israeli jibes that he was impeding the Israeli-Palestinian peace process, Mubarak said in his broadcast on the 25th anniversary of the October 1973 Arab-Israeli War, "those who try to distort facts, and divert the attention away from their intransigence by accusing Egypt, will fail." He added, "Israel must choose between peace and annexing Palestinian land."[17]

By contrast, King Hussein's position has been ambivalent. While Mubarak has maintained peace with Israel only in a limited, formal sense, the Jordanian leader has been eager to transform his peace treaty with Israel—despite its unpopularity among his subjects—into a thriving enterprise. At crucial times—in January 1997 during the talks on Hebron and in October 1998 at the Wye Plantation—he intervened, in essence, to urge Arafat to make concessions. On the other hand, he pressured Netanyahu, successfully, to release Shaikh Ahmad Yasin, and acted as an intermediary to pass on Hamas's offer of a conditional cease-fire with Israel to Netanyahu. Also a majority of his subjects are of Palestinian origin. So, he could not remain immune from their feelings and views for long. The young King Abdallah will most likely follow in his father's footsteps.

Equally importantly, though, the Egyptian and Jordanian leaders will have to take into account the position Washington takes on the issue as May 3, 1999 approaches. At present it is opposed to the idea of a declaration of independence by Arafat without the prior consent of Israel.

If Arafat declares the establishment of the State of Palestine, Netanyahu has the following options, which are not mutually exclusive: military move, political-administrative action, and economic siege. At the very extreme Netanyahu can order the IDF to retake the areas currently under PA control. This is possible, but the ensuing body count, likely to be on the scale of the 1982–85 Lebanese War, will be politically unacceptable to the Israeli public. Indeed the conflict between the IDF and its challengers—Palestinian civilians and the PA armed police—could get so bloody as to result in the posting of UN peace-keeping forces in the Palestinian Territories.[18] Equally seriously, the Israeli-Palestinian violence will draw Egypt into the conflict, and the first victim will be the Egyptian-Israeli peace treaty. If Jordan were to get inducted into the armed hostilities too, then the same thing would happen to the Jordanian-Israeli peace treaty.

A less dramatic military option for Netanyahu is the implementation of a strategy, code-named "Red Hot Steel," devised after the violence of September 1996. It aims at containing the PA controlled areas. The IDF will cut off roads, and freeze Palestinian movement between the population centers. But such a stranglehold cannot be maintained for a lengthy period.

Arguing that Arafat's unilateral act had destroyed the foundation of a mutually agreed settlement, Netanyahu could annex the Israeli-controlled 73 percent of the West Bank, currently labeled area "C." But since annexation would require a majority support in the Knesset he might fail. So he would have to settle for an executive order, taken with the consent of the cabinet—something the Israeli government had done concerning the enlarged East Jerusalem following its victory in the 1967 Arab-Israeli War. (The legislative annexation came later, in 1980.) But, as implied in Mubarak's national broadcast in October 1998, Egypt will challenge this action. This in turn will lead to the breakdown of the Egyptian-Israeli peace treaty, paving the way for an armed conflict between the two countries.

Finally, there is a non-violent option for Israel—imposing an economic siege on the PA-controlled areas. The closures have been such a frequent feature of Palestinian life under Netanyahu's administration that it would not overly tax the IDF and the Border Police. But there will be a qualitative difference from the past. This time around Israel would be strangling the economy of the State of Palestine which would have been recognized by most of the 77 countries that today accept the PA's passports. If these states included Egypt and Jordan—as is highly probable—then they would most likely intervene with humanitarian aid. Outside the region, it is unthinkable that the European Union would just look on while an economic squeeze by Israel led to a human tragedy in Palestine.

Provided the State of Palestine survives its birth pangs, how is it likely to evolve, and how will that affect its relations with Israel? At present, besides the IDF, and the universal conscription of its Jewish citizens, what holds Israel's multi-ethnic and multi-sectarian society together is the sharing of democratic values by all its citizens. What will help consolidate its peace with the Palestinians will be the emergence of a democratic Palestine. This offers a more lasting and secure peace for Israel than a dictatorship, weak or strong, or semi-dictatorship. Though a Palestinian strongman may be able to muzzle the Islamist opposition, and thus make Israel more secure, his success is likely to be temporary rather than permanent, if the final settlement that he secures from Israel is iniquitous and if the pressing problem of Palestinian economic deprivation is not solved satisfactorily and speedily.

Current signals about the democratic behavior of the PA are mixed. Relentless Israeli and American pressures to ensure security of the Jewish state at any cost force Arafat into a dictatorial stance. His egotism, authoritarian behavior, insistence on monopolizing power, and refusal to sign the constitution passed by the Palestinian Legislative Council in September 1996 do not augur well for democracy. Old habits die hard. His political icon remains President Mubarak, hardly a democrat.

But, on balance, the chances of democracy taking root in the Palestinian state are higher than not. Due to historical circumstances, a Palestinian entity was engendered from the bottom up, an aggregation of dispersed power achieved through free and fair elections in a highly politicized and literate society, with Arafat taking charge—quite different from the phenomenon of a political or military leader inheriting an ongoing centralized state like Egypt or Syria.

Secondly, since its inception the Palestinian entity has been dependent for its economic survival on donations from 30 foreign countries, most of them western democracies, committed to upholding civil and human rights. Any persistent or severe violation of these rights will result in the foreign aid being suspended or stopped, a powerful lever.

Finally, the presence of international media in Jerusalem will continue to aid democratic forces among Palestinians. The manner and speed with which the irascibility of Arafat regarding Maher Alami of *Al Quds* and the human rights activist, Bassam Eid, was exposed, illustrated the power of the media and the arduous task faced by the dictatorial forces in the Palestinian administration.[19]

Still, constant vigilance will be needed on all sides to let the seed of democracy strike roots in the Palestinian soil. The most conducive climate for the growth of this plant is the peaceful coexistence between the States of Israel and Palestine— a long term sharing of the Promised Land by Palestinians and Israelis.

Epilogue

The period following the first anniversary of Binyamin Netanyahu's premiership (in June 1997) confirmed his survival skills. In his dealings with the Palestinians in particular and the Arabs in general, he followed a strategy outlined earlier:[1] adopt a hardline, thus drastically reducing Arab expectations—and then yield a little, thereby emerging at the end as a reasonable pragmatist.

In August 1998, Netanyahu made a statement which neatly combined his real view of the Oslo Accord with his political style. "We were not the ones who authored the Oslo agreement, who built it and sanctified it," he said in Hebron. "We are not the ones who longed for it. *This is a flawed, evil accord.* In order to capture the reins of power, we told the nation that we would honor that agreement."[2] In other words, his promise to the Israeli electorate that he would abide by the Oslo Accord was an exercise in opportunism. Having achieved power, therefore, he set out to do what he called a "damage control" job on the agreement,[3] by deliberately alienating and provoking the Palestinians through a series of actions—from opening the tunnel in the Muslim Quarter of Jerusalem's Old City to building the large Jewish settlement at Jabal Abu Ghneim in Greater East Jerusalem. Later, in early 1998, when Yasser Arafat accepted a US proposal for a modest Israeli withdrawal from the West Bank in exchange for specific steps to increase Israeli security, Netanyahu managed to stonewall Washington for many months.

As before, faced with Netanyahu's intransigence, Arafat made one-sided concessions. When he broke off talks and discontinued security cooperation with Israel in mid-March 1997, he said he would resume negotiations only if Israel froze settlement activity and canceled the Har Homa project, and that security cooperation would be linked to progress in peace talks. But soon, under US pressure, he began backtracking. In his May 8 meeting in Gaza with Dennis Ross, Arafat found that, instead of endorsing the European Union's call for an immediate Israeli freeze on Jewish settlements, the American envoy wanted him to drop this demand. Netanyahu argued that settlement expansion was necessitated by natural population growth, although on May 20 *HaAretz* disclosed that 26 percent of the housing units in the Jewish settlements were vacant.[4]

When the Palestinian and Israeli delegations met in Cairo on June 8, Netanyahu's political aide David Bar Ilan, described the encounter as "talks about talks about talks." Soon after, the US House of Representatives' June 13 resolution called on President Clinton to recognize Jerusalem, as currently constituted, as the capital of Israel.

The rising frustration among Palestinians began to worry the Israel Defense Forces. Its secret report, published by the *Yediot Aharonot* on June 24, warned that continued violence in the Palestinian areas could bring about the collapse of the Palestinian Authority. The IDF later concluded that Israeli casualties necessary to retake the PA-controlled areas would be on the same scale as during the Lebanese War of 1982–85.[5]

At home Netanyahu was going through a bad patch. The resignation in mid-June of Dan Meridor, a Likud heavyweight, as finance minister showed that all was not well within his party—at a time when Labor, having elected a new leader, Ehud Barak, was feeling confident. Aware of Labor's low standing among Sephardi Jews, his first public appearance as party leader was in a Sephardi-dominated south Tel Aviv suburb. Opinion polls showed his popularity rating at 52 percent while Netanyahu languished at 26 percent. Buoyed by this, Labor pressed a no-confidence motion in the Netanyahu administration in the Knesset on June 25. Though it failed by 50 votes to 55, 11 of the 66 government supporters had stayed away.

A few days later came even more worrisome news. On June 28 the Arab traders in Hebron found their shopfronts plastered with a poster depicting Prophet Muhammad as a pig. The culprit was a young female settler, Tatiyana Suskin. This led to disturbances in Hebron and Nablus, with Hamas being in the forefront. On July 19, the birthday of Prophet Muhammad, Hamas held a 20,000-strong demonstration. The participants swore allegiance to the Prophet, and warned the Jewish settlers against "playing with fire," a reference to the sacrilegious poster. An indication of Hamas's popularity among the educated youth was illustrated by the fact that it controlled the student unions at the universities in both Hebron and Nablus.

The crisis could not have come at a worse time for Arafat. The PA's standing had taken a knock following the report on May 24 by its General Auditing Office that $326 million, or about 40 percent of the 1996–97 budget, had been misused or wasted by the PA ministries, which now employed 78,000 people, including 35,000 in the police and other security forces.[7] Arafat responded by appointing a National Commission of Inquiry: it concluded two months later that corruption existed at all levels of the PA. This happened at a time when a CPRS poll showed unemployment in the West Bank at 31 percent and in Gaza at 43 percent, with 52 percent saying their economic condition had deteriorated since the 1993 Oslo Accord—four times the figure for those whose condition had improved.

Arafat was warned by Fatah ranks that if he failed to provide leadership to the embittered populace Hamas would play that role and thus broaden its base. But had he given the green light to his Fatah followers to lead the resistance against Israel, he would have angered the Israelis and the US. So he used the discovery by the PA police on July 21 of a "bomb factory" in a Beit Sahour apartment to underline his commitment to combating terrorism. But neither Netanyahu nor Likud was impressed.

On July 24 the Jerusalem municipality, run by Ehud Olmert, a Likud leader, announced that it would allow Irving Moskowitz to build 132 housing units in the East Jerusalem district of Ras al Amoud (population 11,000) just outside the Old City. Moskowitz, an extremist Jewish American millionaire, claimed to have bought 4.2 acres of land from a Jewish religious trust. The local Palestinians said that the land had belonged to the local Ghul family for at least 46 years and that Moskowitz's purchase was fraudulent. Nonetheless the next day he announced his plans to establish a Jewish colony in Ras al Amoud. There was an uproar from the Palestinian side, still recovering from the shock of the Har Homa project. Netanyahu intervened. Accepting his advice, Moskowitz agreed to "postpone" his building plan. Netanyahu boasted that he had fulfilled his election pledge by compelling the PA leadership to take effective steps against terrorism.

On July 30 two suicide bombs exploded at the Mahaneh Yahuda Market in West Jerusalem, killing thirteen Israelis and the two perpetrators. Netanyahu expressed moral outrage and painted the Palestinian leaders as afraid to make tough decisions. His measures were unprecedentedly punitive. Besides the usual sealing of the borders of the West Bank and Gaza Strip with Israel, and the banning of movement by the Palestinians within these territories, he refused to hand over to the PA the tax revenues collected for it by Israel (accounting for nearly two-thirds of the PA's annual budget of about $800 million), froze all PA assets in Israeli banks, and ordered the quasi-independent Israel Broadcasting Authority to jam the Palestine Broadcasting Authority.

Almost all factions in Israel rallied around the government and blamed the PA and Arafat. They ignored the fact that Netanyahu's hardline policies—his flouting of the Oslo Accords in letter (failure to release the Palestinian prisoners, allow a safe corridor between the West Bank and Gaza, permit the opening of an airport in Gaza etc.) and in spirit (the Har Homa settlement)—were creating an environment in which the Islamists were gaining ground. President Ezer Weizman proved to be the exception. When asked whether the bombing was "related" to the proposed Jewish housing project in the Palestinian district of Ras al Amoud, he murmured "Yes."[8]

Arafat followed up his condolences to the relatives of the dead with a promise that the PA would confront "the terrorists... as we did in the past." His adviser on Israeli affairs, Ahmad Tibi, pointed out that "Not even the United States could eliminate terrorism. When Israel had total control of the West Bank and Gaza it could not do so either. Arafat too is not omnipotent, just as Netanyahu isn't."[9] On July 31 Arafat declared a state of emergency and austerity in the PA-controlled areas.

Israel's economic sanctions hurt the already impoverished Palestinians badly. Their GNP, according the World Bank, had dropped by 39 percent during 1995 and 1996. The situation was particularly grim in the Gaza Strip. Up to a quarter of its population of nearly a million lived at or below the poverty line of per capita income of $575 a year. The hopelessness of life, especially among the 30 percent unemployed, could well be imagined.

Such an environment provided plenty of recruits for the military wing of Hamas, the Qassam Brigade, which claimed responsibility for the latest explosion.

Beyond its immediate response to Ras al Amoud, the Qassam Brigade was pursuing a larger agenda. Through its lethal action, it showed that, contrary to his election promise, Netanyahu had failed to deliver the promised "peace with security" to Israelis. It also reckoned, rightly, that he would lean so heavily on Arafat that it would reduce the latter's popularity, thus opening up opportunities for Hamas.

The bombing occurred at a time when Palestinian attention was focused on the disclosures of corruption and mismanagement at high places in Arafat's administration. On July 29 the Legislative Council endorsed the report of the Commission of Inquiry in a vote of 56–4, and called on Arafat to dismiss the current cabinet and replace it with one composed of technocrats and professionals before the Council re-assembled on September 1, put the two accused ministers on trial for corruption, and observe separation of powers between the legislative, executive and judicial branches of the Palestinian Authority, as specified in the Basic Law passed by it (but left unsigned by Arafat). On August 1 when all but two (accused) members of the cabinet resigned, Arafat refused to accept their resignations. The voting, in which half of those either belonging to or allied with Fatah voted with the opposition, reflected the wide gap that had developed between Arafat and his own political base.

To repair the damage, Arafat decided to turn Israel's draconian anti-Palestinian measures into an opportunity to build bridges with his Islamist opponents. In the past, following suicide bombs, he had persecuted Islamists with a vengeance because he believed that the peace process would finally pay off. But now, feeling betrayed by Netanyahu, who wanted him to act as an agent of Israel with nothing in return, he had no incentive to repress Hamas and the Islamic Jihad. Interestingly, this view was shared by Major-General Amos Gilad, deputy head of Aman, Israel's military intelligence. Asked at a cabinet meeting if Arafat would cooperate in smashing the infrastructure of Hamas, Gilad replied that Arafat had no reason to do so as long as he believed that Israel was not complying with the Oslo agreements. "In other words, in your opinion, Arafat will never cooperate in the war against terrorists," said Netanyahu. "That is not what I said," replied Gilad. "I said he would not cooperate as long as he thinks there is no diplomatic process, and Israel is avoiding fulfilling its part of the agreements." This conversation, reported by Zeev Schiff, the highly respected military analyst of *HaAretz*, aptly illustrated Netanyahu's habit of twisting words and events to fit his views.[10]

On the Palestinian side, to set the new tone, the PA's security chief in Gaza, Muhammad Dahlan, announced that the PA's co-operation with IDF was limited to "clarifying the circumstances of the last terrorist act and who stands behind it," and that there would be no return to full co-operation "until Israel understands the limits of its power, control and right to impose orders."[11]

Arafat's chairing of National Unity Forum meetings where Hamas and Islamic Jihad leaders condemned Oslo, confirmed Netanyahu's belief that the Palestinian leader was not serious about ensuring peace with security for Israel. His office announced that the IDF would not redeploy in the nine percent of the West Bank it had promised to do by September 7 so long as the PA refused to repress the Islamic militants. Arafat alleged Netanyahu was using the pretext of security to abrogate the Oslo Accords.

This was the background against which, on September 4, three Islamist bombers blew themselves up at the Ben Yahuda center in West Jerusalem, killing four Israelis and wounding 192. Netanyahu was livid with anger and moral outrage. As before Arafat offered his condolences and repeated his promise to combat terrorism.

Yet there was a difference this time—in both camps. A new poll revealed Palestinian approval for suicide bombs had risen from 21 percent in February to 36 percent.[12] Those Palestinians who in the past criticized Hamas for damaging their future had now fallen silent, since they were getting nothing out of the peace process.

Among Jewish Israelis there was some soul searching, particularly when the next day, in a botched IDF operation in south Lebanon, twelve Israeli soldiers got killed. "Every Israeli is indoctrinated from early childhood that the Arabs understand only the language of force," wrote Haim Baram, a senior Israeli columnist. "Many realize now, perhaps for the first time, that aggression is a double-edged sword, that terror and fear can affect all of us, Arabs and Israelis alike."[13]

Dr. Nurit Peled-Elhanan, the mother of 14-year-old Smadar, killed in the Jerusalem bombing, spoke to *Ma'ariv* on September 7. "I still believe my father was right," said Peled-Elhanan, a daughter of Major-General Mattiyahu Peled, the chairman-founder of the Council for Israeli-Palestinian Peace, who died in 1995. "The latest bombings are a direct result of the repression, subjugation, humiliation and siege that Israel has inflicted upon the Palestinian people. Our government is guilty, doing its utmost to destroy the peace process. It brings upon us death and destruction. I do not criticize the terrorists. They are our creation. Almost every Palestinian family has been hurt by Israel, and they live in squalor and despair. The suicide bombers are our mirror... The government breeds the terrorists. It starts them off... It is the one stealing [Palestinian] land, destroying houses, uprooting trees, erasing villages. It's starving them, humiliating them, oppressing them."

A further, telling comment came from Leah Rabin, the widow of the assassinated Israeli premier. "I have doubts about how much terrorism can be uprooted," she told the IDF Radio on September 11. "We [Zionists] were also terrorists once, and they [the British army] didn't uproot us, and we went on dealing in terrorist activities. Despite all the efforts of the British army... we went on with terrorism."[14]

Rabin then accompanied the visiting US Secretary of State, Madeleine Albright, to lay a wreath at the site of her husband's assassination in Tel Aviv.

At the end of her trip, her first visit to the region, she castigated both sides. Referring to the Palestinian bombs, she said, "There is no moral equivalent between killing people and building houses." Criticizing Israel's withholding of tax returns from the PA, which made it "more difficult to have the kind of political environment that is necessary for this partnership to go forward," she said: "Israel should refrain from unilateral acts, including what Palestinians perceive as the provocative expansion of settlements, land confiscation, home demolitions and confiscations of IDs [in East Jerusalem]. We believe that a time-out for these kinds of unilateral actions will create a climate in which... an accelerated approach can succeed in achieving a final Israeli-Palestinian peace agreement."[15]

Hardly had Albright departed when three families moved in to establish a Jewish settlement in Ras al Amoud. Palestinians rioted, and Peace Now established a "peace camp," but to no avail. Eventually the settler families departed, leaving behind ten yeshiva students to guard and maintain the houses. Netanyahu declared himself "satisfied," and so did the US State Department.

Israel announced on September 23 that it had identified four of the five recent suicide bombers as West Bank residents, contradicting Arafat's claims that they had come from abroad, most likely from Lebanon. Arafat ended the limited PA co-operation with Israel concerning the bombings, and moved against Islamists.

The PA arrested 90 Islamists and shut down sixteen social, educational and charitable institutions run by Hamas, serving an estimated 40,000 Palestinian families.

But the Israeli policies that swelled the ranks of Hamas continued unabated. On September 24 Israel sanctioned 300 more housing units at the Efrat settlement near Bethlehem. The timing could not have been worse for the US State Department. "We are unhappy at that announcement," US Ambassador Martin Indyk told Israeli television. "The Secretary of State is up at the UN at the moment and she is engaged in an almost full-time effort to help Israel, because there is an effort under way to isolate Israel. And it is in that context this announcement comes and it undermines her efforts." (In mid-July the UN General Assembly voted 134–3 to condemn Israel for its non-cooperation with the Secretary-General's envoy concerning the Har Homa settlement.[17])

Soon world attention turned to Amman. On September 25 two Mossad agents carrying fake Canadian passports tried to inject a lethal chemical agent into the ear of Khalid Mashaal, a Jordanian citizen, and the secretary-general of Hamas in Jordan. They were apprehended by Mashaal's bodyguard. The rest of their eight-person unit escaped unscathed. Furious, King Hussein threatened to try the two in court and suspend diplomatic relations with Israel if it failed to supply the antidote for the chemical agent.[19] The next day then-Crown Prince Hassan took the evidence of Mossad's involvement to Netanyahu, and then presented it to President Clinton. In an interview with the London-based *Al Hayat* Hassan described the assassination attempt as "a reckless act carried out by a party that does not want the peace process to continue."

Netanyahu sent his infrastructure minister, Ariel Sharon, to Amman to strike a deal. In exchange for Jordan's release of the Mossad agents, Israel agreed to free Shaikh Ahmad Yasin, the Hamas leader, and 72 other Palestinian activists.[21] Yasin, a 61-year-old quadriplegic with medical problems, serving a fifteen-year sentence, was taken from his jail by helicopter to Amman, and then admitted to the hospital. Among his early visitors were King Hussein and Arafat. In a statement calling for a long struggle against the Israeli occupation of the Palestinian Territories, he showed that he had not given any promise to renounce violence to secure his release. His return to Gaza City on October 6 raised the morale of Hamas. Alluding to the current weakness of the Palestinians as well as the Arab world vis-a-vis Israel, Hamas' Rantisi stated that only suicide bombs redressed the balance. "Every Palestinian knows that without revenge attacks, massacres like that in Hebron in February 1994 [when Baruch Goldstein killed 29 Muslim worshippers] would happen more often."[22]

Referring to Yasin's statement that Islam forbade attacks on innocent civilians, Eric Silver of the London-based *Independent* asked him if "that meant that Hamas was calling off its campaign of terror in Israeli cities." Yasin replied, "Islam tells us not to attack civilians, but it also gives us the right to deal with an enemy the same way that he deals with us. If the enemy attacks civilians, killing them or demolishing their homes... it is our right to defend ourselves and deal with them as they deal with us." Asked if that included suicide bombs, Yasin replied, "We call them martyr operations. God has chosen the martyrs... By their acts they get closer to God." Regarding a ceasefire with Israel, Yasin said, "There could be a temporary truce if they [the Israelis] remove all that remains of occupation, including the settlements. They must release all Palestinian prisoners, open a safe passage between Gaza and the West Bank, and recognize a Palestinian state with its capital in Jerusalem. If we get our rights, the war will end. If we don't, the war will go on."[23]

For Netanyahu, having to free Yasin, the topmost leader of Hamas, an organization he had been relentlessly pressuring Arafat to crush, was a bitter pill to swallow. Earlier, Hamas had put Yasin's release on the top of its list of demands, and the Israeli government had summarily rejected it. Thus Netanyahu provided his critics with a stick to beat him with, especially when it emerged that he had repeatedly telephoned the Mossad chief, Danny Yatom, to execute Mashaal's assassination as a gift for the Jewish New Year (due on September 28) even though the unit assigned the job was not fully ready.[24] Netanyahu appointed a commission to inquire into the episode. Its report submitted in November failed to put the blame for the fiasco on Netanyahu. This disappointed his critics who regretted his unblemished escape from a major crisis once more.

But a far more serious crisis hit Netanyahu that month. At the Likud convention Netanyahu engineered a shift in how candidates were selected, that would benefit Netanyahu but outraged Likud's Knesset members. The resulting crisis was narrowly averted, but while most of the Likud leaders came to detest his lying, opportunistic ways, a growing number of ordinary Israelis began to admire his uncanny knack for extricating himself, from a string of disasters.

Earlier, Netanyahu tried to divert attention away from the deeply embarrassing Mashaal assassination fiasco by accepting the American proposal that the Israelis and the Palestinians confer at the highest level. On October 7 he met Arafat to explore Albright's idea of "time-out" for unilateral actions. But they found their differences unbridgeable. According to Netanyahu, "Time out means continued building in existing settlements to accommodate natural population growth." In other words, no change in Israel's plans for an additional 4,000 housing units in 60 Jewish settlements in the West Bank, not to mention 2,456 units at Har Homa in Greater East Jerusalem. Arafat's position, stated earlier by his PLO deputy, was that "Time out from unilateral steps means freezing all settlement construction in the Occupied Territories for the duration of the final status talks [until May 1999], and cessation of house demolitions, land confiscations, and removal of residency status from the Palestinians in East Jerusalem."[25]

Netanyahu's real thoughts emerged at a religious ceremony on October 21, where he crouched next to Rabbi Yitzhak Kaduri, the 107-year-old ultra-Orthodox rabbi and said, "The left wing has forgotten what it means to be Jews. They think we will put our security in the hands of Arabs—that Arabs will take care of us. We'll give them part of Israel, and they'll take care of us. Whoever heard of such a thing!"[26]

While Netanyahu was doing his utmost to wreck the peace process, Albright was working hard to make a success of the Fourth Middle East and North Africa (MENA) economic conference in Doha, Qatar, in mid-November—a vital part of the multilateral track of the 1991 Peace Conference in Madrid. But her efforts failed. Resisting her pressure, such leading pro-Western Arab states as Saudi Arabia, Egypt and Morocco (which had hosted two earlier MENA economic summits) kept away in protest at Netanyahu's continued stalling of the peace process. The Arab League, in 1997, had called on its members to freeze relations with Israel, and only six attended the MENA conference. Albright realized anew that Netanyahu's obduracy was hurting American national interests in the region; little wonder that in mid-November Clinton refused to see Netanyahu during the latter's visit to the US.

But Albright persisted with her effort to revive the peace process, working on a new security cooperation package. Arafat, having insisted earlier on linking security cooperation and advances on the peace process, now compromised unilaterally by instructing his security chiefs to participate in talks with their Israeli counterparts under the chairmanship of the CIA station chief in Tel Aviv. US State Department spokesman James Rubin announced that they were working on a document which would guarantee Israel security "24 hours a day, seven days a week and 52 weeks a year."

Pledging an "ongoing and continuous struggle against terror" especially against "the civilian infrastructure of those who abuse religion for the purpose of terror," the Memorandum of Understanding (MOU), drafted by the CIA station chief in consultation with top Israeli and Palestinian security officials, formally assigned the mediating role between the parties to the CIA.

But Netanyahu refused to sign it, primarily because it required Israel to keep its extremists under surveillance just as the PA was obliged to do, and secondarily because there was no mention of the PA extraditing "terror suspects" to Israel (partly because Israel was unwilling to concede reciprocity in this matter either). Muhammad Dahlan said, "His rejection is proof that Netanyahu does not want us to reach a security agreement... because then he would have no explanation [left] for foiling the Oslo agreements."[27]

As before Netanyahu gained time by offering contradictory pledges to the diverse segments of his constituency. He secured cabinet agreement for the second withdrawal "in principle" provided the PA kept its side of the bargain. He told the Jewish settlers that since there was only a slim chance of the Palestinians implementing the conditions listed in the Hebron Protocol, his government would be well justified to withhold further redeployment. To counter Washington's pressure, he orchestrated the appearance of full page advertisements in the American press in mid-December urging Clinton to go easy on Israel. By now the Americans for Safe Israel, Zionist Congress of America and American Jewish Committee had emerged as Netanyahu's uncritical supporters.

In early January 1998, Clinton invited Netanyahu and Arafat for separate meetings in Washington to discuss ideas to break the deadlock. Before leaving for the United States, Netanyahu visited an Israeli military base to receive the first of many American F-15I warplanes with all-weather, low-altitude navigation, night-targeting capabilities, and 2,390 mile range, enabling Israel to hit Iranian and Iraqi targets without refueling.

After the resignation of David Levy from his Cabinet, Netanyahu felt freer to pursue his own agenda on the peace process even to the point of standing up to the US president. On the eve of his meeting with Clinton on January 20, Netanyahu met with the Republican US House of Representatives Speaker Newt Gingrich, and the Reverend Jerry Falwell, both leading adversaries of the president. This was his way of telling Clinton that he had other friends in the United States.

Clinton failed to win any serious concessions from Netanyahu.

During his January 22 meeting with Clinton Arafat handed over a letter, detailing how the Palestine National Charter had been amended, and agreed to have the PLO Executive Committee endorse the revised Charter. Afterwards, Clinton said that the purpose of his talks with the two leaders was to see that Israel lived in security, and that "the Palestinians can realize their aspirations to live as a free people"—a statement on which Arafat was later to put an optimistic spin.

A figure of Israeli withdrawal from 10–13 percent of the West Bank as the combined total for the first and second redeployments—versus the aggregate Palestinian expectation of 60 percent—began to emerge in mid-February, when the attention of Washington and the regional capitals was turned to the escalating crisis between Baghdad and the UN concerning the post-Gulf War disarmament of Iraq.

Washington realized once again that its failure to revive the Israeli-Palestinian peace process, dormant for nearly a year, had diminished its standing in the Arab world. The traditionally pro-Washington Saudi Arabia played a key role in ensuring that the chairmanship of the Jeddah-based 55-member Islamic Conference Organization passed to Iran—a state opposed to the US-sponsored peace process in the Middle East. In February, with the exception of Kuwait, all Gulf states refused to let the Pentagon use their soil to bomb Iraq. As the US built up its armada for military strikes against Iraq, there was fear in Israel about possible chemical attacks by Iraq.

In contrast, a poll of Palestinians in mid-February revealed that 94 percent sympathized with Iraq (but not with President Saddam Hussein).[28] Yet the PA banned pro-Iraq demonstrations and cracked down on independent television stations. It took personal diplomacy by UN Secretary-General Kofi Annan to defuse the Iraq-UN crisis. The Clinton administration now tried to repair its dented prestige in the Arab world by leaking some of its ideas on the peace process—a freeze on Jewish settlements and a partial Israeli withdrawal from the West Bank, followed by final status talks. An irked Netanyahu warned on March 2, "An imposed solution is neither desirable nor viable. It simply will not happen." Soon after a dejected Arafat told the Legislative Council (PLC), "The Israeli government is willing to see the peace process become part of the past. Nothing is moving, everything is going backwards."[29]

Disappointed by the United States, Arafat tried to arouse European interest in reviving the peace process. The EU foreign ministers decided to use the forthcoming visit to Jerusalem of Robin Cook, the foreign secretary of Britain, then chairing the EU's presidency, to reassert the EU's role as custodian of the Madrid Peace Conference principle of land for peace, while maintaining its support for Washington's peace-making efforts. Adopting a six-point plan to unblock the peace process, they urged Israel to carry out "substantial, credible and urgent redeployments in the West Bank, and to halt all expansion of the settlements in the Occupied Territories, including East Jerusalem."

Arriving in Jerusalem on March 17, Cook made a point of visiting the Har Homa site at Jabal Abu Ghneim. Here he was greeted by the Israeli cabinet secretary, Danny Niveh. "Welcome to Jerusalem, the capital of Israel," said Niveh. "Well, it is also the capital of the Palestinians," replied Cook. When Amos Radin, the international adviser to Jerusalem municipality, tried to speak, Cook said, "I do not want to hear any briefing from you. I do not recognize your right to be here."[30] Then Cook drove down to an unscheduled site at the foot of Jabal Abu Ghneim, and met Salah Tamari, the PLC member for Bethlehem, and the spokesman for the PA's Emergency Committee for the Defense of the Palestinian Lands. "This is occupied territory since 1967; this is the playground of our youth and we remember it," Tamari said to Cook, who shook his hand. Cook then went to a Palestinian school near the Orient House in East Jerusalem, the local (unofficial) headquarters of the PLO, and laid a wreath to commemorate the Palestinian victims of the 1948 massacre at Deir Yasin. In protest Netanyahu cut short his meeting with Cook to a mere fifteen minutes, and canceled a dinner for him. Unrepentant, Cook said, "My visit to Har Homa was symbolic, to show that one of the biggest obstacles to the peace process is the expansion of settlements. And there has been no progress in the peace process since the decision to build Har Homa."

At the same time Cook stressed that the EU backed Washington's peace-making endeavors. Except that these were getting nowhere. Dissatisfied with the US proposal, centering on an Israeli withdrawal from thirteen percent of the West Bank, on March 10 Netanyahu offered to withdraw from nine percent. Clinton rejected Netanyahu's arguments. Concerned that publication of the American plan would undermine his case, Netanyahu galvanized his supporters in the United States to pressure the White House not to publish it.

"Israel's security needs will not be decided in Paris or London, or even in Washington," Netanyahu declared defiantly. This was the start of a battle of wills between him and Clinton, a confrontation which was to peak in May.

On March 20 *Yediot Aharonot* published the details of the American plan. Israel was required to redeploy from 13.1 percent of the West Bank in three stages, with only one percent to be transferred to A category and the rest to the B category. To compensate the Palestinians, who had been expecting a total of 60 percent, Israel was required to transfer 12 percent of the B area to the A area. In the first stage only two percent was to be transferred to the A category and that also only after the PA had banned anti-Israeli incitement, and agreed to investigate jointly any future incidents of such incitement, and disavowed those clauses of the

Palestine National Charter which called for Israel's destruction.

Ross's visit to the region in late March to sell the finalized American plan to Netanyahu failed. "The peace process is in trouble, we cannot continue this way," said Albright. "One option is that we simply remove ourselves from the process."[31] Her spokesman, James Rubin, summarized the overall situation bleakly. "There is no progress on the interim issues—the airport, the seaport, the industrial park [in Gaza]," he said on March 30. "There is no further redeployment. The Israelis believe that the Palestinians have not done all they could on the security front. There are steps that both sides are taking that we call unilateral steps that prejudge the final status, the permanent status, the ultimate negotiation. There are no multilateral negotiations of significance going on. There is no Syrian-Israeli peace track that's got life in it; same with Lebanon... There is a growing disillusionment among the people about what peace can bring. The permanent status talks haven't begun; they are scheduled to end in a year. These are excruciating issues that are going to take a long time to negotiate. That is why I characterized the peace process as being in dire straits."[32]

Just then US lawmakers joined the fray—on Netanyahu's side. On April 3, 81 US Senators called on Clinton not to change America's traditional role to "using public pressure against Israel," and warned him against publishing the US proposals.

The next day the PA cabinet and the PLO Executive Committee expressed its "positive attitude" to the US plan, urging Washington to publish it. They took this stance primarily because they had been told by then by Egypt, Jordan, the EU and the Israeli Labor Party that the American scheme was the only one that had any chance of success with Netanyahu. Ahmad Abdul Rahman, the PA's cabinet secretary, disclosed that the deal would involve the promise by Israel "not to confiscate land, demolish houses or build new settlements"—implying thereby that Israel would continue to expand the existing Jewish colonies. From then on any negotiations were essentially between Israel and America, and not the Israelis and the Palestinians. Due to Netanyahu's continued refusal to concede anything above nine percent of the West Bank, a stalemate ensued. He angered top American officials, but was unconcerned, knowing the overwhelming backing he had in the US Congress.

One of his uncritical and vocal supporters was Gingrich, whose wife, Marianne, had been vice-president of the Jerusalem-based Israeli Export Development Corporation since September 1994. While forwarding a letter addressed to President Clinton by a majority of the 435 House members on May 7, stating that Israel should not accept the US withdrawal plan, Gingrich accused Clinton of siding with the Palestinians against Israel, one of America's closest allies.[33]

This was a preamble to a week long confrontation. Both Gingrich and Netanyahu were encouraged by the fact that the Lewinsky sex scandal and the continuing Whitewater affair had made Clinton politically vulnerable.

On May 12 Albright became the focus of attack by the Netanyahu camp. "I think it is wrong for the American Secretary of State to become the agent for the Palestinians," said Gingrich. "Our job should be to get the two of them to a table where they find an agreement, not have us pressuring the Israelis to make an agreement."[34]

That day, having met a group of Jewish leaders, who told her that the administration had crossed the line, and that it was wrong of her to set an ultimatum, Albright spoke her mind at the National Press Club. "We had given the parties many weeks to consider our ideas in private," she said "In response primarily to Israeli requests, we allowed more time and then more time and then more time for our suggestions to be studied, considered and discussed." Denying that she had issued ultimatums, she added, "The goodwill that suffused the Mideast two years ago [i.e., before the May 1996 Israeli election] has dissipated and the impasse must be broken to see that the peace process does not die."[35]

Her spokesman explained on May 13 how the US proposals were nearer to the Israeli position than the Palestinian. "Frankly our ideas meet and are virtually identical with the essential elements of the desires of the premier of Israel —namely that we move to accelerated permanent status talks rather than wait for all the interim steps to be taken. Secondly, they require Chairman Arafat to move substantially down from the amount of land [30 percent in each of the two withdrawals] that he was looking to have redeployed to the Palestinian control. And, thirdly, that the redeployment takes place in parallel with an infrastructure to fight terrorism, and that is reciprocal and that is to occur in parallel with further redeployments."

In his meetings with the Israeli lobbyists, Netanyahu said that "We have a letter signed by US Secretary of State Warren Christopher [Albright's predecessor] that Israel, and Israel alone, will make the determinates of redeployment based on its security needs. It cannot be that Israel is expected to do things which will sacrifice and endanger its security." The *Washington Post* editorialized that Albright affirmed Christopher's broad pledge, but added, "It is in the nature of partnership that Israel should take Palestinian concerns into account while following the terms of its agreement, otherwise the peace process cannot move forward."[36]

But Netanyahu was in no mood to listen, especially when he was being so warmly fêted by US lawmakers. "Through a full day of courtesy calls [on May 14], fresh fruit and speech-making at the Capitol, Netanyahu was welcomed with the kind of full-throated, bipartisan heartiness that he rarely receives at home," reported *The New York Times*. "One remark by the committee chairman, Republican Representative Binyamin A. Gilman of New York, seemed to sum up the tone of the day. 'We want you to know that you're not only among friends, but among *mispocha* (Yiddish, family). Congress will continue to stand shoulder to shoulder with Israel regardless of the obstacles that others might place before her.'"[37]

The same day, Martin Indyk, Assistant Secretary of State for Near East, addressed the American Jewish Congress. "I would urge people who at this time of difficulty are worried about what President Clinton might or might not do, I would just urge them to remember that this president did not get the reputation in the Jewish community of being the most pro-Israel president in the history of the [Israeli-American] relationship for nothing, and that he did not achieve this reputation based on the kinds of policies that we have seen previous administrations pursue, and we will not do so," he said.[38]

Commenting on his US visit, Nahum Burnea, a leading columnist in the *Yediot Aharonot*, wrote on May 22: "Netanyahu has no peer when it comes to understanding the American arena. He knows that the US officials, from Albright down, are angry yet helpless. But he also knows he can always beat them because he owns the US Congress."

Gingrich, the third most powerful official in the US after the president and vice-president, was in a combative mood when he arrived in Jerusalem on May 23. In his meetings at the Knesset he reportedly criticized the Clinton administration, and goaded Netanyahu to challenge Clinton.

Referring to media reports that Gingrich was provoking the Israeli government to disagree with the US administration, Rubin, the State Department spokesman, said, "If true, those would be rather stunning comments that would undermine the efforts we are trying to make to advance America's national interests." He added, "I found particularly appalling and outrageous his [earlier] suggestion that the Secretary of State of the United States was an agent for the Palestinians. The Secretary of State is pursuing policies, at the direction of the President, that are designed to advance the national interests of the American people. She is an agent for the American people, and any suggestion that she is an agent of anyone else is an extremely provocative, unjustified and outrageous suggestion."[39]

Netanyahu kept up his defiance of the United States. In June his government allowed the Beit Orot Yeshiva on the Mount of Olives in the annexed Greater East Jerusalem to build 58 new housing units, and topped this with the launch of a plan for "strengthening Jerusalem's status" which would result in the city expanding its size by roughly half—by bringing several Israeli towns and settlements under Jerusalem's municipality. Albright told Netanyahu "that it [his action] was being viewed as something that was not helpful to the peace process, because in this very delicate environment, unilateral actions are not the kind that are helpful."[40] Netanyahu paid no heed.

Palestinian disenchantment with the peace process was growing rapidly. "Netanyahu is killing the idea of peace among Palestinians," said Saeb Erekat, the PA's chief negotiator. "In the Palestinian mind peace is now like a mirage." Soon US officials reached the end of their patience. "The Secretary [of State] has made it clear, and the President concurs, that there is a limit to the degree in which we can participate in a process that does not have utility," said the White House spokesman on July 10.

It was only then that Netanyahu agreed to negotiations between the Israeli and the Palestinian delegations. They met on July 18, 1998—after a gap of sixteen months. The Israelis proposed that all or most of the thirteen percent of the West Bank that the Americans had proposed for transfer to the PA be turned into "a nature reserve" where neither side should be permitted to build. The Palestinians rejected the idea.[41]

The continued stalemate damaged the standing of the PA and Fatah. In April, according to the CPRS poll, the ratings for Fatah declined to 41 percent. That is why in early May Arafat postponed the local elections due in June "until further notice." Erekat, minister of local government, attributed the decision to "unhelpful conditions"—namely, Israel's refusal to redeploy further. "The official explanation is unconvincing," said Professor Ziad Abu Amr, chairman of the PLC's political committee." The PA fears that the outcome will not be guaranteed in favor of it and Fatah."[42] This was so chiefly because Hamas was committed to participating in local elections, and in the prevailing environment these elections were most likely to turn into a referendum on the PA and Arafat, and reveal a sharp drop in their popularity.

The prestige of Hamas was rising not only at home but also in the region. This was highlighted by the reception that Shaikh Yasin received during his foreign tour. While in Cairo for medical treatment, he was invited by King Fahd to perform the *hajj* and undergo medical treatment in Saudi Arabia. At the hospital there he was visited by Crown Prince Abdullah, and in early April performed the *hajj* to Mecca. Addressing fellow-pilgrims at Mount Arafat, he appealed to them to help liberate Palestine and Jerusalem from Israel. His subsequent travels took him not only to Iran, Syria, Iraq and Sudan—regarded as pariah states by Washington—but also to the pro-US Kuwait, Qatar and the United Arab Emirates. Everywhere Yasin was warmly received by government officials as well as ordinary people. In Jeddah, he presided over an emergency meeting of Hamas leaders to discuss the mysterious assassination on March 29 of Muhyi al Din Sharif, a Qassam Brigade member, accused by Israel of involvement in the early 1996 bombings. The PA initially blamed the Shin Beth, but then claimed fellow Hamas activists had murdered Sharif and arrested five suspects, along with detaining fifty more activists.[4]

There were calls in Hamas to challenge the PA, but Yasin reportedly advised restraint, to avoid civil conflict and playing into the hands of Israel. At home, urged by the PLC and secular opposition groups, Hamas agreed to cooperate with the PLC inquiry. Thus Arafat managed to defuse the crisis.

Yet his main predicament, the PA's declining popularity, remained unsolved. One way would have been to respond positively to the PLC's demands—following the revelations of massive corruption in the PA ministries— of replacing the cabinet with a council of technocrats, and prosecuting the criminally corrupt ministers.

But Arafat did not do so. Instead, on August 5, he announced the appointment of nine more ministers, in the name of forging national unity. Hanan Ashrawi, the minister for higher education, resigned in protest. "The new cabinet reflects neither the attitudes nor the structural, procedural and personal reforms that are needed," she said. By concentrating on his Fatah supporters, Arafat won approval of his long-held strategy of placing nationalist resistance to Israel above internal democracy and honest administration.

It was noteworthy that four years after its founding the PA still lacked a constitution. The PLC had produced the Basic Law, setting out the powers and prerogatives of the executive, legislature and judiciary, and submitted it to Arafat for signature. But he had not done so. Apparently, Arafat did not want to function within a constitution which set clear limits to his powers. He wanted to continue ruling by a compendium of PLC legislation and arbitrary decrees, and persist in blurring the lines between the executive, legislative and judicial functions of the PA. This enabled him to defy judicial orders when it suited him (especially pertaining to the release of Islamist activists), exploit the unsolved assassinations of Palestinian militants in an expedient way, and violate civil or human rights if politically necessary.

The US State Department, which never loses an opportunity to trumpet the virtues of democracy and human rights, refrained from criticizing Arafat's refusal to approve and enforce a constitution drafted by an elected legislature. Nor did the European Union, by far the largest foreign donor to the PA. (During 1993–97 the EU had provided $1.2 billion to the PA chiefly for the infrastructure projects.)

Despite corruption, the benefits of this aid in the form of new, asphalted roads and improved or freshly installed sewerage—not to mention the Gaza International Airport at Dahaniya—was by 1998 apparent to a foreign visitor, especially in the Gaza Strip.[46] The PA also created monopolies on flour, fuel, cigarettes, cement, steel, and more in order to generate revenue for itself.

In external affairs there was one forum where the PLO chalked up successes: the UN General Assembly. In mid-March, under the emergency "uniting for peace" session, the Assembly condemned Israel for its Jabal Abu Ghneim settlement by 134–3 (Israel, US and Micronesia). Speaking on behalf of the EU, Britain's ambassador, Sir John Weston, deplored Israel's continued violation of the provisions of the Geneva Convention on Occupied Territories. In early July the PLO had another victory, when the General Assembly agreed, 124–4, to confer on the Palestine Observer Mission almost all the prerogatives of a member state, except a vote, including the right to sponsor resolutions on the Middle East, and speak on any other subject.[47]

On the eve of the fifth anniversary of the 1993 Oslo Accord, the last remnant of the multilateral cooperation—the Regional Bank for Development based in Cairo—collapsed. Washington decided to cut off funding; Israel denied the bank its mandate; and its internationally recruited staff departed. The practice of holding the annual Middle East and North Africa economic conference ended.

The peace camp in Israel was dejected. The rally by the Peace Now group in Tel Aviv on September 13, 1998 drew only 40,000 people, about a quarter of the number that had assembled three years earlier to hear, for the last time, Premier Rabin.

In contrast, the far right was feeling bullish. Fringe groups, including some banned in Israel and considered terrorist by the US, found support from Tzomet and the National Religious Party. Netanyahu's policies enhanced the influence and power of the Orthodox and ultra-Orthodox Jews at the expense of the Conservative, Liberal and Reform Jews, in the process alienating a substantial part of the predominantly non-Orthodox American Jews, who constitute two-thirds of the 8.5 million-strong diaspora. While Netanyahu proved himself to be a master in rallying Jewish American support at crucial moments in his dealings with Clinton, he also increased the degree of disenchantment with Israel that a growing number of American Jews had been feeling. The surveys by the American Jewish Congress showed that between 1997 and 1998 the percentage of US Jews who felt a bond with Israel fell from 75 to 58 percent. "Broad sectors of the American Jewish community that had already been intending to sever their ties with Israel in any case have felt [since 1997] more and more alienated from Israel as a result of its political, religious, cultural and ideological agenda," wrote Professor Avraham Ben-Zvi of the Jaffee Center for Strategic Studies at the Tel Aviv University. "It is a growing belief among a significant majority of American Jews that there is an unbridgeable gap that exists between their world view and the climate of perceived intolerance and dogmatism that has come to increasingly dominate religious and cultural life in Israel." Reflecting this trend, between 1988–97 the contribution of American Jews to the United Jewish Appeal fell from 60 to 40 percent.[49]

The increasing intolerance between secular and religious Jews in Israel had its mirror image in the Netanyahu administration's polices toward Israeli Arabs. The socio-economic gap between Arab and Jewish citizens remained as wide as ever. During 1995–98 the number of Arab professors rose by a mere 12—bringing the total to 24, out of some 6,000.[50] Joblessness among Arabs remained at twice the rate for Jews, showing no sign of decline. The 1996–97 data revealed that Arab children constituted 31 percent of Israel's poor children though Arabs accounted for only 16 percent of the national population.

There was a reversal of the progressive policies adopted by the previous Labor-led administration. During 1992–96, when the education ministry was run by the leftist Meretz, it was decided to change the curriculum and textbooks for the Arabic sector in Israeli schools. With the change of government and Zevulun Hammer of the NRP as the new education minister, "there is little prospect of our manuscripts being published," said Dr. Adel Manna, who had been commissioned to write new history texts.[51]

Two days of clashes between stone-throwing youths and the Border Police that left hundreds injured in the area around Umm al Fahm, highlighted the tensions that existed between Arab citizens and the government, and culminated in a general strike by Israeli Arabs on September 29, 1998.[52]

The strike protested an IDF order issued in May, prohibiting Israeli Arabs from entering their nearby lands and expressed the fear that expropriation of the land for settlement construction was next. "We fear that they are planning to build Jewish settlements on our lands, thus realizing an old housing ministry plan to build a large Jewish city in the area," said an Arab farmer.[53]

Israeli Arabs were further alarmed by the summary of the secret report by Motti Zaken, the prime minister's adviser on Israeli Arabs, published in the *Ma'ariv* on August 16, which described Israeli Arabs as "a strategic threat" to Israel.

There were strategic decisions that Netanyahu had taken to improve his chances of re-election, including appointing Sephardi officials to replace retiring Ashkenazim and Likud members to replace retiring liberals.

These decisions were important as far as they went. But none of them came close to the subject that lies at the very root of the Israeli identity—relations between Israelis and Palestinians. How Netanyahu fares in that field will be the chief criterion by which he will be judged by voters. And there the Wye River Memorandum is likely to be a considerable factor.

The Wye River Memorandum and After

In late September 1998 Albright met separately with Netanyahu and Arafat to persuade them to see President Clinton jointly. This brought Netanyahu and Arafat to the same table after a lapse of a year—a sign of a revival of the peace process. They arrived in Washington on October 15 to finalize a deal. In the interim, to satisfy the far right elements in his coalition, Netanyahu had elevated Ariel Sharon to foreign minister with special responsibility to conduct the final status talks with the PLO.

The venue of the Israeli-Palestinian negotiations was the sprawling Wye River Conference Center set on an old plantation near Washington. The talks, scheduled to end on October 18, dragged on until the 23rd. Working closely with Albright, Clinton arrived daily by helicopter to check the progress. Emulating President Carter's meetings between Israel and Egypt, the Americans conferred alternately with the two sides to bridge the gaps. But there were significant differences from the successful Camp David talks. One was the crucial role played publicly by the CIA director, George Tenet, in the negotiations. Further, unlike Carter, Clinton engaged other American and foreign leaders when the negotiations got bogged down (usually because of Netanyahu's obstructionist attitude). First he included Vice President Al Gore, whose standing as a pro-Israeli politician is even higher than his own, to help break the impasse. On October 20, Clinton called in the late King Hussein, then undergoing cancer treatment in Minnesota, to help reconcile the parties.

Twice the talks seemed on the verge of failure, but survived to end in success. On October 19, a Palestinian threw two grenades at the bus station in Beersheba, injuring 66 Israelis. The negotiations resumed only after Netanyahu had wrung some concessions from Clinton in private. The second crisis came on the morning of October 21, which happened to be Netanyahu's birthday. The previous night Albright phoned Netanyahu to tell him the United States had extracted "as detailed and complete a Palestinian security plan as it thought possible," and that the president wanted to know whether to fly to Wye to finish the job. "We want your comments by the morning," she told him.[55]

Netanyahu was not satisfied with the US-brokered package partly because Arafat refused to agree to extradite the Palestinian suspects to Israel. On the morning of the 21st, he and his delegation began packing their bags and loading them in the vans. According to the official US version, Clinton was unmoved, and told Netanyahu that he had ready a statement to read to the press about the failure, and then the Israeli leader backed down. But, as it emerged later, he stayed on only after he had extracted a further price from Clinton, again in private.

The concessions he won covered the future behavior of Washington in the peace process, monetary help to the Jewish state to "consolidate" the peace, and a further deepening of strategic and military ties between Israel and America. In four letters by Edward Walker, the US ambassador to Israel, to the Israeli cabinet secretary, Washington made an implicit promise that it would not repeat what it did to achieve the Wye Agreement. More specifically, it promised not to adopt any position or express any view about the size of the next Israeli redeployment in the West Bank; reaffirmed that it "opposes and will oppose" a unilateral declaration of Palestinian statehood; agreed that "only Israel can determine its own security needs;" and promised not to attempt to convene another decision-making summit conference "without the prior agreements of both parties."[56] Clinton and Netanyahu agreed that the latter would seek $1.2 billion from Washington to consolidate peace—

bypass-road building, fortifying Jewish settlements, and relocating IDF facilities—and that the former would recommend this to the US Congress.

The top prize for Netanyahu, however, was to be a legally binding Memorandum of Agreement to enhance Israel's "defensive and deterrent capacity," and to upgrade the already extensive strategic, military and technical cooperation between it and the United States. The Agreement requires the United States to consult Israel immediately as to what support or assistance, "diplomatic or otherwise" it can lend Israel in the face of "direct threats to Israel's security arising from the regional deployment of ballistic missiles of intermediate range (500 kilometers/310 miles) or greater." While legally binding, the document does not require the US Senate's approval as it is less than a defense treaty.[57]

In contrast, for the several concessions Arafat made, including accepting Netanyahu's refusal to freeze settlement construction, all he got was a promise of a doubling of US annual grants of $75 million.

Yet the next day, October 22, another impasse developed between the two camps. Clinton called on King Hussein to address the parties in the evening. In a ten minute speech, he made a personal plea for peace, and left the room.

Following a 21-hour non-stop session between Clinton, Netanyahu and Arafat, when they went through the agreement line by line, the Wye River Memorandum was ready for signature on October 23. By then Clinton had invested 80 hours in the negotiations with the two delegations. In late afternoon the document was signed at the White House by Netanyahu and Arafat, witnessed by President Clinton and King Hussein.

Several factors led to the success at Wye. Arafat, the weaker party, had hitched his wagon to the US, and was anxious to show some achievement, territorial and financial, to shore up his diminished popularity among Palestinians. He was aware too that the latest CPRS opinion survey had shown that armed attacks against Israelis had the backing of 51 percent of respondents, the highest figure since the poll was introduced in early 1994. Netanyahu started with the belief that his previous tactics of obstruction and prevarication would succeed as before, and he would be able to blame others for the failure of the talks. But what led him to change course—reluctantly and after squeezing the maximum possible concessions from Clinton—were the prospect of Arafat declaring a sovereign state on May 4, 1999; Clinton's determination not to let him play for time again; and the timing of the summit—on the eve of the US Congressional election when representatives and senators were busy campaigning, and most Jewish leaders were too engrossed in electioneering to rally support for Netanyahu. So the Israeli leader faced the stark choice between rejecting the deal and facing condemnation by the opposition at home and the international community abroad, or accepting it at the risk of dividing his coalition. He chose the latter.

Clinton had the most compelling motivation. He badly wanted success in foreign affairs, especially in the Middle East where public interest is high. He reckoned that if he succeeded at Wye his party would do well in the elections, and that would reduce drastically the chance of his impeachment due to the Monica Lewinsky sex scandal. When the Democrats did well on November 3, the prospect of Clinton's impeachment seemed to recede considerably.

Above all that hung the prospect of Arafat declaring an independent State of Palestine in early May. "Mr. Clinton decided that with the May 4 deadline to implement the Oslo looming—and violence possible if that deadline is missed—passivity was more risky than a failed summit," a senior aide to the president told the *Washington Post*.[58] Little wonder that there was much relief all around when the deal was finally clinched.

At the signing ceremony glowing tributes were paid to Clinton. "He is a warrior for peace," said Netanyahu. "He has this ability to maintain a tireless pace and to nudge and prod and suggest and use a nimble and flexible mind to truly explore the possibilities of both sides, and never just one side. That is a great gift, I think, a precious one and unique one, and it served us well." Netanyahu's words served Clinton well, especially among Jewish American voters and cash contributors.

Arafat was the only one to make points of substance. Alluding to UN Security Council Resolutions 242 and 338, and the principle of land for peace, he said that these should apply to Syria and Lebanon as well. "We have agreed to stop unilateral steps," he added. "And the final status talks are to be finished by the stipulated date of May 4, 1999." He revealed that he was in daily contact with "brothers [President] Mubarak and [his Foreign Minister] Amr Mousa." Among those he thanked were not only Egypt and Jordan but also Russia (the co-sponsor of the Madrid Peace Conference), China, Japan (a substantial aid-donor to the PA), the Non-Aligned Movement, and the European Union. While referring to the Palestinians as "an independent nation," he called for the Palestinian refugees' return to "Palestine." Finally, addressing Israelis, he said, "Your security is our security."

The Wye River Memorandum, effective from November 2, was to be implemented in three phases over a twelve-week period.

A) *Land for Security, and Palestinian Prisoner Release*

Phase I: Weeks 1-2. The PA and "other elements" (meaning the CIA) will prepare a security plan which will include the arrest by the PA of 30 "wanted Palestinian murderers" listed by Israel. The PA will issue a decree outlawing incitement against Israel and Israelis, and a joint Israeli-Palestinian committee will be formed to consider Israel's complaints on this issue. Also the PLO Executive Committee will meet to start the process of amending the Palestine National Charter. If the Palestinians meet these conditions, Israel will complete the first IDF redeployment, and transfer one percent of the West Bank from category C (full Israeli control) to A (full PA civilian control), and two percent from C to B (joint control). It will release the first batch of 250 Palestinian prisoners.

Phase II: Weeks 3-6: The PA will complete a plan for the collection of illegal weapons in its areas, and submit it to the CIA.[59] The PA will also prepare a full list of its armed policemen for the CIA. And the PLO's Central Council will assemble to set the ball rolling for the annulment of the Palestine Charter's objectionable clauses, culminating in a meeting—during Week Six—of "the members of the Palestine National Council" as well as the members of the PLO's Central Council, the Palestinian Legislative Council and the PA cabinet to reaffirm

Arafat's January 22 letter to President Clinton, nullifying each of the Charter's provisions that are inconsistent with the PLO's commitments to renounce terror, and to recognize and live in peace with Israel. Then Israel will transfer five per cent from C to B, and bring that total to seven percent—thus completing nothing more than what it had offered in March 1997 to the Palestinians, which they had rejected summarily as insultingly small. Also Israel will release the second batch of 250 Palestinian prisoners.

Phase III: Week 7-12. The PA will start collecting illegal weapons. Israel will receive a report from the CIA, confirming that the Palestinian police has been reduced from 40,000 to 24,000 as set in the Oslo Accords.[60] Only when Israel is satisfied that the PA police force has been reduced to the agreed size, will it free the final batch of 250 Palestinian prisoners, and transfer another five percent of the West Bank land from C to B, and 14.2 percent from B to A.

If all proceeds as scheduled, Israel will have transferred a total of 13 percent of the West Bank to the PA, with three per cent to be maintained as a nature reserve. Overall the PA will then have full civilian control over 18 percent of the West Bank and joint control over 23 percent. This would leave 59 percent under exclusive Israeli control, several-fold more than what the Palestinians had estimated. In late 1997, Ahmad Tibi, adviser to Arafat on Israeli affairs, said that "after the implementation of the third redeployment [due by August 31, 1998], according to the agreements, all that would remain under Israeli occupation would be... border, East Jerusalem, settlements and specified military locations. These areas, according to our position, comprise only 11 percent of the West Bank. Everything else by then should have been transferred to the PA."[61]

B) *Other Issues*

1. A joint Israeli-Palestinian committee will be set up to discuss the third IDF redeployment in the West Bank.

2. There will be a "timely opening" of the international airport of Gaza to be run jointly by Israel and the PA, with Israel controlling the airspace, and administering security, including the right to vet passenger lists and check passports, and immigration.

3. The two sides will "discuss" the issue of a Gaza seaport with a view to "concluding a deal within 60 days."

4. The parties will negotiate the creation of a 32-kilometer (20-mile) long safe passage corridor for the free movement of Palestinians between the West Bank and Gaza Strip "as soon as possible."

5. Under "Unilateral Actions" the operative sentence reads, "Neither side should initiate or take any steps that will change the status of the West Bank and Gaza prior to the negotiations on the final borders and the powers of the Palestinian entity."

As expected, the ultra-nationalists in Netanyahu's coalition condemned the "territorial compromise" concerning the West Bank. On the defensive, Netanyahu claimed that the Wye Agreement plugged holes in the 1993 Oslo Accord which was "like Swiss cheese," and added, "My mission to Maryland last week was to seek damage control, not peace-making." He overlooked the polls showing 72–80 percent support for the Wye Memorandum among Jewish Israelis.

Netanyahu reverted to his usual prevarication and obfuscation while dealing with his commitments to the Palestinians, and speedy action to placate his far right supporters. On October 26 he told the IDF Radio that Israel had given no promises to freeze Jewish settlements in the West Bank, and would continue to build "for the Jews" in Jerusalem and adjacent to the existing West Bank settlements. He revealed that in the two years of his premiership 12,000 new housing units for Jews had been built, 90 percent of them in the Jerusalem area. On the morning of November 1, the residents of Ras al Amoud awoke to see the 4.2 acre plot, "owned" by Irving Moskowitz, cleared and fenced by barbed wire.

During the next few days Jewish settlers started new construction on eight West Bank hilltops at sites about a mile from the existing settlements while the IDF confiscated 1,130 acres of Palestinian land near the PA-controlled Jenin. Washington offered verbal criticism while Netanyahu found excuses to delay the formal application of the agreement due on November 2.

In contrast, Clinton acted with speed to fulfill his pledges to Netanyahu. Over the weekend of October 31–November 1, they signed the promised agreement to enhance Israel's strategic and deterrent capacity. Uzi Arad, an adviser to Netanyahu, told the *Yediot Aharonot*, "this is the first US-Israel defense agreement signed at the presidential level, and which talks not only about preserving Israel's qualitative edge [over the Arab countries] but also contains a US commitment to reinforce Israel's ability to defend itself against missiles and also strengthen its ability to deter a potential aggressor... In certain spheres, this elevates the US-Israeli cooperation to the level existing between the US and Britain or other NATO states."[62]

Albright lost no time in urging the Arab states to reward Netanyahu for the "sacrifices he had made" by unfreezing their relations with Israel and reviving the multilateral track of the peace process. But she found the response from the traditionally pro-Washington North African and Gulf states "standoffish." The Arab world was particularly incensed by Netanyahu's declaration that he had made no promise to freeze Jewish settlements.

The Palestinians shared the skepticism. A CPRS poll showed that only 19 percent thought Israel would carry out the Wye agreement. While Arafat tried to present it as a success for the Palestinians, 57 percent thought Israel gained more than the PA. On October 29 the Palestinian leadership approved the Wye Memorandum without a vote. So unlike in the Israeli cabinet, where the debate on the agreement was long and acrimonious, the discussion on the Palestinian side was a ritual, the "leadership" merely acting as a rubber-stamp of Arafat.

Prominent among the critics was Ahmad Yasin. "Hamas's military wing will cause more Israeli blood to flow no matter what obstacles are thrown up by the CIA in conjunction with the security services of Netanyahu and Arafat," he said. "As long as there is Israeli occupation and terrorism, resistance will continue."[64]

Significantly, 54 percent of Palestinians opposed the Israeli security provisions of the Wye Memorandum. There was also disquiet about the involvement of the CIA.

"I am afraid our entire security apparatus will become an extra-territorial department of the CIA," said Husam Khader, a Palestinian legislator.[65]

Though the participation of the CIA director, George Tenet, in the Wye negotiations, and his offer to deploy CIA agents to monitor the PA's security guarantees, received much publicity, very little was known of the CIA's secret links with the PA.

These started in late 1995 with the CIA training Palestinian security officials at the counter-intelligence center, run by Rajoub's Preventive Security Service in Jericho. They tightened after the 1996 bombs in Jerusalem. Tenet, then deputy director of the CIA, met Arafat on one-to-one basis, and after the mini-intifada of September 1996, the CIA station chief in Tel Aviv and his subordinates began mediating disputes between the Israeli and Palestinian security services and offering advice. Just then the Paris-based *Al Watan al Arabi* disclosed that the CIA was training Palestinian security forces at its base in North Carolina. The Israelis—whose Mossad had signed a clandestine cooperation agreement with the CIA in 1951—remained content to cooperate with the Americans. In the words of an Israeli official, "The CIA's ongoing counterterrorism efforts in the region make it uniquely situated to judge Israeli and Palestinian claims regarding the arrest, imprisonment and release of suspected terrorists."[66]

The latest accord favored Israel. According to George Friedman, an American intelligence expert, the intelligence-sharing arrangement would enable Israel to manipulate it to its advantage and to access US intelligence sources and methods in the region. By contrast, continued Friedman, the Wye Memorandum exposed Arafat to being labeled "a CIA agent," especially when "he publicly acknowledges that the CIA has completely penetrated his [security] apparatus."[69] Given the history of success that Israeli intelligence agencies had in penetrating the PLO at the top,[70] the formal introduction and legitimization of the CIA's involvement in a small, impoverished Palestinian community can only result in the narrowing of options for its leadership and political-administrative entity.

When the vote on the Wye River Memorandum was finally taken on November 11, the Netanyahu government approved the agreement by eight votes to four with five abstentions, with Sharon voting for it. But approval came with a list of unilateral conditions. "We reserve the right to apply Israeli law to the security areas, the Jerusalem area, and the area of settlement, and to other things that are accepted as vital national interests of Israel," Netanyahu declared. "We took our decision while respecting three principles—security, reciprocity and a determination to maintain the Land of Greater Israel. It is hard for us to give up even one square centimeter of land." Besides reaffirming his resolve to continue "strengthening Jewish settlements in the West Bank and Gaza," he repeated a condition imposed by the cabinet: the third redeployment would not exceed one per cent of the West Bank. The next day, to further placate the ultra-nationalists in the Knesset he invited construction bids for 1,025 housing units at Har Homa, and repeated his pledge, "By the time I have finished my tenure [in 2000] there will be homes in Har Homa."

Netanyahu claimed that the new accord had lowered the Palestinian expectations regarding the final status to the point that the PA would eventually accede to "Israel's vital interests in Judea and Samaria," which, in his view, entailed "annexation of the Jordan Valley and the 144 Jewish settlements and a three kilometer wide security zone along the Green Line." This was in addition to Israel keeping Jerusalem as its "eternal and undivided capital." Dismissing the deadline of November 16, he said that the first withdrawal would take place only after the Knesset's approval of the agreement. When Arafat protested at these unilateral actions, Netanyahu replied haughtily that was the only way his government was prepared to implement the Wye Agreement.

This was a direct provocation. Arafat replied in kind, on an appropriate occasion, November 15, 1998—the 10th anniversary of the declaration of independence by the Palestine National Council. Addressing a rally in Nablus, he said, "We will brandish our guns to extract our right to pray in Jerusalem... because Jerusalem was, is and will continue to be our capital, irrespective of their [Israelis'] whims." Later he said, "We will accept nothing short of an independent Palestinian state with Jerusalem as its capital," and reaffirmed his pledge "to declare our state on 4th of May next year as is our right."

Israeli leaders were incensed. That day, addressing the members of the secular ultra-nationalist Tzomet group, Sharon said, "Go and get the hilltops. Whoever gets there first will have the hills and those you don't grab will end up in their hands." Immediately the Jewish settlers occupied several hilltops near Nablus and Ramallah. At the same time IDF bulldozers uprooted thousands of Palestinian olive groves to build twelve bypass roads, to "protect" the Jewish settlements expected to be "isolated" by the IDF redeployment by enabling the settlers to bypass the Palestinian communities. Like the bypass roads built hurriedly on the eve of the May 1996 elections, the present roads were intended to destroy geographical continuity between the Palestinian areas.

Arafat told visiting German President Roman Herzog on November 17, "Any problems concerning final-status negotiations will be resolved through amicable and peaceful ways and through negotiations, and not through any other means. We will continue to cooperate to confront violence and the use of force."[73]

The next day the Knesset passed the Wye Memorandum, with the conditions attached by the cabinet, by 75 votes to 19, with nine MKs abstaining and 17 absences, including eight ministers. Of the nine ministers voting, two voted against. Nearly three quarters of the Yes votes came from the opposition. The tone of the deliberations, set by Netanyahu, was summarized by Walid Sadiq, an Arab MK, thus: "Instead of the prime minister speaking of joy, peace and happiness, what we heard were words of arrogance and of humiliation for the Palestinian people." Summing up the dominant feeling among the MKs, David Levy stated, "I can say with certainty that this agreement could have been obtained a year ago. And we wouldn't be left, so many of us, with a bitter taste in our mouths." On the rejectionist side, the secretary of the Eretz Israel Front, Michael Kleiner, said, "They [the Netanyahu government] broke the ideological backbone of their movement. The whole exercise of Likud was based on keeping the Eretz Israel undivided. Now what is the difference between Likud and Labor?"[74]

On November 20, the IDF withdrew from 220 square miles in the Jenin-Nablus area. While Arafat claimed that "We managed to shatter the slogan of the Israeli extremists regarding 'the Greater Israel,'" Israeli Defense Minister Mordechai lamented "the slicing up of the land of our fathers," explaining that "in our return to our homeland after 2000 years of exile, changes had occurred there, and another population dwelled in it"[76]—a belated acknowledgment of a glaring fact of history and demography.

On November 24, after Israel's delay of eighteen months, the international airport at Dahaniya in the Gaza Strip, costing $250 million, was finally inaugurated, with planes arriving from Cairo, Amman, Casablanca, Madrid and Amsterdam on the first day. But the Israelis enforced security so strictly that Yasser Arafat's wife, Suha, described the airport as "a branch of Ben Gurion [airport near Tel Aviv] in Gaza."[77]

In any case, the Gaza airport proved to be the last positive development from the Wye Memorandum, for the Palestinians. The immediate point of friction between the two sides concerned the Palestinian prisoners released by Israel as part of the deal. Of the 250 prisoners freed nearly half were common criminals. This upset not only the PA but also ordinary Palestinians, especially those related to the 2,400 still in Israeli jails. Demonstrating outside the Red Cross and Red Crescent offices, they accused Arafat of letting down his own "soldiers." And they often clashed with the IDF troops manning road blocks outside the PA-controlled areas. The popular protest put Arafat on the spot, aware that the wording on the prisoners in the Wye Memorandum was vague. He claimed that Netanyahu had agreed to free political prisoners as had happened before, and that Clinton was witness to this. Netanyahu denied this, accusing Arafat of lying that he had promised to release "murderers of Israelis." By ignoring the street protest Arafat risked losing popular backing at a crucial time. And by backing it he risked providing Netanyahu a pretext to freeze or annul the two remaining IDF pullbacks.

Netanyahu was anxious to save his office, which was becoming increasingly untenable. To secure the support of the NRP's nine MKs for a crucial vote on December 7 Netanyahu adopted a tough line with the PA and instructed his foreign minister, Ariel Sharon, to inform Albright that Israel was suspending the implementation of the Wye Agreement due to the Palestinian violations.

On December 6, 2,400 Palestinian prisoners, including 900 Fatah members, started an open-ended hunger strike. The next day Fatah supporters in Nablus, demonstrating for the prisoner release, clashed with the PA police. The Americans proposed a trilateral committee to go through the prisoners' list, and decide who should be released. Yet despite the crisis Netanyahu rejected the American compromise. Faced with such obduracy, the Palestinian prisoners ended their hunger strike to "sweeten" Clinton's visit to Gaza on December 15.

Clinton's impending trip also impacted Israeli politics. To ensure that the Knesset was not debating a no-confidence motion against the government during his visit, the MKs decided to postpone the final vote on the subject.

On December 7 Netanyahu attempted a series of moves to keep his government intact. It was difficult; by suspending implementation of the Wye Agreement,

Netanyahu had alienated himself decisively from the left and center-left, and by committing himself in writing to further withdrawals from the West Bank, and granting Washington the role of an arbiter, he had, in the eyes of the far right, committed the ultimate betrayal. "Netanyahu discovered that one cannot stand in the air and on the ground at the same time," wrote Sima Kadmon in the *Yediot Aharonot* on December 8. "His tricks were seen for what they are one time too many."

The hard right in Israel was hostile to the US president's December 13–15 visit—especially when it was divided equally between Israel and the PA-administered territories—with Rafi Eitan of Tzomet advising him to stay away, Yitzhak Levy of the NRP calling him "a dupe," and Knesset Speaker Dan Tichon announcing that he would boycott all the public functions organized in Clinton's honor. Fearing heckling by a substantial body of MKs, the cabinet decided not to invite Clinton to address the Knesset.

So Clinton had to settle for addressing a rally of Israeli youths in West Jerusalem on his first day. "One thing and only one thing is predestined: you [Israelis and Palestinians] are bound to be neighbors," Clinton said. "The question is not whether you will live side by side, but how."[80]

His forthcoming visit to the Gaza Strip had already created controversy in Israel. On his return home after the Wye Agreement, Netanyahu had claimed credit for securing Clinton's consent to attend the Palestine National Council session to witness its annulment of the anti-Oslo Accords articles in its Charter. But when his aides realized that Clinton's address to the PNC would be widely seen as boosting the idea of a Palestinian state, he tried to backtrack. He now said that the suggestion had come from Clinton, and that he was in no position to oppose it. (Actually, at Wye he had welcomed Clinton's offer, believing it would pressure Arafat to amend the Palestine National Charter.) In desperation, Netanyahu dissuaded Clinton from flying Air Force One to the Gaza airport, but failed to persuade him to land his helicopter away from the airport as well.

On December 15, Bill Clinton and his wife arrived at the Gaza airport—its control tower draped in a vast US flag—which he inaugurated officially. He received full treatment, a red carpet and a guard of honor. At a meeting for the Palestinian leaders and legislators he said, "For the first time in the history of the Palestinian movement, the Palestinian people and their elected representatives now have a chance to determine their own destiny on their own land. America wants you to succeed, and we will help you create the society you deserve." He expressed sympathy for the Palestinian people who, he said, had suffered "a history of dispossession and dispersal," and called on Israelis to develop "understanding" of their plight.[81] The next day some Israeli commentators equated Clinton's speech with the 1917 Balfour Declaration promising a national homeland for the Jews. "For the first time ever, Clinton equated the suffering, fears, and aspirations of Palestinians with the suffering, fears and aspirations of Israelis," wrote columnist Nahum Barnea in the *Yediot Aharonot*. "At least for some it was an unpalatable declaration."

Accompanied by Arafat, the Clintons went to the hall where the PNC had been in session since morning. As Hillary Rodham Clinton walked through the door there was a thunderous applause. The Palestinian delegates remembered the statement she had made in early May that "the territory the Palestinians currently inhabit, and whatever additional territory they will obtain through peace negotiations, should be considered, and will evolve, into a functioning modern state."[82]

The 950 delegates included most of the 700-strong PNC and the 124-strong Central Council as well as all of the PLC (87 members) and the PA cabinet (34 members) along with the leaders of the organizations of Palestinian students, women, trade unions, professionals etc. Arafat appealed to the assembly "from my heart, for the sake of the Palestinian state and for peace in the Holy Land," to approve the Charter's revision by standing up and raising a hand. All but a few dozen did do so.[83]

Applauding the vote, Clinton said, "You have sent a powerful message not to the government but to the people of Israel." Clinton listed the rewards of the peace process: elections and self-government; Israeli troop redeployments; relations with the United States, and a Palestinian airport. On the negative side, he referred to "the Israeli restrictions on commerce, land confiscations and Israeli settlements." He equated the pain of the Palestinian children whose fathers were in Israeli jails to the pain of the Israeli children whose fathers became victims of the terrorism. Summing up, he said that he sought "legitimate rights for Palestinians" with "real security for Israel."[84]

But, according to a CPRS poll, the PNC vote was at variance with Palestinian opinion. At the time of the PNC's first Charter revision in April 1996, only 34 percent opposed the amendments, now 54 percent did so (with 37 percent backing the revision). Whether Clinton's journey to Gaza was a signal of US recognition of Palestinian self-determination, only 38 percent said Yes, and 56 percent No. (The majority proved right when Clinton said so to Arafat in March in Washington.)[85]

Netanyahu expressed satisfaction with the PNC decision, but did not consider it enough to reverse his government's decision to freeze a further West Bank pull-back by December 18 as required by the Wye Accord. Applauding the vote, Barak accused Netanyahu of pushing Washington into a closer relationship with the Palestinians at the expense of the privileged relationship between Israel and America. The next day Clinton tried to get Netanyahu to reverse his stance on troop pull-back, but failed. With this, the Wye Memorandum entered a period of suspended animation.

So, at the end of a three day trip, Clinton left with the peace process teetering and mistrust seething between Israelis and Palestinians, and a new tension arising between him and Netanyahu.

On December 20, the Israeli cabinet added two further conditions for the PA to meet to gain Israel's enforcement of the Wye Accord: accepting the principle of reciprocity; and collecting and destroying the illegal weapons held by PA officials and civilians, and the detention of murderers, and cooperation with Israel in combating terror, and honoring all other obligations under the Wye Agreement.

The next day the Knesset annulled the electoral law specifying direct election of the prime minister after the next such poll. Then it rejected the government's ultimatum to the PA concerning the Wye Memorandum. Opposing the motion, Barak said, "The prime minister won't teach me about Israel's security. Agreements must be honored. Trust must be renewed. This government has abandoned the peace process which it signed up to [implement]."[86]

Barak decided not to pursue the pending no-confidence motion. He regarded the 60-day period to form a new government insufficient to make an impact on the electorate. Also he reckoned that a longer campaign would expose the weaknesses of the widely expected third candidate for premiership—Amnon Shahak, former chief of military staff.

During the debate on the bill for an early election, Dan Meridor, an ex-colleague of Netanyahu in Likud, denounced him for his "cynicism, manipulation and cockiness."[87] The Knesset adopted the bill and Barak and Netanyahu decided on May 17, 1999 as the date for the elections to the Knesset and prime minister.

Explaining the overwhelming vote for early elections, Gideon Samet of *HaAretz* wrote, "The body politic under the heavy burden of Netanyahu has become so fragmented, so lacking in clear purpose that the urge to turn a new leaf overrode the political instinct of self-preservation."

Among the leaders of the still-to-be-launched Center Party there was no agreement on who the prime ministerial candidate should be: Shahak or Meridor. Their dilemma was solved when Netanyahu sacked Yitzhak Mordechai as defense minister. In the course of the evening news on January 23, Netanyahu read a blistering letter he had just sent to Mordechai. "I have come to realize that your personal ambition supersedes any other consideration," said Netanyahu. "Elected to parliament by Likud voters and appointed minister of defense by a Likud prime minister, you have nevertheless conducted negotiations with opposition parties whose goal is to bring down the Likud government."[88]

Mordechai used the occasion of bidding goodbye to his cabinet colleagues the next day to hit back. He arrived wearing a prayer shawl, and carrying the Hebrew Bible. "Deliver my soul, Oh Lord, from lying lips and a deceitful tongue," he read from the Book of Psalms. "My soul hath long dwelt with him that hateth peace. I am for peace, but when I speak, they are for war." Turning to Netanyahu, he cited the First Book of Samuel where Samuel tells King Saul, "The Lord hath rent the Kingdom of Israel from thee this day, and hath given to another who is better than thee." He then left the room, resigned from the Likud, and visited the Western Wall where he repeated his earlier lines from the scripture for the media.[89]

On January 25, the Center Party founders, respecting the latest poll findings, named Mordechai as their candidate for prime minister; the new party already claimed the loyalty of six MKs.

Born in Iraqi Kurdistan in 1945, Mordechai grew up in the Tiberian region of Israel. After 30 years in the IDF, he joined Likud when it was in the doldrums in the wake of Rabin's assassination in late 1995. Impressed by his charisma, and his habit of citing the Hebrew Bible, many compared him favorably with Menachem Begin, who was popular with the Sephardic working class as well as the religious constituency. He was therefore expected to garner Netanyahu's core constituencies, and take away about a third of his votes, about 17 percent of the total.

As the defense minister in the Netanyahu cabinet, he established himself as a voice of realism and moderation. In external affairs he forged friendly ties not only with the United States, but also with the PA, Jordan and Egypt. A meeting with Clinton at the White House in mid-March raised his stature at home.

Another blow to Netanyahu came from his far right adversary, Benny Begin, who had resigned from the cabinet in February 1997 in protest at the Hebron Protocol. He went ahead with his plans to run for prime minister. He revived Gush Herut, founded by his father, Menachem, in 1948 to establish the biblical Eretz Israel. Benny Begin became Herut's candidate for prime minister. Among others he won the backing of Yitzhak Shamir. In mid-March, when the polls showed eight percent support for Begin as prime minister, Shamir was instrumental in bringing about the merger of Herut with Moledet and the newly formed Tekuma (Rebirth) faction, composed largely of Jewish settlers (who had campaigned vigorously for Netanyahu three years earlier).

The traditional divide between secular and religious Jews had increased. A series of Supreme Court verdicts since late 1998 had angered the Orthodox (forming 15 percent of the Jewish population) and ultra-Orthodox (12 percent). On December 9 the Court ruled that exemption of Orthodox and ultra-Orthodox yeshiva students from the draft was illegal and that it needed to be regulated by the Knesset.[90] Another Court ruling allowed the stores run by kibbutzim on their premises to open on Saturday, the Sabbath.

In early January, in a historic judgment, the Supreme Court declared that Reform and Conservative Jews could not be barred from local Rabbinical Councils, as they had been since the founding of Israel. The Orthodox and ultra-Orthodox leaders hit back, passing a law on January 26 by 50–49, which requires a Reform or Conservative rabbi to declare his allegiance to the Orthodox Chief Rabbinate before taking up his seat on the local Rabbinical Council.[91]

What truly alarmed the Orthodox and ultra-Orthodox rabbis was a district court ruling in December that the government must recognize the conversions to Judaism performed by Reform and Conservative rabbis, which had so far been denied recognition by the government. They appealed the ruling to the Supreme Court, repeating their argument that the Reform and Conservative movements had so diluted Judaism that their adherents could not be regarded as Jews. On February 1 Reform and Conservative leaders petitioned the Supreme Court to hold mixed-sex services in front of the Western Wall, which has been treated as an Orthodox/ultra-Orthodox synagogue where the sexes are segregated.[92]

These judicial reverses goaded the Orthodox and ultra-Orthodox camps into action. Their rabbis summoned a "prayer meeting" in Jerusalem, to enable the rabbis on the state payroll, barred from political activity, to participate.

On February 14, 250,000 Orthodox and ultra-Orthodox men and women demonstrated along Ben Zvi Avenue in Jerusalem. "We accept the [Supreme] Court as long as it deals with relations between man and man," said Menachem Porush, an Orthodox rabbi and leader of Agudat Israel. "But when it deals with relations between man and God, that is different." He described the Supreme Court judges as "dictators," and compared the chief justice, Aharon Barak, to Haman, the Persian King Ahaseurs's prime minister who persecuted the Jews in ancient times.

He threatened "an uprising" if the Supreme Court persisted with its "anti-Semitic decisions." Not to be outdone, Rabbi Ovaida Yosef, the spiritual leader of Shas, described the Supreme Court judges as "wicked, stubborn... empty-headed an evildoers" who were "unclean and desecrated the Sabbath." Summarizing the aim of the "prayer meeting," a participant said, "We want a Jewish state with a Jewish character, based on the Torah and Torah values. What we are complaining about is secular coercion of religious Jews."[93]

Whereas the religious Jews perceived the Supreme Court as an instrument of coercion, the Court saw itself as an agency to ensure that the religious minority did not impose its will on the rest of the Jewish community.

The term "religious coercion" was frequently used by secularists while referring to the actions of the Orthodox and ultra-Orthodox, be it imposing a ban on driving during the Sabbath or "immodest" advertisements. But on February 14 the secular majority proved too complacent to join the counter-demonstration in Jerusalem in impressive numbers, despite the fact that secular Jews, who dominate the political power structure and mainstream media, regarded the Supreme Court as the upholder of law and justice, and a touch-stone of Israeli democracy. Many among them found the language used against the chief justice reminiscent of the rhetorical attacks on prime minister Rabin before his assassination. But the secular counter-demonstration attracted only 50,000. Thus the size of the two demonstrations was inversely proportional to the national constituencies they represented.

Though recent Supreme Court verdicts had accentuated the long-running tensions between the secular and the religious, the reason for the newly-found assertiveness by the Orthodox and ultra-Orthodox could be linked to the installation of Netanyahu as the chief executive. Providing as much parliamentary strength to his administration as his own Likud party, the religious factions had extracted heavy state subsidies for their sectarian institutions from his government and strengthened their power bases. Having exercised political power on an unprecedented scale, the Orthodox and the ultra-Orthodox found it increasingly difficult to accept the robust independence of the Supreme Court.

Shas supporters felt particularly aggrieved on March 17 when, after a nine-year trial, the Jerusalem district court found Rabbi Arye Deri guilty of fraud, breach of public trust and bribe-taking during 1985–90, when he was interior minister. Denouncing the court judges as "partial," Rabbi Yosef declared that Halakha, Jewish Law, held Deri innocent. Deri described his conviction as an assault by the Ashkenazi elite on Sephardim, and added, "God did us great favor that this verdict was passed two months before the elections. We will go to the public, from door to door, and we will see to whom the Israeli people give their trust."[94] Since Sephardi Jews regarded both Barak and Netanyahu as part of the Ashkenazi elite, the gainer would be Mordechai, a Sephardi who also, like Shas, holds moderate views on peace with Arabs.

This will encourage Netanyahu, a hawk at heart, to pursue with greater vigor his policy of Jewish settlement in the West Bank and East Jerusalem. Within days of declaring the date for elections, he had authorized the final go-ahead for construction at Har Homa. He also gave the approval for several high-rise buildings in Ras al Amoud. The settlement activity escalated particularly between Ramallah and Nablus, and was no longer confined to expansion within the established Jewish communities in the West Bank. "We have been troubled by Israel's expansion of existing settlements well beyond their periphery," said the American embassy in Tel Aviv on March 16. But, though the US mission closely monitored the settlement activity, its officials refused to release the data. That would help the Palestinian opposition and undermine Arafat's standing, and would boost Netanyahu's electoral chances by convincing the hardliners that he was still their best bet. More disturbingly, according to the Israeli peace groups, the number of new Jewish settlements in the West Bank established after the Wye Agreement had risen to sixteen. "The trailer communities, blocks of white rectangles atop the highest hills, are as conspicuous as the banks of new house frames that stand beside the established communities," reported Deborah Sontag of *The New York Times* on March 17.

Palestinian, American and Egyptian officials looked on helplessly. Neither Mubarak nor Arafat nor Clinton wanted to highlight the issue of settlements, aware that this would end up helping Netanyahu electorally. So the officials of the PA as well as Egypt and America were resigned to an accelerated Jewish settlement activity in the run-up to the Israeli elections.

So long as the Wye Agreement was being implemented—even in stages— Arafat had an incentive to repress the Islamist opposition and ignore the resulting criticism. Among his critics in the wake of large scale arrests of Hamas members following the signing of the Wye Accord, was Hanan Ashrawi. "We cannot allow a situation where our entire civil system is held hostage to Israeli security," she said. Countering the PA's argument that liberating Palestinian land was more important than civil liberties, she rejoined, "True liberation is contingent upon the creation of a society in which citizens feel safe from arbitrary arrest and violation of their human rights."[95] Despite the widespread arrests of Islamist activists, the opponents of the Wye Agreement attempted to express themselves. But when they held a rally in Hebron in mid-November the PA police fired shots in the air to disperse them.

However, with Israel's failure to carry out its second withdrawal from the West Bank on December 18, followed by its freezing of the Wye Memorandum, public opinion among Palestinians hardened, with support for armed attacks against Israeli targets rising to an unprecedented 53 percent. Arafat moderated his policy toward Islamists somewhat, ending the three-month house arrest of Shaikh Yasin and restoring his telephone lines. But in essence the PA and Islamists remained unreconciled.

Popular attention among Palestinians soon turned to the prisoners held by the PA. According to a Jerusalem-based human rights group, LAW, of the 1,040 untried prisoners in PA jails, mostly on criminal charges, 137 in the West Bank and an unknown number in Gaza, were political prisoners, and most of them had been held for over eighteen months. Of these only 37 (all but one being Islamists) were released at the end of Ramadan on January 19 as demanded by the Palestinian Legislative Council. Israel protested, alleging that five of those freed were involved in bombings that had murdered Israelis and Americans. The United States disputed the claim so far as its citizens were concerned. Yet, on February 3, acting on Netanyahu's advice, President Weizman commuted the sentences of five Israelis, including Amos Popper, who had killed seven Palestinians at random in 1990, from life to 40 years.[96]

By then 48 Islamist prisoners in Nablus and Jericho jails had been on a hunger strike since January 24 in protest at the non-implementation of the PLC resolution for release of all political prisoners by the end of Ramadan. In early February five hunger-strikers were taken to the hospital in Nablus, and Hamas threatened attacks on Zionist targets if anything happened to them on the ground that it was the pressure by Israel that was forcing the PA to act the way it did toward Islamists. On February 6, 3,000 Palestinians, including some PLC members, marched to the local PA office in Hebron, and in Nablus protesters clashed with the PA police.

While the opposition focused on the fate of political prisoners in the PA's custody, PA officials increasingly talked about the importance of May 4, 1999 as an opportunity for a unilateral declaration of independence (UDI) for the State of Palestine, a proposition which, according to a survey of Palestinians in early January, had the backing of 57 percent.

But PA officials did not speak with one voice. An equivocal statement on the issue by Nabil Shaath on January 8 was followed by one by Ahmad Qrei a few days later that an independent state would be declared in May. Egypt and Jordan as well as the Israeli Labor Party let it be known that they were trying to persuade Arafat not to take any action before the May 17 Israeli polls, as the UDI would play into the hands of Netanyahu, far too anxious to implement a robust riposte to Arafat's UDI, and damage the electoral prospects of his rivals.

By late summer 1998 the prospect of the UDI had already come to loom large in the estimations of the Israeli and American officials. A resolve to prevent it had driven Clinton to invest his precious time at the Wye talks.

Launched formally on September 13, 1993 with a Declaration of Principles (DOP), the Oslo Accord focused primarily on interim arrangements between the parties while providing the framework for final status talks and deadlines for both. It specified a five-year transition period after the parties had transformed the DOP into a detailed agreement on the first stage of Palestinian autonomy in the Gaza Strip and Jericho. This happened on May 4, 1994 in Cairo, and led to the establishment of the Palestinian Authority by the PLO. Then on September 28, 1996 came the Oslo II Accord on the second stage of the Palestinian autonomy— in the West Bank—and the arrangement for Palestinian elections.

The tenure of office for the PA presidency and the Palestinian Legislative Council would end on May 3, 1999. This date was also the deadline for the talks on a permanent settlement between the two parties, including the future of Jerusalem, Palestinian refugees, Jewish settlements, borders and relations with neighbors.

The signatories could have extended the five-year period interim period through mutual consent. But with Israel confiscating more land by the day, Arafat could not afford an extension. In any event, Netanyahu did not accept the premise of a deadline. "The only purpose of the agreements is to reach a solution through negotiations," said David Bar-Ilan, his senior spokesman. "There is no time limit, only a target date which obviously cannot be met right now."[97]

Not so, explained Ghassan Khatib, a Palestinian political commentator. "On May 4 no side will be legally bound to the agreement," he said. "Palestinian security services will no longer be obligated to cooperate and coordinate with Israel. The ministers in Arafat's government who serve on the negotiating committees would be legally out of work." More alarmingly, with the expiration of the Oslo Accords, the PA, its president, Arafat, and the PLC will cease to have a legal status. That is why, when Arafat and his chief negotiator, Saeb Erekat, arrived in Washington on March 22, Erekat said, "We are just asking to fill the vacuum, the political and legal vacuum. There are many legal questions related to May 4 that no one is willing to answer."[98]

If Arafat thought that a meeting with Clinton the next day would enlighten him on the legal morass, he was disappointed. Nor did Clinton express his backing for Palestinian self-determination. His spokesman affirmed Clinton's "long-held opposition to any such declaration and said the issue should be resolved through negotiations with Israel," adding that "the special nature of the US role in the region requires that it not stake out positions that ought to be negotiated by the parties." While agreeing that the final status talks should not be open-ended he refused to discuss any time frame. A fortnight later, Igor Ivanov, the foreign minister of Russia, which, as the co-chair of the Madrid Peace Conference, was the co-signatory to the Oslo Accord, urged Arafat not to declare Palestinian independence on May 4, and instead find a way to extend the agreement with Israel.[99]

In the meantime, on March 26 the EU summit in Berlin stated that the Palestinians "have an unqualified right to self-determination, including the option of a state," and expressed its conviction that "the creation of a democratic, viable and peaceful sovereign Palestinian state through negotiations would be the best guarantee of Israeli security." Asserting that "the Palestinian self-determination is not subject to any veto," the EU called on Israel to complete its talks with the Palestinians on their final status within a year—by March 2000. "The [Palestinian] right to statehood is no longer in question," said Ahmad Abdul Rahman, the secretary-general of the PA cabinet. "The EU statement makes clear that negotiations are to lead to statehood."[100]

On the other side, Netanyahu regretted that Europe was trying "to impose a solution that endangered Israel," and added, "such a Palestinian state would be able to raise a large army, use it without limitations, forge alliances with regimes that aim to destroy Israel, and serve as a base of increased terrorism against Israel, and in that way threaten its existence."

Netanyahu's electoral rivals used the EU communiqué to show that his hardline policies had resulted in both the EU and the US distancing themselves from Israel.

In the run-up to the elections, Netanyahu continued to lead his nearest rival Barak, with Mordechai trailing, and Begin at below 10 percent.

Major differences between the 1996 and 1999 polls made the outcome of the prime ministerial contest highly unpredictable. Unlike the former prime ministerial race, limited to two rivals, the latter had four. That made it almost certain that there would be a run-off on June 2.

A major factor in 1996 that slashed support for the incumbent Peres was the bombing campaign by radical Islamists. That the Qassam Brigade was intent on intervening in the 1999 elections became apparent when the news leaked in late March that the PA had tipped off the CIA that the Brigade had assembled explosives in a safe house north of Tel Aviv with a plan to detonate a bomb around the Purim festival, and that the CIA in turn had alerted the Israelis who raided the premises on March 3.[101]

This time, if a suicide bomb went off before the 1999 polls it would favor the incumbent Netanyahu. That is the nightmare not only of Barak but also Arafat and Clinton.

Finally, it is likely that one or more right-wing Israeli groups will approach the Supreme Court after May 3, arguing that since the PA had ceased to have any legal foundation with the expiry of the Oslo Accords, the Israeli government must stop dealing with it. Whether the Court will entertain such an application and what would ensue, if it does, remains to be seen.

Appendix I

United Nations Security Council Resolutions 242 (1967) and 338 (1973)

United Nations Security Council Resolution 242
22 November 1967

The Security Council,

Expressing its continuing concern with the grave situation in the Middle East,

Emphasizing the inadmissibility of the acquisition of territory by war and the need to work for a just and lasting peace in which every State in the area can live in security,

Emphasizing further that all Member States in their acceptance of the Charter of the United Nations have undertaken a commitment to act in accordance with Article 2 of the Charter,

1. Affirms that the fulfillment of Charter principles requires the establishment of a just and lasting peace in the Middle East which include the application of both the following principles: (i) Withdrawal of Israeli armed forces from territories occupied in the recent conflict; (ii) Termination of all claims of states of belligerency and respect for and acknowledgment of the sovereignty, territorial integrity and political independence of every State in the area and their right to live in peace within secure and recognized borders from threats or acts of force;

2. Affirms further necessity (a) For guaranteeing freedom of navigation through international waterways in the area; (b) For achieving a just settlement of the refugee problem; (c) For guaranteeing the territorial inviolability and political independence of every State in the area, through measures including the establishment of demilitarized zones;

3. Requests the Secretary-General to designate a Special Representative to proceed to the Middle East to establish and maintain contacts with the States concerned in order to promote agreement and assist efforts to achieve a peaceful and accepted settlement in accordance with the provisions and principles of this resolution;

4. Requests the Secretary-General to report to the Security Council on the progress of the Special Representative as soon as possible.

—Adopted by unanimous vote

337

United Nations Security Council Resolution 338
22 October 1973

The Security Council

1. Calls upon all parties to the present fighting to cease all firing and terminate all military activity immediately, no later than twelve hours after the moment of adoption of this decision, in the positions they now occupy;

2. Calls upon the parties to start immediately after the ceasefire the implementation of Security Council resolution 242 (1967) in all of its parts;

3. Decides that, immediately and concurrently with the ceasefire, negotiation shall start between the parties concerned under appropriate auspices at establishing a just and durable peace in the Middle East.

—Adopted by fourteen votes to one with one abstention (China)

Appendix II

Letters of Mutual Recognition by Israel and the PLO
exchanged through the Norwegian Foreign Minister,
September 9–10, 1993

From Yasser Arafat, Chairman, Palestine Liberation Organization to
Israeli prime minister Yitzhak Rabin (on September 9, 1993)

Mr. prime minister

The signing of the Declaration of Principles marks a new era in the history of the Middle East. In firm conviction thereof I would like to confirm the following PLO commitments:

The PLO recognizes the right of the State of Israel to exist in peace and security. The PLO accepts the United Nations Security Council Resolutions 242 and 338.

The PLO commits itself to the Middle East peace process and to a peaceful resolution of the conflict between the two sides and declares that all outstanding issues relating to a permanent status will be resolved through negotiations.

The PLO considers the signing of the Declaration of Principles constitutes an historic event, inaugurating a new epoch of peaceful coexistence, free from violence and all other acts which endanger peace and stability. Accordingly, the PLO renounces the use of terrorism and other acts of violence and will assume responsibility over all PLO elements and personnel in order to assure their compliance, prevent violations and discipline violators.

In view of the promise of a new era and the signing of the Declaration of Principles and based on Palestinian acceptance of Security Council Resolutions 242 and 338, the PLO affirms that those articles of the Palestinian Covenant which deny Israel's right to exist and the provisions of the Covenant which are inconsistent with the commitment of this letter are now inoperative and no longer valid. Consequently, the PLO undertakes to submit to the Palestinian National Council for formal approval the necessary changes in regard to the Palestinian Covenant.

Sincerely,

Yasser Arafat, Chairman

Palestine Liberation Organization

From Mr. Yitzhak Rabin to Mr. Yasser Arafat (on September 10, 1993)

Mr. Chairman

In response to your letter of September 9th, 1993 I wish to confirm to you that, in light of the PLO commitments included in your letter, the government of Israel has decided to recognize the PLO as the representative of the Palestinian people and commence negotiations with the PLO within the Middle East peace process.

Yitzhak Rabin
prime minister of Israel

From Mr. Yasser Arafat to Mr. Johan Jorgen Holst,
Norwegian Foreign Minister (on September 10, 1993)

Dear Minister Holst

I would like to confirm to you that, upon signing of the Declaration of Principles, I will include the following positions in my public statements: In light of the new era marked by the signing of the Declaration of Principles, the PLO encourages and calls upon the Palestinian people in the West Bank and Gaza Strip to take part in the steps leading to the normalization of life, rejecting violence and terrorism, contributing to peace and stability and participating actively in the shaping of reconstruction, economic development and co-operation.

Sincerely,
Yasser Arafat, Chairman
Palestine Liberation Organization

Notes

Introduction
   1 Thubron 177.
   2 The detailed information on "Immigration and Absorption" in *Statistical Abstract of Israel,
1994,* a volume of 947 pages, does not break down the figures into "Jews" and "non-Jews" as it does in
all other sections dealing with people. It assumes that all immigrants are Jewish.
   3 Melman 132.
   4 Said 174.
   5 Said 175.

Chapter 1 *The Walled Heart of Jerusalem*
   1 All biblical quotations are from *The Holy Bible: The Old and New Testaments*, conformable to
the edition of 1611, commonly known as the Authorized or King James Version. New York: World
Publishing Company, 1960.
   2 Romann and Weingrod 4.
   3 Thubron 58.
   4 Cited in Eber and O'Sullivan 83.
   5 Elon 182.
   6 McNeill 4.
   7 Benvenisti, *Jerusalem* 12, and Eber and O'Sullivan 81. Muhammad Burqan built a new house
outside Jerusalem on land owned by his relatives. When the Israelis constructed Pisgat Zeev, the third
in the suburban settlement rings to the north of Jerusalem, in 1980, his house ended up in the middle of
a traffic circle.
   8 There is an old, established neighborhood in West Jerusalem called the German Colony. No
attempt has been made yet to rename it.
   9 Cited in Friedman 98.
   10 In 1992 a committee headed by Haim Klugman, director-general of the Justice Ministry, issued
a report which showed that (a) Atreet Cohanim had managed to take over properties in East Jerusalem
using questionable documents; (b) it had been assisted by the Israel Land Administration and the
Custodian of Absentees' Property; and (c) state funds were transferred to it in circuitous ways to pay for
the takeovers, and secrecy maintained. Premir Yitzhak Rabin ordered Miriam Ben Porat, the State
Comptroller, to stop her investigation into the matter. *HaAretz* 16 September 1998. The breakdown was
70 properties by 1987 for an estimated $10 million, and another 53 between January 1988 and the June
1992 general election. Some of the real estate bought by the JRP had belonged to the Jews who had
lived in the Muslim Quarter before 1936. (Friedman 98–104; and my interviews in the Old Town,
February 1995.) Buying the remaining properties in the Muslim Quarter was estimated to cost $100
million. (Friedman 98).
   11 McNeill 6–7.
   12 Interview in February 1995.
   13 Shipler 377.
   14 Friedman 104.

15 *Jerusalem Report* 30 January 1992: 5.
16 It is also the only major Muslim shrine open to non-Muslims.
17 Etzion 2, 5.
18 Menachem Livni, Interrogations (in Hebrew), Court documents, Jerusalem, May 18, 1984.
19 Shipler 107.
20 *Village Voice* November 12, 1985: 22.
21 See also *Time* 16 October 1989: 32.

Chapter 2 *Jerusalem*
    1 Cited in Hiro, *Desert Shield to Desert Storm* 554–5.
    2 The last of the four Conventions—developed by an International Red Cross conference in Stockholm in August 1948 and ratified by United nations members in Geneva on August 12, 1949—was entitled The geneva Convention Relative to the Protection of Civilian Persons in Time of War, 1949. It forbids the Occupying Power to do the following to the Protected Civilians: collective punishment and reprisals; deportation of individuals or groups; hostage-taking; torture; unjustified destruction of property; and discrimination on the grounds of race, religion, national origin or political affiliation. Article 47 states: "Protected persons... shall not be deprived of... the benifits of this Convention by any changes introduced, as the result of the occupation of a territory, into the institutions or the government of the said territory, nor by any agreement concluded between the authorities of the Occupied Territories and the Occupying Power, nor by the annexation of the whole or part of the occupied territory." Article 49 (6) states: "The Occupying Power shall not deport or transfer parts of its own civilian population into the territory it occupies." Cited in Hiro's *Dictionary of the Middle East* 91.
    3 *Financial Times* May 12, 1995.
    4 Romann and Weingrod 46–7.
    5 In late 1993, the Palestinian population of greater East Jerusalem was estimated to be 150,000, and the Jewish population 155,000.
    6 *Guardian* September 5, 1995.
    7 Romann and Weingrod 54.
    8 *Jerusalem Report* June17, 1993: 10.
    9 *Jerusalem Report* June 12, 1993: 12.
    10 The full title of Histadrut is HaHistadrut HaKelalit shel HaOvedim be Eretz Israel, or the General Federation of Workers in the Land of Israel.
    11 Romann and Weingrod 153–4.
    12 *Jerusalem Report* June 12, 1993: 10.
    13 Romann and Weingrod 48.
    14 *Jerusalem Report* 17 June 1993: 12.
    15 *Mainstream* 20 May 1995: 29.
    16 Interview in March 1995.

Chapter 3 *Mea Shearim*
    1 See p 130.
    2 Rabbi Dow Marmur, *Beyond Survival* (London: Darton, Longman & Todd, 1982) 53.
    3 Interview in Jerusalem, March 1995.

Chapter 4 *Mizrachim/Sephardim*
    1 Cited in Smooha 88.
    2 Interview in Tel Aviv, March 1995.
    3 Brook 238–9.
    4 Cited in Smooha 88.
    5 *HaAretz* 21 May 1978.
    6 Kedma means going East; kidma means going forward. That is, "going East" means "going forward," say Kedma's founders, intent on infusing pride among Mizrachim.
    7 Elon, 245.
    8 Kyle and Peters 170–1.

Chapter 5 *The Secular Center*
    1 The Elected Assembly, elected by the members of the Yishuv, (Jewish) Settlement/Community in Palestine, consisted of 170 to 300 members. It elected the National Council, Vaad Leumi, of 23 to 42 members.
    2 See p 41.
    3 Peretz 148.
    4 Cited in Dilip Hiro *Inside the Middle East* 236.
    5 *The Paratroopers' Book* (in Hebrew) (Tel Aviv: Ministry of Defense, 1969) 157–8. Cited in Hiro, *Inside* 204.
    6 Hersh 225–8, 231 and Hiro, *Dictionary* 198. During his first meeting with President Sadat on November 7, 1973, Kissinger reportedly explained the sudden American airlift to Israel as a decision aimed at avoiding a nuclear escalation.
    7 Hiro, *Dictionary* 198.
    8 *Sunday Times* 22 May 1977.
    9 The full title of the Tehiya party was Tenuhat HaTehiya—Brit Ne'emanei Eretz Israel, or The Renaissance Movement—Covenant of the Land of Israel Faithful.
    10 Hiro, *Dictionary* 141.
    11 See p 47.
    12 Cited in Hiro, *Desert Shield* 332.
    13 Hersh 318.
    14 Cited in Ehud Sprinzak's essay "The Israeli Right," in Kyle and Peters 136.
    15 Here are two examples. When a friend asked him why he was wearing only one sneaker, David Levy turned it over, and pointing at the embossed sign on the sole—"TAIWAN"—said, "TIE ONE." As a member of an Israeli delegation, Levy arrived at a White House reception. He soon disappeared. His colleagues found him standing on the roof of the White House, holding a drink in his hand. "What are you doing here?" asked an Israeli aide. "Down there they said 'Drinks on the House,'" Levy replied.
    16 According to the unpublished part of the Shamgar Commission's inquiry into Yitzhak Rabin's assassination, among those who provided posters portraying Rabin as a Nazi SS officer at an opposition rally was Avishai Raviv, an agent of the Shin Beth, who had been planted into Kiryat Arba after Baruch Goldstein's killings of Palestinians, and instructed to establish two extremist groups, Eyal and the Sword of David, with the aim of "hunting down Jewish traitors." When these posters were distributed at the rally against the Oslo II Accord in October 1995, which was addressed by Binyamin Netanyahu, his action was widely criticized. *Observer* 31 March 1996.
    17 Of the 44 Labor MKs, two were Arab; of the 12 Meretz MKs, one. The Rabin government had the backing also of two Jewish MKs who had split from the opposition Tzomet party. Of the remaining Arab MKs, two belonged to Hadash, two to the Arab Democratic Party, and one to Likud.
    18 *Jerusalem Report* 30 November 1995: 17.
    19 *Observer* 3 March 1996.
    20 Cited in *Observer* 3 March 1996.
    21 *Independent* 28 February 1996.
    22 It was not until July 12, 1996 that the representatives of these five countries, meeting in Washington, agreed on procedural matters.
    23 See pp 339.
    24 Cited in *Observer* 28 April 1996. The next day the Labor Party Central Committee voted to remove the clause in its election manifesto which opposed the establishment of a Palestinian state.
    25 *New York Times* 2 June 1996.
    26 A mini-crisis ensued when Netanyahu refused to give any of the important ministries of Defense, Finance or Housing, to Ariel Sharon, whom he regarded "a persistent dissident." This angered Sharon, who had played a crucial role in keeping the secular right-wing united behind Netanyahu, and courting the religious right; successfully. It was only after David Levy had publicly threatened to resign if Sharon was not appointed a minister that Netanyahu relented. It was not until July 8 that Sharon was put in charge of the newly created Ministry of National Infrastructure which—besides railways, ports and military industry—included "bypass roads in the West Bank."
    27 *New York Times* 19 June 1996, and *Middle East International* 21 June 1996: 11.
    28 *The Times* 10 July 1996.

29 *The Times* 8 September 1996.

30 *Al Hayat* 22 September 1996.

31 Cited in *Independent* 30 September 1996.

32 *Middle East International* 4 October 1996: 10.

33 "I do not think that the Arabs who call themselves Palestinians have a right to demand a state," Bentzion Netanyahu said. "It's obvious to me that there isn't a Palestinian people." *HaAretz* Magazine, 18 September 1998: 17–8.

34 *Independent* 1 October 1996.

35 *Independent* 2 October 1996.

36 *International Herald Tribune* 17 December 1996.

37 *Independent* 16 December 1996.

38 *Observer* 19 January 1997.

39 The condemnation was not limited to the Jewish settlers. Yitzhak Shamir, a former Likud Premier, said: "The government's willingness to implement the Oslo Accords is a fatal error. The notion that the decisions of the previous government have to be fulfilled is stupid and malicious." *Observer* 5 January 1997.

40 *The Times* 30 December 1996.

41 See p 26.

42 *Independent* 27 March 1997.

43 *Financial Times* 11 March 1997.

44 *The Times* 17 March 1997, and *Independent* 17 March 1997.

45 *Independent* 1 April 1997.

46 *Independent* 4 April 1997.

47 See p 45 and 142.

48 Interestingly, the earlier Justice Minister, Yaacov Neeman, had to resign when he was charged with pressuring a witness not to give evidence against Arye Deri.

49 Uncharacteristically, Netanyahu was briefly contrite. "About the mistakes that were committed, I am sorry and I will work to correct them," he said. *The Times* 21 April 1997.

Chapter 6 *The Israel Defense Forces*

1 Zahal, Hebrew acronym of Zvai Haganah LeIsrael, Defense Force for Israel.

2 Melman 136.

3 *Davar* 1 April 1994.

4 Interview on Israeli Television, 13 January 1988. It soon proved to be an ineffective gesture.

5 "How did the intifada affect the IDF?" in *Conflict Quarterly* 14. (Summer 1994): 12.

6 Druzes are members of a heterodox Muslim sect which does not feel bound by two of the five pillars of orthodox Islam: fasting during the holy month of Ramadan, and the pilgrimage to Mecca.

7 *HaAretz* 1 May 1992.

8 Cited in *Jerusalem Report* 29 December 1994: 13.

9 Interviews in Jerusalem and Haifa, January-March 1995.

10 Pappe.

11 Rolef 313–6.

12 Elon 191–2.

13 Pappe vii.

14 Pappe 110–1, and Morris 22.

15 Khalidi 861. In addition, the estimates for the "Dissident Groups" of Irgun and Lehi are put respectively at 3,000–5,000 and 200–300. 863.

16 Khalidi 685; and Morris 21–2.

17 Khalidi 865, 867–8.

18 Khalidi 866, 868.

19 See p 66.

20 Morris 291. Though it was in May 1946 that, following the independence of his country, Emir Abdullah of the Emirate of Transjordan changed the name of his realm to the Hashemite Kingdom of Jordan, with himself as king, it was only after March 1948, when he had signed a revised 20-year treaty with Britain, that international recognition of the new status of him and his country followed gradually.

21 Pappe 271.

Chapter 7 *The Double Marginals*
1 Interview in Jerusalem, February 1995.
2 Interview in Haifa, February 1995.
3 Interview in Nazareth, February 1995.
4 Interview in Haifa, February 1995.
5 Morris 1.
6 Morris 288–9.
7 Morris 289–91.
8 Morris 292.
9 Morris 294.
10 Interview with Said Barghouti, February 1995.
11 The PLO publically appealed to Isreali Arabs to vote for the Democratic Front for Peace and Equality. Hiro, *Inside* 197.
12 Said Barghouti, *History of the Middle East, Vol. II*: 210.
13 The eight Arab MKs were divided thus: the ADP 2, the DFPE 2, Labor 2, Meretz 1 and Likud 1. Of these two MKs, one Labor and the other Meretz, were deputy ministers.
14 *Jerusalem Report* 2 July 1994: 19.

Chapter 8 *New Frontiersmen*
1 Cited in *Village Voice* 12 November 1985: 22.
2 Cited in Gideon Aran, "A Mystico-messianic Interpretation of Modern Islaeli History: The Six-Day War as a Key Event in the Development of the Original Religious Culture of Gush Emunim," *Studies in Contemporary Jewry* 4 (1998): 268.
3 See p 75.
4 *Jerusalem Report* 3 October 1991: 7.
5 See p 91.
6 *Jerusalem Report* 3 October 1991: 8. It is worth nothing that it cost Israel $300 million in 1982 to resettle the 6,000 Jews settled earlier in Sinai—that is, $50,000 per settler—following its peace treaty with Egypt.
7 *Jerusalem Report* 9 February 1995: 14. The Jewish construction activity used up 763 hectares, or 4.7 square miles of Palestinian land.
8 Cited in *Newsweek* 16 June 1980: 18.
9 *Jerusalem Report* 3 November 1994: 14.
10 See p 18.
11 Cited in *Village Voice* 12 November 1985: 17.
12 Cited in Shipler 86, 503.
13 El Sayyid Nossair, a 35-year-old Egyptian-American, arrested as the suspected murderer, was found not guilty of murder, but was convicted of possessing an illegal weapon.
14 On my return journey at night from Kiryat Arba to Jerusalem in March 1995, our bus was stoned. The shatterproof windshield was damaged, but nobody was hurt. In September 1998, I traveled from Jerusalem to Kiryat Arba by a bus fitted with a bullet-proof windshield and windows.
15 Whereas most Jews believe that God is sanctified through martyrdom, Rabbi Meir Kahane argued that the final expression of *kiddush HaShem* for the Jews is to decimate their enemies, thus revealing the power of God. "Goldstein did what is written: Whoever comes to kill you, rise up to kill him," said Rabbi Ido Alba of Kiryat Arba. "This is a simple Halacha… Tha Arabs are not afraid of the army, and one of the ways to protect our lives is to make them afraid of us." *Jerusalem Report* 3 November 1994: 15.
16 *Jerusalem Report* 3 November 1994: 15.
17 See pp 17–8.
18 In 1989 some 70,000 settlers were using 40 percent of the water in the Occupied Territories. (Rubenstein 112) Since the early 1980's the IDF had not allowed the Palestinians to dig a new well, banned by a military order, in the West Bank. (Friedman xxiii)
19 *Jerusalem Report* 9 February 1995: 13. Three-fifths pf the Jewish settlers were secular, most of them living within commuting distance from Tel Aviv and Jerusalem. Many of them were reportedly more interested in larger and cheaper housing than in claiming the historic rights of the Jews in Eretz Israel. *Jerusalem Report* 18 November 1993: 209 and *Jerusalem Report* February 1995: 4, 14.

Chapter 9 *The West Bank*

1 Lockman and Benin 108

2 "Membership in, contact with, or expressed support for the aims of a proscribed organization (e.g., the Palestine Liberation Organization or its constituent elements) is grounds for arrest [in Israel or the Occupied Territories]... Educational materials, periodicals, and books originating outside Israel are censored for alleged anti-Jewish or anti-Israeli content and for perceived encouragement of Palestinian nationalism. The occupation authorities maintain a list of forbidden publications... Possession of such publications, many of which are legal in Israel and East Jerusalem, by a West Bank or Gaza Arab is a criminal offense, frequently resulting in fine or imprisonment; however, according to Israeli press reports, the list of forbidden publications is not made public." The US State Department, *Country Reports on Human Rights Practices for 1982*: 1158-9.

3 Lockman and Beinin 108.

4 The title Ansar for a detention camp, which contained Palestinians and Lebanese, was first applied by the Israeli military to a camp in south Lebanon. The name Ansar II was given to the detention camp Israel set up in Gaza City.

5 For an account of the intifada, see Chapter 10.

6 Responding to Palestinian guerrilla attacks, an Israeli armored column with air cover crossed into Jordan at Karameh on March 21, 1968. Instead of retreating, the Palestinians, backed by Jordanian artillery, fought a twelve-hour battle, destroyed many Israeli tanks and halted the IDF advance into Jordan. See further pp 203–4.

7 Though Kiryat Arba today is the second most populous Jewish settlement in the West Bank, after Ariel, an air of defiance remains. As you enter it from Hebron's Ein Bani Salim Road past a white-painted, electronically-controlled steel gate, the large sign in Hebrew reads: "Kiryat Arba/ Zionist-Political Settlement/The more we are pressed, the more we will expand."

8 See p 207. This was a reference to the fighting between the Palestinian commandos and the Jordanian army in September 1970 in which the Palestinians lost.

9 With an altitude of about 3,000 feet, Hebron and its environs are suitable for growing almonds and pistachios.

10 Though, as the owner of the hotel in question, Fayaz Qawasmeh was one of the two parties involved in this historic event, in all these years he had been interviewed only once before despite his fluency in English—by a BBC television researcher. I was the second researcher to interview him on this matter. All accounts so far have originated solely from Rabbi Moshe Levinger or other members of his group in April 1968. In addition to the two versions of the event provided in Chapter 8, here is another, published in the *Jerusalem Report*, a Jerusalem-based fortnightly, on 3 October 1991. "On Passover 1968 ten families led by Rabbi Moshe Levinger checked into Hebron's Arab-owned Park Hotel," reported Yossi Halevi. "They claimed to be Swiss tourists, on pilgrimage to Hebron, the city where Abraham and Sarah are buried. When the holiday ended they refused to leave."

11 Cited in *The Middle East* June 1980: 18.

12 Of the 1.2 million Palestinians in the West Bank in 1994, some 42 percent were registered as refugees with the United Nations Relief and Work Agency for Palestinian Refugees in the Near East (UNRWA). Of these about a quarter lived in refugee camps, and the rest outside.

13 Israel Central Bureau of Statistics, *Statistical Abstract of Israel, 1994* (Jerusalem, 1995) 201, 791. With a 39 percent drop in Palestinan's GNP in 1995 and 1996, the gap between them and the Israelis grew even wider.

14 Lockman and Beinin 225.

15 Lockman and Beinin 225 and *Jerusalem Report* 13 December 1990: 15.

16 Jerusalem Media and Communication Center, *Israeli Obstacles to Economic Development in the Occupied Palestinian Territories* (Jerusalem, 1994) 89.

17 Lockman and Beinin 225.

18 Benvenisti 32.

19 Lockman and Beinin 225.

20 Jerusalem Media and Communication Center 160.

Chapter 10 *Gaza*

1 Cited in Friedman 199.

2 *Jerusalem Report* 13 December 1990: 16.

3 Abu Amr 53.
4 Benvensiti 18.
5 Interview in Jerusalem, February 1995.
6 Cited in *Jerusalem Report* 13 December 1990: 14.
7 Lockman and Beinin 286-91.
8 *Jerusalem Report* 13 December 1990: 14.
9 This standard was originally adopted by the Arabs in 1916 after they had revolted against the Ottoman sultan during World War I. In pre-Islamic poetry in Arabia, white signified good deeds, green fertility, black the enemy who fights, and red the enemy's blood.
10 *Jerusalem Report* 24 October 1991: 22-3.
11 *Middle East International* 8 November 1991: 18.
12 Cited in Friedman 205.
13 Cited in Friedman 193-4.
14 *Jerusalem Report* 24 October 1991: 22.
15 *Jerusalem Report* 13 December 1990: p. 13.
16 The lower figures were provided by the IDF, and the higher by BeTselem, an Israeli human rights monitoring group. *Jerusalem Report* 13 December 1990: 13, 19; and Friedman xxvi.
17 Grossman 14-15.
18 *Jerusalem Report* 13 December 1990: 16, and 29 October 1991: 22.
19 *Jerusalem Report* 13 December 1990: 16.
20 *Jerusalem Report* 13 December 1990: 8.
21 *Jerusalem Report* 13 December 1990: 13.
22 Interview in Ramallah, March 1995.
23 Cited in *Jerusalem Report* 14 March 1991: 26.
24 Cited in *Jerusalem Report* 14 March 1991: 26.
25 *Jerusalem Report* 24 October 1991: 23.
26 *Jerusalem Report* 13 December 1990: 16.
27 Usher 8, and *Middle East International* 18 December 1992: 4.
28 Interview with HaAretz, cited in *Middle East International* 18 December 1992: 4.
29 *Middle East International* 19 March 1993: 8-9.
30 During the Philistine era Gaza was the site of the Temple to pagan god Dagon, which was destroyed by Samson, the jilted strongman.
31 Hassan Ealin was one of the seven leaders of the Popular Front for the Liberation of Palestine in the West Bank and Gaza to have been assassinated by the Shin Beth. Having agreed to release them in 1985 as part of a prisoner exchange, the Israeli government reckoned that they were too dangerous to be allowed to live as free men and decided to kill them.
32 Friedman 197-201.
33 *Jerusalem Post Magazine* 17 February 1995: 15-16.
34 *Jerusalem Post Magazine* 17 February 1995: 16.

Chapter 11 *The Palestine Liberation Organization*
1 Anybody born of a Palestinian father, irrespective of his place of residence, was entitled to become a Palestine National Council member.
2 Interview at Birzeit University, Birzeit, January 1995.
3 Yasser Arafat kept on making brief clandestine visits to the West Bank until early 1969, just before being elected Chairman of the Palestine Liberation Organization in February.
4 Michael C. Hudson, *Arab Politics: The Search for Legitimacy*, (New haven: Yale University Press, 1977) 302.
5 Gowers and Walker 83, citing Mohamed Heikal, a confidant of President Nasser, who was present at the meeting.
6 Hirst 314.
7 Abu Iyad (with Eric Rouleau), *My Home, My Land: A Narrative of the Palestinian Struggle* (New York: Times Books, 1981) 135-6.
8 Cited in Hiro, *Inside* 55.
9 *Guardian* 10 June 1974.
10 Cited in Shemesh 259.

11 Cited in Hirst 335.

12 On December 16, 1991, at the American initiative, the United Nations General Assembly revoked Resolution 3379 by 111 votes to 25, with 13 abstentions.

13 Sandra Mackey, *Lebanon: Death of a Nation* (New york: Congdon and Weed 1989) 178.

14 Hiro, *Lebanon, Fire and Embers: A History of the Lebanese Civil War* (New York: St. Martin's Press 1993) 89; and Mohamed Heikal, *Secret Channels* (London: Harper Collins 1996) 355.

15 Cited in E. Sahliyeh, *The PLO after the Lebanon War* (Boulder, CO: Westview Press 1986) 165.

16 *Washington Post* 25 December 1983.

17 The Sinai II Agreement between Egypt and Israel, brokered by Washington and primarily concerning disengagement in the Sinai, was signed on September 4, 1975. It consisted of three published and four secret documents. Of the latter, three concerned the United States and Israel, including reaffirmation of America's earlier commitment to help Israel maintain military superiority over its Arab neighbors, and a guarantee of oil deliveries to Israel from Iran, then ruled by a pro-western monarch, or mainland United States. Hiro, *Dictionary* 302.

18 Gowers and Walker 337-8.

19 Foreign Broadcasting Information Service, Washington, DC, 11 December 1984.

20 Raviv and Melman 394.

21 Raviv and Melman 395-7.

22 *Sunday Times* 24 April 1988.

23 Raviv and Melman 397.

24 Lockman and Beinin 396 397. George Habash of the Popular Front for the Liberation of Palestine, while opposed to the political communique and the declaration of the founding of the State of Palestine, stated that he would abide by the decision of the majority.

25 Cited in Heikal 394-5.

26 *Washington Post* 15 December 1988.

27 Cited in Hiro, *Desert Shield* 79.

28 Cited in Hiro, *Desert Shield* 505.

29 Cited in *Jerusalem Report* 28 March 1991: 10.

30 Cited in Gowers and Walker 444.

31 *Mideast Mirror* 11 February 1991.

32 *Jerusalem Report* 11 March 1993: 24-6; and Walid Khalidi, *At a Critical Juncture: the United States and the Palestinian People*, (Washington, DC: Center for Contemporary Arab Studies, Georgetown University 1989) 23. The PLO also paid compensation to those whose houses were demolished by the IDF.

33 *Guardian* 1 July 1992.

34 Cited in *Jerusalem Post* 13 January 1995.

35 Cited in *Jerusalem Post* 13 January 1995.

36 It was the same table on which the Camp David Accords were signed in September 1978.

37 *The Times* 14 September 1993.

38 *Guardian* 8 and 12 November 1993; *Middle East International* 19 November 1993: 3; *Jerusalem Report* 30 December 1993: 20; and *Observer* 20 March 1994. Adnan Yasin's wife died soon after his arrest in November 1993.

39 *Independent* 9 October 1993.

40 Cited in *Guardian* 12 November 1993. Of the 107 central council members, 25 radicals boycotted the meeting. The rest split thus: 63 for the accord, 8 against, with 11 abstentions. *Guardian* 13 October 1993.

41 *Guardian* 8 and 12 November 1993; *Middle East International* 19 November 1993: 3; and *Jerusalem Report* 30 December 1993: 20.

42 *Los Angeles Times* 28 September 1993.

43 Cited in *Middle East International* 26 August 1994: 6.

Chapter 12 *The Palestinian Authority*

1 *The Times* 26 May 1994. For the text of the Cairo Agreement, see Usher, 104-15.

2 *Guardian* 2 July 1994, and *Middle East International* 8 July 1994: 3.

3 In reply to a question at a cabinet meeting Rabin confirmed on September 18, 1994 that

"Palestinian Authority security personnel" operated throughout the West Bank with "Israel's knowledge and in co-operation with Israel's security forces to safeguard Israel's security interests." Cited in *Middle East International* 1 March 1996: 16.

4 *Observer* 3 September 1995.

5 *Al Quds* 12 January 1995.

6 *Jerusalem Report* 18 May 1995: 34.

7 A few days later Force 17, acting on Yasser Arafat's orders, abducted Bassam Eid, an Israeli Arab human rights activist resident in East Jerusalem who had led the campaign for Maher Alami's release, and took him to the Force's Ramallah headquarters for interrogation. Eid's ordeal lasted a day.

8 Cited in Usher 69.

9 Cited in *Middle East International* 14 April 1995: 3.

10 See Usher 109-10.

11 In a similar partisan move, soon after his arrival in Gaza City in July 1994, Arafat had dismissed the local council—consisting of all PLO factions, Islamists and the representatives of refugees, landowners and professionals—nominated by mayor Mansour Shawwa, his appointee, and replaced it with a council consisting exclusively of six Fatah members.

12 Cited in Usher 71.

13 *Jerusalem Post* 5 February 1995.

14 Funds for the policemen above the 9,000 limit fixed by the Cairo Agreement, and other security organizations such as the PSS, came most probably from the accounts of Fatah, which were managed secretly by Arafat.

15 *Jerusalem Post* 20 February 1995.

16 *Al Quds* 31 January 1995.

17 *Jerusalem Report* 2 November 1995: 17.

18 Interview in Gaza, March 1995.

19 Commenting on Arafat's inclusion of Nabil Shaath, a millionaire, in the Fatah list for Khan Yunis, Ziad Saleh, a local unemployed engineer, said: "What's Shaath's revolutionary background? When our children were throwing stones, his children were shopping in London and Paris." *Observer* 14 January 1996.

20 When Samiha Khalil tried to hold a rally at Al Najah University in Nablus, the guards acting on "orders from high up," barred the entry of her supporters as well as reporters. *Observer* 14 January 1996.

21 Cited in *Middle East International* 16 February 1996: 7.

22 Cited in *Independent* 20 January 1996 and *New Statesman and Society* 27 January 1996: 6.

23 The team "Palestinian national authority" can be traced back to the June 1974 resolution by the Palestine National Council. See p 208.

24 *Guardian* 24 June 1996.

25 See p .

26 *HaAretz* 24 June 1996.

27 This meeting, however, did not take place until October 9, a month after Netanyahu and Arafat had met for the first time.

28 *Observer* 1 September 1996.

29 See p .

30 *Independent* 10 October 1996.

31 Cited in *Middle East International* 25 October 1996.

32 *Yediot Aharonot* 15 December 1996.

33 Cited in *Independent* 13 January 1997.

34 Cited in *Midde East International* 25 October 1996: 5.

35 *International Herald Tribune* 4 March 1997, and *Independent* 4 March 1997.

36 *Sunday Times* 23 March 1997, and *Independant* 24 March 1997.

37 *Independent* 12 April 1997.

38 Cited in *Independent* 3 April 1997.

39 The "Uniting for Peace" device was fashioned by the US in the 1950s to circumvent frequent Soviet vetoes at the UN Security Council.

40 Article I, "Aim of the Negotiations," of the Oslo Accord states: "It is inderstood that the interim arrangements are an integral part of the whole peace process and that the negotiations on the permanant status will lead to the implementation of Security Council Resolutions 242 and 338."

Chapter 13 *Islamist Opposition*

1 1398 was the Islamic year.

2 See the last Quranic verse in Chapter 1, p 20. All Quranic verses are from Arthur J. Arberry, The Koran Interpreted, Oxford University Press, Oxford and New York, 1964.

3 The other co-founders of Hamas were Abdul Fattah Dukhan, a teacher; Isa Nashshar, an engineer; Dr. Abdul Aziz Rantisi, a physician; Muhammad Shamaa, a teacher; Shaikh Salah Shihada, a professor; and Ibrahim al Yazuri, a pharmacist.

4 Shipler 177.

5 Cited in Shaked and Shaby 87.

6 Cited in Abu Amr 80–3.

7 *Middle East International* 8 November 1991: 17–9, and Abu Amr 78.

8 Abu Amr 69–70.

9 *Al Sirat* (Arabic, The Path) June 1998: 10.

10 Cited in Abu Amr 74.

11 *Al Islam wa Falastin* 30 December 1988: 23.

12 Abu Amr 89.

13 See p 194.

14 See p 238.

15 *Jerusalem Post* 27 January 1995.

16 The explosions occured a few hundred yards from the Beit Lid jail where Shaikh Ahmad Yasin of Hamas was held. "It caused me pain," he told the mass circulation Hebrew daily, *Ma'ariv*, on January 2, 1995. "However, the Israeli occupation and violence against Palestinians are the cause, not the effect, pf Palestinian violent resistance. Don't ask me to denounce violence as long as I am under your occupation and persecution. The end of violence would have to be bilateral, not unilateral."

17 *Jerusalem Times* 26 January 1995.

18 *Jerusalem Post* 27 January 1995.

19 *Al Islam wa Falastin* 5 June, 1998: 14. By the early 1990's suicide bombing had been adopted by Sri Lanka's Tamil rebels, Hindu by religion, fighting for an independant state. One of their activists assassinated Indian prime minister Rajiv gandhi in May 1991 this way. And in early 1996 a suicide truck-bombing in front of the Central Bank of Sri Lanka in downtown Colombo killed 72 people and devastated a large area.

20 Qutb 21, Cited in Hiro, *Holy Wars: The Rise of Islamic Fundamentalism* (New York: Routledge 1989) 67.

21 Tawfiq al Tayab, *After the two Catastrophes* (Cairo: Al Mukhtor al Islami, 1979).13.

22 Cited in *Observer* 3 September 1995.

23 Cited in *Observer* 3 September 1995.

24 Jerusalem Report 27 July 1995: 32–3.

25 Guardian 8 January 1996.

26 The figure of 68 included 21 Israelis killed at Beit Lid by the explosions caused by the activists of the Islamic Jihad, to which Yahya Ayash did not belong; the remaining 47 consisting of the victims in Afula (8), Hadera (5), Tel Aviv (22), Ramat Gan (7) and Jerusalem (5).

27 *Observer* 28 January 1996; and *Sunday Times* 7 January 1996.

28 *Jerusalem Report* 27 July 1995: 33.

29 Cited in *Observer* 10 March 1996.

30 Cited in *Sunday Times* 10 March 1996.

31 *Ma'ariv* 2 June 1995.

32 *Independant* 6 March 1996.

33 During the border closure in early 1995, for instance, many Palestine cars and communal taxis from Ramallah entered Jerusalem either via a long, circuitous asphalted route or backroad pedestrian tracks.

34 Cited in *Middle East International* 15 March 1996: 4.

Chapter 15 *Summing Up the Past, Surmising the Future*
1 Cited in Thubron 163.
2 Foreign Office
>2nd November 1917
>Dear Lord Rothschild
>I have much pleasure in conveying to you on behalf of His majesty's government the following declaration of our sympathy with Jewish Zionist aspirations which has been submitted to, and approved by, the Cabinet. "His Majesty's government view with favour the establishment in Palestine of a National Home for the Jewish people, and will use their best endeavours to facilitate the achievement of this object, it being clearly understood that nothing shall be done which may prejudice the civil and religious rights of existing non-Jewish communities in Palestine, or the rights and political status enjoyed by Jews in any other country." I should be grateful if you would bring this declaration to the knowledge of the Zionist Federation.
>Yours sincerely,
>(Arthur James Balfour)

3 See further, Dilip Hiro, *Between Marx and Muhammad: The Changing Face of Central Asia* (New York: HarperCollins 1994) 305.
4 Interview in Jerusalem, January 1995.
5 Interview in Haifa, February 1995.
6 Interview in Jerusalem, February 1995.
7 *Jerusalem Report* 30 November 1995: 14.
8 Interview in Jerusalem, February 1995.
9 Interview in Haifa, February 1995.
10 Elon 243-5.
11 See pp 112–3.
12 *Washington Post* 20 November 1998.
13 See p 196–7.
14 Interview in Kiryat Arba, March 1995.
15 *The Times* 23 December 1997.
16 Interview in Jerusalem, March 1995.
17 *International Herald Tribune* 6 October 1998.
18 Already the Temporary International Presence in Hebron (TIBH), introduced by the UN Security Council in May 1994, following the Ibrahimi Mosque Massacre, continues.
19 See p 237.

Epilogue
1 See p.106.
2 *HaAretz* 26 August 1998.
3 *Washington Post*, 25 October 1998.
4 These figures, culled from the US National Security Agency's satellite pictures, were confirmed by Edward Abingdon, the American consul-general in Jerusalem.
5 *Financial Times* 1 August 1997.
6 Cited in *Middle East International* 11 July 1997: 6.
7 A survey by the Center for Palestinian Research and Studies, released on June 16, 1997, showed that 63 percent believed that there was corruption in the PA. This happened at a time when the same poll showed unemployment in the West Bank at 31 percent and in gaza at 43 percent, with 52 percent saying their economic condition had deteriorated since the 1993 Oslo Accord—four times the figure for those whose condition had improved.
8 Cited in *Middle East International*, 8 August 1997: 5.
9 *The Times*, 2 August 1997.
10 *HaAretz* 26 September 1997.
11Cited in *Middle East International*, August 8: p. 6.
12 However, 56 percent disapproved. *Independent* 26 September 1997.
13 *Middle East International* 12 September 1997: 5.

14 Cited in *Independent* 12 September 1997.

15 Cited in *Middle East International* 26 September 1997: 8.

16 See p.13.

17 The General Assembly resolution further called on Israel to reverse all its illegal actions against the Palestinian residents of East Jerusalem.

18 Cited in *Independent* 26 September 1997.

19 The chemical agent was Fentanyl, a synthetic opiate. One of the agents lunged at Mashaal's left ear with his hand wrapped in a white bandage with a small lead-colored protuberance in the palm. *New York Times* 15 October 1997. The same team hadcarried out the assassination of the Islamic Jihad leader, Fathi Shikaki, in Malta two years earlier. See p.270.

20 *Al Hayat* 4 October 1997.

21 There were then 3,650 Palestinian prisoners in Israel, including 800 under administrative detention.

22 Cited in *Independent* 1 October 1997.

23 *Independent* 23 October 1997.

24 *Sunday Times* 5 October 1997.

25 Cited in *Middle East International* 10 October 1997: 8.

26 *Observer* 26 October 1997.

27 Cited in *Middle East International* 10 October 1997: 3. The crisis could not have come at a worse time for Arafat. The PA's standing had taken a knock following the report on May 24 by its General Auditing Office that $326 million, or about 40 percent of the 1996–97 budget, had been misused or wasted by the PA ministries, now employing 78,000 people, including 35,000 working for the police and other security forces.[7] Arafat responded by appointing a National Commission of Inquiry, which it concluded two months later that corruption existed at all levels of the PA. This happened at a time when a CPRS poll showed unemployment in the West Bank at 31 percent and in Gaza at 43 percent, with 52 percent saying their economic condition had deteriorted since the 1993 Oslo Accord—four times the figure for those whose condition had improved.

28 Only 4 percent based their support for Iraq on Saddam Hussein's policies. *Middle East International* 17 February 1998: 9.

29 *Jerusalem Times* 14 March 1998.

30 *Times* 18 March 1998.

31 *Times* 30 March 1998.

32 Cited in *Middle East International*, April 10, 1998: p. 6.

33 *The Times* 8 May 1998.

34 Cited in *Washington Post* 27 May 1998.

35 *Washington Post* 13 May 1998.

36 *Washington Post* 25 May 1998.

37 *New York Times* 15 May 1998.

38 *Washington Post* 8 June 1998.

39 On the same day Mike McCurry, the White House spokesman, said, "Gingrich's suggestion that the Secretary of State is loyal to anyone but to the people of the United States of America is offensive. He has injected a high degree of partisanship in his comments." *Washington Post* 27 May 1998.

40 *New York Times* 22 June 1998.

41 In private, Netanyahu and Arafat activated a secret channel, with their respective confidantes—Yitzhak Molcho, a lawyer, and Ahmad Qrei, the PLC Speaker—meeting alternatively at each other's homes, and drafting a handwritten deal that three of the thirteen percent Israeli withdrawal would cover a nature reserve in the Judean desert. *Washington Post* 5 November 1998.

42 Interview in Ramallah, September 1998.

43 Interview in Gaza, September 1998.

44 *Middle East International* 8 May 1998: 4.

45 After the 1993 Oslo Accord, besides the killing of six Fatah Eagles in Gaza in March 1994 by an IDF undercover unit, Israel had carried out the assassinations of five Palestinians, including Hani Abid, Mahmoud Khwaja, Kamal Khalid and Yahya Ayash. See p. 267 and p. 272.

46 Among other things the main north-south road in the Gaza Strip had been fully repaired and widened, and the squalid Palestine Square in Gaza City had been transformed beyond recognition. In

Hebron the municipal building had been given a face-lift. Author's visits in September 1998.

47 *Times* 8 July 1998, and *Middle East International* 17 July 1998: 5.

48 *HaAretz* 16 September 1998. The TMF's attempt to lay a foundation stone on the Temple Mount in October 1990 led to a riot in which 17 Palestinians were shot dead by Israel's security forces. See p. 22.

49 Cited in *HaAretz* 17 September 1998.

50 See p. 117.

50 *HaAretz* 17 September 1998.

51 Interview in *Jerusalem*, September 1998. See also p. 160.

52 It was the worst violence of its kind since March 30, 1976. See p. 138.

53 *HaAretz* 18 September 1998.

54 Jibril Rajoub alleged that Sarsour, a construction worker, had murdered Rabbi Raanan in Hebron's Tel Rumaida settlement on 20 August, and injured 14 IDF soldiers in a grenade attack on September 30. According to the *HaAretz* of October 21, the Shin Beth officials confirmed that they had tried to recruit Sansour (who had a record of arrests during the intifada), and had three meetings with him in August and September. Sarsour reportedly told his interrogators that he was a Shin Beth agent at the time of killing Raanan. After that murder he contacted a senior Hamas leader in Hebron who recruited him for the Qassam Brigade which tutored him in th handling of hand grenades. *Guardian* 22 October 1998.

55 *Washington Post* 4 November 1998.

56 *Washington Post* 4 November 1998. Fuller texts of these letters were published in the *HaAretz*.

57 A formal US-Israeli defense treaty would go down badly in Israel which, wedded to the doctrine of self-reliance, has in the past acted militarily to pre-empt attack, and wants to maintain its freedom of unilateral action. *New York Times* 2 November 1998.

58 October 22, 1998.

59 According to the Israeli authorities, the PA has purchased about half of the 150,000 illegal rifles and pistols in the Palestinian territories, either smuggled from Egypt through tunnels to Gaza or Jordan across the Dead Sea, or stolen from IDF bases by Israeli criminals. In the past few years the IDF has discovered and destroyed a dozen tunnels from Egypt into Gaza near the Rafah crossing, some of them large enough to accommodate anti-tank missiles and rocket-propelled grenades. *Jerusalem Report* 16 April 1998: 28–9.

60 According to the Oslo Accords, the PA was to have 20,000 armed policemen, equipped with 11,000 Kalashnikovs, 4,000 pistols and 240 mortars. But these agreements did not mention security and intelligence services. By 1998 the PA had nine such organizations, with most of their personnel bearing arms.

61 Cited in *Middle East International* 19 December 1997: 5. The breakdown of the 11 percent was: borders 3 percent, East Jerusalem 1 per cent, Jewish settlements 6 percent, and IDF locations 1 percent.

62 *Middle East International* 27 November 1998: 12.

63 Reuters 26 October 1998; *Washington Post* October 1998; and AssociatedPress 5 November 1998.

64 *Washington Post* 24 October 1998.

65 Cited in *Middle East International* 30 October 1998: 7.

66 Cited in *Washington Post* 30 September 1998.

67 See p. 314.

68 Cited in *Washington Post* 30 September 1998.

69 *International Herald Tribune* 27 October 1998.

70 See pp. 227-28.

71 November 12, 1998.

72 BBC News, November 15, 1998. Arafat told the Fatah congress, "Our great intifada went on for seven years. If they [the Israelis] don't want to continue on the path of peace, we will start it all over again, but I tell them we have made the peace of the brave out of conviction." *International Herald Tribune* 16 November 1998.

73 *Middle East International* 18 November 1998.

74 *New York Times* 19 November 1998.

75 Cited in *Middle East International* 27 November 1998: 15.

76 *Washington Post*, 23 November 1998.

77 *New York Times* 4 February 1999.

78 *International Herald Tribune* 4 December 1998, and *New York Times* 5 December 1998.

79 *Middle East International* 11 December 1998: 11.

80 *New York Times* 14 Dec 1998.

81 *Washington Post* 16 December 1998; and *Middle East International* 25 December 1998: 15–6. Of the 87 Palestinian legislators (one, Haidar Abdul Shafi, had resigned), 22 boycotted the reception in protest at Washington's mealy-mouthed policy toward the Palestinians.

82 Cited in *Daily Telegraph* 15 December 1998.

83 Meeting in Gaza earlier, the Palestine Central Council had by 81–7 votes approved Arafat's letter of January 20, 1998 to Clinton in which the offending paragraphs of the Charter were declared revoked. *International Herald Tribune* 11 December 1998.

84 *Associated Press* 15 December 1998, and *Agence France-Presse* 15 December 1998.

85 The poll was taken on January 7–9,1999.

86 *International Herald Tribune* 22 December 1998.

87 *New York Times* 22 December 1998.

88 *New York Times* 25 January 1999.

89 *Middle East International* 29 January 1999: 8.

90 At any given time there were 31,000 such students. *New York Times* 10 December 1998.

91 *International Herald Tribune* 27 January 1998.

92 Also the members of the Women of the Wall petitioned the Supreme Court to be allowed to wear a prayer shawl and read the Torah in front of the Wall. *New York Times* 2 February 1999.

93 *New York Times* 15 and 23 February 1999; *Washington Post* 15 February 1999; and *Middle East International* 12 March: 7.

94 *Washington Post* 18 March 1999, and *Middle East Internationa*, 26 March: 9.

95 Cited in *Middle East International* 30 October 1998: 7.

96 On February 22 at a panel discussion organized by the Jewish Council for Public Affairs in Washington, when Israeli ambassador, Zalman Shoval, repeated Netanyahu's charge, Martin Indyk, US Assistant Secretary for Near East, said, "We checked your information, we checked their [PA] information, and we got our own information, and it's simply not true. On the basis that they [PA] did not have any grounds for holding them, they released them. Israel releases people as well." Cited in *Middle East International* 12 March 1999: 8.

97 *Associated Press* 23 March 1999.

98 *Associated Press* 23 March 1999.

99 *Associated Press* 23 March 1999; Washington Post, 24 March 1999; and *Daily Telegraph* 6 April 1999. In mid-March both houses of the US Congress had passed resolutions saying the Palestinian UDI was unacceptable to them.

100 *International Herald Tribune* 27–28 March 1999.

Works Cited

Abu Amr, Ziad. *Islamic Fundamentalism in the West Bank and Gaza.* Bloomington: Indiana University Press, 1994.

Alwash, Naji. *The Arab Resistance in Palestine, 1917-1948* (in Arabic). Beirut: Dar al Mashriq, 1973.

Arberry, Arthur J. *The Koran Interpreted.* New York: Oxford University Press, 1964.

Asali, K.J. *Jerusalem in History.* New York: Olive Branch Press, 1990.

Beit-Hallahmi, Binyamin. *Original Sins: Reflections on the History of Zionism and Israel.* New York: Olive Branch Press, 1993.

Bennis, Phyllis and Moushabeck, Michel. *Beyond the Storm: A Gulf Crisis Reader.* New York: Olive Branch Press, 1991.

Benvenisti, Meron. *Demographic, Economic, Legal, Social and Political Developments in the West Bank.* Jerusalem: The West Bank Data Base Project, 1987.

Benvenisti, Meron. *Jerusalem: A Study of a Polarized Community, Research Paper 3.* Jerusalem: The West Bank Data Base Project, 1983.

Brook, Stephen. *Winner Takes All: A Season in Israel.* London: Picador, 1991.

Central Bureau of Statistics. *Statistical Abstract of Israel 1994.* Tel Aviv: government Publishing House, 1995.

Eber, Shirley, and O'Sullivan, Kevin. *Israel and the Occupied Territories: The Rough Guide.* London: Harrap Columbus, 1989.

Elon, Amos. *The Israelis: Founders and Sons.* New York: Holt, Rinehart & Winston, 1971. Jerusalem: Adam Publishers, 1981.

Etzion, Yehuda. *The Temple Mount (in Hebrew).* Jerusalem: E. Capsi, 1985.

Friedman, Robert I. *Zealots for Zion: Inside Israel's West Bank Settlement Movement.* New York: Random House, 1993.

Gee, John. *Unequal Conflict: The Palestinians and Israel.* New York: Olive Branch Press, 1998.

Gowers, Andrew and Walker, Tony. *Arafat: The Biography.* London: Virgin Books, 1994.

Grossman, David. *The Yellow Wind.* New York: Dell Publishing, 1989.

Hadawi, Sami. *Bitter Harvest: A Modern History of Palestine.* New York: Olive Branch Press, 1991.

Heikal, Mohamed. *Secret Channels*. London: HarperCollins, 1996.

Hersh, Seymour. *The Samson Option: Israel's Nuclear Arsenal And American Foreign Policy.* New York: Random House, 1991.

Hiro, Dilip. *Desert Shield to Desert Storm: The Second Gulf War.* New York: Routledge/London: HarperCollins, 1992.

Hiro, Dilip. *Dictionary of the Middle East*, New York: St Martin's Press/London: Macmillan, 1996.

Hiro, Dilip. *Inside the Middle East.* New York: McGraw-Hill/London: Routledge & Kegan Paul, 1982.

Hirst, David. *The Gun and the Olive Branch: The Roots of Violence in the Middle East.* London: Faber & Faber, 1978.

The Holy Bible: The Old and New Testaments, conformable to the edition of 1611, commonly known as the Authorized or King James Version. Cleveland and New York: World Publishing Company, 1960.

Jerusalem Media and Communication Center. *Israeli Military Orders in the Occupied Palestinian West Bank, 1967-1992.* Jerusalem: Second Edition, 1995.

Jerusalem Media and Communication Center. *Israeli Obstacles to Economic Development in the Occupied Palestinian Territories.* Jerusalem, 1994.

Kaufman, Gerald. *Inside the Promised Land: A Personal View of Today's Israel.* Aldershot: Wildwood House, 1986.

Khalidi, Walid. *From Haven to Conquest: Readings in Zionism and the Palestinian Problem until 1948.* Beirut: The Institute of Palestine Studies, 1971.

Kyle, Keith, and Peters, Joel (eds). *Whither Israel? The Domestic Challenges.* London and New York: I.B. Tauris, 1994.

Lockman, Zachary and Beinin, Joel (eds). *Intifada: The Palestinian Uprising Against Israeli Occupation.* London and New York: I.B. Tauris, 1990.

Lynd, Staughton, Staughton, Alice, and Bahour, Sam. *Homeland: Oral Histories of Palestine and Palestinians.* New York: Olive Branch Press, 1994.

Massoulie, Francois. *Middle East Conflicts.* New York: Olive Branch Press, 1998.

McGowan, Dan and Ellis, Marc. *Remembering Deir Yassin: The Future of Israel and Palestine.* New York: Olive Branch Press, 1998.

McNeill, Graham. *An Unsettling Affair: Housing Conditions, Tenancy Regulations and the Coming of the Messiah in the Old City of Jerusalem.* Birzeit: Birzeit University, 1990.

Melman, Yossi. *The New Israelis.* New York: Carol Publishing Group, 1993.

Morris, Benny. *The Birth of the Palestinian Refugee Problem, 1947-1949.* Cambridge and New York: Cambridge University Press, 1987.

Nasser, Jamal and Heacock, Roger (eds). *Intifada: Palestinians at the Crossroads.* New York: Birzeit University & Praeger, 1991.

Pappe, Ilan. *The Making of the Arab-Israeli Conflict, 1947-51.* New York: I.B. Tauris, 1994.

Peretz, Don. *The Government and Politics of Israel.* Boulder, CO: Westview Press/ United Kingdom: Dawson, 1979.

Qutb, Sayyid. *Signposts along the Road (in Arabic).* Beirut: Dar al Mashriq, 1986.

Raviv, Dan, and Melman, Yossi. *Every Spy a Prince: The Complete History of*

Israel's Intelligence Community. New York: Houghton Mifflin, 1991.

Rolef, Susan Hattis (ed.). *The Political Dictionary of the State of Israel*. Jerusalem: Jerusalem Publishing House, 1993.

Romann, Michael and Weingrod, Alex. *Living Together Separately: Arabs and Jews in Contemporary Jerusalem*. Princeton, N.J.: Princeton University Press, 1991.

Rubinstein, Danny. *People of Nowhere: The Palestinian Vision of Home*. New York: Times Books, 1991.

Said, Edward W. *The Question of Palestine*. New York: Pantheon/London: Routledge & Kegan Paul, 1980.

Schiff, Zeev and Ya'ari, Ehud. *Intifada: The Palestinian Uprising—Israel's Third Front*. New York: Simon and Schuster, 1990.

Shaked, Rony and Shaby, Aviva. *Hamas (in Hebrew)*, Jerusalem: Ketter Publications, 1994.

Shemesh, Moshe. *The Palestinian Entity, 1959-1974: Arab Politics and the PLO*. London: Frank Cass, 1988.

Shipler, David K., *Arab and Jew: Wounded Spirits in a Promised Land*, Penguin Books, New York, 1987.

Smooha, Sammy. *Israel: Pluralism and Conflict*. Boston: Routledge & Kegan Paul, 1978.

Sprinzak, Ehud. *The Ascendance of Israel's Radical Right*. New York: Oxford University Press, 1991.

Thubron, Colin. *Jerusalem*. London: Century Hutchinson, 1986.

Usher, Graham. *Palestine in Crisis*. London: Pluto Press, 1995.

Index

A

al Abadleh, Qusai, 246
Abbas, Mahmoud, 93, 104, 211, 224, 231, 255, 276
Abdul Hakim, see al Samra, Abdul Hakim
Abdul Malik ibn Marwan, 16
Abdullah al Hashem (Jordanian King), 128-9, 227, 289
Abid, Hani, 238, 267
Abidin, Abdul Qadir, 241
Abraham (Old Testament), 1-2, 17, 21, 147-9, 152, 158, 163, 165-8, 171, 280-5
Abram (Old Testament), 280-81, 283
Absentee Property Law 1950 (Israel), 8
Abu al Abbas, see Zaidan, Muhammad Abbas
Abu Abdullah, see Hussein ibn Talal (Jordanian King)
Abu Aied, Jibril, 195
Abu Aied, Mufeed, 195-6
Abu Alaa, see Ahmad Qrei
Abu Ali, Mansour, 173
Abu Ammar, see Arafat, Yasser
Abu Amr, Ziad, 183, 260, 262
Abu Hatzeria, Baruch, 49
Abu al Hol, see Hamid, Hayil Abdul
Abu Ismail, 222
Abu Iyad, see Khalaf, Salah
Abu Jihad, see Wazir, Khalil
Abu Khalif, Amjad, 170
Abu Mazen, see Abbas, Mahmoud
Abu Musa, see Margha, Muhammad Said Musa
Abu Musammeh, Sayyid, 269
Abu Namous, Ahmad, 190
Abu Namous, Baraaka, 190-1
Abu Namous, Harb, 233
Abu Namous, Imad, 190
Abu Namous, Jamal, 190
Abu Namous, Muhammad Harb, 190

Abu Namous, Ziad Muhammad, 190
Abu Nidal, see Banna, Sabri
Abu Sweieh, Muhammad, 188
Abu Tur, 37
Abu Uday, see Hussein, Saddam
Abu Wardeh, Majid, 273-4, 276
Abu Wardeh, Muhammad, 99, 276
Abu Zaid, Hamza, 220
Acre, xxii, xxiii
Adabiya, 77
Adam (Old Testament), 166
Administered Territories, see Occupied Territories
After the Two Catastrophes, 268
Afula, 264
al Agha, Zakaria, 233
Aghazarian, Albert, 203, 294
Agranat, Shimon, 78
Agudat Israel, 41
Ahdut HaAvodah-Poale Zion, 75
Ahmad, Sabiha, 170
Alami, Maher, 237, 303
Alba, Ido, 156
Alexander the Great, 174, 182, 287
Alfersey, Taniya, 127
Algeria, 202, 204, 211-2
Allenby Bridge, 235
Allenby, Edmund, 182
Allied Powers (World War I), 287-8
Allon Plan, 159
Allon, Yigal, 74, 75, 77-9, 96, 150, 157, 299
Aloni, Shulamit, 141
Altalena, 66-7, 81
Alumot kibbutz, 79
Alwash, Naji, 140
Amaleks (Old Testament), 14, 154-5
Aman, 104, 107, 216
American Colony Hotel (Jerusalem), 24, 34, 37, 119, 132
American Jews, 48, 50, 107, 108, 157

American University in Beirut, 197, 205, 223
American University in Cairo, 182, 195
Amir, Yigal, 95-6
Amitel, Meir, 49
Amman, 34, 107, 133, 158, 161, 180, 184, 190, 195, 205, 206, 213-4, 221, 224, 241, 270
Ansar I, 232
Ansar III, 163, 176, 190
Aqaba, 71, 73, 287
Aqabat Jabr, 236
Aql, Imad, 264
Al Aqsa Mosque, 1, 9, 13, 16, 19, 20-3, 28, 35, 165, 192, 241, 249, 284, 300
Arab Democratic Party (Israel), 140, 142
Arab Deterrent Force, 210
Arab Higher Committee (Palestinian), 202
Arab Israelis, see Israeli Arabs
Arab Jews, 50-1, 54, 56, 283, see also Mizrachim and Sephardim
Arab League, 99, 127-30, 184, 202, 206-8, 210, 219, 248, 250, 251, 253-4, 260, 269, 301
Arab Liberation Army, 130
Arab Nationalist Movement, 197
Arab Revolt, 191
Arab Studies Center (East Jerusalem), 223
Arab-Israeli War I (1948-9), 6, 11, 13, 29, 32, 37, 43, 49, 66, 68, 71, 75, 78-9, 81, 84, 126-9, 133, 135, 138, 171, 175, 178, 181, 183, 201-2, 205, 227, 261, 294, 298
Arab-Israeli War II, see Suez War
Arab-Israeli War III, see June 1967 War
Arab-Israeli War IV, see October 1973 War
Arabic language, 13, 15, 30-4, 37, 49, 53, 56, 59, 68, 73, 134-5, 137, 140-1, 162, 165, 167-71, 188, 216, 226, 231, 242-3, 252, 256, 266, 269, 288
Arafat, Yasser, 88, 90, 93-5, 97-9, 101-2, 104-12, 114-6, 127, 142-3, 155, 168, 171, 173, 187-8, 192-3, 195, 200-30, 232-55, 262-3, 265, 267, 269, 270-2, 274-9, 291, 297, 301-3
Arayshe, Tahrir, 177
Arens, Moshe, 90, 93, 219, 258
Argov, Shlomo, 211
Ariel, 109
Ariel, Israel, 19
Ariel, Uri, 151
al Arif, Arif, 286
Al Arish, 182, 289
Arlosoroff, Chaim, 65
Armenia, 288
Armenian Quarter, 10
Arnon, Naom, 146, 156, 167
Arnon, Tsafair, 13

Asfour, Hassan, 230
Ashdod, 95
Asher (Old Testament), 283
Asher, David, 38
Ashkenazim, xii, xx, 3, 39, 42, 45-6, 48-61, 88-9, 92, 122, 139, 148, 284, 295, see also Mizrachim
Ashqelon, 97, 247, 273
Ashrawi, Emile, 223
Ashrawi, Hanan, 222-4, 242-3, 246
Assad, Hafiz, 207, 210, 213
Assad, Rifaat, 213
Associated Press, 265
Assyrians, 283, 285
Aswan High Dam, 70
Atalai, Elhanoun Aron, 14
Atara Le Yoshna, 8, 10
Athens, 206
Atreet Cohanim Yeshiva, see Yeshiva Atreet Cohanim
Atzmona, 199
Aviner, Shlomo Haim, 10
Avineri, Shlomo, 59
Awali River, 213
Ayash, Yahya, 97, 99, 264, 271, 273
Ayubi, Salah al Din, see Saladin
Azerbaijan, 288
Al Azhar University (Gaza City), 106, 200, 279
Azzam Pasha, Abdul Rahman, 128

B

Baal, 21
Baath Socialist Party (Syria), 202, 206
Babylon and Babylonians (Old Testament), 2-3, 283, 285
Badawi, Amjad, 177
Baghdad, 45, 49, 54, 115, 125, 185, 192, 210-1, 214, 219, 221-2
Bahar, Ahmad, 270
Baker, James, 109, 221, 252, 254
Balawi, Abdul Hakkam, 227, 245
Balfour, Arthur James, xxvi, 288
Balfour Declaration (1917), 142, 205, 221, 287-8
Banna, Hassan al, 257
Baqaa (Jerusalem), 28, 38
Bar Lev, Chaim, 149
Bar Shalom, Menachem, 9
Bar Yohai, Shimon, 48
Barak, Ehud, 98
Barghouti, Iyad, 174
Barghouti, Said, 137, 141
Basle, xxvi, 66, 208, 285, 287
Battle of Karameh, 163, 204-5, 235
Baybar (Ottoman Sultan), 166
al Bayed, Walid, 175

Beddawi, 213
Beersheba, 163, 176-7, 190, 216
Begin, Benny, 64
Begin, Menachem, 9, 43-4, 51-2, 64, 66-7, 72-5, 81-7, 92-3, 111, 148, 157, 195, 210-1, 225, 291
Beilin, Yossi, 93, 112, 115, 224-5, 254, 297
Beinin, Joel (American author), 185
Beinin, Joel (Western Wall visitor), 2
Beirut, xxii, xxv, 85-6, 100-1, 125, 129, 133, 140, 197, 202, 205, 207, 211-2, 215, 223, 227, 247, 262, 266, 287
Beit El (Jewish Settlement), 154, 158, 183
Beit El (Old Testament), 147, 149, 280
Beit Hanoun, 239
Beit Lahiya, 97, 195-6, 200, 271
Beit Lehem, see Bethlehem
Beit Lid, 23, 94, 239, 266
Beit al Muquddus, see Jerusalem
Beit Shean, 92
Ben Eliezer, Binyamin, 159
Ben Gurion, David, xxi, 41, 43, 49-51, 62, 65-73, 79, 81, 83-4, 96, 130-1, 136-7, 204, 208, 291
Ben Nahuman, Moshe, 5, 12
Ben Shoshan, Yeshua, 17
Beni Israel, 20, 283-5
Benvensiti, Meron, 6, 180
Beqaa Valley, 100
Bethlehem, xxvi, 6, 29, 74, 97, 105, 113, 115, 147, 149, 159, 177, 191, 234, 237, 244, 253, 272
BeTselem, 269
Bhatia, Shyam, 269
Bir Nabala, 237-8
The Birth of the Palestinian Refugee Problem, 1947, 125
Birzeit University, 176, 183, 203, 222-3, 264
Black Panther Party (Israel), 51, 139
Black September, 164, 207
Bnei Akiva, 17, 148
Bnei Beraq, 45
Bonaporte, Napoleon, 287
Boutros-Ghali, Boutros, 240
Bratslav (Ukraine), 13, 39-40
Bratslavic (Jewish sect), 39
Britain and British, xii-iii, xxvi, xxvii, 5-6, 9, 11, 15, 30, 32-3, 51, 53-4, 62, 72, 75, 78, 80-1, 83, 85-6, 99, 124, 126-30, 136, 137, 140-1, 145, 147, 154, 161, 166, 174, 178, 182, 187, 200, 202, 205,-6, 211, 220, 232, 257, 266, 274, 284, 286-92, 296, 298-9
British White Paper (1939), 65
Brook, Stephen, 51
Bulan, 284

Bulganin, Nikolai, 71
al Buraq, 20-1
al Bureij, 200-1
Burqah, 275
Burqan, Muhammad, 7
Bush, George, 189, 248, 252
Buzaglo, Meir, 46, 54

C

Cairo, 17, 70, 73, 76, 94, 104, 107, 114, 180-2, 195-6, 201-2, 205-6, 211, 222, 224, 231-6, 238-9, 243, 247-9, 251, 256-7, 264, 271, 295
Cairo Agreement (May 1994), 232-5, 238, 243, 247, 264, 295
Camp David (Maryland, USA), 83, 86, 88-9, 162
Camp David Accords (1978), 9, 83, 86, 88, 139, 162, 182, 210, 225, 229
Canaan (Old Testament), 156, 171, 281-2, 285
Cardova, Rubin, 40
Carter, James, 83, 252
Catholics, 210, 292
Cave of Machpela (Old Testament), 165-7; *see also* Tomb of the Patriarchs
Central Powers (World War I), 288
Chafets, Zeev, 293
Chamoun, Camille, 210
Cheney, Dick, 174
Cheshin, Amir, 36
Chetrit, Sami, 50, 54
Chicago, 246
Chief Rabbinate (Israel), 41-2, 67
Chosroes II (Persian Emperor), 21
Christian Quarter (Jerusalem), 9, 12
Christianity and Christians, 5, 16, 31, 49, 166, 174, 178, 182, 209, 210, 237, 244, 260, 284, 292
Christopher, Warren, 99, 103, 277
Church of God (Christian sect), 16
Church of Resurrection, see Church of the Holy Sepulchre
Church of the Holy Sepulcher, 1, 12, 16
von Clausewitz, Karl, 130
Clinton, Bill, 99, 195
Club des Pins (Algeria), 215, 217
Cohen, Erik, 59
Cohen, Galia, 149
Cohen, Stuart, 123
Collusion Across the Jordan, 129
Communist Party of the Soviet Union, 208
Copenhagen, xxiii
Comprehensive Interim Agreement (Israeli-Palestinian, see Oslo II Accord
Compulsory Service Law 1949 (Israel), 120
Constituent Assembly (Israel), 67

Costa Rica, 30
Council of the Jewish Communities in Judea, Samaria and Gaza, 151
Cromwell, Oliver, 292
Crusades and Crusaders, 1, 4-5, 16, 23, 37, 166, 171, 174, 182, 250
Cyprus, 266, 289
Czechoslovakia, 128, 130, 290

D

Dababesh, Faraj, 265
Dahlan, Muhammad, 104, 234, 236
Damascus, xxiii, 34, 73, 99, 104, 185, 202-3, 211, 213-4, 262-3, 265-8, 270, 273
Damascus Gate (Jerusalem), 1, 28, 30, 34-5
Dan (Old Testament), 283
Dan, Matityahu HaCohen, 9
Darawshe, Abdul Wahab, 140
Darie, 175
Darwish, Abdullah Nimr, 144
David (Old Testament), 149, 156, 165, 284
Dawayma, 178
Day of Equality, 140
Day of Housing, 140
Day of Peace, 140
Day of the Land, 115, 139, 140, 175
Dayan, Moshe, 6, 69, 71-3, 78, 150, 157, 163
Declaration of Establishment of Israel, xix, 42, 66, 142
Declaration of Independance of Israel, see Declaration of the Establishment of Israel
Declaration of Principles, see Oslo Accord
Deheisheh, xxvi, 177, 179, 191, 293
Deir Aban, xxvi
Deir Yasin, 66, 81, 240
Democratic Front for Peace and Equality (Israel), 139, 142
Democratic Front for the Liberation of Palestine, 193, 206, 210, 254, 265
Democratic Movement for Change, 80, 83, 87
Democratic Palestinian Union, 229-30
Denmark, 231
Deri, Arye, 45-6, 117, 142
Detroit, 246
Deuteronomy, 285
Dhaka, xxiii
diaspora (Jewish), xx, 58-9, 61, 125, 133, 290, 296-7
diaspora (Palestinian), xxiii, xxv, 206, 215, 222, 241, 298
Dimona, 79, 216
Dimra, 200
Dinitz, Simcha, 77

Diodoros I, 241
Dome of the Chain, 19
Dome of the Rock, xxvii, 1, 9, 15-9, 153, 156, 190, 241, 268, 292
Dresden, 212
Druze, 64, 124, 134, 143-4
Dung Gate (Jerusalem), 1, 30

E

Ealin, Abdul Qadir, 196
East Europe, 43, 57, 66, 68, 130
East Jerusalem, 6, 18-9, 21, 22, 24-7, 29-34, 36-7, 74-5, 84, 89, 104, 108-9, 113, 143, 145, 151, 156, 159, 171, 178, 184-5, 189, 195, 202, 22-3, 229, 237, 244-6, 248, 249, 250, 255, 265, 269-70, 294, 298-9, 302, 304, see also Greater East Jerusalem
East Talpiyot, xxvii, 25, 31
Eban, Abba, 73
Edot Mizrachim, see Mizrachim
Education Ministry (Israel), 31, 34, 141-2, 319
education system (Israel), 135
Efrat, xxvi, xxvii, 309
Egypt and Egyptians, xxi, 60, 65-7, 70-9, 83-4, 90, 96, 108, 127-8, 130, 146, 162, 174, 181-2, 195, 197, 199, 201, 204-6, 210-1, 214, 220, 232, 235, 239, 248-9, 253, 257, 261, 267, 277, 281, 287, 289-90, 301-3
Egyptian-Israeli Peace Treaty (1979), 17, 84, 164, 302
Ein Hilwa, 133, 135
Eisenhower, Dwight, 71
Eitan, Raphael, 85
Elazar, David, 77-8
Elijah (Old Testament), 21
Elon, Amos, 7, 55, 126, 295
Elon Moreh, 17, 83, 149, 157-8
Eppel, David, 53
Eretz Israel, xxi, xxii, xxv, 9, 17, 59, 82, 95, 102-3, 106, 113-4, 137, 146-8, 150, 158, 179, 284, 295, 299, 301
Erez, 98, 104, 182, 183, 196, 198, 200
Esharif, Muhyi al Din, 270
Eshkol, Levi, 72, 82, 134
Ethiopian Jews, 199, 283
Etzion, Yehuda, 16, 17, 19
Euphrates River, 17, 281
European Jews, 34, 48, 50, 283, 287-90, see also Ashkenazim
European Union, 27, 250, 302, 304
Events in Jerusalem, 33
ex-Soviet Jews, see Russian immigrants (Jewish)

F

Falashas, *see* Ethiopian Jews
Falastinuna: Nida al Hayat, 201
Faluji, Imad, 268, 273
Fatah, 97, 169, 175-6, 178, 193, 195-6,
    200-9, 211-3, 215-7, 223, 225, 229,
    230, 235-6, 238, 242-7, 250, 252, 257,
    262, 264-5, 267, 279
Fatah Hawks, 193, 238, 264
Al Fawwar, 273-4
Financial Times, 217
First Temple, 2, 11, 147, 256
Flower Gate (Jerusalem), 30
Force 17 (Palestinian), 204, 214, 235
Force 18 (Palestinian), 235
Ford, Gerald, 209
Fourth Geneva Convention, 30, 189, 219,
    250, 254, 262
Franjieh, Suleiman, 210
French Hill, 25
Friedman, Robert, 11, 198
*From Haven to Conquest: Readings in
    Zionism and the Palestinian Problem*, 129
Fuchs, Pinchas, 157

G

Gabriel (Old Testament), 21
Gad (Old Testament), 283
Gailani, Rashid, 54
Gal, Reuven, 125
Galanta, Abraham, 48
Galilee, 45, 48-9, 71, 126, 130, 133, 138-
    9, 202
Galili, Israel, 75, 77
Gaza Center for Rights and Law, 239
Gaza City, xxiii, 99, 101, 106, 110, 182-3,
    190, 195-200, 204, 232-4, 238-9, 241,
    251, 253, 256, 258, 264, 267-9, 271-2,
    276-7, 279
Gaza Regional Council, 198
Gaza Strip, xxii-v, 12, 22-3, 70-1, 74-5,
    82, 84-5, 88-9, 93-4, 98, 105-6, 110,
    123-4, 139, 143, 150, 152, 157, 179-80,
    183-6, 194-5, 197-201, 205, 225, 227,
    229, 232-3, 235-8, 240, 246-7, 251,
    256-8, 260, 262-5, 267, 269, 272-3,
    275-8, 290, 293, 296, 298-9, 301
Gemayel, Amin, 86
Gemayel, Bashir, 85
Genesis (Old Testament), 148, 156, 158,
    165, 280-3
Geneva, 25, 30, 78, 89, 187, 189, 209,
    218-9, 250, 254, 262
Geneva Convention relative to Protection of
    Civilian Persons in Times of War, *see*
    Fourth Geneva Convention

Gere (Jewish sect), 41
Germany, 82, 90, 99, 119, 149, 154, 201-
    2, 274, 287-8, 290
Gesher, 103, 113
Ghazali, Said, 265
Gillon, Karmi, 97-8
Gilo, 25
Givat HaMitvar, *see* French Hill
Givat HaSinai, 164
Givat Mamre, 149, 165, 299
Glubb, John, 130
Golan Heights, 10, 18, 74-6, 84, 103, 248
Goldstein, Baruch Kapal, 155
Goldstein, Miriam, 155
Goliath (Old Testament), 128
Goren, Shlomo, 46
The Government and Politics of Israel, 68
Gowers, Andrew, 217
Grapes of Wrath operation, 100-1
Greater East Jerusalem, xxiii, 6, 24, 32, 34,
    36-7, 108-9, 143, 145, 151, 156, 159,
    195, 229, 244-6, 250, 265, 298, *see
    also* East Jerusalem
Greater Syria, 283
Greek Orthodox Church, 12-3
Grossman, David, 191
Gulf of Aqaba, 71, 73, 287
Gulf of Suez, 77
Gulf states, 197, 204, 211, 217, 220-1,
    274, 296
Gulf War (1991), 26, 90-2, 123, 151, 173-4,
    184, 192, 220-1, 247-8, 296
Gus, Avi, 53
Gush Emunim, 13, 17, 79, 83, 148, 150,
    157, 345
Gush Qatif, 198-9, 237

H

HaAretz, 145
Habad (Jewish sect), *see* Lubanvitch (Jewish
    sect)
Habash, George, 205, 229
Habib, Philip, 212
Habibi, Emile Shukri, 133
Hadash, *see* Democratic Front for Peace and
    Equality
Hadashot, 224
Hadera, 264
Hadi, Mahdi Abdul, 184
Haetzni, Eliakim, 299
Hafiz, Khadija, 170
Haganah, 66, 71, 78-9, 81, 84, 126,
    129-30, 136-7, 147
Hagar (Old Testament), 281-2
Hague Convention, 150
Hai (Old Testament), 280
Haifa xviii, 48, 63, 66, 127, 133-4, 140,

147, 192, 196
Haifa University, 53, 127, 132, 135, 137, 291
al Haj, Majid, 135, 140
Halacha, 39, 41-2, 154, 156
Halevi, Yossi, 28, 34, 151, 186, 188, 193
Halhoul, 154, 162, 253
Hamad, Hisham, 238
Hamad, Kamal, 97, 272
Hamad, Osama, 271
Haman (Old Testament), xvii, 154
Hamas, xxiv-v, 94-5, 97-9, 102, 115-6, 140-1, 143, 154, 175, 185-8, 193-4, 225, 227, 229, 230, 234-5, 237-8, 240, 247, 249, 250, 253-8, 260-5, 268-79, 294, 296
Hamid, Hayil Abdul, 220
Hanegbi, Tzahi, 99, 114, 117
Hani, Abdul, 240, 277
Har Homa, 26, 113-6, 252-5, 278
al Haram al Khalil, see Tomb of the Patriarchs
al Haram al Sharif, see Noble Sanctuary
Haredim, see ultra-Orthodox Jews
Hassadim, 39-41
Hassan, Khalid 206, 215
Hawatmeh, Nayif, 208
Hebrew language, 38
Hebrew University (Jerusalem), 26, 47, 55, 121, 127, 132, 137, 141, 162, 290
Hebron, 17, 18, 29-30, 74, 94, 101-2, 104-5, 108-14, 117-8, 144, 146-50, 152-8, 160-6, 168-9, 171-2, 175, 178, 194, 231, 236, 244, 248-9, 251-3, 262, 264, 273, 275, 278, 290-1, 297, 301
Hendel, Zvi, 199
Herod Antipas (Roman Governor), 2
Herod the Great (Roman Emperor), 126, 165
Herod's Gate (Jerusalem), 30
Herut, 51, 81, 86, 92
Herzl, Theodor, xxvi, 126
Herzliya, 147
Herzog, Chaim, 227
Himnutta Company, 12
Hintlian, George, 10, 192
Hirschfield, Yair, 225
Histadrut, xvii, 31, 37, 52, 65, 75
history books, 24, 54, 137, 141
History of the Middle East, 142
History of Palestine, Volumes VI-VII, 291
Hizbollah, 100-2, 278
Holland, 76, 146
Holocaust, 4, 41, 50, 54, 119-20, 126, 290
Holocaust Day, 119-20
Homs, 223
Horovitz, David, 191
Hourani, Abdullah, 240
Housing Ministry (Israel), 9, 319

Hudson, Michael C., 204
Hungary, 68, 288
Hussein, ibn Talal (Jordanian King), 73, 88-9, 94, 163, 178, 187, 192, 202, 206-8, 213-5, 217, 220, 228, 241, 251, 259, 301
Hussein, Saddam, 90, 189, 192, 219
al Husseini clan (Gaza Strip), 201
al Husseini clan (Jerusalem), 15, 222
Husseini, Abdul Qadir, 222
Husseini, Faisal, 27, 222-4, 233, 243
Husseini, Muhammad Amin, 222
Hyrcanus, John (Hasmonean King), 165

I

Ibrahim, *see* Abraham
Ibrahimi Mosque (Hebron), *see* Tomb of the Patriarchs
Immigration and Absorption Ministry (Israel), xxvii, 92, 151
intifada, xxii, xxiv-v, xxvii, 10, 14, 28, 34, 88-90, 105-6, 123-4, 138-41, 144, 153-4, 163, 170, 172, 175, 177, 183-96, 198-200, 215-7, 219-20, 223, 230, 232, 234, 236, 241, 244, 249, 257-64, 266, 268-9, 274, 278, 293, 296
Intifada, 185-7, 215
In the Land of Israel, 290
India, 167, 182, 287-9
Interior Ministry (Israel), 196
Iran, 99, 102, 118, 220, 263, 268, 270, 277, 293
Iraq, xxi, 54, 55, 66-7, 90, 118, 128, 130, 171, 184, 189, 209, 210-2, 219, 220-1, 236, 283, 287, 289
Iraqi Jews, 54
Irbid, 207
Irgun, 66-7, 75, 81, 86, 130, 137, 291
Isa, Malik al Muzzam, 5
Isaac (Old Testament), 1-2, 165-6, 280-5
Isaac's Mosque (Hebron), 167
Isawiya, 37
Ishaq, *see* Isaac
Ishaqiye Mosque (Hebron), *see* Isaac's Mosque (Hebron)
Ishmael (Old Testament), *see* Ismail (Old Testament)
Islam, xxvii, 16, 19-20, 49, 141, 144, 165, 169, 174, 178, 256-7, 259, 260-1, 272, 279, 283-4, 294
Al Islam wa Falastin, 261, 266
Islamic Bloc, 169-71, 279
Islamic Center, 185, 257-9, 262-3, 293
Islamic College (Hebron), *see* Islamic University (Hebron)
Islamic Conference Organization, 16, 253, 300, 312
Islamic fundamentalism, 174, 258, 293

Islamic Jihad (Palestine), 4, 23, 94, 97-8, 102, 104, 116, 140-1, 178-9, 184, 194, 227, 235, 237-40, 247, 249, 256, 258, 260, 264, 266-8, 270-1, 274, 275-9
Islamic Movement (Israel), 144-5, 258, 263, 272
Islamic Resistance Movement (Palestine), *see* Hamas
Islamic University (Gaza City), 237, 256, 261, 276
Islamic University (Hebron), 292
Ismail (Old Testament), 1
Israel Broadcasting Authority, 53, 306
Israel Defense Forces (IDF), xxi, 4, 9, 10, 15, 17, 19, 21-3, 29, 44, 66-9, 71-3, 77-81, 83, 85-6, 88, 94, 97-8, 100-1, 103, 105-6, 109-15, 118-9, 120-6, 130-1, 134, 136-8, 144, 150, 152, 154, 157-8, 161-4, 166-3, 175-6, 178, 181-4, 186-96, 198-201, 203-4, 211-3, 216, 218, 223, 231-40, 242-4, 247, 249, 251, 255, 257-8, 261-6, 268, 270, 273-7, 292, 294, 296, 298-9, 301-2
Israel Land Administration, 8
Israeli Arabs, 6, 12-3, 26, 31, 64, 68, 73, 101-3, 132-4, 137-40, 142-4, 184, 188, 224, 238, 250, 275, 291-2, 294-5
Israeli Association of Civil Rights, 227
Israeli Invasion of Lebanon (1978), 100, 124, 211
Israeli Invasion of Lebanon (1982), *see* Lebanon War (1982)
Israeli Obstacles to Economic Development in the Occupied Palestinian Territories, 180
Israeli-Palestine Liberation Organization Accord, *see* Oslo Accord (September 1993)
The Israelis: Founders and Sons, 55, 128
Israelites, *see* Beni Israel
Istanbul, 65
Al Istiqlal, 238, 267-8
Italy, 85, 99, 231, 266, 288

J

Jaabari, Amani , 170
Jabal al Muqabar, 21, 31
Jabaliya camp, xxiv, 183, 185, 188, 234, 264
Jaber, Abdul Hamid, 164
Jaber, Badran Bader, 161
Jaber, Fathi, 161
Jaber, Hamida, 164
Jabotinsky, Vladimir Zeev, 59, 81
Jacob (Old Testament) 2, 24, 158, 165-7, 280, 282-4
Jaffa, xxii, xxiii, 34-5, 114, 144, 201, 261, 273, 290

Jaffa Gate (Jerusalem), 1, 15, 30, 35, 294
Jalazoun, 175-9, 187
Japan, 99, 288,
Jarash, xxiii
Jarrar, Bassam, 262, 280
Javne, 261
Jayousi, Faizeh, 192
Jenin, 74, 175, 178, 203, 244
Jericho, 93, 94, 148, 178, 229, 232-3, 235-7
Jerusalem, xxiii, xxvii, 1-9, 11-2, 14, 16, 18-9, 21-2, 24-40, 44-7, 50-1, 53-4, 62, 64, 66, 71-2, 74-5, 77-8, 80-1, 83-4, 89, 92, 94-8, 102-9, 113-9, 121, 126-7, 132, 143, 145-6, 150-1, 153, 156, 158-9, 165, 167, 169, 171, 178, 181-5, 188-9, 191-3, 195, 199, 201-2, 209, 213-4, 218, 221-3, 225, 229-30, 234-7, 241-2, 244--50, 252-3, 255-6, 258-9, 263, 265-6, 269-70, 273, 275-6, 285-7, 291, 293-4, 297-303, *see also* East Jerusalem, Greater East Jerusalem and West Jerusalem
Jerusalem, *sanjak* of, 287
Jerusalem 3000, 27, 29, 294
Jerusalem Post, 33, 108, 156, 266
Jerusalem Post Magazine, 199
Jerusalem Reclamation Project, 9
Jerusalem Report, 28, 34, 132, 151, 159, 181, 188, 191, 193, 235-6, 273, 293, 300
Jesus Christ, 1
Jewish Agency, xxvii, 65-6, 127
Jewish Defense League (United States), 152
Jewish fundamentalists, 279-80
Jewish mysticism, *see kabbala*
Jewish National Fund, 12, 41, 294, 297
Jewish nationalism, xvii, 59-60, 81, 108, 286
Jewish Quarter (Jerusalem), 2, 4-8, 11, 14, 19, 29, 31, 34-6, 146-7, 153
Jewish Quarter Restoration and Development Corporation, 7
Jewish settlements and settlers, xxvii, 10, 12, 14, 17-8, 22-6, 29-30, 32, 34, 36, 66, 78, 90-2, 94-5, 102-3, 105-6, 108-10, 112, 126, 147, 149, 150-60, 162-3, 166, 168, 170, 173, 183, 195, 197-9, 224-6, 229-31, 237, 240, 242-4, 248-52, 254, 269, 275-7, 292, 297-9
Jewish Underground, 18
Jews, 49, 58, *see also* American Jews, Arab Jews, European Jews, Indian Jews, Iraqi Jews, Moroccan Jews and Yemeni Jews
Jibril, Ahmad, 205
Jneid, 162, 176
Johnson, Lyndon, 79

Jora, 257
Jordan, xxi, xxiii, 29-33, 62, 66-7, 71,
  73-4, 83, 88-9, 94, 96, 103, 106, 108,
  113, 115, 127-8, 130, 133, 147-8, 150,
  158, 171, 174-5, 178, 187, 195-6, 198,
  201-4, 206-8, 213-5, 217-20, 227,
  235-6, 241, 246, 248, 253, 257,
  259-60, 262-3, 268, 270, 272, 274,
  277, 284, 286-7, 289, 301-2
Jordan Valley, 113, 150, 158-9, 299, 300
Jordanian-Israeli Peace Treaty (1994), 94,
  302
Joshua (Old Testament), 156, 158, 165
Joudeh, Jamal, 173
Judah, Kingdom of, 165, 283, 285
Judaism, 3, 4, 9, 16, 38-9, 41-2, 45, 48,
  60, 64, 67, 126, 133, 146, 279, 284
Judaistic fundamentalism, *see* Jewish
  fundamentalism
Judaistic laws (Israel), *see* Religious laws
Judea, 10, 18, 24, 147-9, 151, 158, 162,
  224, 326
Judges (Old Testament), 156
Jumblat, Kamal, 210
June 1967 War, xxi, xxv, 29, 72, 78, 113,
  124, 168, 185, 197, 205, 223, 290, 298
Jupiter, 21
Juul, Mona, 93, 104, 225

K

kabbala, 48-9
Kach, 153, 293
Kadume, 79, 157
Kahalani, Avigdor, 103, 118
Kahan, Yitzhak, 86
Kahane, Baruch, 153
Kahane Chai, 153, 155, 293
Kahane, Meir, 153
Kaleb, 156
Karaki, Abdul Karim, 21-2
Karameh, 163, 203-5, 218, 235, 346
Katchta, Shaul, 49
Kedma schools, 54-5
Kennedy, John, 79
Kessar, Yisrael, 52
Kfar Darom, 106, 198, 240
Kfar Etzion, 148, 159
Kfar Giladi, 126
Kfar Zechariah, 90
Khadam, 167
Al Khadr, 95
Khadr (Old Testament), *see* Elijah (Old
  Testament)
Khalaf, Karim, 162
Khalaf, Salah, 200-1, 206, 208, 211, 218,
  220
Khalidi, Walid, 129

Al Khalil al Rahman, *see* Hebron
Khalil, Samiha, 245, 349
Khan Yunis, xxiii, 194, 199, 201, 233,
  240, 261, 277, 279
Khartoum, 224, 263, 270
Khatib, Rouhi, 30
Khaykin, Yona, 153
Khazar, *see* Khazaria, Kingdom of
Khazaria, Kingdom of, 284
Kheil, Kamal, 239
Khomeini, Ruhollah, 267
*Khomeini: The Islamic Solution and
  Alternative*, 267
Khushniya, 76
kibbutzim, xviii, 41, 80, 122, 294
Kidre, Khalid, 269, 276
Kinda tribe, 284
King David Hotel (Jerusalem), 81
Kiryat Arba 17-8, 110, 144, 146-50, 152-8,
  163-8, 170, 172, 292, 299
Kiryat Gan, 169
Kiryat HaYovel, 28
Kiryat Shimona, 100
Kissinger, Henry, 76
Kollek, Teddy, 27, 32
kollel, 42-3
Kook, Avaraham Yitzhak HaCohen, 148
Kook, Zvi Yehuda, 11, 148
Koran, *see* Quran
Kosygin, Alexei, 76
Kotel, *see* Western Wall
Kuttab, Daoud, 194
Kuwait, 22, 26, 90, 184-5, 189, 192, 196,
  201-2, 220-1, 241, 247

L

Labor Party (Israel), 51, 57, 63, 69, 74-5,
  78-9, 224-5, 293
Labor-Mapam bloc, 78, 87
al Lakhim, Abu Wahid al Bikri, 11
Lalor, Paul, 187
Lamdan, Yaacov, 126
Land of Israel, *see* Eretz Israel
Landover, Joel, 3
Larnaca, 214
Larsen, Terje Rod, 93, 104, 225, 240
Lass, Yoram, 62
Lavon, Pinchas, 70
Law of Return (1950), 68
League of National Liberation (Palestine), 133
League of Nations, xxvi, 219, 287-8
Leah (Old Testament), 165, 167, 283
Lebanese Civil War (1975–90), 213
Lebanese Front, 210
Lebanon, xxi-iii, xxv, 66-7, 84-8, 96,
  99-100, 102-3, 107, 124-5, 128-9, 133,
  140, 148, 150, 153, 162, 172, 174,

184, 194-5, 202, 204, 207-8, 210-1, 213,-4, 220, 225, 228, 236, 247, 261-2, 263-4, 266, 268, 270, 272, 274, 278, 287, 290
Lebanon War (1982), 84, 86-7
Lehi, 17, 66, 68, 81, 86, 130, 137, 291
Leor, Israel, 77
Levi (Old Testament), 283
Levinger, Miriam, 148, 172
Levinger, Moshe, 17, 146, 148, 152, 158, 169
Levy, David, 12, 51, 52, 60, 64, 86, 92
Levy, Moshe, 52
Liberal Party (Israel), 73
Libinskin, Zeev, 158
Libya, 210, 211, 212, 270
Liebowitz, Efrat, 19
Likud, 9, 25-7, 43-4, 47, 51-2, 57, 59-60, 64, 74-5, 78, 80-2, 84-7, 89, 91-3, 95, 97-9, 103, 107-8, 112-3, 117-8, 139, 143, 146-7, 149-51, 157, 160, 162, 164, 194, 210, 219, 224, 230, 275, 297-8
Lion's Gate (Jerusalem), 30
Livni, Menachem, 17, 156, 292
Lockman, Zachary, 185
Lod, 71, 177, 194, 205
London, 5, 70-1, 73, 88, 104, 172, 216, 221, 232, 269, 288-9, 290, 292
Lubanvitch (Jewish sect), 8
Lydda, 205

M

Maalot Dafna, 25
Ma'ariv, 60, 114-5, 117, 273-4
Maccabees, 285
Mackey, Sandra, 212
Madrid, 60, 91, 93, 109, 113, 118, 152, 193, 222-3, 225, 228-9, 238, 243, 248, 249, 252, 254, 262-3, 298
Mafdal, *see* National Religious Party (Israel)
Maher, Captain, 176
Mahmoud, Omar, 171
Majd al Kurum, 133
Maki, 46, 51-2, 58, 63, 69, 83, 85, 93, 95, 114, 127, 133-4, 136, 138, 144, 150, 160, 172, 189, 191, 212, 215-7, 227-8, 294, 301
The Making of the Arab-Israeli Conflict, 127
Mamelukes, 5, 182
Manna, Adel, 132, 141, 143-4, 184, 292, 319
Mansion House (Gaza City), 232, 234, 246
Mapai, 41, 42, 50, 65, 67-9, 75, 79-80, 204
Mapam, 68, 78, 82, 87, 134, 138
Margha, Muhammad Said Musa, 213

Marj al Zuhur, 261, 263
Marmur, Dow, 42
Maronite Christians, 85, 210
Marsden, Eric, 80
Marseilles, 230
martyrdom, 266-7, 277
Masada, 125-6
masorti, 58
Masri, Munib, 233
McNeill, Graham, 9
Mea Shearim, 3, 14, 37-41, 46
Mecca, 1, 20, 165, 222
Medad, Yisrael, 153
Medina, 20, 165
Megged, Aharon, 96
Meir, Golda, xxv, 74-5, 90, 198
Meiri, Yehoshua, 224
Melamed, Zalman, 154
Melman, Yossi, xxi, 120, 216
Meretz 44, 91, 102-3, 112, 141, 160, 238
Merkaz Harav Kook Yeshiva, *see* Yeshiva Merkaz HaRav Kook
Middle East Peace Conference (Geneva, 1977), 78, 91
Middle East Peace Conference (Madrid, 1991), 26, 109, 118, 160, 184, 222-3, 226, 248
Mideast Mirror, 221
Milhem, Muhammad, 162
military (Israel), *see* Israel Defense Forces
Milson, Menachem, 162
Mintz, Abraham, 17
Mitnagdim, 39-41
Mizrachim, xx, xxi, 39, 45, 47-61, 103, 284
Mizrahi, 41-2, 48
Mizrahi, Chaim, 154
Moledet, 89, 147
Montefiore, Moses, 5
Morag, 198
Moroccan Jews, 49
Morocco, 38, 49, 51, 90, 92, 220, 301
Morris, Benny, 125-7, 129-30, 136
Moscow, 68, 76-7, 152, 208, 290
Moses (Old Testament), 20, 43, 156, 165, 280, 284-5
Mossad, 86, 115, 214, 216-7, 227-8, 230, 270
Mosul, 289
Mount Ebal, 158
Mount Meron, 48
Mount Moriah, 2, 9-11, 17
Mount Scopus, 26, 121
Moyne, Lord, 86
Mubarak, Hosni, 99, 106, 110, 214, 228, 239, 249, 251-2, 277, 301-3

Muhammad (Prophet), 1, 20-1, 165, 280, 284
Muhammad Suri, xxii
Multinational Force (in Lebanon), 86
Musaaid, Hussein, 177
Muslim Brotherhood, 144, 185, 257-9, 261-2, 267, 293
Muslim Quarter (Jerusalem) 8-10, 13-4, 23, 35, 105, 118, 158, 249
Muslims, 1, 5, 9, 16, 20-1, 23, 30-1, 34-5, 134, 141, 165-70, 172-4, 178, 209-10, 241-2, 256-7, 264, 267-8, 275, 279-80, 283, 289, 293, 295

N

Nabatiya, 100
Nablus, xxiii, 1, 17, 30, 74, 79, 83, 105, 109, 116, 133, 147-9, 157, 162, 171-3, 176, 223, 234, 244, 254, 272, 279
Nabulsi, Khalid, 172
Na'emanei Har HaBeit, *see* Temple Mount Faithful
Nahal Qatif D., 198
Nahar al Khalil (Hebron), 149, 168
Nahuman of Bratslav, 13, 40
Nahumanides, *see* Ben Nahuman, Moshe
Al Najah University, 171, 173
Nakhichevan, 288
Naphtali (Old Testament), 283
Naqoura, 100
Nasser, Abdul Gamal (Egyptian president), 70, 73, 197, 202, 204-5, 207, 267
Nasser, Imad, 172
Natanya, 23, 94, 121, 143, 147, 239, 266
National Committee for Heads of Arab Local Authorities (Israel), 139
National Guidance Committee (Palestinian), 162, 172
National Liberation Front (Algeria), 202
National Reconciliation Agreement (Palestinian), 240
National Religious Party (Israel), 17, 42, 89, 91, 103, 138, 148, 150, 158
Natsche, Mustafa Abdul Nabi, 168, 231, 233
Navon, Yitzhak, 52
Nazareth, 134, 137, 144, 345
Nazis, 119, 154
Nebuchadnezzar (Old Testament), 283
Negev, 18, 45, 68, 70, 78-9, 121, 130, 144, 176-7, 216, 284, 299
Netanyahu, Bentzion, 106
Netanyahu, Binyamin, 39, 64, 92-3, 95, 97, 101-17, 230, 248-53, 255, 275, 278, 297-2
Netivot, 49
Neturei Karta, 41

Netzarim, 106, 198-9, 238
Neve Dekalim, 198-9
Neve Yaacov, 25-6
The New Israelis, xxi
New Testament, 286
New Town (Jerusalem), 5
New York, 12, 38, 65, 72, 152-3, 157, 209, 246, 252,
New York Times, 11, 19, 102, 108, 213, 252, 258
Night Journey and Ascension (Quran), 28
Noah (Old Testament), 20
Noble Sanctuary, 9, 15, 105, 250
North Korea, 69
North Yemen, 127, 212
Northern Ireland, 291-2
Norway, 231
nuclear weapons (Israel), xxii, 71, 77, 79, 90, 130, 216
Nuseirat, 188

O

Obeid, Ramez, 275
al Obeidiah of Bertinoro, 5
Observer, 269
Occupied Homeland (Palestinian), *see* Occupied Territories
Occupied Territories, xxii, xxv, 12, 17-8, 22, 74-6, 80-3, 89-91, 94-5, 139, 144, 150-1, 153, 159, 161-2, 179-80, 184-6, 189, 192-4, 208, 213-5, 218-21, 223, 228-31, 240, 247, 250, 254, 258, 260, 263, 274, 293, *see also* East Jerusalem, Gaza Strip, Greater East Jerusalem, and West Bank
October 1973 War, xxiv, 76, 84, 138, 208
Odysseus Elytis, 214
Ofer, Avraham, 80
Ofra, 17
oil, 19, 76, 172, 174, 206-7, 211, 221, 274, 287, 289, 296
Oklahoma City, 292
Old City (Jerusalem), xix, 1, 4-10, 18-9, 22, 26, 28-31, 33-6, 40, 104-5, 108, 118, 158, 171, 178, 201, 203, 249-50, 278, 294
Old Testament, 43, 128, 154, 158, 171, 283, 286
Old Town (Jerusalem), *see* Old City (Jerusalem)
Olmert, Ehud, 27, 39, 44, 113, 245, 250
Omar ibn Khattab (Caliph), 15, 19, 166, 237
Omari, Fakhri, 220
Organization of Arab Petroleum Exporting Countries, 76

Oriental Jews, *see* Mizrachim and Sephardim
Orthodox Jews, 1, 8, 37, 41-2, 101, 158, 198, 318
Oslo 97, 226, 230, 233
Oslo Accord (September 1993), 26, 28, 93-5, 97-8, 101, 104, 106, 108, 115-6, 151, 173, 176, 179, 184, 198, 226, 229, 230, 233-7, 239, 243, 245, 247, 250, 255-6, 263-5, 269, 271, 278, 280, 292, 294, 296-7, 299-301
Oslo I Accord, *see* Oslo Accord (September 1993)
Oslo II Accord (September 1995), 95, 97-8, 109-12, 244-5, 247, 251-2, 255, 270, 297-8, 301 *see also* Cairo Agreement (May 1994)
Ottoman empire, 70, 166, 182, 287-8, 291
Oudieh, Nahiz Muhammad, 195
Oz, Amos, 290

P

Pakistan, 289
Palestine Broadcasting Authority, 99, 233, 241
Palestine Broadcasting Station (British), 133
Palestine Communist Party, 133, 210, 215
Palestine Liberation Army, 197, 205, 207, 211, 223, 235
Palestine Liberation Front, 185, 188, 205, 220
Palestine Liberation Organization (PLO), xxiv-v, 12, 26, 29, 85, 88-91, 93-5, 102, 125, 139, 140, 142-3, 151-2, 154-5, 159, 161, 168, 173, 177-8, 184-7, 189-90, 193-5, 197-200, 202-3, 205-31, 233, 236-7, 240, 243, 247, 250, 258-60, 262-5, 267, 271-2, 275-7, 291, 293-300
Palestine National Charter, 110, 202, 251, 294
Palestine National Council, 88-9, 101, 185, 202, 205, 208, 211, 214-5, 217-8, 246-7, 259, 262-3, 295, 300
Palestine National Front, 161, 210
Palestine National Fund, xxv, 206
Palestine People's Party, 229-30
Palestine Struggle Front, 210, 229, 230
Palestine Students' Federation, 201
Palestine War (1948–49), *see* Arab-Israeli War I (1948-9)
Palestinian Academic Society for the Study of International Affairs, 184
Palestinian Authority (PA), 93-5, 97-9, 104-6, 108-10, 115-6, 142-3, 171, 190, 196, 199, 217, 224, 231-47, 249-53, 255, 265, 267, 269, 270-1, 273-9, 295, 298, 300-3

Palestinian Economic Council for Development and Reconstruction, 247
Palestinian Forces Alliance, 263, 265
Palestinian National Authority, *see* Palestinian Authority
Palestinian Territories, *see* Gaza Strip, Greater East Jerusalem, and West Bank
Pappe, Ilan, 127, 129, 291, 294
The Paratrooper's Book, 72
Paris, 70, 73, 79, 86, 227-8, 230, 245
Park Hotel (Hebron), *see* Nahar al Khalil
Peace Now (Israeli group), 83, 86, 95-6, 290
Peel Commission, 1937 (British), 65
Peres, Shimon, 63, 69, 72, 75, 78-80, 83, 87-9, 91, 93-103, 107, 112, 114, 116, 118, 150, 157, 173, 184, 215, 217, 219, 224-6, 229-30, 244, 246, 248-9, 270, 272, 274-5, 277, 299
Peretz, Don, 68
Peretz, Yitzhak, 45
Perez de Cuellar, Javier, 189
Perry, Yaacov, 234
Phalange militia (Lebanese), 85
Pisgat Zeev, 25
Plonsk, 65
Poale Zion, 65, 75
Political Dictionary of the State of Israel, 128-9
Popular Front for the Liberation of Palestine, 162, 175, 193, 197, 204-5, 210, 254, 265
Popular Front for the Liberation of Palestine-General Command, 184
Port Said, 31, 71, 182
Port Suez, 77
Portugal, 76
Preventive Security Service (Palestinian), 98, 104, 235, 245, 253, 269
Psagot, 242-3
Pundak, Ron, 225
Pundak, Yitzhak, 194

Q

Qaddumi, Farouq, 206, 229, 237
Qalqilya, 244
Qana, 100
Qana massacre, 102
Qassam Brigade, 98-9, 237, 239, 247, 253, 258, 262, 264-5, 273-8
Qassam, Izz al Din, 140
Qassam militia, 275
Qawasmeh, Fahd, 162, 168, 172
Qawasmeh, Fayaz, 149, 169, 173
Qrei, Ahmad, 225, 228, 233, 244, 247
Al Quds, *see* Jerusalem
Al Quds, 24, 30, 33, 218, 236-7, 303
Al Quds Palestinian Arab Radio, 185

al Qudwa, Muhammad Abdul Raouf, *see*
Arafat, Yasser
Al Quds al Sharif, *see* Jerusalem
Quran, 15, 20-1, 172, 190, 246, 256, 259-
61, 266, 272, 279-80, 284
Qutb, Sayyid, 267

R

Rabbinical Councils, 42
Rabbo, Abdul, 21
Rabbo, Yasser Abd, 230
Rabin, Leah, 80
Rabin, Yitzhak, xxv, 26, 29, 72-4, 78-80,
84, 87-9, 91, 93-7, 101, 112, 116,
118, 123, 139-40, 142-3, 155-63, 183,
186-7, 194-5, 216-7, 224-8, 230, 234,
237-40, 243, 260, 262, 264, 270,
291-3, 299
Rachel (Old Testament), 283
Rafah, 75, 181-2, 191, 193, 196, 235, 267
Rafat, 264, 271-2
Rafi, xvi-ii, xxii, 1-4, 10-1, 13, 38-9,
62-4, 132, 146, 155-7, 165, 167
Rafi (Israeli group), 72-3, 75, 79
Rahat, 144
Raja, Amin, 177
Rajoub, Jibril, 98, 234, 236
Rakah, 138-9
Ramadan War, *see* October 1973 War
Ramallah, 28, 99, 104-5, 147, 154, 158,
162, 175, 176, 178, 187, 222-3, 244-
5,
262, 264, 275-6
Ramat Allon, 25
Ramat Eshkol, 24-5
Ramat Gan, 94-5, 149, 270
Ramban, *see* Ben Nahuman, Moshe
Ramle, xxvi, 71, 201, 237, 267
Rantisi, Abdul Aziz, 261-2, 264
Raphael, Eitan, 85
Raviv, Dan, 216
Reagan, Ronald, 211
Rebecca (Old Testament), 165
Rechis Shuafat, 26
Red Crescent, 32, 258
Reform Judaism, 67
Rehovot, 157
Religious Affairs Ministry (Israel), 33, 42, 105
Religious laws (Israel), 39-41, 43, 67, 154,
156, 169, 284, 286
Remembrance Day, 119
Reuben (Old Testament), 283
Revisionist Zionism and Zionists, 59, 65-6,
81-2, 125, 152
Rishon LeZion, 115, 176, 185, 188
RMBN, *see* Ramban

The Road to Oslo, 224
Rock of Foundation, 21
Rock of Heaven, 21
Rogers Peace Plan, 76
Rogers, William, 25, 75
Rohan, Michael Dennis, 16
Rojeib, 149, 157
Rome, 228, 234-5
Ross, Dennis, 106, 229, 249
Rothschild, Danny, 263
Route One (Jerusalem), 28, 30, 32, 34
Rubinstein, Amnon, 141
Russia, 11, 40, 99, 125-6, 288
Russian immigrants (Jewish), 91-2, 151

S

Sabbath (Jewish), xviii, 2, 11, 23, 34,
41-2, 44, 46, 67, 121, 153, 266
Sabra, 73, 86, 293
Sabri, Ekrima Said, 241
Sadat, Anwar, 9, 76, 83, 127, 210
Saeer, 164
Safed, 48, 50, 291
al Safi, Abu Jamil, 175
al Safi, Marouf, 177
al Safi, Riyad, 175
Said, Edward W., xxvi, xxvii
Saida, 170-1, 175
Saint John's Hospice (Jerusalem), 9, 12-3
saint worship (Jewish), 49
Saiqa, 210
Sakal, Shlomo, 183-4
Sakura, Anwar, 266
Saladin, 1, 16, 22-3, 166
Salah al Din, *see* Saladin
Salah al Din Street (Jerusalem), 28, 34
Salamin, Ali, 19
Sali, Baba, 49
El Salvador, 30
al Samra, Abdul Hakim, 243
Samaria, 10, 18, 24, 147-9, 151, 158, 162,
224
Samed Foundation, 211, 247
al Samra, Abdul Hakim, 182, 232, 268, 276,
278, 181
Samson Unit, 195, 264
Samu, 203
Samuel, Herbert, 288
San Remo Agreement, 288
Sarah (Old Testament), 165, 167, 281-2
Sarahneh, Ibrahim Hussein, 273-6
Sarai (Old Testament), 281
Sarid, Yossi, 238
Saudi Arabia, 16, 19, 118, 127, 196, 204,
301
Saul (Old Testament), 156, 165

Savir, Uri, 225
Sayeret, 92, 216
Sayeret Matkal, 92, 216
SBC (company), 12
Schach, Eliezer, 45, 89
Schiff, Zeev, 98, 124, 192
Schmemann, Serge, 102
Schneerson, Menach M., 8
Second Temple, xvii, 2, 4, 8, 16, 147, 285
Sede Boqer, xviii
Segev, Yitzhak, 258
Sephardim, 64, 80, 84, 87, 89, 92, 122, 284, 295, see also Mizrachim
settlements and settlers, see Jewish settlements and settlers
Shaath, Nabil, 225, 233, 243, 245, 265
Shaati, 198
Shabak, see Shin Beth
Shabbat (Jewish), see Sabbath (Jewish)
Shafi, Abdul Haidar, 223-4, 228, 234, 238, 240, 243, 245-7, 258
Shaheen, Abu Ali, 203
Shaheen, Habib, 175
Shaikh Radwan, 239
Shakaa, Bassam, 162, 172
Shaker, Salah, 266
Shami, Abdullah, 266
Shamir, Moshe, 149
Shamir, Yitzhak, 10, 60, 63, 66, 75, 84, 86-93, 151, 187-8, 193, 219, 221, 223-4, 260, 291
Shankl, Ahmad, 177
Sharaka, Mustafa, 177
Sharett, Moshe, 70, 75
Sharia and Sharia courts, 28, 33, 169
Sharm al Shaikh, 71, 73-4, 99, 277
Sharnoubi, Riad Karim, 275
Sharon, Ariel, 9-10, 14, 72, 76, 82, 84-92, 123, 125, 151, 160, 187, 197-8, 211-13, 253, 258, 297, 299
Shas, 45-7, 52, 89, 91, 103, 117, 142
Shavit, Yaacov, 290
Shawwa, Rashid, 197-8
Shcharansky, Natan, 103
Shechem (Old Testament), 1, 30, 147-8, 157-8, 171, 280, see also Nablus
Shikaki, Fathi Abdul Aziz, 266-7
Shin Beth, xxii, 18-9, 35, 97-8, 104, 107, 114, 118, 124, 138, 154, 156, 172, 184-5, 189, 197, 234, 236, 239, 258, 267, 270-2, 274, 293
Shinkar Committee, 168
Shipler, David K., 11, 19
Shlaim, Avi, 129
Shomron, Dan, 110, 186

Al Shuab, 170
Shuafat, 19, 26
Shultz, George, 88, 218
Shultz Peace Plan, 88-9
Shuqairi, Ahmad, 202
Sidon, 133
Siftawi, Ala, 267
Signposts along the Road, 267
Silwadi, Fadlallah, 22
Silwan, 22
Simeon (Old Testament), 283
Sinai II Agreement (Egyptian-Israeli), 214
Sinai Campaign, see Suez War (1956)
Sinai Peninsula, 17, 70, 74, 287-8
Singer, Joel, 225, 233
Singer, Rafi, 120
Siso, David, 48
Smooha, Sammy, 53
Sneh, Ephraim, 224
Social-cultural Changes in the Middle East, Vol, VIII, 142
socialist Zionists, 42
Solomon (Old Testament), 2, 11, 141, 284
Sourani, Raji, 239
South Africa, 134, 209
South Korea, 69
South Lebanon Army, 88, 125
Soviet Union, 64, 68, 70, 76-7, 81, 84, 90, 130, 173, 208, 219, 268, 287, 290, 293, 296, 298
Spain, 5, 50, 99, 166, 292
Stalin, Joseph, 288
State Education Law 1953 (Israel), 137
Stephen's Gate (Jerusalem), 30
Stern, Avraham, 86
Stern Gang/Group, see Lehi
Strauss, Franz, 79
Students of Yahya Ayash, 273
Stuttgart, 201-2
Subtenants, 134
Sudan, 270
Suez Canal, 70, 74, 76, 84, 182, 287-9, 295
Suez War (1956), xxi, 69-73, 84, 144, 201, 290
suicide bombs, 97, 270
Suleiman, Muhammad Yusuf, xxvi
Suleiman the Magnificent (Ottoman Sultan), 1
Sunday Times, 216
Supreme Muslim Council (Palestinian), 15
Supreme Surveillance Committee of Arab Affairs (Israel), 140
Suq Alloon, 15
Suq al Huzor, 14
Susser, Leslie, 159, 300
Syria and Syrians, xxi, xxv, xxiii, 66-7, 71-3, 76, 78, 83, 85-6, 90, 99, 100,

103, 113, 124, 126, 128, 133, 174,
202, 204-5, 207-8, 210, 212-3, 220,
223, 235, 263, 270, 272, 274, 283,
287, 297, 303

T

Taba, 244
Taba Agreement (September 1995), *see* Oslo
    II Accord (September 1995)
Tabsin, Awad, 177
Taiba, 143, 178
Tal, Ron, 184, 268
Talmud, 11, 40, 155, 286
Talouli, Muhammad, 200
Talpiyot, 25, 31, 38
Tami, 52
Tamimi, Rajab, 172
Tarqumiya, 154
al Tayib, Tawfiq, 268
Tehiya, 89, 149
Tekoa, 147
Tel Aviv, xvi, 4, 29-30, 50, 54, 63-4, 66,
    77, 80, 86, 90, 94-8, 104, 107, 109-10,
    115-7, 120, 128, 146-7, 149, 157-9,
    169, 176, 188, 192, 196, 228, 238-9,
    247, 253, 265, 270, 275-6, 278, 291,
    299
Tel Hai, 125-6
Temple Institute, 8, 19
Temple Mount, *see* Noble Sanctuary
Temple Mount Faithful, 8, 22, 189
Temporary International Presence in Hebron,
    231
terrorism and terrorists, 4, 17-9, 23, 28, 81,
    89, 93-5, 98-9, 102-3, 107, 113,
    115-6, 148, 152, 156, 162, 170, 172,
    184, 193-5, 198, 207, 214, 216-20,
    223-5, 237-40, 247, 253, 255, 265-7,
    270, 275-9, 291-2, 295, 300, *see also*
    suicide bombs
Terzi, Zehdi, 209
Third Temple, 9, 16, 18-9, 22
Third Way (Israeli group), 103
Thubron, Colin, xix
Tiberias, 50, 291
Tibi, Ahmad, 143
Tiran Straits, 73-4
Titus (Roman Emporer), xvii, 2
Toledano, Nissim, 194, 262
Tomb of the Patriarchs, 29, 94, 112, 144,
    152, 154, 161, 165-6, 172, 231
Torah, 3, 9-11, 38-46, 95, 153, 155-6, 158,
    167, 280, 285
Torah Chaim, 158
Touma, Emile, 139
Tov, Israel Baal Shem, 40
Transition Law 1949 (Israel), 67

Transjordan, *see* Jordan
Tripartite Declaration, 69
Tripoli (Lebanon), 213
Trumpeldor, Yosef, 125
Tsagrat al Abid, 164
Tulkarm, 192, 244, 263
Tunis, xxiii, xxv, 94, 115, 186, 211-2,
    215-7, 219-21, 224, 227-30, 232-3,
    236, 244, 247, 262-3
Tunisia, 185, 212, 215, 227
Turkey, 5, 99, 166, 288
Tyre, 100, 174
Tzomet, 44, 89, 103

U

ultra-Orthodox Jews, 1, 3, 8-9, 13, 33,
    37-44, 46, 58, 89, 101-2, 270
ultranationalism and ultranationalists (Jewish),
    112, 250-1
Umedi, Eli, 14
Umm al Fahm, 144
Al Umma, 236
Unit 805 (Israel), 121
United Arab List (Israel), 112
United National Leadership (Palestinian),
    185, 187, 215, 259
United Nations Palestine Partition Plan (1947),
    6, 30, 41, 66-8, 81, 126-7, 133, 205,
    218, 222, 290
United Nations Relief and Works Agency for
    Palestian Refugees in the Near East (1949),
    175, 221
United Religious Front (Israel), 41, 67
United States, 9, 25, 27, 30, 69-70, 74-8,
    84-5, 90, 92-3, 99-100, 103, 111,
    113-4, 119, 131, 143, 173, 187, 189,
    195, 211, 214, 217-20, 222, 226, 231,
    252, 254, 266, 272, 276, 287-8, 290,
    292, 296
United States Consulate, 119
United Torah Judaism, 45
Ur, 171
Usrat al Jihad, 144

V

Vanunu, Mordechai, 216
Vespasian, Flavia, 171
Via Dolorosa (Jerusalem), 35, 105
Village Councils (West Bank), 162
Vilna, 40
Vilnai, Matan, 233
Vilnius, 41
Vishnitz (Jewish sect), 41
Voice of Palestine Radio, 99
Voice of the Palestine Liberation Organization
    Radio, 185, 215, 219-20

W

Al Wad Street (Jerusalem), 10, 14, 105
Wadi Ara, 133
Wadi al Ghurous, 164
Wadi al Hussein, 164
Wadi Joz, 28
Wailing Wall, *see* Western Wall
al Walid ibn Abdul Malik (Caliph), 16
Walker, Tony, 217
War of Attrition (1969–70), 76, 184, 206
War of Establishment of Israel, 127, *see also* Arab-Israeli War I (1948–49)
War of Independance (Israel), *see* War of Establishment of Israel
War of Independence (United States), *see* American Revolution
Washington, 68-9, 73, 76-7, 80, 84-5, 89, 91, 103-4, 106, 108, 111, 113, 116, 142, 151, 189, 214, 219, 226, 229, 249, 251-2, 254-5, 288, 301
Al Watan, 268-70
Watt, Micah, 3
Wazir, Intissar, 233, 245
Waxman, Nachshon, 237, 265
Wazir, Khalil, 186, 200-1, 209, 216, 227, 236
Weingrod, Alex, 4, 26, 32, 36-7
Weizman, Ezer, 73, 75, 81, 89, 98, 155, 217
Weizmann, Chaim, 75
West Bank, xx, xxii-vii, 29-33, 75, 78, 82-5, 88-5, 98, 100, 102-4, 106, 108-4, 123-4, 129, 132, 138-9, 144-5, 147-4, 156-61, 163, 169, 171, 173, 175, 178-80, 184-8, 190-2, 194, 197-8, 201, 203, 207-8, 210, 213, 215, 220-1, 223-5, 227, 229, 233, 236, 238, 242-7, 249, 251-2, 255, 257, 259-60, 262, 264-5, 269, 270-7, 280, 290-1, 297-302
West Germany, 82, 90, 202
West Jerusalem, 4, 6, 25, 27-37, 62
Western Wall, xix, 1, 2, 4-6, 10, 15, 21-2, 28, 42, 57, 165, 167, 268
WEVD Radio (New York), 38
Wilson, Woodrow, 288
Winternitz, Helen, 186, 189, 190, 192
World Bank, 70, 240, 247
World War I, 65, 126, 137, 182, 287-8
World War II, 41, 65-6, 71, 75, 174, 178, 212, 287, 289
World Zionist Organization, xxvi, 5, 41, 65-6, 287

Y

Yaacov (Old Testament), *see* Jacob
Ya'ari, Ehud, 192, 235, 238

Yad Vashem, 4, 119
Yadin, Yigal, 80
Yadlin, Asher, 80
Yahadut HaTorah HaMeuhedat, *see* United Torah Judaism
Yamit, 75, 164
Yaron, Michael, 119
Yasin, Adnan, 227, 229
Yasin, Ahmad, 175, 194, 234, 237, 257, 260, 273-4, 301
Yasin, Hani, 230
Yediot Aharonot, 23, 112, 227, 251
Yellin-Mor, Nathan, 66
The Yellow Wind, 191
Yemeni, Ben Dror, 60
Yemeni Jews, 58
Yerushalayim, *see* Jerusalem
Yeshiva Atreet Cohanim, 8-9, 12-14, 17
Yeshiva Merkaz HaRav Kook, 148, 158
Yeshiva Shuvia Banin, 8, 13, 15
Yeshiva Yavne, 95
Yeshivath Torah Hagin, 10
Yiddish, xvii, 42, 59
Yisrael BeAliya, 103
Yitzhak (Old Testament), *see* Isaac
Yom Kippur War, *see* October 1973 War
Yoram, Avi, 157
Yossi, 181, 191, 193
Young Israeli Synagogue, 15
Yusuf, Nasser, 233, 237-8

Z

Zahar, Mahmoud, 256, 260, 270, 272, 274, 278, 294
Zaidan, Muhammad Abbas, 188
Zangezur, 288
Zarnuqa, 267
Zebulin (Old Testament), 283
Zechariah (Old Testament), 8, 77, 90
Zeevi, Rachavam, 147
Zefat, *see* Safed
Zion, 3, 135, 156, 286, 299
Zion Gate (Jerusalem), 30
Zionism and Zionists, xxi, xxvi, 5, 9, 16-7, 35-6, 41-2, 50-1, 53-5, 57-9, 63, 65-6, 68, 72-3, 79, 81-2, 84, 86, 103, 106, 112, 125-30, 133-5, 137-42, 148-9, 152, 155, 170, 173-4, 178, 187, 202, 204-6, 208-9, 222, 227, 240, 260, 268, 272-3, 277, 279-80, 285-8, 290-1, 293-5
Zionist Congress, 65, 208, 285, 287, 311
Zionist Organization, xv, xxvi, 5, 17, 65, 287, *see also* World Zionist Organization
Zogby, James, 246
Zubaidi, Nasr Mahmoud, 175